CompTIA® Network+ N10-008 Cert Guide, Deluxe Edition

Anthony Sequeira, CCIE #15626
Michael D. Taylor, Sim Software Author

Pearson IT Certification

Pearson

CompTIA® Network+ N10-008 Cert Guide, Deluxe Edition

Anthony Sequeira, CCIE #15626
Michael D. Taylor, Sim Software Author

ISBN-13: 978-0-13-758530-4

ISBN-10: 0-13-758530-6

Library of Congress Control Number: 2021913554

1 2021

Trademarks

Editor-in-Chief
Mark Taub

Director, ITP Product Management
Brett Bartow

Managing Editor
Sandra Schroeder

Development Editor
Christopher Cleveland

Project Editor
Mandie Frank

Copy Editor
Kitty Wilson

Technical Editor
Chris Crayton

Editorial Assistant
Cindy Teeters

Designer
Chuti Prasertsith

Composition
codeMantra

Indexer
Ken Johnson

Proofreader
Charlotte Kughen

Warning and Disclaimer

This book is designed to provide information about IT networking in the scope of the CompTIA Network+ exam. Every effort has been made to make this book as complete and as accurate as possible, but no warranty or fitness is implied.

The information is provided on an "as is" basis. The author shall have neither liability nor responsibility to any person or entity with respect to any loss or damages arising from the information contained in this book or from the use of the discs or programs that may accompany it.

The opinions expressed in this book belong to the author and are not necessarily those of Pearson.

Special Sales

For information about buying this title in bulk quantities, or for special sales opportunities (which may include electronic versions; custom cover designs; and content particular to your business, training goals, marketing focus, or branding interests), please contact our corporate sales department at corpsales@pearsoned.com or (800) 382-3419.

For government sales inquiries, please contact governmentsales@pearsoned.com.

For questions about sales outside the U.S., please contact intlcs@pearson.com.

Figure	**Attribution**
Figure 2-1	Courtesy of Cisco Systems, Inc
Figure 2-2	Courtesy of Cisco Systems, Inc
Figure 2-3	Courtesy of Cisco Systems, Inc
Figure 2-4	Courtesy of Cisco Systems, Inc
Figure 2-5	Courtesy of Cisco Systems, Inc
Figure 2-6	Courtesy of Cisco Systems, Inc
Figure 2-7	Courtesy of Cisco Systems, Inc
Figure 2-8	Courtesy of Cisco Systems, Inc
Figure 2-10	Courtesy of Cisco Systems, Inc
Figure 2-11	Courtesy of Cisco Systems, Inc
Figure 2-12	Courtesy of Cisco Systems, Inc
Figure 2-13	Courtesy of Cisco Systems, Inc
Figure 2-14	Courtesy of Cisco Systems, Inc
Figure 2-15	Courtesy of Cisco Systems, Inc
Figure 2-16	Screenshot of Configuring a vNIC © 2021, Oracle and/or its affiliates
Figure 2-17	Courtesy of Cisco Systems, Inc
Figure 2-18	Screenshot of Configuring a Virtual Switch © Microsoft 2021
Figure 2-19	Courtesy of Cisco Systems, Inc
Figure 2-20	Courtesy of Cisco Systems, Inc
Figure 2-21	Courtesy of Cisco Systems, Inc
Figure 2-22	Courtesy of Cisco Systems, Inc
Figure 2-23	Courtesy of Cisco Systems, Inc
Figure 4-4	Courtesy of Cisco Systems, Inc
Figure 4-5	Courtesy of Cisco Systems, Inc
Figure 4-6	Courtesy of Cisco Systems, Inc
Figure 4-7	Screenshot of Windows Control Panel © Microsoft 2021
Figure 4-8	Screenshot of Network and Internet Control Panel © Microsoft 2021
Figure 4-9	Screenshot of Network and Sharing Center © Microsoft 2021
Figure 4-10	Screenshot of Network Connections Window © Microsoft 2021
Figure 4-11	Screenshot of Local Area Connection Status Window © Microsoft 2021
Figure 4-12	Screenshot of Local Area Connection Properties © Microsoft 2021
Figure 4-13	Screenshot of Internet Protocol Version 4 (TCP/IPv4) Properties © Microsoft 2021

Contents at a Glance

Table of Contents

ONLINE ELEMENTS:

APPENDIX C   Memory Tables

APPENDIX D   Memory Tables Answer Key

APPENDIX E   Study Planner

Exam Essentials Interactive Study Guide

Key Terms Flash Cards Application

Instructional Videos

Performance-Based Exercises

Comptia Network+ N10-008 Hands-On Lab Simulator Software

About the Authors

Anthony Sequeira (CCIE No. 15626) began his IT career in 1994 with IBM in Tampa, Florida. He quickly formed his own computer consultancy, Computer Solutions, and then discovered his true passion: teaching and writing about networking technologies. Anthony lectured to massive audiences around the world while working for Mastering Computers. Anthony has never been happier in his career than he is now, as a senior technical instructor for Splunk. He is an avid tennis player, a private pilot, and a semi-professional poker player, and he loves anything at all to do with technology.

Lab Simulator Author: Network+ Certified since 2003, **Michael D. Taylor** currently serves as Computer Sciences Program Director for a career college in the eastern United States where he has taught for the past twenty years. In his role as a technical instructor, he won the Instructor of the Year award from his superiors and Instructor of the Quarter award from students multiple times.

Dedication

This book is dedicated to my wife, Joette Sequeira, who made this book, and all the rest of them, possible.

Acknowledgments

I cannot thank Brett Bartow and Chris Cleveland enough for their patience as I created this latest edition of the text.

About the Technical Reviewer

Chris Crayton (MCSE) is an author, technical consultant, and trainer. In the past, he has worked as a computer technology and networking instructor, information security director, network administrator, network engineer, and PC specialist. Chris has authored several print and online books on PC repair, CompTIA A+, CompTIA Security+, and Microsoft Windows. He has also served as technical editor and content contributor on numerous technical titles for several leading publishing companies. Chris holds numerous industry certifications, has been recognized with many professional teaching awards, and has served as a state-level SkillsUSA competition judge.

We Want to Hear from You!

As the reader of this book, *you* are our most important critic and commentator. We value your opinion and want to know what we're doing right, what we could do better, what areas you'd like to see us publish in, and any other words of wisdom you're willing to pass our way.

We welcome your comments. You can email or write to let us know what you did or didn't like about this book—as well as what we can do to make our books better.

Please note that we cannot help you with technical problems related to the topic of this book.

When you write, please be sure to include this book's title and author as well as your name and email address. We will carefully review your comments and share them with the author and editors who worked on the book.

Email: community@informit.com

Reader Services

Register your copy of *CompTIA® Network+ N10-008 Cert Guide* at www.pearsonitcertification.com for convenient access to downloads, updates, and corrections as they become available. To start the registration process, go to **www.pearsonitcertification.com/register** and log in or create an account.* Enter the product ISBN 9780137585304 and click **Submit**. When the process is complete, you will find any available bonus content under Registered Products.

* Be sure to check the box indicating that you would like to hear from us to receive exclusive discounts on future editions of this product.

Introduction

The CompTIA Network+ certification is a popular certification for those entering the computer networking field. Although many vendor-specific networking certifications are popular in the industry, the CompTIA Network+ certification is unique in that it is vendor neutral. The CompTIA Network+ certification often acts as a stepping-stone to more specialized and vendor-specific certifications, such as those offered by Cisco Systems.

On the CompTIA Network+ exam, the topics are mostly generic in that they can apply to networking equipment regardless of vendor. Although the CompTIA Network+ certification is vendor neutral, network software and systems are implemented by multiple independent vendors. Therefore, several of the exercises, examples, and simulations in this book include using particular vendors' configurations and technologies, such as Microsoft Windows operating systems or Cisco Systems routers and switches. More detailed training for a specific vendor's software and hardware can be found in books and training specific to that vendor.

Who Should Read This Book?

This book was written with two audiences in mind: those who want to learn all they can about networking technology and those who want to pass the CompTIA Network+ exam. I think that both groups are going to be very impressed with the breadth of technologies this book details. Although it would be impossible to cover every topic in networking today, this book manages to cover all the massive areas that make networking an exciting field that many people want to learn.

Readers will range from people who are attempting to attain a position in the IT field to people who want to keep their skills sharp or perhaps retain their job when facing a company policy that mandates they take the new exams. This book is also for those who want to acquire additional certifications beyond the Network+ certification (for example, the Cisco Certified Network Associate [CCNA] certification and beyond). The book is designed to enable an easy transition to future certification studies.

Resources

This book comes with a wealth of digital resources to help you review, practice, and assess your knowledge. The end of each chapter contains a review section that references several of these tools, and you should be sure to use them as you complete each chapter to help reinforce what you are learning. You can use them again after you finish the book to help review and make sure you are fully prepared for the exam.

Here's a list of resources available on the companion website/via download instructions in the back of the book:

- Interactive glossary flash card application

- Interactive exam essentials appendix

- Performance-based exercises

- CompTIA Network+ Hands-on Lab Simulator Software for exam N10-008

- The Pearson Test Prep practice test software with enhanced remediation features

- Free copies of the eBook version of the text in PDF, EPUB, and Kindle formats

- Video training on key exam topics

- Memory table review exercises and answer keys

- A study planner tool

- Instructions to redeem your Network+ certification exam voucher, which provides a 10% discount on the exam

To access the companion website, follow these steps:

Step 1.   Go to **http://www.pearsonitcertification.com/register.**

Step 2.   Either log in to your account if you have an existing account already or create a new account.

Step 3.   Enter the print book ISBN (9780137585304) and click **Submit**.

Step 4.   Answer the challenge questions to validate your purchase.

Step 5.   In your account page, click the **Registered Products** tab and then click the **Access Bonus Content** link.

Pearson Test Prep Practice Test Software

The companion website that accompanies this book includes the Pearson Test Prep practice test engine, which is software that displays and grades a set of exam-realistic practice test questions. Using the Pearson Test Prep practice test engine, you can either study by going through the questions in study mode or take a simulated CompTIA Network+ exam that mimics real exam conditions. The software also has a flash card mode that allows you to challenge yourself to answer the questions without seeing the multiple-choice answers.

Premium Edition

This Deluxe Edition comes complete with a free version of the Premium Edition eBook and Practice Test. To access the eBook files and the practice test access code, follow these steps:

Step 1. Open your web browser and go to www.pearsonitcertification.com

Step 2. Sign in to your account.

Step 3. On your account page, in the upper-right corner, enter the Digital Product Voucher code that is printed on the insert card in the sleeve in the back of your book in the Digital Product Voucher field and click Submit Your Code.

Step 4. The Premium Edition eBook and Practice Test will now be populated on your account page under Digital Purchases. You will see links to refresh and download your eBook files under the product listing. You will aslo see links to access the desktop and online versions of the Pearson Test Prep practice test software and the access code you will need to activate your exam.

The Pearson Test Prep software is available both online and as a Windows desktop application that you can run offline. The online version can be accessed at www. pearsontestprep.com. This version can be used on any device that has an Internet connection, including desktop computers, laptop computers, tablets, and smartphones. It is optimized for viewing on screens as small as a standard iPhone screen. The desktop application can be downloaded and installed from the companion website.

NOTE The desktop Pearson Test Prep application is a Windows-based application, so it is only designed to run on Windows. Although it can be run on other operating systems using a Windows emulator, other operating systems are not officially supported for the desktop version. If you are using an OS other than Windows, you might want to consider using the online version of Pearson Test Prep instead.

Accessing the test engine is a two-step process. The first step is to either install the software on your desktop or access the online version website. However, the practice exam (that is, the database of CompTIA Network+ exam questions) is not available to you until you take the second step: Register the unique access code that accompanies your book.

NOTE The code listed on the slip of paper in the sleeve in the back of your book is NOT your Pearson Test Prep access code. It is the digital product voucher code that gives you access to the free version of the Premium Edition eBook and Practice Test. Follow the instructions above to redeem that code on our web site, which will provide the access code needed to register your exam.

Installing the Pearson Test Prep Software

If you choose to use the Windows desktop version of the practice test software, you will need to download the installers from the companion website.

The software installation process is similar to other wizard-based installation processes. If you have already installed the Pearson Test Prep practice test software from another Pearson product, you do not need to reinstall the software. Just launch the software on your desktop and proceed to activate the practice exam from this book by using the access code on your account page on our website after you redeem your Premium Edition eBook and Practice Test digital product voucher in the back of this book. The following steps outline the installation process:

Step 1. Download the software to your computer from the companion website.

Step 2. Extract all files from the .zip file you downloaded.

Step 3. Launch the installer from the extracted files folder.

Step 4. Respond to the wizard-based prompts.

The installation process gives you the option to activate your exam with the access code on your account page after you redeem the digital product voucher in the back of this book. This process requires that you establish a Pearson website login. You need this login to activate the exam, so please register when prompted. If you already have a Pearson website login, you do not need to register again; just use your existing login.

Activating and Downloading the Practice Exam

The second step to accessing your practice exam product is to activate the product using the unique access code found on your account page after you redeem the digital product voucher in the back of this book. You must follow this step regardless of which version of the product you are using—the online version or the Windows desktop version. The following steps walk you through how to activate your exam on each platform.

Windows Desktop Version:

1. Start the Pearson Test Prep Practice Test software from the Windows Start menu or from your desktop shortcut icon.

2. To activate and download the exam associated with this book, on the My Products or Tools tab, click the **Activate** button.

3. At the next screen, enter the *access code* from your account page after you redeem the digital product voucher in the back of this book, and then click the **Activate** button. The activation process downloads the practice exam to your machine.

4. Click **Next** and then click **Finish**.

Online Version:

1. On a device with an active Internet connection, open your browser of choice and go to the website **www.pearsontestprep.com**.

2. Select **Pearson IT Certification** as the product group.

3. Enter the email address and password associated with your account and click **Login**.

4. In the middle of the screen, click the **Activate New Product** button.

5. Enter the access code from your account page after you redeem the digital product voucher in the back of this book and click the **Activate** button.

After the activation process is complete, the My Products tab should list your new exam. If you do not see the exam, make sure that you selected the **My Products** tab on the menu. At this point, the software and practice exam are ready to use. Simply select the exam and click the **Exams** button.

To update an exam that you have already activated and downloaded, simply select the **Tools** tab and click the **Update Products** button. Updating your exams ensures that you have the latest changes and updates to the exam data.

If you want to check for updates to the Pearson Cert Practice Test exam engine software, simply select the **Tools** tab and click the **Update Application** button to ensure that you are running the latest version of the exam engine.

NOTE The online version always contains the latest updates to the exam questions, so there is never a need to update when you're using that version.

Activating Other Exams

The exam software installation process and the registration process both occur only once. Then, for each new exam, only a few steps are required. For example, if you buy another new Pearson IT Certification Cert Guide, you can extract the activation code from the sleeve in the back of that book, start the exam engine (if it's not still up and running), and perform the activation steps from the previous list.

Goals and Methods

The goal of this book is to assist you in learning and understanding the technologies covered in the Network+ N10-008 blueprint from CompTIA. This book also helps you prepare for the N10-008 version of the CompTIA Network+ exam.

To aid you in mastering and understanding the Network+ certification objectives, this book uses the following methods:

- **Opening topics list:** This list spells out the Network+ objectives and topics that are covered in the chapter.

- **Foundation topics:** At the heart of a chapter, the sections under "Foundation Topics" explain the topics from hands-on and theory-based standpoints. These sections include in-depth descriptions, tables, and figures that build your knowledge so that you can pass the N10-008 exam. Each chapter is broken into multiple sections.

- **Key topics:** The "Review All Key Topics" section indicates important figures, tables, and lists of information that you need to review for the exam. Key Topic icons are sprinkled throughout each chapter, and a table at the end of each chapter lists the important parts of the text called out by these icons.

- **Memory tables:** You can find memory tables on the book's companion website in Appendixes C and D. Use them to help memorize important information.

- **Key terms:** Key terms without definitions are listed at the end of each chapter. Write down the definition of each term and check your work against the definitions in the Glossary. On the companion website, you will find a flash card application with all the glossary terms separated by chapter, and you can use it to study key terms as well.

- **Exercises:** This book comes with 40 performance-based practice exercises that are designed to help you prepare for the hands-on portion of the Network+ exam. These exercises are available on the companion website. Make sure you do the exercises as you complete each chapter and again when you have completed the book and are doing your final preparation.

- **Hands-on labs:** These hands-on exercises, which are an important part of this book, include matching, drag and drop, and simulations. In addition to reading this book, you should go through all the exercises included with the book. These interactive hands-on exercises provide examples, additional information, and insight about a vendor's implementation of the technologies. To perform the labs, simply install the CompTIA Network+ N10-008 Hands-on Lab Simulator software. This software is a Windows and Mac desktop application. You should be sure to install the software prior to reading the book because each chapter will indicate what labs you should perform. To install the software, follow these steps:

Step 1. Go to the companion website for the book. (Refer to the "Resources" section for how to access the companion website. or follow the instructions on the insert card in the sleeve in the back of the book.)

Step 2. Click the link to download the CompTIA Network+ N10-008 Hands-on Lab Simulator software.

Step 3. Once you have downloaded the software to your computer, extract all the files from the .zip file.

Step 4. Launch the installer from the extracted files.

Step 5. Respond to the wizard-based prompts.

NOTE You will need the access code for the Network Simulator printed on the insert card in the sleeve in the back of the book to activate the software during registration.

- **Practice exams:** This book comes complete with several full-length practice exams available to you in the Pearson Test Prep practice test software, which you can download and install from the companion website. The Pearson Test Prep software is also available to you online, at www.PearsonTestPrep. com. You can access both the online and desktop versions using the access code printed on the card in the sleeve in the back of this book. Be sure to run through the questions in Exam Bank 1 as you complete each chapter in study mode. When you have completed the book, take a full practice test using Exam Bank 2 questions in practice exam mode to test your exam readiness.

- **Exam essentials:** This book includes an exam essentials appendix that summaries the key points from every chapter. This review tool is available in print and as an interactive PDF on the companion website. Review these essential exam facts after each chapter and again when you have completed the book. This makes a great review summary that you can mark up as you review and master each concept.

For current information about the CompTIA Network+ certification exam, visit https://certification.comptia.org/certifications/network.

Strategies for Exam Preparation

This book comes with a study planner tool on the companion website. It is a spreadsheet that helps you keep track of the activities you need to perform in each chapter and helps you organize your exam preparation tasks. As you read the chapters in this book, jot down notes with key concepts or configurations in the study planner. Each chapter ends with a summary and series of exam preparation tasks to help you reinforce what you have learned. These tasks include review exercises such as reviewing key topics, completing memory tables, defining key terms, answering review questions, and performing hands-on labs and exercises. Make sure you perform these tasks as you complete each chapter to improve your retention of the material and record your progress in the study planner.

The book concludes with Chapter 26, "Final Preparation," which offers you guidance on your final exam preparation and provides you with some helpful exam advice. Make sure you read over that chapter to help assess your exam readiness and identify areas where you need to focus your review.

Make sure you complete all the performance-based question exercises and hands-on labs associated with this book. The exercises and labs are organized by chapter, making it easy to perform them after you complete each section. These exercises help you reinforce what you have learned, offer examples of some popular vendors' methods for implementing networking technologies, and provide additional information to assist you in building real-world skills and preparing you for the certification exam.

Download the current exam objectives by submitting a form on the following web page: https://www.comptia.org/certifications/network.

Use the practice exam, which is included on this book's companion website. As you work through the practice exam, use the practice test software reporting features to note the areas where you lack confidence and then review the related concepts. After you review those areas, work through the practice exam a second time and rate your skills. Keep in mind that the more you work through the practice exam, the more familiar the questions become, and the less accurately the practice exam judges your skills.

After you work through the practice exam a second time and feel confident with your skills, schedule the real CompTIA Network+ exam (N10-008).

CompTIA Network+ Exam Topics

Table I-1 lists general exam topics (*objectives*) and specific topics under each general topic (*subobjectives*) for the CompTIA Network+ N10-008 exam. This table lists the primary chapter in which each exam topic is covered. Note that many objectives and subobjectives are interrelated and are addressed in multiple chapters in the book.

Table I-1   CompTIA Network+ Exam Topics

Chapter	N10-008 Exam Objective	N10-008 Exam Subobjective
1 The OSI Model and Encapsulation	1.0 Networking Fundamentals	1.1 Compare and contrast the Open Systems Interconnection (OSI) model layers and encapsulation concepts.
2 Network Topologies and Types	1.0 Networking Fundamentals	1.2 Explain the characteristics of network topologies and network types.
3 Network Media Types	1.0 Networking Fundamentals	1.3 Summarize the types of cables and connectors and explain which is the appropriate type for a solution.
4 IP Addressing	1.0 Networking Fundamentals	1.4 Given a scenario, configure a subnet and use appropriate IP addressing schemes.
5 Common Ports and Protocols	1.0 Networking Fundamentals	1.5 Explain common ports and protocols, their application, and encrypted alternatives.
6 Network Services	1.0 Networking Fundamentals	1.6 Explain the use and purpose of network services.
7 Corporate and Datacenter Architectures	1.0 Networking Fundamentals	1.7 Explain basic corporate and datacenter network architecture.
8 Cloud Concepts	1.0 Networking Fundamentals	1.8 Summarize cloud concepts and connectivity options.
9 Various Network Devices	2.0 Network Implementations	2.1 Compare and contrast various devices, their features and their appropriate placement on the network.
10 Routing Technologies and Bandwidth Management	2.0 Network Implementations	2.2 Compare and contrast routing technologies and bandwidth management concepts.
11 Ethernet Switching	2.0 Network Implementations	2.3 Given a scenario, configure and deploy common Ethernet switching features.
12 Wireless Standards	2.0 Network Implementations	2.4 Given a scenario, install and configure the appropriate wireless standards and technologies.
13 Ensure Network Availability	3.0 Network Operations	3.1 Given a scenario, use the appropriate statistics and sensors to ensure network availability.

Chapter	N10-008 Exam Objective	N10-008 Exam Subobjective
14 Organizational Documents and Policies	3.0 Network Operations	3.2 Explain the purpose of organizational documents and policies.
15 High Availability and Disaster Recovery	3.0 Network Operations	3.3 Explain high availability and disaster recovery concepts and summarize which is the best solution.
16 Common Security Concepts	4.0 Network Security	4.1 Explain common security topics.
17 Common Types of Attacks	4.0 Network Security	4.2 Compare and contrast common types of attacks.
18 Network Hardening Techniques	4.0 Network Security	4.3 Given a scenario, apply network hardening techniques.
19 Remote Access Methods	4.0 Network Security	4.4 Compare and contrast remote access methods and security implications.
20 Physical Security	4.0 Network Security	4.5 Explain the importance of physical security.
21 A Network Troubleshooting Methodology	5.0 Network Troubleshooting	5.1 Explain the network troubleshooting methodology.
22 Troubleshoot Common Cabling Problems	5.0 Network Troubleshooting	5.2 Given a scenario, troubleshoot common cable connectivity issues and select the appropriate tools.
23 Network Software Tools and Commands	5.0 Network Troubleshooting	5.3 Given a scenario, use the appropriate network software tools and commands.
24 Troubleshoot Common Wireless Issues	5.0 Network Troubleshooting	5.4 Given a scenario, troubleshoot common wireless connectivity issues.
25 Troubleshoot General Network Issues	5.0 Network Troubleshooting	5.5 Given a scenario, troubleshoot general networking issues.

How This Book Is Organized

Although this book could be read cover to cover, it is designed to be flexible and allow you to easily move between chapters and sections of chapters to cover just the material that you need more work with. However, if you do intend to read all the chapters, the order in the book is an excellent sequence to use:

- **Chapter 1: The OSI Model and Encapsulation**—The OSI model is an extremely powerful guide you can use as you design, implement, and trouble-shoot networks.

- **Chapter 2: Network Topologies and Types**—This chapter explores the many types of networks and topologies used in enterprises today.

- **Chapter 3: Network Media Types**—This chapter drills deep into the media that connects networks today.

- **Chapter 4: IP Addressing**—Addressing of systems is critical in networks, and this chapter covers the addressing used with IPv4 and IPv6.

- **Chapter 5: Common Ports and Protocols**—This chapter introduces many of the common ports and protocols in use today.

- **Chapter 6: Network Services**—The network is the plumbing that carries the data and services you require. This chapter examines some of the many services that you will encounter in networks today.

- **Chapter 7: Corporate and Datacenter Architectures**—Today's corporate enterprise networks and the datacenters that are common in networks today are the subject of this chapter.

- **Chapter 8: Cloud Concepts**—This chapter explores key principles of the cloud, which has become common in networks today.

- **Chapter 9: Various Network Devices**—This chapter explores some of the various devices found in networks today.

- **Chapter 10: Routing Technologies and Bandwidth Management**—Moving packets from one network to another is the job of a router. This chapter ensures that you are well versed in the many technologies that operate in this category.

- **Chapter 11: Ethernet Switching**—Wireless is great, but Ethernet still rules the access layer. This chapter explores Ethernet in depth.

- **Chapter 12: Wireless Standards**—Wireless networking is here to stay. This chapter provides you with details on important topics such as security and emerging technologies.

- **Chapter 13: Ensure Network Availability**—There are many tools available today to help you ensure that a network is running smoothly. This chapter details many of them.

- **Chapter 14: Organizational Documents and Policies**—This chapter discusses many of the documents and policies that are found in enterprises today. Those that could impact the IT department are the focus of this chapter.

- **Chapter 15: High Availability and Disaster Recovery**—Making sure the network is always available is the subject of this chapter.

- **Chapter 16: Common Security Concepts**—This chapter explores the fundamentals of network security.

- **Chapter 17: Common Types of Attacks**—This chapter covers the most common types of attacks in the cybersecurity landscape today.

- **Chapter 18: Network Hardening Techniques**—This chapter explores the methods of hardening the network and its devices against the most common attacks.

- **Chapter 19: Remote Access Methods**—This chapter explores the many types of remote access that are possible today.

- **Chapter 20: Physical Security**—This chapter explores the important topic of physical security for a network.

- **Chapter 21: A Network Troubleshooting Methodology**—Whereas other chapters just touch on network troubleshooting, this chapter makes it the focus.

- **Chapter 22: Troubleshoot Common Cabling Problems**—This chapter examines the most common issues with network media and what you can do to detect and resolve these issues.

- **Chapter 23: Network Software Tools and Commands**—This chapter explores many of the common tools and commands you can use to troubleshoot a network.

- **Chapter 24: Troubleshoot Common Wireless Issues**—This chapter explores the most common issues with wireless networks.

- **Chapter 25: Troubleshoot General Network Issues**—This chapter explores common general network issues and how you can quickly detect and resolve them.

This chapter covers the following topics related to Objective 1.1 (Compare and contrast the Open Systems Interconnection [OSI] model layers and encapsulation concepts) of the CompTIA Network+ N10-008 certification exam:

- OSI model
  - Layer 1—Physical
  - Layer 2—Data link
  - Layer 3—Network
  - Layer 4—Transport
  - Layer 5—Session
  - Layer 6—Presentation
  - Layer 7—Application
- Data encapsulation and decapsulation within the OSI model context
  - Ethernet header
  - Internet Protocol (IP) header
  - Transmission Control Protocol (TCP)/User Datagram Protocol (UDP) headers
  - TCP flags
  - Payload
  - Maximum transmission unit (MTU)

CHAPTER 1

The OSI Model and Encapsulation

Way back in 1977, the International Organization for Standardization (ISO) developed a subcommittee to focus on the interoperability of multivendor communications systems. This is fancy language for getting network "thingies" to communicate with each other, even if different companies made those network "thingies." What sprang from this subcommittee was the ***Open Systems Interconnection (OSI) reference model*** (also referred to as the *OSI model* or the *OSI stack*). Thanks to this model, you can talk about any networking technology and categorize that technology as residing at one or more of the seven layers of the model.

This chapter defines those seven layers and offers examples of what you might find at each layer. It also contrasts the OSI model with another model—the TCP/IP stack, also known as the Department of Defense (DoD) model—that focuses on Internet Protocol (IP) communications.

Foundation Topics

The Purpose of Reference Models

Throughout this book, various protocols and devices that play a role in your network (and your networking career) are introduced. To better understand how a technology fits in, it helps to have a common point of reference against which various technologies from different vendors can be compared. Understanding the OSI model is useful in troubleshooting networks.

One of the most common ways of categorizing the function of a network technology is to say at what layer (or layers) of the OSI model that technology runs. Understanding how that technology performs a certain function at a certain layer of the OSI model helps you determine whether one device is going to be able to communicate with another device, which might or might not be using a similar technology, at that layer of the OSI reference model.

For example, when your end-user device connects to a web server on the Internet, your service provider assigns your device an IP address. Similarly, the web server to which you are communicating has an IP address. As described in this chapter, an IP address lives at Layer 3 (the network layer) of the OSI model. Because your device and the web server use a common protocol (that is, IP) at Layer 3, they are capable of communicating with one another.

Notice also in this example that you are interested in receiving the data from the web server, which will be web pages filed with text and graphics and maybe even videos. This is the information you are really after. You (typically) do not care about the IP addresses in use or any of the other information required by the network devices to make this transfer happen. In technical terms, you are interested in the *payload* of the packets sent from the web server. The *payload* provides a simple and generic method of describing the data itself, which is separate and distinct from any of the other information required for proper transmission.

Personally, I have been in the computer-networking industry since 1996, and I have had the OSI model explained in many classes I have attended and books I have read. From this, I have taken away a collection of metaphors to help describe the operation of the different layers of the OSI model. Some of the metaphors involve sending a letter from one location to another or placing a message in a series of envelopes. These are often excellent metaphors for encapsulation and decapsulation (covered later in this chapter), but they do not work all that well for the OSI model in general. My favorite way to describe the OSI model is to simply think of it as being analogous to a bookshelf, such the one shown in Figure 1-1.

FIGURE 1-1   A Bookshelf Is Analogous to the OSI Model

If you were to look this or any other bookshelf in my home office, you would see that I have organized diverse types of books on different shelves. One shelf holds my collection of technical books, another shelf holds the books I wrote for Pearson and other publishers, another shelf holds books regarding self-improvement and finance. I have grouped similar books together on each shelf, just as the OSI model groups similar protocols and functions together in a layer.

A common pitfall my readers meet when studying the OSI model is to try to neatly fit all the devices and protocols in their network into one of the OSI model's seven layers. However, not every technology fits perfectly into these layers. In fact, some networks might not have any technologies running at one or more of these layers. This reminds me of my favorite statement about the OSI model. It comes from Rich Seifert's book *The Switch Book*. In that book, Rich reminds us that the OSI model is a *reference* model, not a *reverence* model. That is, no cosmic law states that all technologies must cleanly plug into the model. So, as you discover the characteristics of the OSI model layers throughout this chapter, remember that these layers are like shelves for organizing similar protocols and functions, not immutable laws.

> **NOTE** When first studying the OSI model, my students quickly realize that the model was created for the reasons described earlier. Later in their information technology (IT) careers, they realize the biggest value of the OSI model to them: to aid in troubleshooting network problems. Check out my video in the Additional Resources section at the end of this chapter, where I walk you through exactly how this is true!

The OSI Model

As previously described, the OSI model consists of seven layers:

- **Layer 1:** The physical layer
- **Layer 2:** The data link layer
- **Layer 3:** The network layer
- **Layer 4:** The transport layer
- **Layer 5:** The session layer
- **Layer 6:** The presentation layer
- **Layer 7:** The application layer

Graphically, we depict these layers with Layer 1 at the bottom of the stack, as shown in Figure 1-2.

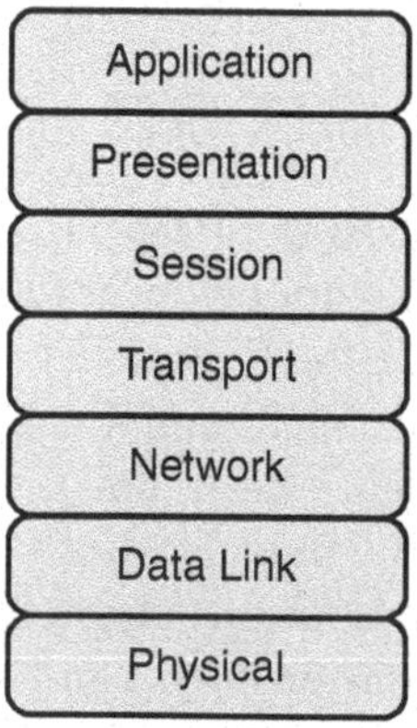

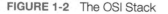

| Application |
| Presentation |
| Session |
| Transport |
| Network |
| Data Link |
| Physical |

FIGURE 1-2 The OSI Stack

NOTE Various mnemonics are available to help memorize these layers in their proper order. A top-down (that is, starting at the top of the stack with Layer 7 and working your way down to Layer 1) memory aid is *All People Seem To Need Data Processing*. Another common technique is *Please Do Not Throw Sausage Pizza Away*, which begins at Layer 1 and works up to Layer 7.

At the physical layer, binary expressions (that is, a series of 1s and 0s) represent data. A binary expression is created using bits, where a bit is a single 1 or a single 0. At upper layers, however, bits are grouped together, into what is known as a ***protocol data unit (PDU)*** or a *data service unit*.

Engineers tend to use the term *packet* generically to refer to these PDUs. However, PDUs might have an added name, depending on their OSI layer. Figure 1-3 illustrates these PDU names. A common memory aid for these PDUs is *Some People Fear Birthdays*, where the *S* in *Some* reminds us of the *S* in *Segments*. The *P* in *People* reminds us of the *P* in *Packets*, and the *F* in *Fear* reflects the *F* in *Frames*. Finally, the *B* in *Birthdays* reminds us of the *B* in *Bits*. (If you have never heard this memory aid before, I am not that surprised as I invented it!)

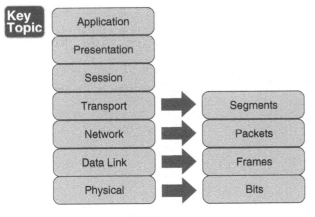

Key Topic

FIGURE 1-3   PDU Names

Layer 1: The Physical Layer

The concern of the ***physical layer***, as shown in Figure 1-4, is the transmission of bits on the network along with the physical and electrical characteristics of the network.

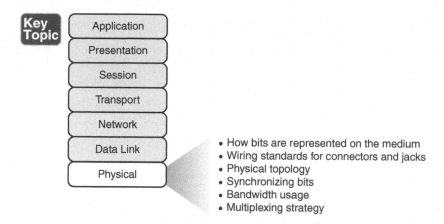

FIGURE 1-4   Layer 1: The Physical Layer

The physical layer defines the following:

■ **How to represent bits on the medium:** Data on a computer network is represented as a binary expression. Chapter 4, "IP Addressing," discusses binary in much more detail. Electrical voltage (on copper wiring) or light (carried via fiber-optic cabling) can represent these 1s and 0s.

For example, the presence or absence of voltage on a wire portrays a binary 1 or a binary 0, respectively, as illustrated in Figure 1-5. Similarly, the presence or absence of light on a fiber-optic cable renders a 1 or 0 in binary. This type of approach is called *current state modulation*.

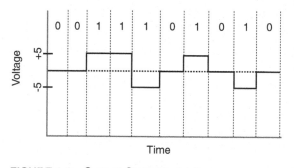

FIGURE 1-5   Current State Modulation

An alternative approach to portraying binary data is *state transition modulation,* as shown in Figure 1-6, where the transition between voltages or the presence of light shows a binary value.

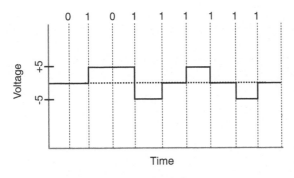

FIGURE 1-6   Transition Modulation

NOTE   Other modulation types you might be familiar with from radio include amplitude modulation (AM) and frequency modulation (FM). AM uses a variation in a waveform's amplitude (that is, signal strength) to portray the original signal. FM uses a variation in frequency to stand for the original signal.

- **Wiring standards for connectors and jacks:** Chapter 3, "Network Media Types," describes several standards for network connectors. For example, the TIA/EIA-568-B standard describes how to wire an RJ-45 connector for use on a 100BASE-TX Ethernet network, as shown in Figure 1-7.

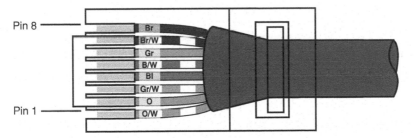

FIGURE 1-7   TIA/EIA-568-B Wiring Standard for an RJ-45 Connector

- **Physical topology:** Layer 1 devices view a network as a physical topology (as opposed to a logical topology). Examples of a physical topology include bus, ring, and star topologies, as described in Chapter 2, "Network Topologies and Types."

- **Synchronizing bits:** For two networked devices to successfully communicate at the physical layer, they must agree on when one bit stops and another bit starts. Specifically, the devices need a method to synchronize the bits.

Two basic approaches to bit synchronization are *asynchronous* and *synchronous* synchronization:

- **Asynchronous:** With this approach, a sender states that it is about to start transmitting by sending a start bit to the receiver. When the receiver sees this, it starts its own internal clock to measure the next bits. After the sender transmits its data, it sends a stop bit to say that it has finished its transmission.

- **Synchronous:** This approach synchronizes the internal clocks of the sender and the receiver to ensure that they agree on when bits begin and end. A common approach to make this synchronization happen is to use an external clock (for example, a clock provided by a service provider). The sender and receiver then reference this external clock.

- **Bandwidth usage:** The two fundamental approaches to bandwidth usage on a network are *broadband* and *baseband*:

  - **Broadband:** Broadband technologies divide the bandwidth available on a medium (for example, copper or fiber-optic cabling) into different channels. A sender can then transmit different communication streams over the various channels. For example, consider frequency-division multiplexing (FDM) used by a cable modem. Specifically, a cable modem uses certain ranges of frequencies on the cable coming into your home from the local cable company to carry incoming data, another range of frequencies for outgoing data, and several other frequency ranges for various TV stations.

  - **Baseband:** Baseband technologies use all the available frequencies on a medium to send data. Ethernet is an example of a networking technology that uses baseband.

- **Multiplexing strategy:** Multiplexing allows multiple communications sessions to share the same physical medium. Cable TV, as previously mentioned, allows you to receive multiple channels over a single physical medium (for example, a coaxial cable plugged into the back of your television). Here are some of the most common approaches to multiplexing:

  - *Time-division multiplexing (TDM):* TDM supports different communication sessions (for example, different telephone conversations in a telephony network) on the same physical medium by causing the sessions to take turns. For a brief period, defined as a *time slot*, data from the first session is sent, followed by data from the second session. This continues until all sessions have had a turn, and the process repeats.

- **Statistical time-division multiplexing (StatTDM):** A downside to TDM is that each communication session receives its own time slot, even if one of the sessions does not have any data to send at the moment. To make more efficient use of available bandwidth, StatTDM dynamically assigns time slots to communications sessions on an as-needed basis.

- **Frequency-division multiplexing (FDM):** FDM divides a medium's frequency range into channels, and different communication sessions send their data over different channels. As previously described, this approach to bandwidth usage is called *broadband*.

- **Orthogonal frequency-division multiplexing (OFDM):** OFDM encodes digital data onto multiple carrier frequencies. OFDM is very popular today and is used in wideband digital communication. This makes OFDM useful in applications such as digital television and audio broadcasting, DSL Internet access, wireless networks, powerline networks, and 4G/5G mobile communications.

Examples of devices defined by physical layer standards include hubs, wireless access points, and network cabling.

NOTE Hubs are not used in modern computer networks. So why are we even bothering to mention them? Well, they really did help give rise to our modern switches. A hub interconnects PCs in a LAN; it is considered a physical layer device because it takes bits coming in on one port and retransmits those bits out all other ports. At no point does the hub interrogate any addressing information in the data as our modern switches do.

Layer 2: The Data Link Layer

The *data link layer* is concerned with the following:

- Packaging data into frames and transmitting those frames on the network

- Ensuring that frames do not exceed the *maximum transmission unit (MTU)* of the physical media

- Performing error detection/correction

- Uniquely finding network devices with addresses

- Handling flow control

> **NOTE**   Network interfaces use the MTU to define the largest packet size the interface will forward. For example, a 1500-byte packet could not be forwarded via a router interface with an MTU of 1470 bytes.

Data link layer processes, collectively referred to as *data link control (DLC)*, are illustrated in Figure 1-8.

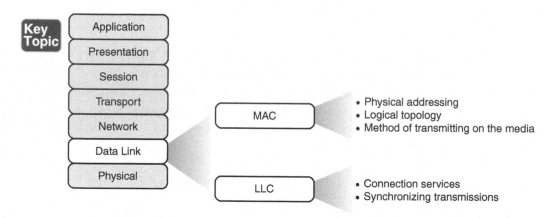

FIGURE 1-8   Layer 2: The Data Link Layer

In fact, the data link layer is distinct from the other layers in that it has two sublayers: MAC and LLC.

Media Access Control

Characteristics of the Media Access Control (MAC) sublayer of the data link layer include the following:

- **Physical addressing:** A common example of a Layer 2 address is a MAC address, which is a 48-bit address assigned to a device's network interface card (NIC). MAC addresses are written in hexadecimal notation (for example, 58:55:ca:eb:27:83). The first 24 bits of the 48-bit address are the *vendor code*. The IEEE Registration Authority assigns a manufacturer one or more unique vendor codes. You can use the list of vendor codes at https://standards.ieee. org/develop/regauth/oui/oui.txt to identify the manufacturer of a networking device, based on the first half of the device's MAC address. The last 24 bits of a MAC address are assigned by the manufacturer, and they act as a serial number for the device. No two MAC addresses in the world should have the same value.

- **Logical topology:** Layer 2 devices view a network as a logical topology. Examples of logical topologies include bus and ring topologies, as described in Chapter 2.

- **Method of transmitting on the media:** With several devices connected to a network, there needs to be some strategy for deciding when a device sends on the media. Otherwise, multiple devices might send at the same time and interfere with one another's transmissions.

Logical Link Control

Characteristics of the Logical Link Control (LLC) sublayer of the data link layer include the following:

- **Connection services:** When a device on a network receives a message from another device on the network, that recipient device can give feedback to the sender in the form of an acknowledgment message. The two main functions provided by these acknowledgment messages are as follows:

  - **Flow control:** Limits the amount of data a sender can send at one time; this prevents the sender from overwhelming the receiver with too much information.

  - **Error control:** Allows the recipient of data to let the sender know whether the expected data frame was not received or whether it was received but is corrupted. The recipient figures out whether the data frame is corrupt by mathematically calculating a checksum of the data received. If the calculated checksum does not match the checksum received with the data frame, the recipient of the data draws the conclusion that the data frame is corrupted and can then notify the sender via an acknowledgment message.

- **Synchronizing transmissions:** Senders and receivers of data frames need to coordinate when a data frame is being transmitted and should be received. The three methods of performing this synchronization are detailed here:

  - **Isochronous:** With isochronous transmission, network devices look to a common device in the network as a clock source, which creates fixed-length time slots. Network devices can determine how much free space, if any, is available within a time slot and then insert data into an available time slot. A time slot can accommodate more than one data frame. Isochronous transmission does not need to provide clocking at the beginning of a data string (as does synchronous transmission) or for every data frame (as does asynchronous transmission). As a result, isochronous transmission uses little overhead compared to asynchronous or synchronous transmission methods.

- **Asynchronous:** With asynchronous transmission, network devices reference their own internal clocks, and network devices do not need to synchronize their clocks. Instead, the sender places a start bit at the beginning of each data frame and a stop bit at the end of each data frame. These start and stop bits tell the receiver when to monitor the medium for the presence of bits.

An additional bit, called the *parity bit*, might also be added to the end of each byte in a frame to detect an error in the frame. For example, if even parity error detection (as opposed to odd parity error detection) is used, the parity bit (with a value of either 0 or 1) would be added to the end of a byte, causing the total number of 1s in the data frame to be an even number. If the receiver of a byte is configured for even parity error detection and receives a byte where the total number of bits (including the parity bit) is even, the receiver can conclude that the byte was not corrupted during transmission.

NOTE   Using a parity bit to detect errors might not be effective if a byte has more than one error (that is, if more than one bit has been changed from its original value).

- **Synchronous:** With synchronous transmission, two network devices that want to communicate between themselves must agree on a clocking method to show the beginning and ending of data frames. One approach to providing this clocking is to use a separate communications channel over which a clock signal is sent. Another approach relies on specific bit combinations or control characters to indicate the beginning of a frame or a byte of data.

Like asynchronous transmissions, synchronous transmissions can perform error detection. However, rather than using parity bits, synchronous communication runs a mathematical algorithm on the data to create a *cyclic redundancy check (CRC)*. If the sender and the receiver calculate the same CRC value for the same chunk of data, the receiver can conclude that the data was not corrupted during transmission.

Examples of devices defined by data link layer standards include switches, bridges, and NICs.

NOTE   NICs are not entirely defined at the data link layer because they are partially based on physical layer standards, such as a NIC's network connector.

Layer 3: The Network Layer

The *network layer*, as shown in Figure 1-9, is primarily concerned with forwarding data based on logical addresses.

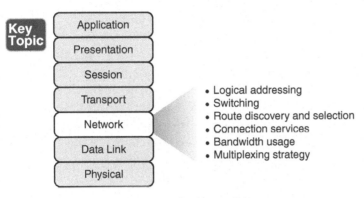

FIGURE 1-9   Layer 3: The Network Layer

Although many network administrators think of routing and IP addressing when they hear about the network layer, this layer is actually responsible for a variety of tasks:

- **Logical addressing:** Whereas the data link layer uses physical addresses to make forwarding decisions, the network layer uses logical addressing to make forwarding decisions. A variety of routed protocols (for example, AppleTalk and IPX) have their own logical addressing schemes, but by far the most widely deployed routed protocol is Internet Protocol (IP). Chapter 4 discusses IP addressing in detail.

- **Switching:** Engineers often associate the term *switching* with Layer 2 technologies; however, the concept of switching also exists at Layer 3. Switching, at its essence, is making decisions about how data should be forwarded. At Layer 3, three common switching techniques exist:

  - **Packet switching:** With packet switching, a data stream is divided into packets. Each packet has a Layer 3 header that includes source and destination Layer 3 addresses. Another term for packet switching is *routing*, which is discussed in more detail in Chapter 10, "Routing Technologies and Bandwidth Management."

  - **Circuit switching:** Circuit switching dynamically brings up a dedicated communication link between two parties for those parties to communicate.

    As a simple example of circuit switching, think of making a phone call from your home to a business. In fact, let's go "old school" and pretend you have a traditional landline servicing your phone, the telephone company's switching equipment interconnects your home phone with the phone system of the business you are calling. This interconnection (that is, *circuit*) exists only for the duration of the phone call.

■ **Message switching:** Unlike packet switching and circuit switching technologies, message switching is usually not well suited for real-time applications because of the delay involved. Specifically, with message switching, a data stream is divided into messages. Each message is tagged with a destination address, and the messages travel from one network device to another network device on the way to their destination. Because these devices might briefly store the messages before forwarding them, a network using message switching is sometimes called a *store-and-forward* network. Metaphorically, you could visualize message switching like routing an email message, where the email message might be briefly stored on an email server before being forwarded to the recipient.

■ **Route discovery and selection:** Because Layer 3 devices make forwarding decisions based on logical network addresses, a Layer 3 device might need to know how to reach various network addresses. For example, a common Layer 3 device is a router. A router can maintain a routing table indicating how to forward a packet based on the packet's destination network address.

A router can have its routing table populated via manual configuration (that is, by entering static routes), via a dynamic routing protocol (for example, OSPF or EIGRP), or simply by being directly connected to certain networks.

NOTE Routing protocols are discussed in Chapter 10.

■ **Connection services:** Just as the data link layer offers connection services for flow control and error control, connection services also exist at the network layer. Connection services at the network layer can improve the communication reliability if the data link's LLC sublayer is not performing connection services. The following functions are performed by connection services at the network layer:

■ **Flow control (also known as congestion control):** Helps prevent a sender from sending data more rapidly than the receiver is capable of receiving it.

■ **Packet reordering:** Allows packets to be placed in the proper sequence as they are sent to the receiver. This might be necessary because some networks support load balancing, where multiple links are used to send packets between two devices. Because multiple links exist, packets might arrive out of order.

Examples of devices found at the network layer include routers and multilayer switches. The most common Layer 3 protocol in use, and the protocol on which the Internet is based, is IPv4. However, IPv6 is beginning to be more common on networks today.

Layer 4: The Transport Layer

The *transport layer*, as shown in Figure 1-10, acts as a dividing line between the upper layers and lower layers of the OSI model. Specifically, messages are taken from upper layers (Layers 5–7) and are encapsulated into segments for transmission to the lower layers (Layers 1–3). Similarly, data streams coming from lower layers are decapsulated and sent to Layer 5 (the session layer), or some other upper layer, depending on the protocol.

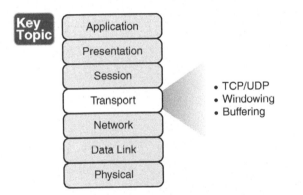

FIGURE 1-10   Layer 4: The Transport Layer

Two common transport layer protocols are TCP and UDP:

- *Transmission Control Protocol (TCP)*: TCP is a connection-oriented transport protocol. Connection-oriented transport protocols offer reliable transport, in that if a segment is dropped, the sender can detect the drop and retransmit the dropped segment. Specifically, a receiver acknowledges segments that it receives. Based on those acknowledgments, a sender can decide which segments were successfully received and which segments need to be transmitted again.

- *User Datagram Protocol (UDP)*: UDP is a connectionless transport protocol. Connectionless transport protocols offer unreliable transport, in that if a segment is dropped, the sender is unaware of the drop, and no retransmission occurs.

Just as Layer 2 and Layer 3 offer flow control services, flow control services also exist at Layer 4. Two common flow control approaches at Layer 4 are windowing and buffering:

- **Windowing:** TCP communication uses windowing, in that one or more segments are sent at one time, and a receiver can attest to the receipt of all the segments in a window with a single acknowledgment. In some cases, as illustrated in Figure 1-11, TCP uses a sliding window, where the window size begins with one segment. If there is a successful acknowledgment of that one segment (that is, the receiver sends an acknowledgment asking for the next segment), the window size doubles to two segments. Upon successful receipt of those two segments, the next window holds four segments. This exponential increase in window size continues until the receiver does not acknowledge successful receipt of all segments within a certain amount of time—known as the *round-trip time* (RTT), which is sometimes called *real transfer time*—or until a configured maximum window size is reached.

Key Topic

Window Size 1

Segment 1 →

← ACK 2

Window Size 2

Sender

Segment 2 →

Segment 3 →

← ACK 4

Receiver

Window Size 4

Segment 4 →

Segment 5 →

Segment 6 →

Segment 7 →

← ACK 8

FIGURE 1-11 TCP Sliding Window

- **Buffering:** With buffering, a device (for example, a router) uses a chunk of memory (sometimes called a *buffer* or a *queue*) to store segments if bandwidth is not available to send those segments. A queue has finite capacity, however, and can overflow (that is, drop segments) in the event of sustained network congestion.

In addition to TCP and UDP, Internet Control Message Protocol (ICMP) is another transport layer protocol you are likely to meet. ICMP is used by utilities such as ping and traceroute, which are discussed in Chapter 23, "Network Software Tools and Commands."

Layer 5: The Session Layer

The *session layer*, as shown in Figure 1-12, is responsible for setting up, maintaining, and tearing down sessions. You can think of a session as a conversation that needs to be treated separately from other sessions to avoid the intermingling of data from different conversations.

Key Topic

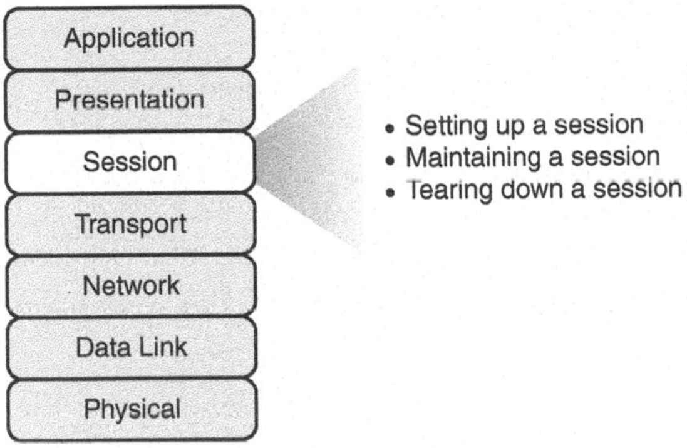

| Application |
| Presentation |
| Session |
| Transport |
| Network |
| Data Link |
| Physical |

- Setting up a session
- Maintaining a session
- Tearing down a session

FIGURE 1-12   Layer 5: The Session Layer

Here is a detailed look at the functions of the session layer:

- **Setting up a session:** Examples of the procedures involved in setting up a session include the following:

    - Checking user credentials (for example, username and password)

    - Assigning numbers to a session's communication flows to uniquely find each one

    - Negotiating services needed during the session

    - Negotiating which device begins sending data

- **Maintaining a session:** Examples of the procedures involved in supporting a session include the following:

    - Transferring data

    - Reestablishing a disconnected session

    - Acknowledging receipt of data

- **Tearing down a session:** A session can be disconnected based on agreement of the devices in the session. Alternatively, a session might be torn down because one party disconnects (either intentionally or because of an error condition). If one party disconnects, the other party can detect a loss of communication with that party and tear down its side of the session.

Session Initiation Protocol (SIP) is an example of a session layer protocol, which can help set up, support, and tear down a voice or video connection. Keep in mind, however, that not every network application neatly maps directly to all seven layers of the OSI model. The session layer is one of those layers where it might not be possible to name what protocol in each scenario is running in it. Network Basic Input/ Output System (NetBIOS) is one example of a session layer protocol.

NOTE NetBIOS is an application programming interface (API) developed in the early 1980s to enable computer-to-computer communication on a small LAN (specifically, PC-Network, which was IBM's LAN technology at the time). Later, IBM needed to support computer-to-computer communication over larger Token Ring networks. As a result, IBM enhanced the scalability and features of NetBIOS with a NetBIOS emulator named NetBIOS Extended User Interface (NetBEUI).

Layer 6: The Presentation Layer

The *presentation layer*, as shown in Figure 1-13, formats the data being exchanged and secures that data with encryption.

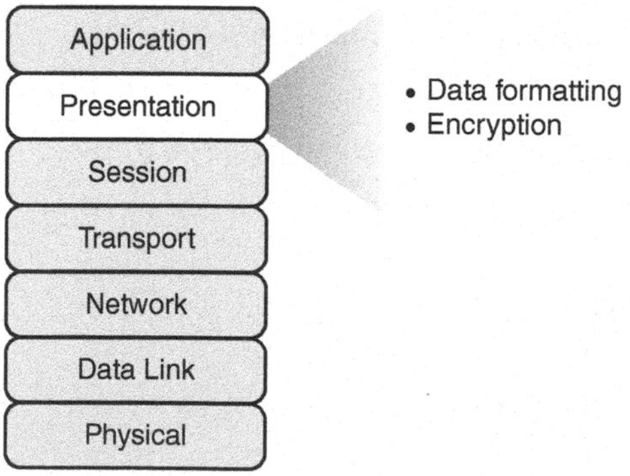

FIGURE 1-13   Layer 6: The Presentation Layer

The following list describes the functions involved in data formatting and encryption in more detail:

- **Data formatting:** As an example of how the presentation layer handles data formatting, consider how text is formatted. Some applications might format text using American Standard Code for Information Interchange (ASCII), while other applications might format text using Extended Binary Coded Decimal Interchange Code (EBCDIC). The presentation layer handles formatting the text (or other types of data, such as multimedia or graphics files) in a format that allows compatibility between the communicating devices.

- **Encryption:** Imagine that you are sending sensitive information over a network (for example, your credit card number or bank password). If a malicious user were to intercept your transmission, they might be able to obtain this sensitive information. To add a layer of security for such transmissions, encryption can be used to scramble (encrypt) the data in such a way that if the data were intercepted, a third party would not be able to unscramble (decrypt) it. However, the intended recipient would be able to decrypt the transmission.

Encryption is discussed in detail in Chapter 16, "Common Security Concepts."

Layer 7: The Application Layer

The *application layer*, as shown in Figure 1-14, gives application services to a network. An important (and often-misunderstood) concept is that end-user applications (such as Microsoft Word) live at the application layer. Instead, the application layer supports services used by end-user applications. For example, email is an application layer service that does exist at the application layer, whereas Microsoft Outlook (an example of an email client) is an end-user application that does not live at the application layer. Another function of the application layer is advertising available services.

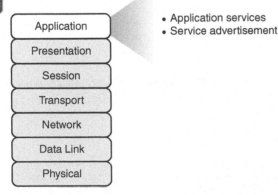

FIGURE 1-14 Layer 7: The Application Layer

The following list describes the functions of the application layer in more detail:

- **Application services:** Examples of the application services living at the application layer include file sharing and email.

- **Service advertisement:** Some applications' services (for example, some networked printers) periodically send out advertisements, making their availability known to other devices on the network. Other services, however, register themselves and their services with a centralized directory (for example, Microsoft Active Directory), which can be queried by other network devices seeking such services.

Recall that even though the application layer is numbered as Layer 7, it is at the top of the OSI stack because its networking functions are closest to the end user.

The TCP/IP Stack

The ISO developed the OSI reference model to be generic, in terms of what protocols and technologies could be categorized by the model. However, most of the traffic on the Internet (and traffic on corporate networks) is based on the TCP/IP protocol suite. Therefore, a more relevant model for many network designers and administrators to reference is a model developed by the U.S. Department of Defense (DoD). This model is known as the *DoD model*, or the ***TCP/IP stack***.

> **NOTE**   An older protocol known as Network Control Protocol (NCP) was similar to TCP/IP. NCP was used on ARPANET (the predecessor to the Internet), and it provided features like those offered by the TCP/IP suite of protocols on the Internet, although they were not as robust.

Layers of the TCP/IP Stack

The TCP/IP stack has only four defined layers, as opposed to the seven layers of the OSI model. Figure 1-15 contrasts these two models.

The TCP/IP stack is composed of the following layers:

- **Network interface:** The TCP/IP stack's ***network interface layer*** encompasses the technologies offered by Layers 1 and 2 (the physical and data link layers) of the OSI model.

> **NOTE**   Some literature refers to the network interface layer as the *network access layer*.

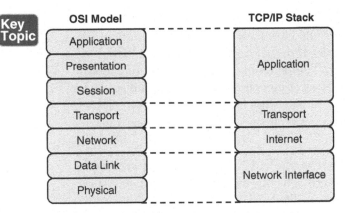

FIGURE 1-15   TCP/IP Stack

- **Internet:** The *Internet layer* of the TCP/IP stack maps to Layer 3 (the network layer) of the OSI model. Although multiple routed protocols live at the OSI model's network layer, the Internet layer of the TCP/IP stack focuses on IP as the protocol to be routed through a network. Figure 1-16 shows the format of an IP version 4 (IPv4) packet.

Version	Header Length	Type of Service	Total Length	
Identification			IP Flags	Fragment Offset
TTL		Protocol	Header Checksum	
Source Address				
Destination Address				
IP Option (Variable Length)				

FIGURE 1-16   IPv4 Packet Format

Notice that there are fields in the IP packet header for both source and a destination IP addresses. The Protocol field shows the transport layer protocol from which the packet was sent or to which the packet should be sent. Also of note is the Time-to-Live (TTL) field. The value in this field is decremented by 1 every time this packet is routed from one IP network to another (that is, when it passes through a router). If the TTL value ever reaches 0, the packet is discarded from the network. This behavior helps prevent routing loops. As a common practice, the OSI layer numbers 1, 2, and 3 are still used when referring to physical, data link, and network layers of the TCP/IP stack, even though the TCP/IP stack does not explicitly separate the physical and data link layers.

- **Transport:** The *transport layer* of the TCP/IP stack maps to Layer 4 (the transport layer) of the OSI model. The two primary protocols found at the TCP/IP stack's transport layer are TCP and UDP.

Figure 1-17 details the structure of a TCP segment. Notice the fields for source and destination ports. As described later in this chapter, these ports identify to which upper-layer protocol data should be forwarded or from which upper-layer protocol the data is being sent.

Source Port	Destination Port
Sequence Number	
Acknowledgment Number	

Offset	Reserved	TCP Flags	Window

Checksum	Urgent Pointer
TCP Options Option (Optional)	

FIGURE 1-17   TCP Segment Format

Also notice the field for window size. The value in this field determines how many bytes a device can receive before expecting an acknowledgment. As previously described, this feature offers flow control.

The header of a TCP segment also contains sequence numbers for segments. With sequence numbering, if segments arrive out of order, the recipient can put them back in the proper order based on the sequence numbers.

The acknowledgment number in the header shows the next sequence number the receiver expects to receive. This is a way for the receiver to let the sender know that all segments up to and including that point have been received. Due to the sequencing and acknowledgements, TCP is considered to be a *connection-oriented* transport layer protocol.

> **NOTE** You might have noticed that both the ***IP header*** and the ***TCP header*** make use of a Flags field. Including this field is a very common technique in networking to permit the data unit to convey specific settings. For example, the IP header uses the IP Flags field (3 bits) to help manage (or prevent) fragmentation. ***TCP flags*** are used to indicate a particular connection state or provide additional information. They are often used for troubleshooting purposes or to control how a particular connection is handled.

Figure 1-18 presents the structure of a UDP segment. UDP is a connection-less, unreliable protocol. UDP lacks the sequence numbering, window size, and acknowledgment numbering present in the header of a TCP segment. The UDP segment's header simply contains source and destination port numbers, a UDP checksum (which is an optional field used to detect transmission errors), and the segment length (measured in bytes).

Source Port	Destination Port
UDP Length	UDP Checksum

FIGURE 1-18 UDP Segment Format

Because a ***UDP header*** is much smaller than a TCP header, UDP is a good candidate for the transport layer protocol for applications that need to maximize bandwidth and do not require acknowledgments (for example, audio or video streams).

- **Application:** The biggest difference between the TCP/IP stack and the OSI model is at the TCP/IP stack's ***application layer***. This layer addresses concepts described by Layers 5, 6, and 7 (the session, presentation, and application layers) of the OSI model.

With the reduced complexity of a four-layer model like the TCP/IP stack, network designers and administrators can more easily categorize a given networking technology into a specific layer. For example, although SIP was shown earlier as a session layer protocol within the OSI model, you would have to know more about the behavior of SIP to properly categorize it in that model. However, with the TCP/IP stack, you could quickly figure out that SIP is a higher-level protocol that gets encapsulated inside TCP, and you could thus classify SIP in the application layer of the TCP/IP stack.

Common Application Protocols in the TCP/IP Stack

Application layer protocols in the TCP/IP stack are identifiable by unique port numbers. For example, when you enter a web address in an Internet browser, you are (by default) communicating with that remote web address using TCP port 80. Specifically, Hypertext Transfer Protocol (HTTP), which is the protocol used by web servers, uses TCP port 80. Therefore, the data you send to that remote web server has a destination port number of 80. That data is encapsulated into a TCP segment at the transport layer. That segment is further encapsulated into a packet at the Internet layer and sent out on the network using an underlying network interface layer technology such as Ethernet.

NOTE Thanks to awareness of network security today, you do not see HTTP (port 80) actually being used on the Internet very much anymore. It has been replaced with a secured version, HTTPS, which uses TCP port 443 in its operation.

Consider the example illustrated in Figure 1-19. When you send traffic to the remote website, the packet you send out to the network needs not only the destination IP address (172.16.1.2 in this example) of the web server and the destination port number for HTTP (that is, 80) but also the source IP address of your computer (10.1.1.1 in this example). Because your computer is not acting as a web server, its port is not 80. Instead, your computer selects a source port number greater than 1023. In this example, let's imagine that the client PC selects the source port 1248.

Key Topic

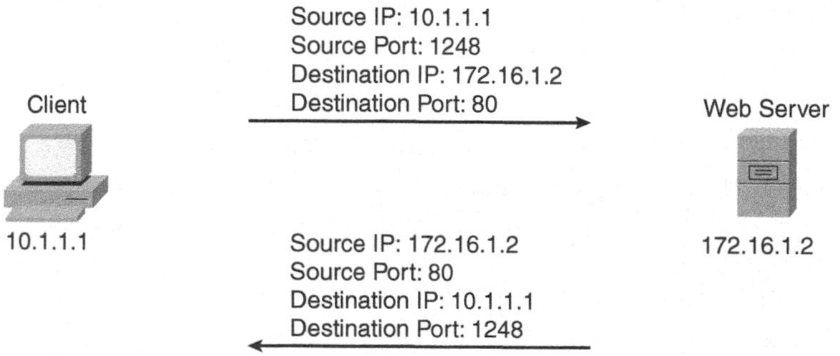

Client

Source IP: 10.1.1.1
Source Port: 1248
Destination IP: 172.16.1.2
Destination Port: 80 →

Web Server

10.1.1.1

Source IP: 172.16.1.2
Source Port: 80
Destination IP: 10.1.1.1
← Destination Port: 1248

172.16.1.2

FIGURE 1-19   Example: Port Numbers and IP Addresses

Notice that when the web server sends content back, the IP addresses and port numbers have now switched, with the web server as the source and your PC as the destination. With both source and destination port numbers, along with source and destination IP addresses, two-way communication becomes possible.

NOTE Ports numbered 1023 and below are called *well-known* ports, and ports numbered above 1023 are called *ephemeral* ports. The maximum value of a port is 65,535. Well-known port number assignments are available at https://www.iana.org/assignments/port-numbers.

Real-World Case Study

Bob, a manager of the networking team at Acme, Inc. is paying extra attention to the specific words he uses as he talks to his team in preparation for the implementation of the network. When referring to transport protocols such as the connection-oriented TCP and the connectionless UDP, the word Bob uses to describe those protocol data units is *segment*.

In discussing the applications that the company will be using over its network, Bob notes that many of these applications will be using TCP at the transport layer. This includes HTTPS for secure web traffic and Simple Mail Transfer Protocol (SMTP) and Internet Access Message Protocol (IMAP) for email services.

The company will use the Secure Shell (SSH) protocol, which also uses TCP at the transport layer, as a secure method to remotely connect to and manage its network devices. A common connectionless UDP protocol is Domain Name System (DNS), which will be used thousands of times a day to translate a friendly name like http://www.pearson.com to an IP address that is reachable over the network. Another protocol based on UDP that will be used often is Dynamic Control Host Protocol (DHCP), which assigns client computers on the network an IP address that is required for sending and receiving Layer 3 packets.

For the traffic on the LAN, the Ethernet cables and electronic signals being sent as bits going over those cables represent Layer 1 from an OSI perspective. On the LAN, they will be using Ethernet technology, and as a result, the Layer 2 frames that are sent on the LAN will be encapsulated and sent as Ethernet Layer 2 frames.

For datagrams being sent across the serial WAN connections provided by the service provider, it is likely that either Point-to-Point Protocol (PPP) or High-Level Data Link Control (HDLC) encapsulation will be used for the Layer 2 frames. On both the LAN and the WAN, at Layer 3 (the network layer), IPv4 will be used for host addressing and defining networks. The same Layer 1, Layer 2, and Layer 3 infrastructure is also capable of transporting IPv6, if desired.

Inside the Layer 3 IP headers, each packet contains the source and destination address, in addition to the information to tell the receiving network device about which Layer 4 transport protocol is encapsulated or carried inside the Layer 3 packet. When a network device receives the packet and opens it up to look at the contents, this process is called *decapsulation*. As the recipient decapsulates and looks at the Layer 4 information, it identifies the application layer protocol or service being used. A segment going to a web server is likely to have a TCP destination port of 80 or 443, depending on whether encryption is being used for a secure connection. A DNS request uses a UDP destination port of 53.

Summary

Here are the main topics covered in this chapter:

- The ISO's OSI reference model consists of seven layers: physical (Layer 1), data link (Layer 2), network (Layer 3), transport (Layer 4), session (Layer 5), presentation (Layer 6), and application (Layer 7). The purpose of each layer is presented, along with examples of technologies present at the individual layers, as it pertains to networking.

- The TCP/IP stack is presented as an alternative model to the OSI reference model. The TCP/IP stack consists of four layers: network interface, Internet, transport, and application. These layers are compared with the seven layers of the OSI model.

- Data encapsulation and decapsulation within the OSI model context are covered.

- This chapter discusses how port numbers are used to associate data at the transport layer with a proper application layer protocol.

Exam Preparation Tasks

Review All the Key Topics

Review the most important topics from this chapter, noted with the Key Topic icon in the outer margin of the page. Table 1-1 lists these key topics and the page number where each is found.

Table 1-1 Key Topics for Chapter 1

Key Topic Element	Description	Page Number
List	Layers of the OSI model	6
Figure 1-3	Protocol data unit (PDU) names	7
Figure 1-4	Layer 1: The physical layer	8
Figure 1-8	Layer 2: The data link layer	12
Figure 1-9	Layer 3: The network layer	15
Figure 1-10	Layer 4: The transport layer	17
Figure 1-11	TCP sliding window	18
Figure 1-12	Layer 5: The session layer	19
Figure 1-13	Layer 6: The presentation layer	20
Figure 1-14	Layer 7: The application layer	21
Figure 1-15	TCP/IP stack	23
Figure 1-16	IPv4 packet format	23
Figure 1-17	TCP segment format	24
Figure 1-18	UDP segment format	25
Figure 1-19	Example: Port numbers and IP addresses	26
Table 1-1	Application layer protocols/applications	29

Define Key Terms

Define the following key terms from this chapter and check your answers in the Glossary:

Open Systems Interconnection (OSI) reference model, protocol data unit (PDU), IP header, TCP header, UDP header, TCP flags, payload, maximum transmission unit (MTU), current state modulation, state transition modulation, cyclic redundancy check (CRC), physical layer, data link layer, network layer, transport layer (OSI model), session layer, presentation layer, application layer (OSI model), network interface layer, Internet layer, transport layer (TCP/IP stack), application layer (TCP/IP stack), time-division multiplexing (TDM), Transmission Control Protocol (TCP), User Datagram Protocol (UDP), TCP/IP stack

Complete Chapter 1 Hands-On Labs in Network+ Simulator Lite

- TCP/IP Protocols and Their Functions
- Network Application Protocols
- OSI Model Layer Functions
- OSI Model Layer and Network Devices

Additional Resources

Troubleshooting with the OSI Model: https://youtu.be/kdFOCleUkVE

The OSI Model Challenge: https://ajsnetworking.com/osiquiz1

Review Questions

The answers to these review questions appear in Appendix A, "Answers to Review Questions."

1. Which layer of the OSI reference model contains the MAC and LLC sublayers?
   a. Network layer
   b. Transport layer
   c. Physical layer
   d. Data link layer

2. Which approach to bandwidth usage consumes all the available frequencies on a medium to transmit data?
   a. Broadband
   b. Baseband
   c. Time-division multiplexing
   d. Simplex

3. Windowing is provided at what layer of the OSI reference model?
   a. Data link layer
   b. Network layer
   c. Transport layer
   d. Physical layer

4. IP addresses reside at which layer of the OSI reference model?

    a. Network layer

    b. Session layer

    c. Data link layer

    d. Transport layer

5. Which of the following is a connectionless transport layer protocol?

    a. IP

    b. TCP

    c. UDP

    d. SIP

6. What setting ultimately controls the size of packets that are moving through the modern network?

    a. TTL

    b. MTU

    c. SSH

    d. CSMA/CD

7. What is the range of well-known TCP and UDP ports?

    a. Below 2048

    b. Below 1024

    c. 16,384–32,768

    d. Above 8192

8. What port number is used by HTTPS?

    a. 80

    b. 443

    c. 69

    d. 23

9. What value is decremented by one for each router hop on the network?

    a. Count

    b. Type

    c. TTL

    d. Dead timer

10. Windowing is a technology that applies to which transport layer protocol?

   a. UDP

   b. FTP

   c. ICMP

   d. TCP

11. What happens to data as it moves from the upper layers to the lower layers of the OSI model on a host system?

   a. The data moves from the physical layer to the application layer.

   b. The data is encapsulated with a header at the beginning and a trailer at the end.

   c. The header and trailer are stripped off through decapsulation.

   d. The data is sent in groups of segments that require two acknowledgments.

12. Which layer of the OSI reference model is responsible for ensuring that frames do not exceed the maximum transmission unit (MTU) of the physical media?

   a. Network layer

   b. Transport layer

   c. Physical layer

   d. Data link layer

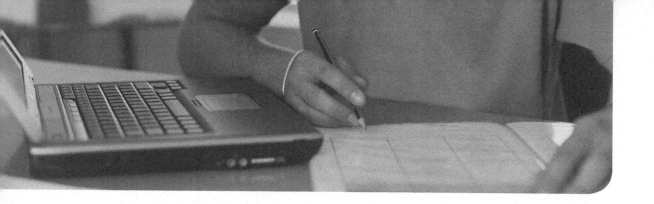

This chapter covers the following topics related to Objective 1.2 (Explain the characteristics of network topologies and network types) of the CompTIA Network+ N10-008 certification exam:

- Mesh
- Star/hub-and-spoke
- Bus
- Ring
- Hybrid
- Network types and characteristics
  - Peer-to-peer
  - Client-server
  - Local area network (LAN)
  - Metropolitan area network (MAN)
  - Wide area network (WAN)
  - Wireless local area network (WLAN)
  - Personal area network (PAN)
  - Campus area network (CAN)
  - Storage area network (SAN)
  - Software-defined wide area network (SDWAN)
  - Multiprotocol label switching (MPLS)
- Multipoint generic routing encapsulation (mGRE)
- Service-related entry point
  - Demarcation point
  - Smartjack
- Virtual network concepts
  - vSwitch
  - Virtual network interface card (vNIC)
  - Network function virtualization (NFV)
  - Hypervisor
- Provider links
  - Satellite
  - Digital subscriber line (DSL)
  - Cable
  - Leased line
  - Metro-optical

CHAPTER 2

Network Topologies and Types

What comes to mind when you think of a computer network? Is it the Internet? Is it email? Is it the wireless connection that lets you print to your printer from your laptop? Is it the smart thermostat and lights in your home?

Whatever your current perception of a computer network, this chapter just might help you expand your thought process in this regard. Be aware that although you think of computer networks as interconnecting computers, today's computer networks interconnect a variety of devices in addition to just computers. Examples include game consoles, video-surveillance devices, IP-based telephones, tablets, and smartphones. Therefore, throughout this book, think of the term *computer network* as being synonymous with the more generic term *network*, because these terms are used interchangeably.

The goal of this chapter is to acquaint you with the purpose of a network and help you categorize a given network based on criteria such as geography, topology, and the location of the network's resources.

Foundation Topics

Defining a Network

The movie *Field of Dreams* featured the statement "If you build it, he will come." This statement most certainly applies to the evolution of network-based services in modern-day networks. Computer networks are no longer relegated to allowing a group of computers to access a common set of files stored on a computer chosen as a *file server*. Instead, with the building of high-speed, highly redundant networks, network architects are seeing the wisdom of placing a variety of traffic types on a single network. Examples include voice and video, in addition to data. As you will learn in this chapter, the Internet of Things (IoT) means that just about everything wants to join your network, from the lights in your home to many of your household appliances.

One could argue that a network is the sum of its parts. So, as you begin your study of networking, you should start to gain a basic understanding of fundamental networking components, including such entities as the client, server, hub, switch, and router, as well as the media used to interconnect these devices.

The Purpose of Networks

The basic purpose of a network is to make connections. These connections might be between a PC and a printer or between a laptop and the Internet, as just a couple of examples. However, the true value of a network comes from the traffic flowing over those connections. Consider a sampling of applications that can travel over a network's connections:

- File sharing between two computers

- Video chatting between computers located in different parts of the world

- Surfing the Web (for example, to use social media sites, watch streaming video, listen to an Internet radio station, or do research for a school term paper)

- Instant messaging (IM) between computers with IM software installed

- Email

- Voice over IP (VoIP), to replace traditional telephony systems

A term given to a network transporting multiple types of traffic (for example, voice, video, and data) is a *converged network*. A converged network might offer significant cost savings to organizations that previously supported separate network infrastructures for voice, data, and video traffic. This convergence also potentially reduces staffing costs because only a single network needs to be supported, rather than separate networks for separate traffic types.

Network Types and Characteristics

As you might be sensing at this point, not all networks look the same. They vary in many ways. One criterion by which networks are classified is how geographically dispersed the network's components are. For example, a network might interconnect devices within an office, or a network might interconnect a database at a corporate headquarters location with a remote sales office on the opposite side of the globe.

Based on the geographic dispersion of network components, you can classify networks into various categories, including the following:

- *Local area network (LAN)*

- *Wide area network (WAN)*

- *Wireless local area network (WLAN)*

- *Storage area network (SAN)*

- *Campus area network (CAN)*

- *Metropolitan area network (MAN)*

- *Personal area network (PAN)*

In addition to discussing these categories, this section also discusses SD-WAN and mGRE technologies, which help create network *overlays*, which permit virtualization of network topologies. The "traditional" hardware and software of the network make up what is termed the *underlay*.

LAN

A LAN interconnects network components within a local area (for example, within a building). Examples of common LAN technologies you are likely to meet include Ethernet (that is, IEEE 802.3) and wireless networks (that is, IEEE 802.11). Figure 2-1 illustrates an example of a LAN.

NOTE IEEE stands for *Institute of Electrical and Electronics Engineers*, which is an internationally recognized standards body.

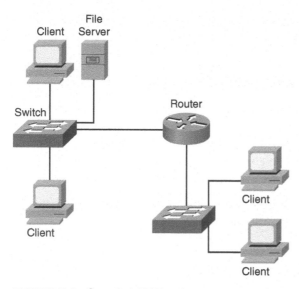

FIGURE 2-1   Sample LAN Topology

WAN

A WAN interconnects network components that are geographically separated. For example, a corporate headquarters might have multiple WAN connections to remote office sites. Multiprotocol Label Switching (MPLS) and Asynchronous Transfer Mode (ATM) are examples of WAN technologies. Figure 2-2 depicts a simple WAN topology, which interconnects two geographically distant locations.

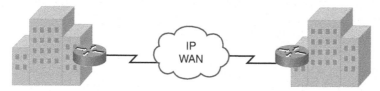

FIGURE 2-2   Sample WAN Topology

WLAN

A local area network made up of wireless networking devices is a wireless local area network (WLAN).

SAN

You can construct a high-speed, highly reliable network for the express purpose of transmitting stored data. This network is called a storage area network (SAN).

Other Categories of Networks

Although LAN and WAN are the most common terms used to categorize computer networks based on geography, other categories include campus area network (CAN), metropolitan area network (MAN), and personal area network (PAN).

CAN

The first time I discovered a CAN-type topology was at a major university. The university covered several square miles and had several dozen buildings. Many of these buildings were running individual LANs, and these building-centric LANs were interconnected. The interconnection of these LANs created another network type: a campus area network (CAN). Besides being common on university campuses, CANs are often used in industrial parks and business parks.

MAN

More widespread than a CAN and less widespread than a WAN, a metropolitan area network (MAN) interconnects locations scattered throughout a metropolitan area. Imagine, for example, that a business in Chicago has a location near O'Hare Airport, another location near the Navy Pier, and another location in the Willis Tower (previously known as the Sears Tower). If a service provider could interconnect those locations using a high-speed network, such as a 10Gbps (that is, 10 billion bits per second) network, the interconnection of those locations would form a MAN. One example of a MAN technology is Metro Ethernet, which features much higher speeds than the traditional WAN technologies that were used in the past to connect such locations.

PAN

A personal area network (PAN) is a network whose scale is even smaller than a LAN. For example, a connection between a PC and a digital camera via a universal serial bus (USB) cable could be considered a PAN. Another example is a PC connected to an external hard drive via a USB 3.0 or Thunderbolt connection. A PAN, however, is not necessarily a wired connection. A Bluetooth connection between your cell phone and your car's audio system is considered a wireless PAN (WPAN). The main distinction of a PAN is that its range is typically limited to just a few meters.

Software-Defined Wide Area Network (SD-WAN)

Almost every major networking vendor now offers a *software-defined wide area network (SD-WAN)* product. Cisco Systems, for example, currently has two of these solutions in its portfolio: the Cisco SD-WAN that Cisco acquired through the purchase of Viptela and the SD-WAN that is part of Cisco's Meraki acquisition.

An SD-WAN provides a simple policy and profile approach to managing the WAN. It also provides tools that enable new levels of visibility into and control over the use of the varied WAN circuits in the typical enterprise today.

Multiprotocol Label Switching

Multiprotocol Label Switching (MPLS) is growing in popularity as a WAN technology used by service providers. This growth in popularity is due in part to MPLS's capability to support multiple protocols on the same network—for example, an MPLS network can accommodate users connecting via Frame Relay or ATM on the same MPLS backbone—and MPLS's capability to perform traffic engineering (which allows traffic to be dynamically routed within an MPLS cloud, based on current load conditions of specific links and availability of alternate paths).

MPLS inserts a 32-bit header between Layer 2 and Layer 3 headers. Because this header is shimmed between the Layer 2 and Layer 3 headers, it is sometimes referred to as a *shim header*. Also, because the MPLS header resides between the Layer 2 and Layer 3 headers, MPLS is considered to be a Layer 2½ technology.

The 32-bit header contains a 20-bit label that is used to make forwarding decisions within an MPLS cloud. The process of routing MPLS frames through an MPLS cloud is referred to as *label switching*.

Figure 2-3 shows a sample MPLS network. Table 2-1 defines the various MPLS network elements shown in the figure.

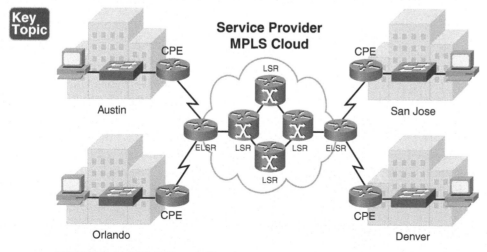

FIGURE 2-3 MPLS Sample Topology

Table 2-1   MPLS Network Elements

Element	Description
CPE	A customer premises equipment (CPE) device resides at a customer site. A router, for example, could be CPE that connects a customer with an MPLS service provider.
CE	A customer edge (CE) router is a customer router that provides the connectivity between the customer network and the service provider network. CE routers use static or dynamic routing protocols but do not run MPLS. The MPLS function occurs in the service provider network.
ELSR	An edge label switch router (ELSR) resides at the edge of an MPLS service provider's cloud and interconnects a service provider to one or more customers.
PE	A provider edge (PE) router is the MPLS service provider's router that connects to the customer router. PE is another name for ELSR.
LSR	A label switch router (LSR) resides as part of a service provider's MPLS cloud and makes frame-forwarding decisions based on labels applied to frames.
P	A provider (P) router is a service provider internal router that doesn't directly interface with the customer routers. A P router is internal to the service provider's network.

An MPLS frame does not maintain the same label throughout the MPLS cloud. Rather, an LSR receives a frame, examines the label on the frame, makes a forwarding decision based on the label, places a new label on the frame, and forwards the frame to the next LSR. This process of label switching is more efficient than routing based on Layer 3 IP addresses. The customer using a provider's network and the MPLS transport across that network is not normally aware of the details of the exact MPLS forwarding that is done by the service provider.

Multipoint Generic Routing Encapsulation (mGRE)

Normally, the flexible GRE encapsulation protocol is a point-to-point type of technology. *Multipoint generic routing encapsulation (mGRE)* variation of GRE is a multipoint technology. In fact, when you create a GRE tunnel, you specify source and destination interfaces for the tunnel. When you create an mGRE tunnel interface, all you specify is the source interface. You do not specify a destination because there are multiple, dynamic peers.

mGRE is one of the key technologies in the Dynamic Multipoint VPN (DMVPN) solution. mGRE makes the tunnels that are formed dynamically between spokes and hubs (and between spokes and spokes). The mGRE tunnels are secured with Internet Protocol Security (IPsec) virtual private network (VPN) technology.

Networks Defined Based on Resource Location

Another way to categorize networks is based on where the network resources reside. For example, a *client/server network* is a collection of PCs all sharing files stored on a centralized server. However, if those PCs had their operating system (for example, Microsoft Windows 10 or macOS) configured for file sharing, they could share files from one another's hard drives. This is referred to as a *peer-to-peer network* because the peers (the PCs in this example) make resources available to other peers. The following sections describe client/server and peer-to-peer networks in more detail.

Client/Server Networks

Figure 2-4 illustrates an example of a **client/server network**, where a dedicated file server gives shared access to files, and a networked printer is available as a resource to the network's clients. Client/server networks are commonly used by businesses. Because resources are found on one or more servers, administration is simpler than administration of network resources on multiple peer devices.

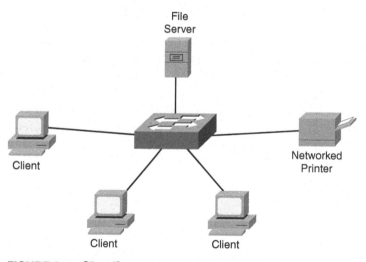

FIGURE 2-4   Client/Server Network Example

The performance of a client/server network can be better than that of a peer-to-peer network because resources can be located on dedicated servers rather than on a PC running a variety of end-user applications. You can simplify backups because fewer locations must be backed up. However, client/server networks come with the extra expense of dedicated server resources. Table 2-2 lists the benefits and drawbacks of client/server networks.

Table 2-2 Characteristics, Benefits, and Drawbacks of Client/Server Networks

Characteristics	Benefits	Drawbacks
Client devices (for example, PCs) share a common set of resources (for example, file or print resources) located on one or more dedicated servers.	Client/server networks can easily scale, which might require the purchase of additional client licenses.	Because multiple clients might rely on a single server for their resources, the single server can become a single point of failure in the network.
Resource sharing is made possible via dedicated server hardware and network operating systems.	Administration is simplified because parameters such as file-sharing permissions and other security settings can be administered on a server as opposed to on multiple clients.	Client/server networks can cost more than peer-to-peer networks. For example, client/server networks might require the purchase of dedicated server hardware and a network OS with an appropriate number of licenses.

NOTE A server in a client/server network could be a computer running a network operating system (NOS) such as Linux Server or one of the Microsoft Windows Server operating systems. Alternatively, a server might be a host making its file system available to remote clients via the Network File System (NFS) service, which was originally developed by Sun Microsystems.

NOTE A variant of the traditional server in a client/server network, where the server provides shared file access, is network-attached storage (NAS). A NAS device is a mass storage device that attaches directly to a network. Rather than running an advanced NOS, a NAS device usually makes files available to network clients via a service such as NFS.

Peer-to-Peer Networks

Peer-to-peer networks allow interconnected devices (for example, PCs) to share their resources with one another. Those resources could be, for example, files or printers. As an example of a peer-to-peer network, consider Figure 2-5, where each of the peers can share files on its own hard drive, and one of the peers has a directly attached printer that can be shared with the other peers in the network.

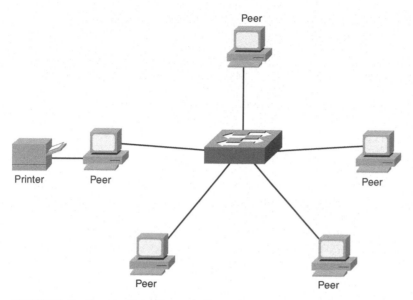

FIGURE 2-5   Peer-to-Peer Network Example

Peer-to-peer networks tend to be used in smaller businesses and in homes. The popularity of peer-to-peer networks is fueled in part by client operating systems that support file and print sharing. Scalability for peer-to-peer networks is a concern, however. Specifically, as the number of devices (that is, peers) increases, the administration burden increases. For example, a network administrator might have to manage file permissions on multiple devices, as opposed to on a single server. Table 2-3 lists the characteristics, benefits, and drawbacks of peer-to-peer networks.

Key Topic

Table 2-3   Characteristics, Benefits, and Drawbacks of a Peer-to-Peer Network

Characteristics	Benefits	Drawbacks
Client devices (for example, PCs) share their resources (for example, file and printer resources) with other client devices.	Peer-to-peer networks can be installed easily because resource sharing is made possible by the clients' operating systems, and knowledge of advanced networking operating systems is not required.	Scalability is limited because of the increased administration burden of managing multiple clients.
Resource sharing is made available through the clients' operating systems.	Peer-to-peer networks usually cost less than client/server networks because there is no requirement for dedicated server resources or advanced NOS software.	Performance might not be as strong as in a client/server network because the devices providing network resources might be performing other tasks not related to resource sharing (for example, word processing).

> **NOTE**   Some networks have characteristics of both peer-to-peer and client/server
> networks. For example, all PCs in a company might point to a centralized server for
> accessing a shared database in a client/server topology. However, these PCs might
> simultaneously share files and printers with one another in a peer-to-peer topology.
> Such a network, which has a mixture of client/server and peer-to-peer characteristics,
> is called a *hybrid* network.

Networks Defined by Topology

In addition to classifying networks based on the geographic placement of their
components, another approach to classifying a network is to use the network's topology. Looks can be deceiving, however. You need to be able to distinguish between a
physical topology and a logical topology.

Physical Versus Logical Topology

Even if a network appears to be a star topology (that is, where the network components all connect to a centralized device, such as a switch), the traffic might be
flowing in a circular pattern through all the network components attached to the
centralized device. The actual traffic flow determines the *logical topology*, whereas
the way components are physically interconnected determines the *physical topology*.

For example, consider Figure 2-6, which shows a collection of computers connected to
a Token Ring media access unit (MAU). From a quick inspection of Figure 2-6, you can
conclude that the devices are physically connected in a star topology, where the connected
devices radiate out from a centralized aggregation point (the MAU in this example).

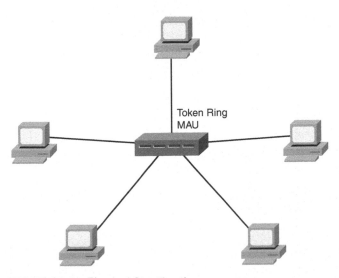

Token Ring
MAU

FIGURE 2-6   Physical Star Topology

Now contrast the physical topology in Figure 2-6 with the logical topology illustrated in Figure 2-7. Although you can see that the computers physically connect to a centralized MAU, when you examine the flow of traffic through (or in this case, around) the network, you see that the traffic flow actually loops around and around the network. The traffic flow dictates how to classify a network's logical topology. In this instance, the logical topology is a *ring topology* because the traffic circulates around the network as if circulating around a ring.

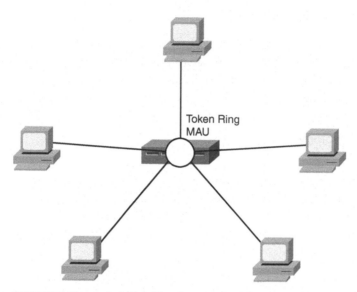

FIGURE 2-7   Logical Ring Topology

NOTE   Before you run out and try to purchase a Token Ring network for your LAN, keep in mind that you'll only see this technology in networking museums now!

Bus Topology

A *bus topology*, as depicted in Figure 2-8, typically has a cable running through the area that requires connectivity, and devices that need to connect to the network tap into this cable. Early Ethernet networks relied on bus topologies.

A network tap might be in the form of a T connector (used in older 10BASE2 networks) or a vampire tap (used in older 10BASE5 networks). Figure 2-9 shows an example of a T connector.

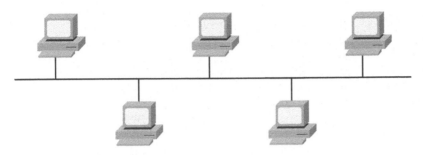

FIGURE 2-8 Bus Topology

FIGURE 2-9 T Connector

A bus and all devices connected to that bus make up a *network segment*. A single network segment is a single collision domain, which means that all devices connected to the bus might try to gain access to the bus at the same time, resulting in an error condition known as a *collision*. Table 2-4 shows some of the primary characteristics, benefits, and drawbacks of a bus topology.

Key Topic

Table 2-4 Characteristics, Benefits, and Drawbacks of a Bus Topology

Characteristics	Benefits	Drawbacks
One cable is used per network segment.	Less cable is needed to install a bus topology than is required with other topologies.	Because a single cable is used per network segment, the cable is potentially a single point of failure.

Characteristics	Benefits	Drawbacks
To support appropriate electrical characteristics of the cable, the cable requires a terminator (of a specific resistance) at each end of the cable.	Depending on the media used by the bus, a bus topology can be less expensive than other topologies.	Troubleshooting a bus topology can be difficult because problem isolation might require inspection of multiple network taps to make sure they either have a device connected or are properly terminated.
Bus topologies were popular in early Ethernet networks.	Installation of a network based on a bus topology is easier than with some other topologies, which might require extra wiring to be installed.	Adding devices to a bus might cause an outage for other users on the bus.
Network components tap directly into the cable via a connector such as a T connector or a vampire tap.	—	An error condition existing on one device on the bus can affect performance of other devices on the bus.
—	—	A bus topology does not scale well because all devices share the bandwidth available on the bus. Also, if two devices on the bus simultaneously request access to the bus, an error condition results.

Ring Topology

Figure 2-10 provides an example of a ***ring topology***, where traffic flows in a circular fashion around a closed network loop (that is, a ring). Typically, a ring topology sends data, in a single direction, to each connected device in turn, until the intended destination receives the data. Token Ring networks relied on a ring topology.

Token Ring was not the only popular ring-based topology popular in networks in the 1990s. Fiber Distributed Data Interface (FDDI) was another variant of a ring-based topology. Most FDDI networks (which, as the name suggests, have fiber optics as the media) used not just one ring but two. These two rings sent data in opposite directions, resulting in *counter-rotating rings*. One benefit of counter-rotating rings was that if a fiber broke, the stations on each side of the break could interconnect their two rings to create a single ring capable of reaching all stations on the ring.

Because a ring topology allows devices on the ring to take turns transmitting on the ring, contention for media access was not a problem, as it was for a bus topology. If a network had a single ring, however, the ring was potentially a single point of failure. If the ring was broken at any point, data stopped flowing. Table 2-5 lists some of the primary characteristics, benefits, and drawbacks of a ring topology.

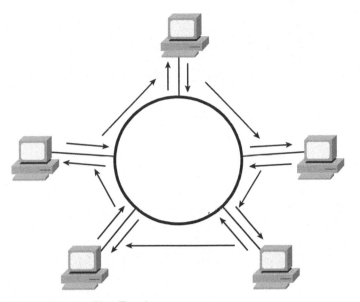

FIGURE 2-10 Ring Topology

Table 2-5 Characteristics, Benefits, and Drawbacks of a Ring Topology

Characteristics	Benefits	Drawbacks
Devices are interconnected by connecting to a single ring or, in some cases (such as with FDDI), a dual ring.	A dual-ring topology adds a layer of fault tolerance. Therefore, if a cable break occurs, connectivity to all devices can be restored.	A break in a ring when a single ring topology is used results in a network outage for all devices connected to the ring.
Each device on a ring includes both a receiver (for the incoming cable) and a transmitter (for the outgoing cable).	Troubleshooting is simplified in the event of a cable break because each device on a ring contains a repeater. When the repeater on the far side of a cable break does not receive any data within a certain amount of time, it reports an error condition, typically in the form of an indicator light on a network interface card (NIC).	Rings have scalability limitations. Specifically, a ring has a maximum length and a maximum number of attached stations. Once either of these limits is exceeded, a single ring might need to be divided into two interconnected rings. A network maintenance window might need to be scheduled to perform this ring division.
Each device on the ring repeats the signal it receives.	—	Because a ring must be a complete loop, the amount of cable required for a ring is usually higher than the amount of cable required for a bus topology serving the same number of devices.

Star Topology

Figure 2-11 shows a sample *star topology* with a hub at the center of the topology and a collection of clients individually connected to the hub. Notice that a star topology has a central point from which all attached devices radiate. In LANs in the early 1990s, that centralized device was typically a hub. Modern networks, however, usually have a switch located at the center of the star.

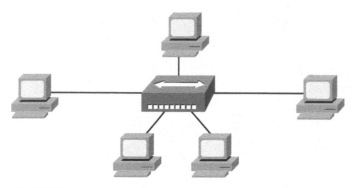

FIGURE 2-11   Star Topology

The star topology is the most popular physical LAN topology in use today, with an Ethernet switch at the center of the star and unshielded twisted-pair (UTP) cable used to connect from the switch ports to clients.

Table 2-6 identifies some of the primary characteristics, benefits, and drawbacks of a star topology.

Key Topic

Table 2-6   Characteristics, Benefits, and Drawbacks of a Star Topology

Characteristics	Benefits	Drawbacks
Devices have independent connections to a central device (for example, a hub or a switch).	A cable break impacts only the device connected via the broken cable and not the entire topology.	More cable is required for a star topology than for bus or ring topologies because each device requires its own cable to connect back to the central device.
Star topologies are commonly used with Ethernet technologies (described in Chapter 3).	Troubleshooting is relatively simple because a central device in the star topology acts as the aggregation point for all the connected devices.	Installation can take longer for a star topology than for a bus or ring topology because more cable runs must be installed.

Hub-and-Spoke Topology

When interconnecting multiple sites (for example, multiple corporate locations) via WAN links, a *hub-and-spoke topology* may be used, with a WAN link from each remote site (that is, a *spoke site*) to the main site (that is, the *hub site*). This approach, an example of which is shown in Figure 2-12, is similar to the star topology used in LANs.

With WAN links, a service provider is paid a recurring fee for each link. Therefore, a hub-and-spoke topology helps minimize WAN expenses by not directly connecting any two spoke locations. If two spoke locations need to communicate with each other, their communication is sent via the hub location. Table 2-7 describes the characteristics, benefits, and drawbacks of a hub-and-spoke WAN topology.

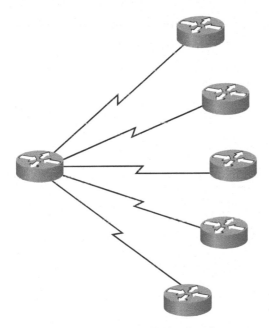

FIGURE 2-12   Hub-and-Spoke Topology

Table 2-7   Characteristics, Benefits, and Drawbacks of a Hub-and-Spoke WAN Topology

Characteristics	Benefits	Drawbacks
Each remote site (that is, a spoke) connects to a main site (that is, the hub) via a WAN link.	Costs are reduced (as compared to with a full-mesh or partial-mesh topology) because a minimal number of links is used.	Suboptimal routes must be used between remote sites because all intersite communication must travel via the main site.

Characteristics	Benefits	Drawbacks
Communication between two remote sites travels through the hub site.	Adding one or more additional sites is easy (compared to in a full-mesh or partial-mesh topology) because only one link needs to be added per site.	Because all remote sites converge on the main site, this hub site is potentially a single point of failure.
—	—	Because each remote site is reachable by only a single WAN link, the hub-and-spoke topology lacks redundancy.

Full-Mesh Topology

Whereas a hub-and-spoke WAN topology lacks redundancy and suffers from suboptimal routes, a *full-mesh topology*, as shown in Figure 2-13, directly connects every site to every other site.

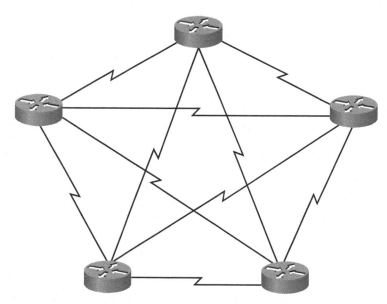

FIGURE 2-13   Full-Mesh Topology

Because each site connects directly to every other site, an optimal path can be selected, as opposed to relaying traffic via another site. Also, a full-mesh topology is highly fault tolerant. By inspecting Figure 2-13, you can see that multiple links in the topology could be lost, and every site might still be able to connect to every other site. Table 2-8 summarizes the characteristics, benefits, and drawbacks of a full-mesh topology.

Key Topic

Table 2-8 Characteristics, Benefits, and Drawbacks of a Full-Mesh WAN Topology

Characteristics	Benefits	Drawbacks
Every site has a direct WAN connection to every other site.	An optimal route exists between any two sites.	A full-mesh network can be difficult and expensive to scale because the addition of one new site requires a new WAN link between the new site and every other existing site.
The number of required WAN connections can be calculated with the formula $w = n \times (n - 1) / 2$, where w = the number of WAN links and n = the number of sites. For example, a network with 10 sites would require 45 WAN connections to form a fully meshed network: $45 = 10 \times (10 - 1) / 2$.	A full-mesh network is fault tolerant because one or more links can be lost, and reachability between all sites might still be maintained.	—
—	Troubleshooting a full-mesh network is relatively easy because each link is independent of the other links.	—

Partial-Mesh Topology

A partial-mesh WAN topology, as depicted in Figure 2-14, is a hybrid of the previously described hub-and-spoke topology and full-mesh topology. Specifically, a *partial-mesh topology* can be designed to offer an optimal route between selected sites while avoiding the expense of interconnecting every site to every other site.

When designing a partial-mesh topology, a network designer must consider network traffic patterns and strategically add links interconnecting sites that have higher volumes of traffic between themselves. Table 2-9 highlights the characteristics, benefits, and drawbacks of a partial-mesh topology.

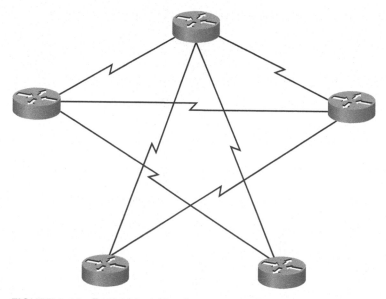

FIGURE 2-14   Partial-Mesh Topology

Table 2-9   Characteristics, Benefits, and Drawbacks of a Partial-Mesh Topology

Characteristics	Benefits	Drawbacks
Selected sites (that is, sites with frequent intersite communication) are interconnected via direct links, whereas sites that have less-frequent communication can communicate via another site.	A partial-mesh topology provides optimal routes between selected sites with higher intersite traffic volumes while avoiding the expense of interconnecting every site to every other site.	A partial-mesh topology is less fault tolerant than a full-mesh topology.
A partial-mesh topology uses fewer links than a full-mesh topology and more links than a hub-and-spoke topology for interconnecting the same number of sites.	A partial-mesh topology is more redundant than a hub-and-spoke topology.	A partial-mesh topology is more expensive than a hub-and-spoke topology.

NOTE   There are plenty of network topologies today that use a variety of different design approaches. This often results in several approaches being used in one solution. We often term this a *hybrid* approach.

Service-Related Entry Points

An important aspect of the network topology is the *service-related entry point*. Two possibilities of which you should be aware for the Network+ exam are the demarcation point and the smartjack.

A *demarcation point* (also known as a *demarc* or a *demarc extension*) is the point in a telephone network where the maintenance responsibility passes from a telephone company to the subscriber (unless the subscriber has purchased inside wiring maintenance). This demarc is typically located in a box mounted to the outside of a customer's building (for example, a residential home). This box is called a *network interface device* (*NID*).

A *smartjack* is a type of network interface device that adds circuitry. This circuitry adds such features as converting between framing formats on a digital circuit (for example, a T1 circuit), supporting remote diagnostics, and regenerating a digital signal.

Virtual Network Concepts

A major data center paradigm shift is underway. This shift is away from a company having its own data center (with its raised flooring and large air conditioning system) containing multiple physical servers, each of which offer a specific service (for example, email, DNS services, or Microsoft Active Directory).

Virtual Servers

The computing power available in a single high-end server is often sufficient to handle the tasks of multiple independent servers. With the advent of virtualization, multiple servers (which might be running different operating systems) can run in virtual server instances on one physical device. For example, a single high-end server might be running an instance of a Microsoft Windows Server providing Microsoft Active Directory (AD) services to an enterprise, while simultaneously running an instance of a Linux server acting as a corporate web server, and at the same time acting as a Oracle Solaris UNIX server providing corporate DNS services. Figure 2-15 illustrates the concept of a virtual server. Although the virtual server in the figure uses a single NIC to connect to an Ethernet switch, many virtual server platforms support multiple NICs. Having multiple NICs offers increased throughput and load balancing.

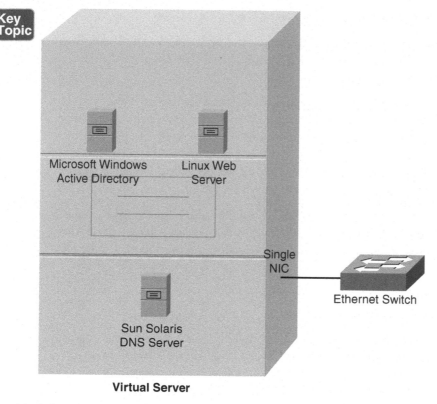

Virtual Server

FIGURE 2-15   Virtual Server

NOTE   Although the example in Figure 2-15 uses a Linux-based web server, web servers can run on a variety of operating system platforms. For example, Microsoft Windows servers support a web server application called *Internet Information Services (IIS)*, which was previously known as Internet Information Server.

Virtualization is possible with servers thanks to specialized software called a hypervisor. The *hypervisor* takes physical hardware and abstracts it for the virtual server. The extent of virtualization is amazing, and even the NIC of each virtual server can be represented virtually (*virtual network interface card [vNIC]*). Figure 2-16 shows some of the configuration options for a vNIC in a virtualized environment. Notice that technologies such as VLANs and QoS (in this case, bandwidth management) are still possible in the virtualized world.

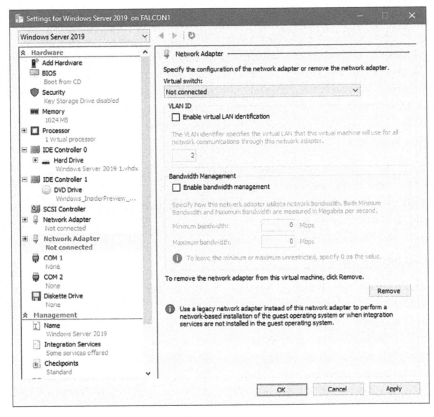

FIGURE 2-16   Configuring a vNIC

The networks and systems supporting virtual servers also commonly have network-attached storage (NAS), where disk storage is delivered as a service over the network. A technology for network storage is IP-based Small Computer System Interface (iSCSI). With iSCSI, a client using the storage is referred to as an *initiator*, and the system providing the iSCSI storage is called the iSCSI *target*. The networks supporting iSCSI are often configured to support larger-than-normal frame sizes, referred to as *jumbo frames*.

Fibre Channel is another technology that can deliver storage services over a network. Thanks to high-speed Ethernet options today, you can even configure Fibre Channel over Ethernet (FCoE) to run a unified network for your SAN and non-storage-data traffic.

NOTE   A less commonly encountered communication technology, InfiniBand (IB), permits high-speed, low-latency communications between supercomputers.

Virtual Routers and Firewalls

Most of the vendors that create physical routers and firewalls also have an offering that includes virtualized routers and firewalls. The benefit of using a virtualized firewall or router is that the same features of routing and security can be available in the virtual environment as in the physical environment. As part of interfacing with virtual networks, virtual network adapters can be used. For connectivity between the virtual world and the physical one, physical interfaces can be used to connect to the logical virtual interfaces.

Virtualization is pervasive in networking today. In fact, virtualization is now used to implement almost all network functionality. There is actually a term for this approach: *network function virtualization (NFV)*. NFV can include security, storage, compute, and monitoring services.

Virtual Switches (vSwitches)

One potential trade-off you make with the previously described virtual server scenario is that all servers belong to the same IP subnet, which could have Quality of Service (QoS) and security implications. If these server instances ran on separate physical devices, they could be attached to different ports on an Ethernet switch. These switch ports could belong to different VLANs, which could place each server in a different broadcast domain.

Fortunately, some virtual servers allow you to still have Layer 2 control (for example, VLAN separation and filtering). This Layer 2 control is made possible by the virtual server not only virtualizing instances of servers but also virtualizing a Layer 2 switch. Figure 2-17 depicts a virtual switch (*vSwitch*). Notice that the servers logically reside on separate VLANs, and frames from those servers are appropriately tagged when traveling over a trunk to the attached Ethernet switch.

Figure 2-18 shows just how easy it is to configure a virtual switch in a network today. This is an example of the Hyper-V management software made available by Microsoft.

Virtual Desktops

Key Topic

Another emerging virtualization technology is virtual desktops. Today's users are more mobile than ever before, and they need access to information traditionally stored on their office computers' hard drives from a variety of other locations. For example, a user might be at an airport using their smartphone and need access to a document they created on their office computer. With virtual desktops, a user's data is stored in a data center rather than on an office computer's hard drive. By providing authentication credentials, the user can establish a secure connection between the centralized repository of user data and their device, as shown in Figure 2-19, thus allowing the user to remotely access the desired document.

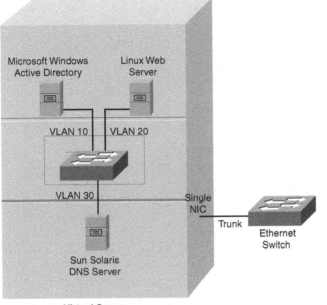

Virtual Server

FIGURE 2-17   Virtual Server with a vSwitch

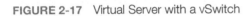

FIGURE 2-18   Configuring a Virtual Switch

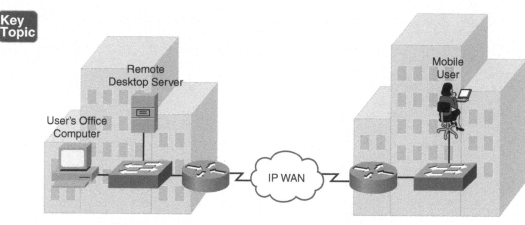

FIGURE 2-19   Virtual Desktop Topology

Other Virtualization Solutions

Although the previously discussed virtualization technologies—that is, virtual servers, virtual switches, and virtual desktops—are described as residing at a corporate location (that is, *on-site*), some service providers offer *off-site* options. Specifically, if a service provider's customer did not want to house and maintain its own data center, these virtualization technologies could be located at a service provider's data center, and the customer could be billed based on usage patterns. Such a service provider offering is called *network as a service* (NaaS), implying that network features can be provided by a service provider, just as a telephony service provider offers access to the public switched telephone network (PSTN), and an ISP offers access to the public Internet.

Provider Links

One type of network categorization is based on the provider link. There are many options here, including satellite, DSL, cable, and SONET.

Satellite

Many rural locations lack the option of connecting to an IP WAN or to the Internet via physical media (for example, a DSL modem or a broadband cable modem connection). For such locations, a *satellite* WAN connection, as illustrated in Figure 2-20, might be an option.

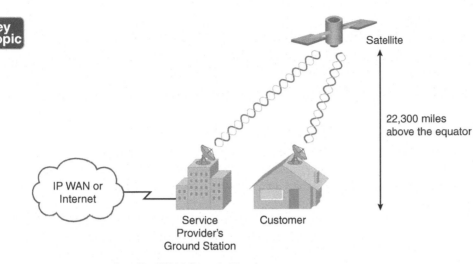

FIGURE 2-20 Satellite WAN Sample Topology

Most satellites used for WAN connectivity are in orbit above the earth's equator, about 22,300 miles high. Therefore, a customer in North America, for example, with a clear view of the southern sky would be able to install a satellite dish and establish a line-of-sight communication path with the orbiting satellite. The satellite would then relay transmissions back and forth between the customer's site and the service provider's ground station. The ground station could then provide connectivity, via physical media, to an IP WAN or to the Internet.

Two significant design considerations need to be taken into account:

- **Delay:** Radio waves travel at the speed of light, which is 186,000 miles per second, or 3×10^8 meters per second. This speed is specifically the speed of light (and radio waves) in a vacuum; however, for the purposes of this discussion, assume that these known values, even though, technically, the speed of light (and radio waves) is a bit slower when traveling through air than when traveling through a vacuum. Although these are fast speeds, consider the distance between a customer and the satellite. If a customer were located 2000 miles north of the equator, the approximate distance between the customer site and the satellite could be calculated using the Pythagorean theorem: $d^2 = 2000^2 + 22{,}300^2$. Solving the equation for d, which is the distance between the customer and the satellite, yields a result of approximately 22,390 miles.

  A transmission from a customer to a destination on the Internet (or an IP WAN) would have to travel from the customer to the satellite, from the satellite to the ground station, and then out to the Internet (or IP WAN). The propagation delay alone introduced by bouncing a signal off the satellite is approximately 241 ms—that is, $(22,390 \times 2) / 186,000 = .241$ seconds $= 241$ ms). In addition, there are other delay components, such as processing delay (by the satellite and other networking devices), making the one-way delay greater than one-fourth of a second and, therefore, the round-trip delay greater than one-half of a second. Such delays are not conducive to latency-sensitive applications such as voice over IP (VoIP).

- **Sensitivity to weather conditions:** Because communication between a customer's satellite dish and an orbiting satellite must travel through the earth's atmosphere, weather conditions can impede communications. For example, if a thunderstorm is near the customer location, that customer might temporarily lose connectivity with their satellite.

Based on these design considerations, even though satellite WAN technology offers tremendous flexibility in terms of geographic location, more terrestrial-based solutions are preferred.

Digital Subscriber Line

A provider link that used to be commonplace in many residential and small business locations is ***digital subscriber line (DSL).*** *DSL installations are becoming more and more rare, but they do still exist. For example, I still rely on one that acts as a backup WAN circuit in my small office/home office (SOHO) environment.*

DSL is a group of technologies that provide high-speed data transmission over existing telephone wiring. DSL has several variants that differ in data rates and distance limitations:

- **Asymmetric DSL (ADSL):** ADSL is a popular Internet-access solution for residential locations. Figure 2-21 shows a sample ADSL topology. Note that ADSL allows an existing analog telephone to share the same line used for data for simultaneous transmission of voice and data.

  Also notice in Figure 2-21 that the maximum distance from a DSL modem to a DSL access multiplexer (DSLAM) is 18,000 feet. This limitation stems from a procedure telephone companies have used for decades to change the impedance of telephone lines.

  Here is a brief history: If wires in a telephone cable run side-by-side for several thousand feet, capacitance builds up in the line (which can cause echo). To counteract this capacitance, after 18,000 feet of cable, telephone companies insert a *load coil*, which adds inductance to the line. Electrically speaking, inductance is the opposite of capacitance. So, by adding a load coil, much of the built-up capacitance in a telephone cable is reduced. However, ADSL signals cannot cross a load coil, so there is a 18,000-foot distance limitation for ADSL.

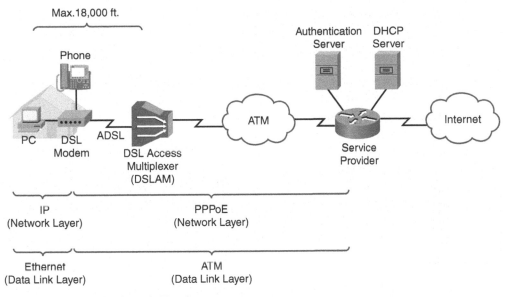

FIGURE 2-21   ADSL Sample Topology

Figure 2-21 also shows how a telephone line leaving a residence terminates on a DSLAM. A DSLAM acts as an aggregation point for multiple connections, and it connects via an ATM network back to a service provider's router. The service provider authenticates user credentials, given via Point-to-Point Protocol over Ethernet (PPPoE), using an authentication server. Also, the service provider has a DHCP server to hand out IP address information to end-user devices (for example, a PC or a wireless router connected to a DSL modem).

The term *asymmetric* in asymmetric DSL indicates that the upstream and downstream speeds can be different. Typically, downstream speeds are greater than upstream speeds in an ADSL connection.

The theoretical maximum downstream speed for an ADSL connection is 8Mbps, and the maximum upstream speed is 1.544Mbps (the speed of a T1 circuit).

- **Symmetric DSL (SDSL):** Whereas ADSL has asymmetric (unequal) upstream and downstream speeds, by definition, SDSL has symmetric (equal) upstream and downstream speeds. Another distinction between ADSL and SDSL is that SDSL does not allow simultaneous voice and data on the same phone line. Therefore, SDSL is less popular in residential installations because an additional phone line is required for data. Although service providers vary, a typical maximum upstream/downstream data rate for an SDSL connection is 1.168Mbps. Also, SDSL connections are usually limited to a maximum distance of 12,000 feet between a DSL modem and its DSLAM.

- **Very High Bit-Rate DSL (VDSL):** VDSL boasts a much higher bandwidth capacity than ADSL or SDSL, with a common downstream limit of 52Mbps and a limit of 12Mbps for upstream traffic.

  VDSL's distance limitation is 4000 feet of telephone cable between a cable modem and a DSLAM. This constraint might seem too stringent for many potential VDSL subscribers, based on their proximity to their closest telephone central office (CO). However, service providers and telephone companies offering VDSL service often extend their fiber-optic network into their surrounding communities. This allows VDSL gateways to be located in multiple communities. The 4000 feet limitation then becomes a distance limitation between a DSL modem and the nearest VDSL gateway, thus increasing the number of potential VDSL subscribers.

Cable Modem

Cable television companies have a well-established and wide-reaching infrastructure for television programming. This infrastructure might contain both coaxial and fiber-optic cabling. Such an infrastructure is called a *hybrid fiber-coax* (*HFC*) distribution network. These networks can designate specific frequency ranges for upstream and downstream data transmission. The device located in a residence (or a business) that can receive and transmit in those data frequency ranges is known as a *cable modem*, as illustrated in Figure 2-22.

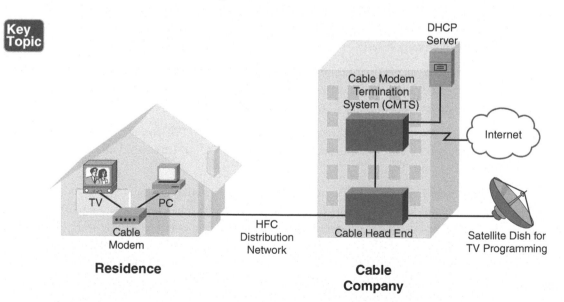

FIGURE 2-22   Cable Modem Sample Topology

The frequency ranges typically given for upstream and downstream data are as follows:

- **Upstream data frequencies:** 5MHz to 42MHz

- **Downstream data frequencies:** 50MHz to 860MHz

Although the theoretical maximum upstream/downstream bandwidth limits are greater (and are dependent on the HFC distribution network in use), most upstream speeds are limited to around 20Mbps, with downstream speeds limited to around 200Mbps. As HFC distribution networks continue to evolve, greater bandwidth capacities will be available. The current theoretical maximums are 1Gbps upstream and 10Gbps downstream. In my SOHO, for example, the main WAN connection using cable modem technology offers 300Mbps down and 100Mbps up. Of course, I pay extra for these faster speeds. As I write this, my service provider is trying to convince me to upgrade (and pay more) for 400Mbps download speeds and 400Mbps upload speeds.

The frequencies dedicated to data transmission are specified by a Data Over Cable Service Interface Specification (DOCSIS) version. Although DOCSIS is an international standard, European countries use their own set of frequency ranges, known as *Euro-DOCSIS*.

Leased Line

Often referred to as a dedicated leased line, a ***leased line*** is typically a *point-to-point* connection interconnecting two sites. All the bandwidth on that dedicated leased line is available to those sites. This means that, unlike with a packet-switched connection, the bandwidth of a dedicated leased line connection does not need to be shared among multiple service provider customers.

WAN technologies used with dedicated leased lines include digital circuits, such as T1, E1, T3, and E3. These circuits can use multiplexing technology to simultaneously carry multiple conversations in different 64Kbps channels. A single 64Kbps channel is called a *Digital Signal 0 (DS0)*. When one of these circuits comes into your location, it terminates on a device called a channel service unit/data service unit (CSU/DSU). Also, be aware that a common Layer 2 protocol used on dedicated leased lines is Point-to-Point Protocol (PPP). A common connection type used to connect to a CSU/DSU is an RJ-48C, which looks like an RJ-45(Ethernet) connector.

> **NOTE** High-Level Data Link Control (HDLC) is another protocol used on dedicated leased lines, though it is less common than PPP. HDLC lacks many of the features of PPP, and in its standards-based implementation, it can only support a single Layer 3 protocol on a circuit. However, Cisco has its own HDLC implementation in which the HDLC header has a protocol field, thus allowing the simultaneous transmission of multiple Layer 3 protocols.

T1

T1 circuits were originally used in telephony networks, with the intent of one voice conversation being carried in a single channel (that is, a single DS0). A T1 circuit is composed of 24 DS0s, which is called a *Digital Signal 1 (DS1)*. The bandwidth of a T1 circuit is 1.544Mbps:

- The size of a T1 frame = 193 bits (that is, 24 channels × 8 bits per channel + 1 framing bit = 193 bits).

- The *Nyquist theorem* needs 8000 samples to be sent per second for a voice conversation (that is, a rate at least twice the highest frequency of 4000Hz).

- Total bandwidth = 193-bit frames × 8000 samples per second = 1.544Mbps.

In a T1 environment, more than one frame is sent at once. Here are two popular approaches to grouping these frames:

- **Super Frame (SF):** Combines 12 standard 193-bit frames into a *super frame*.

- **Extended Super Frame (ESF):** Combines 24 standard 193-bit frames into an *extended super frame*.

T1 circuits are popular in North America and Japan.

E1

An E1 circuit contains 32 channels, in contrast to the 24 channels on a T1 circuit. Only 30 of those 32 channels, however, can transmit data (or voice or video). Specifically, the first of those 32 channels is reserved for framing and synchronization, and the seventeenth channel is reserved for signaling (that is, setting up, maintaining, and tearing down a call).

Because an E1 circuit has more DS0s than a T1, it has a higher bandwidth capacity. Specifically, an E1 has a bandwidth capacity of 2.048Mbps (8000 samples per second, as required by the Nyquist theorem, and 8 bits per sample × 32 channels = 2,048,000 bits per second).

Unlike a T1 circuit, an E1 circuit does not group frames in an SF or an ESF. Rather, an E1 circuit groups 16 frames in a *multiframe*.

E1 circuits are popular outside North America and Japan.

T3

In the same T-carrier family of standards as T1, a T3 circuit offers an increased bandwidth capacity. Whereas a T1 circuit combines 24 DS0s into a single physical connection to offer 1.544Mbps of bandwidth, a T3 circuit combines 672 DS0s into a single physical connection, delivered to the customer over coaxial cable, which is called a *Digital Signal 3 (DS3)*. A T3 circuit has a bandwidth capacity of 44.7Mbps.

E3

Just as a T3 circuit provides more bandwidth than a T1 circuit, an E3 circuit's available bandwidth of 34.4Mbps is significantly more than the 2.048Mbps of bandwidth offered by an E1 circuit. A common misconception is that the bandwidth of E3 is greater than the bandwidth of T3 because E1's bandwidth is greater than T1's bandwidth. However, that is not the case; a T3 has greater bandwidth (that is, 44.7Mbps) than an E3 (that is, 34.4Mbps).

Metro-optical

Telecommunications networks today are often divided into a three-tier hierarchy, consisting of the access section, the metropolitan section, and the long-haul section. This metropolitan section clearly plays an important role and connects to both the access section and the long-haul section. Typically, this portion of the telecommunication network covers an area of 10 to 100 km and is often based on a SONET ring architecture. While this section is described using many different terms, CompTIA (and your author) like the term metro-optical for the technology used in this part of the WAN.

Synchronous Optical Network

Synchronous Optical Network (SONET) is a Layer 1 technology that uses fiber-optic cabling as its media. Because SONET is a Layer 1 technology, it can be used to transport various Layer 2 encapsulation types, such as ATM. Also, because SONET uses fiber-optic cabling, it offers high data rates, typically in the 155Mbps to 10Gbps range, and long-distance limitations, typically in the 20 km to 250 km range. Optical Carrier transmission rates, such as OC3 (close to 155Mbps) and OC12 (close to 622Mbps), are examples of specifications for digital signal transmission bandwidth.

> **NOTE**   The term *SONET* is often used synonymously with the term *Synchronous Digital Hierarchy* (*SDH*), which is another fiber-optic multiplexing standard. Although these standards are similar, SONET is usually seen in North America, whereas SDH has greater worldwide popularity.

SONET networks can vary in their physical topology. For example, a SONET network can connect as many as 16 other devices in a linear fashion (similar to a bus topology) or in a ring topology. A metropolitan area network (MAN), as depicted in Figure 2-23, often uses a ring topology. The ring might circumnavigate a large metropolitan area. A site within that MAN could then connect to the nearest point on the SONET ring.

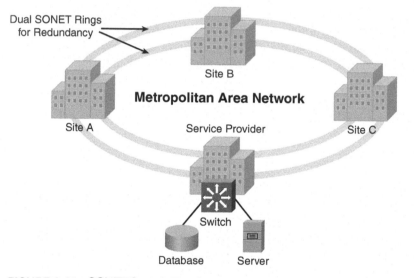

FIGURE 2-23   SONET Sample Topology

> **NOTE**   A SONET network uses a single wavelength of light, along with time-division multiplexing (TDM), to support multiple data flows on a single fiber. This approach differs from dense wavelength-division multiplexing (DWDM), which is another high-speed optical network technology commonly used in MANs. DWDM uses as many as 32 light wavelengths on a single fiber, where each wavelength can support as many as 160 simultaneous transmissions using more than 8 active wavelengths per fiber. Coarse wavelength-division multiplexing (CWDM) uses fewer than 8 active wavelengths per fiber.

NOTE Another optical WAN technology to be aware of is passive optical network (PON), which allows a single fiber cable to service as many as 128 subscribers. This is made possible via unpowered (that is, passive) optical splitters.

Real-World Case Study

The headquarters for Acme, Inc. is located on a single floor of a downtown building. Acme also has two branch offices, Branch1 and Branch2, that are in remote locations. The company wants to do file sharing, instant messaging, email, and voice on its own private networks when possible. It also wants connectivity to the Internet.

At the headquarters location, Acme sets up a LAN with UTP (Cat 6a) cabling, with the clients and servers connected to a central switch. This forms a physical star topology. For connectivity between HQ and its two branch offices, the company uses a service provider (SP) for WAN connectivity.

The SP provides logical, point-to-point connections between the headquarters office and both of the branch locations. Physically, the path between the headquarters and each branch office is going through several routers in the SP's network. For the time being, Branch1 and Branch2 do not have direct connectivity to each other, so branch-to-branch traffic must pass through the headquarters site (hub and spoke).

Next year, as more funds are available, the company can add WAN connectivity directly between Branch1 and Branch2. This will change the WAN topology from hub and spoke to full mesh.

Summary

Here are the main topics covered in this chapter:

- One way to classify networks is by their geographic dispersion. Specifically, these network types are identified in this chapter: LAN, WAN, CAN, MAN, PAN, WLAN, SAN, and SD-WAN.

- Another approach to classifying networks is based on a network's topology. Examples of network types, based on topology, include bus, ring, star, hybrid (partial mesh), full mesh, and hub and spoke. This chapter also provides information on the various wireless topologies available.

- This chapter contrasts client/server and peer-to-peer networks.

- Multiprotocol label switching (MPLS) and multipoint generic routing encapsulation (mGRE) are detailed.

- Service-related entry points such as demarcation point and smartjack are covered.

- This chapter presents virtual networking components, including virtual network interface card (vNIC), virtual switch (vSwitch), network function virtualization (NFV), and hypervisor.

- This chapter covers provider links, including satellite, DSL, cable, leased line, and metro-optical.

Exam Preparation Tasks

Review All the Key Topics

Review the most important topics from this chapter, noted with the Key Topic icon in the outer margin of the page. Table 2-10 lists these key topics and the page number where each is found.

Table 2-10 Key Topics for Chapter 2

Key Topic Element	Description	Page Number
List	Network types, as defined by geography	37
Figure 2-3	Service provider MPLS cloud	40
Table 2-2	Characteristics, benefits, and drawbacks of a client/server network	43
Table 2-3	Characteristics, benefits, and drawbacks of a peer-to-peer network	44
Table 2-4	Characteristics, benefits, and drawbacks of a bus topology	47
Table 2-5	Characteristics, benefits, and drawbacks of a ring topology	49
Table 2-6	Characteristics, benefits, and drawbacks of a star topology	50
Table 2-7	Characteristics, benefits, and drawbacks of a hub-and-spoke topology	51
Table 2-8	Characteristics, benefits, and drawbacks of a full-mesh topology	53
Table 2-9	Characteristics, benefits, and drawbacks of a partial-mesh topology	54
Figure 2-17	Virtual server with a virtual switch	58
Figure 2-19	Virtual desktop topology	60
Figure 2-20	Satellite WAN topology	61
List	DSL variants	62
Figure 2-22	Cable modem sample topology	64

Complete Tables and Lists from Memory

Print a copy of Appendix C, "Memory Tables," or at least the section for this chapter and complete as many of the tables as possible from memory. Appendix D, "Memory Tables Answer Key," includes the completed tables and lists so you can check your work.

Define Key Terms

Define the following key terms from this chapter and check your answers in the Glossary:

local area network (LAN), wide area network (WAN), campus area network (CAN), metropolitan area network (MAN), personal area network (PAN), wireless local area network (WLAN), storage area network (SAN), logical topology, physical topology, bus topology, ring topology, star topology, hub-and-spoke topology, full-mesh topology, partial-mesh topology, hybrid, client/server network, peer-to-peer network, demarcation point, smartjack, network function virtualization (NFV), hypervisor, satellite, digital subscriber line (DSL), cable, leased line, *metro-optical*, software-defined wide area network (SD-WAN), Multiprotocol Label Switching (MPLS), multipoint generic routing encapsulation (mGRE), vSwitch, virtual network interface card (vNIC)

Complete Chapter 2 Hands-On Labs in Network+ Simulator Lite

- Network Topologies

Additional Resources

Wide Area Network (WAN) Topologies: https://www.youtube.com/watch?v=9WkZT0YMZ70

MPLS Basics: https://www.youtube.com/watch?v=mMu4iPWI1m8

Review Questions

The answers to these review questions appear in Appendix A, "Answers to Review Questions."

1. What DSL variant has a distance limitation of 18,000 feet between a DSL modem and its DSLAM?

   a. HDSL

   b. ADSL

   c. SDSL

   d. VDSL

2. What kind of network do many cable companies use to service their cable modems with both fiber-optic and coaxial cabling?

   a. Head-end

   b. DOCSIS

   c. Composite

   d. HFC

3. Which of these components is used to make virtualization possible in the server environment by permitting multiple systems to use the underlying hardware of the host system?

   a. vNIC

   b. vSwitch

   c. SD-WAN

   d. Hypervisor

4. Which technology allows enterprises to leverage a combination of transport services such as MPLS, 5G, LTE, or broadband to securely connect users to applications?

   a. mGRE

   b. SD-WAN

   c. Smartjack

   d. Demarcation

5. A company has various locations in a city interconnected using Metro Ethernet connections. This is an example of what type of network?

   a. WAN

   b. CAN

   c. PAN

   d. MAN

6. A network formed by interconnecting a PC to a digital camera via a USB cable is considered what type of network?

   a. WAN

   b. CAN

   c. PAN

   d. MAN

7. Which of the following physical LAN topologies requires the most cabling?

   a. Bus

   b. Ring

   c. Star

   d. WLAN

8. Which of the following topologies offers the highest level of redundancy?

   a. Full mesh

   b. Hub and spoke

   c. Bus

   d. Partial mesh

9. How many WAN links are required to create a full mesh of connections between five remote sites?

   a. 5

   b. 10

   c. 15

   d. 20

10. Which of the following are advantages of a hub-and-spoke WAN topology as compared to a full-mesh WAN topology? (Choose two.)

    a. Lower cost

    b. Optimal routes

    c. More scalable

    d. More redundancy

11. Which type of network is based on network clients sharing resources with one another?

    a. Client/server

    b. Client/peer

    c. Peer-to-peer

    d. Peer-to-server

12. Which of the following is an advantage of a peer-to-peer network as compared with a client/server network?

    a. More scalable

    b. Less expensive

    c. Better performance

    d. Simplified administration

13. What network type would help facilitate communications when large video or audio files need to be housed and transferred through the network?

    a. WLAN

    b. CAN

    c. PAN

    d. SAN

This chapter covers the following topics related to Objective 1.3 (Summarize the types of cables and connectors and explain which is the appropriate type for a solution) of the CompTIA Network+ N10-008 certification exam:

- Copper
  - Twisted pair
    - Cat 5
    - Cat 5e
    - Cat 6
    - Cat 6a
    - Cat 7
    - Cat 8
  - Coaxial/RG-6
  - Twinaxial
  - Termination standards
    - TIA/EIA-568A
    - TIA/EIA-568B
- Fiber
  - Single-mode
  - Multimode
- Connector types
  - Local connector (LC), straight tip (ST), subscriber connector (SC), mechanical transfer (MT), registered jack (RJ)
    - Angled physical contact (APC)
    - Ultra-physical contact (UPC)
  - RJ11
  - RJ45
  - F-type connector
  - Transceivers/media converters
  - Transceiver type
    - Small form-factor pluggable (SFP)
    - Enhanced form-factor pluggable (SFP+)
    - Quad small form-factor pluggable (QSFP)
    - Enhanced quad small form-factor pluggable (QSFP+)
- Cable management
  - Patch panel/patch bay

- Fiber distribution panel
- Punchdown block
    - 66
    - 110
    - Krone
    - Bix
- Ethernet standards
    - Copper
        - 10BASE-T
        - 100BASE-TX
        - 1000BASE-T
        - 10GBASE-T
        - 40GBASE-T
    - Fiber
        - 100BASE-FX
        - 100BASE-SX
        - 1000BASE-SX
        - 1000BASE-LX
        - 10GBASE-SR
        - 10GBASE-LR
        - Coarse wavelength division multiplexing (CWDM)
        - Dense wavelength division multiplexing (DWDM)
        - Bidirectional wavelength division multiplexing (WDM)

Network Media Types

Many modern networks have a daunting number of devices, and it is your job to understand the function of each device and how it works with the others. To create a network, these devices need some sort of interconnection. An interconnection uses one of a variety of media types. This chapter dives into the world of physical media. You will learn about classic media technologies that set the stage for the modern, high-speed media used in networks today. You will also learn about the connectors used for this media and the main aspects of cable management.

Copper and Fiber Media and Connectors

A network is an interconnection of devices. Those interconnections occur over some type of media. The media might be physical, such as a copper or fiber-optic cable. Alternatively, the media might be the air, through which radio waves propagate (as is the case with wireless networking technologies).

This section examines copper and fiber physical media types and the connectors they commonly use.

Coaxial Cable

Coaxial cable (referred to as *coax*) consists of two conductors. As illustrated in Figure 3-1, one of the conductors is an inner insulated conductor. This inner conductor is surrounded by another conductor that is sometimes made of a metallic foil or woven wire.

FIGURE 3-1   Coaxial Cable

Because the inner conductor is shielded by the metallic outer conductor, coaxial cable is resistant to electromagnetic interference (EMI). For example, EMI occurs when an external signal is received on a wire and might result in a corrupted data transmission. As another example, EMI occurs when a wire acts as an antenna and radiates electromagnetic waves, which might interfere with data transmission on another cable. Coaxial cables have an associated characteristic impedance that needs to be balanced with the device (or terminator) with which the cable connects.

NOTE   The term *electromagnetic interference (EMI)* is sometimes used interchangeably with the term *radio frequency interference (RFI)*.

There are three common types of coaxial cables:

- **RG-59:** Typically used for short-distance applications, such as carrying composite video between two nearby devices. This cable type has loss characteristics such that it is not right for long-distance applications. RG-59 cable has a characteristic impedance of 75 ohms.

- **RG-6:** Used by local cable companies to connect individual homes to the cable company's distribution network. Like RG-59 cable, RG-6 cable has a characteristic impedance of 75 ohms.

- **RG-58:** Has loss characteristics and distance limitations like those of RG-59. However, the characteristic impedance of RG-58 is 50 ohms, and this type of coax was popular with early 10BASE2 Ethernet networks.

Although RG-58 coaxial cable was commonplace in early computer networks (that is, 10BASE2 networks), coaxial cable's role in modern computer networks is as the media used by cable modems. Cable modems are commonly installed in residences to provide high-speed Internet access over the same connection used to receive multiple television stations.

NOTE Far less popular is **twinaxial** cabling, commonly called *twinax*. This is very similar to coaxial cable, but it uses two inner conductors instead of one.

Common connectors used on coaxial cables include the following:

Key Topic

- **BNC:** A Bayonet Neill-Concelman (BNC) connector (*British Naval Connector* in some literature) can be used for a variety of applications, including as a connector in a 10BASE2 Ethernet network. A BNC coupler could be used to connect two coaxial cables together back-to-back.

- **F-connector:** An F-connector is often used for cable TV (including cable modem) connections. Notice that some, including CompTIA, refer to it simply as *F-type connector*.

Figure 3-2 shows what both of these connectors look like.

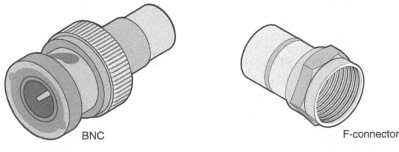

BNC   F-connector

FIGURE 3-2 Coaxial Cable Connectors

Twisted-Pair Cable

Today's most popular LAN media type is *twisted-pair* cable, in which individually insulated copper strands are intertwined. Two categories of twisted-pair cable are shielded twisted pair (STP) and unshielded twisted pair (UTP). A UTP coupler could be used to connect two UTP cables, back-to-back. Also, for adherence to fire codes, you might need to select plenum-rated cable versus nonplenum cable.

To define industry-standard pinouts and color coding for twisted-pair cabling, the TIA/EIA-568 standard was developed. The first iteration of the TIA/EIA-568 standard, which was released in 1991, has come to be known as the *TIA/EIA-568A* standard.

NOTE   The TIA/EIA acronym comes from Telecommunications Industry Association/Electronic Industries Alliance.

In 2001, an updated standard was released, which became known as *TIA/EIA-568B*. Interestingly, the pinout of these two standards is the same. However, the color coding of the wiring is different. 568B is the more commonly used standard in the United States.

Shielded Twisted Pair

If wires in a cable are not twisted or shielded, the cable can act as an antenna, which might receive or transmit EMI. To help prevent this type of behavior, the wires (which are individually insulated) can be twisted together in pairs.

If the distance between the twists is less than a quarter of the wavelength of an electromagnetic waveform, the twisted pair of wires will not radiate that wavelength or receive EMI from that wavelength (in theory, if the wires were perfect conductors). However, as frequencies increase, wavelengths decrease.

One option for supporting higher frequencies is to surround a twisted pair in a metallic shielding, similar to the outer conductor in a coaxial cable. This type of cable is referred to as a *shielded twisted-pair (STP) cable*.

Figure 3-3 shows an example of STP cable. The outer conductors shield the copper strands from EMI; however, the drawback of STP is that the addition of the metallic shielding adds to the expense of the cable.

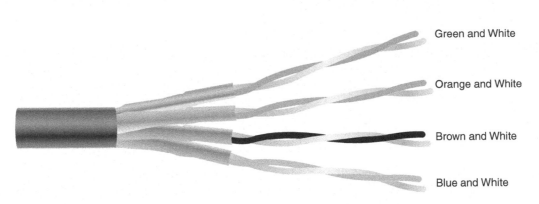

FIGURE 3-3 Shielded Twisted Pair

Unshielded Twisted Pair

Another way to block EMI from the copper strands making up a twisted-pair cable is to twist the strands more tightly (that is, more twists per centimeter). With the strands wrapped tightly around each other, the wires insulate each other from EMI.

Figure 3-4 illustrates an example of UTP cable. Because UTP is less expensive than STP, it has grown in popularity since the mid-1990s to become the media of choice for most LANs.

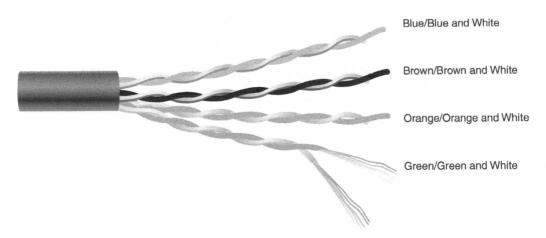

FIGURE 3-4 Unshielded Twisted Pair

UTP cable types vary in their data-carrying capacity. Common categories of UTP cabling include the following:

- **Category 5:** Category 5 (*Cat 5*) cable is commonly used in Ethernet 100BASE-TX networks, which carry data at a rate of 100Mbps. However,

Cat 5 cable can carry ATM traffic at a rate of 155Mbps. Most Cat 5 cables consist of four pairs of 24-gauge wires. Each pair is twisted, with a different number of twists per meter. However, on average, one pair of wires has a twist every 5 cm.

- **Category 5e:** Category 5e (*Cat 5e*) cable is an updated version of Cat 5 that is commonly used for 1000BASE-T networks, which carry data at a rate of 1Gbps. Cat 5e cable offers reduced crosstalk compared to Cat 5 cable.

- **Category 6:** Like Cat 5e cable, Category 6 (*Cat 6*) cable is commonly used for 1000BASE-T Ethernet networks. Some Cat 6 cable is made of thicker conductors (for example, 22-gauge or 23-gauge wire), although some Cat 6 cable is made from the same 24-gauge wire used by Cat 5 and Cat 5e. Cat 6 cable has thicker insulation and offers reduced crosstalk compared with Cat 5e.

- **Category 6a:** Category 6a (*Cat 6a*), or augmented Cat 6, supports twice as many frequencies as Cat 6 and can be used for 10GBASE-T networks, which can transmit data at a rate of 10 billion bits per second (10Gbps).

- **Category 7:** *Cat 7* is not an IEEE standard, and it is not very popular as a result. This very strict specification supports 10Gbps over 100 m using copper media.

- **Category 8:** *Cat 8* is capable of 40Gbps speeds. As you might guess, however, this speed comes at a cost. Cat 8 supports distances of only 30 to 36 m, depending on the patch cables used. These short distances and very high speeds are ideal for connections in a data center between high-speed multilayer switches.

Although other wiring categories exist, the ones presented in this list are the categories most commonly seen in modern networks.

Most UTP cabling used in today's networks is considered to be *straight-through*, meaning that the RJ45 jacks at each end of a cable have matching pinouts. For example, pin 1 in an RJ45 jack at one end of a cable uses the same copper conductor as pin 1 in the RJ45 jack at the other end of a cable.

However, some network devices cannot be interconnected with a straight-through cable. For example, consider two PCs interconnected with a straight-through cable. Because the network interface cards (NICs) in these PCs use the same pair of wires for transmission and reception, when one PC sends data to the other PC, the receiving PC would receive the data on its transmission wires rather than its reception wires. For such a scenario, you can use a crossover cable, which swaps the transmit and receive wire pairs between the two ends of a cable.

NOTE   A crossover cable for Ethernet devices is different from a crossover cable used for a digital T1 circuit. Specifically, an Ethernet crossover cable has a pin mapping of $1 \rightarrow 3, 2 \rightarrow 6, 3 \rightarrow 1$, and $6 \rightarrow 2$, whereas a T1 crossover cable has a pin mapping of $1 \rightarrow 4, 2 \rightarrow 5, 4 \rightarrow 1$, and $5 \rightarrow 2$. Another type of cable is the rollover cable, which is used to connect to a console port to manage a device such as a router or switch. The pin mapping for a rollover cable is $1 \leftrightarrow 8, 2 \leftrightarrow 7, 3 \leftrightarrow 6, 4 \leftrightarrow 5$. The end of the cable looks like an RJ45 eight-pin connector.

NOTE   A traditional port found in a PC's NIC is called a *media-dependent interface* (*MDI*). If a straight-through cable connects a PC's MDI port to an Ethernet switch port, the Ethernet switch port needs to swap the transmit pair of wires (that is, the wires connected to pins 1 and 2) with the receive pair of wires (that is, the wires connected to pins 3 and 6).

Therefore, a traditional port found on an Ethernet switch is called a *media-dependent interface crossover* (*MDIX*), and it reverses the transmit and receive pairs. However, if you want to interconnect two switches, where both switch ports used for the interconnection are MDIX ports, the cable needs to be a crossover cable.

Fortunately, most modern Ethernet switches have ports that can automatically detect whether they need to act as MDI ports or MDIX ports and make the appropriate adjustments. This eliminates the necessity of using straight-through cables for some Ethernet switch connections and crossover cables for other connections. With this *Auto-MDIX* feature, you can use either straight-through cables or crossover cables.

Twisted-Pair Cable Connectors

Common connectors used on twisted-pair cables are as follows:

- *RJ45*: A type 45 registered jack (RJ45) is an eight-pin connector found in most Ethernet networks. However, most Ethernet implementations only use four of the eight pins.

- *RJ11*: A type 11 registered jack (RJ11) has the capacity to be a six-pin connector. However, most RJ11 connectors have only two or four conductors. An RJ11 connector is found in most home telephone networks. However, most home phones use only two of the six pins.

- **DB-9 (RS-232):** A nine-pin D-subminiature (DB-9) connector is an older connector used for low-speed asynchronous serial communications, such as a PC to a serial printer, a PC to a console port of a router or switch, or a PC to an external modem. Do not confuse the DB-9 with a DB-25. The DB-25 connector was also used for the serial or parallel ports of early personal computers.

Figure 3-5 shows what these connectors look like.

FIGURE 3-5 Twisted-Pair Cable Connectors

Plenum Versus Nonplenum Cable

If a twisted-pair cable is to be installed under raised flooring or in an open-air return, fire codes must be considered. For example, imagine that there was a fire in a building. If the outer insulation of a twisted-pair cable caught on fire or started to melt, it could release toxic fumes. If those toxic fumes were released in a location such as an open-air return, those fumes could be spread throughout a building, posing a huge health risk.

To mitigate the concern of pumping poisonous gas throughout a building's heating, ventilation, and air conditioning (HVAC) system, *plenum* cabling can be used. The outer insulator of a plenum twisted-pair cable is not only fire retardant; in addition, some plenum cabling uses a fluorinated ethylene polymer (FEP) or a low-smoke polyvinyl chloride (PVC) to minimize dangerous fumes.

NOTE Check with your local fire codes before installing network cabling.

Fiber-Optic Cable

An alternative to copper cabling is fiber-optic cabling, which sends light (instead of electricity) through an optical fiber (typically made of glass). Using light instead of electricity makes fiber optics immune to EMI. Also, depending on the Layer 1 technology being used, fiber-optic cables typically have greater range (that is, a greater maximum distance between networked devices) and greater data-carrying capacity.

Lasers are often used to inject light pulses into a fiber-optic cable. However, lower-cost light-emitting diodes (LEDs) are also available. Fiber-optic cables are generally classified according to their diameter and fall into one of two categories: multimode fiber (MMF) and single-mode fiber (SMF).

The wavelengths of light also vary between MMF and SMF cables. Usually, wavelengths of light in an MMF cable are in the range 850–1300 nm, where nm stands for nanometers. (A nanometer is one-billionth of a meter.) Conversely, the wavelengths of light in an SMF cable are usually in the range 1310–1550 nm. A fiber coupler could be used to connect two fiber cables, back-to-back.

Multimode Fiber

When a light source, such as a laser, sends light pulses into a fiber-optic cable, what keeps the light from simply passing through the glass and being dispersed into the surrounding air? The trick is that fiber-optic cables use two different types of glass. There is an inner strand of glass (that is, a *core*) surrounded by an outer *cladding* of glass, similar to the construction of the previously mentioned coaxial cable.

The light injected by a laser (or LED) enters the core, and the light is prevented from leaving that inner strand and going into the outer cladding of glass. Specifically, the indexes of refraction of these two different types of glass are so different that if the light attempts to leave the inner strand, it hits the outer cladding and bends back on itself.

To better understand this concept, consider a straw in a glass of water, as shown in Figure 3-6. Because air and water have different indexes of refraction (that is, light travels at a slightly different speeds in air and water), the light that bounces off the straw and travels to our eyes is bent by the water's index of refraction. When a fiber-optic cable is manufactured, dopants are injected into the two types of glasses, making up the core and cladding to give them significantly different indexes of refraction, thus causing any light attempting to escape to be bent back into the core.

The path that light takes through a fiber-optic cable is called a *mode of propagation*. The diameter of the core in a multimode fiber is large enough to permit light to enter the core at different angles, as depicted in Figure 3-7. If light enters at a steep angle, it bounces back and forth much more frequently on its way to the far end of the cable than does light that enters the cable perpendicularly. If pulses of light representing different bits travel down the cable using different modes of propagation, it is possible that the bits (that is, the pulses of light representing the bits) will arrive out of order at the far end (where the pulses of light, or absence of light, are interpreted as binary data by photoelectronic sensors).

FIGURE 3-6   Example: Refractive Index

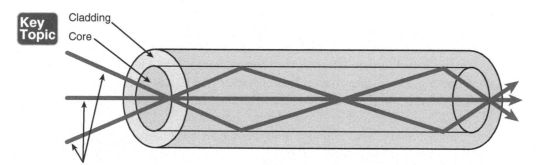

FIGURE 3-7   Light Propagation in Multimode Fiber

For example, say that the pulse of light representing the first bit intersects the core at a steep angle and bounces back and forth many times on its way to the far end of the cable, while the light pulse representing the second bit intersects the core perpendicularly and does not bounce back and forth very much. With all of its bouncing, the first bit has to travel further than the second bit, and so the bits might arrive out of order. This condition is known as *multimode delay distortion*. To mitigate multimode delay distortion, ***multimode fiber (MMF)*** is typically limited to shorter distances than SMF.

Single-Mode Fiber

Single-mode fiber (SMF) eliminates the issue of multimode delay distortion by having a core with a diameter so small that it only permits one mode (that is, one path) of propagation, as shown in Figure 3-8. With the issue of multimode delay distortion mitigated, SMF typically can be run for longer distances than MMF.

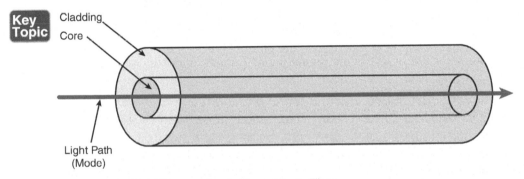

FIGURE 3-8   Light Propagation in Single-Mode Fiber

A potential downside to SMF, however, is cost. Because SMF has to be manufactured to very exacting tolerances, you usually pay more for a given length of single-mode fiber-optic cabling. However, for some implementations where greater distances are required, the cost is an acceptable trade-off for reaching greater distances.

Fiber-Optic Cable Connectors

Some common connectors used on fiber-optic cables are as follows:

- **ST:** A ***straight tip* (ST)** *connector* is sometimes referred to as a *bayonet connector*, because of the long tip extending from the connector. ST connectors are most commonly used with MMF. You connect an ST connector to a terminating device by pushing the connector into the terminating equipment and then twisting the connector housing to lock it in place.

- **SC:** Different literature defines an SC connector as *subscriber connector (SC)*, *standard connector*, or *square connector*. You connect an SC connector by pushing it into the terminating device; you can remove it by pulling the connector from the terminating device. This connector type has slight variants within the industry, with the major types being APC, UPC, and MTRJ. Always consult with the vendor or an IT staff member regarding the exact requirements.

- **LC:** You connect a *Lucent connector*, *little connector*, or **local connector (LC)** to a terminating device by pushing the connector into the terminating device. You can remove it by pressing the tab on the connector and pulling it out of the terminating device.

- **MTRJ:** The most unique characteristic of a *media termination recommended jack (MTRJ)* or **mechanical transfer (MT) registered jack (RJ)** connector is that two fiber strands (a transmit strand and a receive strand) are included in a single connector. You connect an MTRJ connector by pushing it into the terminating device; you can remove it by pulling the connector from the terminating device.

Figure 3-9 shows what these connectors look like.

Fiber Connector Polishing Styles

Fiber-optic cables have different types of mechanical connections. The type of connection impacts the quality of the fiber-optic transmission. Listed from basic to better, the options include physical contact (PC), *ultra physical contact (UPC)*, and *angled physical contact (APC)*, which refer to the polishing styles of fiber-optic connectors. The different polish of the fiber-optic connectors results in different performance of the connector. The less back reflection, the better the transmission. The PC back reflection is –40 dB, the UPC back reflection is around –55 dB, and the APC back reflection is about –70 dB.

Ethernet and Fiber Standards

A popular implementation of Ethernet, in the early days, was called *10BASE5*. The 10 in 10BASE5 referred to network throughput, specifically 10Mbps (that is, 10 million [mega] bits per second). The BASE in 10BASE5 referred to baseband, as opposed to broadband. Finally, the 5 in 10BASE5 indicated the distance limitation of 500 m. The cable used in 10BASE5 networks, illustrated in Figure 3-10, was a larger diameter than most types of media. In fact, this network type became known as *thicknet*.

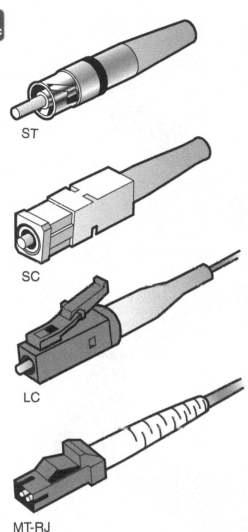

The ST connector uses a half-twist bayonet type of lock.

The SC uses a push-pull connector similar to common audio and video plugs and sockets.

LC connectors have a flange on top, similar to an RJ-45 connector, that aids secure connection.

MT-RJ is a popular connector for two fibers in a very small form factor.

FIGURE 3-9   Common Fiber-Optic Connectors

Another early Ethernet implementation was 10BASE2. From the previous analysis of 10BASE5, you might conclude that 10BASE2 was a 10Mbps baseband technology with a distance limitation of 200 meters. That is almost correct. However, 10BASE2's actual distance limitation was 185 m. The cabling used in 10BASE2 networks was significantly thinner and therefore less expensive than 10BASE5 cabling. As a result, 10BASE2 cabling, illustrated in Figure 3-11, was known as *thinnet* or *cheapernet*.

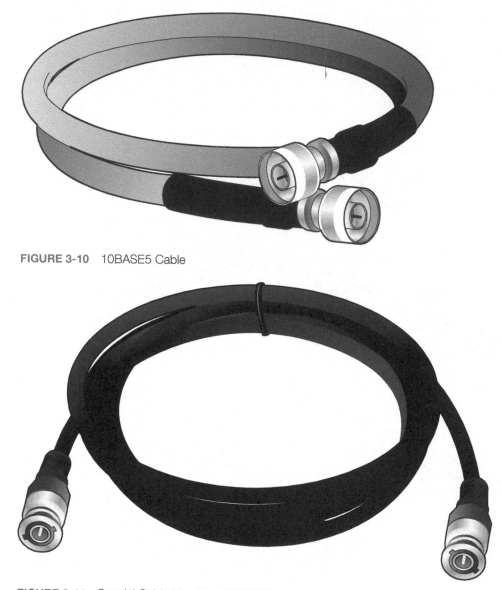

FIGURE 3-10   10BASE5 Cable

FIGURE 3-11   Coaxial Cable Used for 10BASE2

10BASE5 and 10BASE2 networks are rarely, if ever, seen today. The cabling used by these legacy technologies quickly faded in popularity with the advent of UTP cabling. The 10Mbps version of Ethernet that relied on UTP cabling, an example of which is provided in Figure 3-12, is known as *10BASE-T*. Notice that the "T" in 10BASE-T refers to twisted-pair cabling.

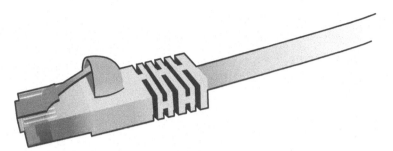

FIGURE 3-12   UTP Cable Used for 10BASE-T

Distance and Speed Limitations

To understand the bandwidth available on networks, you need to understand a few terms. You should already know that a *bit* refers to one of two values. These values are represented using binary math, which uses only the numbers 0 and 1. On a cable such as twisted-pair cable, a bit could be represented by the absence or presence of voltage. Fiber-optic cables, however, might represent a bit with the absence or presence of light.

The bandwidth of a network is measured in terms of how many bits the network can transmit during a 1-second period of time. For example, if a network has the capacity to send 10,000,000 (that is, 10 million) bits in a 1-second period of time, the bandwidth capacity is said to be 10 megabits (that is, millions of bits) per second (or *Mbps*). Table 3-1 defines common bandwidths supported on distinct types of Ethernet networks.

Table 3-1   Ethernet Bandwidth Capacities

Ethernet Type	Bandwidth Capacity
Standard Ethernet	10Mbps: 10 million bits per second (that is, 10 megabits per second)
Fast Ethernet	100Mbps: 100 million bits per second (that is, 100 megabits per second)
Gigabit Ethernet	1Gbps: 1 billion bits per second (that is, 1 gigabit per second)
10-Gigabit Ethernet	10Gbps: 10 billion bits per second (that is, 10 gigabits per second)
100-Gigabit Ethernet	100Gbps: 100 billion bits per second (that is, 100 gigabits per second)

The type of cabling used in an Ethernet network influences the bandwidth capacity and the distance limitation of the network. For example, fiber-optic cabling often has a higher bandwidth capacity and can be run longer distances than twisted-pair cabling.

As mentioned earlier in this chapter, because of the issue of multimode delay distortion, SMF usually has a longer distance limitation than MMF.

Although not comprehensive, Table 3-2 lists a number of Ethernet standards, along with the media type, bandwidth capacity, and distance limitation for each.

Table 3-2 Types of Ethernet

Ethernet Standard	Media Type	Bandwidth Capacity	Distance Limitation
10BASE5	Coax (thicknet)	10Mbps	500 m
10BASE2	Coax (thinnet)	10Mbps	185 m
10BASE-T	Cat 3 (or higher) UTP	10Mbps	100 m
100BASE-TX	Cat 5 (or higher) UTP	100Mbps	100 m
100BASE-FX	MMF	100Mbps	2 km
100BASE-SX	MMF	100Mbps	850 nm
1000BASE-T	Cat 5e (or higher) UTP	1Gbps	100 m
1000BASE-TX	Cat 6 (or higher) UTP	1Gbps	100 m
1000BASE-SX	MMF	1Gbps	550 km
1000BASE-LX	SMF	1Gbps	5 km
1000BASE-LH	SMF	1Gbps	10 km
1000BASE-ZX	SMF	1Gbps	70 km
10GBASE-SR	MMF	10Gbps	26–400 m
10GBASE-LR	SMF	10Gbps	10–25 km
10GBASE-ER	SMF	10Gbps	40 km
10GBASE-SW	MMF	10Gbps	300 m
10GBASE-LW	SMF	10Gbps	10 km
10GBASE-EW	SMF	10Gbps	40 km
10GBASE-T	Cat 6a (or higher)	10Gbps	100 m
40GBASE-T	Cat 8	40Gbps	30 m
100GBASE-SR10	MMF	100Gbps	125 m
100GBASE-LR4	SMF	100Gbps	10 km
100GBASE-ER4	SMF	100Gbps	40 km

NOTE   Two often-confused terms are *100BASE-T* and *100BASE-TX*. 100BASE-T is not a specific standard. Rather, 100BASE-T is a category of standards and includes 100BASE-T2 (which uses two pairs of wires in a Cat 3 cable), 100BASE-T4 (which uses four pairs of wires in a Cat 3 cable), and 100BASE-TX. 100BASE-T2 and 100BASE-T4 were early implementations of 100Mbps Ethernet and are no longer used. Therefore, you can generally use the terms *100BASE-T* and *100BASE-TX* interchangeably.

Similarly, the term *1000BASE-X* is not a specific standard. Rather, 1000BASE-X refers to all Ethernet technologies that transmit data at a rate of 1Gbps over fiber-optic cabling. Additional and creative ways of using Ethernet technology include IEEE 1901-2013, which could be used for Ethernet over HDMI cables and Ethernet over existing power lines to avoid having to run a separate cabling just for networking.

Transceivers

When you want to uplink one Ethernet switch to another, you might need different connectors (for example, for MMF, SMF, or UTP) for different installations. Fortunately, some Ethernet switches have one or more empty slots in which you can insert a gigabit interface converter (GBIC). GBICs are interfaces that have a bandwidth capacity of 1Gbps and are available with MMF, SMF, and UTP connectors. This allows you to have flexibility in the uplink technology you use in an Ethernet switch.

A smaller variant of a regular GBIC is the ***small form-factor pluggable (SFP)***, which is sometimes called a *mini-GBIC*. And to show the variety of ***transceivers*** you might encounter today, even this SFP has many variations, including the following:

- *Enhanced form-factor pluggable (SFP+)*
- *Quad small form-factor pluggable (QSFP)*
- *Enhanced quad small form-factor pluggable (QSFP+)*

Multiplexing in Fiber-Optic Networks

Remember, as mentioned in Chapters 1, "The OSI Model and Encapsulation," and 2, "Network Topologies and Types," that multiplexing allows multiple communications sessions to share the same physical medium. At this point, you need to be familiar with three different approaches common with fiber networking:

- *Dense wavelength-division multiplexing (DWDM)*: DWDM uses as many as 32 light wavelengths on a single fiber, where each wavelength can support as many as 160 simultaneous transmissions using more than eight active wavelengths per fiber.

- *Coarse wavelength-division multiplexing (CWDM)*: CWDM uses fewer than eight active wavelengths per fiber.

- *Bidirectional wavelength-division multiplexing (WDM)*: This approach multiplexes a number of optical carrier signals onto a single optical fiber by using different wavelengths. Using this technique enables bidirectional communications over one strand of fiber and increases the overall capacity.

Cable Management

After deciding what type of media you are going to use in your network (for example, UTP, STP, MMF, or SMF), you should install that media as part of an organized cable distribution system. Typically, cable distribution systems are hierarchical in nature.

Consider the example profiled in Figure 3-13. In this example, cable from end-user offices runs back to common locations within the building. These locations are sometimes referred to as *wiring closets*. Cables in these locations might terminate in a *patch panel*, or *patch bay*. The patch panel might consist of some sort of cross-connect block wired into a series of ports (for example, RJ45 ports), which can be used to quickly interconnect cables coming from end-user offices with a network device, such as an Ethernet switch. A common term for cross-connect blocks is *punchdown blocks*. This term indicates how you physically connect the media— "punching" the media into the appropriate slot.

The fiber connections into a wiring closet can terminate into a *fiber distribution panel*, also known as a fiber-optic patch panel. This cable management component is mainly used for accommodating fiber cable terminations, connections, and patching. The two major categories of fiber distribution panels are wall mount and rack mount types.

A building might have multiple patch panels (for example, on different floors of the building). Common locations where cables from nearby offices terminate are often called *intermediate distribution frames* (IDFs).

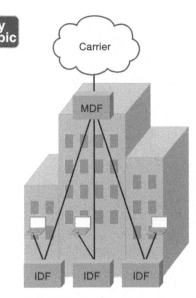

FIGURE 3-13   Example: Cable Distribution System

The two most popular types of cross-connect blocks found an IDF are detailed here:

- *66 block*: 66 blocks were traditionally used in corporate environments for cross-connecting phone system cabling. As 10Mbps LANs grew in popularity, in the late 1980s and early 1990s, these termination blocks were used to cross-connect Cat 3 UTP cabling. The electrical characteristics (specifically, cross-talk) of a 66 block, however, do not support higher-speed LAN technologies, such as 100Mbps Ethernet networks. Figure 3-14 illustrates a 66 block.

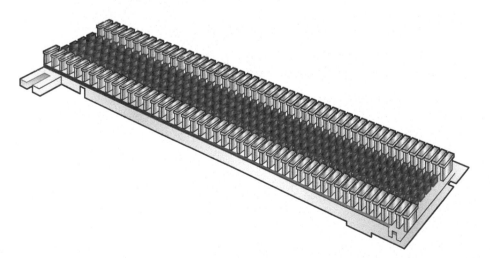

FIGURE 3-14   66 Block

- **110 block:** Because 66 blocks are subject to a lot of crosstalk (that is, interference between different pairs of wires) for higher-speed LAN connections, 110 blocks are often used to terminate cable (for example, a Cat 5e cable) used for higher-speed LANs. Figure 3-15 illustrates a 110 block.

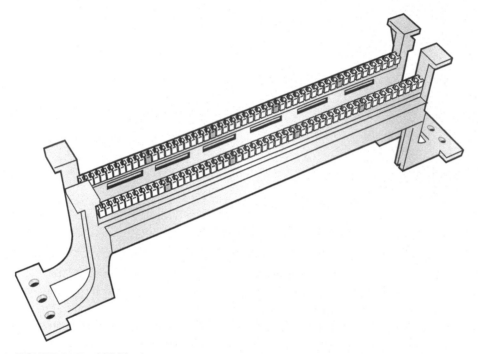

FIGURE 3-15   110 Block

There are two other cross-connect blocks you should be familiar with:

- **Krone (or Krone LSA-PLUS):** Krone, a proprietary European alternative to 110 block, is used not only in data environments but in television broadcasting.

- **BIX (or Building Industry Cross-connect):** A BIX terminates 25 pairs (that is, 50 wires). The 25 pairs may be punched down to one side of a "wafer" that is then inserted into a metal frame with the punched-down side against the wall, so you only see the unused side.

The centralized distribution frame, which connects out to multiple IDFs, is called the *main distribution frame (MDF)*.

NOTE   You will learn more about IDFs and MDFs in Chapter 14, "Organizational Documents and Policies," which covers the importance of documenting these designs and implementations as part of operational excellence for your organization.

Media Converters

Due to the wide variety of copper and fiber cabling used by different network devices, you might need one or more *media converters*. Examples of media converters include the following:

- MMF to Ethernet
- SMF to Ethernet
- Fiber to coaxial
- SMF to MMF

Real-World Case Study

Acme, Inc. is analyzing their physical media implementations and the performance they are achieving in their Ethernet-based LAN. The decision has been made to retain portions of the Cat 5e-based media, which is capable of 1Gbps speeds. Other areas of the network, particularly those that must deal with aggregate bandwidth demands, are being upgraded to Cat 8. Remember, Category 8 is capable of 40Gbps speeds. Cat 8 supports distances of only 30 to 36 m, depending on the patch cables used.

For Acme, these short distances and very high speeds are ideal for connections between high-speed multilayer switches that make up a good part of the distribution and core layers of the LAN.

Summary

Here are the main topics covered in this chapter:

- There are many different options today when it comes to copper and fiber media and connectors. This section of the chapter explored many of these in great detail.

- This chapter also covered the different options for multiplexing in fiber-optic environments.

- Finally, this chapter examined some typical component types for cable management.

Exam Preparation Tasks

Review All the Key Topics

Review the most important topics from this chapter, noted with the Key Topic icon in the outer margin of the page. Table 3-3 lists these key topics and the page number where each is found.

Key Topic

Table 3-3 Key Topics for Chapter 3

Key Topic Element	Description	Page Number
List, Figure 3-2	Common coaxial connectors	81
List	Categories of UTP cabling	83
List, Figure 3-5	Twisted-pair cable connectors	85
Figure 3-7	Light propagation in multimode fiber	88
Figure 3-8	Light propagation in single-mode fiber	89
List, Figure 3-9	Common fiber-optic connectors	91
Table 3-1	Ethernet bandwidth capacities	93
Table 3-2	Types of Ethernet	94
Figure 3-13	Cable distribution system example	97

Complete Tables and Lists from Memory

Print a copy of Appendix C, "Memory Tables," or at least the section for this chapter and complete as many of the tables as possible from memory. Appendix D, "Memory Tables Answer Key," includes the completed tables and lists so you can check your work.

Define Key Terms

Define the following key terms from this chapter and check your answers in the Glossary:

twisted pair, Cat 5, Cat 5e, Cat 6, Cat 6a, Cat 7, Cat 8, coaxial/RG-6, twinaxial, TIA/EIA-568A, TIA/EIA-568B, single-mode fiber (SMF), multimode fiber (MMF), local connector (LC), straight tip (ST) connector, subscriber connector (SC), mechanical transfer (MT), registered jack (RJ), angled physical contact

(APC), ultra-physical contact (UPC), RJ11, RJ45, F-type connector, transceiver, media converter, small form-factor pluggable (SFP), enhanced form-factor pluggable (SFP+), quad small form-factor pluggable (QSFP), enhanced quad small form-factor pluggable (QSFP+), patch panel/patch bay, fiber distribution panel, punchdown block, 66 block, 110 block, Krone, Bix, 10BASE-T, 100BASE-TX, 1000BASE-T, 10GBASE-T, 40GBASE-T, 100BASE-FX, 100BASE-SX, 1000BASE-SX, 1000BASE-LX, 10GBASE-SR, 10GBASE-LR, coarse wavelength-division multiplexing (CWDM), dense wavelength-division multiplexing (DWDM), bidirectional wavelength-division multiplexing (WDM)

Complete Chapter 3 Hands-On Labs in Network+ Simulator Lite

- Network Cabling
- Identify Common Cat5 Wiring Problems
- Create a Straight Cable and Test It
- Create a Crossover Cable
- Create a Console Cable

Additional Resources

Fundamentals of Fiber Optic Cabling: https://youtu.be/-VYhfR8Fv2I

Real World Cabling: https://www.youtube.com/watch?v=CV3-is8Yd8U

Review Questions

The answers to these review questions appear in Appendix A, "Answers to Review Questions."

1. Which of the following categories of UTP cabling are commonly used for 1000BASE-T networks? (Choose two.)

    a. Cat 5

    b. Cat 5e

    c. Cat 6

    d. Cat 6f

2. Which type of cable might be required for installation in a drop ceiling that is used as an open-air return duct?

   a. Riser

   b. Plenum

   c. Multimode

   d. Twinaxial

3. Which of the following is the eight-pin connector found in most Ethernet networks?

   a. RJ11

   b. RJ45

   c. DB-9

   d. ST

4. What are the two major categories of fiber-optic media? (Choose two.)

   a. Straight-through

   b. Single-mode

   c. Unshielded

   d. Multimode

5. What is the speed of Fast Ethernet?

   a. 1Mbps

   b. 100Mbps

   c. 1Gbps

   d. 10Gbps

6. What is a common fiber-optic cable management component for terminating many connections?

   a. A fiber distribution panel

   b. An IDF

   c. A 110 block

   d. A plenum

7. What Ethernet UTP cable was the first standard cable to carry data at speeds of 1Gbps?

    a. Cat 4

    b. Cat 5

    c. Cat 5e

    d. Cat 6

8. What type of connector is often used for cable TV (including cable modem) connections?

    a. Krone

    b. BIX

    c. F-type

    d. UPC

9. Which standards were developed to define industry-standard pinouts and color coding for twisted-pair cabling? (Choose two.)

    a. CWDM

    b. TIA/EIA-568A

    c. DWDM

    d. TIA/EIA-568B

10. What fiber type would you use if the requirements to be met included an SMF media type, 1Gbps bandwidth capacity, and a distance limitation of 5 km?

    a. 1000BASE-LX

    b. 1000BASE-SX

    c. 1000BASE-TX

    d. Thicknet

This chapter covers the following topics related to Objective 1.4 (Given a scenario, configure a subnet and use appropriate IP addressing schemes) of the CompTIA Network+ N10-008 certification exam:

- Public vs. private
  - RFC1918
  - Network address translation (NAT)
  - Port address translation (PAT)
- IPv4 vs. IPv6
  - Automatic Private IP Addressing (APIPA)
  - Extended unique identifier (EUI-64)
  - Multicast
  - Unicast
  - Anycast
  - Broadcast
  - Link local
  - Loopback
  - Default gateway
- IPv4 subnetting
  - Classless (variable-length subnet mask)

- Classful
  - A
  - B
  - C
  - D
  - E
  - Classless Inter-Domain Routing (CIDR) notation
- IPv6 concepts
  - Tunneling
  - Dual stack
  - Shorthand notation
  - Router advertisement
  - Stateless address autoconfiguration (SLAAC)
- Virtual IP (VIP)
- Subinterfaces

CHAPTER 4

IP Addressing

When two devices on a network want to communicate, they need logical addresses (that is, Layer 3 addresses, as described in Chapter 1, "The OSI Model and Encapsulation"). Most modern networks use Internet Protocol (IP) addressing. Therefore, the focus of this chapter is IP.

This chapter covers two versions of IP: IP version 4 (IPv4) and IP version 6 (IPv6). First, it discusses how IP concepts apply to IPv4. This discussion introduces you to how IP addresses are represented in binary notation. You will learn about the structure of an IPv4 address and learn to distinguish between different categories of IPv4 addresses.

Next, this chapter details various options for assigning IP addresses to end stations. As you will see, one of the benefits of IP addressing is that you have flexibility in how you can subdivide a network address into multiple subnets. This discussion of subnetting is a bit mathematical, and multiple practice exercises are provided to help solidify these concepts in your mind.

Although IPv4 is the most widely deployed Layer 3 addressing scheme in today's networks, its scalability limitation is causing available IPv4 addresses to quickly become depleted. Fortunately, a newer version of IP, IPv6, is scalable beyond anything you will need in your lifetime. So, after focusing on the foundation of IP addressing laid by IPv4, this chapter concludes by introducing you to the fundamental characteristics of IPv6 addressing.

Foundation Topics

Binary Numbering

Chapter 1 describes how a network transmits data as a series of binary 1s and 0s. Similarly, IP addresses are represented as series of binary digits (that is, *bits*). An IPv4 address consists of 32 bits, and an IPv6 address has a whopping 128 bits.

Later in this chapter, you will need to be able to convert between the decimal representation of a number and that number's binary equivalent. This skill is needed for things such as subnet mask calculations. This section describes this mathematical procedure and provides you with practice exercises.

Principles of Binary Numbering

You are accustomed to using base 10 numbering on a day-to-day basis. In a base 10 numbering system, you have 10 digits, in the range 0 through 9, at your disposal. Binary numbering, however, uses a base 2 numbering system, where there are only two digits: 0 and 1.

Because computer systems divide 32-bit IPv4 addresses into four 8-bit octets each, this discussion focuses on converting between 8-bit binary numbers and decimal numbers. To convert a binary number to decimal, you can create a table like Table 4-1.

Key Topic

Table 4-1   Binary Conversion Table

128	64	32	16	8	4	2	1

Note the structure of this table. There are eight columns, representing the 8 bits in an octet. The column headings are the powers of 2, from 0 to 7, beginning in the rightmost column. Specifically, 2 raised to the power of 0 (2^0) is 1. (In fact, any number raised to the power of 0 is 1.) If you raise 2 to the first power (2^1), that equals 2, and 2 raised to the second power (that is, 2^2, or 2×2) is 4. This continues through 2 raised to the power of 7 (that is, 2^7, or $2 \times 2 \times 2 \times 2 \times 2 \times 2 \times 2$), which equals 128. You can use this table for converting binary numbers to decimal and decimal numbers to binary. The skill of binary-to-decimal and decimal-to-binary conversion is critical for working with subnet masks, as discussed later in this chapter.

Converting a Binary Number to a Decimal Number

To convert a binary number to a decimal number, you populate the previously described binary table with the given binary digits. Then you add up the column heading values for the columns that contain a binary 1.

For example, consider Table 4-2. Only the 128, 16, 4, and 2 columns contain a 1, and all the other columns contain a 0. If you add all the column headings containing a 1 in their column (that is, 128 + 16 + 4 + 2), you get the result 150. Therefore, you can conclude that the binary number 10010110 equates to the decimal value 150.

Table 4-2 Binary Conversion Example 1

128	64	32	16	8	4	2	1
1	0	0	1	0	1	1	0

Converting a Decimal Number to a Binary Number

To convert numbers from decimal to binary, staring with the leftmost column, ask the question, "Is this number equal to or greater than the column heading?" If the answer to that question is no, place a 0 in that column and move to the next column. If the answer is yes, place a 1 in that column and subtract the value of the column heading from the number you are converting. When you then move to the next column (to your right), again ask yourself, "Is this number (which is the result of your earlier subtraction) equal to or greater than the column heading?" This process continues (to the right) for all the remaining column headings.

For example, say that you want to convert the number 167 to binary. The following steps walk you through the process:

Step 1. Ask the question, "Is 167 equal to or greater than 128?" Because the answer is yes, you place a 1 in the 128 column, as shown in Table 4-3, and subtract 128 from 167, which yields the result 39.

Table 4-3 Binary Conversion Example 2: Step 1

128	64	32	16	8	4	2	1
1							

Step 2. Now that you are done with the 128 column, move (to the right) to the 64 column. Ask the question, "Is 39 equal to or greater than 64?" Because the answer is no, you place a 0 in the 64 column, as shown in Table 4-4, and continue to the next column (the 32 column).

Table 4-4   Binary Conversion Example 2: Step 2

128	64	32	16	8	4	2	1
1	0						

Step 3.   Under the 32 column, ask the question, "Is 39 equal to or greater than 32?" Because the answer is yes, you place a 1 in the 32 column, as shown in Table 4-5, and subtract 32 from 39, which yields the result 7.

Table 4-5   Binary Conversion Example 2: Step 3

128	64	32	16	8	4	2	1
1	0	1					

Step 4.   Now you are under the 16 column and ask, "Is 7 equal to or greater than 16?" Because the answer is no, you place a 0 in the 16 column, as shown in Table 4-6, and move to the 8 column.

Table 4-6   Binary Conversion Example 2: Step 4

128	64	32	16	8	4	2	1
1	0	1	0				

Step 5.   As with the 16 column, the number 7 is not equal to or greater than 8. So, you place a 0 in the 8 column, as shown in Table 4-7.

Table 4-7   Binary Conversion Example 2: Step 5

128	64	32	16	8	4	2	1
1	0	1	0	0			

Step 6.   Because 7 is greater than or equal to 4, you place a 1 in the 4 column, as shown in Table 4-8, and subtract 4 from 7, yielding 3 as the result.

Table 4-8   Binary Conversion Example 2: Step 6

128	64	32	16	8	4	2	1
1	0	1	0	0	1		

Step 7.   Now under the 2 column, you ask the question, "Is 3 greater than or equal to 2?" Because the answer is yes, you place a 1 in the 2 column, as shown in Table 4-9, and subtract 2 from 3, yielding 1 as the result.

Table 4-9 Binary Conversion Example 2: Step 7

128	64	32	16	8	4	2	1
1	0	1	0	0	1	1	

Step 8. Finally, in the rightmost column (that is, the 1 column), you ask whether the number 1 is greater than or equal to 1. Because it is, you place a 1 in the 1 column, as shown in Table 4-10.

Table 4-10 Binary Conversion Example 2: Step 8

128	64	32	16	8	4	2	1
1	0	1	0	0	1	1	1

You can now conclude that the decimal number 167 equates to the binary value 10100111. In fact, you can check your work by adding up the values for the column headings that contain a 1 in their column. In this example, the 128, 32, 4, 2, and 1 columns contain a 1. If you add these values, the result is 167 (that is, 128 + 32 + 4 + 2 + 1 = 167).

Binary Numbering Practice

Because binary number conversion is a skill developed through practice, you will now be challenged with a few conversion exercises. The first two exercises ask you to convert a binary number to a decimal number, and the last two exercises ask you to convert a decimal number to a binary number.

Binary Conversion Exercise 1

Using Table 4-11 as a reference, convert the binary number 01101011 to a decimal number.

Table 4-11 Binary Conversion Exercise 1: Base Table

128	64	32	16	8	4	2	1

Write your answer here: _____

Binary Conversion Exercise 1: Solution

Given the binary number 01101011 and filling in a binary conversion table, as shown in Table 4-12, you find that the 64, 32, 8, 2, and 1 columns contain a 1.

Each of the other columns contains a 0. By adding up the column headings for the columns that contain a 1 (that is, 64 + 32 + 8 + 2 + 1), you get the decimal value 107.

Table 4-12 Binary Conversion Exercise 1: Solution Table

128	64	32	16	8	4	2	1
0	1	1	0	1	0	1	1

Binary Conversion Exercise 2

Using Table 4-13 as a reference, convert the binary number 10010100 to a decimal number.

Table 4-13 Binary Conversion Exercise 2: Base Table

128	64	32	16	8	4	2	1

Write your answer here: _____

Binary Conversion Exercise 2: Solution

Given the binary number 10010100 and filling in a binary conversion table, as shown in Table 4-14, you find that the 128, 16, and 4 columns contain a 1. Each of the other columns contains a 0. By adding up the column headings for the columns that contain a 1 (that is, 128 + 16 + 4), you get the decimal value 148.

Table 4-14 Binary Conversion Exercise 2: Solution Table

128	64	32	16	8	4	2	1
1	0	0	1	0	1	0	0

Binary Conversion Exercise 3

Using Table 4-15 as a reference, convert the decimal number 49 to a binary number.

Table 4-15 Binary Conversion Exercise 3: Base Table

128	64	32	16	8	4	2	1

Write your answer here: _____

Binary Conversion Exercise 3: Solution

You can begin your conversion of the decimal number 49 to a binary number by asking the following questions and performing the following calculations:

1. Is 49 greater than or equal to 128? No. Put a 0 in the 128 column.

2. Is 49 greater than or equal to 64? No. Put a 0 in the 64 column.

3. Is 49 greater than or equal to 32? Yes. Put a 1 in the 32 column and subtract 32 from 49. 49 – 32 = 17.

4. Is 17 greater than or equal to 16? Yes. Put a 1 in the 16 column and subtract 16 from 17. 17 – 16 = 1.

5. Is 1 greater than or equal to 8? No. Put a 0 in the 8 column.

6. Is 1 greater than or equal to 4? No. Put a 0 in the 4 column.

7. Is 1 greater than or equal to 2? No. Put a 0 in the 2 column.

8. Is 1 greater than or equal to 1? Yes. Put a 1 in the 1 column.

Combining these 8 binary digits, you form the binary number 00110001, as shown in Table 4-16. Verify your work by adding the values of the column headings whose columns contain a 1. In this case, columns 32, 16, and 1 each contain a 1. By adding these values (that is, 32 + 16 + 1), you get the value 49.

Table 4-16   Binary Conversion Exercise 3: Solution Table

128	64	32	16	8	4	2	1
0	0	1	1	0	0	0	1

Binary Conversion Exercise 4

Using Table 4-17 as a reference, convert the decimal number 236 to a binary number.

Table 4-17   Binary Conversion Exercise 4: Base Table

128	64	32	16	8	4	2	1

Write your answer here: _____

Binary Conversion Exercise 4: Solution

You can begin your conversion of the decimal number 236 to a binary number by asking the following questions and performing the following calculations:

1. Is 236 greater than or equal to 128? Yes. Put a 1 in the 128 column and subtract 128 from 236. 236 − 128 = 108.

2. Is 108 greater than or equal to 64? Yes. Put a 1 in the 64 column and subtract 64 from 108. 108 − 64 = 44.

3. Is 44 greater than or equal to 32? Yes. Put a 1 in the 32 column and subtract 32 from 44. 44 − 32 = 12.

4. Is 12 greater than or equal to 16? No. Put a 0 in the 16 column.

5. Is 12 greater than or equal to 8? Yes. Put a 1 in the 8 column and subtract 8 from 12. 12 − 8 = 4.

6. Is 4 greater than or equal to 4? Yes. Put a 1 in the 4 column and subtract 4 from 4. 4 − 4 = 0.

7. Is 0 greater than or equal to 2? No. Put a 0 in the 2 column.

8. Is 0 greater than or equal to 1? No. Put a 0 in the 1 column.

By combining these 8 binary digits, you form the binary number 11101100, as shown in Table 4-18. You can verify your work by adding the values of the column headings whose columns contain a 1. In this case, columns 128, 64, 32, 8, and 4 each contain a 1. By adding these values (that is, 128 + 64 + 32 + 8 + 4), you get the value 236.

Table 4-18   Binary Conversion Exercise 4: Solution Table

128	64	32	16	8	4	2	1
1	1	1	0	1	1	0	0

IPv4 Addressing

Although IPv6 is increasingly being adopted in corporate networks, IPv4 is by far the most popular Layer 3 addressing scheme in today's networks. For brevity in this section, the term *IPv4 address* is used interchangeably with the more generic term *IP address*.

Devices on an IPv4 network use unique IP addresses to communicate with one another. Metaphorically, you can relate this to sending a letter through the postal service. You place a destination address on an envelope containing the letter, and in the upper-left corner of the envelope, you place your return address. Similarly, when an IPv4 network device sends data on a network, it places both a destination IP address and a source IP address in the packet's IPv4 header.

IPv4 Address Structure

An IPv4 address is a 32-bit address. However, rather than write out each individual bit value, you write the address in **dotted-decimal notation**. Consider the IP address 10.1.2.3. Notice that this IP address is divided into four separate numbers, separated by periods. Each number represents one-fourth of the IP address. Specifically, each number represents an 8-bit portion of the 32 bits in the address. Because each of these four divisions of an IP address represents 8 bits, these divisions are called *octets*. For example, Figure 4-1 shows the binary representation of the 10.1.2.3 IP address. In Figure 4-1, notice that the 8 leftmost bits of 00001010 equate to the decimal value 10. (The calculation for this is described in the previous section.) Similarly, 00000001 in binary equates to 1 in decimal, and 00000010 in binary equals 2 in decimal. Finally, 00000011 yields the decimal value 3.

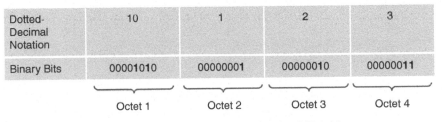

FIGURE 4-1   Binary Representation of a Dotted-Decimal IP Address

Interestingly, an IP address is composed of two types of addresses: a network address and a host address. Specifically, a group of contiguous left-justified bits represent the network address, and the remaining bits (that is, a group of contiguous right-justified bits) represent the address of a host on a network. The IP address component that determines which bits refer to the network and which bits refer to the host is called the **subnet mask**. You can think of the subnet mask as a dividing line separating an IP address's 32 bits into a group of network bits (on the left) and a group of host bits (on the right).

A subnet mask typically consists of a series of contiguous 1s followed by a set of contiguous 0s. In total, a subnet mask contains 32 bits, which correspond to the 32 bits found in an IPv4 address. The 1s in a subnet mask correspond to network bits in an IPv4 address, and 0s in a subnet mask correspond to host bits in an IPv4 address.

For example, consider Figure 4-2. The 8 leftmost bits of the subnet mask are 1s, and the remaining 24 bits are 0s. As a result, the 8 leftmost bits of the IP address represent the network address, and the remaining 24 bits represent the host address.

Key Topic	Dotted-Decimal Notation	10	1	2	3
	IP Address (in Binary)	00001010	00000001	00000010	00000011
	Subnet Mask	11111111	00000000	00000000	00000000

Network Bits   Host Bits

FIGURE 4-2 Dividing an IP Address into a Network Portion and a Host Portion

When you write a network address, all host bits are set to 0s. Once again, consider the example shown in Figure 4-2. The subnet mask in this example is an *8-bit subnet mask*, meaning that the 8 leftmost bits in the subnet mask are 1s. If the remaining bits are set to 0, as shown in Figure 4-3, the network address is 10.0.0.0.

Network Address (in Dotted Decimal)	10	0	0	0
Network Address (in Binary)	00001010	00000000	00000000	00000000
Subnet Mask	11111111	00000000	00000000	00000000

Network Bits   Host Bits

FIGURE 4-3 Network Address Calculation

When writing a network address, or an IP address for that matter, you need to provide more detail than just a dotted-decimal representation of an IP address's 32 bits. For example, just being told that a device has IP address 10.1.2.3 does not tell you the network on which the IP address resides. To know the network address, you need to know the subnet mask, which could be written in dotted-decimal notation or in *prefix notation* (also known as *slash notation*). In the example with the IP address 10.1.2.3 and an 8-bit subnet mask, the IP address could be written as 10.1.2.3 255.0.0.0 or 10.1.2.3 /8. Similarly, the network address could be written as 10.0.0.0 255.0.0.0 or 10.0.0.0 /8.

Classes of Addresses

Although for an IP address (or a network address) you need subnet mask information to determine which bits represent the network portion of the address, there are default subnet masks with which you should be familiar. The default subnet mask for a given IP address is solely determined by the value in the IP address's first octet. Table 4-19 shows the default subnet masks for various ranges of IP addresses.

Key Topic

Table 4-19 IP Address Classes

Address Class	Value in First Octet	Classful Mask (Dotted Decimal)	Classful Mask (Prefix Notation)
Class A	1–126	255.0.0.0	/8
Class B	128–191	255.255.0.0	/16
Class C	192–223	255.255.255.0	/24
Class D	224–239	—	—
Class E	240–255	—	—

These IP address ranges, which you should memorize, are referred to as different *classes* of addresses. Class A, B, and C addresses are assigned to network devices. Class D addresses are used as destination IP addresses (that is, not assigned to devices sourcing traffic) for multicast networks, and Class E addresses are reserved for experimental use. The default subnet masks associated with address Classes A, B, and C are called ***classful masks***.

For example, consider the IP address 172.16.40.56. If you are told that this IP address uses its classful mask, you should know that it has subnet mask 255.255.0.0, which is the classful mask for a Class B IP address. You should know that 172.16.40.56 is a Class B IP address, based on the value of the first octet (172), which falls in the Class B range 128–191.

NOTE You might have noticed that in the ranges of values in the first octet, the number 127 seems to have been skipped. The reason is that 127 is used as a ***loopback*** IP address, which is a locally significant IP address representing the device itself. For example, if you are working on a network device and want to verify that the device has a TCP/IP stack loaded, you can try to ping IP address 127.1.1.1. If you receive ping responses, you can conclude that the device is running a TCP/IP stack.

The nonprofit corporation Internet Corporation for Assigned Names and Numbers (ICANN) globally manages publicly routable IP addresses. ICANN does not directly assign a block of IP addresses to your Internet service provider (ISP) but rather assigns a block of IP addresses to a regional Internet registry. One example of a regional Internet registry is the American Registry for Internet Numbers (ARIN), which acts as an Internet registry for North America.

The Internet Assigned Numbers Authority (IANA) is yet another entity responsible for IP address assignment. The ICANN operates IANA and is responsible for IP address assignment outside North America.

> **NOTE** Some literature references the *Internet Network Information Center* (*InterNIC*), which was the predecessor to ICANN and existed until September 18, 1998.

When an organization is assigned one or more publicly routable IP addresses by its service provider, that organization often needs more IP addresses to accommodate all of its devices. One solution is to use private IP addressing within an organization, in combination with **Network Address Translation (NAT)**. Remember, specific Class A, B, and C networks have been designated for private use. Although these networks are routable (with the exception of the 169.254.0.0–169.254.255.255 address range) within the organization, ISPs do not route these private networks over the public Internet. Table 4-20 shows the IP networks reserved for internal use.

Key Topic

Table 4-20 Private IP Networks

Address Class	Address Range	Default Subnet Mask
Class A	10.0.0.0–10.255.255.255	255.0.0.0
Class B	172.16.0.0–172.31.255.255	255.255.0.0
Class B	169.254.0.0–169.254.255.255	255.255.0.0
Class C	192.168.0.0–192.168.255.255	255.255.255.0

> **NOTE** The 169.254.0.0–169.254.255.255 address range is not routable. Addresses in this range are only usable on their local subnet and are dynamically assigned to network hosts using Automatic Private IP Addressing (APIPA), which is discussed later in this chapter.

NAT, which is available on routers, allows private IP addresses used within an organization to be translated into a pool of one or more publicly routable IP addresses.

Types of Addresses

For the real world and for the Network+ exam, you need to be familiar with the following categories of IPv4 addresses (and even more, which we will discuss later): unicast, broadcast, and multicast. The following sections describe these types of addresses in detail.

Unicast

Most network traffic is ***unicast*** in nature, meaning that traffic travels from a single source device to a single destination device. Figure 4-4 illustrates an example of a unicast transmission.

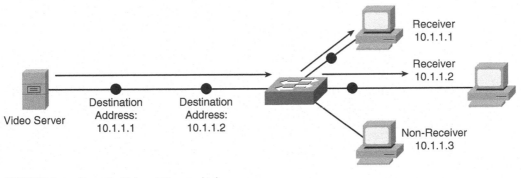

FIGURE 4-4   Sample Unicast Transmission

Broadcast

Broadcast traffic travels from a single source to all destinations on a network (that is, a *broadcast domain*). It might seem as though the broadcast address 255.255.255.255 would reach all hosts on all interconnected networks. However, 255.255.255.255 targets all devices on a single network—specifically, the network local to the device sending a packet destined for 255.255.255.255. Another type of broadcast address is a *directed broadcast address*, which targets all devices in a remote network. For example, the address 172.16.255.255 /16 is a directed broadcast address targeting all devices in the 172.16.0.0 /16 network. Figure 4-5 illustrates an example of a broadcast transmission.

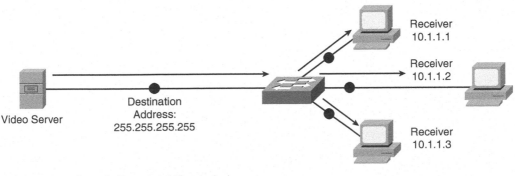

FIGURE 4-5   Sample Broadcast Transmission

Multicast

Multicast technology offers an efficient mechanism for a single host to send traffic to multiple specific destinations. For example, say that a network has 100 users, and 20 of those users want to receive a video stream from a video server. With a unicast solution, the video server would have to send 20 individual streams, 1 for each recipient. Such a solution could consume a significant amount of network bandwidth and put a heavy processor burden on the video server.

With a broadcast solution, the video server would only have to send the video stream once; however, it would be received by every device on the local subnet, even devices not wanting to receive the video stream. Even though a lot of the devices do not want to receive the video stream, they still must pause what they are doing and take time to check each of these unwanted packets.

As shown in Figure 4-6, multicast offers a compromise, allowing the video server to send the video stream only once and sending the video stream only to devices on the network that want to receive the stream. Multicast is possible thanks to the use of a Class D address. A Class D address, such as 239.1.2.3, represents the address of a *multicast group*. The video server could, in this example, send a single copy of each video stream packet destined for 239.1.2.3. Devices wanting to receive the video stream could join the multicast group. Based on the device request, switches and routers in the topology could then dynamically determine out of which ports the video stream should be forwarded.

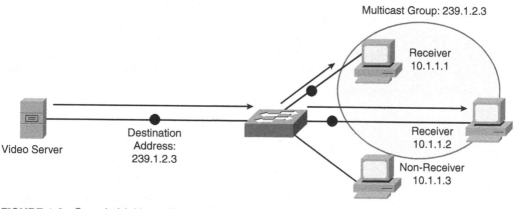

FIGURE 4-6 Sample Multicast Transmission

Assigning IPv4 Addresses

At this point in the discussion, you should understand that networked devices need IP addresses. However, beyond just an IP address, what extra IP address–related information needs to be provided to a device, and how does an IP address get assigned to a device?

This section begins by discussing various parameters that might be assigned to a network device, followed by discussions covering various approaches to assigning IP addresses to devices.

IP Addressing Components

As discussed in the previous section, an IP address has two portions: a network portion and a host portion. A subnet mask is required to delineate between these two portions.

In addition, if traffic is destined for a different subnet than the subnet on which the traffic originates, a *default gateway* needs to be defined. A default gateway routes traffic from the sender's subnet toward the destination subnet. Chapter 10, "Routing Technologies and Bandwidth Management," covers the concept of routing.

Another consideration is that end users typically do not type in the IP address of the destination device with which they want to connect (for example, a web server on the Internet). Instead, end users typically type in fully qualified domain names (FQDNs), such as www.ajsnetworking.com. When connecting to devices on the public Internet, a Domain Name System (DNS) server translates an FQDN into the corresponding IP address.

For a very long time, in a company's internal network (that is, an intranet), a Microsoft Windows Internet Name Service (WINS) was used to convert the names of network devices into their corresponding IP addresses. For example, say that you attempted to navigate to the shared folder \\server1\hrdocs. A WINS server could be used to resolve the network device name server1 to a corresponding IP address. The path \\server1\hrdocs is in *universal naming convention* (*UNC*) form, where you are specifying a network device name (in this case, server1) and a resource available on that device (in this case, hrdocs). Companies today use DNS even for internal network name resolution.

To summarize, network devices (for example, an end-user PC) can benefit from a variety of IP address parameters, such as the following:

- IP address
- Subnet mask
- Default gateway
- Server address

Remember as well that an IP address no longer needs to be assigned to a single entity or interface. A *virtual IP (VIP) address* is commonly used and can fulfill many purposes, such as the following:

- Provide key addresses used in address translation.

- Represent any actual IP address assigned to a network device interface.

- Permit the sending of traffic to multiple different network devices, all configured to respond based on the virtual IP address.

A concept that is very similar to the virtual IP address is the *subinterface*. This is a handy interface capability supported by most router and switch manufacturers that allows you to create many virtual interfaces out of a single physical interface. Example 4-1 demonstrates the creation of a subinterface on a Cisco router and the assignment of an IP address there. This is done after enabling and providing an IP address to the physical interface.

Example 4-1   Creating a Subinterface on a Router and Assigning an IP Address

```
interface gi0/0
no shutdown
ip address 10.10.10.10 255.255.255.0
!
interface gi0/0.100
ip address 10.100.100.10 255.255.255.0
```

NOTE   If a physical interface is enabled and in an up/up state, the subinterface should also be enabled, and its IP address should be functional on the network.

Static Configuration

A simple way of configuring a PC with, for example, IP address parameters is to statically configure that information. For example, on a PC running Microsoft Windows as the operating system, you can navigate to the Control Panel, as shown in Figure 4-7, and click **Network and Internet**.

In the Network and Internet control panel, click *Network and Sharing Center*, as shown in Figure 4-8.

You can then click the *Change adapter settings* link, as shown in Figure 4-9.

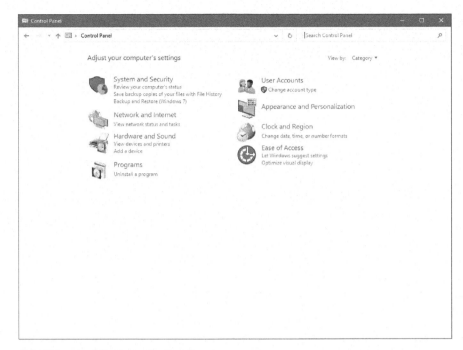

FIGURE 4-7   Windows Control Panel

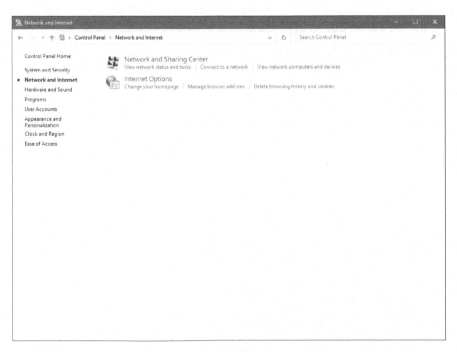

FIGURE 4-8   Network and Internet Control Panel

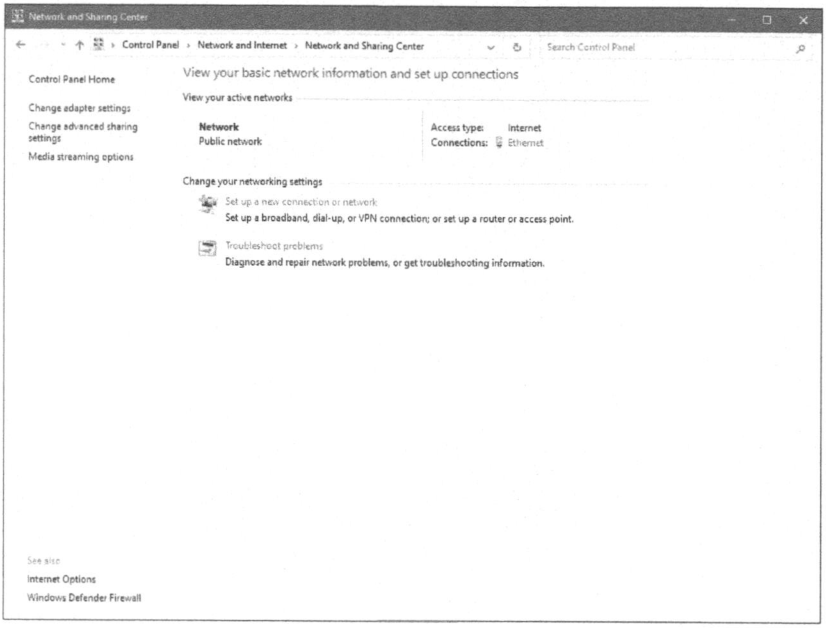

FIGURE 4-9   Network and Sharing Center

In the *Network Connections* window, double-click the network adapter whose settings you want to change, as shown in Figure 4-10.

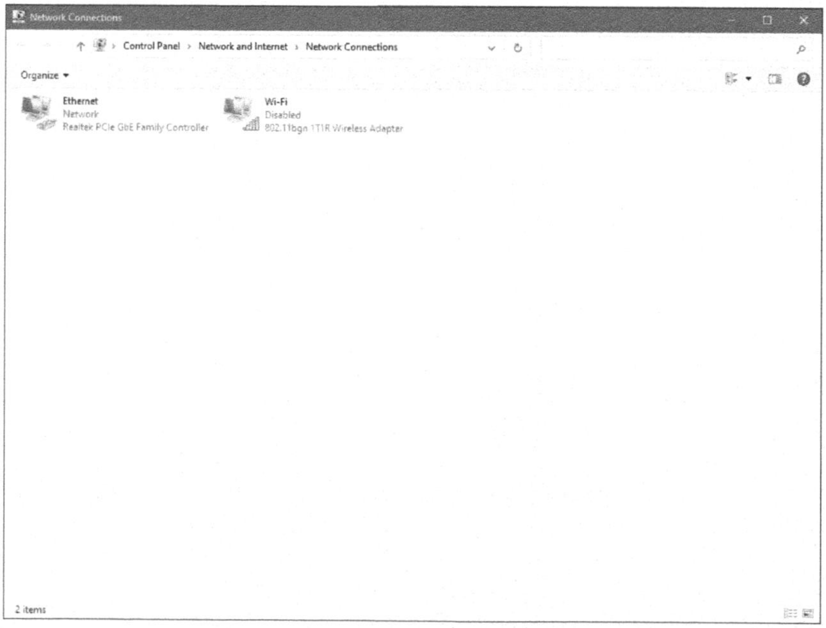

FIGURE 4-10   Network Connections Window

You are then taken to the Local Area Connection Status window, as shown in Figure 4-11, where you can click the *Properties* button.

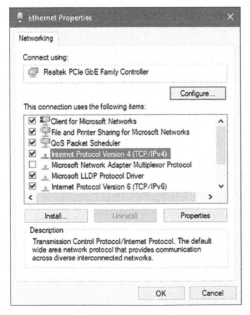

FIGURE 4-11   Local Area Connection Status Window

As shown in Figure 4-12, you can highlight *Internet Protocol Version 4 (TCP/IPv4)* and click the *Properties* button.

FIGURE 4-12   Local Area Connection Properties

You can enter an IP address, a subnet mask, a default gateway, and DNS server information into the Internet Protocol Version 4 (TCP/IPv4) Properties window, shown in Figure 4-13. Although DNS server information can be entered in this window, more advanced DNS options and WINS options are available by clicking the **Advanced** button.

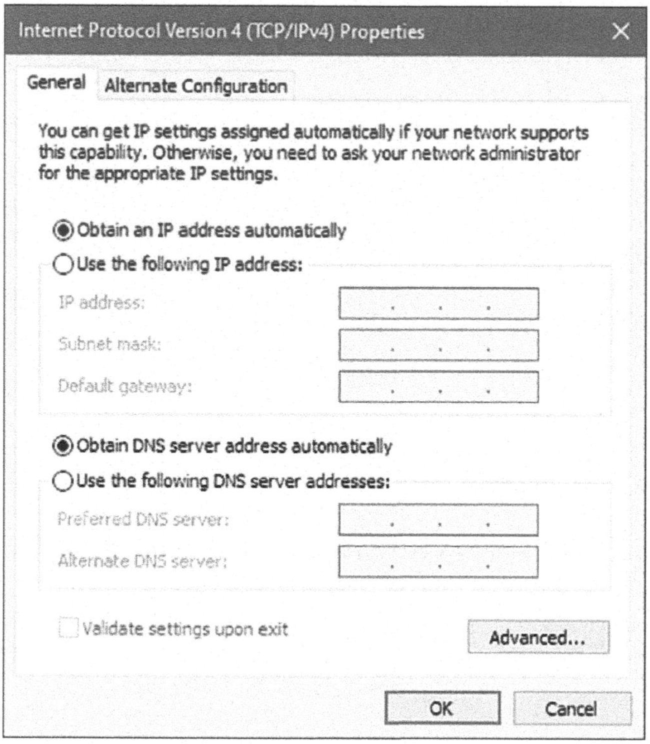

FIGURE 4-13   Internet Protocol Version 4 (TCP/IPv4) Properties

By clicking the *DNS* tab in the Advanced TCP/IP Settings window, as shown in Figure 4-14, you can add, remove, or reorder DNS servers, and you can adjust various other DNS parameters. Recall that a DNS server converts an FQDN to an IP address. Also, although Figure 4-13 shows the same IP address for the default gateway and a DNS server, these are not always located on the same device.

Similarly, you can configure Windows Internet Name Service (WINS) servers in the WINS tab of the Advanced TCP/IP Settings window, as shown in Figure 4-15. Much like a DNS server, a WINS server converts a NetBIOS computer name to a corresponding IP address.

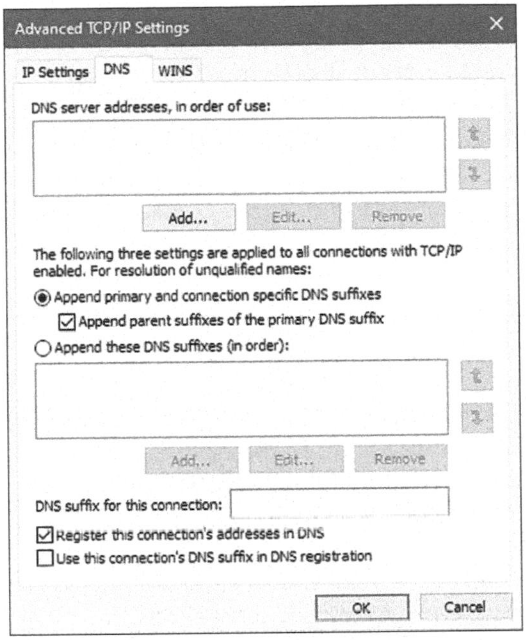

FIGURE 4-14 Advanced TCP/IP Settings: DNS Tab

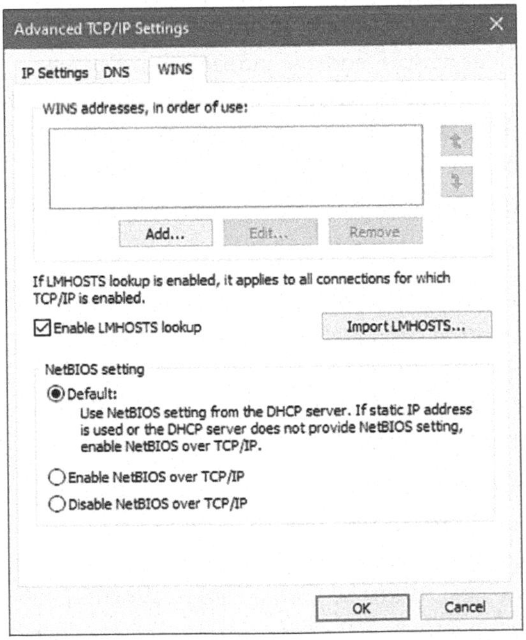

FIGURE 4-15 Advanced TCP/IP Settings: WINS Tab

Dynamic Configuration

Statically assigning IP address information to individual networked devices can be time-consuming, error-prone, and lacking in scalability. Instead of using static IP address assignments, many corporate networks dynamically assign IP address parameters to their devices. An early choice for performing this automatic assignment of IP addresses was the *Bootstrap Protocol (BOOTP)*. Currently, however, the most popular approach for dynamic IP address assignment is *Dynamic Host Configuration Protocol (DHCP)*.

BOOTP

Engineers developed BOOTP as a method of assigning IP address, subnet mask, and default gateway information to diskless workstations. In the early days of Microsoft Windows (for example, Microsoft Windows 3.1), Microsoft Windows did not natively support TCP/IP. To include TCP/IP support, an add-on TCP/IP application (for example, Trumpet Winsock) could be run. Such an application would typically support BOOTP.

When a device needed to obtain IP address information, a BOOTP broadcast would be sent out from the device needing an IP address. If a BOOTP server (BOOTPS) received the broadcast, it could match the source MAC address in the received frame (the MAC address from the device wanting to obtain an IP address) with a corresponding IP address in a database stored on the BOOTP server. The BOOTPS would then respond to the requesting client with IP address information. Because BOOTP requests were based on broadcasts, by default, a BOOTP request could not propagate beyond a device's local subnet. However, most enterprise-class routers can be configured to forward selected broadcast types, including BOOTP broadcasts.

DHCP

DHCP offers a more robust solution to IP address assignment than does BOOTP. DHCP does not require a statically configured database of MAC-address-to-IP-address mappings. Also, DHCP has a wide variety of options beyond basic IP address, subnet mask, and default gateway parameters. For example, a DHCP server can educate a DHCP client about the IP address of a TFTP server from which a configuration file could be downloaded.

In Chapter 6, "Network Services," you will learn more about the operation of DHCP. For now, it is important to realize that, as with BOOTP, DHCP's initial request is a broadcast, requiring a client's local router be configured to appropriately forward DHCP requests to a DHCP server if that DHCP server is not on the local subnet of the requesting client.

In setting up a DHCP server, you would identify a range of IP addresses to hand out, and this would be referred to as the *scope*. In addition, a DHCP server can be configured to have reservations, so that a specific IP address is reserved for a specific Layer 2 Ethernet MAC address. The lease time can also be configured and is usually set to one day. The DHCP server also provides options such as DNS server addresses, the default gateway to use, domain suffixes to use, and more. If a DHCP client is not on the same subnet as a DHCP server, a router or another device that is connected to the same subnet as the DHCP client can be configured as a DHCP relay agent. The device takes the discover packet from the client (broadcast) and routes it to the DHCP server (unicast). This feature is also sometimes referred to as *IP helper*.

As an example of DHCP client configuration, in Microsoft Windows 10, you can select the ***Obtain an IP address automatically*** and ***Obtain DNS server address automatically*** options in the Internet Protocol Version 4 (TCP/IPv4) Properties window, as shown in Figure 4-16.

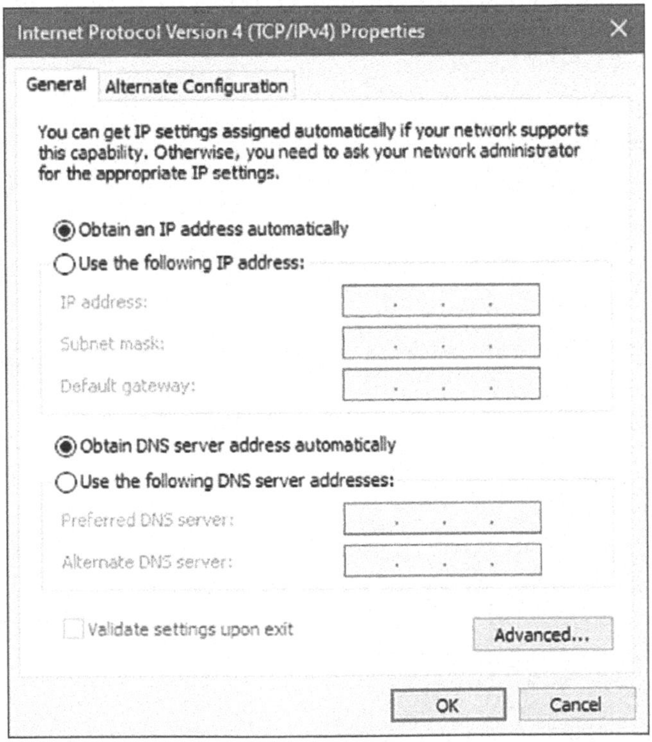

FIGURE 4-16   Configuring Microsoft Windows 10 to Obtain IP Address Information via DHCP

> **NOTE**   A protocol made obsolete by BOOTP and DHCP is Reverse Address Resolution Protocol (RARP). Whereas Address Resolution Protocol (ARP) requests a MAC address that corresponds to a known IP address, RARP requested an IP address (from a preconfigured host) that corresponded to a station's MAC address. Although RARP did allow a station to dynamically obtain an IP address, both BOOTP and DHCP offer additional features.

Automatic Private IP Addressing

If a networked device does not have a statically configured IP address and is unable to contact a DHCP server, it still might be able to communicate on an IP network thanks to *Automatic Private IP Addressing (APIPA)*. The APIPA feature allows a networked device to self-assign an IP address from the 169.254.0.0/16 network. Note that this address is usable only on the device's local subnet. (The IP address is not routable.)

As shown in Figure 4-17, Microsoft Windows 10 defaults to APIPA if a client is configured to automatically obtain IP address information and that client fails to obtain IP address information from a DHCP server.

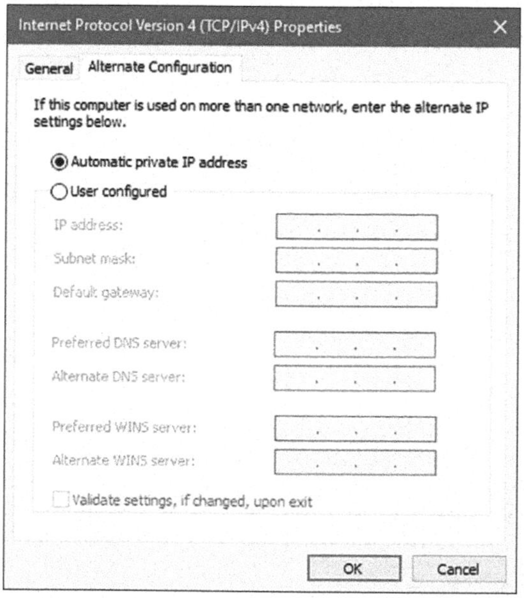

FIGURE 4-17   APIPA Configuration Enabled by Default

APIPA was designed as a solution for quickly setting up a localized network without the need to configure a DHCP server or the need to statically assign IP address information. However, there remains a need for devices on this localized network to perform name resolution and discover network services. Fortunately, these needs are covered by Zero Configuration (Zeroconf). *Zeroconf* is a technology supported on most modern operating systems and performs three basic functions:

- **Assigning link-local IP addresses:** A *link-local* IP address is a nonroutable IP address usable only on a local subnet. APIPA is an example of a technology that assigns link-local IP addresses.

- **Resolving computer names to IP addresses:** Multicast Domain Name System (mDNS) is an example of a technology that can resolve computer names to their corresponding IP addresses on a local subnet, without the aid of a DNS server or a WINS server.

- **Locating network services:** Examples of service discovery protocols include the standards-based Service Location Protocol (SLP), Microsoft's Simple Service Discovery Protocol (SSDP), and Apple's DNS-based Service Discovery (DNS-SD).

If devices supporting these three Zeroconf features are interconnected on a local subnet, they can dynamically obtain link-local IP addresses, resolve one another's names to IP addresses, and discover services available on a network.

Subnetting

Earlier in this chapter, you were introduced to the purpose of a subnet mask and the default subnet masks for the various IP address classes. Default subnet masks (that is, classful subnet masks) are not always the most efficient choice. Fortunately, you can add additional network bits to a subnet mask (thereby extending the subnet mask) to create subnets within a classful network. This section explains why you might want to perform this process and describes how you mathematically perform subnet calculations.

Purpose of Subnetting

Consider the number of assignable IP addresses in the various classes of IP addresses shown in Table 4-21. Recall that the host bits of an IP address cannot be all 0s (which represents the network address) or all 1s (which represents the directed broadcast address). Therefore, the number of assignable IP addresses in a subnet can be determined by the following formula:

Number of assignable IP addresses in a subnet $= 2^h - 2$

where h is the number of host bits in a subnet mask.

Table 4-21   Assignable IP Addresses

Address Class	Assignable IP Addresses
Class A	16,777,214 (2^{24}–2)
Class B	65,534 (2^{16}–2)
Class C	254 (2^{8}–2)

Suppose that you decide to use a private Class B IP address (for example, 172.16.0.0/16) for your internal IP addressing. For performance reasons, you would not want to support as many as 65,534 hosts in a single broadcast domain. Therefore, a best practice with such a network address is to subnet the network (thereby extending the number of network bits in the network's subnet mask) into additional subnetworks. In fact, you could subnet your major network address space and then further subnet one of your unused subnet addresses! This practice, known as *Variable-Length Subnet Masking (VLSM)*, allows you to design the network the best way possible in terms of the number of IP addresses required in different areas. Of course, this network also uses a variety of subnet masks to accomplish this task.

Subnet Mask Notation

As previously mentioned, the number of bits in a subnet mask can be represented in dotted-decimal notation (for example, 255.255.255.0) or in prefix notation (for example, /24). As a reference, Table 4-22 shows valid subnet masks in dotted-decimal notation and the corresponding prefix notation.

Table 4-22   Dotted-Decimal and Prefix-Notation Representations for IPv4 Subnets

Dotted-Decimal Notation	Prefix Notation
255.0.0.0	/8 (classful subnet mask for Class A networks)
255.128.0.0	/9
255.192.0.0	/10
255.224.0.0	/11
255.240.0.0	/12
255.248.0.0	/13
255.252.0.0	/14
255.254.0.0	/15
255.255.0.0	/16 (classful subnet mask for Class B networks)
255.255.128.0	/17
255.255.192.0	/18
255.255.224.0	/19

Dotted-Decimal Notation	Prefix Notation
255.255.240.0	/20
255.255.248.0	/21
255.255.252.0	/22
255.255.254.0	/23
255.255.255.0	/24 (classful subnet mask for Class C networks)
255.255.255.128	/25
255.255.255.192	/26
255.255.255.224	/27
255.255.255.240	/28
255.255.255.248	/29
255.255.255.252	/30

Recall that any octet with a value of 255 contains eight 1s. Also, you should memorize valid octet values for an octet and the corresponding number of 1s (that is, continuous, left-justified 1s) in that octet, as shown in Table 4-23. Based on this information, you should be able to see the dotted-decimal notation of a subnet mask and quickly determine the corresponding prefix notation.

Key Topic

Table 4-23 Subnet Octet Values

Subnet Octet Value	Number of Contiguous Left-Justified Ones
0	0
128	1
192	2
224	3
240	4
248	5
252	6
254	7
255	8

For example, consider the subnet mask 255.255.192.0. Because each of the first two octets has a value of 255, you know that you have sixteen 1s from the first two octets. You then recall that a value of 192 in the third octet requires two 1s from that octet. By adding the sixteen 1s from the first two octets to the two 1s from the third octet, you can determine that the subnet mask 255.255.192.0 has the corresponding prefix notation /18.

To help you develop the skill of making these calculations quickly, work through the following two exercises.

Subnet Notation: Practice Exercise 1

Given the subnet mask 255.255.255.248, what is the corresponding prefix notation?

_____

Subnet Notation: Practice Exercise 1 Solution

Given the subnet mask 255.255.255.248, you should recognize that the first three octets, each containing a value of 255, represent twenty-four 1s. To those twenty-four 1s, you add five additional 1s, based on your memorization of how many contiguous, left-justified 1s in an octet are required to produce various octet values. The sum of 24 bits (from the first three octets) and the 5 bits (from the fourth octet) gives you a total of 29 bits. Therefore, you can conclude that a subnet mask with dotted-decimal notation 255.255.255.248 has equivalent prefix notation /29.

Subnet Notation: Practice Exercise 2

Given the subnet mask /17, what is the corresponding dotted-decimal notation?

_____

Subnet Notation: Practice Exercise 2 Solution

You know that each octet contains 8 bits. So, given the subnet mask /17, you can count by 8s to determine that there are eight 1s in the first octet, eight 1s in the second octet, and one 1 in the third octet. You already knew that an octet containing all 1s has the decimal value 255. From that knowledge, you conclude that each of the first two octets has the value 255. Also, based on your memorization of Table 4-23, you know that one 1 (that is, a left-justified 1) in an octet has the decimal equivalent value 128. Therefore, you can conclude that a subnet mask with prefix notation /17 can be represented in dotted-decimal notation as 255.255.128.0.

Extending a Classful Mask

The way to take a classful network (that is, a network using a classful subnet mask) and divide that network into multiple subnets is by adding 1s to the network's classful subnet mask. However, the class of the IP address does not change, regardless of the new subnet mask. For example, if you took the 172.16.0.0/16 network and subnetted it into multiple networks using a 24-bit subnet mask (172.16.0.0/24, 172.16.1.0/24, 172.16.2.0/24, …), those networks would still be Class B networks.

Specifically, the class of a network is entirely determined by the value of the first octet. The class of a network has nothing to do with the number of bits in a subnet, which makes this an often-misunderstood concept. For example, the network 10.2.3.0/24 has the subnet mask of a Class C network (that is, a 24-bit subnet mask). However, the 10.2.3.0/24 network is a Class A network because the value of the first octet is 10. It is simply a Class A network that happens to have a 24-bit subnet mask.

Borrowed Bits

When you add bits to a classful mask, the bits you add are referred to as *borrowed bits*. The number of borrowed bits you use determines how many subnets are created and the number of usable hosts per subnet.

Calculating the Number of Created Subnets

To determine the number of subnets created when adding bits to a classful mask, you can use the following formula:

Number of created subnets = $2s$

where s is the number of borrowed bits.

For example, let's say you subnetted the 192.168.1.0 network with a 28-bit subnet mask, and you want to determine how many subnets were created. First, you determine how many borrowed bits you have. Recall that the number of borrowed bits is the number of bits in a subnet mask beyond the classful mask. In this case, because the first octet in the network address has the value 192, you can conclude that this is a Class C network. Also recall that a Class C network has 24 bits in its classful (that is, its default) subnet mask. Because you now have a 28-bit subnet mask, the number of borrowed bits can be calculated as follows:

Number of borrowed bits = Bits in custom subnet mask – Bits in classful
subnet mask

Number of borrowed bits = 28 – 24 = 4

Now that you know you have 4 borrowed bits, you can raise 2 to the power of 4 (2^4, or $2 \times 2 \times 2 \times 2$), which equals 16. From this calculation, you conclude that subnetting 192.168.1.0/24 with a 28-bit subnet mask yields 16 subnets.

Calculating the Number of Available Hosts

Earlier in this section, you saw the formula for calculating the number of available (that is, assignable) host IP addresses, based on the number of host bits in a subnet mask. Here again is the formula:

Number of assignable IP address in a subnet = $2h - 2$

where h is the number of host bits in the subnet mask.

Using the previous example, let's say you want to determine the number of available host IP addresses in one of the 192.168.1.0/28 subnets. First, you need to determine the number of host bits in the subnet mask. Because you know that an IPv4 address consists of 32 bits, you can subtract the number of bits in the subnet mask (28, in this example) from 32 to determine the number of host bits:

Number of host bits = 32 − Number of bits in subnet mask

Number of host bits = 32 − 28 = 4

Now that you know the number of host bits, you can apply it to the previously presented formula:

Number of assignable IP addresses in a subnet = $2h - 2$

where h is the number of host bits in the subnet mask.

Number of assignable IP addresses in a subnet = $2^4 - 2 = 14$

From this calculation, you can conclude that each of the 192.168.1.0/28 subnets has 14 usable IP addresses.

To reinforce your skill with these calculations, you are now challenged with a few practice exercises.

Basic Subnetting Practice: Exercise 1

Using a separate sheet of paper, solve the following scenario:

Your company has been assigned the 172.20.0.0/16 network for use at one of its sites. You need to use a subnet mask that will accommodate 47 subnets while simultaneously accommodating the maximum number of hosts per subnet. What subnet mask will you use?

Basic Subnetting Practice: Exercise 1 Solution

To determine how many borrowed bits are required to accommodate 47 subnets, you can write out a table that lists the powers of 2, as shown in Table 4-24. In fact, you might want to sketch out a similar table on the dry-erase card you are given when you take the Network+ exam.

Table 4-24 Number of Subnets Created by a Specified Number of Borrowed Bits

Borrowed Bits	Number of Subnets Created (2^s, Where s Is the Number of Borrowed Bits)
0	1
1	2
2	4
3	8
4	16
5	32
6	64
7	128
8	256
9	512
10	1024
11	2048
12	4096

In this example, where you want to support 47 subnets, 5 borrowed bits are not enough, and 6 borrowed bits are more than enough. Because 5 borrowed bits are not enough, you round up and use 6 borrowed bits.

The first octet in the network address 172.20.0.0 has the value 172, which means you are dealing with a Class B address. Because a Class B address has 16 bits in its classful mask, you can add the 6 borrowed bits to the 16-bit classful mask, which results in a 22-bit subnet mask.

One might argue that although a 22-bit subnet mask would accommodate 47 subnets, so would a 23-bit subnet mask or a 24-bit subnet mask. Although that is true, recall that the scenario said you should have the maximum number of hosts per subnet. This suggests that you should not use more borrowed bits than necessary. Therefore, you can conclude that to meet the scenario's requirements, you should use a subnet mask of /22, which could also be written as 255.255.252.0.

Basic Subnetting Practice: Exercise 2

Using a separate sheet of paper, solve the following scenario:

Your company has been assigned the 172.20.0.0/16 network for use at one of its sites. You need to calculate a subnet mask that will accommodate 100 hosts per subnet while maximizing the number of available subnets. What subnet mask will you use?

Basic Subnetting Practice: Exercise 2 Solution

To determine how many host bits are required to accommodate 100 hosts, you can write out a table that shows the number of hosts supported by a specific number of hosts bits, as shown in Table 4-25. As with the previous example, you might want to sketch out a similar table on the dry-erase card you are given when taking the Network+ exam.

Key Topic

Table 4-25   Number of Supported Hosts, Given a Specified Number of Host Bits

Host Bits	Number of Supported Hosts ($2^h - 2$, Where h Is the Number of Host Bits)
2	2
3	6
4	14
5	30
6	62
7	126
8	254
9	510
10	1022
11	2046
12	4094

In this example, where you want to support 100 hosts, 6 host bits are not enough, and 7 host bits are more than enough. Because 6 host bits are not enough, you round up and use 7 host bits.

Because an IPv4 address has 32 bits and you need 7 host bits, you can calculate the number of subnet bits by subtracting the 7 host bits from 32 (that is, the total number of bits in an IPv4 address). This results in a 25-bit subnet mask (that is, 32 total bits – 7 host bits = 25 subnet mask bits). Therefore, you can conclude that to meet the scenario's requirements, you should use a subnet mask of /25, which could also be written as 255.255.255.128.

Calculating New IP Address Ranges

Now that you can calculate the number of subnets created based on a given number of borrowed bits, the next logical step is to calculate the IP address ranges making up those subnets. For example, if you subnetted 172.25.0.0/16 with a 24-bit subnet mask, the resulting subnets would be as follows:

172.25.0.0/24

172.25.1.0/24

172.25.2.0/24

...

172.25.255.0/24

Let's consider how such a calculation is performed. Notice in the previous example that you count by 1 in the third octet to calculate the new networks. To decide in what octet you start counting and by what increment you count, a new term needs to be defined. The *interesting octet* is the octet that contains the last 1 in the subnet mask.

In this example, the subnet mask is a 24-bit subnet mask, which has the dotted-decimal equivalent 255.255.255.0 and the binary equivalent 11111111.11111111.111 11111.00000000. From any of these subnet mask representations, you can determine that the third octet is the octet to contain the last 1 in the subnet mask. Therefore, you will be changing the value of the third octet to calculate the new networks.

Now that you know the third octet is the interesting octet, you need to know by what increment you will be counting in that octet. This increment is known as the **block size**, and you can calculate it by subtracting the subnet mask value in the interesting octet from 256. In this example, the subnet mask has the value 255 in the interesting octet (that is, the third octet). If you subtract 255 from 256, you get the result 1 (that is, 256 – 255 = 1). The first subnet is the original network address, with all of the borrowed bits set to 0. After this first subnet, you start counting by the block size (1 in this example) in the interesting octet to calculate the remainder of the subnets.

The process just described for calculating subnets can be summarized as follows:

Step 1.   Determine the interesting octet by determining the last octet in the subnet mask to contain a 1.

Step 2.   Determine the block size by subtracting the decimal value in the subnet's interesting octet from 256.

Step 3.   Determine the first subnet by setting all the borrowed bits (which are bits in the subnet mask beyond the bits in the classful subnet mask) to 0.

Step 4.   Determine additional subnets by taking the first subnet and counting by the block size increment in the interesting octet.

To reinforce this procedure, consider another example. Say that a 27-bit subnet mask is applied to the network address 192.168.10.0/24. To calculate the created subnets, you can perform the following steps:

Step 1.   The subnet mask /27 (in binary) is 11111111.11111111.11111111.111000 00. The interesting octet is the fourth octet because the fourth octet contains the last 1 in the subnet mask.

Step 2.   The decimal value of the fourth octet in the subnet mask is 224 (11100000 in decimal). Therefore, the block size is 32 (256 − 224 = 32).

Step 3.   The first subnet is 192.168.10.0/27—the value of the original 192.168.10.0 network with the borrowed bits (the first 3 bits in the fourth octet) set to 0.

Step 4.   Counting by 32 (the block size) in the interesting octet (the fourth octet) allows you to calculate the remaining subnets:

192.168.10.0

192.168.10.32

192.168.10.64

192.168.10.96

192.168.10.128

192.168.10.160

192.168.10.192

192.168.10.224

Now that you know the subnets created from a classful network given a subnet mask, the next logical step is to determine the usable addresses within those subnets. Recall that you cannot assign an IP address to a device if all the host bits in the IP address are set to 0 because an IP address with all host bits set to 0 is the address of the subnet itself.

Similarly, you cannot assign an IP address to a device if all the host bits in the IP address are set to 1 because an IP address with all host bits set to 1 is the directed broadcast address of a subnet.

By excluding the network and directed broadcast addresses from the 192.168.10.0/27 subnets (as previously calculated), you can determine the usable addresses shown in Table 4-26.

Key Topic

Table 4-26   Usable IP Address Ranges for the 192.168.10.0/27 Subnets

Subnet Address	Directed Broadcast Address	Usable IP Addresses
192.168.10.0	192.168.10.31	192.168.10.1–192.168.10.30
192.168.10.32	192.168.10.63	192.168.10.33–192.168.10.62
192.168.10.64	192.168.10.95	192.168.10.65–192.168.10.94
192.168.10.96	192.168.10.127	192.168.10.97–192.168.10.126
192.168.10.128	192.168.10.159	192.168.10.129–192.168.10.158
192.168.10.160	192.168.10.191	192.168.10.161–192.168.10.190
192.168.10.192	192.168.10.223	192.168.10.193–192.168.10.222
192.168.10.224	192.168.10.255	192.168.10.225–192.168.10.254

To help develop your subnet-calculation skills, you are now challenged with a few practice subnetting exercises.

Advanced Subnetting Practice: Exercise 1

Using a separate sheet of paper, solve the following scenario:

Based on your network design requirements, you determine that you should use a 26-bit subnet mask applied to your 192.168.0.0/24 network. You now need to calculate each of the created subnets. In addition, you want to know the broadcast address and the range of usable addresses for each of the created subnets.

Advanced Subnetting Practice: Exercise 1 Solution

As described earlier, you can go through the following four-step process to determine the subnet address:

Step 1.   The subnet mask /26 (in binary) is 11111111.11111111.11111111.1100 0000. The interesting octet is the fourth octet because the fourth octet contains the last 1 in the subnet mask.

Step 2.   The decimal value of the fourth octet in the subnet mask is 192 (11000000 in decimal). Therefore, the block size is 64 (256 – 192 = 64).

Step 3.   The first subnet is 192.168.0.0/26—the value of the original 192.168.0.0 network with the borrowed bits (the first 2 bits in the last octet) set to 0.

Step 4.   Counting by 64 (the block size) in the interesting octet (the fourth octet) allows you to calculate the remaining subnets, resulting in the following subnets:

192.168.0.0

192.168.0.64

192.168.0.128

192.168.0.192

The directed broadcast addresses for each of these preceding subnets can be calculated by adding 63 (that is, one less than the block size) to the interesting octet for each subnet address. Excluding the subnet addresses and directed broadcast addresses, you can calculate a range of usable addresses, the results of which are shown in Table 4-27.

Table 4-27   Usable IP Address Ranges for the 192.168.0.0/26 Subnets

Subnet Address	Directed Broadcast Address	Usable IP Addresses
192.168.0.0	192.168.0.63	192.168.0.1–192.168.0.62
192.168.0.64	192.168.0.127	192.168.0.65–192.168.0.126
192.168.0.128	192.168.0.191	192.168.0.129–192.168.0.190
192.168.0.192	192.168.0.255	192.168.0.193–192.168.0.254

Advanced Subnetting Practice: Exercise 2

Using a separate sheet of paper, solve the following scenario:

In the network shown in Figure 4-18, the 172.16.0.0/16 network is subnetted using a 20-bit subnet mask. Notice that two VLANs (two subnets) are configured; however, one of the client PCs is assigned an IP address that is not in that PC's VLAN. Which client PC is assigned an incorrect IP address?

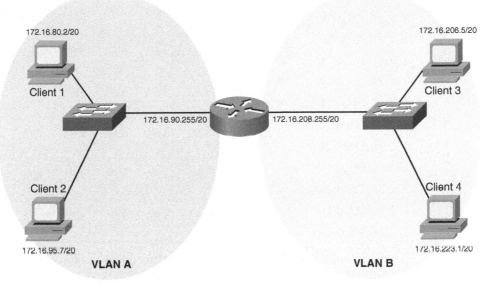

172.16.80.2/20

172.16.206.5/20

Client 1

Client 3

172.16.90.255/20   172.16.208.255/20

Client 2

Client 4

172.16.95.7/20

172.16.223.1/20

VLAN A   **VLAN B**

FIGURE 4-18 Topology for Advanced Subnetting Practice: Exercise 2

Advanced Subnetting Practice: Exercise 2 Solution

To determine which client PC is assigned an IP address outside its local VLAN, you need to determine the subnets created by the 20-bit subnet mask applied to the 172.16.0.0/16 network:

Step 1. The interesting octet for a 20-bit subnet mask is the third octet because the third octet is the last octet to contain a 1 in the 20-bit subnet mask (11111111.11111111.11110000.00000000, which could also be written as 255.255.240.0).

Step 2. The decimal value of the third octet in the subnet mask is 240. Therefore, the block size is 16 (256 – 240 = 16).

Step 3. The first 172.16.0.0/20 subnet is 172.16.0.0 (172.16.0.0/20 with the 4 borrowed bits in the third octet set to 0).

Step 4. Beginning with the first subnet, 172.16.0.0/20, and counting by the block size 16 in the interesting octet yields the following subnets:

172.16.0.0/20

172.16.16.0/20

172.16.32.0/20

172.16.48.0/20

172.16.64.0/20

172.16.80.0/20

172.16.96.0/20

172.16.112.0/20

172.16.128.0/20

172.16.144.0/20

172.16.160.0/20

172.16.176.0/20

172.16.192.0/20

172.16.208.0/20

172.16.224.0/20

172.16.240.0/20

Based on the IP addresses of the router interfaces, you can figure out the subnets for VLAN A and VLAN B. Specifically, the router interface in VLAN A has the IP address 172.16.90.255/20. Based on the previous listing of subnets, you can determine that this interface resides in the 172.16.80.0/20 network, whose range of usable addresses is 172.16.80.1–172.16.95.254. Then you can examine the IP addresses of Client 1 and Client 2 to determine whether their IP addresses reside in that range of usable addresses.

Similarly, for VLAN B, the router's interface has an IP address of 172.16.208.255/20. Based on the previous subnet listing, you notice that this interface has an IP address that is part of the 172.16.208.0/20 subnet. As you did for VLAN A, you can check the IP address of Client 3 and Client 4 to decide whether their IP addresses live in VLAN B's range of usable IP addresses (that is, 172.16.208.1–172.16.223.254). Table 4-28 shows these comparisons.

Table 4-28 IP Address Comparison for Advanced Subnetting Practice: Exercise 2

Client	VLAN	Range of Usable Addresses	Client IP Address	Is Client in Range of Usable Addresses?
Client 1	A	172.16.80.1–172.16.95.254	172.16.80.2	Yes
Client 2	A	172.16.80.1–172.16.95.254	172.16.95.7	Yes
Client 3	B	172.16.208.1–172.16.223.254	172.16.206.5	No
Client 4	B	172.16.208.1–172.16.223.254	172.16.223.1	Yes

The comparison in Table 4-28 reveals that Client 3 (with IP address 172.16.206.5) does not have an IP address in VLAN B's subnet (with the usable address range 172.16.208.1–172.16.223.254).

Additional Practice

If you want to continue practicing these concepts, make up your own subnet mask and apply it to a classful network of your choosing. Then you can calculate the created subnets, the directed broadcast IP address for each subnet, and the range of usable IP addresses for each subnet.

To check your work, you can use a subnet calculator. An example of such a calculator is the free Advanced Subnet Calculator, available for download from https://www. solarwinds.com/free-tools/advanced-subnet-calculator, as shown in Figure 4-19.

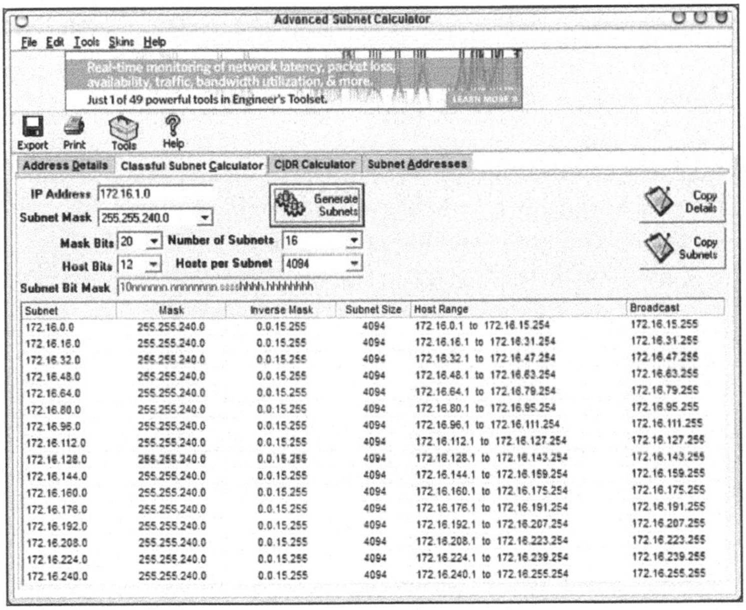

FIGURE 4-19   Free IP Address Manager

NOTE   As you read through different networking literature, you might come across other approaches to performing subnetting. Various shortcuts exist (including the one presented in this chapter), and some approaches involve much more binary math. The purpose of this section is not to provide an exhaustive treatment of all available subnetting methods but to show a quick and easy approach to performing subnet calculations in the real world and for the Network+ certification exam.

Classless Interdomain Routing

Whereas subnetting is the process of extending a classful subnet mask (that is, adding 1s to a classful mask), *classless interdomain routing (CIDR)* does just the opposite. Specifically, CIDR shortens a classful subnet mask by removing 1s from the classful mask. As a result, CIDR allows contiguous classful networks to be aggregated. This process is sometimes called *route aggregation*.

A typical use of CIDR is by a service provider summarizing multiple Class C networks that are assigned to the provider's various customers. For example, imagine that a service provider is responsible for advertising the following Class C networks:

192.168.32.0/24

192.168.33.0/24

192.168.34.0/24

192.168.35.0/24

The service provider could advertise all four networks with the single route advertisement 192.168.32.0/22. To calculate this advertisement, convert the values in the third octet (that is, the octet where the values start to differ) to binary, as shown in Figure 4-20. Then determine how many bits the networks have in common. The number of common bits then becomes the number of bits in the CIDR mask.

Key Topic

Network Address	1st Octet	2nd Octet	3rd Octet	4th Octet
192.168.32.0	11000000	10101000	001000 00	00000000
192.168.33.0	11000000	10101000	001000 01	00000000
192.168.34.0	11000000	10101000	001000 10	00000000
192.168.35.0	11000000	10101000	001000 11	00000000

All Networks Have 22 Bits in Common

FIGURE 4-20 CIDR Calculation Example

Because all four of the network addresses have the first 22 bits in common, and because setting the remaining bits to 0 (11000000.10101000.00100000.00000000) creates the network address 192.168.32.0, these networks can be summarized as 192.168.32.0/22.

Address Translation

As described earlier in this chapter, some IP addresses are routable through the public Internet, and other IP addresses are considered private and are intended for use within an organization. Network Address Translation (NAT) allows *private IP addresses* (as defined in RFC 1918) to be translated into Internet-routable IP addresses (that is, public IP addresses). This section examines the operation of basic NAT and a variant called *Port Address Translation (PAT)*. Address translation can also be done for specific ports associated with an IP address. When this is done, it's often referred to as *port forwarding*.

NOTE If RFC 1918 is not the most famous document in our field, it is certainly in the top five. *RFC 1918* was so important and had such a major impact on TCP/IP networks that we often refer to *private IP addresses* as simply RFC 1918 addresses.

NAT

Consider Figure 4-21, which shows a basic NAT topology. Note that, even though the IP networks 172.16.1.0/24 and 192.168.1.0/24 are actually private IP networks, for this discussion, assume that they are publicly routable IP addresses. The reason for the use of these private IP addresses to represent public IP addresses is to avoid using an entity's registered IP addresses in the example.

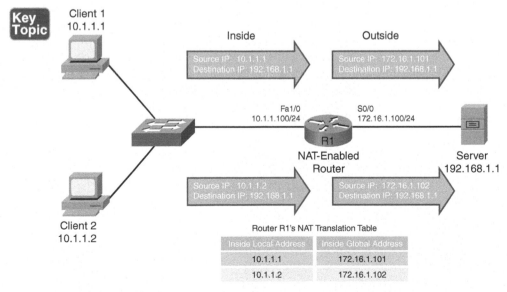

FIGURE 4-21 Basic NAT Topology

In the topology shown in Figure 4-21, two clients with private IP addresses 10.1.1.1 and 10.1.1.2 want to communicate with a web server on the public Internet. The server's IP address is 192.168.1.1. Router R1 is configured for NAT. As an example, router R1 takes packets coming from 10.1.1.1 destined for 192.168.1.1 and changes the source IP address in the packets' headers to 172.16.1.101 (which we assume is a publicly routable IP address for the purposes of this discussion). When the server at IP address 192.168.1.1 receives traffic from the client, the server's return traffic is sent to the destination address 172.16.1.101. When router R1 receives traffic from the outside network destined for 172.16.1.101, the router translates the destination IP address to 10.1.1.1 and forwards the traffic to the inside network, where client 1 receives the traffic. Similarly, client 2's IP address 10.1.1.2 is translated into the IP address 172.16.1.102.

Table 4-29 introduces the terminology used when describing the various IP addresses involved in a translation.

Key Topic

Table 4-29 Names of NAT IP Addresses

NAT IP Address	Definition
Inside local	A private IP address referencing an inside device
Inside global	A public IP address referencing an inside device
Outside local	A private IP address referencing an outside device
Outside global	A public IP address referencing an outside device

As a memory aid, remember that *inside* always refers to an inside device (source), and *outside* always refers to an outside device (destination). Also, think of the word *local* being similar to the Spanish word *loco*, meaning crazy. That is what a local address could be thought of. It is a crazy, made-up address (a private IP address that is not routable on the Internet). Finally, let the *g* in *global* remind you of the *g* in *good*, because a global address is a good (routable on the Internet) IP address.

Based on these definitions, Table 4-30 categorizes the IP addresses shown in Figure 4-21.

Table 4-30 Classifying the NAT IP Addresses in Figure 4-21

NAT IP Address	NAT IP Address
Inside local	10.1.1.1
Inside local	10.1.1.2
Inside global	172.16.1.101
Inside global	172.16.1.102
Outside local	None
Outside global	192.168.1.1

NAT does not always have to be between private and public addresses. For example, NAT could be implemented between two private address ranges or two public address ranges.

Whether an inside local address is randomly assigned an inside global address from a pool of available addresses or is assigned an address from a static configuration determines the type of NAT in use. These two approaches to NAT are called *DNAT* and *SNAT*:

- **DNAT:** In the preceding example, the inside local addresses were automatically assigned an inside global address from a pool of available public addresses. This approach to NAT is referred to as Dynamic NAT (DNAT). This is often referred to as "many-to-many," as many inside local users (a network) are mapped to a pool of inside global addresses.

- **SNAT:** Sometimes, you want to statically configure the inside global address assigned to a specific device inside your network. For example, you might have an email server inside your company and want other email servers on the Internet to send email messages to your server. Those email servers on the Internet need to point to a specific IP address, not one that was randomly picked from a pool of available IP addresses. In such a case, you can statically configure the mapping of an inside local address (the IP address of your internal email server) to an inside global address (the IP address to which email servers on the Internet will send email for your company). This approach to NAT is referred to as Static NAT (SNAT). This is often called a "one-to-one" mapping.

PAT

A challenge with basic NAT is that there is a one-to-one mapping of inside local addresses to inside global addresses, meaning that a company would need as many publicly routable IP addresses as it had internal devices needing IP addresses. This does not scale well because, often, a service provider provides a customer with only a single IP address or a small block of IP addresses.

Fortunately, many routers support *Port Address Translation (PAT)*, which allows multiple inside local addresses to share a single inside global address (a single publicly routable IP address). For this reason, PAT is referred to as "many-to-one." In Chapter 1, you learned about how IP communications rely on port numbers. As a review, when a client sends an IP packet, not only does that packet have a source and destination IP address, it has a source and destination port number. PAT leverages these port numbers to track separate communication flows.

For instance, consider Figure 4-22. Unlike in the example shown in Figure 4-21, in which each inside local address is translated to its own inside global address, the example shown in Figure 4-22 has only one inside global address. This single inside global address is shared among all the devices inside a network. The different communication flows are kept separate in router R1's NAT translation table by considering port numbers.

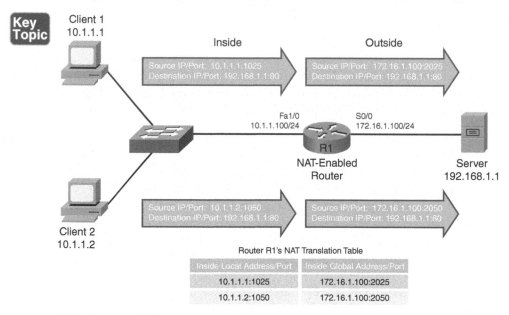

FIGURE 4-22   PAT Topology

When Client 1 sends a packet to the web server (with IP address 192.168.1.1), the client's ephemeral port number (its selected source port, which is greater than 1023) is 1025. Router R1 notes that port number and translates the inside local address 10.1.1.1 with port number 1025 to the inside global address 172.16.1.100 with port number 2025. When Client 2 sends a packet to the same web server, its inside local address 10.1.1.2 with port number 1050 is translated into the inside global address 172.16.1.100 with port number 2050.

Notice that both Client 1 and Client 2 have their inside local addresses translated into the same inside global address, 172.16.1.100. Therefore, when the web server sends packets back to Client 1 and Client 2, those packets are destined for the same IP address (172.16.1.100). However, when Router R1 receives those packets, it knows to which client each packet should be forwarded based on the destination port number. For example, if a packet from the web server (192.168.1.1) arrived at Router R1 with destination IP address 172.16.1.100 and destination port number 2050, Router R1 would translate the destination IP address to 10.1.1.2 and port number 1050, which would be forwarded to Client 2.

IP Version 6

With the global proliferation of IP-based networks, available IPv4 addresses are rapidly becoming extinct. Fortunately, IPv6 provides enough IP addresses for many generations to come. This section introduces IPv6's address structure and discusses some of its unique characteristics.

Need for IPv6

With the worldwide depletion of IP version 4 (IPv4) addresses, many organizations have migrated, are in the process of migrating, or are considering migrating their IPv4 addresses to IPv6 addresses. IPv6 dramatically increases the number of available IP addresses. In fact, IPv6 offers approximately 5×10^{28} IP addresses for each person on the planet.

Beyond the increased address space, IPv6 offers many other features:

- Simplified header:

    - The IPv4 header uses 12 fields.

    - The IPv6 header uses 5 fields.

- No broadcasts

- No fragmentation (performs MTU discovery for each session)

- Can coexist with IPv4 during a transition:

    - *Dual stack* (running IPv4 and IPv6 simultaneously on a network interface or device)

    - IPv6 over IPv4 (tunneling IPv6 over an IPv4 tunnel)

Even if you are designing a network based on IPv4 addressing, it is a good practice to consider how readily an IPv6 addressing scheme could be overlaid on that network at some point in the future. Using Teredo *tunneling*, an IPv6 host could provide IPv6 connectivity even when the host is directly connected to an IPv4-only network. Miredo is a client that can be used to implement the Teredo protocol and is included in many versions of Linux. IPv6/IPv4 tunneling is often referred to as 6to4 or 4to6 tunneling, depending on which protocol is being tunneled (IPv4 or IPv6). These are just some of the many tunneling mechanisms devised to ensure a smooth transition from IPv4 to IPv6. In fact, thanks to dual stack and tunneling features, it is very unlikely that you will see IPv4 ever completely go away in your lifetime.

IPv6 Address Structure

An IPv6 address has the following address format, where *X* is a hexadecimal digit in the range of 0 to F:

XXXX:XXXX:XXXX:XXXX:XXXX:XXXX:XXXX:XXXX

A hexadecimal digit is 4 bits in size (4 binary bits can represent 16 values). Notice that an IPv6 address has eight fields, and each field contains four hexadecimal digits. The following formula reveals why an IPv6 address is a 128-bit address:

4 bits per digit × 4 digits per field × 8 fields = 128 bits in an IPv6 address

IPv6 addresses can be difficult to work with because of their size. Fortunately, the following rules (often collectively referred to as *shorthand notation*) exist for abbreviating these addresses:

Key Topic

- Leading 0s in a field can be omitted.

- Contiguous fields containing all 0s can be represented with a double colon. (Note that this can be done only once for a single IPv6 address.)

For example, consider the following IPv6 address:

ABCD:0123:4040:0000:0000:0000:000A:000B

Using the rules for abbreviation, the IPv6 address can be rewritten as follows:

ABCD:123:4040::A:B

An exciting feature of IPv6 is the Extended Unique Identifier (*EUI-64*) format, which permits a device to automatically populate the low-order 64 bits of an IPv6 address based on an interface's MAC address. You will read more about this capability later in this chapter.

IPv6 Address Types

The following are some of the many unique aspects of IPv6 addressing and interesting address types:

- IPv6 globally routable unicast addresses start with the first four hex characters in the range 2000 to 3999.

- An IPv6 link-local address is also used on each IPv6 interface. The link-local address begins with FE80.

- Multicast addresses begin with FF as the first two hex characters.

- IPv6 can use autoconfiguration to discover the current network and select a host ID that is unique on that network. Automatic generation of a unique host ID is made possible through a process known as EUI-64, which uses the 48-bit MAC address on the device to aid in the generation of the unique 64-bit host ID. Notice that the autoconfiguration capabilities described here permit you to create an IPv6 network free of DHCP-type services. The ability of IPv6 to replace the need for DHCP services like this is known as stateless address autoconfiguration (SLAAC).

- IPv6 can also use a special version of DHCP for IPv6. Not surprisingly, this version is called *DHCPv6*.

- The protocol that is used for *network discovery*—that is, to discover the network address and learn the Layer 2 addresses of neighbors on the same network—is Neighbor Discovery Protocol (NDP).

NDP is hugely important in IPv6. It defines five ICMPv6 packet types for important jobs:

- **Router Solicitation:** Hosts inquire with Router Solicitation messages to locate routers on an attached link.

- *Router Advertisement*: Routers advertise their presence together with various link and Internet parameters, either periodically or in response to a Router Solicitation message.

- **Neighbor Solicitation:** Neighbor solicitations are used by nodes to determine the link layer address of a neighbor or to verify that a neighbor is still reachable via a cached link layer address.

- **Neighbor Advertisement:** Neighbor advertisements are used by nodes to respond to a Neighbor Solicitation message.

- **Redirect:** Routers may inform hosts of a better first-hop router for a destination.

IPv6 Data Flows

IPv6 uses three types of data flows:

- Unicast

- Multicast

- Anycast

Just like in IPv4, IPv6 uses special address types for these data flows. The following sections summarize the characteristics of each address type.

Unicast

With unicast, a single IPv6 address is applied to a single interface, as illustrated in Figure 4-23. The communication flow can be thought of as a one-to-one communication flow.

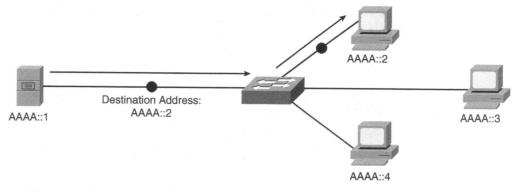

FIGURE 4-23   IPv6 Unicast Example

In Figure 4-23, a server (AAAA::1) is sending traffic to a single client (AAAA::2).

Multicast

With multicast, a single IPv6 address (a multicast group) can represent multiple devices on a network, as shown in Figure 4-24. The communication flow is a one-to-many communication flow.

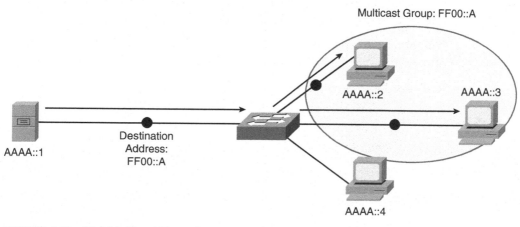

FIGURE 4-24   IPv6 Multicast Example

In Figure 4-24, a server (AAAA::1) is sending traffic to a multicast group (FF00::A).
Two clients (AAAA::2 and AAAA::3) have joined this group. Those clients receive
the traffic from the server, and any client that did not join the group (for example,
AAAA::4) does not receive the traffic.

IPv6 replaces broadcast behavior with multicast, thanks to the "all nodes" multicast
group. This reserved address is FF01:0:0:0:0:0:0:1 (FF01::1). All IPv6 nodes join this
group. This is a simple and efficient method for sending traffic to all nodes.

Anycast

With *anycast*, a single IPv6 address is assigned to multiple devices, as illustrated in
Figure 4-25. It is a one-to-nearest (from the perspective of a router's routing table)
communication flow.

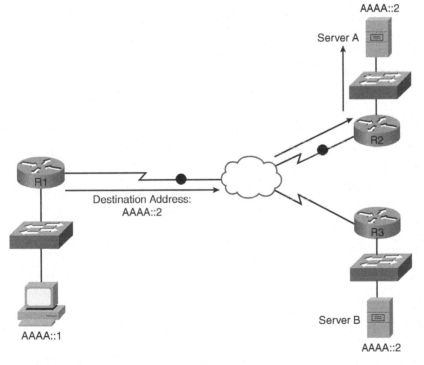

FIGURE 4-25   IPv6 Anycast Example

In Figure 4-25, a client with IPv6 address AAAA::1 wants to send traffic to destination IPv6 address AAAA::2. Notice that two servers (Server A and Server B) have
the IPv6 address AAAA::2. In the figure, the traffic destined for AAAA::2 is sent to
Server A, via Router R2, because the network on which Server A resides appears
to be closer than the network on which Server B resides, from the perspective of
Router R1's IPv6 routing table.

NOTE   Remember that the dreaded broadcast frames and packets from IPv4 do not exist in an IPv6-only network. IPv6 uses only unicasts, multicasts, and anycasts, as described in this section. With IPv6, if you want to send a frame or packet to all nodes in the local network, you use the all-nodes IPv6 multicast address.

Real-World Case Study

Acme, Inc. has decided to use private IP addresses for its internal LAN and for the WAN. The company will use the private block 10.0.0.0/8 and create enough subnets to cover the number of VLANs it will be using on the LANs at the headquarters site and at each of the remote offices. The association between the Layer 2 VLANs and the Layer 3 IP subnets will be one-to-one, with each VLAN having its own associated subnet.

The company will have nine VLANs and will use a couple subnets for the WAN connections. For the VLANs, the company plans to use the network mask /12, which will offer enough subnets to meet its needs based on the starting mask /8 for the Class A private address 10.0.0.0/8.

For the WAN connectivity Acme is purchasing from a service provider for connectivity between the remote branch offices and the headquarters site, the company will use /30 masks, which will allow for two hosts on each of the WAN connections. This is enough for each device at the end of the point-to-point WAN connections.

To connect its LANs to the Internet, Acme plans to use NAT, which is going to be performed by its service provider so that traffic going to the Internet will appear to be coming from a globally routable IP address and not from a private address. (You'll learn more about NAT in Chapter 6.)

Summary

Here are the main topics covered in this chapter:

- A binary math tutorial is provided to give you a basic understanding of why binary math is necessary for working with subnet masks.

- The characteristics of IPv4 are presented, including IPv4's address format and a descriptions of unicast, broadcast, and multicast data flows.

- This chapter examines various approaches for assigning IP address information to network devices, including static assignment, dynamic assignment (with BOOTP and DHCP), and APIPA (a Zeroconf component).

- Multiple examples and practice exercises are provided for various subnet calculations.

- This chapter covers address translation technologies that assist with the short-age of IPv4 addresses and the migration or integration with other IP address space. It discusses NAT and PAT, which are two related forms of address translation.

- The characteristics of IPv6 are highlighted, including the IPv6 address format and IPv6 data flows (unicast, multicast, and anycast).

Exam Preparation Tasks

Review All the Key Topics

Review the most important topics from this chapter, noted with the Key Topic icon in the outer margin of the page. Table 4-31 lists these key topics and the page number where each is found.

Table 4-31 Key Topics for Chapter 4

Key Topic Element	Description	Page Number
Table 4-1	Binary conversion table	106
Section	Converting a decimal number to a binary number	107
Figure 4-2	Dividing an IP address into a network portion and a host portion	114
Table 4-19	IP address classes	115
Table 4-20	Private IP networks	116
List	Basic functions of Zeroconf	129
Table 4-22	Dotted-decimal and prefix-notation representations for IPv4 subnets	130
Table 4-23	Subnet octet values	131
Formula	Number of created subnets	133
Formula	Number of borrowed bits	133
Formula	Number of host bits	134
Formula	Number of assignable IP addresses in a subnet	134
Table 4-24	Number of subnets created by a specified number of borrowed bits	135
Step list	Steps for calculating subnets	138

Key Topic Element	Description	Page Number
Table 4-25	Number of supported hosts, given a specified number of host bits	136
Figure 4-20	CIDR calculation example	144
List	Rules for abbreviating IPv6 addresses	150
List	List of NDP packets	151
Figure 4-21	Basic NAT topology	145
Table 4-29	Names of NAT IP addresses	146
List	DNAT and SNAT	147
Figure 4-22	PAT topology	148
List	Types of IPv6 data flows	151

Complete Tables and Lists from Memory

Print a copy of Appendix C, "Memory Tables," or at least the section for this chapter and complete as many of the tables as possible from memory. Appendix D, "Memory Tables Answer Key," includes the completed tables and lists so you can check your work.

Define Key Terms

Define the following key terms from this chapter and check your answers in the Glossary:

classful mask, private IP address, Network Address Translation (NAT), Port Address Translation (PAT), loopback, octet, prefix notation, slash notation, dotted-decimal notation, subnet mask, default gateway, Variable-Length Subnet Masking (VLSM), Bootstrap Protocol (BOOTP), Dynamic Host Configuration Protocol (DHCP), Zeroconf, link-local, Automatic Private IP Addressing (APIPA), borrowed bits, block size, classless interdomain routing (CIDR), unicast, multicast, anycast, tunneling, dual stack, Router Advertisement, neighbor discovery, DHCPv6, EUI-64, RFC 1918, virtual IP (VIP) address, subinterface

Complete Chapter 4 Hands-On Labs in Network+ Simulator Lite

- IPv4 Address Types and Classes
- Configuring a Client Network Adapter with an IPv4 Address
- IPv6 Addressing Terminology

- Truncating IPv6 Addresses

- Intermediate IPv4 Addressing Practice

- IPv6 Address Placement

- Configuring a Network Adapter with an IPv6 Address

- IPv6 Router Gateway Addressing

Additional Resources

Subnetting—Hosts per Subnet: https://www.ajsnetworking.com/subnetting

Subnetting—What Mask to Use: https://www.ajsnetworking.com/subnetting2

Subnetting—"I Feel the Need, the Need for Speed":
https://www.ajsnetworking.com/subnetting3

Review Questions

The answers to these review questions appear in Appendix A, "Answers to Review Questions."

1. What is the binary representation of the decimal number 117?

   a. 10110101

   b. 01110101

   c. 10110110

   d. 01101001

2. What is the decimal equivalent of the binary number 10110100?

   a. 114

   b. 190

   c. 172

   d. 180

3. What is the class of IP address 10.1.2.3/24?

   a. Class A

   b. Class B

   c. Class C

   d. Class D

4. What type of IPv4 address is 239.1.2.3?

   a. Unicast

   b. Experimental

   c. Private use only

   d. Multicast

5. Which of the following are dynamic approaches to assigning routable IP addresses to networked devices? (Choose two.)

   a. BOOTP

   b. APIPA

   c. Zeroconf

   d. DHCP

6. How many assignable IP addresses exist in the 172.16.1.10/27 network?

   a. 30

   b. 32

   c. 14

   d. 64

7. What is the prefix notation for the subnet mask 255.255.255.240?

   a. /20

   b. /24

   c. /28

   d. /29

8. Your company has been assigned the 192.168.30.0/24 network for use at one of its sites. You need to use a subnet mask that will accommodate seven subnets while simultaneously accommodating the maximum number of hosts per subnet. What subnet mask should you use?

   a. /24

   b. /26

   c. /27

   d. /28

9. A client with IP address 172.16.18.5/18 belongs to what network?

    a. 172.16.0.0/18

    b. 172.16.64.0/18

    c. 172.16.96.0/18

    d. 172.16.128.0/18

10. How can the following IPv6 address be condensed?

    2009:0123:4040:0000:0000:000:000A:100B

    a. 2009::123:404:A:100B

    b. 2009::123:404:A:1B

    c. 2009:123:4040::A:100B

    d. 2009:0123:4040::0::000A:100B

11. What technology allows for the automatic assignment of the host portion of an IPv6 address?

    a. Dual stack

    b. EUI-64

    c. Neighbor discovery

    d. Anycast

12. When you are configuring PAT as part of your address translation configuration, what is the source IP address used for translation with a large potential number of inside hosts?

    a. The IP address on the physical outside interface

    b. The IP address on a loopback interface

    c. The IP address on the physical interface with the lowest interface identifier

    d. The IP address automatically assigned to the backplane on the device

13. What capability supported by most router and switch manufacturers allows you to create many virtual interfaces out of a single physical interface?

    a. Shorthand notation

    b. Router advertisement

    c. Tunneling

    d. Subinterface

14. What specifically does NAT allow to be translated into Internet-routable IP addresses?

    a. Virtual IP addresses

    b. RFC 1918 private IP addresses

    c. APIPA addresses

    d. Variable-length subnet masks

15. What can IPv6 networks use to assign IP addresses?

    a. SLAAC

    b. CIDR

    c. Port address translation

    d. Classless inter-domain routing notation

This chapter covers the following topics related to Objective 1.5 (Explain common ports and protocols, their application, and encrypted alternatives) of the CompTIA Network+ N10-008 certification exam:

- File Transfer Protocol (FTP): Ports 20/21
- Secure Shell (SSH): Port 22
- Secure File Transfer Protocol (SFTP): Port 22
- Telnet: Port 23
- Simple Mail Transfer Protocol (SMTP): Port 25
- Domain Name System (DNS): Port 53
- Dynamic Host Configuration Protocol (DHCP): Ports 67/68
- Trivial File Transfer Protocol (TFTP): Port 69
- Hypertext Transfer Protocol (HTTP): Port 80
- Post Office Protocol v3 (POP3): Port 110
- Network Time Protocol (NTP): Port 123
- Internet Message Access Protocol (IMAP): Port 143
- Simple Network Management Protocol (SNMP): Ports 161/162

- Lightweight Directory Access Protocol (LDAP): Port 389
- Hypertext Transfer Protocol Secure (HTTPS) [Secure Socket Layer (SSL)]: Port 443
- HTTPS [Transport Layer Security (TLS)]: Port 443
- Server Message Block (SMB): Port 445
- Syslog: Port 514
- SMTP TLS: Port 587
- Lightweight Directory Access Protocol (over SSL) (LDAPS): Port 636
- IMAP over SSL: Port 993
- POP3 over SSL: Port 995
- Structured Query Language (SQL) Server: Port 1433
- SQLnet: Port 1521
- MySQL: Port 3306
- Remote Desktop Protocol (RDP): Port 3389
- Session Initiation Protocol (SIP): Ports 5060/5061

- IP protocol types
  - Internet Control Message Protocol (ICMP)
  - TCP
  - UDP
  - Generic Routing Encapsulation (GRE)

- Internet Protocol Security (IPSec)
  - Authentication Header (AH)/Encapsulating Security Payload (ESP)
- Connectionless vs. connection-oriented

Common Ports and Protocols

This chapter might initially look like a reference chapter, and it can certainly serve that function. It also prepares you for more in-depth explanations of many of these protocols in later chapters of this book.

Foundation Topics

Ports and Protocols

I know it might be very intimidating to look at this section of the chapter and realize just how many different protocols (and ports) are needed in a typical network today. Resist the urge to panic! Through study and practice, you will master these different protocols and the ports they use.

DHCP (Dynamic Host Configuration Protocol)

You can use *Dynamic Host Configuration Protocol (DHCP)* to dynamically assign IP address information (for example, IP address, subnet mask, DNS server IP address, and default gateway IP address) to a network device. DHCP uses UDP ports 67 and 68 in its operation.

DNS (Domain Name System)

Domain Name System (DNS) resolves domain names to corresponding IP addresses. It uses both TCP and UDP in its operation. The port used in both cases is port 53.

FTP (File Transfer Protocol)

File Transfer Protocol (FTP) can be used to transfer files with a remote host (which typically requires authentication of user credentials). It uses TCP ports 20 and 21 in its operation.

H.323

H.323 is a signaling protocol that provides multimedia communications over a network. It uses port 1720.

HTTP

Hypertext Transfer Protocol (HTTP) retrieves content from a web server. This protocol operates using TCP port 80. Many web server administrators liked to move the protocol to port 8080 in an attempt to circumvent the massive number of attacks against the default port 80. Today, it is hard to find websites that are running HTTP because HTTPS is now the de facto standard for web servers.

HTTPS

Hypertext Transfer Protocol over SSL (HTTPS) is used to securely retrieve content from a web server. This secure version of HTTP uses TCP port 443 in its operation. HTTPS was originally made possible by the *Secure Socket Layer (SSL)* protocol. *Transport Layer Security (TLS)* is the latest version of this technology. Because TLS is closely related to SSL, we often simply say that HTTPS is made possible by SSL/TLS.

IMAP

Internet Message Access Protocol (IMAP) retrieves email from an email server. You should note that this is only one option of many for the retrieval of email from such servers. IMAP uses TCP port 143 in its operation.

IMAP over SSL

IMAP does not have any way to provide security for the communications. As a result, it did not take long for the more secure *IMAP over SSL* to be created. This protocol uses TCP port 993 in its operation.

LDAP

Lightweight Directory Access Protocol (LDAP) provides directory services (for example, a user directory that includes username, password, email, and phone number information) to network clients. TCP port 389 is used in its operation.

LDAPS

Lightweight Directory Access Protocol over SSL (LDAPS) is the secure version of LDAP. It operates over TCP port 636.

MGCP

Media Gateway Control Protocol is used as a call control and communication protocol for voice over IP networks. MGCP uses port 2427 for both TCP and UDP in its operation.

MySQL

MySQL is an open-source relational database management system (RDBMS) with a client/server model. RDBMS is a software or service used to create and manage databases based on a relational model. MySQL uses TCP port 3306 in its operation.

NTP

Network devices use *Network Time Protocol (NTP)* to synchronize their clocks with a time server (that is, an NTP server). This protocol relies on UDP port 123 in its operation.

POP3

Post Office Protocol Version 3 (POP3) retrieves email from an email server. POP3 uses TCP port 110 in its operation.

POP3 over SSL

POP3 is another important networking protocol that does not feature support for built-in security. As a result, *POP3 over SSL* was developed. This secure protocol uses TCP port 995 in its operation.

RDP

Remote Desktop Protocol (RDP) is a Microsoft protocol that allows a user to view and control the desktop of a remote computer. This remote access technology uses both TCP and UDP port 3389 in its operation.

SFTP

Secure FTP (SFTP) provides FTP file transfer service over an SSH connection. Just like SSH, this secure protocol uses TCP port 22 in its operation.

SIP

Session Initiation Protocol (SIP) is used to create and end sessions for one or more media connections, including voice over IP calls. SIP can use both TCP and UDP ports 5060 and 5061 in its operation.

SMB

Server Message Block (SMB) is used to share files, printers, and other network resources. You should note that this protocol is used by Microsoft clients. UNIX and Linux systems use NFS for accessing file shares. Older versions of SMB used both UDP and TCP port 3020. Today, newer versions of SMB (after Windows 2000) use port 445 on top of a TCP stack in order to communicate over the Internet.

SMTP

Simple Mail Transfer Protocol (SMTP) is used for sending email throughout a network. This protocol uses TCP port 25 in its operation.

SMTP TLS

SMTPS, also called *SMTP TLS*, uses TCP port 465 in its operation. This is the secure version of SMTP.

SNMP

Simple Network Management Protocol (SNMP) is used to monitor and manage network devices. SNMP uses UDP ports 161 and 162 in its operation.

SSH

Secure Shell (SSH) is used to securely connect to a remote host (typically via a terminal emulator). SSH has become the new de facto standard method of remote access for devices that use a command-line interface. SSH uses TCP port 22 in its operation.

SQLnet

SQLnet (or SQL*NET or NET8) is Oracle's networking software, which allows remote data access between programs and an Oracle database or among multiple Oracle databases. Applications and databases can be distributed physically to different machines and can continue to communicate as if they were local. SQLnet relies on TCP port 1521 in its operation.

Structured Query Language (SQL) Server

You can use the SQL language to run powerful queries against data that is stored in databases. *Structured Query Language (SQL) Server* can use TCP and UDP in its operation. Port 1433 was reserved for this Microsoft invention.

Syslog

Syslog is the standard used by network devices (and other computer systems) to report on status information and events. This data is often called *machine data*. Storing and analyzing this information can be very important. Syslog uses UDP port 514 in its operation.

Telnet

Telnet is used to connect to a remote host (typically via a terminal emulator). This protocol should only be used in a lab or practice environment because this remote access protocol does not provide security. The alternative to this protocol that you should use in production is SSH. Telnet uses TCP port 23 in its operation.

TFTP

Trivial File Transfer Protocol (TFTP) transfers files with a remote host (and does not require authentication of user credentials). TFTP uses UDP port 69 in its operation.

Protocol/Port Summary

Table 5-1 provides a summary of protocols and their assigned ports

Table 5-1   Port Assignments for Commonly Used Protocols

Protocol	Description	Port Assignment
DHCP (Dynamic Host Configuration Protocol)	Dynamically assigns IP address information (for example, IP address, subnet mask, DNS server IP address, and default gateway IP address) to a network device	UDP 67, 68
DNS (Domain Name System)	Resolves domain names to corresponding IP addresses	TCP/UDP 53
FTP (File Transfer Protocol)	Used to transfer files with a remote host (typically requires authentication of user credentials)	TCP 20, 21
H.323	A signaling protocol that provides multimedia communications over a network	TCP 1720
HTTP (Hypertext Transfer Protocol)	Used to retrieve content from a web server	TCP 80
HTTPS (Hypertext Transfer Protocol Secure)	Used to securely retrieve content from a web server	TCP 443
IMAP (Internet Message Access Protocol)	Retrieves email from an email server	TCP 143
IMAP over SSL	The secure version of IMAP	TCP 993
LDAP (Lightweight Directory Access Protocol)	Provides directory services (for example, a user directory that includes username, password, email, and phone number information) to network clients	TCP 389

Protocol	Description	Port Assignment
LDAPS (Lightweight Directory Access Protocol over SSL)	The secure version of LDAP	TCP 636
MGCP (Media Gateway Control Protocol)	Used as a call control and communication protocol for voice over IP networks	TCP/UDP 2427
MySQL	An open-source relational database management system (RDBMS) with a client/server model	3306
NTP (Network Time Protocol)	Used by a network device to synchronize its clock with a time server (NTP server)	UDP 123
POP3 (Post Office Protocol Version 3)	Retrieves email from an email server	TCP 110
POP3 over SSL	The secure version of POP3, used to retrieve email from an email server	TCP 995
RDP (Remote Desktop Protocol)	A Microsoft protocol that allows a user to view and control the desktop of a remote computer	TCP/UDP 3389
SFTP (Secure FTP)	Provides FTP file transfer service over an SSH connection	TCP 22
SIP (Session Initiation Protocol)	Used to create and end sessions for one or more media connections, including voice over IP calls	TCP/UDP 5060, 5061
SMB (Server Message Block)	Used to share files, printers, and other network resources	TCP/UDP 3020, TCP 445
SMTP (Simple Mail Transfer Protocol)	Used for sending email throughout the network	TCP 25
SMTP over TLS	Secure version of SMTP	TCP 587
SNMP (Simple Network Management Protocol)	Used to monitor and manage network devices	UDP 161, 162
SQL (Structured Query Language) Server	SQL used to run powerful queries against data that is stored in databases	TCP/UDP 1433
SQLnet	Oracle's networking software that allows remote data access between programs and an Oracle database or among multiple Oracle databases	TCP 1521
SSH (Secure Shell)	Used to securely connect to a remote host (typically via a terminal emulator)	TCP 22

Protocol	Description	Port Assignment
Syslog	The standard used by network devices (and other computer systems) to report on status information and events	UDP 514
Telnet	Used to connect to a remote host (typically via a terminal emulator)	TCP 23
TFTP (Trivial File Transfer Protocol)	Used to transfer files with a remote host (does not require authentication of user credentials)	UDP 69

IP Protocol Types

As you have probably realized, there are many, many protocols that are considered part of the TCP/IP protocol suite. This section provides an overview of several of the IP protocol types used within TCP/IP. Many of these protocols are discussed in detail in other chapters.

Transmission Control Protocol (TCP)

The transport layer of the OSI model offers an important protocol for reliable transport. What does *reliable transport* mean, in networking terms? It means that if a segment is dropped, the sender can detect that drop and retransmit the dropped segment. Specifically, a receiver acknowledges segments that it receives. Based on those acknowledgments, a sender can decide which segments were successfully received and which segments need to be transmitted again.

User Datagram Protocol (UDP)

UDP can be considered an opposite approach to *TCP*. Unlike TCP, UDP offers unreliable transport. This means that if a segment is dropped, the sender is unaware of the drop, and no retransmission occurs.

NOTE   The reliability of TCP versus the unreliability of UDP is often referred to as *connectionless* versus *connection-oriented* communications. You might use the analogy of a phone call versus a postcard. With a phone call (which represents TCP), as you send messages, you ensure that the connection remains strong and that communications are clear. For example, you might ask "can you hear me now?" as you move to a different part of the house for a better cell connection. In fact, you begin the connection with a "hello" and end the connection with a "goodbye." UDP operates more like a postcard: There is no connection maintained at all. You drop the postcard in the mail and hope that it reaches its destination.

Internet Control Message Protocol (ICMP)

In addition to TCP and UDP, *Internet Control Message Protocol (ICMP)* is another transport layer protocol you are likely to meet. ICMP is used by utilities such as ping and traceroute.

Generic Routing Encapsulation (GRE)

Generic Routing Encapsulation (GRE), as its name implies, is a multipurpose, simple tunneling protocol that you might call on in a wide variety of circumstances. For example, let's say you have traffic that you want to protect over an IPsec tunnel, but this traffic is multicast traffic. IPsec does not support securing this type of traffic. That is where GRE can come into play. The multicast can be encapsulated inside GRE, and then this GRE traffic can be protected by IPsec. This is just one example of many where GRE can come in handy.

Internet Protocol Security (IPsec)

Internet Protocol Security (IPsec) is a complex suite of protocols that are used to create secured connections between network systems. In fact, IPsec is quickly becoming the de facto standard for VPN connections. IPsec features the use of *Authentication Header (AH)* and *Encapsulating Security Payload (ESP)*. As you would guess, AH handles authentication functions, while ESP takes care of encryption.

TCP/IP Suite Protocol Summary

Table 5-2 provides a summary of the TCP/IP suite protocols described so far in this chapter.

Key Topic

Table 5-2   TCP/IP Suite Selected Summary

Protocol	Complete Protocol Name	Description
IPsec	Internet Protocol Security	A complex suite of protocols that are used to create secured connections between network systems
GRE	Generic Routing Encapsulation	A tunneling protocol used to encapsulate a wide variety of network layer protocols inside virtual point-to-point links or point-to-multipoint links over an IP network
IP	Internet Protocol	A connectionless protocol used to move data around a network.

Protocol	Complete Protocol Name	Description
TCP	Transmission Control Protocol	A connection-oriented protocol that offers flow control, sequencing, and retransmission of dropped packets.
UDP	User Datagram Protocol	A connectionless alternative to TCP used for applications that do not require the functions offered by TCP.
FTP	File Transfer Protocol	A protocol for uploading and downloading files to and from a remote host. It also accommodates basic file management tasks.
SFTP	Secure File Transfer Protocol	A protocol for securely uploading and downloading files to and from a remote host. Based on SSH security.
TFTP	Trivial File Transfer Protocol	A file transfer protocol that does not have the security or error checking of FTP. TFTP uses UDP as a transport protocol and therefore is connectionless.
SMTP	Simple Mail Transfer Protocol	A mechanism for transporting email across networks.
HTTP	Hypertext Transfer Protocol	A insecure protocol for retrieving files from a web server.
HTTPS	Hypertext Transfer Protocol Secure	A secure protocol for retrieving files from a web server.
POP3/IMAP4	Post Office Protocol Version 3/Internet Message Access Protocol Version 4	Used to retrieve email from the server on which it is stored. Can only be used to retrieve mail and not to send mail.
Telnet	Telnet	Allows sessions to be opened on a remote host. Considered insecure.
SSH	Secure Shell	Allows secure sessions to be opened on a remote host.
ICMP	Internet Control Message Protocol	Used on IP-based networks for error reporting, flow control, and route testing.
NTP	Network Time Protocol	Used to communicate time synchronization information between devices.
NNTP	Network News Transfer Protocol	Facilitates the access and downloading of messages from newsgroup servers.
SCP	Secure Copy Protocol	Allows files to be copied securely between two systems. Uses Secure Shell (SSH) technology to provide encryption services.

Protocol	Complete Protocol Name	Description
LDAP	Lightweight Directory Access Protocol	A protocol used to access and query directory services systems such as Microsoft Active Directory.
IGMP	Internet Group Management Protocol	Provides a mechanism for systems within the same multicast group to register and communicate with each other.
DNS	Domain Name System	Resolves hostnames to IP addresses.
DHCP	Dynamic Host Configuration Protocol	Automatically assigns TCP/IP information.
SNMP	Simple Network Management Protocol	Used in network management systems to monitor network-attached devices for conditions that may need attention from an administrator.
TLS	Transport Layer Security	A security protocol designed to ensure privacy between communicating client/server applications.
SIP	Session Initiation Protocol	An application-layer protocol designed to establish and maintain multimedia sessions such as Internet telephony calls.

Summary

Here are the main topics covered in this chapter:

■ The focus of this straightforward chapter is to ensure you are well versed in the most common protocols we will work with in the network today. Notice that these protocols are often recognized by their well-known port numbers. When you hear 443 – you should immediately think about HTTPS traffic.

■ This chapter also covers the most important IP protocol types in use today including TCP, UDP, ICMP, GRE, and IPsec.

Exam Preparation Tasks

Review All the Key Topics

Review the most important topics from this chapter, noted with the Key Topic icon in the outer margin of the page. Table 5-3 lists these key topics and the page number where each is found.

Table 5-3   Key Topics for Chapter 5

Key Topic Element	Description	Page Number
Table 5-1	Summary of protocols/ports	170
Table 5-2	TCP/IP suite selected summary	173

Complete Tables and Lists from Memory

Print a copy of Appendix C, "Memory Tables," or at least the section for this chapter and complete as many of the tables as possible from memory. Appendix D, "Memory Tables Answer Key," includes the completed tables and lists so you can check your work.

Define Key Terms

Define the following key terms from this chapter and check your answers in the Glossary:

File Transfer Protocol (FTP), Secure Shell (SSH), Secure File Transfer Protocol (SFTP), Telnet, Simple Mail Transfer Protocol (SMTP), Domain Name System (DNS), Dynamic Host Configuration Protocol (DHCP), Trivial File Transfer Protocol (TFTP), Hypertext Transfer Protocol (HTTP), Post Office Protocol Version 3 (POP3), Network Time Protocol (NTP), Internet Message Access Protocol (IMAP), Simple Network Management Protocol (SNMP), Lightweight Directory Access Protocol (LDAP), Hypertext Transfer Protocol over SSL (HTTPS), Secure Socket Layer (SSL), Transport Layer Security (TLS), Server Message Block (SMB), Syslog, SMTP TLS, Lightweight Directory Access Protocol over SSL (LDAPS), IMAP over SSL, POP3 over SSL, Structured Query Language (SQL) Server, SQLnet, MySQL, Remote Desktop Protocol (RDP), Session Initiation Protocol (SIP), Internet Control Message Protocol (ICMP), TCP, UDP, Generic Routing Encapsulation (GRE), Internet Protocol Security (IPSec), Authentication Header (AH), Encapsulating Security Payload (ESP), connectionless, connection-oriented

Complete Chapter 5 Hands-On Labs in Network+ Simulator Lite

- Matching Well-Known Port Numbers
- TCP/IP Protocols and Their Functions

Additional Resources

IP, ICMP, UDP, and TCP: https://www.ajsnetworking.com/udp-and-tcp/

OSI and Things That Use It Quiz: https://www.ajsnetworking.com/osi-and-things-that-use-it-quiz/

Review Questions

The answers to these review questions are in Appendix A, "Answers to Review Questions."

1. What protocol is considered the de facto standard when it comes to secure access to remote systems for management purposes?

   a. Telnet

   b. SSH

   c. IPSec

   d. IMAP

2. You are interested in dynamically assigning the IP address information in your IPv4-based network infrastructure. What protocol can you use to accomplish this?

   a. DNS

   b. TFTP

   c. FTP

   d. DHCP

3. What global hierarchical system is used to resolve names to IP addresses?

   a. TFTP

   b. DHCP

   c. NTP

   d. DNS

4. What port and protocol are used by HTTPS? (Choose two.)

   a. TCP

   b. UDP

   c. 443

        d. 123

        e. 8080

        f. 80

5. What is the port and protocol used by Syslog? (Choose two.)

        a. TCP

        b. UDP

        c. 148

        d. 514

        e. 240

6. What protocol do ping and traceroute use in their operation?

        a. IPsec

        b. DNS

        c. ICMP

        d. DHCP

7. Which incoming email protocols are encrypted and secure because they use SSL/TLS sessions? (Choose two.)

        a. POP3 over SSL

        b. IMAPS

        c. SMTP

        d. POP

8. You need to establish an authenticated and encrypted connection between a client and a host system. What should you use?

        a. Telnet

        b. SSH

        c. LDAP

        d. LDAPS

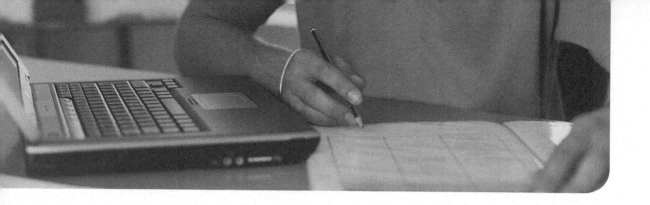

This chapter covers the following topics related to Objective 1.6 (Explain the use and purpose of network services) of the CompTIA Network+ N10-008 certification exam:

- DHCP
  - Scope
  - Exclusion ranges
  - Reservation
  - Dynamic assignment
  - Static assignment
  - Lease time
  - Scope options
  - Available leases
  - DHCP relay
  - IP helper/UDP forwarding
- DNS
  - Record types
    - Address (A)
    - Canonical name (CNAME)
    - Mail exchange (MX)
    - Authentication, authorization, accounting, auditing (AAAA)
    - Start of authority (SOA)
  - Pointer (PTR)
  - Text (TXT)
  - Service (SRV)
  - Name server (NS)
- Global hierarchy
  - Root DNS servers
  - Internal vs. external
  - Zone transfers
  - Authoritative name servers
  - Time to live (TTL)
  - DNS caching
  - Reverse DNS/reverse lookup/forward lookup
  - Recursive lookup/iterative lookup
- NTP
  - Stratum
  - Clients
  - Servers

CHAPTER 6

Network Services

While there are many network services available today, three services are so commonplace that we encounter them at every turn in the modern network: DHCP, DNS, and NTP. In this chapter, you'll learn the important basics of these critical network components.

Foundation Topics

DHCP

Statically assigning IP address information to individual networked devices can be time-consuming, error prone, and subject to scalability problems. Instead of using static IP address assignments, many corporate networks dynamically assign IP address parameters to their devices. This is typically referred to as *dynamic address assignment*. The alternative approach is referred to as manual assignment, or *static assignment*.

An early choice for performing automatic assignment of IP addresses was Bootstrap Protocol (BOOTP). Currently, however, the most popular approach for dynamic IP address assignment is the use of Dynamic Host Configuration Protocol (*DHCP*).

Engineers developed BOOTP as a method of assigning IP address, subnet mask, and default gateway information to diskless workstations. In the early days of Microsoft Windows (for example, Microsoft Windows 3.1), Microsoft Windows did not natively support TCP/IP. To include TCP/IP support, an add-on TCP/IP application (for example, Trumpet Winsock) could be run. Such an application would typically support BOOTP.

DHCP offers a more robust solution to IP address assignment than does BOOTP. DHCP does not require a statically configured database of MAC-address-to-IP-address mappings. Also, DHCP has a wide variety of options beyond basic IP address, subnet mask, and default gateway parameters. For example, a DHCP server can educate a DHCP client about the IP address of a TFTP server from which a configuration file could be downloaded.

Figure 6-1 illustrates the exchange of messages that occurs as a DHCP client obtains IP address information from a DHCP server. The list that follows describes these steps in further detail:

Step 1.   When a DHCP client initially boots, it has no IP address, default gateway, or other such configuration information. Therefore, the way a DHCP client initially communicates is by sending a broadcast message (that is, a DHCPDISCOVER message to the destination address 255.255.255.255) in an attempt to discover a DHCP server.

Step 2.   When a DHCP server receives a DHCPDISCOVER message, it can respond with a unicast DHCPOFFER message. Because the DHCP-DISCOVER message is sent as a broadcast, more than one DHCP server might respond to this discover request. However, the client typically selects the server that sent the first DHCPOFFER response received by the client.

Step 3. The DHCP client communicates with this selected server by sending a unicast DHCPREQUEST message, asking the DHCP server to provide IP configuration parameters.

Step 4. The DHCP server responds to the client with a unicast DHCPACK message. This DHCPACK message contains a collection of IP configuration parameters.

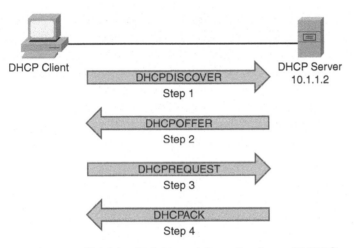

FIGURE 6-1   Obtaining IP Address Information from a DHCP Server

Notice that in step 1, the DHCPDISCOVER message is sent as a broadcast. By default, a broadcast cannot cross a router boundary. Therefore, if a client resides on a different network than the DHCP server, the client's next-hop router should be configured as a DHCP relay agent, which allows a router to relay DHCP requests to either a unicast IP address or a directed broadcast address for a network. The DHCP relay agent is often referred to as an *IP helper*, or simply a *DHCP relay*.

Using a DHCP relay agent allows you to centrally locate a DHCP server that can simultaneously service many different TCP/IP subnets in your enterprise infrastructure. This is often a very desirable configuration because centralizing this information often makes it easier to manage. Of course, the risk in this configuration is that you must ensure that the DHCP relay agents are configured properly and that they are available; otherwise, the client broadcasts for DHCP services will not be successful.

NOTE   This technology has an amazing number of different names for this technology, including IP helper, DHCP relay, DHCP relay agent, relay agent, and UDP forwarder.

A DHCP server can be configured to assign IP addresses to devices belonging to different subnets. Specifically, a DHCP server can determine the source subnet of a DHCP request and select an appropriate address pool from which to assign an address. One of these address pools (which typically corresponds to a single subnet) is called a *scope*.

When a network device is assigned an IP address from an appropriate DHCP scope, that assignment is not permanent. Rather, it is a temporary assignment referred to as a *lease*. Although most client devices on a network work well with this dynamic addressing, some devices (for example, servers) might need to be assigned specific IP addresses. Fortunately, you can configure a DHCP reservation, where a specific MAC address is mapped to a specific IP address that will not be assigned to any other network device. This static addressing approach is referred to as a DHCP *reservation*.

Another frequent configuration you might make in a DHCP implementation is to configure an *exclusion range*. This is a portion of the address pool that you never want leased out to clients in the network. Perhaps you have numbered your servers 192.168.1.1–192.168.1.10. Because the servers are statically configured with these addresses, you exclude these addresses from the 192.168.1.0/24 pool of addresses. Your DHCP server then leases out addresses beginning at the first available in the range; in this example, that would be 192.168.1.11.

NOTE   A method for remembering the four main steps of DHCP is to think of the acronym DORA: discover, offer, request, and acknowledge.

As an example of DHCP client configuration, in Microsoft Windows 10, you can select the **Obtain an IP address automatically** and **Obtain DNS server address automatically** options in the Internet Protocol Version 4 (TCP/IPv4) Properties window, as shown in Figure 6-2.

Perhaps you have noticed that DHCP dynamically assigns IP addresses and subnet masks to clients, but they need more IP addressing information than that in order to communicate properly on the network. For example, clients need DNS server addresses, they need a default gateway assigned, and they might even need the IP addresses associated with other key services, such as NTP and TFTP servers on the network. Your DHCP server can provide all this required IP addressing information. You enable this as part of the *scope options* you can configure on the DHCP server.

The *scope* is the addresses that your DHCP server will lease out to clients. The scope options include the additional address information that must be distributed and can also include settings such as the ***lease time***. Most DHCP servers permit a client to retain IP address information for 24 hours by default. If you have an environment with relatively few available addresses (and, therefore, few ***available leases***), you can set the lease time to a shorter duration so that clients cannot retain the address information for excessive time periods.

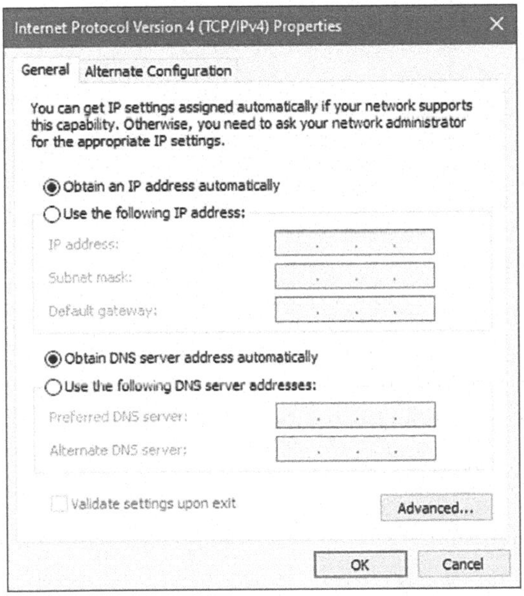

FIGURE 6-2   Configuring Microsoft Windows 10 to Obtain IP Address Information via DHCP

DNS

A Domain Name System (***DNS***) server performs the task of resolving a domain name (for example, www.ciscopress.com) to a corresponding IP address (for example, 10.1.2.3). Because routers (or multilayer switches) make their forwarding decisions based on Layer 3 information (for example, IP addresses), an IP packet needs to contain IP address information, not DNS names. However, we humans recall meaningful names more readily than we recall 32-bit numbers.

As shown in Figure 6-3, an end user who wants to navigate to the www.ciscopress.com website enters that fully qualified domain name (FQDN) into a web browser; however, the browser cannot immediately send a packet destined for www.ciscopress.com. First, the end user's computer needs to resolve the FQDN www.ciscopress.com to a corresponding IP address, which can be inserted as the destination IP address in an IP packet. This resolution is made possible by a DNS server, which maintains a database of local FQDNs and their corresponding IP addresses, in addition to pointers to other servers that can resolve IP addresses for other domains.

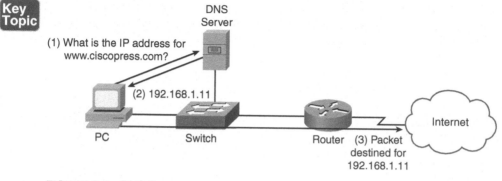

FIGURE 6-3   DNS Server

A FQDN is a series of strings, delimited by a period (such as www.ciscopress.com). The rightmost part of the FQDN is the top-level domain. Examples of top-level domains include .com, .mil, and .edu, as shown in Figure 6-4. Although there are many other top-level domains, these are among the most common top-level domains in the United States.

Lower-level domains can point upward to higher-level DNS servers to resolve nonlocal FQDNs, as illustrated in Figure 6-4.

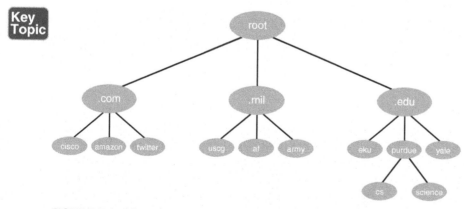

FIGURE 6-4   Hierarchical Domain Name Structure

DNS follows this strict hierarchy. And because public DNS is shared around the globe, we like to refer to the system as having a *global hierarchy*. In fact, the top-level domains include country references. For example, to enjoy a version of the Amazon.com domain tailored to India, you can visit www.amazon.in.

In addition to the global hierarchy of the DNS name system, the organization of DNS servers throughout the world follows a global hierarchy. The following DNS server types exist:

- **Root DNS servers:** These authoritative name servers serve the DNS root zone; they are a network of hundreds of servers in many countries around the world.

- **Internal DNS servers:** These servers exist inside organization to resolve the names of private hosts and servers within the organizations. These servers can also forward requests for outside resources to the appropriate external DNS servers when internal clients need to access external resources.

- **External DNS servers:** These servers reside outside an organization (typically on the public Internet) and can resolve names of systems that are located outside the organization.

- **Authoritative name server:** This DNS server is usually the last step in the journey for an IP address. The authoritative name server contains information specific to the domain name it serves (for example, ajsnetworking.com). The authoritative name server is able to resolve queries thanks to the records it contains.

A DNS server's database contains not only FQDNs and corresponding IP addresses but also *DNS record types*. For example, a mail exchange (MX) record would be the record type for an email server. As a few examples, Table 6-1 lists a collection of common DNS record types.

Key Topic

Table 6-1 Common DNS Record Types

Record Type	Description
A	An *address* record (that is, A record) maps a hostname to an IPv4 address.
AAAA	An IPv6 address record (that is, AAAA record) maps a hostname to an IPv6 address.
CNAME	A *canonical name* record (that is, CNAME record) is an alias of an existing record that allows multiple DNS records to map to the same IP address.
MX	A *mail exchange* record (that is, MX record) maps a domain name to an email (or message transfer agent) server for that domain.
NS	A *name server* record (that is, NS record) delegates a DNS zone to use the given authoritative name server.

Record Type	Description
PTR	A *pointer* record (that is, PTR record) points to a canonical name. A PTR record is commonly used when performing a reverse DNS lookup to determine what domain name is associated with a known IP address.
SOA	A *start of authority* record (that is, SOA record) provides authoritative information about a DNS zone, such as email contact information for the zone's administrator, the zone's primary name server, and various refresh timers.
SRV	A *service* location record (that is, SRV record) is used for newer protocols instead of creating protocol-specific records such as MX records.
TXT	A *text* record (that is, TXT record) originally for arbitrary human-readable text in a DNS record. Since the early 1990s, however, this record has carried machine-readable data, such as data specified by RFC 1464, opportunistic encryption, Sender Policy Framework (SPF), or DomainKeys Identified Email (DKIM).

A potential challenge when setting up DNS records is when you want to point to the IP address of a device that might change its IP address. For example, if you have a cable modem or digital subscriber line (DSL) modem in your home, that device might obtain its IP address from your service provider via DHCP. As a result, if you add the IP address of your cable modem or DSL modem to a DNS record (to allow users on the Internet to access one or more devices inside your network), that record could be incorrect if your device obtains a new IP address from your service provider.

To overcome this challenge, you can use dynamic DNS (DDNS). A DDNS provider supplies software you run on one of your PCs that monitors the IP address of the device referenced in the DNS record (such as your cable modem or DSL modem). If the software detects a change in the monitored IP address, that change is reported to your service provider, which is also providing DNS service.

Another option is IP address management (IPAM), which is a means of planning, tracking, and managing the Internet Protocol address space used in a network. IPAM integrates DNS and DHCP so that each is aware of changes in the other (for instance, DNS knowing of the IP address taken by a client via DHCP and updating itself accordingly).

Yet another DNS variant is Extension Mechanisms for DNS (EDNS). The original specification for DNS had size limitations that prevented the addition of certain features, such as security. EDNS supports these additional features while maintaining backward compatibility with the original DNS implementation. Rather than using new flags in the DNS header, which would negate backward compatibility, EDNS sends optional pseudo-resource records between devices supporting EDNS.

These records can use 16 new DNS flags. If a legacy DNS server were to receive one of these optional records, the record would simply be ignored. Therefore, backward compatibility is maintained, while new features can be added for newer DNS servers.

When you enter a web address into your browser in the form https://*FQDN* (for example, https://www.ajsnetworking.com), notice that you not only indicate the FQDN of your web address but also specify that you want to access that location by using the HTTPS protocol. Such a string, which indicates both an address (for example, www.ajsnetworking.com) and a method for accessing that address (for example, https://), is called a *uniform resource locator* (*URL*).

Here are some other DNS concepts that you should be familiar with for the latest Network+ exam:

- *Zone transfers*: Because DNS servers will always need to be available (to make the Internet function), it is a common approach to use primary and secondary backup name servers. In order to keep the primary and secondary servers in sync with each other and updated with the same information, DNS zone transfers can be performed. There are multiple types of zone transfers, including full zone transfers and incremental zone transfers.

- *DNS time to live (TTL)*: Do not confuse DNS TTL with the TTL that is in an IP packet header. Whereas the TTL in an IP packet header is a loop-prevention mechanism to ensure that a packet does not circulate endlessly on an IP network, the DNS TTL specifies the number of seconds a DNS server (or client) caches name resolution entries without having to perform a search of the DNS database. As you might guess, there is a lot of *DNS caching* going on in the *global DNS system* (both on servers and on clients). This is why name resolution for popular destinations like google.com appears to happen instantaneously.

NOTE The caching of DNS resolution information is another reason changes in the global DNS system can take hours, or even days, to be fully propagated. All the cached information must age out (that is, the TTL must expire), and new information must be requested.

- *Forward lookup*: You might not have realized this, but when you have a DNS server resolve a name (such as ajsnetworking.com) into an IP address, you are having the DNS server perform a forward lookup. This is common scenario is a forward lookup, and it is what DNS was invented to perform.

- *Reverse lookup*: DNS servers are also able to perform reverse lookups. As you might guess, this is when the client has the IP address of the resource and needs the resolution to work in reverse: The client is looking for the name that goes with the IP address.

- *Recursive lookup*: In this type of DNS query, the client instructs the DNS server to respond with an answer (if possible), and the client does not want to be referred to another DNS server. Contrast this with the iterative (or nonrecursive) query type covered next.

- *Iterative lookup*: In this type of DNS query, the client indicates that it would like the answer from the DNS server, or it will take a referral to another DNS server that might have the answer.

NTP

Network Time Protocol (*NTP*) is the final critical service we examine in this chapter. This protocol might be easy for you to overlook—or at least not think of as being very important. After all, who cares if the time is a bit off on your network devices?

For many reasons, it is actually very important that network devices possess times that are as accurate as possible. Perhaps the biggest reason is the fact that devices can then stamp Syslog and other messages with the accurate time. This can often be critical for helping you catch and prevent security attacks against your network or for helping you troubleshoot faults that are occurring as a result of failed components or configurations.

Another reason you typically need accurate time is that many services cannot properly integrate with other network services if the time is not within a certain threshold between the devices.

The configuration of NTP involves three main components:

- *Client*: Your network device is typically the NTP client and is consuming the correct time from an NTP server system.

- *Server*: The network node that provides the correct time to NTP clients. The most common servers these days are located regionally on the Internet.

- *Stratum*: The stratum is an important value in NTP operations. It is like a hop count and measures how far the client is from the accurate time source. The larger the stratum value, the more chance the time on the client could be inaccurate because it is more hops away from the accurate time source.

NTP does not require connection-oriented transport. As a result, NTP relies on UDP at the transport layer. Specifically, NTP uses UDP port 123.

Real-World Case Study

Acme, Inc. has been busy improving the DHCP implementation in the main end-user locations of the network. These improvements have involved increasing the availability of centralized DHCP server nodes. This increase in the availability has been made possible by the use of DHCP Relay Agents. These strategically placed network nodes ensure DHCP broadcasts from client systems can be routed effectively to the DHCP servers of Acme, Inc.

The DHCP enhancements also include the setting and configuration of key network parameters through the DCHP information disseminated using the scope options feature.

Acme, Inc. has also improved the dissemination of accurate time by configuring all network nodes with fallback NTP servers to use should the main, Internet-based NTP server fail.

Summary

Here are the main topics covered in this chapter:

- This chapter covered DHCP in detail for you. This protocol still dominates networks today in the area of IP address (and parameter) assignment dynamically.

- This chapter also covered DNS systems. DNS is critical for a network system, especially one that is connected to the Internet and requires access to remote resources. Resolving "friendly" names against an IP address is a fundamental necessity of the modern network.

- This chapter concluded with a look at the Network Time Protocol (NTP). Ensuring network nodes all agree on the correct time is another fundamental necessity in the typical network.

Exam Preparation Tasks

Review All the Key Topics

Review the most important topics from this chapter, noted with the Key Topic icon in the outer margin of the page. Table 6-2 lists these key topics and the page number where each is found.

Table 6-2 Key Topics for Chapter 6

Key Topic Element	Description	Page Number
Steps	Steps of DHCP	182
Figure 6-3	DNS server	186
Figure 6-4	Hierarchical domain name structure	186
Table 6-1	Common DNS record types	187
List	NTP components	190

Complete Tables and Lists from Memory

Print a copy of Appendix C, "Memory Tables," or at least the section for this chapter and complete as many of the tables as possible from memory. Appendix D, "Memory Tables Answer Key," includes the completed tables and lists so you can check your work.

Define Key Terms

Define the following key terms from this chapter and check your answers in the Glossary:

address (A), IPv6 address record (AAAA), available lease, canonical name (CNAME), client, DHCP, DHCP relay, DNS, DNS caching, dynamic address assignment, lease, reservation, exclusion range, internal DNS server, external DNS server, IP helper, lease time, mail exchange (MX), name server (NS), global DNS system, NTP, pointer (PTR), DNS record type, recursive lookup, iterative lookup, reverse lookup, forward lookup, root DNS server, scope, scope option, server, service (SRV), start of authority (SOA), static assignment, stratum, text (TXT), DNS time to live (TTL), zone transfer

Complete Chapter 6 Hands-On Labs in Network+ Simulator Lite

- DHCP Technology
- Network Application Protocols
- Application Layer Network Server Descriptions
- Internet of Things
- Details of DHCP Client Address Configuration Process

Additional Resources

DHCP and DHCP Relay: https://www.youtube.com/watch?v=efGkjWfVfA8

NTP – As Easy as 1, 2, 3: https://youtu.be/LtMWTmQqRfA

Review Questions

The answers to these review questions are in Appendix A, "Answers to Review Questions."

1. What is the name of the DHCP message that a client sends when it needs to obtain IP address information? This message is the first step in the four-way DHCP process.

   a. DHCP OFFER

   b. DHCP REQUEST

   c. DHCP DISCOVER

   d. DHCP ACK

2. Where might you set the lease duration for a DHCP server that is servicing many clients in the network?

   a. The zone record

   b. Scope options

   c. The DHCP forwarder

   d. The relay agent

3. What type of DNS message is often used to perform reverse lookups?

   a. PTR

   b. SRV

   c. TXT

   d. MX

4. What value in DNS dictates how long a DNS server or client might cache DNS name resolution information?

   a. Hop count

   b. Increment duration

   c. Backoff timer

   d. TTL

5. What port and protocol are used by NTP? (Choose two.)

   a. TCP

   b. UDP

   c. 69

   d. 443

   e. 123

6. Which component of NTP is a measure of how far the NTP client is from the server?

   a. Administrative distance

   b. Stratum

   c. MED

   d. Metric

This chapter covers the following topics related to Objective 1.7 (Explain basic corporate and datacenter network architecture) of the CompTIA Network+ N10-008 certification exam:

- Three-tiered
  - Core
  - Distribution/aggregation layer
  - Access/edge
- Software-defined networking
  - Application layer
  - Control layer
  - Infrastructure layer
  - Management plane
- Spine and leaf
  - Software-defined network
  - Top-of-rack switching
  - Backbone

- Traffic flows
  - North-South
  - East-West
- Branch office vs. on-premises datacenter vs. colocation
- Storage area networks
  - Connection types
    - Fibre Channel over Ethernet (FCoE)
    - Fibre Channel
    - Internet Small Computer Systems Interface (iSCSI)

CHAPTER 7

Corporate and Datacenter Architectures

In today's complex networks, we really need tested and validated models and blueprints that we can follow in order to ensure that we build the best network architecture possible. This chapter examines some classic and newer models for building both corporate and datacenter architectures.

Foundation Topics

The Three-Tiered Network Architecture

For a very long time now in networking, we have had the concept of building a network in tiers. Doing so allows you to separate the logical functions of the network and target the appropriate hardware and software at the correct areas. For example, you do not want to consider a switch that is designed to permit users to access the network in the same way that you would consider a switch for moving traffic through the core of the network. We begin this section by examining one of the most classic (and still used) models for network architecture: the classic three-tiered design.

Perhaps the very first thing you need to understand about this model (shown in Figure 7-1) is that in addition to being called the classic or classical model, it is also referred to as the hierarchical network model. Whatever you call it, notice that it is built with three layers: the access layer (which is the layer closest to the end users), the distribution layer, and the core layer.

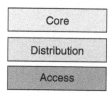

FIGURE 7-1   The "Classic" *Three-Tiered Network Architecture*

Different names are often used for these layers. For example, the core layer might be called the backbone layer, and the distribution layer is often referred to as the aggregation layer. Finally, the access layer might be called the workstation or edge layer. You can clearly see what is happening here: Engineers often use names that say more about what is happening at the various layers of the model.

The Access/Edge Layer

The *access/edge layer* ensures that authorized users can access the network with ease and in a high-bandwidth fashion. In addition to providing a guide for what equipment is appropriate at the access layer, the classic three-tiered model gives you a sense of what technologies are needed at certain layers.

Devices commonly found at the access layer include the following:

- End-user devices such as laptops, desktops, tablets, and smartphones

- Relatively inexpensive Layer 2 switches (that is, access layer switches)

- Wireless access points (APs)

Common technologies found at the access layer include the following:

- Layer 2 switching

- Spanning Tree Protocol (STP)

- Power over Ethernet (PoE)

- Voice virtual local area network (VLAN) technologies

- Quality of service (QoS) functions

- Port security

- VLAN access control lists (VACLs)

The Distribution/Aggregation Layer

A consistent trend in networking decade after decade has been the fact that more and more of the data that users need to access is located remotely. More and more traffic is being sent outside the local network infrastructure. As cloud technology continues to take hold, remote data access will become even more common.

The *distribution/aggregation layer* is critical in the design of a network. This layer is responsible for connecting the access layer and the many devices inside it to the rest of the world and the valuable data that must be accessed.

At this layer, you typically find the following network devices:

- High-speed routers

- High-speed multilayer switches

- Firewalls

- Intrusion prevention devices

- Proxy servers

NOTE Network engineers often try to remove overhead from the access and core layers and add it to the distribution layer.

The distribution layer is famous for its use of the following technologies:

- Security

- Policy

- Routing

- Load balancing

- Redundancy

- Summarization

The Core Layer

You've no doubt heard that three things are important in real estate: location, location, and location. Well, when it comes to the core layer of the classic design, three things are important as well: speed, speed, and speed. The *core layer* is responsible for moving massive amounts of data in an enterprise network—often between a datacenter (or even datacenters) and the main employee locations.

Even in today's remote work environment, there are still core network devices that are crucial to a properly operating IT organization. The core layer is home to very high-speed routers and multilayer switches (or even high-speed Layer 2 switches). (Remember, it is all about speed.)

The following types of technologies exist at the core layer:

- Redundancy

- Bandwidth aggregation

- Traffic policing and/or shaping

NOTE   Many organizations are just too small to really need a three-tiered model. Such organizations can often successfully implement a classic two-tier model, which is often referred to as a *collapsed core design*. In this approach, the core and distribution layers are merged together for the sake of simplicity (as well as cost savings).

Software-Defined Networking

Artificial intelligence (AI) and computers are not going to be eliminating the need for you (a human) in the network any time soon. While *software-defined*

networking (SDN) allows you to add more and more automation and orchestration to a network, there will still be a need for you and your skills.

Software-defined networking, which has been around for a very long time, is making a huge resurgence and being implemented in many parts of large and small networks today. For example, consider your wireless LAN. Perhaps you are using lightweight access points and wireless LAN controllers (WLCs). If so, you are seeing a very strict separation of the data layer, from the management plane, from the control layer. The WLC is the primary control layer intelligence of the solution. (The specific SDN layers are covered in more detail later in this chapter.)

SDN is changing the landscape of traditional networks. A well-implemented software-defined network allows the administrator to implement features, functions, and configurations without the need to do command-line configuration on the individual network devices. The front end that the administrator interfaces with can alert the administrator to what the network is currently doing, and then, through that same graphical user interface, the administrator can indicate what he or she wants done; behind the scenes, the software-defined network implements the detailed configurations across multiple network devices.

A key component in most software-defined networking solutions is an SDN controller. This appliance-based device is responsible for distributing control plane instructions to network devices downstream for configuration and management.

While many different approaches can be taken to SDN, almost everyone agrees that the best strategy is to separate the network into different discrete planes or layers of operation:

- *Application layer*: This is where all the technology that involves the applications resides. Today, it is not uncommon for an application to be powered by tiny microservices running as containers in a heavily virtualized cloud environment. But of course, there are plenty of other options for powering this layer. Many of them can even be much more traditional.

- *Control layer*: Although this layer (or plane) of operation is often described as the "brains" of the operation, you are still the true brains of the operation. In fact, you are likely to use a "single pane of glass" solution that provides the correct application programming interface (API) calls to the controller. The controller turns these API commands into calls to the network devices in order to monitor or configure them properly. The API calls from you to the controller are referred to as *northbound* operations, and the commands from the controller to the network devices are referred to as *southbound operations*. The controller is always considered to be in the middle. Examples of control layer functions include routing and switching intelligence, and common control layer protocols include Open Shortest Path First (OSPF), Border Gateway Protocol (BGP), and Rapid Spanning Tree Protocol (RSTP).

NOTE   Northbound and southbound, or *north–south traffic flows*, are not the only descriptors for traffic flows in an SDN environment. There are also eastbound and westbound traffic flows, or *east–west traffic flows*. Virtual machines (VMs) and/or containers communicate with each other over east–west flows, and this is the bulk of the traffic flow today.

- *Infrastructure layer*: The infrastructure layer contains the hardware and software that powers the enterprise. In it, you often find legacy and dated technologies. This infrastructure is now being controlled in a new and exciting way.

- *Management layer*: It is necessary to perform a lot of routine maintenance in a network, and the management plane is for these boring tasks.

All the layers of operation are critically important, and each plays an important role. The layers of operation work seamlessly together as one to get the various jobs done.

Spine and Leaf

The classic hierarchical model for building an enterprise network is excellent for building an enterprise network. But what about for different kinds of network locations in an organization, such as a datacenter? Certainly, different models might be more appropriate in a datacenter, where traffic is different and traffic patterns are not always as expected. Different models are used for different network locations. One that has become quite famous is called the *spine and leaf* topology or network model.

One of the reasons the spine and leaf topology has gained popularity in the datacenter is that vendors such as Cisco Systems rely on it for new technologies they are rolling out. Cisco created the Application Centric Infrastructure (ACI) for SDN in the datacenter. As its name directly communicates, ACI takes a very application-centric (software as a service [SaaS]) approach to the control and management of network design, bringing automation and orchestration to the SaaS engine of the private datacenter.

Figure 7-2 shows a simple spine and leaf network design.

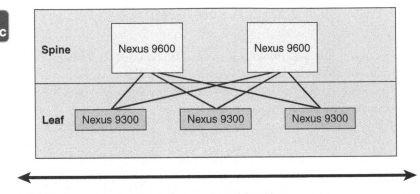

FIGURE 7-2   The Cisco ACI Spine and Leaf Design

Notice that this model consists of just two layers: the spine and the leaf layers.

NOTE   Some engineers call the spine layer the core layer or the *backbone* layer.

One thing that can really surprise long-time Cisco fans is just how inflexible Cisco is when it comes to the spine and leaf topology that powers the Cisco ACI solution. Cisco makes it very clear exactly which devices must be used at each layer of the model. Figure 7-2 shows Cisco Nexus 9600s at the spine layer and Cisco Nexus 9300s at the leaf layer. Cisco will continue to produce different classes of devices that will fit in these layers, but you can expect that the ACI solution will always require particular Cisco devices.

There is also no flexibility in how you connect the spine and leaf topology. Each leaf node *must* connect to each spine node—and that is it. The spine nodes do not directly connect to each other, and the leaf nodes do not directly connect to each other. Rather, each leaf must connect to each spine. This inflexibility brings several benefits:

- There is no doubt about how you should connect the equipment. It is actually refreshing to be told exactly how the Gigabit Ethernet segments must be constructed, leaving no room for doubt or experimentation.

- There is completely predicable data pathing in the system. VMs (or containers) are hosted on systems that connect to leaf nodes. When a VM that connects to the leaf layer needs to communicate with another VM on the same leaf device, it does not need to transit to the spine layer; when a VM on one leaf needs to communicate to a VM on another leaf device, it is *always* one hop away; there is exactly one spine device that must be transited.

- The latency is predictable, due in large part to the predictability of the data pathing.

- Monitoring and expanding the topology is simple. If you need to connect more hosts (hardware) to connect more containers and VMs, you can just add a leaf device; if you need more overall bandwidth and processing power for the solution, you can just add a new spine.

NOTE The Cisco ACI approach is actually a variation of an earlier technological approach called *top-of-rack switching*, or end-of-rack switching. In this design, multiple physical components act as one network device. For example, with the end-of-rack switching design, there are physical switches in each datacenter rack for connectivity, but the control layer (or plane) intelligence and the "real" switching engine are located at the end of a row of racks in the datacenter. This larger physical device is controlling the behavior of the distributed switches in the racks. They function logically as one big device. Specifically, the smaller switches in the racks act like line cards inserted in the chassis of a bigger and more powerful switch. ACI functions similarly, with leaf nodes appearing to the solution as part of the spine devices.

Storage Area Networks

There are many approaches to storing data in networks today, including the following:

- Network-attached storage (NAS)
- Directly attached storage
- Storage area networks (SANs)

Networks and systems supporting virtual servers commonly have NAS, where disk storage is delivered as a service over the network. As this approach evolved to include more efficiency and more features, the idea for a network dedicated to storing data was born.

A *storage area network (SAN)* is a high-speed, very specialized network that is designed to store massive amounts of data and make that data available quickly when clients and/or servers request it.

Originally, *Fibre Channel* was the technology that ruled the SAN space. Unlike Ethernet, Fibre Channel is designed for very low-latency, guaranteed lossless connectivity. In contrast, with UDP in an Ethernet environment, it is easy to contend with packet loss and delays. This is not the case in a SAN environment.

To make SANs even more accessible and flexible, they began to be created to support *Internet Small Computer System Interface (iSCSI)*. With iSCSI, which is an IP-based technology for network storage, a client using the storage is referred to as an *initiator*, and the system providing the iSCSI storage is called the iSCSI *target*. Networks supporting iSCSI are often configured to support larger-than-normal frame sizes, referred to as *jumbo frames*.

NOTE   Less commonly encountered these days in SANs is InfiniBand (IB), a communication technology that permits high-speed, low-latency communications between supercomputers.

Network convergence is often the goal today. For example, voice and video and data networks are successfully combined today. These very different types of communications can all be sent over the same network. Converging different forms of traffic on a network extended to SAN and LAN traffic thanks to a remarkable invention: *Fibre Channel over Ethernet (FCoE)*. Just like it sounds, this technology allows Ethernet to encapsulate Fibre Channel frames and carry them over a high-speed Ethernet infrastructure. Modifications were made to the Ethernet standards for FCoE to provide the level of service required in the SAN for Fibre Channel.

NOTE   As you might guess, Ethernet needs to be truly high speed in order to have a chance at providing FCoE services. In the Cisco implementation, 10Gbps Ethernet is required for FCoE! This might sound crazy and too difficult to accommodate, but keep in mind that FCoE is mostly used with datacenters, where 10Gbps and even 40Gbps Ethernet links are becoming common.

Deciding on an Architecture

Many options are available in networking today, and this chapter only scratches the surface, discussing what you need to know for the Network+ exam.

One of your first big decision points when designing modern networks has to do with the physical locations of your hardware and software. Early on, you are likely to find yourself choosing among the following options:

- Branch office locations hosting services

- On-premises datacenter designs hosting services

- Colocation designs where the services are hosted using your own equipment and the equipment of a provider

- Cloud-based designs where you provide the data, and everything else is provided by the cloud vendor

A lot of factors are involved in this decision process, including levels of control, budgets, security, and IT staff expertise.

Real-World Case Study

Acme, Inc. is starting to redesign portions of the enterprise network as well as the datacenter. More specialized modules are being incorporated into the enterprise network, such as an emphasis on Software Defined Networking solutions.

In the datacenter, Acme, Inc. is implementing a spine/leaf architecture to foster an SDN environment for SaaS application management and deployment in the private cloud.

Acme, Inc. has also implemented a SAN in the datacenter. This SAN connects to the enterprise network thanks to FCoE that has been implemented in key distribution areas.

Summary

Here are the main topics covered in this chapter:

- This chapter covered the classic three-tiered network architecture. This simple design includes the access, distribution, and core layers.

- This chapter also examined the popular trend of Software Defined Networking (SDN). This approach to the network often features a centralized controller that uses APIs to accept commands from you and your team, and then uses APIs to deliver configurations to the network infrastructure. Notice this is taking advantage of the separation of the modern network in different planes of operation. There is typically a data plane, a control plane, and a management plane.

- This chapter also covered Storage Area Networks and the technologies that are typically featured in these very specialized network areas.

Exam Preparation Tasks

Review All the Key Topics

Review the most important topics from this chapter, noted with the Key Topic icon in the outer margin of the page. Table 7-1 lists these key topics and the page number where each is found.

Key Topic

Table 7-1 Key Topics for Chapter 7

Key Topic Element	Description	Page Number
Section	The three-tiered network architecture	198
Section	Software-defined networking	200
Figure 7-2	The Cisco ACI spine and leaf solution	203
Section	Storage area networks	204
List	Physical locations of hardware	205

Define Key Terms

Define the following key terms from this chapter and check your answers in the Glossary:

three-tiered architecture, core layer, access/edge layer, distribution/aggregation layer, software-defined networking (SDN), application layer, control layer, infrastructure layer, management layer, spine and leaf, top-of-rack switching, backbone, north–south traffic flows, east–west traffic flows, storage area network (SAN), Fibre Channel, Internet Small Computer System Interface (iSCSI), Fibre Channel over Ethernet (FCoE)

Additional Resources

5 SDN Concepts You've Gotta Know: https://www.youtube.com/watch?v=RdCLmakGZL0

Intro to SANs: https://www.youtube.com/watch?v=4RsLUTJ_Qtk

Review Questions

The answers to these review questions appear in Appendix A, "Answers to Review Questions."

1. Which layer of the three-tiered model is most concerned with speed?

   a. Access/edge

   b. Distribution/aggregation

   c. Policy

   d. Core

2. Which layer of the three-tiered model is most likely to feature large amounts of security and load balancing and is also often responsible for setting policy?

   a. Access/edge

   b. Distribution/aggregation

   c. Workstation

   d. Core

3. How is connectivity for the Cisco ACI spine and leaf model implemented?

   a. Each spine device connects to every other device.

   b. Each leaf device connects to each spine device.

   c. Each spine device connects to every other spine device.

   d. Each leaf device must connect to each other leaf device.

4. Which of the following is an example of an east-west traffic flow in a modern datacenter?

   a. A client requesting email from a datacenter SaaS email solution

   b. A container requesting services provided by another container in the solution

   c. A client uploading large numbers of archive files for storage

   d. The downloading of a large number of archive files from a SAN

5. What convergence technology seeks to unify the SAN and the LAN?

   a. Fibre Channel

   b. IB

   c. iSCSI

   d. FCoE

6. BGP is an example of a technology found in what layer/plane of operation in a modern network?

   a. Management

   b. Control

   c. Data

   d. Policy

This chapter covers the following topics related to Objective 1.8 (Summarize cloud concepts and connectivity options) of the CompTIA Network+ N10-008 certification exam:

- Deployment models
    - Public
    - Private
    - Hybrid
    - Community
- Service models
    - Software as a service (SaaS)
    - Infrastructure as a service (IaaS)
    - Platform as a service (PaaS)
    - Desktop as a service (DaaS)
- Infrastructure as code
    - Automation/orchestration
- Connectivity options
    - Virtual private network (VPN)
    - Private-direct connection to cloud provider
- Multitenancy
- Elasticity
- Scalability
- Security implications

CHAPTER 8

Cloud Concepts

It is not just a fad. It is not just marketing hype. Cloud computing is the future, and it is exploding in usage and usefulness. In this chapter, you will learn about some of the most foundational and critical topics in the vast field of cloud computing today.

Foundation Topics

Deployment Models

Virtualized services and solutions are often offered by service providers as *cloud computing*. A company purchasing cloud computing services has several options to choose from:

- **Private cloud**: Private cloud services include systems that only have interactions and communications with other devices inside the same private cloud or system.

- **Public cloud**: Public cloud services interact with devices on public networks such as the Internet and potentially other public clouds. The three largest public cloud providers are Amazon Web Services (AWS), Microsoft Azure, and Google Cloud Platform.

- **Hybrid cloud**: With hybrid cloud services, some private cloud services interact with public clouds.

- **Community cloud**: Community cloud services are used by individuals, companies, or entities with similar interests. A community cloud is typically a partnership between many different cloud vendors or organizations. An excellent example of a community cloud is cloud.gov in the United States. This community cloud provides a wide variety of services to employees of the U.S. government. These services are offered in the community cloud by several different public cloud vendors.

When an organization requires scalability, wants reduced costs, lacks in-house administrative personnel trained in cloud technologies, and has a complex network, a public cloud is the best deployment model to use. The advantages of using a public cloud include the following:

- Lower infrastructure, maintenance, and administrative costs

- Greater hardware efficiency

- Reduced implementation times

- Availability of short-term usage

When an organization needs to maintain strict control of business-critical data or is in a highly regulated businesses, such as the financial industry, a private cloud is typically the best choice.

A hybrid cloud environment is the best choice when an organization offers services that need to be configured for diverse vertical markets or has varying needs. Hybrid clouds are also ideal for organizations migrating to public clouds because they can ensure interoperability and efficiencies across the different environments.

The community cloud option is best suited for organizations that want to increase cross-organizational or collaborative processes when in-house implementation is not possible due to conditions such as geographically distributed participants, fluctuating resource requirements, or resource limitations.

Service Models

Cloud services are typically offered using one of several "as a service" models, which are usually offered on a pay-as-you-go basis. This is similar to the model used with utilities in the home (for example, electricity, Internet).

The following are a few of the service models that are available as part of cloud computing:

- *Infrastructure as a service (IaaS)*: With IaaS, the company rents virtualized servers (which are hosted by a service provider) and runs specific applications on those servers.

- *Software as a service (SaaS)*: With SaaS, the details of the servers are hidden from the customer, and the customer's experience is similar to the experience of using a web-based application.

- *Platform as a service (PaaS)*: PaaS provides a development platform for companies that are developing applications and want to focus on creating the software without having to worry about the servers and infrastructure that are being used for that development.

> **NOTE** Countless "as a service" designations have been established. For example, *desktop as a service (DaaS)* refers to cloud-hosted OS desktops made available to cloud clients. The term everything as a service (XaaS) is often used to describe the vast array of cloud services available now that the use of cloud approaches has exploded in popularity.

Key Cloud Concepts

We could easily fill a book this size with details of cloud technology, but for the Network+ exam, you need to know the following key aspects:

- Infrastructure as code
- Connectivity options
- Multitenancy
- Elasticity
- Scalability
- Security implications

Infrastructure as Code (IaC)

One of the most exciting developments in technology today is *infrastructure as code (IaC)*. When your infrastructure in the cloud is all virtualized, it can be easily created (and destroyed) as well as maintained by using scripts (code). This makes it possible for you to "spin up" test environments or pilot tests with ease. Think about how much easier it is to create a duplicate site for high availability (HA) needs when using IaaS and IaC than when using physical devices.

The large public cloud providers make it simple for you to implement IaC. They provide tools (such as CloudFormation from AWS) that permit you to easily generate the code required to script the creation of useful (and even complex) infrastructures. Thanks to this capability, you can easily automate—and even orchestrate—common networking tasks that used to take weeks or months to carry out. For example, say that you need to spin up 50 servers for a test project. Thanks to IaC, you can now do this with a few clicks of the mouse instead of using a massive (and often) expensive deployment of physical servers.

There is a difference between automation and orchestration:

- *Automation* refers to the automated completion of a task or tasks.
- *Orchestration* refers to the scheduling and monitoring of many different automations. It is, basically, automating the automation.

NOTE   IaC is also known as *programmable infrastructure* to indicate that the infrastructure configuration can be incorporated into application code. IaC enables DevOps teams to test applications in production-like environments from the beginning of the development cycle.

Connectivity Options

As more and more technology has appeared in the cloud (both public and private), secured connectivity has become crucial. Secure protocols such as HTTPS, TLS, and SSH are necessary when accessing most cloud resources. Fortunately, massive cloud providers such as AWS make it simple to securely connect using a wide variety of methods, including hardware *virtual private network (VPN)* appliances located at your corporate or home office. Although your applications and servers might be sharing physical equipment with other customers of AWS, great pains are taken to ensure that this multitenancy (described in the next section) does not come at the cost of security.

AWS and other large public cloud providers go a step further, allowing customers to purchase AWS Direct Connect circuits. These circuits are private, dedicated leased lines directly into the AWS infrastructure. When you use AWS Direct Connect, your traffic does not co-mingle with that of other AWS customers or other Internet users at all. Of course, these types of connections can be expensive.

Multitenancy

If you ask engineers why they are hesitant to move to the public cloud, they are likely to say that they are worried about security. When they react this way, it is almost always because they are thinking about *multitenancy*. This is a fancy term for the fact that the physical servers in the public cloud infrastructure are hosting workloads for many different customers. Your virtual machines (VMs) might be located on exactly the same physical server as the VMs of your biggest competitor. Multitenancy requires you to have great faith that the cloud provider has done excellent setup of security work to ensure that the VMs of one customer are completely hidden from other customers.

NOTE When you have the money to spend and need the certainty, you can purchase a fully dedicated hosting solution. In such a situation, the cloud provider leases to you your own dedicated hardware in their cloud—and this hardware is not shared with other customers.

Elasticity

Elasticity is another extremely compelling reason to move to the cloud. Elasticity means that a cloud solution can scale (up or down or in or out) as needed based on demand. Scaling up or down means adding or subtracting resources to provide larger or smaller systems. Scaling in or out refers to allowing systems to clone themselves or terminate themselves, as needed.

NOTE   The National Institute of Standards and Technology (NIST) includes rapid elasticity as one of the five key characteristics that define what *cloud* truly means. The other four characteristics are on-demand self-service, broad network access, resource pooling, and measured service.

Elasticity is truly incredible. When your cloud offers you rapid elasticity (and it should!), your network infrastructure and services offered can grow and shrink along with demand. This is incredibly exciting for many reasons, but perhaps the two biggest reasons are the fact that you do not have to worry (as much) about your infrastructure failing under a large load, and you do not have to worry about over-provisioned resources when demand is low.

Scalability

It should be no surprise that if your cloud solution can grow and shrink as needed (elasticity), it has no problem demonstrating great scalability. *Scalability* refers to a solution's ability to grow with need or demand. Cloud technology today can do even better than this: It can grow or shrink as needed.

Cloud Security

Your public cloud provider will most likely make it very clear to you that your cloud security with a public cloud is a shared responsibility model. For example, AWS will secure your virtual machine from other customers' virtual machines, but it is up to you to properly secure the operating system (OS) inside the VM, and it is your responsibility to control access to and from the VM.

Here are just some of the main security concerns with moving to the cloud:

- Data breaches
- Account hijacking
- Insider threats
- Malware injection
- Abuse of cloud services
- Insecure APIs
- Denial of service (DoS) attacks
- Insufficient due diligence

Notice that many of these concerns apply to non-cloud environments as well.

Real-World Case Study

Acme, Inc. is considering a move to the cloud with some key services they are having problems scaling from their on-prem, local datacenter. Specifically, Acme, Inc. is considering a public cloud implementation for the streaming of new training videos globally. They need these movies to be delivered in a format that is based on the bandwidth of the access device.

Acme, Inc. is also investigating the changes in the security posture of the organization with this move. Specifically, they are exploring their security responsibilities in this new solution compared to the security responsibilities of the cloud provider.

Summary

Here are the main topics covered in this chapter:

- This chapter covered the deployment models often seen with cloud in networking today. These include private, public, hybrid, and community clouds.

- This chapter also covered the service models seen today with cloud, including SaaS, IaaS, and PaaS.

- Finally, this chapter covered key cloud concepts you should be aware of, including infrastructure as code, connectivity options, multitenancy, elasticity and scalability, and security implications.

Exam Preparation Tasks

Review All the Key Topics

Review the most important topics from this chapter, noted with the Key Topic icon in the outer margin of the page. Table 8-1 lists these key topics and the page number where each is found.

Table 8-1 Key Topics for Chapter 8

Key Topic Element	Description	Page Number
List	Deployment models	212
List	As a service models	213
List	Key cloud concepts	214
Section	Elasticity	215
Section	Security implications	216

Define Key Terms

Define the following key terms from this chapter and check your answers in the Glossary:

public cloud, private cloud, hybrid cloud, community cloud, software as a service (SaaS), infrastructure as a service (IaaS), platform as a service (PaaS), desktop as a service (DaaS), infrastructure as code (IaC), automation, orchestration, virtual private network (VPN), multitenancy, elasticity, scalability

Complete Chapter 8 Hands-On Labs in Network+ Simulator Lite

- Contrast Virtualization Technologies and Services
- Using Cloud Storage
- Workstation Virtualization

Additional Resources

Google Cloud Platform: Deploying Cloud Marketplace Solutions to Google Kubernetes Engine (GKE): https://www.ajsnetworking.com/gcp-compute/

Cloud Versus Outsourcing: https://www.ajsnetworking.com/comptia-cloud-essentials-cloud-vs-outsourcing/

Review Questions

The answers to these review questions appear in Appendix A, "Answers to Review Questions."

1. What type of cloud deployment model features many customers consuming resources from a single provider?

    a. Public

    b. Private

    c. Community

    d. Hybrid

2. What type of "as a service" model features a powerful cloud environment targeted at developers who need to test and deploy updates to their applications?

   a. IaaS

   b. SaaS

   c. PaaS

   d. DaaS

3. Which cloud characteristic refers to the ability to dynamically scale resources as needed during times of great demand as well as in times of low demand?

   a. Scalability

   b. Elasticity

   c. On-demand

   d. Centralized

4. Which of the following are popular options when it comes to ensuring security of cloud-based data in transit? (Choose two.)

   a. Public Internet

   b. VPN

   c. Direct private connection

   d. RDP

5. Which term refers to your company's data being stored on shared physical servers in the public cloud infrastructure?

   a. Infrastructure as code

   b. Multitenancy

   c. Automation

   d. Orchestration

This chapter covers the following topics related to Objective 2.1 (Compare and contrast various devices, their features, and their appropriate placement on the network) of the CompTIA Network+ N10-008 certification exam:

- Networking Devices
  - Layer 2 switch
  - Layer 3 capable switch
  - Router
  - Hub
  - Access point
  - Bridge
  - Wireless LAN controller
  - Load balancer
  - Proxy server
  - Cable modem
  - DSL modem
  - Repeater
  - Voice gateway
  - Media converter
  - Intrusion prevention system (IPS)/intrusion detection system (IDS) device

- Firewall
- VPN headend
- Networked devices
  - Voice over Internet Protocol (VoIP) phone
  - Printer
  - Physical access control devices
  - Cameras
  - Heating, ventilation, and air conditioning (HVAC) sensors
  - Internet of Things (IoT)
    - Refrigerator
    - Smart speakers
    - Smart thermostats
    - Smart doorbells
  - Industrial control systems/ supervisory control and data acquisition (SCADA)

CHAPTER 9

Various Network Devices

Modern networks can include a daunting number of devices, and it is your job to understand the function of each device and how it works with the others. To create a network, these devices need some sort of interconnection, using one of a variety of media types. This chapter begins by delving into the many networking devices that make up a typical enterprise (or even small home office) network.

Next, this chapter covers network devices that rely on the network to accomplish some of their tasks. For example, Internet of Things components rely on the underlying network to transfer the data they collect from their environment. Without this underlying network, the data would need to be manually extracted from each device, which would just not be practical in most scenarios.

Foundation Topics

Networking Devices

This chapter begins with a fairly detailed look at the networking devices that work together to determine the success or failure of your IT infrastructure. You might not have every one of these devices in your network. In fact, many of the devices mentioned here are now considered legacy but may still come up on the Network+ exam.

Hubs

A *hub* (specifically, an Ethernet hub) lives at Layer 1 of the OSI model. As a result, a hub does not make forwarding decisions. Instead, a hub receives bits on one port and then retransmits those bits out all other ports (that is, all ports on the hub other than the port on which the bits were received). Because of this basic function, a hub is also called a *bit spitter* or a *repeater*.

Hubs are most often connected to other network devices via UTP cabling; however, some early versions of Ethernet hubs (prior to the popularization of Ethernet switches) supported fiber-optic connections.

The three basic types of Ethernet hubs are as follows:

- **Passive hub:** This type of hub does not amplify (that is, electrically regenerate) received bits.

- **Active hub:** This type of hub regenerates incoming bits as they are sent out all the ports on a hub other than the port on which the bits were received.

- **Smart hub:** The term *smart hub* usually implies an active hub with enhanced features, such as support for Simple Network Management Protocol (SNMP).

A significant downside to hubs—and the main reason they have largely been replaced with *switches*—is that all ports on a hub belong to the same collision domain. A *collision domain* represents an area on a LAN on which there can be only one transmission at a time. Because multiple devices can reside in the same collision domain, as is the case with multiple PCs connected to a hub, if two devices transmit at the same time, those transmissions *collide* and have to be retransmitted.

Because of the collision domain issue and the inefficient use of bandwidth (that is, bits being sent out all ports rather than only the port needing the bits), hubs are rarely used in modern LANs. However, they are an important piece of the history of

Ethernet networks and share some of the characteristics of different areas of modern Ethernet networks. For example, a wireless access point (AP) is much like a hub, in that all the wireless devices associated with the AP belong to the same collision domain.

In Figure 9-1, notice that the PCs depicted are interconnected using an Ethernet hub, but they are all in the same collision domain. As a result, only one of the connected PCs can transmit at any one time. This characteristic of hubs can limit the scalability of hub-based LANs.

Keep in mind that all the devices on a hub belong to the same broadcast domain, which means that a broadcast sent into the hub will be propagated out all of the ports on the hub (other than the port on which the broadcast was received).

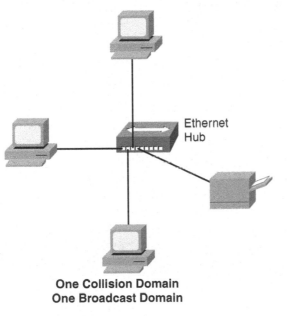

One Collision Domain
One Broadcast Domain

FIGURE 9-1   Ethernet Hub

Bridges

A **bridge** joins two or more LAN segments, typically two Ethernet LAN segments. Each LAN segment is in a separate collision domain, as shown in Figure 9-2. As a result, an Ethernet bridge can be used to scale Ethernet networks to a larger number of attached devices.

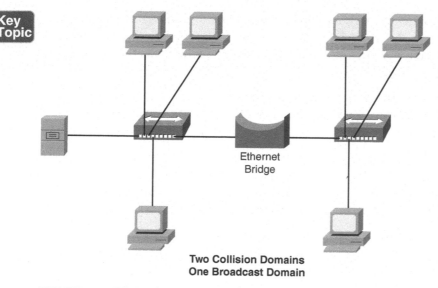

Two Collision Domains
One Broadcast Domain

FIGURE 9-2 Ethernet Bridge

Unlike a hub, which blindly forwards received bits, a bridge (specifically, an Ethernet bridge in this discussion) makes intelligent forwarding decisions based on the destination MAC address in a frame. Specifically, a bridge analyzes source MAC address information on frames entering the bridge and populates an internal MAC address table based on the learned information. Then, when a frame enters the bridge destined for a MAC address known by the bridge's MAC address table to reside off a specific port, the bridge can intelligently forward the frame out the appropriate port. (This operation is logically the same as switch operation, and a more detailed description is presented in the upcoming discussion on switches.) Because a bridge makes forwarding decisions based on Layer 2 information (that is, MAC addresses), a bridge is considered to be a Layer 2 device.

Although a bridge segments a LAN into multiple collision domains (that is, one collision domain per bridge port), all ports on a bridge belong to the same broadcast domain. To understand this concept, think about the destination MAC address in a broadcast frame. At Layer 2, the destination MAC address of a broadcast frame is FFFF.FFFF.FFFF in hexadecimal notation. Also, recall that a bridge filters frames (that is, sends frames only out necessary ports) if the bridge has previously learned the destination MAC address in its MAC address table. Because no device on a network will have the MAC address FFFF.FFFF.FFFF, a bridge will never enter that MAC address in its MAC address table. As a result, broadcast frames are *flooded* out all bridge ports other than the port that received the frame.

Bridges were popular in the mid- to late 1980s and early 1990s, but they have largely been replaced with switches due to price, performance, and features. From a performance perspective, a bridge makes its forwarding decisions in software, whereas a switch makes its forwarding decisions in hardware, using application-specific integrated circuits (ASICs). Not only do these ASICs help reduce the cost of switches, they enable switches to offer a wider array of features. In fact, this book you are holding discusses a variety of these switch features, including VLANs, trunks, port mirroring, Power over Ethernet (PoE), Power over Ethernet Plus (PoE+), and 802.1X authentication.

Layer 2 Switch

Like a bridge, a switch (specifically, a *Layer 2 Ethernet switch* in this discussion) can dynamically learn the MAC addresses attached to various ports by looking at the source MAC addresses on frames coming into a port. For example, if switch port Gigabit Ethernet 1/1 received a frame with source MAC address DDDD.DDDD. DDDD, the switch could conclude that MAC address DDDD.DDDD.DDDD resides off port Gigabit Ethernet 1/1. In the future, if the switch receives a frame destined for MAC address DDDD.DDDD.DDDD, the switch would only send that frame out port Gigabit Ethernet 1/1.

Initially, however, a switch is unaware of what MAC addresses reside off which ports (unless MAC addresses have been statically configured). Therefore, when a switch receives a frame destined for a MAC address not yet present in the switch's MAC address table, the switch floods that frame out all the switch ports except the port on which the frame was received. Similarly, broadcast frames (that is, frames with destination MAC address FFFF.FFFF.FFFF) are always flooded out all switch ports except the port on which the frame was received. As mentioned earlier in this chapter, in the discussion on bridges, the reason broadcast frames are always flooded is that no endpoint will have MAC address FFFF.FFFF.FFFF, which means that the FFFF.FFFF.FFFF MAC address will never be learned in a switch's MAC address table.

To illustrate how a switch's MAC address table becomes populated, consider an endpoint named PC1 that wants to form an SSH connection with a server. Also, assume that PC1 and its server both reside on the same subnet (that is, no routing is required to get traffic between PC1 and its server). Before PC1 can establish an SSH session to its server, PC1 needs to know the IP address (that is, the Layer 3 address) and the MAC address (Layer 2 address) of the server. The IP address of the server is typically known or is resolved via a Domain Name System (DNS) lookup. In this example, assume that the server's IP address is known. To properly form an SSH segment, however, PC1 needs to know the server's Layer 2 MAC address. If PC1 does not already have the server's MAC address in its Address Resolution Protocol

(ARP) cache, PC1 can send an ARP request in an attempt to learn the server's MAC address, as shown in Figure 9-3.

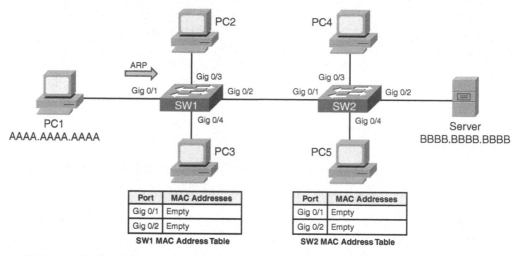

FIGURE 9-3 Endpoint Sending an ARP Request

When switch SW1 sees PC1's ARP request enter port Gigabit 0/1, PC1's MAC address AAAA.AAAA.AAAA is added to switch SW1's MAC address table. Also, because the ARP request is a broadcast, its destination MAC address is FFFF.FFFF. FFFF. Because the MAC address FFFF.FFFF.FFFF is not known to switch SW1's MAC address table, switch SW1 floods a copy of the incoming frame out all switch ports other than the port on which the frame was received, as shown in Figure 9-4.

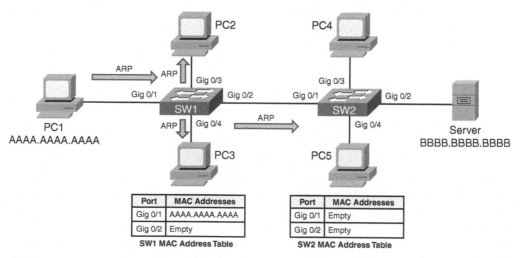

FIGURE 9-4 Switch SW1 Flooding the ARP Request

When switch SW2 receives the ARP request over its Gig 0/1 trunk port, the source
MAC address AAAA.AAAA.AAAA is added to switch SW2's MAC address table, as
illustrated in Figure 9-5. Also, using behavior similar to that of switch SW1, switch
SW2 floods the broadcast.

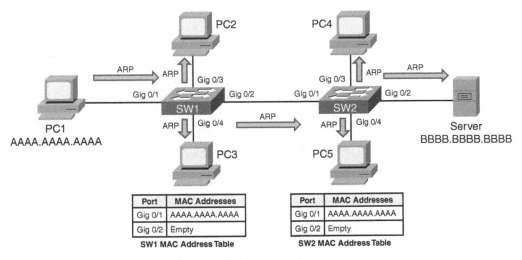

FIGURE 9-5   Switch SW2 Flooding the ARP Request

The server receives the ARP request and responds with an ARP reply, as shown in
Figure 9-6. Unlike the ARP request, however, the ARP reply frame is not a broad-
cast frame. The ARP reply, in this example, has a destination MAC address AAAA.
AAAA.AAAA, which makes the ARP reply a unicast frame.

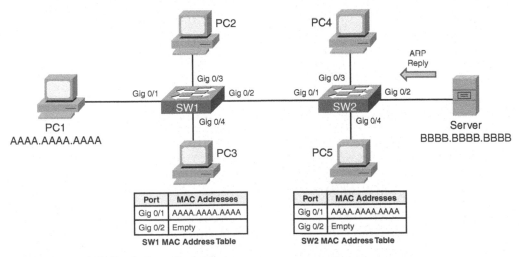

FIGURE 9-6   ARP Reply Sent from a Server

Upon receiving the ARP reply from the server, switch SW2 adds the server's MAC address BBBB.BBBB.BBBB to its MAC address table, as shown in Figure 9-7. Also, the ARP reply is only sent out port Gig 0/1 because switch SW1 knows that the destination MAC address AAAA.AAAA.AAAA is available off port Gig 0/1.

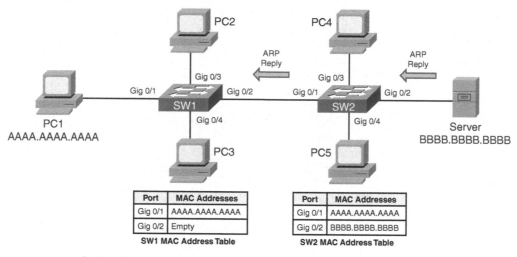

FIGURE 9-7 Switch SW2 Forwarding the ARP Reply

When receiving the ARP reply in its Gig 0/2 port, switch SW1 adds the server's MAC address BBBB.BBBB.BBBB to its MAC address table. Also, like switch SW2, switch SW1 now has an entry in its MAC address table for the frame's destination MAC address AAAA.AAAA.AAAA. Therefore, switch SW1 forwards the ARP reply out port Gig 0/1 to the endpoint of PC1, as illustrated in Figure 9-8.

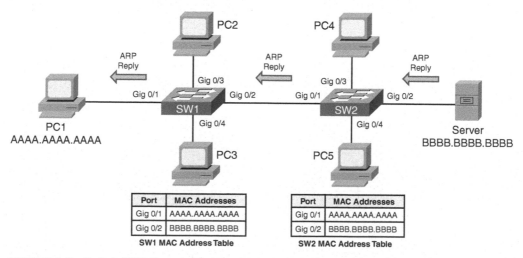

FIGURE 9-8 Switch SW1 Forwarding the ARP Reply

After receiving the server's ARP reply, PC1 knows the MAC address of the server. Therefore, PC1 can now properly construct an SSH segment destined for the server, as depicted in Figure 9-9.

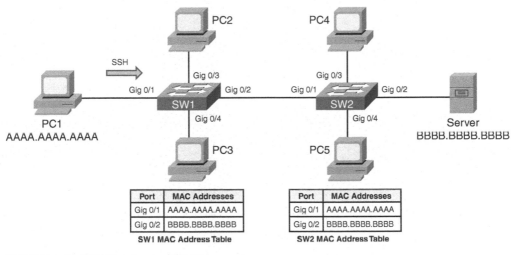

FIGURE 9-9 PC1 Sending an SSH Segment

Switch SW1 has the server's MAC address BBBB.BBBB.BBBB in its MAC address table. Therefore, when switch SW1 receives the SSH segment from PC1, that segment is forwarded out of switch SW1's Gig 0/2 port, as shown in Figure 9-10.

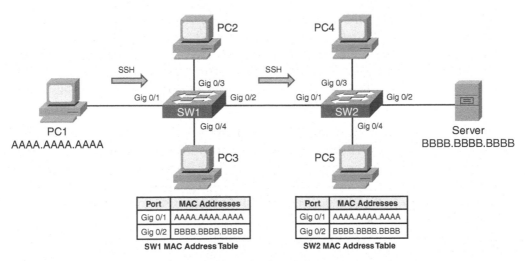

FIGURE 9-10 Switch SW1 Forwarding the SSH Segment

With behavior similar to that of switch SW1, switch SW2 forwards the SSH segment out of its Gig 0/2 port. This forwarding, shown in Figure 9-11, is possible because switch SW2 has an entry for the segment's destination MAC address BBBB. BBBB.BBBB in its MAC address table.

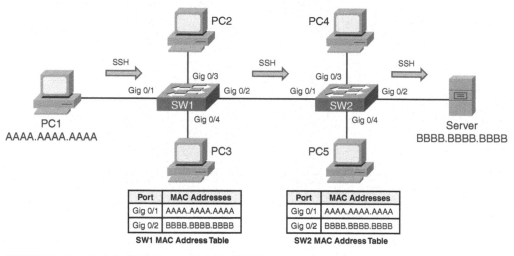

FIGURE 9-11   Switch SW2 Forwarding the SSH Segment

Finally, the server responds to PC1, and a bidirectional SSH session is established between PC1 and the server, as illustrated in Figure 9-12. Because PC1 learned the server's MAC address as a result of its earlier ARP request and stored that result in its local ARP cache, the transmission of subsequent Telnet segments does not require additional ARP requests. However, if unused for a period of time, entries in a PC's ARP cache can time out. Therefore, the PC would have to broadcast another ARP frame if it needed to send traffic to the same destination IP address. The sending of the additional ARP frames adds a small amount of delay when reestablishing a session with that destination IP address.

As shown in Figure 9-13, as on a bridge, each port on a switch represents a separate collision domain. Also, all ports on a switch belong to the same broadcast domain, with one exception: when the ports on a switch have been divided into separate virtual LANs (VLANs). Remember that each VLAN represents a separate broadcast domain, and for traffic to travel from one VLAN to another, that traffic must be routed by a Layer 3 device.

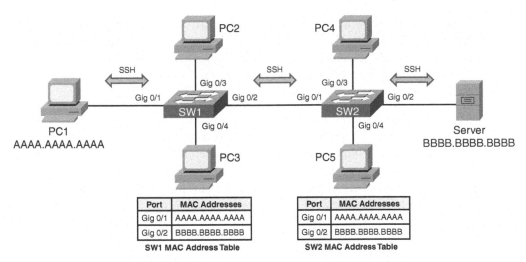

Port	MAC Addresses
Gig 0/1	AAAA.AAAA.AAAA
Gig 0/2	BBBB.BBBB.BBBB

SW1 MAC Address Table

Port	MAC Addresses
Gig 0/1	AAAA.AAAA.AAAA
Gig 0/2	BBBB.BBBB.BBBB

SW2 MAC Address Table

FIGURE 9-12   Bidirectional SSH Session Between PC1 and the Server

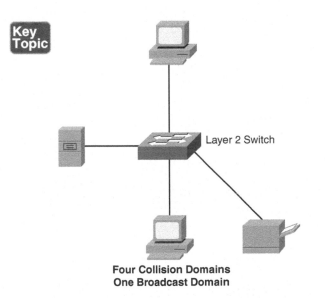

Layer 2 Switch

**Four Collision Domains
One Broadcast Domain**

FIGURE 9-13   Switch Collision and Broadcast Domains

Layer 3 Capable Switch

Whereas a Layer 2 switch makes forwarding decisions based on MAC address information, a *multilayer switch* can make forwarding decisions based on upper-layer information. For example, a multilayer switch could function as a router and make forwarding decisions based on destination IP address information. Some literature refers to a multilayer switch as a ***Layer 3 capable switch*** because of the switch's capability to make forwarding decisions like a router. The term *multilayer switch* is more accurate, however, because many multilayer switches have policy-based routing features that allow upper-layer information (for example, application port numbers) to be used in making forwarding decisions.

Figure 9-14 makes the point that a multilayer switch can be used to interconnect not just network segments but entire networks. Remember that logical Layer 3 IP addresses are used to assign network devices to different logical networks. For traffic to travel between two networked devices that belong to different networks, that traffic must be *routed*. (That is, a device, such as a multilayer switch, has to make a forwarding decision based on Layer 3 information.)

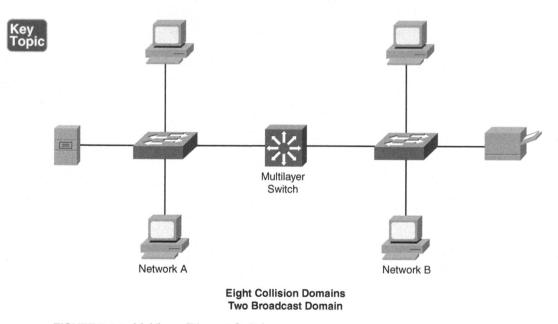

Eight Collision Domains
Two Broadcast Domain

FIGURE 9-14 Multilayer Ethernet Switch

As on a Layer 2 switch, each port on a multilayer switch represents a separate collision domain; however, a characteristic of a multilayer switch (and a router) is that it can become a boundary of a broadcast domain. Although all ports on a Layer 2 switch belong to the same broadcast domain, if configured as such, all ports on a multilayer switch can belong to different broadcast domains.

Routers

A *router* is a Layer 3 device, which means it makes forwarding decisions based on logical network address (for example, IP address) information. Although a router is considered to be a Layer 3 device, like a multilayer switch, it has the capability to consider high-layer traffic parameters, such as quality of service (QoS) settings, in making forwarding decisions.

As shown in Figure 9-15, each port on a router is a separate collision domain and a separate broadcast domain. At this point in the discussion, routers are beginning to sound much like multilayer switches. So, why would network designers select a router rather than a multilayer switch in their design?

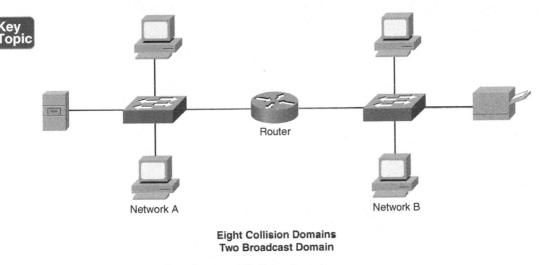

Key
Topic

Router

Network A

Network B

Eight Collision Domains
Two Broadcast Domain

FIGURE 9-15   Router Broadcast and Collision Domains

One reason a router is preferable to a multilayer switch in some cases is that routers are usually more feature rich and support a broader range of interface types. For example, if you need to connect a Layer 3 device out to your Internet service provider (ISP) using a serial port, you will be more likely to find a serial port expansion module for your router than for your multilayer switch.

Table 9-1 summarizes the characteristics of the network infrastructure devices discussed so far in this chapter.

Key Topic

Table 9-1 Network Infrastructure Device Characteristics

Device	Number of Collision Domains Possible	Number of Broadcast Domains Possible	OSI Layer of Operation
Hub	1	1	1
Bridge	1 per port	1	2
Switch	1 per port	1 per port	2
Multilayer switch	1 per port	1 per port	3+
Router	1 per port	1 per port	3+

Access Points

If you examine the sample network topology shown in Figure 9-16, you will notice that wireless clients gain access to a wired network by communicating via radio waves with a wireless *access point (AP)*. The AP can then be hardwired to a LAN.

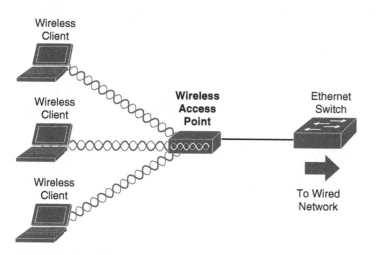

FIGURE 9-16   A Wireless Access Point in a Network

Wireless LANs include multiple standards that support various transmission speeds and security features. However, you need to understand, at this point, that all wireless devices connecting to the same AP are considered to be on the same *shared network segment*, which means that only one device can send data to and receive data from an AP at any one time.

Wireless LAN Controller

Access points tend to come in two major types: autonomous and lightweight. Lightweight access points do not have the control plane intelligence built in to perform their functions for the network. These devices are controlled by *wireless LAN controllers (WLCs)*. WLCs are specialized network devices that permit the central control and management of large numbers of lightweight access points. WLCs simplify the administration of your access points, and they can also assist you dramatically in the monitoring and ongoing maintenance of the wireless infrastructure.

Load Balancer

Load balancers are important specialized network devices that can assist with performance and high availability of key network devices and services. For example, a load balancer can sit in front of a fleet of web servers in a data center. When a large volume of requests come in from clients for the content of those web servers, the load balancer can ensure that the requests are intelligently distributed to the web servers. Often this intelligent distribution can be based on the resources available for each web server. More requests can be sent to those web servers that have the most available resources of the group. As you might expect, the load balancer can also check the health of the nodes periodically and intelligently prevent the forwarding of web requests to servers that are sickly.

Cable Modem

As discussed in Chapter 2, "Network Topologies and Types," cable television companies have a well-established and wide-reaching infrastructure for television programming. These companies can designate specific frequency ranges for upstream and downstream data transmission. A device located in a residence (or a business) that can receive and transmit in those data frequency ranges is known as a *cable modem*. Figure 9-17 shows a typical cable modem that you might find in a small office/home office (SOHO) environment today.

DSL Modem

Recall from Chapter 2 that an alternative to cable high-speed Internet is DSL. While this technology is getting harder and harder to find in today's WAN environments, you may discover it at a SOHO location or remote branch. In such a case, a *DSL modem* is the local device that makes the data transfers possible.

FIGURE 9-17   A Cable Modem

VPN Headend

Companies with locations spread across multiple sites often require secure communications between those sites. One option is to purchase multiple WAN connections to interconnect those sites. Sometimes, however, a more cost-effective option is to create secure connections through an untrusted network, such as the Internet. Such a secure tunnel is called a *virtual private network* (*VPN*). Depending on the VPN technology being used, the devices that terminate the ends of a VPN tunnel might be required to perform heavy processing. For example, consider a company headquarters location with VPN connections to each of 100 remote sites. The device at the headquarters terminating these VPN tunnels might have to perform encryption and authentication for each tunnel, resulting in a heavy processor burden on that device.

Although several router models can terminate a VPN circuit, a dedicated device, called a *VPN headend*, or *VPN concentrator*, can be used instead. A VPN headend device performs the processor-intensive process required to terminate multiple VPN tunnels. Figure 9-18 shows a sample VPN topology, with a VPN concentrator at each corporate location.

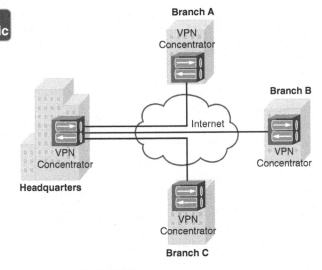

FIGURE 9-18   VPN Concentrator

The term *encryption* refers to the capability of a device to scramble data from a sender in such a way that the data can be unscrambled by the receiver but not by any other party that might intercept the data. Because a VPN concentrator is able to encrypt data, it is considered to belong to a class of devices called *encryption devices*, which are devices (such as routers, firewalls, and VPN concentrators) capable of participating in an encrypted session.

Proxy Servers

Some clients are configured to forward their packets, which are seemingly destined for the Internet, to a ***proxy server***. The proxy server receives the client's request, and on behalf of that client (that is, as that client's proxy), the proxy server sends the request out to the Internet. When a reply is received from the Internet, the proxy server forwards the response on to the client. Figure 9-19 illustrates the operation of a proxy server.

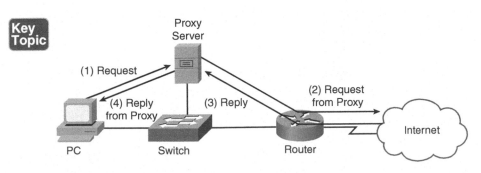

FIGURE 9-19   Proxy Server Operation

What possible benefit could come from such an arrangement? Security is one benefit. Specifically, because all requests going out to the Internet are sourced from the proxy server, the IP addresses of network devices inside the trusted network are hidden from the Internet.

Yet another benefit could come in the form of bandwidth savings because many proxy servers perform content caching. For example, without a proxy server, if multiple clients all visited the same website, the same graphics from the home page of the website would be downloaded multiple times (one time for each client visiting the website). However, with a proxy server performing content caching, when the first client navigates to a website on the Internet, and the Internet-based web server returns its content, the proxy server not only forwards this content to the client requesting the web page but stores a copy of the content on its hard drive. Then, when a subsequent client points its web browser to the same website, after the proxy server determines that the page has not changed, the proxy server can locally serve up the content to the client, without having to once again consume Internet bandwidth to download all the graphic elements from the Internet-based website.

As a final example of a proxy server benefit, some proxy servers can perform content filtering to restrict clients from accessing certain URLs. For example, many companies use content filtering to prevent their employees from accessing popular social networking sites and promote productivity.

> **NOTE**   A reverse proxy receives requests on behalf of a server or servers and replies back to the clients on behalf of those servers. Reverse proxie scan also be used with load-balancing and caching to better utilize a group of servers providing scalability and high availability.

Firewalls

A network *firewall* is most often implemented as a network security appliance. As depicted in Figure 9-20, a firewall stands guard at the door of your network, protecting it from malicious Internet traffic.

For example, a *stateful firewall* allows traffic to originate from an inside network (that is, a trusted network) and go out to the Internet (an untrusted network). Likewise, return traffic coming back from the Internet to the inside network is allowed by the firewall. However, if traffic originates from a device on the Internet (that is, not returning traffic), the firewall blocks that traffic.

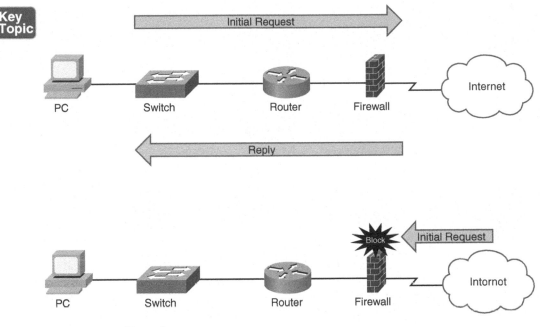

FIGURE 9-20 Firewall

Intrusion Detection and Prevention

When an attacker launches an attack against a network, *intrusion detection system (IDS)* and *intrusion prevention system (IPS)* technologies are often able to recognize the attack and respond appropriately. Attacks might be recognizable by comparing incoming data streams against a database of well-known attack signatures. Other mechanisms for detecting attacks include policy-based and anomaly-based approaches. In addition to dedicated network-based intrusion prevention system (NIPS) sensors, IPS software can be installed on a host to provide a host-based intrusion prevention system (HIPS) or host-based intrusion detection system (HIDS) solution.

IDS Versus IPS

Both IDS and IPS devices can recognize network attacks; they differ primarily in their network placement. Specifically, whereas an IDS device receives a copy of traffic to be analyzed, an IPS device resides inline with the traffic, as illustrated in Figure 9-21.

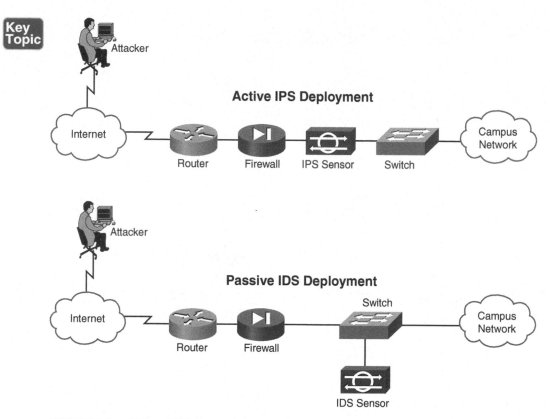

FIGURE 9-21   IDS and IPS Network Placement

Because the analyzed traffic does not flow through the IDS device, the IDS device is considered to be *passive*, and the IPS device is considered to be *active*. Both the IDS and the IPS devices can send alerts to, for example, a management station. Although an IDS device can also communicate with a security appliance or a router to prevent subsequent attack packets, the initially offending traffic reaches its destination. Conversely, an IPS device can drop the traffic inline, thus preventing even the first malicious packet from reaching its intended target.

The previous discussion of IDS versus IPS devices might seem to suggest that IPS devices should always be used instead of IDS devices. However, in some network environments, these two solutions complement one another. For example, an IDS device can add value to a network that already employs an IPS device by verifying that the IPS device is still operational. The IDS device might also identify suspicious traffic and send alerts about that traffic without having the IPS device drop the traffic.

IDS and IPS Device Categories

IDS and IPS devices can be categorized based on how they detect malicious traffic. Alternatively, IPS devices can be categorized based on whether they run on a network device or on a host.

Consider the following approaches to detecting malicious traffic:

- Signature-based detection

- Policy-based detection

- Anomaly-based detection

The following sections describe these methods in detail.

Signature-Based Detection

The primary method used to detect and prevent attacks using IDS or IPS technologies is signature based. A signature could be a string of bytes that, in a certain context, triggers detection. For example, attacks against a web server typically take the form of URLs. Therefore, URLs could be searched for a certain string that would identify an attack against a web server.

As another example, the IDS or IPS device could search for a pattern in the MIME header of an email message. However, because signature-based IDS/IPS is, as its name suggests, based on signatures, the administrator needs to routinely update the signature files.

Policy-Based Detection

Another approach to IDS/IPS detection is policy based. With a policy-based approach, the IDS/IPS device needs a specific declaration of the security policy. For example, you could write a network access policy that identifies which networks can communicate with other networks. The IDS/IPS device could then recognize out-of-profile traffic that does not conform to the policy and report that activity. Policy-based detection could also identify unencrypted channels and plaintext credentials and insecure protocols such as Telnet, SNMPv1, HTTP, FTP, SLIP, and TFTP. Secure protocols such as SSH, SNMPv3, TLS/SSL, HTTPS, SFTP, and IPsec should be used when possible to protect the confidentiality of the data flows on the network.

Anomaly-Based Detection

A third approach to detecting or preventing malicious traffic is anomaly based. This approach is prone to false positives because a *normal* condition is difficult to measurably define. However, there are a couple of options for detecting anomalies:

- **Statistical anomaly detection:** This approach involves watching network traffic patterns over a period of time and dynamically building a baseline. Then, if traffic patterns significantly vary from the baseline, an alarm can be triggered.

- **Nonstatistical anomaly detection:** This approach allows an administrator to define what traffic patterns are supposed to look like. However, imagine that Microsoft releases a large update for its Windows 10 OS, and your company has hundreds of computers that are configured to automatically download that service pack. If multiple employees turn on their computers at approximately the same time tomorrow morning, and multiple copies of the service pack simultaneously start to download from https://www.microsoft.com, the IDS/IPS device might consider that traffic pattern to be significantly outside the baseline. As a result, the nonstatistical anomaly detection approach could lead to a false positive (that is, an alarm being triggered in the absence of malicious traffic). However, an anomaly-based IPS may be able to indicate abnormal behavior, compared to the baseline of normal activity, which could assist you in discovering a new type of attack that is being used against your network. A zero-day attack is an attack that exploits a previously unknown vulnerability.

> **NOTE**   Anomaly-based detection is also known as *behavior-based detection*.

Networking Device Summary

Table 9-2 provides a summary of the networking devices discussed in this chapter.

Table 9-2   Networking Device Summary

Device	Description	Key Points
Hub	Connects devices on an Ethernet twisted-pair network	A hub does not perform any tasks besides signal regeneration. It simply forwards data to all nodes connected to it.
Bridge	Connects two network segments	A bridge operates at the data link layer, and it filters, forwards, or floods an incoming frame based on the packet's MAC address.

Device	Description	Key Points
Switch	Connects devices on a twisted-pair network	A switch forwards data to its destination by using the MAC address embedded in each packet. It only forwards data to nodes that need to receive it.
Router	Connects networks	A router uses the software-configured network address to make forwarding decisions.
Repeater (booster/wireless extender)	Amplifies a wireless signal to make it stronger	This increases the distance that the client system can be placed from the access point and still be on the network.
Modem	Provides serial communication capabilities across phone lines	Modems modulate the digital signal into analog at the sending end and perform the reverse function at the receiving end.
Firewall	Provides controlled data access between networks	Firewalls can be hardware or software based. They are an essential part of a network's security strategy.
Multilayer switch	Functions as a switch or router	Operates on Layers 2 and 3 of the OSI model as a switch and can perform router functionality.
Load balancer	Distributes network load	Load balancing increases redundancy and performance by distributing the load to multiple servers.
VPN concentrator	Increases remote-access security	Establishes a secure connection (tunnel) between the sending and receiving network devices.
AP	Used to create a wireless LAN and to extend a wired network	Uses the wireless infrastructure network mode to provide a connection point between WLANs and a wired Ethernet LAN.
IDS/IPS	Detects and prevents intrusions	Monitors the network and attempts to detect/prevent intrusion attempts.
Media converter	Connects two dissimilar types of network media	Can be used for ■ Single-mode fiber to Ethernet ■ Single-mode to multimode fiber ■ Multimode fiber to Ethernet ■ Fiber to coaxial
WLC	Used with branch/remote office deployments for wireless authentication	When an AP boots, it authenticates with a controller before it can start working as an AP.

Networked Devices

This section discusses some of the many networked devices that work together to make end users happy.

Voice over IP Protocols and Components

A *voice over IP (VoIP)*–enabled network digitizes speech into packets and transmits those packets across a data network. This allows voice, data, and even video to share the same medium. In a network with unified communications (UC) such as voice, video, and data, specialized UC servers, controllers, devices, and *voice gateways* are also likely to be used. In a cloud computing environment, they may be virtualized as well. Figure 9-22 shows a sample VoIP network topology. Not only can a VoIP network provide significant cost savings over a traditional PBX solution, many VoIP networks offer enhanced services (for example, integration with video conferencing applications and calendaring software to determine availability) not found in traditional corporate telephony environments.

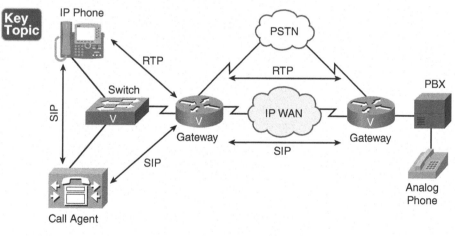

FIGURE 9-22   Sample VoIP Network Topology

Table 9-3 defines the VoIP devices and protocols shown in Figure 9-22.

Table 9-3   VoIP Network Elements

Protocol/Device	Description
IP phone	An IP phone is a telephone with an integrated Ethernet connection. Although users speak into a traditional analog handset (or headset) on the IP phone, the IP phone digitizes the user's speech, packetizes it, and sends it out over a data network (via the IP phone's Ethernet port). While an IP phone is a common example of a VoIP endpoint, an alternative is software running on a computer.

Protocol/Device	Description
Call agent	A call agent is a repository for a VoIP network's dial plan. For example, when a user dials a number from an IP phone, the call agent analyzes the dialed digits and determines how to route the call toward the destination.
Gateway	A gateway in a VoIP network acts as a translator between two different telephony signaling environments. In Figure 9-22, both gateways interconnect a VoIP network with the PSTN. Also, the gateway on the right interconnects a traditional PBX with a VoIP network.
PBX	A private branch exchange (PBX) is a privately owned telephone switch traditionally used in corporate telephony systems. Although a PBX is not typically considered a VoIP device, it connects into a VoIP network through a gateway, as shown in Figure 9-22.
Analog phone	An analog phone is a traditional telephone, like the ones individuals used to have in their homes. Even though an analog phone is not typically considered a VoIP device, it can connect to a VoIP network via a VoIP adapter or, as shown in Figure 9-22, via a PBX, which is connected to a VoIP network.
SIP	Session Initiation Protocol (SIP) is a signaling, setup, and management protocol used with voice and video sessions over IP networks. SIP, in conjunction with other protocols, specifies the encoder/decoder (codec) that will be used for voice and video connections over the network.
RTP	Real-Time Transport Protocol (RTP) is a protocol that carries voice and interactive video. Notice in Figure 9-22 that the bidirectional RTP stream does not flow through the call agent.

Printer

While networked printers were once considered gems of convenience for the office environment, they were not even contemplated for home or small offices for many years. Today, it is rare to find a printer that does not have networking capabilities. Printers used in home or small offices are typically wireless and easy to use on a network.

Physical Access Control Devices

In high-security environments, there are typically many networked devices that help control and monitor physical access. Devices that might be included in this category of *physical access control devices* include the following:

- An access control panel (also known as a controller)

- An access control vestibule (formerly known as a mantrap), such as a door, a turnstile, a parking gate, an elevator, or another physical barrier

- A reader installed near an entrance

- Locking hardware, such as electric door strikes and electromagnetic locks

- A magnetic door switch for monitoring door position

- Request-to-exit (RTE) devices for allowing egress

Cameras

Today, many networks use cameras for monitoring and/or security. These cameras, called IP cameras, are digital video cameras that receive control data and send image data via an IP network. They are commonly used for surveillance, but unlike analog closed-circuit television (CCTV) cameras, they require no local recording device— only a local area network. Most IP cameras are webcams, but the term *IP camera* or *netcam* usually applies only to cameras that can be directly accessed over a network connection, usually used for surveillance.

Heating, Ventilation, and Air Conditioning (HVAC) Sensors

Heating, ventilation, and air conditioning (HVAC) is the technology you most likely appreciate every day for your indoor and vehicular environmental comfort. The goal of HVAC systems is to provide thermal comfort and acceptable indoor air quality.

HVAC devices are frequently connected to networks in modern enterprise infrastructures. Providing connectivity to the HVAC system through an **HVAC sensor** is extremely beneficial from a maintenance and configuration standpoint. In addition, such connectivity is also of huge benefit when it comes time to carefully monitor the system and compile monitoring data in a central location for any analysis that might be required.

Technologies for the Internet of Things

Many wireless technologies (or technologies related to wireless) come in to play to make the **Internet of Things (IoT)** a reality. IoT refers to the trend today to connect everyday objects to the Internet in order to make them "smart." In my home, I speak to my Amazon Echo (Alexa) speaker to have it control the lights, for example. This Internet-connected speaker and the lights are perfect examples of IoT in action.

Smart devices abound today. They include the following:

- Refrigerators

- Smart speakers

- Smart thermostats

- Smart doorbells

You should be aware of the following key technologies that help make the modern IoT a reality:

- **Z-Wave:** This wireless communications protocol is used primarily for home automation. It is a mesh network using low-energy radio waves to communicate from appliance to appliance. Z-Wave is used with devices such as lighting control systems, security systems, thermostats, windows, locks, swimming pools, and garage door openers.

- **ANT+:** This is a wireless protocol for monitoring sensor data such as a person's heart rate or a car's tire pressure, as well as for controlling systems such as indoor lighting and entertainment appliances such as televisions. ANT+ is designed and maintained by the ANT+ Alliance, which is owned by Garmin.

- **Bluetooth:** Bluetooth is a wireless technology that allows devices to communicate over a short distance. Bluetooth is often used to create personal area networks (PANs), and it also enables communications for the IoT.

- **NFC:** Near field communication (NFC) is a set of communication protocols that enables two electronic devices to transfer information. Typically, one of these devices is a portable device such as a smartphone. NFC devices must be close to each other (within 4 cm, or 1.6 inches). NFC devices are used in contactless payment systems, such as with credit cards and electronic ticket smartcards, and allow mobile payment to replace/supplement these systems.

- **IR:** Infrared (IR) is another wireless technology that permits data transmission over short ranges among computer peripherals and personal digital assistants. These devices usually conform to standards published by IrDA, the Infrared Data Association. Remote controls and IrDA devices use infrared light-emitting diodes (LEDs) to emit infrared radiation that is focused by a plastic lens into a narrow beam.

- **RFID:** Radio-frequency identification (RFID) uses electromagnetic fields to automatically identify and track tags attached to objects. The tags contain electronically stored information. Passive tags collect energy from a nearby RFID reader's interrogating radio waves. An active tag has a local power source such as a battery and may operate at hundreds of meters from the RFID reader. Unlike with a barcode, an RFID tag need not be within the line of sight of the reader, so it may be embedded in the tracked object.

- **802.11:** As detailed in Chapter 12, "Wireless Standards," IEEE 802.11 is a set of Media Access Control and physical layer specifications for implementing wireless local area network (WLAN) computer communication in the 900MHz and 2.4GHz, 3.6GHz, 5GHz, 6 GHz, and 60GHz frequency bands. Obviously, these technologies play a great role in the IoT because many appliances and common objects communicate over 802.11 wireless signals to reach a main hub. This is how most smart lights function, for example.

Industrial Control Systems/Supervisory Control and Data Acquisition (SCADA)

- A *supervisory control and data acquisition (SCADA)* system is used to control remote equipment and to monitor that equipment. It might be part of an *industrial control system (ICS)* that is used to manage a power plant or water treatment facility. Networked devices like these with distributed control systems (DCSs) may have devices such as programmable logic controllers (PLCs) and remote terminal units (RTUs) that are proprietary and may require specialized training to learn and troubleshoot.

Real-World Case Study

Acme, Inc. has decided that to keep pace with growing customer demand, it will use software as a service (SaaS) from a cloud provider for its primary business application. This will allow the company to focus on its business and use the application instead of managing and maintaining that application.

There will be some desktop computers in the office for the users, and those computers will be networked using UTP cabling that goes to a switch. The switches on each floor of the building will be secured in a locked intermediate distribution frame (IDF) in a wiring closet on each floor. For the interconnections between the switches on each of the floors, multimode fiber-optic cabling is used. When purchasing hardware and fiber-optic cabling, Acme, Inc. will want to make sure that the fiber-optic connector type matches the correct fiber interface type on the switches. In the basement of the building is an area for Acme, Inc. to use as its own dedicated main distribution frame (MDF). From the MDF, there will be cabling that goes to the demarcation point for the service provider for the WAN and Internet connectivity provided by the service provider. This connectivity will be used to access cloud services (SaaS specifically) from the service provider and for WAN and Internet access.

Inside the building, a few of the users have mobile devices. To facilitate network access for these mobile users, wireless APs, which are physically connected through UTP cabling to the switches on each floor, will be used. Hubs will not be used because they are not very secure or effective and because all network traffic is sent to every other port on a hub, whereas a switch only forwards unicast frames to the other ports that need to see that traffic. To consolidate hardware in the MDF, multilayer switches will be used to provide not only Layer 2 forwarding of frames based on MAC addresses but also Layer 3 forwarding of packets based on IP addresses (routing). On the LAN, Acme, Inc. intends to use a set of redundant servers near the MDF to provide services such as DHCP, DNS, and time synchronization to each of its offices on each floor. The servers can coordinate DNS and time synchronization with other servers on the public Internet. The local servers can also be used for network authentication to control user access to the network regardless of the source, including wireless, wired, and VPN. Instead of purchasing multiple physical servers, the company is going to virtualize the servers onto specialized hardware that is fault tolerant. With this solution, the company can easily add more logical servers without purchasing a physical system for every new server. This could include unified communications servers that may be involved with voice, video, and other types of streaming data.

A VPN device will also be installed in the MDF to allow users who are connected to the Internet from their home or other locations to build a secure VPN remote access connection over the Internet to the corporate headquarters. Instead of buying a dedicated VPN device such as a concentrator, Acme, Inc. is going to use a firewall that has this VPN capability integrated as part of its services.

Summary

Here are the main topics covered in this chapter:

- This chapter contrasts the roles of various networking device infrastructure components, including switches, routers, and wireless LAN controllers.

- This chapter provides examples of specialized network devices and explains how they can enhance a network. These devices include VPN concentrators, firewalls, DNS servers, DHCP servers, proxy servers, and IPS and IDS devices.

- This chapter discusses technologies often found with the Internet of Things (IoT) today.

- This chapter introduces VoIP and describes some of the protocols and hardware components that make up a VoIP network.

Exam Preparation Tasks

Review All the Key Topics

Review the most important topics from this chapter, noted with the Key Topic icon in the outer margin of the page. Table 9-4 lists these key topics and the page number where each is found.

Key Topic

Table 9-4 Key Topics for Chapter 9

Key Topic Element	Description	Page Number
Figure 9-2	Ethernet bridge	224
Figure 9-13	Layer 2 Ethernet switch	231
Figure 9-14	Multilayer Ethernet switch	232
Figure 9-15	Router	233
Table 9-1	Network device characteristics	234
Figure 9-17	Cable modem	236
Figure 9-18	VPN concentrator	237
Figure 9-19	Proxy server operation	237
Figure 9-20	Firewall	239
Figure 9-21	IDS/IPS network placement	240
List	Approaches for detecting malicious traffic	241
Figure 9-22	Sample VoIP network topology	244
Table 9-2	Networking device summary	242
Table 9-3	VoIP network elements	244
List	Internet of Things (IoT) technologies	246

Complete Tables and Lists from Memory

Print a copy of Appendix C, "Memory Tables," or at least the section for this chapter and complete as many of the tables as possible from memory. Appendix D, "Memory Tables Answer Key," includes the completed tables and lists so you can check your work.

Define Key Terms

Define the following key terms from this chapter and check your answers in the Glossary:

switch, router, multilayer switch, Layer 2 Ethernet switch, Layer 3 capable switch, hub, access point (AP), bridge, wireless LAN controller (WLC), load balancer, proxy server, cable modem, DSL modem, repeater, voice gateway, media converter, intrusion detection system (IDS), intrusion prevention system (IPS), firewall, VPN headend, voice over IP (VoIP), physical access control device,

HVAC sensor, Internet of Things (IoT), industrial control system (ICS), supervisory control and data acquisition (SCADA)

Additional Resources

Network Devices, Part 1: https://www.youtube.com/watch?v=CdoG4tWNPqs

What is VoIP: https://youtu.be/SYJfO99nOmo

Review Questions

The answers to these review questions appear in Appendix A, "Answers to Review Questions."

1. Which of the following is a VoIP signaling protocol used to set up, maintain, and tear down VoIP phone calls?

    a. MX

    b. RJ-45

    c. SIP

    d. IMAP

2. Which network infrastructure device primarily makes forwarding decisions based on Layer 2 MAC addresses?

    a. Router

    b. Switch

    c. Hub

    d. Multilayer switch

3. A router operating at Layer 3 primarily makes its forwarding decisions based on what address?

    a. Destination MAC address

    b. Source IP address

    c. Source MAC address

    d. Destination IP address

4. Identify two differences between an Ethernet bridge and an Ethernet switch. (Choose two.)

    a. Switches use ASICs to make forwarding decisions, whereas bridges make their forwarding decisions in software.

    b. Bridges typically operate faster than switches.

    c. Switches usually have higher port densities than bridges.

    d. Bridges can base their forwarding decisions on logical network layer addresses.

5. In a router that has 12 ports, how many broadcast domains does the router have?

    a. None

    b. 1

    c. 2

    d. 12

6. In a switch that has 12 ports, how many collision domains does the switch have?

    a. None

    b. 1

    c. 2

    d. 12

7. What IoT technology is specialized for monitoring sensor data and is owned by Garmin?

    a. Z-Wave

    b. ANT+

    c. Bluetooth

    d. RFID

8. What networking device often uses signatures to help protect a network from known malicious attacks?

    a. Wireless LAN controller

    b. Media converter

    c. Proxy server

    d. IPS

9. What device can act as both a content cache and a URL filter and is typically configured in the client browser of an end-user system?

   a. Wireless LAN controller

   b. Media converter

   c. Proxy server

   d. IPS

10. You are using a network firewall in your enterprise infrastructure. This firewall requires you to define which connections are permitted outbound. Once you do so, the appropriate and expected return data flows are dynamically allowed through the firewall. What firewall characteristic does this scenario describe?

    a. Stateless

    b. Stateful

    c. Deterministic

    d. Zone-based

This chapter covers the following topics related to Objective 2.2 (Compare and contrast routing technologies and bandwidth management concepts) of the CompTIA Network+ N10-008 certification exam:

- Routing
  - Dynamic routing
  - Protocols
    - Routing Information Protocol (RIP)
    - Open Shortest Path First (OSPF)
    - Enhanced Interior Gateway Routing Protocol (EIGRP)
    - Border Gateway Protocol (BGP)
  - Link state vs. distance vector vs. hybrid
  - Static routing
  - Default route
  - Administrative distance
  - Exterior vs. interior
  - Time to live
- Bandwidth management
  - Traffic shaping
  - Quality of service (QoS)

CHAPTER 10

Routing Technologies and Bandwidth Management

In Chapter 4, "IP Addressing," you learned how Internet Protocol (IP) networks can be divided into subnets. Each subnet is its own broadcast domain, and the device that separates broadcast domains is a router (which this text considers synonymous with a multilayer switch). A multilayer switch is a network device that can perform the Layer 2 switching of frames as well as the Layer 3 routing of IP packets. Multilayer switches generally use dedicated chips to perform these functions and, as a result, may be faster than traditional routers in forwarding packets.

For traffic to flow between subnets, the traffic has to be routed; this routing is a router's primary job. This chapter discusses how routing occurs and introduces a variety of approaches for performing routing, including dynamic routing, static routing, and default routing. The chapter also breaks down the various categories of routing protocols and provides specific examples of each.

The chapter concludes with a discussion of various bandwidth management topics, including a discussion of QoS concepts, such as traffic shaping.

Foundation Topics

Routing

To understand basic routing processes, consider Figure 10-1. In this topology, PC1 needs to send traffic to Server1. Notice that these devices are on different networks. In this topology, how does a packet from the source IP address 192.168.1.2 get routed to the destination IP address 192.168.3.2?

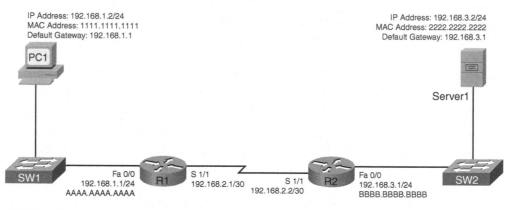

FIGURE 10-1   Basic Routing Topology

It might help to walk through this process systematically:

Key Topic

Step 1.   PC1 compares its IP address and subnet mask 192.168.1.2/24 with the destination IP address and subnet mask 192.168.3.2/24. PC1 concludes that the destination IP address resides on a remote subnet. Therefore, PC1 needs to send the packet to its default gateway, which could have been manually configured on PC1 or dynamically learned via Dynamic Host Configuration Protocol (DHCP). In this example, PC1 has the default gateway 192.168.1.1 (router R1). However, to construct a Layer 2 frame, PC1 also needs the MAC address of its default gateway. PC1 sends an ***Address Resolution Protocol (ARP)*** request for router R1's MAC address. After PC1 receives an ARP reply from router R1, PC1 adds router R1's MAC address to its ARP cache. PC1 now sends its data in a frame destined for Server1, as shown in Figure 10-2.

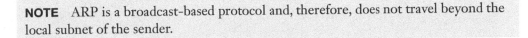

NOTE   ARP is a broadcast-based protocol and, therefore, does not travel beyond the local subnet of the sender.

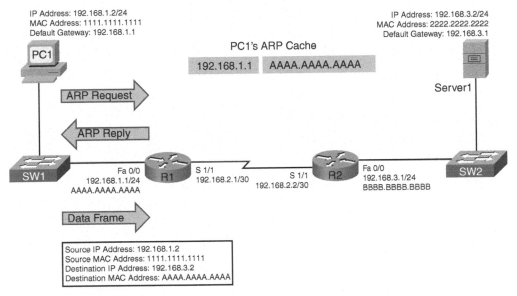

FIGURE 10-2   Basic Routing: Step 1

Step 2.   Router R1 receives the frame sent from PC1 and interrogates the IP header. An IP header contains a *Time-to-Live (TTL)* field, which is decremented once for each router hop. Therefore, router R1 decrements the packet's TTL field. If the value in the TTL field is reduced to 0, the router discards the frame and sends a "time exceeded" Internet Control Message Protocol (ICMP) message back to the source. As long as the TTL has not been decremented to 0, router R1 checks its routing table to determine the best path to reach network 192.168.3.0/24. In this example, router R1's routing table has an entry stating that network 192.168.3.0/24 is accessible via interface Serial 1/1. Note that ARP is not required for serial interfaces because these interface types do not have MAC addresses. Router R1, therefore, forwards the frame out its Serial 1/1 interface, as shown in Figure 10-3.

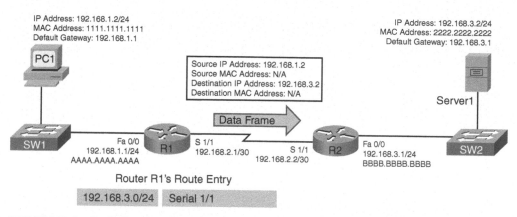

FIGURE 10-3 Basic Routing: Step 2

Step 3. When router R2 receives the frame, it decrements the TTL in the IP header, just as router R1 did. Again, as long as the TTL has not been decremented to 0, router R2 interrogates the IP header to determine the destination network. In this case, the destination network 192.168.3.0/24 is directly attached to router R2's Fast Ethernet 0/0 interface. Similar to the way PC1 sent out an ARP request to determine the MAC address of its default gateway, router R2 sends an ARP request to determine the MAC address of Server1. After an ARP reply is received from Server1, router R2 forwards the frame out its Fast Ethernet 0/0 interface to Server1, as illustrated in Figure 10-4.

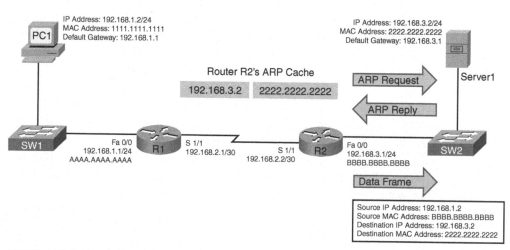

FIGURE 10-4 Basic Routing: Step 3

The previous steps identified two router data structures:

- **IP routing table:** When a router needed to route an IP packet, it consulted its IP routing table to find the best match. The best match is the route that has the longest prefix. Specifically, a route entry with the longest prefix is the most specific network. For example, imagine that a router has an entry for network 10.0.0.0/8 and for network 10.1.1.0/24. Also, imagine that the router is seeking the best match for destination address 10.1.1.1/24. The router would select the 10.1.1.0/24 route entry as the best entry because that route entry has the longest prefix (/24 is longer than /8, which is a more specific entry).

- **Layer 3 to Layer 2 mapping:** In the previous example, router R2's ARP cache contained Layer 3 to Layer 2 mapping information. Specifically, the ARP cache had a mapping that said MAC address 2222.2222.2222 corresponded to IP address 192.168.3.2.

As shown in the preceding example, routers rely on their internal routing table to make packet-forwarding decisions. So how does a router's routing table become populated with entries? That is the focus of the next section.

Sources of Routing Information

A router's routing table can be populated from various sources. As an administrator, you could statically configure a route entry. A route could be learned via a *dynamic routing* protocol (for example, OSPF or EIGRP), or a router could know how to get to a specific network because the router is physically attached to that network.

Directly Connected Routes

A router that has an interface directly participating in a network knows how to reach that specific destination network. For example, consider Figure 10-5.

In Figure 10-5, router R1's routing table knows how to reach the 192.168.1.0/24 and 192.168.2.0/30 networks because router R1 has an interface physically attached to each network. Similarly, router R2 has interfaces participating in the 10.1.1.0/30 and 192.168.2.0/30 networks and therefore knows how to reach those networks. The entries currently shown to be in the routing tables of routers R1 and R2 are called *directly connected routes*.

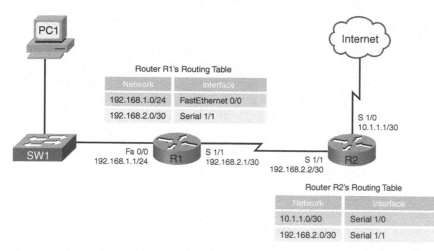

FIGURE 10-5   Directly Connected Routes

Static Routes

It is also possible to statically configure routes in a router's routing table. Continuing to expand on the previous example, consider router R1. As shown in Figure 10-6, router R1 does not need knowledge of each route on the Internet. Specifically, router R1 already knows how to reach devices on its locally attached networks. All router R1 really needs to know at this point is how to get out to the rest of the world. As you can see from Figure 10-6, any traffic destined for a nonlocal network (for example, any of the networks available on the public Internet) can simply be sent to router R2. Because R2 is the next router hop along the path to reach all those other networks, router R1 could be configured with a *default static route*, which says, "If traffic is destined for a network not currently in the routing table, send that traffic out interface Serial 1/1."

NOTE   A static route does not always reference a local interface. Instead, a static route might point to a *next-hop IP address* (that is, an interface's IP address on the next router to which traffic should be forwarded). The network address of a default route is 0.0.0.0/0.

Similarly, router R2 can reach the Internet by sending traffic out its Serial 1/0 interface. However, router R2 does need information about how to reach the 192.168.1.0/24 network available off router R1. To educate router R2 about how this network can be reached, a network administrator can add a static route pointing to 192.168.1.0/24 to router R2's routing table.

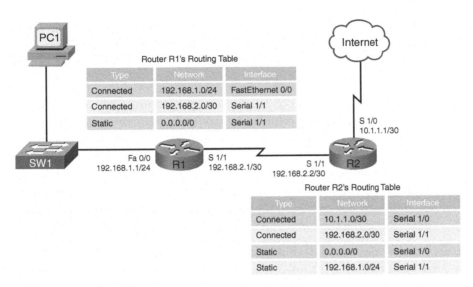

FIGURE 10-6   Static Routes

Dynamic Routing Protocols

In complex networks, such as the topology shown in Figure 10-7, static routing does not scale well. Fortunately, a variety of dynamic routing protocols are available that allow a router's routing table to be updated as network conditions change.

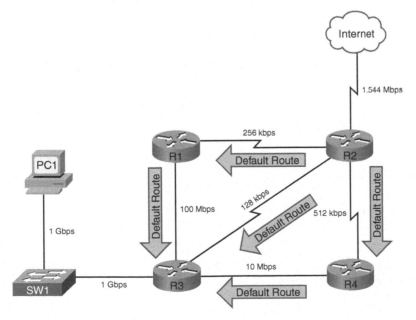

FIGURE 10-7   Dynamic Routes

In Figure 10-7, router R2 is advertising a default route to its neighbors (routers R1, R3, and R4). What happens if PC1 wants to send traffic to the Internet? PC1's default gateway is router R3, and router R3 has received three default routes. Which one does it use?

Router R3's path selection depends on the dynamic routing protocol being used. As you will see later in this chapter, a routing protocol such as Routing Information Protocol (RIP) would make the path selection based on the number of routers that must be used to reach the Internet (that is, *hop count*). Based on the topology presented, router R3 would select the 128Kbps link (where Kbps stands for kilobits per second, meaning thousands of bits per second) connecting to router R2 because the Internet would be only one hop away. If router R3 instead selected a path pointing to either router R1 or R4, the Internet would be two hops away.

However, based on the link bandwidths, you can see that the path from router R3 to router R2 is suboptimal. Unfortunately, RIP does not consider available bandwidth when making its route selection. Some other protocols, such as Open Shortest Path First (OSPF), can consider available bandwidth when making their routing decisions.

Dynamic routes also allow a router to reroute around a failed link. For example, in Figure 10-8, router R3 prefers to reach the Internet via router R4. However, the link between routers R3 and R4 goes down. Thanks to a dynamic routing protocol, router R3 knows of two other paths to reach the Internet, and it selects the next-best path, which is via router R1 in this example. This process of failing over from one route to a backup route is called *convergence*.

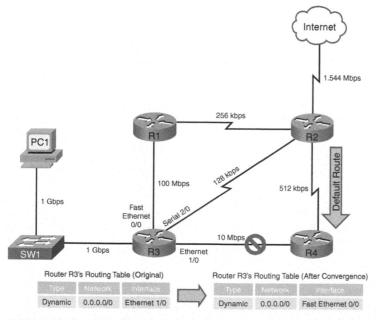

FIGURE 10-8 Route Redundancy

Routing Protocol Characteristics

Before examining the characteristics of routing protocols, we need to look at the important distinction between a *routing protocol* and a *routed protocol*:

- A **routing protocol** (for example, RIP, OSPF, or EIGRP) is a protocol that advertises route information between routers.

- A **routed protocol** is a protocol with an addressing scheme (for example, IP) that defines different network addresses. Traffic can then be routed between defined networks, perhaps with the assistance of a routing protocol.

This section looks at routing protocol characteristics, such as how believable a routing protocol is compared to other routing protocols. In addition, in the presence of multiple routes, different routing protocols use different **metrics** to determine the best path. A distinction is made between **interior gateway protocols (IGPs)** and **exterior gateway protocols (EGPs)**. Finally, this section discusses different approaches to making route advertisements.

Believability of a Route

If a network is running more than one routing protocol (maybe as a result of a corporate merger), and a router receives two route advertisements from different routing protocols for the same network, which route advertisement does the router believe? Interestingly, some routing protocols are considered to be more believable that others. For example, a Cisco router would consider EIGRP to be more believable than RIP.

The index of believability is called **administrative distance (AD)**. Table 10-1 shows the AD values for various sources of routing information. Note that lower AD values are more believable than higher AD values.

Key Topic

Table 10-1   Administrative Distance

Routing Information Source	AD Value
Directly connected network	0
Statically configured network	1
EIGRP	90
OSPF	110
RIP	120
External EIGRP	170
Unknown or unbelievable	255 (considered to be unreachable)

Metrics

Some networks might be reachable via more than one path. If a routing protocol knows of multiple paths to reach such a network, which route (or routes) does the routing protocol select? Actually, it varies depending on the routing protocol and what that routing protocol uses as a *metric* (that is, a value assigned to a route). Lower metrics are preferred over higher metrics.

Some routing protocols support load balancing across equal-cost paths; this is useful when a routing protocol knows of more than one route to reach a destination network and those routes have equal metrics. EIGRP can even be configured to do load balancing across unequal-cost paths.

Different routing protocols can use different parameters in their calculation of a metric. The specific parameters used for a variety of routing protocols are presented later in this chapter.

Interior Versus Exterior Gateway Protocols

Routing protocols can also be categorized based on the scope of their operation. Interior gateway protocols (IGPs) operate within an autonomous system, where an autonomous system is a network under a single administrative control. Conversely, exterior gateway protocols (EGPs) operate between autonomous systems.

Consider Figure 10-9. Routers R1 and R2 are in one autonomous system (AS 65002), and routers R3 and R4 are in another autonomous system (AS 65003). Within those autonomous systems, an IGP is used to exchange routing information. However, router ISP1 is a router in a separate autonomous system (AS 65001) that is run by a service provider. An EGP (typically, Border Gateway Protocol) is used to exchange routing information between the service provider's autonomous system and each of the other autonomous systems.

Route Advertisement Method

Another characteristic of a routing protocol is how it receives, advertises, and stores routing information. The two fundamental approaches are *distance vector* and *link state*.

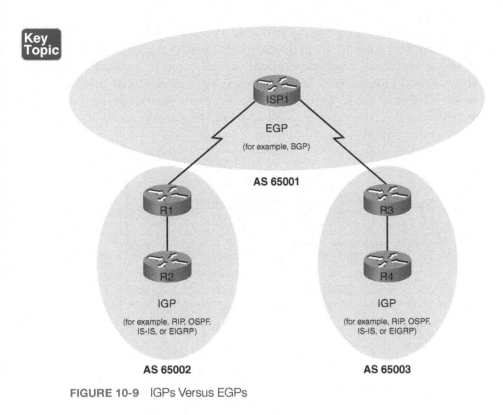

FIGURE 10-9   IGPs Versus EGPs

Distance Vector

A *distance-vector routing protocol* sends a full copy of its routing table to its directly attached neighbors. This is a periodic advertisement, meaning that even if there have been no topological changes, a distance-vector routing protocol will, at regular intervals, advertise again its full routing table to its neighbors.

Obviously, this periodic advertisement of redundant information is inefficient. Ideally, you want a full exchange of route information to occur only once and subsequent updates to be triggered by topological changes.

Another drawback to distance-vector routing protocols is the time they take to converge, which is the time required for all routers to update their routing tables in response to a topological change in a network. *Hold-down timers* can speed the convergence process. After a router makes a change to a route entry, a hold-down timer prevents any subsequent updates for a specified period of time. This approach helps stop flapping routes (which are routes that oscillate between being available and unavailable) from preventing convergence.

Yet another issue with distance-vector routing protocols is the potential of a routing loop. To illustrate, consider Figure 10-10. In this topology, the metric being used is *hop count*, which is the number of routers that must be crossed to reach a network. As one example, router R3's routing table has a route entry for network 10.1.1.0/24 available off router R1. For router R3 to reach that network, two routers must be transited (routers R2 and R1). As a result, network 10.1.1.0/24 appears in router R3's routing table with a metric (hop count) of 2.

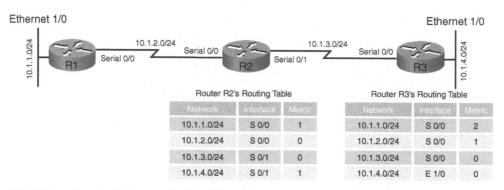

FIGURE 10-10   Routing Loop: Before Link Failure

Continuing with the example, imagine that interface Ethernet 1/0 on router R3 goes down. As shown in Figure 10-11, router R3 loses its directly connected route (with a metric of 0) to network 10.1.4.0/24. However, router R2 had a route to 10.1.4.0/24 in its routing table (with a metric of 1), and this route was advertised to router R3. Router R3 adds this entry for 10.1.4.0 to its routing table and increments the metric by 1.

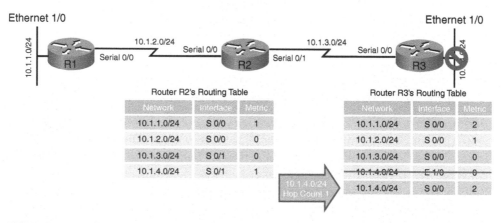

FIGURE 10-11   Routing Loop: After Link Failure

The problem with this scenario is that the 10.1.4.0/24 entry in router R2's routing table was due to an advertisement router R2 received from router R3. Now, router R3 is relying on that route, which is no longer valid. The routing loop continues as router R3 advertises its newly learned route 10.1.4.0/24 with a metric of 2 to its neighbor, router R2. Because router R2 originally learned the 10.1.4.0/24 network from router R3, when it sees router R2 advertising that same route with a metric of 2, the network gets updated in router R2's routing table to have a metric of 3, as shown in Figure 10-12.

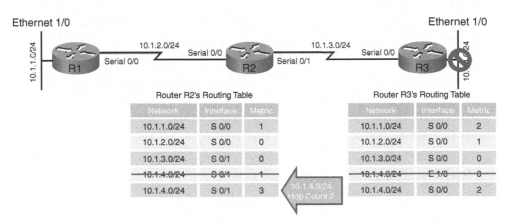

FIGURE 10-12 Routing Loop: Routers R2 and R3 Incrementing the Metric for 10.1.4.0/24

The metric for the 10.1.4.0/24 network continues to increment in the routing tables for both routers R2 and R3 until the metric reaches a value considered to be an unreachable value (for example, 16 in the case of RIP). This process is referred to as a *routing loop*.

Distance-vector routing protocols typically use one of two approaches for preventing routing loops:

- *Split horizon:* The split-horizon feature prevents a route learned on one interface from being advertised back out that same interface.

- *Poison reverse:* The poison-reverse feature causes a route received on one interface to be advertised back out that same interface with a metric that is considered to be infinite.

In the previous example, either approach would have prevented router R3 from adding the 10.1.4.0/24 network to its routing table based on an advertisement from router R2.

Link State

Rather than having neighboring routers exchange their full routing tables with one another, a *link-state* routing protocol allows routers to build a topological map of the network. Then, much like a Global Positioning System (GPS) device in a car, a router can execute an algorithm to calculate an optimal path (or paths) to a destination network.

Routers send *link-state advertisements (LSAs)* to advertise the networks they know how to reach. Routers then use those LSAs to construct the topological map of a network. The algorithm that runs against this topological map is *Dijkstra's shortest path first* algorithm.

Unlike distance-vector routing protocols, *link-state routing protocols* exchange full routing information only when two routers initially form their adjacency. Then routing updates are sent in response to changes in the network, as opposed to being sent periodically. Also, link-state routing protocols benefit from shorter convergence times compared to distance-vector routing protocols.

Routing Protocol Examples

Key Topic

Now that you understand some of the characteristics that distinguish one routing protocol from another, this section contrasts some of the most popular routing protocols used in modern networks:

- *Routing Information Protocol (RIP)*: RIP is a distance-vector routing protocol that uses the metric *hop count*. The maximum number of hops between two routers in an RIP-based network is 15. Therefore, a hop count of 16 is considered to be infinite. Also, RIP is an IGP.

- *Open Shortest Path First (OSPF)*: OSPF is a link-state routing protocol that uses the metric *cost*, which is based on the link speed between two routers. OSPF is a popular IGP because of its scalability, fast convergence, and vendor interoperability.

- **Intermediate System-to-Intermediate System (IS-IS):** This link-state routing protocol is similar in operation to OSPF. It uses a configurable, yet dimensionless, metric associated with an interface and runs Dijkstra's shortest path first algorithm. Although IS-IS is an IGP that offers the scalability, fast convergence, and vendor-interoperability benefits of OSPF, it has not been as widely deployed as OSPF.

- *Enhanced Interior Gateway Routing Protocol (EIGRP)*: EIGRP is a Cisco-proprietary protocol that is popular in Cisco-only networks but less popular in mixed-vendor environments. Like OSPF, EIGRP is an IGP that offers fast convergence and scalability. EIGRP is more challenging to classify as a distance-vector or a link-state routing protocol.

By default, EIGRP uses bandwidth and delay in its metric calculation; however, other parameters can be considered, including reliability, load, and maximum transmission unit (MTU) size. Using delay as part of the metric, EIGRP can take into consideration the latency caused by the slowest links in the path.

Some literature calls EIGRP an *advanced distance-vector* routing protocol, and some literature calls it a **hybrid routing protocol** (mixing characteristics of both distance-vector and link-state routing protocols). EIGRP uses information from its neighbors to help select an optimal route (like distance-vector routing protocols). However, EIGRP also maintains a database of topological information (like a link-state routing protocol). The algorithm EIGRP uses for its route selection is not Dijkstra's shortest path first algorithm. Instead, EIGRP uses Diffusing Update Algorithm (DUAL).

- *Border Gateway Protocol (BGP)*: BGP is the only EGP in widespread use today. In fact, BGP is considered to be the routing protocol that runs the Internet, which is an interconnection of multiple autonomous systems. Although some literature classifies BGP as a distance-vector routing protocol, it can more accurately be described as a *path-vector* routing protocol, meaning that it can use as its metric the number of autonomous system hops that must be transited to reach a destination network, as opposed to a number of required router hops. BGP's path selection is not solely based on autonomous system hops, however. BGP can consider a variety of other parameters. Interestingly, none of those parameters are based on link speed. In addition, although BGP is incredibly scalable, it does not quickly converge in the event of a topological change.

NOTE   When studying for the Network+ exam, be sure to focus on RIP, OSPF, EIGRP, and BGP as these are the dynamic routing protocols that the exam is sure to cover.

Table 10-2 compares the key characteristics of dynamic routing protocols.

Table 10-2 Comparing Dynamic Routing Protocols

Routing Protocol	IGP or EGP	Type	Metric
RIP	IGP	Distance vector	Hop count
OSPF	IGP	Link state	Cost (based on bandwidth)
EIGRP	IGP	Hybrid	Composite (bandwidth and delay by default)
BGP	EGP	Path vector	Path attributes

A network can simultaneously support more than one routing protocol through the process of *route redistribution*. For example, a router could have one of its interfaces participating in an OSPF area of the network and have another interface participating in an EIGRP area of the network. This router could then take routes learned via OSPF and inject those routes into the EIGRP routing process. Similarly, EIGRP-learned routes could be redistributed into the OSPF routing process.

Bandwidth Management

While the main concern with routing is ensuring that data packets (as well as control plane packets) reach their rightful destinations, it is the job of *quality of service* (QoS) to ensure that packets do not suffer from long delays (latency) or, worse, dropped packets.

QoS is actually a suite of technologies that allows you to strategically optimize network performance for select traffic types. For example, in today's converged networks (that is, networks simultaneously transporting voice, video, and data), some applications (for example, voice) might be more intolerant of delay (or *latency*) than other applications; for example, an FTP file transfer is less latency sensitive than a VoIP call. Fortunately, through the use of QoS technologies, you can identify which traffic types need to be sent first, how much bandwidth to allocate to various traffic types, which traffic types should be dropped first in the event of congestion, and how to make the most efficient use of the relatively limited bandwidth of an IP WAN. This section introduces QoS and a collection of QoS mechanisms.

NOTE Do not get confused by the many uses we have for the word converged in networking. It all depends on the context. For example, when speaking about the network in general and what data it can carry, a converged network is one that includes multiple forms of traffic—for example VoIP and data traffic. When we are speaking of a single routing protocol—converged means the device has learned of all the updates that have been in the routing protocol's information.

Introduction to QoS

A lack of bandwidth is the overshadowing issue for most network quality problems. Specifically, when there is a lack of bandwidth, packets might suffer from one or more of the symptoms listed in Table 10-3.

Table 10-3 Three Categories of Quality Issues

Issue	Description
Delay	Delay is the time required for a packet to travel from source to destination. You might have witnessed delay on the evening news when the news anchor is talking via satellite to a foreign news correspondent. Because of the satellite delay, the conversation begins to feel unnatural.
Jitter	Jitter is the uneven arrival of packets. For example, imagine a VoIP conversation where packet 1 arrives at a destination router. Then, 20 ms later, packet 2 arrives. After another 70 ms, packet 3 arrives, and then packet 4 arrives 20 ms behind packet 3. This variation in arrival times (that is, *variable delay*) is not due to dropped packets, but the jitter might be interpreted by the listener as dropped packets.
Drops	Packet drops occur when a link is congested and a router's interface queue overflows. Some types of traffic, such as UDP traffic carrying voice packets, are not retransmitted if packets are dropped.

Fortunately, QoS features available on many routers and switches can recognize important traffic and then treat that traffic in a special way. For example, you might want to allocate 128Kbps of bandwidth for your VoIP traffic and give that traffic priority treatment.

Consider water flowing through a series of pipes with varying diameters. The water's flow rate through those pipes is limited to the water's flow rate through the pipe with the smallest diameter. Similarly, as a packet travels from source to destination, its effective bandwidth is the bandwidth of the slowest link along that path. For example, in Figure 10-13, notice that the slowest link speed is 256Kbps. This weakest link becomes the effective bandwidth between client and server.

Because the primary challenge of QoS is a lack of bandwidth, the logical question is, "How do we increase available bandwidth?" A knee-jerk response to that question is often "Add more bandwidth." However, more bandwidth often comes at a relatively high cost.

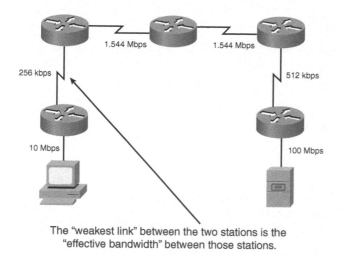

The "weakest link" between the two stations is the
"effective bandwidth" between those stations.

FIGURE 10-13   Effective Bandwidth of 256Kbps

Think of your network as a highway system in a large city. During rush hour, the lanes of the highway are congested; during other periods of the day, the lanes might be underutilized. Instead of just building more lanes to accommodate peak traffic rates, the highway engineers might add a carpool lane to give higher priority to cars with two or more occupants. Similarly, you can use QoS features to give your mission-critical applications higher-priority treatment in times of network congestion.

QoS Configuration Steps

The mission statement of QoS could read something like this: "To categorize traffic and apply a policy to those traffic categories, in accordance with a QoS policy." Understanding this underlying purpose of QoS can help you better understand the three basic steps involved in QoS configuration:

Step 1.   Determine network performance requirements for various traffic types. For example, consider these design recommendations for voice, video, and data traffic:

- **Voice:** No more than 150 ms of one-way delay; no more than 30 ms of jitter; and no more than 1% packet loss.

- **Video:** No more than 150 ms of one-way delay for interactive voice applications (for example, video conferencing); no more than 30 ms of jitter; and no more than 1% of packet loss.

- **Data:** Applications have varying delay and loss requirements. Therefore, data applications should be categorized into predefined *classes* of traffic, where each class is configured with specific delay and loss characteristics.

Step 2.   Categorize traffic into specific categories. For example, you might have a category named *Low Delay* for voice and video packets in that category. You might also have a *Low Priority* class for traffic such as music downloads from the Internet.

Step 3.   Document your QoS policy and make it available to your users. Then, for example, if users complain that their network gaming applications are running slowly, you can point them to your corporate QoS policy, which describes how applications such as network gaming have *best-effort* treatment, while VoIP traffic receives *priority* treatment.

The actual implementation of these steps varies based on the specific device you are configuring. In some cases, you might be using the command-line interface (CLI) of a router or switch. In other cases, you might have some sort of graphical user interface (GUI) through which you configure QoS on your routers and switches.

QoS Components

QoS features are categorized into one of the three categories shown in Table 10-4.

Key Topic

Table 10-4   Three Categories of QoS Mechanisms

Issue	Description
Best effort	Best-effort treatment of traffic does not truly provide QoS to that traffic because there is no reordering of packets. Best effort uses a first-in, first-out (FIFO) queuing strategy, where packets are emptied from a queue in the same order in which they entered the queue.
Integrated Services (IntServ)	IntServ is often referred to as *hard QoS* because it can make strict bandwidth reservations. IntServ uses signaling among network devices to provide bandwidth reservations. Resource Reservation Protocol (RSVP) is an example of an IntServ approach to QoS. Because IntServ must be configured on every router along a packet's path, the main drawback of IntServ is its lack of scalability.
Differentiated Services (DiffServ)	DiffServ, as its name suggests, differentiates between multiple traffic flows. Specifically, packets are marked, and routers and switches can then make decisions (for example, dropping or forwarding decisions) based on those markings. Because DiffServ does not make an explicit reservation, it is often called *soft QoS*. Most modern QoS configurations are based on the DiffServ approach.

Figure 10-14 summarizes these three QoS categories.

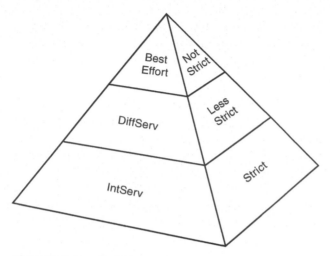

FIGURE 10-14   QoS Categories

QoS Mechanisms

As previously mentioned, a DiffServ approach to QoS marks traffic. However, for markings to impact the behavior of traffic, a QoS tool must reference those markings and alter the packets' treatment based on them. The following is a collection of commonly used QoS mechanisms:

- Classification
- Marking
- Congestion management
- Congestion avoidance
- Policing and shaping
- Link efficiency

While all of these mechanisms can be considered important, this chapter focuses on the main bandwidth management tools policing and traffic shaping.

Policing and Traffic Shaping

Key Topic

Instead of making a minimum amount of bandwidth available for specific traffic types, you might want to limit available bandwidth. Both *traffic policing* and *traffic shaping* tools can accomplish this objective. Collectively, these tools are called *traffic conditioners*.

Policing can be used in either the inbound or the outbound direction, and it typically discards packets that exceed the configured rate limit, which you can think of as a *speed limit* for specific traffic types. Because policing drops packets, resulting in retransmissions, it is recommended for higher-speed interfaces.

Shaping buffers (and therefore delays) traffic exceeding a configured rate. Therefore, shaping is recommended for slower-speed interfaces.

Because traffic shaping (and policing) can limit the speed of packets exiting a router, a question arises: "How do you send traffic out of an interface at a rate that is less than the physical clock rate of the interface?" For this to be possible, shaping and policing tools do not transmit all the time. Specifically, they send a certain number of bits or bytes at line rate, and then they stop sending until a specific timing interval (for example, one-eighth of a second) is reached. After the timing interval is reached, the interface again sends a specific amount of traffic at the line rate. It stops and waits for the next timing interval to occur. This process continually repeats, allowing an interface to send an average bandwidth that might be below the physical speed of the interface. This average bandwidth is called the *committed information rate* (CIR). The number of bits (the unit of measure used with shaping tools) or bytes (the unit of measure used with policing tools) that is sent during a timing interval is called the *committed burst* (Bc). The timing interval is written as *Tc*.

For example, imagine that you have a physical line rate of 128Kbps, but the CIR is only 64Kbps. Also, assume that there are eight timing intervals in a second (that is, Tc = 1/8 second = 125 ms), and during each of those timing intervals, 8000 bits (the committed burst parameter) are sent at the line rate. Therefore, over the period of a second, 8000 bits are sent (at the line rate) eight times, for a grand total of 64,000 bits per second, which is the CIR. Figure 10-15 illustrates this shaping of traffic to 64Kbps on a line with a rate of 128Kbps.

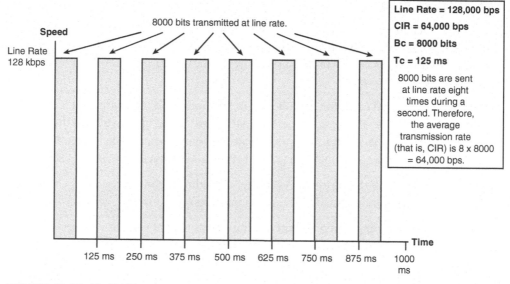

FIGURE 10-15   Traffic Shaping

If all the Bc bits (or bytes) are not sent during a timing interval, there is an option to *bank* those bits and use them during a future timing interval. The parameter that allows this storing of unused potential bandwidth is called the *excess burst (Be)* parameter. The Be parameter in a shaping configuration specifies the maximum number of bits or bytes that can be sent in excess of the Bc during a timing interval, if those bits are indeed available. For those bits or bytes to be available, they must have gone unused during previous timing intervals. Policing tools, however, use the Be parameter to specify the maximum number of bytes that can be sent during a timing interval. Therefore, in a policing configuration, if the Bc equals the Be, no excess bursting occurs. If excess bursting occurs, policing tools consider this excess traffic to be *exceeding traffic*. Policing tools consider traffic that conforms to (that is, does not exceed) a specified CIR to be *conforming traffic*.

The relationship between the Tc, Bc, and CIR is given with this formula: *CIR = Bc / Tc*. Alternatively, the formula can be written as *Tc = Bc / CIR*. Therefore, if you want a smaller timing interval, you can configure a smaller Bc.

Real-World Case Study

Acme, Inc. has decided to use a link-state routing protocol for dynamic routing between its LANs and the remote offices, which are connected over the WANs. The link-state protocol the company has chosen is OSPF. Each of the routers that has connections to the LAN and WAN subnets will learn about and advertise OSPF routes with its OSPF neighbors.

The branch offices will have a default route that points toward the headquarters' routers, and at the headquarters' site, they will use a default route that points toward the service provider. Acme, Inc. itself will not be using BGP, but its WAN and Internet service provider, which is interacting with other service providers, will use BGP.

The WAN connection to one of the remote offices is very low bandwidth and is prone to becoming congested with traffic. It also occasionally drops all connection to the remote office's router. Acme, Inc. has decided to use traffic shaping as part of the QoS configuration to attempt to ensure that the link is used more sparingly and is not overwhelmed with traffic during key business hours.

Summary

Here are the main topics covered in this chapter:

- This chapter discusses how routers forward traffic through a network based on source and destination IP addresses.

- This chapter also covers the sources of route information used to populate a router's routing table. These sources include directly connected routes, statically configured routes, and dynamically learned routes.

- This chapter distinguishes between routed protocols (for example, IP) and routing protocols (such as OSPF or EIGRP).

- Some routing sources are more trustworthy than other routing sources, based on their administrative distances.

- Different routing protocols use different metrics to select the best route in the presence of multiple routes.

- This chapter distinguishes between IGPs (which run within an autonomous system) and EGPs (which run between autonomous systems).

- This chapter contrasts the behavior of distance-vector and link-state routing protocols and shows how split horizon and poison reverse can prevent routing loops in a distance-vector routing protocol environment.

- This chapter describes today's most popular routing protocols (including RIP, OSPF, IS-IS, EIGRP, and BGP), along with their characteristics.

- This chapter reviews various QoS technologies, with an emphasis on traffic shaping, which can limit the rate of data transmission on a WAN link to the CIR.

Exam Preparation Tasks

Review All the Key Topics

Review the most important topics from this chapter, noted with the Key Topic icon in the outer margin of the page. Table 10-5 lists these key topics and the page number where each is found.

Table 10-5 Key Topics for Chapter 10

Key Topic Element	Description	Page Number
Step list	Basic routing process	256
Table 10-1	Administrative distance	263
Figure 10-9	IGPs versus EGPs	265
List	Preventing routing loops	267
List	Routing protocol examples	268
Step list	QoS configuration	272
Table 10-4	Three categories of QoS mechanisms	273
Section	Limiting available bandwidth through traffic policing and traffic-shaping tools	275

Complete Tables and Lists from Memory

Print a copy of Appendix C, "Memory Tables," or at least the section for this chapter and complete as many of the tables as possible from memory. Appendix D, "Memory Tables Answer Key," includes the completed tables and lists so you can check your work.

Define Key Terms

Define the following key terms from this chapter and check your answers in the Glossary:

Address Resolution Protocol (ARP), Time-to-Live (TTL), default static route, next-hop IP address, routed protocol, routing protocol, administrative distance (AD), metric, interior gateway protocol (IGP), exterior gateway protocol (EGP), distance-vector routing protocol, link-state routing protocol, hold-down timer, split horizon, poison reverse, link-state advertisement (LSA), Routing Information Protocol (RIP), Open Shortest Path First (OSPF), Enhanced Interior

Gateway Routing Protocol (EIGRP), Border Gateway Protocol (BGP), route redistribution, quality of service (QoS), traffic shaping, traffic policing, dynamic routing, hybrid routing protocol

Complete Chapter 10 Hands-On Labs in Network+ Simulator Lite

- Connecting to the Router's Console Port

- Configuring an Ethernet Interface on a Router

- Connecting Two Routers to Each Other

- Verifying a Router-to-Router Connection with Cisco Discovery Protocol

- Static and Default Routing

- Configuring Dynamic Routing

- Reading a Routing Table

Additional Resources

An OSPF Review: https://www.ajsnetworking.com/an-ospf-review/

EIGRP's Composite Metric: https://www.ajsnetworking.com/eigrp-metric

Review Questions

The answers to these review questions appear in Appendix A, "Answers to Review Questions."

1. If a PC on an Ethernet network attempts to communicate with a host on a different subnet, what destination IP address and destination MAC address will be placed in the packet/frame header sent by the PC?

   a. **Destination IP: IP address of the default gateway. Destination MAC: MAC address of the default gateway.**

   b. **Destination IP: IP address of the remote host. Destination MAC: MAC address of the default gateway.**

   c. **Destination IP: IP address of the remote host. Destination MAC: MAC address of the remote host.**

        d. Destination IP: IP address of the remote host. Destination MAC: MAC address of the local PC.

2. What protocol is used to request a MAC address that corresponds to a known IPv4 address on the local network?

    a. IGMP

    b. TTL

    c. ICMP

    d. ARP

3. What is the network address and subnet mask of a default route?

    a. 255.255.255.255/32

    b. 0.0.0.0/32

    c. 255.255.255.255/0

    d. 0.0.0.0/0

4. What routing protocol characteristic indicates the believability of the routing protocol (compared to other routing protocols)?

    a. Weight

    b. Metric

    c. Administrative distance

    d. SPF algorithm

5. Which of the following are distance-vector routing protocol features that can prevent routing loops? (Choose two.)

    a. Reverse path forwarding (RPF) check

    b. Split horizon

    c. Poison reverse

    d. Rendezvous point

6. Which of the following is a distance-vector routing protocol with a maximum usable hop count of 15?

    a. BGP

    b. EIGRP

    c. RIP

    d. OSPF

7. Which of the following routing protocols is an EGP?

    a. BGP

    b. EIGRP

    c. RIP

    d. OSPF

8. What is the term for unpredictable variation in delay in a modern network?

    a. Congestion

    b. Contention

    c. Jitter

    d. Serialization delay

9. The RSVP protocol is associated with which overall approach to QoS in a modern network?

    a. DiffServ

    b. IntServ

    c. FIFO

    d. Best effort

10. What QoS tool seeks to smooth out bandwidth utilization by buffering excess packets?

    a. Traffic policing

    b. Traffic shaping

    c. Weighted Random Early Detection (WRED)

    d. Integrated Services (IntServ)

This chapter covers the following topics related to Objective 2.3 (Given a scenario, configure and deploy common Ethernet switching features) of the CompTIA Network+ N10-008 certification exam:

- Data virtual local area network (VLAN)

- Voice VLAN

- Port configurations

  - Port tagging/802.1Q

  - Port aggregation

    - Link Aggregation Control Protocol (LACP)

  - Duplex

  - Speed

  - Flow control

  - Port mirroring

  - Port security

  - Jumbo frames

  - Auto-medium-dependent interface crossover (MDI-X)

- Media access control (MAC) address tables

- Power over Ethernet (PoE)/Power over Ethernet plus (PoE+)

- Spanning Tree Protocol

- Carrier-sense multiple access with collision detection (CSMA/CD)

- Address Resolution Protocol (ARP)

- Neighbor Discovery Protocol

CHAPTER 11

Ethernet Switching

Odds are, when you are working with local area networks (LANs), you are working with Ethernet as the Layer 1 technology. Back in the mid-1990s, there was tremendous competition between technologies such as Ethernet, Token Ring, and Fiber Distributed Data Interface (FDDI). Today, however, you can see that Ethernet is the clear winner of those Layer 1 wars.

Of course, over the years, Ethernet has evolved. Several Ethernet standards exist in modern LANs, with a variety of distance and speed limitations. This chapter begins by reviewing the fundamentals of Ethernet networks, including a collection of Ethernet speeds and feeds. This chapter also delves into many of the features available with some Ethernet switches.

Foundation Topics

Principles of Ethernet

Xerox Corporation developed Ethernet in 1973, with the goal of creating a technology to allow computers to connect with laser printers. A quick survey of almost any corporate network reveals that Ethernet rose well beyond its humble beginnings; today it is used to interconnect devices such as computers, printers, wireless access points, servers, switches, routers, video game systems, and more. This section discusses early Ethernet implementations and limitations as well as modern Ethernet throughput and distance specifications.

Ethernet Origins

In the network industry literature, you might come upon the term *IEEE 802.3* (where IEEE refers to the Institute of Electrical and Electronics Engineers standards body). In general, you can use the term *IEEE 802.3* interchangeably with the term **Ethernet**. However, be aware that these technologies have some subtle distinctions. For example, an Ethernet frame is a fixed-length frame, whereas the 802.3 frame length can vary.

A popular implementation of Ethernet in the early days was called *10BASE5*. The 10 in 10BASE5 referred to network throughput, specifically 10Mbps (that is, 10 megabits [million bits] per second). The BASE in 10BASE5 referred to baseband, as opposed to broadband. Finally, the 5 in 10BASE5 indicated the distance limitation of 500 meters. The cable used in 10BASE5 networks, as shown in Figure 11-1, was a larger diameter than most types of media. In fact, this network media type became known as *thicknet*.

Another early Ethernet implementation was 10BASE2. From the previous analysis of 10BASE5, you might conclude that 10BASE2 was a 10Mbps baseband technology with a distance limitation of 200 meters. That is almost correct. However, 10BASE2's actual distance limitation was 185 meters. The cabling used in 10BASE2 networks was significantly thinner and therefore less expensive than 10BASE5 cabling (see Figure 11-2). As a result, 10BASE2 cabling was known as *thinnet* or *cheapernet*.

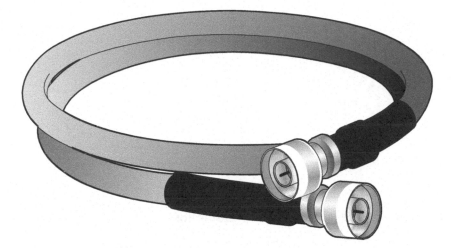

FIGURE 11-1   10BASE5 Cable

FIGURE 11-2   Coaxial Cable Used for 10BASE2

10BASE5 and 10BASE2 networks were quickly replaced with UTP cabling. The 10Mbps version of Ethernet that relied on UTP cabling, an example of which is provided in Figure 11-3, is known as *10BASE-T*, where the T refers to twisted-pair cabling.

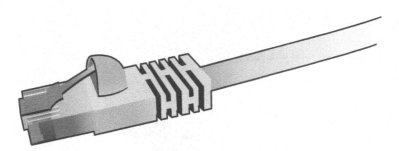

FIGURE 11-3   UTP Cable Used for 10BASE-T

Carrier-Sense Multiple Access with Collision Detection

Ethernet was based on the philosophy that all networked devices should be eligible, at any time, to transmit on a network. In contrast, Token Ring used a *deterministic* media access approach. Specifically, Token Ring networks passed a token around a network in a circular fashion, from one networked device to the next. Only when a networked device was in possession of that token was it eligible to send on the network.

Recall from Chapter 2, "Network Topologies and Types," the concept of a bus topology. An example of a bus topology is a long cable (such as thicknet or thinnet) running the length of a building, with various networked devices tapping into that cable to gain access to the network. Figure 11-4 depicts an Ethernet network using a shared bus topology.

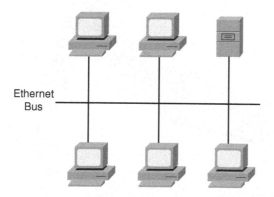

Ethernet
Bus

FIGURE 11-4   Ethernet Network Using a Shared Bus Topology

In this topology, all devices are directly connected to the network and are free to transmit at any time, if they have reason to believe no other transmission currently exists on the wire. Ethernet permits only a single frame to be on a network segment at any one time. So, before a device in this network transmits, it listens to the wire to see if there is currently any traffic being transmitted. If no traffic is detected, the networked device transmits its data. However, what if two devices simultaneously have data to send? If they both listen to the wire at the same time, they could simultaneously, and erroneously, conclude that it is safe to send their data. However, when both devices simultaneously send their data, a *collision* occurs (see Figure 11-5), and data corruption results.

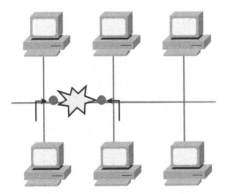

FIGURE 11-5   Collision on an Ethernet Segment

Fortunately, Ethernet was designed with a mechanism to detect collisions and allow the devices whose transmissions collided to retransmit their data at different times. Specifically, after the devices notice that a collision occurred, they independently set a random *back-off timer*. Each device waits for this random amount of time to elapse before again trying to transmit. Here is the logic: Because each device certainly picked a different amount of time to back off from transmitting, their transmissions should not collide the next time these devices transmit, as illustrated in Figure 11-6.

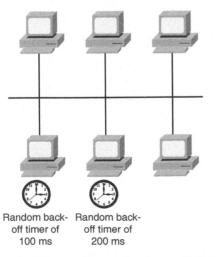

Random back-off timer of 100 ms   Random back-off timer of 200 ms

FIGURE 11-6   Recovering from a Collision with Random Back-off Timers

The procedure used by Ethernet to decide whether it is safe to transmit, detect collisions, and retransmit if necessary is called **_carrier-sense multiple access with collision detection (CSMA/CD)_**.

Let's break down CSMA/CD into its constituent components:

- **Carrier sense:** A device attached to an Ethernet network can listen to the wire, prior to transmitting, to make sure a frame is not being transmitted on the network segment.

- **Multiple access:** Unlike with a deterministic method of network access (for example, the method used by Token Ring), all Ethernet devices simultaneously have access to an Ethernet segment.

- **Collision detection:** If a collision occurs (perhaps because two devices were simultaneously listening to the network and simultaneously concluded that it was safe to send), Ethernet devices can detect that collision and set random back-off timers. After each device's random timer expires, the device again tries to transmit its data.

Despite Ethernet's CSMA/CD feature, Ethernet segments still suffer from scalability limitations. Specifically, the likelihood of collisions increases as the number of devices on a shared Ethernet segment increases.

An alternate approach is CSMA/CA, where CA refers to _collision avoidance_. This technology is common in wireless networks and was made famous by Token Ring in early LANs.

With wired Ethernet, devices on a shared Ethernet segment belong to the same _collision domain_. One example of a shared Ethernet segment is a 10BASE5 or 10BASE2 network with multiple devices attaching to the same cable. On that cable, only one device can send at any one time. Therefore, all devices attached to the thicknet or thinnet cable are in the same collision domain.

Similarly, devices connected to an Ethernet hub are in the same collision domain (see Figure 11-7). A hub is a Layer 1 device and does not make forwarding decisions. Instead, a hub takes bits in on one port and sends them out all the other hub ports except the one on which the bits were received.

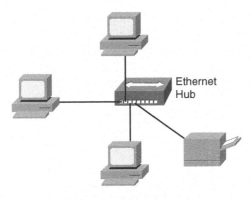

One Collision Domain

FIGURE 11-7   Shared Ethernet Hub: One Collision Domain

Ethernet switches dramatically increase the scalability of Ethernet networks by creating multiple collision domains (see Figure 11-8). In fact, every port on an Ethernet switch is in its own collision domain.

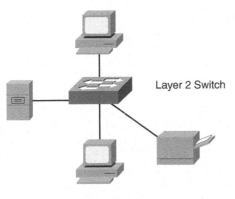

Four Collision Domains

FIGURE 11-8   Ethernet Switch: One Collision Domain per Port

Ethernet switches have a less obvious but powerful benefit: Because a switch port connects to a single device, there is no chance of collision. With no chance of collision, collision detection is no longer needed, and with collision detection disabled, network devices can run in *full-duplex* mode rather than *half-duplex* mode. In full-duplex mode, a device can simultaneously send and receive at the same time.

When multiple devices are connected to the same shared Ethernet segment, such as a Layer 1 hub, CSMA/CD must be enabled. As a result, the network must work in half-duplex mode, which means that only a single networked device can transmit or receive at any one time. In half-duplex mode, a networked device cannot simultaneously send and receive, so the device makes inefficient use of the network's bandwidth.

Another important mechanism in an Ethernet network is flow control. *Flow control* is a mechanism for temporarily stopping the transmission of data on Ethernet-based networks. The goal of this mechanism is to avoid packet loss in the presence of network congestion.

Distance and Speed Limitations

To understand the bandwidth available on networks, you need to understand a few terms. You should already know that a *bit* refers to one of two values, represented using binary math, which uses only the numbers 0 and 1. On a cable such as twisted-pair cable, a bit could be represented by the absence or presence of voltage. Fiber-optic cable, however, might represent a bit with the absence or presence of light.

The bandwidth of a network is measured in terms of how many bits the network can transmit during a 1-second period of time. For example, if a network has the capacity to send 10,000,000 (that is, 10 million) bits in a 1-second period of time, the bandwidth capacity is said to be 10 megabits (that is, millions of bits) per second (or *Mbps*). Table 11-1 defines common bandwidths supported on distinct types of Ethernet networks.

Key Topic

Table 11-1 Ethernet Bandwidth Capacities

Ethernet Type	Bandwidth Capacity
Standard Ethernet	10Mbps: 10 million bits per second (that is, 10 megabits per second)
Fast Ethernet	100Mbps: 100 million bits per second (that is, 100 megabits per second)
Gigabit Ethernet	1Gbps: 1 billion bits per second (that is, 1 gigabit per second)
10-Gigabit Ethernet	10Gbps: 10 billion bits per second (that is, 10 gigabits per second)
100-Gigabit Ethernet	100Gbps: 100 billion bits per second (that is, 100 gigabits per second)

The type of cabling used in an Ethernet network influences the bandwidth capacity and the distance limitation of the network. For example, fiber-optic cabling often has a higher bandwidth capacity and a longer distance limitation than twisted-pair cabling.

When it comes to the size of a frame the media can send, there is a Maximum Transmission Unit (MTU) value the media can accommodate. You can even configure support for *jumbo frames*, which are Ethernet frames with more than 1500 bytes of payload (the limit set by the IEEE 802.3 standard).

In Chapter 3, "Network Media Types," you learned about single-mode fiber (SMF) and multimode fiber (MMF). Because of the issue of multimode delay distortion, SMF usually has a longer distance limitation than MMF.

When you want to uplink one Ethernet switch to another, you might need different connectors (for example, MMF, SMF, or UTP) for different installations. Fortunately, some Ethernet switches have one or more empty slots in which you can insert a gigabit interface converter (GBIC). GBICs are interfaces that have a bandwidth capacity of 1Gbps and are available with MMF, SMF, and UTP connectors. This allows you to have flexibility in the uplink technology you use in an Ethernet switch.

The various interface converters are commonly called *transceivers*. Two common characteristics of fiber-optic transceivers are that they are bidirectional and full-duplex. This means they can send data in both directions (bidirectional), and they can do so simultaneously (full-duplex).

NOTE   A smaller variant of a regular GBIC is a small form-factor pluggable (SFP), which is sometimes called a *mini-GBIC*. Variations of a SFP include SFP+ and QSFP.

Although not comprehensive, Table 11-2 lists multiple Ethernet standards, along with the media type, bandwidth capacity, and distance limitation of each.

Key Topic

Table 11-2   Types of Ethernet

Ethernet Standard	Media Type	Bandwidth Capacity	Distance Limitation
10BASE5	Coax (thicknet)	10Mbps	500 m
10BASE2	Coax (thinnet)	10Mbps	185 m
10BASE-T	Cat 3 (or higher) UTP	10Mbps	100 m
100BASE-TX	Cat 5 (or higher) UTP	100Mbps	100 m
100BASE-FX	MMF	100Mbps	2 km
1000BASE-T	Cat 5e (or higher) UTP	1Gbps	100 m
1000BASE-TX	Cat 6 (or higher) UTP	1Gbps	100 m
1000BASE-SX	MMF	1Gbps	550 km
1000BASE-LX	SMF	1Gbps	5 km
1000BASE-LH	SMF	1Gbps	10 km

Ethernet Standard	Media Type	Bandwidth Capacity	Distance Limitation
1000BASE-ZX	SMF	1Gbps	70 km
10GBASE-SR	MMF	10Gbps	26 m–400 m
10GBASE-LR	SMF	10Gbps	10–25 km
10GBASE-ER	SMF	10Gbps	40 km
10GBASE-SW	MMF	10Gbps	300 m
10GBASE-LW	SMF	10Gbps	10 km
10GBASE-EW	SMF	10Gbps	40 km
10GBASE-T	Cat 6a (or higher)	10Gbps	100 m
40GBASE-T	Cat8	40Gbps	30 m
100GBASE-SR10	MMF	100Gbps	125 m
100GBASE-LR4	SMF	100Gbps	10 km
100GBASE-ER4	SMF	100Gbps	40 km

NOTE   Two often-confused terms are *100BASE-T* and *100BASE-TX*. 100BASE-T itself is not a specific standard. Rather, 100BASE-T is a category of standards and includes 100BASE-T2 (which uses two pairs of wires in a Cat 3 cable), 100BASE-T4 (which uses four pairs of wires in a Cat 3 cable), and 100BASE-TX. 100BASE-T2 and 100BASE-T4 were early implementations of 100Mbps Ethernet and are no longer used. Therefore, you can generally use the terms *100BASE-T* and *100BASE-TX* interchangeably.

Similarly, the term *1000BASE-X* is not a specific standard. Rather, 1000BASE-X refers to all Ethernet technologies that transmit data at a rate of 1Gbps over fiber-optic cabling. Additional and creative ways of using Ethernet technology include IEEE 1901-2013, which could be used for Ethernet over HDMI cables and Ethernet over existing powerlines to avoid having to run a separate cabling just for networking.

Ethernet Switch Features

Beyond basic frame forwarding, many Layer 2 Ethernet switches offer a variety of other features to enhance such things as network performance, redundancy, security, management, flexibility, and scalability. Although the specific features offered by a switch vary, this section introduces you to some of the most common features of switches.

Virtual LANs

In a basic switch configuration, all ports on a switch belong to the same *broadcast domain*. In such an arrangement, a broadcast received on one port gets forwarded out all other ports.

Also, from a Layer 3 perspective, all devices connected in a broadcast domain have the same *network address*. Chapter 4, "IP Addressing," gets into the binary math involved in assigning IP addresses (that is, logical Layer 3 addresses) to networked devices. A portion of that address is the address of the network to which that device is attached. The remainder of that address is the address of the device itself. Devices that have the same network address belong to the same network, or *subnet*.

Say that you decide to place PCs from different departments within your company into their own subnet. One reason you might want to do this is for security purposes. For example, by having the Accounting department in a separate subnet (that is, a separate broadcast domain) from the Sales department, devices in one subnet will not see the broadcasts being sent on the other subnet.

Another reason that you might want to do this is to make the overall network segment more efficient. Remember that excessive broadcast frames can cause a network to suffer, and there are plenty of operations that rely on broadcasts to function properly. *Address Resolution Protocol (ARP)* is a great example of such an operation. ARP is a broadcast-based solution that permits a system to discover the MAC address that coordinates to a particular IP address. IPv6 eliminates this challenge altogether with the introduction and use of *Neighbor Discovery Protocol (NDP)*. As you might guess, NDP is not broadcast based. This is fortunate, as broadcasts are not supported in IPv6.

The PCs belonging to the different departments in your company are scattered across multiple floors in a building (see Figure 11-9). The Accounting and Sales departments each have a PC on each floor of a building. Because the wiring for each floor runs back to a wiring closet on that floor, to support these two subnets using a switch's default configuration, you need to install two switches on each floor. For traffic to travel from one subnet to another subnet, that traffic has to be routed, meaning that a device such as a multilayer switch or a router forwards traffic based on a packet's destination network addresses. So, in this example, the Accounting department switches are interconnected and then connect to a router, and the Sales department switches are connected similarly.

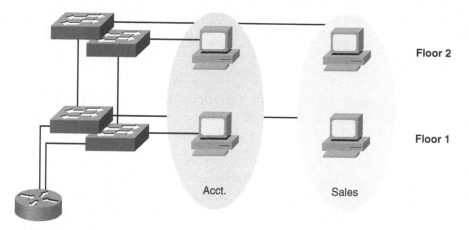

FIGURE 11-9 Example: All Ports on a Switch Belonging to the Same Subnet

The design described here lacks efficiency because you must install at least one switch per subnet. A more efficient design would be to logically separate a switch's ports into different broadcast domains. Then, an Accounting department PC and a Sales department PC could connect to the same switch, even though those PCs belong to different subnets. Fortunately, *virtual LANs (VLANs)* make such a design possible.

With VLANs, as illustrated in Figure 11-10, a switch can have its ports logically divided into more than one broadcast domain (that is, more than one subnet or VLAN). Then, devices that need to connect to those VLANs can connect to the same physical switch, but they remain logically separate from one another.

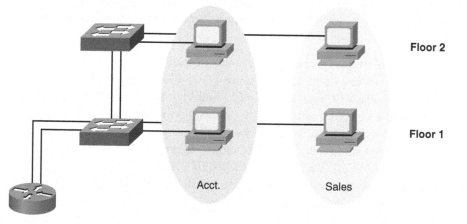

FIGURE 11-10 Example: Ports on a Switch Belonging to Different VLANs

VLANs are very handy with another popular configuration requirement in many modern network environments: You can use a special-purpose VLAN termed a *voice VLAN* to segment and provide network access for VoIP packets. These packets need access to the data network for transport, and they also need special priority treatment to ensure that the voice call quality always remains excellent. Using a voice VLAN is an ideal segmentation strategy for all these needs.

One challenge with VLAN configuration in large environments is the need to configure identical VLAN information on all switches. Manually performing this configuration is time-consuming and error prone. However, switches from Cisco Systems support VLAN Trunking Protocol (VTP), which allows a VLAN created on one switch to be propagated to other switches in a group of switches (that is, a VTP domain). VTP information is carried over a *trunk connection*, as discussed in the next section.

Switch Configuration for an Access Port

Configurations used on a switch port may vary, based on the manufacturer of the switch. Example 11-1 shows a sample configuration on an access port (without trunking) on a Cisco Catalyst switch. A line with a leading ! is a comment used to document the next line(s) of the configuration.

Notice in this configuration the use of port security, which is a small but useful step in securing a network. In this configuration example, the port can learn only two MAC addresses—perhaps the MAC address of a VoIP phone and the computer that connects to that phone.

Example 11-1 Switch Access Port Configuration

```
! Move into configuration mode for interface gig 0/21
SW1(config)# interface GigabitEthernet0/21


! Add a text description of what the port is used for
SW1(config-if)# description Access port in Sales VLAN 21


! Define the port as an access port, and not a trunk port
SW1(config-if)# switchport mode access


! Assign the port to VLAN 21
SW1(config-if)# switchport access vlan 21
```

```
! Enable port security
SW1(config-if)# switchport port-security

! Control the number of MAC addresses the switch may learn
! from device(s) connected to this switch port
SW1(config-if)# switchport port-security maximum 2

! Restrict any frames from MAC addresses above the 2 allowed
SW1(config-if)# switchport port-security violation restrict

! Set the speed to 1,000 Mbps (1 Gigabit per second)
SW1(config-if)# speed 1000

! Set the duplex to full
SW1(config-if)# duplex full

! Configure the port to begin forwarding without waiting the
! standard amount of time normally set by Spanning Tree Protocol
SW1(config-if)# spanning-tree portfast
```

Trunks

One challenge with carving up a switch into multiple VLANs is that several switch ports (that is, one port per VLAN) could be consumed by connecting a switch to a switch or a switch to a router. A more efficient approach is to allow traffic for multiple VLANs to travel over a single connection, as shown in Figure 11-11. This type of connection is called a *trunk*.

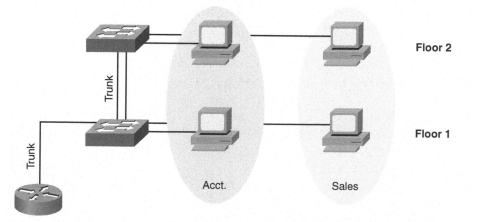

FIGURE 11-11   Example: Trunking Between Switches

The most popular trunking standard today is IEEE 802.1Q, which is often referred to as *dot1q*. One of the VLANs traveling over an 802.1Q trunk is called a *native VLAN*. Frames belonging to the native VLAN are sent unaltered over the trunk (untagged/no tag). However, to distinguish other VLANs from one another, the remaining VLANs are tagged.

NOTE   IEEE 802.1Q is often called *tagging* or *port tagging*.

Specifically, a nonnative VLAN has 4 tag bytes (where a *byte* is a collection of 8 bits) added to the Ethernet frame (that is, tagged frame). Figure 11-12 shows the format of an IEEE 802.1Q header with these 4 bytes.

Key Topic

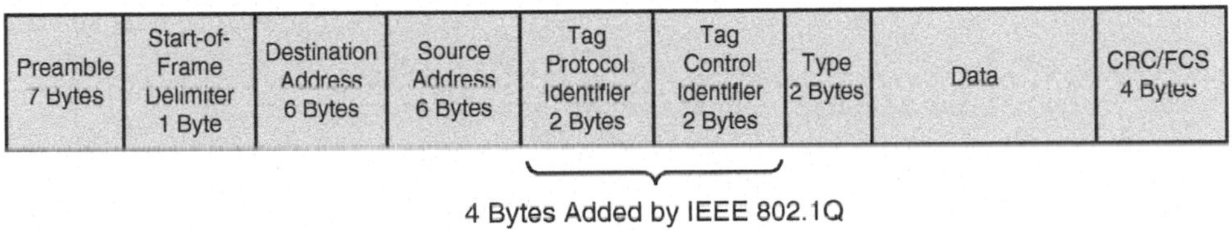

Preamble 7 Bytes	Start-of-Frame Delimiter 1 Byte	Destination Address 6 Bytes	Source Address 6 Bytes	Tag Protocol Identifier 2 Bytes	Tag Control Identifier 2 Bytes	Type 2 Bytes	Data	CRC/FCS 4 Bytes

4 Bytes Added by IEEE 802.1Q

FIGURE 11-12   IEEE 8021Q Header

One of these bytes contains a VLAN field, which indicates to which VLAN a frame belongs. The devices (for example, switch, multilayer switch, router) at each end of a trunk interrogate that field to determine to which VLAN an incoming frame is associated. As you can see by comparing Figures 11-9, 11-10, and 11-11, VLAN and trunking features allow switch ports to be used far more efficiently than merely relying on a default switch configuration.

NOTE   What type of Ethernet media do you use for a trunk link? Well, it used to be that you needed a special Ethernet cable called a *crossover cable* a trunk link. This is no longer the case in most networks as switches now support *auto-medium-dependent interface crossover* (*MDI-X*) technology. This technology essentially permits a switch to detect the type of Ethernet cable used (straight-through versus crossover) and adjust accordingly so that communication between the two network devices (switches in this case) is successful.

Switch Configuration for a Trunk Port

Example 11-2 shows a sample configuration on a trunk port on a Cisco Catalyst switch. A line with a leading ! is a comment used to document the next line(s) of the configuration.

Example 11-2 Sample Trunk Port Configuration

```
! Go to interface config mode for interface Gig 0/22
SW1(config)# interface GigabitEthernet0/22


! Add a text description
SW1(config-if)# description Trunk to another switch


! Specify that this is a trunk port
SW1(config-if)# switchport mode trunk


! Specify the trunking protocol to use
SW1(config-if)# switchport trunk encapsulation dot1q


! Specify the native VLAN to use for un-tagged frames
SW1(config-if)# switchport trunk native vlan 5


! Specify which VLANs are allowed to go on the trunk
SW1(config-if)# switchport trunk allowed vlan 1-50
```

Spanning Tree Protocol

Administrators of corporate telephone networks often boast about their telephone systems—that is, private branch exchange (PBX) systems—having *five nines* availability. Five nines availability means that a system is up and functioning 99.999% of the time, which translates to only about 5 minutes of downtime per year.

Traditionally, corporate data networks struggled to compete with corporate voice networks in terms of availability. Today, however, many networks that traditionally carried only data now carry voice, video, and data. Therefore, availability is an especially important design consideration.

To improve network availability at Layer 2, many networks have redundant links between switches. However, unlike Layer 3 packets, Layer 2 frames lack a Time-to-Live (TTL) field. As a result, a Layer 2 frame can circulate endlessly through a looped Layer 2 topology. Fortunately, IEEE 802.1D *Spanning Tree Protocol (STP)* allows a network to physically have Layer 2 loops while strategically blocking data from flowing over one or more switch ports to prevent the looping of traffic.

In the absence of STP, if a network has parallel paths, two significant symptoms include corruption of a switch's MAC address table and broadcast storms, where frames loop over and over throughout the switched network. An enhancement to the original STP is *802.1w*, which is also called *Rapid Spanning Tree Protocol (RSTP)* because it does a quicker job of adjusting to network conditions, such as the addition or removal of Layer 2 links in the network.

Shortest Path Bridging (SPB; IEEE 802.1aq) is a protocol that is more scalable than STP in larger environments (with hundreds of switches interconnected).

Corruption of a Switch's MAC Address Table

A switch's MAC address table can dynamically learn what MAC addresses are available off its ports. However, in the case of an STP failure, a switch's MAC address table can become corrupted (see Figure 11-13).

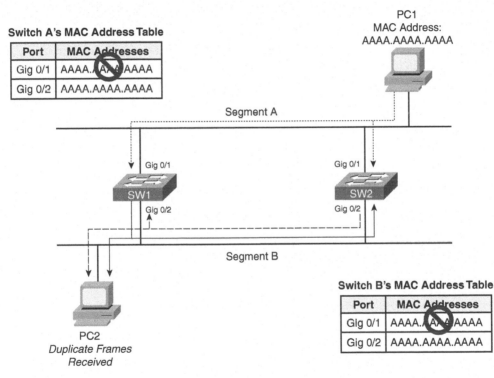

FIGURE 11-13   MAC Address Table Corruption

In Figure 11-13, PC1 is transmitting traffic to PC2. When the frame sent from PC1 is transmitted on segment A, the frame is seen on the Gig 0/1 ports of switches SW1 and SW2, causing both switches to add an entry to their MAC address tables, associating MAC address AAAA.AAAA.AAAA with port Gig 0/1. Because STP is not functioning, both switches then forward the frame out on segment B. As a result, PC2 receives two copies of the frame. Also, switch SW1 sees the frame forwarded out of switch SW2's Gig 0/2 port. Because the frame has source MAC address

AAAA.AAAA.AAAA, switch SW1 incorrectly updates its MAC address table, indicating that MAC address AAAA.AAAA.AAAA resides off port Gig 0/2. Similarly, switch SW2 sees the frame forwarded on to segment B by switch SW1 on its Gig 0/2 port. Therefore, switch SW2 also incorrectly updates its MAC address table.

Broadcast Storms

As previously mentioned, when a switch receives a broadcast frame (that is, a frame destined for MAC address FFFF.FFFF.FFFF), the switch floods the frame out all switch ports other than the port on which the frame was received. Because a Layer 2 frame does not have a TTL field, a broadcast frame endlessly circulates through the Layer 2 topology, consuming resources on both switches and attached devices (for example, user PCs).

Figure 11-14 and the following list illustrate how a broadcast storm can form in a Layer 2 topology when STP is not functioning correctly:

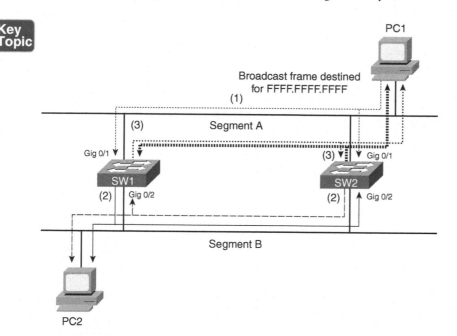

FIGURE 11-14 Broadcast Storm

Step 1.   PC1 sends a broadcast frame on to segment A, and the frame enters each switch on port Gig 0/1.

Step 2.   Both switches flood a copy of the broadcast frame out their Gig 0/2 ports (that is, on to segment B), causing PC2 to receive two copies of the broadcast frame.

Step 3.   Both switches receive a copy of the broadcast frame on their Gig 0/2
ports (that is, from segment B) and flood the frame out their Gig 0/1
ports (that is, on to segment A), causing PC1 to receive two copies of the
broadcast frame.

This behavior continues as the broadcast frame copies continue to loop through the
network. The performance of PC1 and PC2 is affected because they also continue to
receive copies of the broadcast frame.

STP Operation

STP prevents Layer 2 loops—which might result in a broadcast storm or corruption
of a switch's MAC address table—from occurring in a network. Switches in an STP
topology are classified as one of the following:

- **Root bridge:** A root bridge is a switch elected to act as a reference point for
  a spanning tree. The switch with the lowest bridge ID (BID) is elected as the
  root bridge. The BID is made up of a priority value and a MAC address.

- **Nonroot bridge:** All other switches in the STP topology are nonroot bridges.

Figure 11-15 illustrates root bridge election in a network. Notice that in this case,
the bridge priorities are both 32768; therefore, the switch with the lowest MAC
address (that is, SW1) is elected as the root bridge.

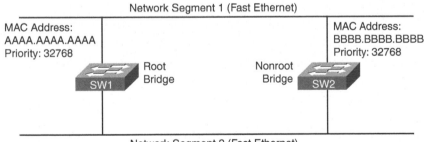

FIGURE 11-15   Root Bridge Election

Ports that interconnect switches in an STP topology are categorized as one of the
port types described in Table 11-3.

Key Topic

Table 11-3 STP Port Types

Port Type	Description
Root port	Every nonroot bridge has a single root port, which is the port on that switch that is closest to the root bridge in terms of cost.
Designated port	Every network segment has a single designated port, which is the port on that segment that is closest to the root bridge in terms of cost. Therefore, all ports on a root bridge are designated ports.
Nondesignated port	Nondesignated ports block traffic to create a loop-free topology.

Figure 11-16 illustrates these port types. Notice that both links are equal in this case, with a cost of 19, because both links are Fast Ethernet links; therefore, the root port for switch SW2 is selected because it has the lowest port ID.

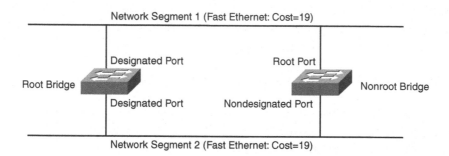

FIGURE 11-16   Identifying STP Port Roles

Figure 11-17 shows a similar topology to Figure 11-16. In Figure 11-17, however, the top link is running at a speed of 10Mbps, whereas the bottom link is running at a speed of 100Mbps. Because switch SW2 seeks to get back to the root bridge (that is, switch SW1) with the least cost, port Gig 0/2 on switch SW2 is selected as the root port.

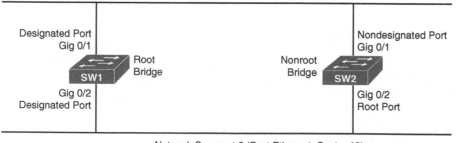

FIGURE 11-17   STP with Different Port Costs

Specifically, port Gig 0/1 has a cost of 100, and Gig 0/2 has a cost of 19. Table 11-4 shows the port costs for various link speeds.

Table 11-4   STP Port Cost

Link Speed	STP Port Cost
10Mbps (Ethernet)	100
100Mbps (Fast Ethernet)	19
1Gbps (Gigabit Ethernet)	4
10Gbps (10-Gigabit Ethernet)	2

NOTE   A new standard for STP port costs, called *long STP*, will be increasingly adopted over the coming years because of link speeds exceeding 10Gbps. Long STP values range from 2,000,000 for 10Mbps Ethernet to as little as 2 for 10Tbps (that is, 10 terabits [trillion bits] per second).

Nondesignated ports do not forward traffic during normal operation but do receive bridge protocol data units (BPDUs). Switches exchange STP information in the form of BPDUs, which contain useful information for STP elections, path cost calculation, link suppression, and loop detection. If a link in the topology goes down, the nondesignated port detects the link failure and determines whether it needs to transition to the forwarding state.

If a nondesignated port needs to transition to the forwarding state, it does not do so immediately. Rather, it transitions through the following states:

- **Blocking:** The port remains in the blocking state for 20 seconds by default. During this time, the nondesignated port evaluates BPDUs in an attempt to determine its role in the spanning tree.

- **Listening:** The port moves from the blocking state to the listening state and remains in this state for 15 seconds by default. During this time, the port sources BPDUs, which inform adjacent switches of the port's intent to forward data.

- **Learning:** The port moves from the listening state to the learning state and remains in this state for 15 seconds by default. During this time, the port begins to add entries to its MAC address table.

- **Forwarding:** The port moves from the learning state to the forwarding state and begins to forward frames.

Link Aggregation

If all ports on a switch are operating at the same speed (for example, 1Gbps), the ports most likely to experience congestion are ports connecting to another switch or router. For example, imagine a wiring closet switch connected (via Fast Ethernet ports) to multiple PCs. That wiring closet switch has an uplink to the main switch for a building. Because this uplink port aggregates multiple 100Mbps connections and the uplink port is also operating at 100Mbps, it can quickly become congested if multiple PCs are transmitting traffic that needs to be sent over that uplink, as shown in Figure 11-18.

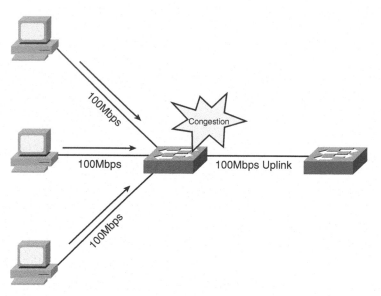

FIGURE 11-18 Uplink Congestion

To help alleviate congested links between switches, you can (on some) switch models logically combine multiple physical connections into a single logical connection over which traffic can be sent. This feature, which is illustrated in Figure 11-19, is called *link aggregation*.

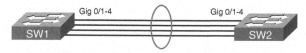

FIGURE 11-19 Link Aggregation

Although vendor-proprietary solutions for link aggregation have existed for some time, some solutions faced a couple of common issues:

- Each link in the logical bundle was a potential single point of failure.

- Each end of the logical bundle had to be manually configured.

In 2000, the IEEE ratified the 802.3ad standard for link aggregation. This standard supports *Link Aggregation Control Protocol* (*LACP*). Unlike some of the older vendor-proprietary solutions, LACP supports automatic configuration and prevents an individual link from becoming a single point of failure. Specifically, with LACP, if a link fails, that link's traffic is forwarded over a different link. The Cisco Systems implementation of LACP is called *EtherChannel*. Groups of interfaces that make up an EtherChannel bundle are often referred to as a *link aggregation group* (*LAG*). An EtherChannel group can be configured to act as a Layer 2 access port and support only a single VLAN, or it can be configured to act as a Layer 2 802.1Q trunk and support multiple VLANs of the LAG. A LAG can also be configured as a Layer 3 routed interface if the switch supports that feature. In the case of a Layer 3 Ether-Channel, an IP address would be applied to the logical interface that represents the LAG. Another term related to LACP and LAGs is *port bonding*, which also refers to the same concept of grouping multiple ports and using them as a single logical interface.

LACP Configuration

Example 11-3 shows a sample configuration of LACP on a Cisco switch. A line with a leading ! is a comment used to document the next line(s) of the configuration.

Example 11-3   LACP Configuration

```
! Move to interface that will be part of the LACP group
SW1(config)# interface GigabitEthernet0/16


! Assign this interface to the LACP group 1
SW1(config-if)# channel-group 1 mode active


! Move to the other interface(s) that will be part of
! the same group
SW1(config-if)# interface GigabitEthernet0/17
SW1(config-if)# channel-group 1 mode active


! Configure the group of interfaces as a logical group
! Configuration here will also apply the individual
```

```
! interfaces that are part of the group
SW1(config-if)# interface Port-channel 1


! Apply the configuration desired for the group
! LACP groups can be access or trunk ports depending
! on how the configuration of the logical port-channel interface
! In this example the LAG will be acting as a trunk
SW1(config-if)# switchport mode trunk
SW1(config-if)# switchport trunk encapsulation dot1q
```

Power over Ethernet

Some switches not only transmit data over a connected UTP cable but use that cable to provide power to an attached device. For example, say that you want to mount a wireless access point (AP) on the ceiling. Although no electrical outlet is available near the AP's location, you can, as an example, run a Cat 6 UTP plenum cable above the drop ceiling and connect it to the AP. Some APs allow the switch at the other end of the UTP cable to provide power over the same wires that carry data. Examples of other devices that might benefit from receiving power from an Ethernet switch include security cameras and IP phones.

The switch feature that gives power to attached devices is called *Power over Ethernet (PoE)*, and it is defined by the IEEE 802.3af standard. As shown in Figure 11-20, the PoE feature of a switch checks for 25,000 ohms of resistance in the attached device. To check the resistance, the switch applies as much as 10V of direct current (DC) across specific pairs of wires (that is, pins 1 and 2 combine to form one side of the circuit, and pins 3 and 6 combine to form the other side of the circuit) connecting back to the attached device and checks to see how much current flows over those wires. For example, if the switch applies 10V DC across those wires and notices 0.4 mA (milliamps) of current, the switch concludes that the attached device has 25,000 ohms of resistance across those wires (based on the formula $E = IR$, where E represents voltage, I represents current, and R represents resistance). The switch could then apply power across those wires.

Key Topic — Switch applies 2.8V–10V DC to two pairs of leads to detect a 25,000 Ohm resistor in the attached device

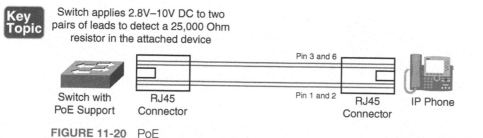

FIGURE 11-20   PoE

Next, the switch must determine how much power the attached device needs. The switch makes this determination by applying 15.5V–20.5V DC (making sure that the current never exceeds 100 mA) to the attached device for a brief period of time (less than one-tenth of a second). The amount of current flowing to the attached device tells the switch the *power class* of the attached device. The switch then knows how much power should be made available on the port connecting to the device requiring power, and it begins supplying an appropriate amount of voltage (in the range 44V–57V) to the attached device.

The IEEE 802.3af standard can supply a maximum of 15.4W (watts) of power. However, the later standard IEEE 802.3at offers as much as 32.4W of power, enabling PoE to support a wider range of devices, such as power-hungry IP video cameras. This newer standard for PoE is often referred to as ***Power over Ethernet Plus (PoE+)***.

Port Monitoring

For troubleshooting purposes, you might want to analyze packets flowing over a network. To capture packets (that is, store copies of packets on a local hard drive) for analysis, you could attach a *network sniffer* to a hub. Because a hub sends bits received on one port out all other ports, the attached network sniffer sees all traffic entering the hub.

Several standalone network sniffers are available. However, a low-cost way to perform packet capture and analysis is to use software such as Wireshark (www.wireshark.org), as shown in Figure 11-21.

A challenge arises, however, if you connect a network sniffer (for example, a laptop running the Wireshark software) to a switch port rather than to a hub port. Because a switch, by design, forwards frames out ports containing the frames' destination addresses, a network sniffer attached to one port would not see traffic destined for a device connected to a different port.

For example, in Figure 11-22, traffic enters a switch on port 1 and, based on the destination MAC addresses, exits via port 2. However, a network sniffer is connected to port 3 and is unable to see (and therefore capture) the traffic flowing between ports 1 and 2.

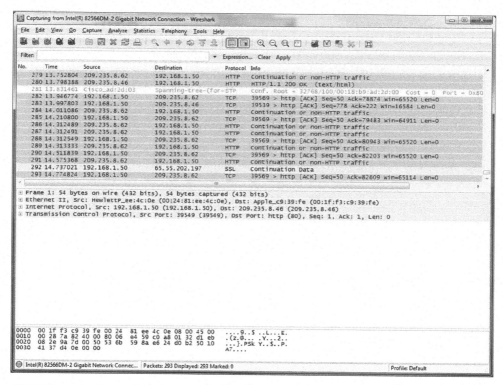

FIGURE 11-21   Example: Wireshark Packet-Capture Software

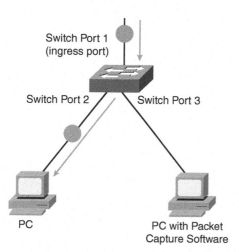

FIGURE 11-22   Example: Network Sniffer Unable to Capture Traffic

Fortunately, some switches support a *port mirroring* feature, which makes a copy of traffic seen on one port and sends that duplicated traffic out another port (to which a network sniffer could be attached). As shown in Figure 11-23, this switch is configured to mirror traffic on port 2 to port 3, allowing a network sniffer to capture the packets that need to be analyzed. Depending on the switch, locally captured traffic could be forwarded to a remote destination for centralized analysis of that traffic.

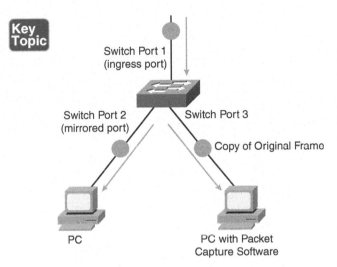

Key Topic

Switch Port 1
(ingress port)

Switch Port 2
(mirrored port)

Switch Port 3

Copy of Original Frame

PC

PC with Packet
Capture Software

FIGURE 11-23 Example: Network Sniffer with Port Mirroring Configured on the Switch

Port Mirroring Configuration

Example 11-4 shows a sample configuration from a Cisco Catalyst switch that captures all the frames coming in on port Gig 0/1 and forwards them to port Gig 0/3.

Example 11-4 Port Mirroring Configuration

```
SW1(config)# monitor session 1 source interface Gi0/1
SW1(config)# monitor session 1 destination interface Gi0/3
```

User Authentication

For security purposes, some switches require users to *authenticate* themselves (that is, provide credentials, such as a username and password, to prove who they are) before gaining access to the rest of the network. A standards-based method of enforcing user authentication is IEEE 802.1X.

With 802.lX enabled, a switch requires a client to authenticate before communicating on the network. After the authentication occurs, a key is generated that is shared between the client and the device to which it attaches (for example, a wireless LAN controller or a Layer 2 switch). The key then encrypts traffic coming from and being sent to the client.

Figure 11-24 illustrates the three primary components of an 802.1X network, which are described in the following list:

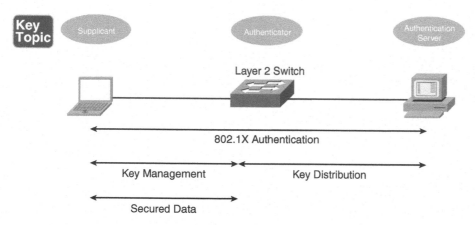

FIGURE 11-24   8021X User Authentication

- **Supplicant:** The supplicant is the device that wants to gain access to a network.

- **Authenticator:** The authenticator forwards the supplicant's authentication request on to an authentication server. After the authentication server authenticates the supplicant, the authenticator receives a key that is used to communicate securely during a session with the supplicant.

- **Authentication server:** The authentication server (for example, a Remote Authentication Dial-In User Service [RADIUS] server) checks a supplicant's credentials. If the credentials are acceptable, the authentication server notifies the authenticator that the supplicant is allowed to communicate on the network. The authentication server also gives the authenticator a key that can be used to securely transmit data during the authenticator's session with the supplicant.

An even more sophisticated approach to admission control is the Network Access Control (NAC) feature offered by some authentication servers. Beyond just checking credentials, NAC can check characteristics of the device seeking admission to the network. The client's operating system (OS) and version of antivirus software are examples of these characteristics.

Management Access and Authentication

To configure a managed switch, you could use Secure Shell (SSH) or connect directly to the console port of the switch. An unmanaged switch is one that does not support the use of an IP address or a console port to connect to for management purposes. When possible, using a separate network for management of a managed switch is desired. This is referred to as *out-of-band* (*OOB*) management when the management traffic is kept on a separate network from the user traffic. To use remote SSH access, SSH must be enabled on the switch and the switch must have an IP address and default gateway configured so it can reply to the SSH requests when the administrator using SSH is not on the same local network as the switch. Example 11-5 shows a sample configuration for IP and management access on a Cisco Catalyst switch. A line with a leading ! is a comment used to document the next line(s) of the configuration.

Example 11-5   Management Access

```
! Move to the logical Layer 3 interface that will
! receive the management IP address for the switch
SW1(config)# interface vlan 1

! Configure an IP address that is available for the
! switch to use
SW1(config-if)# ip address 172.16.55.123 255.255.255.0
SW1(config-if)# exit

! Configure a domain name, required for creating the
! keys used for SSH cryptography
SW1(config)# ip domain-name pearson.com

! Create the public/private key pair SSH can use
SW1(config)# crypto key generate rsa modulus 1024

! Specify the version of SSH to allow
SW1(config)# ip ssh version 2

! Create a user account on the local switch
SW1(config)# username admin privilege 15 secret pears0nR0cks!
```

```
! Move to the logical VTY lines used for SSH access
SW1(config)# line vty 0 15


! Allow only SSH on the logical range 16 VTY lines (0 - 15)
SW1(config-line)# transport input ssh


! Require using an account from the local switch to log in
SW1(config-line)# login local
SW1(config-line)# exit


! Set the default gateway the switch can use when communicating
! over an SSH session with an administrator who is on a different
! network than the switch's interface VLAN 1
SW1(config)# ip default-gateway 172.16.55.1


! Move to the console port of the switch
SW1(config)# line console 0


! Require authentication using the local switch before allowing
! access to the switch through the console port
SW1(config-line)# login local
```

NOTE   The virtual terminal (VTY) lines (lines 0–15 in Example 11-5) allow for 16 simultaneous connections to the switch by administrators. If more simultaneous connections are required, additional VTY lines could be configured on the switch.

First-Hop Redundancy

Many devices, such as PCs, are configured with default gateways. The *default gateway* parameter identifies the IP address of a next-hop router. As a result, if that router were to become unavailable, devices that relied on the default gateway's IP address would be unable to send traffic off their local subnet, even if a backup router existed.

Fortunately, a variety of technologies are available for providing first-hop redundancy. One such technology is Hot Standby Router Protocol (HSRP), which is a Cisco-proprietary protocol. HSRP can run on routers or multilayer switches.

HSRP uses virtual IP addresses and virtual MAC addresses. One router, known as the *active router*, services requests destined for the virtual IP and virtual MAC addresses. Another router, known as the *standby router*, can service such requests in the event that the active router becomes unavailable. Figure 11-25 illustrates a sample HSRP topology.

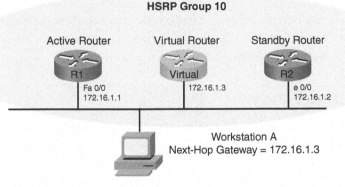

FIGURE 11-25   Sample HSRP Topology

In Figure 11-25, notice that router R1 is acting as the active router, and router R2 is acting as the standby router. When workstation A sends traffic destined for a remote network, it sends traffic to its default gateway, 172.16.1.3, which is the virtual IP address shared by the HSRP routers. When router R1 is the active router, it assumes the virtual IP and virtual MAC addresses, and it forwards the traffic off the local network. However, if R2 notices that R1 has become unavailable (based on the fact that hello messages are no longer received from router R1), R2 transitions to the active router role and assumes the virtual IP and virtual MAC addresses. With default timer settings, the time required to fail over to router R2 is approximately 10 seconds. However, timers can be adjusted such that the failover time is as little as 1 second.

NOTE   Cisco has another proprietary first-hop redundancy protocol called *Gateway Load Balancing Protocol* (*GLBP*). Whereas GLBP and HSRP are Cisco-proprietary solutions, *Virtual Router Redundancy Protocol* (*VRRP*) and *Common Address Redundancy Protocol* (*CARP*) are open-standard options for first-hop redundancy.

Other Switch Features

Switch features, such as those previously described, vary widely by manufacturer, and some switches offer a variety of security features. For example, MAC filtering might be supported, which allows traffic to be permitted or denied based on a device's MAC address. Other types of traffic filtering might also be supported, based on criteria such as IP address information (for multilayer switches).

For monitoring and troubleshooting purposes, interface *diagnostics* might be accessible. This diagnostic information might include various error conditions, such as late collisions or cyclic redundancy check (CRC) errors, which might indicate a duplex mismatch.

Some switches also support *quality of service* (*QoS*) settings, which make it possible to forward traffic based on the traffic's priority markings. Also, some switches have the ability to perform marking and remarking of traffic priority values.

Real-World Case Study

Acme, Inc. has made some decisions regarding the setup of its LAN. For connections from the client machines to the switches in the wiring closets (the intermediate distribution frames), it will use unshielded twisted-pair Category 6a cabling with the switch ports configured as access ports and set to 1000Mbps to match the Gigabit Ethernet capabilities of the client computers that will be connecting to the switches.

Multiple VLANs will be used. The computers that are being used by the Sales department will be connected to ports on a switch that are configured as access ports for the specific VLAN for Sales. Computers used by Human Resources will connect to switch ports that are configured as access ports for the Human Resources VLAN. There will be separate IP subnetworks associated with each of the VLANs.

To provide a fault-tolerant default gateway for the clients in each of the VLANs, a first-hop redundancy protocol will be used, such as HSRP, GLBP, or VRRP.

The fiber connections that will go vertically through the building and connect the switches in the IDFs to the MDF (main distribution frame) in the basement will be running at 1Gbps each, and multiple fiber cables will be used. LACP will be used for these vertical connections to make the multiple fiber links work together as part of one logical EtherChannel interface. For the LACP connections between the IDFs and MDF to support multiple VLANs, the LAG will be configured as a trunk using 802.1Q tagging. Routing between the VLANs will be done by multilayer switches that are located near the MDF.

Spanning tree will be enabled on the switches so that in the event of parallel paths between switches, a Layer 2 loop can be prevented.

To support IP-based telephones in the offices, the switches will also provide PoE+, which can supply power to the IP phones over the Ethernet cables that run between the switch in the IDF and the IP phones.

In case protocol analysis needs to be done, the switches that will be purchased need to support port mirroring so that frames from one port can be captured and forwarded to an alternate port for analysis.

To authenticate devices that are connecting to the switch ports, 802.1X can be used. To authenticate administrators who are connecting to switches for management, authentication can be forced at the logical VTY lines. SSH will be enabled and enforced because it is a secure management protocol. The switches will be given their own IP address, in addition to a default gateway, to use so that they can be remotely managed. Local user accounts will be created on the switches so that local authentication can be implemented as each administrator connects either to the console or via SSH.

Summary

Here are the main topics covered in this chapter:

- This chapter describes the origins of Ethernet, including a discussion of Ethernet's CSMA/CD features.

- This chapter compares a variety of Ethernet standards in terms of media type, network bandwidth, and distance limitation.

- This chapter covers various features that might be available on modern Ethernet switches, including VLANs, trunking, STP, link aggregation, PoE, and PoE+.

Exam Preparation Tasks

Review All the Key Topics

Review the most important topics from this chapter, noted with the Key Topic icon in the outer margin of the page. Table 11-5 lists these key topics and the page number where each is found.

Table 11-5 Key Topics for Chapter 11

Key Topic Element	Description	Page Number
List	Components of CSMA/CD	288
Table 11-1	Ethernet bandwidth capacities	290
Table 11-2	Types of Ethernet	291
Figure 11-12	IEEE 802.1Q tag bytes	297
Figure 11-14	A broadcast storm	300
List	STP operation	301

Key Topic Element	Description	Page Number
List	STP switch classification	
Table 11-3	STP port types	302
Table 11-4	STP port cost	303
List	STP port states	303
Figure 11-20	Power over Ethernet	306
Figure 11-23	Network sniffer and port mirroring example	309
Figure 11-24	802.1X User Authentication	310
List	IEEE 802.1X network components	

Complete Tables and Lists from Memory

Print a copy of Appendix C, "Memory Tables," or at least the section for this chapter and complete as many of the tables as possible from memory. Appendix D, "Memory Tables Answer Key," includes the completed tables and lists so you can check your work.

Define Key Terms

Define the following key terms from this chapter and check your answers in the Glossary:

Ethernet, collision, carrier-sense multiple access with collision detection (CSMA/CD), full-duplex, half-duplex, virtual LAN (VLAN), trunk, Spanning Tree Protocol (STP), Rapid Spanning Tree Protocol (RSTP), root port, designated port, nondesignated port, link aggregation, Power over Ethernet (PoE), Power over Ethernet plus (PoE+), supplicant, authenticator, authentication server

Complete Chapter 11 Hands-On Labs in Network+ Simulator Lite

- Using ARP to Discover the MAC Address
- Troubleshooting VLAN Client Connection Issues
- Connect to Switch Console Port Using PuTTY
- Connect to a Switch and Reconfigure the Hostname and Password
- Configure an IP Address and Default Gateway setting on a Switch

- Switch Management via Telnet

- Configuring Port Security

Additional Resources

Migrating from STP to RSTP: https://www.ajsnetworking.com/cisco-migrating-from-stp-to-rstp/

VLAN Trunking Protocol Version 3: https://www.ajsnetworking.com/vlan-trunking-protocol-vtp-version-3/

Review Questions

The answers to these review questions appear in Appendix A, "Answers to Review Questions."

1. What is the distance limitation of a 1000BASE-T Ethernet network?

   a. 100 m

   b. 185 m

   c. 500 m

   d. 2 km

2. If two devices simultaneously transmit data on an Ethernet network and a collision occurs, what does each station do in an attempt to resend the data and avoid another collision?

   a. Each device compares the other device's priority value (determined by IP address) with its own, and the device with the highest priority value transmits first.

   b. Each device waits for a clear-to-send (CTS) signal from the switch.

   c. Each device randomly picks a priority value, and the device with the highest value transmits first.

   d. Each device sets a random back-off timer, and a device attempts retransmission after the timer expires.

3. What kind of media is used by 100GBASE-SR10 Ethernet?

   a. UTP

   b. MMF

   c. STP

   d. SMF

4. Which of the following statements are true regarding VLANs? (Choose two.)

   a. A VLAN has a single broadcast domain.

   b. For traffic to pass between two VLANs, that traffic must be routed.

   c. Because of a switch's MAC address table, traffic does not need to be routed to pass between two VLANs.

   d. A VLAN has a single collision domain.

5. What name is given to a VLAN on an IEEE 802.1Q trunk whose frames are not tagged?

   a. Native VLAN

   b. Default VLAN

   c. Management VLAN

   d. VLAN 0

6. In a topology running STP, every network segment has a single _____ port, which is the port on that segment that is closest to the root bridge in terms of cost.

   a. Root

   b. Designated

   c. Nondesignated

   d. Nonroot

7. What is the IEEE standard for link aggregation?

   a. 802.1Q

   b. 802.3ad

   c. 802.1d

   d. 802.3af

8. What is the maximum amount of power a switch is allowed to provide per port, according to the IEEE 802.3af standard?

   a. 7.7W

   b. 15.4W

   c. 26.4W

   d. 32.4W

9. What switch feature allows you to connect a network sniffer to a switch port and tells the switch to send a copy of frames seen on one port out the port to which your network sniffer is connected?

   a. Port interception

   b. Port duplexing

   c. Port mirroring

   d. Port redirect

10. Which IEEE 802.1X component checks the credentials of a device wanting to gain access to a network?

    a. Supplicant

    b. Authentication server

    c. Access point

    d. Authenticator

This chapter covers the following topics related to Objective 2.4 (Given a scenario, install and configure the appropriate wireless standards and technologies) of the CompTIA Network+ N10-008 certification exam:

- 802.11 standards
  - a
  - b
  - g
  - n (WiFi 4)
  - ac (WiFi 5)
  - ax (WiFi 6)
- Frequencies and range
  - 2.4GHz
  - 5GHz
- Channels
  - Regulatory impacts
- Channel bonding
- Service set identifier (SSID)
  - Basic service set
  - Extended service set
  - Independent basic service set (Ad-hoc)
  - Roaming

- Antenna types
  - Omni
  - Directional
- Encryption standards
  - WiFi Protected Access (WPA)/ WPA2 Personal [Advanced Encryption Standard (AES)/ Temporal Key Integrity Protocol (TKIP)]
  - WPA/WPA2 Enterprise (AES/TKIP)
- Cellular technologies
  - Code-division multiple access (CDMA)
  - Global System for Mobile Communications (GSM)
  - Long-Term Evolution (LTE)
  - 3G, 4G, 5G
- Multiple input, multiple output (MIMO) and multi-user MIMO (MU-MIMO)

CHAPTER 12

Wireless Standards

The popularity of wireless LANs (WLANs) has exploded over the past decade, allowing users to roam within a WLAN coverage area, take their laptops and tablets with them, and maintain network connectivity as they move throughout a building or campus environment. Many other devices can also take advantage of wireless networks, such as gaming consoles, smartphones, and printers.

This chapter introduces WLAN technology, along with various wireless concepts, components, and standards. It also presents WLAN design considerations, followed by a discussion of WLAN security.

Foundation Topics

Introducing Wireless LANs

This section introduces the basic building blocks of WLANs and discusses how WLANs connect to a wired local area network (LAN). Various design options, including antenna design, frequencies, and communications channels, are discussed, along with a comparison of today's major wireless standards, which are all some variant of IEEE 802.11.

WLAN Concepts and Components

Wireless devices, such as laptops, tablets, and smartphones, often have built-in wireless cards that allow those devices to communicate on a WLAN. But what is the device to which they communicate? It could be another laptop or device with a wireless card. This would be an example of an *ad hoc* WLAN. However, enterprise-class WLANs, and even most WLANs in homes, are configured in such a way that a wireless client connects to some sort of wireless base station, such as a wireless access point (AP) or a wireless router. Many companies offer WiFi as a service, and users in range of an AP can use the AP as a *hotspot*, indicating that WiFi is available through the AP.

> **NOTE**   A much fancier term for an ad hoc network that you should be aware of is *independent basic service set* (IBSS) *WLAN*.

This communication might be done using a variety of antenna types, frequencies, and communication channels. The following sections consider some of these elements in more detail.

Wireless Routers

Consider the basic WLAN topology shown in Figure 12-1. Such a WLAN might be found in a residence whose Internet access is provided by a high-speed cable modem. In this topology, a wireless router and switch are shown as separate components. However, in many residential networks, a wireless router integrates switch ports and wireless routing functionality into a single device.

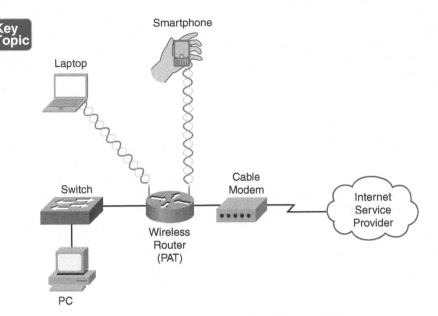

FIGURE 12-1 Basic WLAN Topology with a Wireless Router

In Figure 12-1, the cable modem obtains an IP address via DHCP from the Internet service provider (ISP). The wireless router behind the modem also uses DHCP to provide IP addresses to LAN devices attaching to it wirelessly or through a wired connection. The process through which a wireless client (for example, a laptop or a smartphone) attaches with a wireless router (or wireless AP) is called *association*. All wireless devices associating with a single AP share a collision domain. Therefore, for scalability and performance reasons, WLANs might include multiple APs. The router then uses Port Address Translation (PAT) to allow packets to leave the LAN and head to the Internet.

Wireless Access Point

Although a wireless access point (AP) interconnects a wired LAN with a WLAN, it does not interconnect two networks (for example, the service provider's network and an internal network). Figure 12-2 shows a typical deployment of an AP.

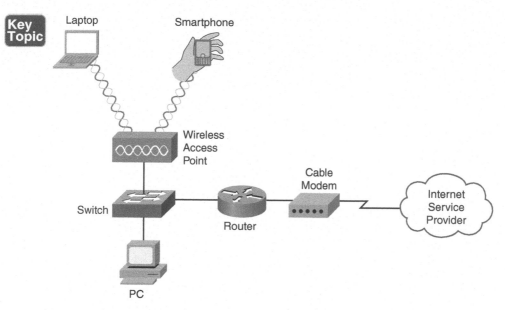

FIGURE 12-2   Basic WLAN Topology with a Wireless AP

In Figure 12-2, the AP connects to the wired LAN, and the wireless devices that connect to the wired LAN via the AP are on the same subnet as the AP. (No Network Address Translation [NAT] or PAT is being performed.) This is acting as a wireless bridge between the wireless clients connected to the AP and the wired devices connected to the switch in the same Layer 2 domain.

To manage multiple APs, a company uses a wireless LAN controller (WLC) for centralized management and control of the APs. A Cisco model 5760 WLC is an example of a network controller for multiple APs. The protocols used to communicate between an AP and a WLC could be the older Lightweight Access Point Protocol (LWAPP) or the more current Control and Provisioning of Wireless Access Points (CAPWAP). With a WLC, VLAN pooling can be used to assign IP addresses to wireless clients from a pool of IP subnets and their associated VLANs.

Antennas

The coverage area of a WLAN is largely determined by the type of antenna used on a wireless AP or a wireless router. Although some lower-end, consumer-grade wireless APs have fixed antennas, higher-end, enterprise-class wireless APs often support various antenna types.

Design goals to keep in mind when selecting an antenna include the following:

■ The required distance between an AP and a wireless client

- The coverage area pattern (For example, the coverage area might radiate out in all directions, forming a spherical coverage area around an antenna, or an antenna might provide increased coverage in only one or two directions.)

- The type of environment—either indoor or outdoor

- The need to avoid interference with other APs

The strength of the electromagnetic waves being radiated from an antenna is referred to as *gain*, and it involves a measurement of both direction and efficiency of a transmission. For example, the gain measurement for a wireless AP's antenna transmitting a signal is a measurement of how efficiently the power being applied to the antenna is converted into electromagnetic waves being broadcast in a specific direction. Conversely, the gain measurement for a wireless AP's antenna receiving a signal is a measurement of how efficiently the received electromagnetic waves arriving from a specific direction are converted back into electricity leaving the antenna.

Gain is commonly measured using the dBi unit of measure, where *dB* stands for *decibels*, and *i* stands for *isotropic*. A decibel, in this context, is a ratio of radiated power to a reference value. In the case of dBi, the reference value is the signal strength (power) radiated from an isotropic antenna, which represents a theoretical antenna that radiates an equal amount of power in all directions (in a spherical pattern). An isotropic antenna is considered to have gain of 0 dBi.

Here is the most common formula used for antenna gain:

$$GdBi = 10 * \log^{10} (G)$$

Based on this formula, an antenna with a peak power gain of 4 (*G*) would have a gain of 6.02 dBi. Antenna theory can become mathematical, heavily relying on the use of Maxwell's equations. However, generally speaking, if one antenna has 3 dB more gain than another antenna, it has approximately twice the effective power.

Antennas are classified not just by their gain but also by their coverage area. There are two broad categories of antennas, based on coverage area:

- **Omnidirectional:** An *omnidirectional antenna* (sometimes simply called an *omni*) radiates power at relatively equal power levels in all directions; it is somewhat similar to a theoretical isotropic antenna. Omnidirectional antennas, an example of which is depicted in Figure 12-3, are popular in residential WLANs and small office/home office (SOHO) locations.

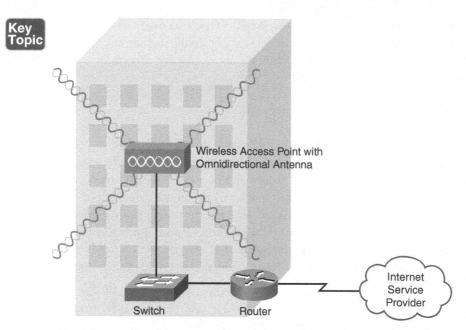

FIGURE 12-3   Omnidirectional Antenna Coverage

■ **Unidirectional:** A *unidirectional antenna* can focus its power in a specific direction, thus avoiding potential interference with other wireless devices and perhaps reaching greater distances than are possible with omnidirectional antennas. One application for unidirectional antennas is interconnecting two nearby buildings, as shown in Figure 12-4.

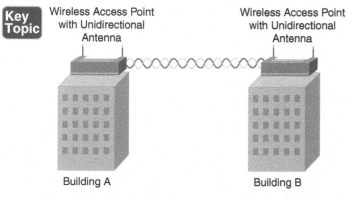

FIGURE 12-4   Unidirectional Antenna Coverage

Another consideration for antenna installation is the horizontal or vertical orientation of the antenna. For best performance, if two wireless APs communicate with one another, they need to have matching antenna orientations (that is, their *polarity* needs to be the same).

Frequencies and Channels

Later in this chapter, you will learn more about a variety of wireless standards, which are all variants of the IEEE 802.11 standard. As you contrast one standard with another, a characteristic to watch out for is the frequencies at which these standards operate. Although there are some country-specific variations, certain frequency ranges (or *frequency bands*) have been reserved internationally for industrial, scientific, and medical purposes. These frequency bands are called the *ISM bands*, where ISM derives from *i*ndustrial, *s*cientific, and *m*edical.

Two of these bands are commonly used for WLANs. Specifically, WLANs use the range of frequencies in the 2.4GHz–2.5GHz range (commonly referred to as the *2.4GHz band*) or in the 5.725GHz–5.875GHz range (commonly referred to as the *5GHz band*). In fact, some WLANs support a mixed environment, where 2.4GHz devices run alongside 5GHz devices.

NOTE The latest wireless standard, 802.11ax (WiFi 6), takes WiFi operation to the 6 GHz frequency. WiFi 6 uses up to 14 additional 80MHz channels or 7 additional super-wide 160MHz channels in the 6GHz band. This new technology is ideal for applications such as high-definition video streaming and virtual reality.

Within each band are specific frequencies (or *channels*) at which wireless devices operate. To avoid interference, nearby wireless APs should use frequencies that do not overlap with one another. You can use wireless survey tools such as AirMagnet from Fluke Networks to analyze what is currently in use so you can set up a new wireless system that does not compete for the frequencies that are already in use. Those same tools can also help you identify **wireless channel** utilization in existing and new wireless networks. Regarding channel selection, merely selecting different channels is not sufficient because transmissions on one channel spill over into nearby channels. Site survey tools can collect data to show the relative strength of signals in the areas being serviced by the APs. This output can be color-coded and overlaid on top of the floor plan and is often referred to as a *heat map* of the wireless signals.

Consider, for example, the 2.4GHz band. Here, channel frequencies are separated by 5MHz (with the exception of channel 14, which has 12MHz of separation from channel 13). However, a single channel's transmission can spread over a frequency range of 22MHz. As a result, channels must have five channels of separation (5 × 5MHz = 25MHz, which is greater than 22MHz). You can see from Figure 12-5 that, in the United States, you could select the nonoverlapping channels 1, 6, and 11.

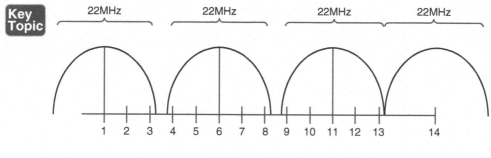

Channel

FIGURE 12-5   Nonoverlapping Channels in the 2.4GHz Band

NOTE   Even though some countries use channel 14 as a nonoverlapping channel, it is not supported in the United States.

As a reference, Table 12-1 shows the specific frequencies for each of the channels in the 2.4GHz band.

Table 12-1   Channel Frequencies in the 2.4GHz Band

Channel	Frequency (GHz)	Recommended as a Nonoverlapping Channel
1	2.412	Yes
2	2.417	No
3	2.422	No
4	2.427	No
5	2.432	No
6	2.437	Yes
7	2.442	No
8	2.447	No
9	2.452	No
10	2.457	No
11	2.462	Yes
12	2.467	No
13	2.472	No
14	2.484	Yes (not supported in the United States)

The 5GHz band has more channels than the 2.4GHz band. Table 12-2 lists the recommended nonoverlapping channels for the 5GHz band in the United States. Note that additional channels are supported in some countries.

Table 12-2 Nonoverlapping Channels in the 5GHz Band Recommended for Use in the United States

Channel	Frequency (GHz)
36	5.180
40	5.200
44	5.220
48	5.240
52	5.260*
56	5.280*
60	5.300*
64	5.320*
100	5.500**
104	5.520**
108	5.540**
112	5.560**
116	5.580**
136	5.680**
140	5.700**
149	5.745
153	5.765
157	5.785
161	5.805
165	5.825

*Must support dynamic frequency selection to prevent interference with RADAR.

**Must be professionally installed.

CSMA/CA

You learned about *carrier-sense multiple access with collision detection* (CSMA/CD) technology in Chapter 11, "Ethernet Switching." WLANs use a similar technology called carrier-sense multiple access with collision avoidance (CSMA/CA). Just as CSMA/CD is needed for half-duplex Ethernet connections, CSMA/CA is needed for WLAN connections because of their half-duplex operation. Similar to the way an Ethernet device listens to an Ethernet segment to determine whether a frame exists on the segment, a WLAN device listens for a transmission on a wireless channel to determine whether it is safe to transmit. In addition, the collision-avoidance part of the CSMA/CA algorithm causes wireless devices to wait for a random back-off time before transmitting.

Transmission Methods

In the previous section, you learned about the frequencies used for various wireless channels. However, you need to be aware that each of those frequencies is considered to be the *center frequency* of a channel. In actual operation, a channel uses more than one frequency, which is a transmission method called *spread spectrum*. These frequencies are, however, very close to one another, which results in a *narrowband transmission*.

Here are the three variations of spread-spectrum technology to be aware of for your study of WLANs:

- **Direct-sequence spread spectrum (DSSS):** DSSS modulates data over an entire range of frequencies by using a series of symbols called *chips*. A chip is shorter in duration than a bit, meaning that chips are transmitted at a higher rate than is the actual data. These chips encode not only the data to be transmitted but also what appears to be random data. Although both parties involved in a DSSS communication know which chips represent actual data and which chips do not, if a third party intercepted a DSSS transmission, it would be difficult for that party to eavesdrop on the data because they would not easily know which chips represented valid bits. DSSS is more subject to environmental factors than FHSS and OFDM because of its use of an entire frequency spectrum.

- **Frequency-hopping spread spectrum (FHSS):** FSSS allows the participants in a communication to hop between predetermined frequencies. Security is enhanced because the participants can predict the next frequency to be used, but a third party cannot easily predict the next frequency. FHSS can also provision extra bandwidth by simultaneously using more than one frequency.

- **Orthogonal frequency-division multiplexing (OFDM):** Whereas DSSS uses a high modulation rate for the symbols it sends, OFDM uses a relatively slow modulation rate for symbols. This slower modulation rate, combined with the simultaneous transmission of data over 52 data streams, helps OFDM support high data rates while resisting interference between the various data streams.

NOTE WiFi 6 features the latest enhancements in technology and uses the latest spread-spectrum technology, called *orthogonal frequency-division multiple access (OFDMA)*. OFDMA provides sophisticated scheduling techniques to provide better performance in highly congested WiFi environments.

WLAN Standards

Most modern WLAN standards are variations of the original IEEE 802.11 standard, which was developed in 1997. This original standard supported a DSSS implementation and an FHSS implementation, both of which operated in the 2.4GHz band. However, with supported speeds of 1Mbps or 2Mbps, the original 802.11 standard lacks sufficient bandwidth to meet the needs of today's WLANs. The most popular variants of the 802.11 standard in use today are 802.11a, 802.11b, 802.11g, 802.11n, 802.11ac, and 802.11ax, as described in detail in the following sections.

802.11a

The *802.11a* WLAN standard, which was ratified in 1999, supports speeds as high as 54Mbps. Other supported data rates (which can be used if conditions are not suitable for the 54Mbps rate) include 6Mbps, 9Mbps, 12Mbps, 18Mbps, 24Mbps, 36Mbps, and 48Mbps. The 802.11a standard uses the 5GHz band and uses the OFDM transmission method. Interestingly, 802.11a never gained widespread adoption because it was not backward compatible with 802.11b, whereas 802.11g was backward compatible. However, it is worth noting that 802.11a is a possible alternative to 802.11b/g, as the 2.4GHz band is often far more crowded than the 5GHz band.

802.11b

The *802.11b* WLAN standard, which was ratified in 1999, supports speeds as high as 11Mbps. However, 5.5Mbps is another supported data rate. The 802.11b standard uses the 2.4GHz band and uses the DSSS transmission method.

802.11g

The *802.11g* WLAN standard, which was ratified in 2003, supports speeds as high as 54Mbps. Like 802.11a, 802.11g also supports data rates of 6Mbps, 9Mbps, 12Mbps, 18Mbps, 24Mbps, 36Mbps, and 48Mbps. However, like 802.11b, 802.11g operates in the 2.4GHz band, which allows it to offer backward compatibility to 802.11b devices. 802.11g can use either the OFDM or the DSSS transmission method.

802.11n (WiFi 4)

The *802.11n* WLAN standard, which was ratified in 2009, supports a wide variety of speeds, depending on its implementation. Although the speed of an 802.11n network could exceed 300Mbps (through the use of channel bonding, which is discussed shortly), many 802.11n devices on the market have speed ratings in the 130Mbps–150Mbps range. An 802.11n WLAN can operate in the 2.4GHz band, the 5GHz band, or both simultaneously. 802.11n uses the OFDM transmission method.

One way 802.11n achieves superior throughput is through the use of a technology called *multiple input, multiple output (MIMO)*. MIMO uses multiple antennas for transmission and reception. These antennas do not interfere with one another, thanks to MIMO's use of *spatial multiplexing*, which encodes data based on the antenna from which the data will be transmitted. Both reliability and throughput are increased by MIMO's simultaneous use of multiple antennas.

Yet another technology implemented by 802.11n is *channel bonding*. With channel bonding, two *wireless bands* are logically bonded together, forming a band with twice the bandwidth of an individual band. Some literature refers to channel bonding as *40MHz mode*, which is the bonding of two adjacent 20MHz bands into a 40MHz band.

The 802.11n High Throughput (HT) standard defines modes for ensuring that older a/b/g devices and newer 802.11n devices avoid collisions with each other.

NOTE The IEEE finally accepted the fact that using the standard identification codes for describing wireless to nontechnical end users makes no sense, and it is now using simpler names for recent standards. For example, 802.11n is called WiFi 4, 802.11ac is WiFi 5, and 802.11ax is WiFi 6.

802.11ac (WiFi 5)

802.11ac is a 5GHz standard that uses more simultaneous streams than 802.11n and features *multi-user MIMO (MU-MIMO)*. A single 80MHz stream supports 433Mbps.

802.11ax (WiFi 6)

802.11ax (WiFi 6) is up to 30% faster than WiFi 5 (802.11ac), but even more exciting are its lower latency, more simultaneously deliverable data, and improved power efficiency. WiFi 6 is the first iteration of 802.11 to include OFDMA (which is an improvement on OFDM). OFDMA can transmit data to multiple devices at the same time. It does so by splitting traffic into smaller packets to eliminate queueing. Also, WiFi 6 adds MU-MIMO capabilities to upstream connections. The net effect of this is to allow more devices on one network at the same time.

802.11x Standard Summary

Table 12-3 provides a reference to help you contrast the characteristics of the 802.11 standards.

Key Topic

Table 12-3 Characteristics of 802.11 Standards

Standard	Band	Maximum Bandwidth	Transmission Method	Maximum Range
802.11	2.4GHz	1Mbps or 2Mbps	DSSS or FHSS	20 m indoors/100 m outdoors
802.11a	5GHz	54Mbps	OFDM	35 m indoors/120 m outdoors
802.11b	2.4GHz	11Mbps	DSSS	32 m indoors/140 m outdoors
802.11g	2.4GHz	54Mbps	OFDM or DSSS	32 m indoors/140 m outdoors
802.11n	2.4GHz or 5GHz (or both)	> 300Mbps (with channel bonding)	OFDM	70 m indoors/250 m outdoors
802.11ac	5GHz	> 3Gbps (with MU-MIMO and several antennas)	OFDM	70 m indoors/250 m outdoors
802.11ax	2.4GHz, 5GHz, 6GHz	9.6 Gbps	OFDMA	70 m indoors/250 m outdoors

Others forms of wireless technologies are in a group termed *cellular* because the technology is used on cell phones (among other mobile devices). Some cellular phone technologies, such as ***Long-Term Evolution (LTE)***, which supports a 100Mbps data rate for mobile devices and a 1Gbps data rate for stationary devices, can be used to connect a mobile device such as a smartphone to the Internet.

Other technologies for cellular phones include the older 2G (Edge), which offers slow data rates. 2G was improved upon with *3G*, in addition to the newer *4G*, *5G*, LTE, and Evolved High-Speed Packet Access (HSPA+).

Tethering allows a smartphone's data connection to be used by another device, such as a laptop. Also, mobile hotspots are growing in popularity because these devices connect to a cell phone company's data network and make that data network available to nearby devices (typically, a maximum of five devices) via wireless networking technologies. For example, multiple passengers in a car can share a mobile hotspot and have Internet connectivity from their laptops or tablets while riding down the road.

Code-division multiple access (CDMA) and *Global System for Mobile Communications (GSM)* are the two major radio systems used in cell phones. GSM uses time-division multiple access (TDMA) in its operation.

Deploying Wireless LANs

A variety of installation options and design considerations are involved in designing and deploying WLANs. This section delves into the available options and provides you with some best practice recommendations.

Types of WLANs

WLANs can be categorized based on their use of wireless APs. The three main categories are *independent basic service set (IBSS or ad hoc)*, *basic service set (BSS)*, and *extended service set (ESS)*. An IBSS WLAN operates in an ad hoc fashion, whereas BSS and ESS WLANs operate in infrastructure mode. The following sections describe these three types of WLANs in detail.

IBSS

As shown in Figure 12-6, a WLAN can be created without the use of an AP. Such a configuration, called an IBSS, is said to work in an ad hoc fashion. An ad hoc WLAN is useful for temporary connections between wireless devices. For example, you might temporarily interconnect two laptop computers to transfer a few files.

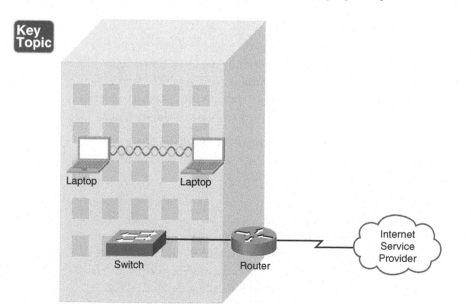

FIGURE 12-6   Independent Basic Service Set (IBSS) WLAN

BSS

Figure 12-7 depicts a WLAN using a single AP. A WLAN that has just one AP is called a BSS WLAN. BSS WLANs are said to run in *infrastructure mode* because wireless clients connect to an AP, which is typically connected to a wired network infrastructure. BSS networks are often used in residential and SOHO locations, where the signal strength provided by a single AP is sufficient to service all the WLAN's wireless clients.

Key Topic

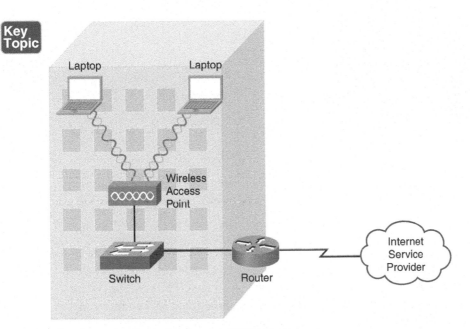

FIGURE 12-7   Basic Service Set (BSS) WLAN

ESS

Figure 12-8 illustrates a WLAN using two APs. A WLAN containing more than one AP is called an *ESS WLAN*. Like BSS WLANs, ESS WLANs operate in infrastructure mode. When you have more than one AP, it is important to prevent one AP from interfering with another. Specifically, the previously discussed nonoverlapping channels (channels 1, 6, and 11 for the 2.4GHz band) should be selected for adjacent wireless coverage areas.

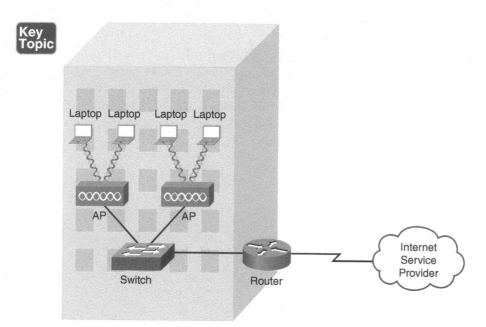

FIGURE 12-8   Extended Service Set (ESS) WLAN

Mesh Topology

A mesh wireless network is a collection of wireless devices that may not use central-ized control (but instead features decentralized management). The combined wire-less coverage range defines the range of the network. This could also be referred to as a *mesh cloud*. Additional wireless technologies (besides WiFi) could be used to build a mesh wireless topology. This type of network could be used for hosts to communicate with other devices in the mesh, or the network could provide a gate-way to the Internet or other networks.

Sources of Interference

A major issue for WLANs is radio frequency interference (RFI) caused by other devices using frequencies similar to those of the WLAN devices. Also, physical obstacles can impede or reflect WLAN transmissions. The following are some of the most common sources of interference:

- **Other WLAN devices:** Earlier in this chapter, you read about nonoverlap-ping channels for both the 2.4GHz and 5GHz bands. If two or more WLAN devices are in close proximity and use overlapping channels, those devices could interfere with one another.

- **Cordless phones:** Several models of cordless phones operate in the 2.4GHz band and can interfere with WLAN devices. However, if you need cordless phones to coexist in an environment with WLAN devices using the 2.4GHz band, consider the use of Digital Enhanced Cordless Telecommunications (DECT) cordless phones. Although the exact frequencies used by DECT cordless phones vary based on country, DECT cordless phones do not use the 2.4GHz band. For example, in the United States, DECT cordless phones use frequencies in the range 1.92GHz–1.93GHz.

- **Microwave ovens:** Older microwave ovens, which might not have sufficient shielding, can emit relatively high-powered signals in the 2.4GHz band, resulting in significant interference with WLAN devices operating in the 2.4GHz band.

- **Wireless security system devices:** Most wireless security cameras operate in the 2.4GHz frequency range, which can cause potential issues with WLAN devices.

- **Physical obstacles:** In electromagnetic theory, radio waves cannot propagate through a perfect conductor. So, although metal filing cabinets and large appliances are not perfect conductors, they are sufficient to cause degradation of a WLAN signal. For example, a WLAN signal might hit a large air conditioning unit, causing the radio waves to be reflected and scattered in multiple directions. Not only does this limit the range of the WLAN signal, but radio waves carrying data might travel over different paths. This *multipath issue* can cause data corruption. Concrete walls, metal studs, and even window film can reduce the quality of the wireless network signals.

- **Signal strength:** The range of a WLAN device is a function of the device's signal strength. Lower-cost consumer-grade APs do not typically allow administrative adjustment of signal strength. However, enterprise-class APs often allow signal strength to be adjusted to ensure sufficient coverage of a specific area, while avoiding interference with other APs using the same channel.

As you can see from this list, most RFI occurs in the 2.4GHz band rather than the 5GHz band. Therefore, depending on the wireless clients you need to support, you might consider using the 5GHz band, which is an option with the newer wireless standards. With the increased use of wireless, both coverage and capacity-based planning should be done to provide acceptable goodput. *Goodput* refers to the number of useful information bits that the network can deliver (not including overhead for the protocols being used). Another factor is the density (that is, the ratio of users to APs), which, if too high, could harm performance of the network. Areas expecting high density include classrooms, hotels, and hospitals. Device or bandwidth saturation could impact performance.

Wireless AP Placement

A WLAN using more than one AP (that is, an ESS WLAN) requires careful planning to prevent the APs from interfering with one another while still servicing a desired coverage area. Specifically, an overlap of coverage between APs should exist to allow uninterrupted *roaming* from one WLAN *cell* (which is the coverage area provided by an AP) to another. However, those overlapping coverage areas should not use overlapping frequencies.

Figure 12-9 shows how nonoverlapping channels in the 2.4GHz band can have overlapping coverage areas to provide seamless roaming between AP coverage areas. A common WLAN design recommendation is to have 10% to 15% overlap of coverage between adjoining cells.

Key Topic

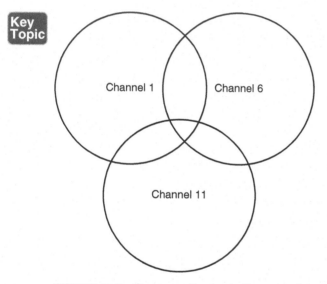

Channel 1   Channel 6

Channel 11

FIGURE 12-9   Coverage Overlap in Coverage Areas for Nonoverlapping Channels

If a WLAN has more than three APs, the APs are deployed in a honeycomb fashion to allow an overlap of AP coverage areas while avoiding an overlap of identical channels. The example in Figure 12-10 shows an approach to channel selection for adjoining cells in the 2.4GHz band. Notice that cells using the same nonoverlapping channels (channels 1, 6, and 11) are separated by another cell. For example, notice that none of the cells using channel 11 overlap another cell using channel 11.

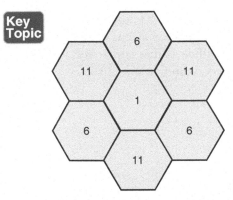

FIGURE 12-10   Nonoverlapping Coverage Cells for the 2.4GHz Band

NOTE   Although a honeycomb channel assignment scheme can be used for the 5GHz band, identical channels should be separated by at least two cells rather than by a single cell, as shown in Figure 12-10 for the 2.4GHz band.

Securing Wireless LANs

WLANs introduce some unique concerns to a network. For example, improperly installing wireless APs is roughly equivalent to putting an Ethernet port in a building's parking lot, where someone can drive up and access your network. Fortunately, various features are available to harden the security of your WLAN, as discussed in this section.

Security Issues

In the days when dial-up modems were popular, malicious users could run a program on a computer to call all phone numbers in a certain number range. Phone numbers that answered with modem tone became targets for later attacks. This type of reconnaissance was known as *war dialing*. A modern-day variant of war dialing is *war driving*, where potentially malicious users drive around looking for unsecured WLANs. These users might be identifying unsecured WLANs for nefarious purposes or simply looking for free Internet access. Devices such as cell phones, laptops, tablets, and gaming and media devices could act as wireless clients as well as be used in a wireless attack because they have potential WiFi access to the network.

Other WLAN security threats include the following:

■ **War chalking:** Once an open WLAN (that is, a WLAN whose SSID and authentication credentials are known) is found in a public place, a user might write a symbol on a wall (or some other nearby structure) to let others know the characteristics of the discovered network. This practice, which is a variant of the decades-old practice of hobos leaving symbols as messages to fellow hobos, is called *war chalking*. Figure 12-11 shows common war-chalking symbols.

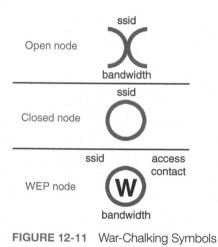

FIGURE 12-11   War-Chalking Symbols

> **NOTE**   Just as technologies evolve, so do computer criminals. War flying features the use of mobile devices in conjunction with drones or other aircraft to find wireless networks.

- **WEP and WPA security cracking:** As discussed later in this chapter, various security standards are available for encrypting and authenticating a WLAN client with an AP. Two of the less secure standards are Wired Equivalent Privacy (WEP) and *WiFi Protected Access (WPA)*. Although WPA is considered more secure than WEP, utilities are available on the Internet for cracking each of these approaches to wireless security. By collecting enough packets transmitted by a secure AP, these cracking utilities can use mathematical algorithms to determine the preshared key (PSK) configured on a wireless AP with which an associating wireless client must also be configured.

- **Rogue access point:** A malicious user may set up an AP called a *rogue access point* to which legitimate users can connect. The malicious user might then use a packet sniffer (which displays information about unencrypted traffic, including the traffic's data and header information) to eavesdrop on communications flowing through the rogue AP. To cause unsuspecting users to connect to the rogue AP, the malicious user could configure the AP with the same *service set identifier (SSID)* used by a legitimate AP. When a rogue AP is configured with the SSID of a legitimate AP, the rogue AP is commonly referred to as an *evil twin*.

NOTE   An SSID is a string of characters identifying a WLAN. APs participating in the same WLAN (that is, in an ESS) can be configured with identical SSIDs. An SSID shared among multiple APs is called an *extended service set identifier* (*ESSID*).

Approaches to WLAN Security

A WLAN that does not require authentication or provide encryption for wireless devices (for example, a publicly available WLAN, such as the ones in many airports) is said to be using *open authentication*. To protect such a WLAN's traffic from eavesdroppers, a variety of security standards and practices have been developed, including the following:

- **MAC address filtering:** An AP can be configured with a list of MAC addresses that are permitted to associate with the AP. If a malicious user attempts to connect via a laptop whose MAC address is not on the list of trusted MAC addresses, that user is denied access. One drawback to MAC address filtering is the administrative overhead required to keep an approved list of MAC addresses up to date. Another issue with MAC address filtering is that a knowledgeable user could falsify the MAC address of a wireless network card, making a device appear to be approved.

- **Disabling SSID broadcast:** An SSID can be broadcast by an AP to let users know the name of the WLAN. For security purposes, an AP might be configured not to broadcast its SSID. However, knowledgeable users could still determine the SSID of an AP by examining captured packets.

- **Preshared key:** To encrypt transmission between a wireless client and an AP (in addition to authenticating a wireless client with an AP), both the wireless client and the AP could be preconfigured with a matching string of characters (a PSK, as previously described). The PSK could be used as part of a mathematical algorithm to encrypt traffic, such that if an eavesdropper intercepted the encrypted traffic, they would not be able to decrypt the traffic without knowing the PSK. Although using a PSK can be effective in providing security for a small network (such as a SOHO network), it lacks scalability. For example, in a large corporate environment, the compromise of a PSK would necessitate the reconfiguration of all devices configured with that PSK. WLAN security based on PSK technology is called *Personal mode*.

NOTE The latest WPA security approach (WPA3) running in Personal mode replaces the PSK approach with a more secure method of authentication called Simultaneous Authentication of Equals (SAE).

- **IEEE 802.1X:** Rather than having all devices in a WLAN configured with the same PSK, a more scalable approach is to require all wireless users to authenticate using their own credentials (for example, a username and password). Allowing users to have their own credentials prevents the compromising of one password from impacting the configuration of all wireless devices. IEEE 802.1X is a technology that allows wireless clients to authenticate with an authentication server—typically, a Remote Authentication Dial-In User Service (RADIUS) server. Figure 12-12 shows a wireless implementation of IEEE 802.1X.

NOTE WLAN security based on IEEE 802.1X and a centralized authentication server such as RADIUS is called *Enterprise mode*.

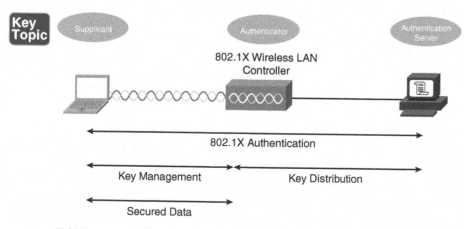

FIGURE 12-12   IEEE 802.1X Security for a WLAN

NOTE   IEEE 802.1X works in conjunction with Extensible Authentication Protocol (EAP) to perform its job of authentication. A variety of EAP types exist, including Lightweight Extensible Authentication Protocol (LEAP), EAP-Flexible Authentication via Secure Tunneling (EAP-FAST), EAP-Transport Layer Security (EAP-TLS), EAP-Tunneled Transport Layer Security (EAP-TTLS), Protected EAP–Generic Token Card (PEAP-GTC), and Protected EAP–Microsoft Challenge Handshake Authentication Protocol Version 2 (PEAP-MSCHAPv2). Although these EAP types differ in their procedures, the overriding goal for all the EAP types is to securely authenticate a supplicant and provide the supplicant and the authenticator a session key that can be used during a single session in the calculation of security algorithms (for example, encryption algorithms).

Security Standards

Key Topic

When you're configuring a wireless client for security, the most common security standards from which you can select are as follows:

- Wired Equivalent Privacy (WEP)

- WiFi Protected Access (WPA)

- WiFi Protected Access Version 2 (WPA2)

NOTE   While it is not widely implemented at the time of this writing, remember that WPA3 technology is now available and makes further improvements in WLAN security.

The sections that follow describe these standards in detail.

WEP

The original 802.11 standard addresses security; however, the security is a WEP key. With WEP, an AP is configured with a static WEP key. Wireless clients that need to associate with an AP are configured with an identical key (making this a PSK approach to security). The 802.11 standard specifies a 40-bit WEP key, which is considered to be a relatively weak security measure.

Because a WEP key is a static string of characters, it could be compromised with a brute-force attack, in which an attacker attempts all possible character combinations until a match for the WEP key is found. Another concern, however, is that WEP uses RC4 as its encryption algorithm.

NOTE   RC4 (which stands for "Ron's Code" or "Rivest Cipher" because it was developed by Ron Rivest of RSA Security) is sometimes pronounced *arc four*.

RC4 uses a 24-bit initialization vector (IV), which is a string of characters added to the transmitted data, such that the same plaintext data frame will never appear as the same WEP-encrypted data frame. However, the IV is transmitted in plaintext. So, because a malicious user can see the IV in plaintext, if they use packet-capture software and capture enough packets having the same WEP key, they can use a mathematical algorithm to determine the static WEP key (which can be performed with WEP-cracking software available on the Internet).

Some WEP implementations support the use of a longer WEP key (for example, 128 bits instead of 40 bits), making a WEP key more difficult to crack; however, both the wireless clients and their AP must support the longer WEP key.

WPA

The WiFi Alliance, a nonprofit organization formed to certify interoperability of wireless devices, developed its own security standard, WPA, to address the weaknesses of WEP. Here are some of the security enhancements offered by WPA:

- WPA operating in Enterprise mode can require a user to be authenticated before keys are exchanged.

- In Enterprise mode, the keys used between a wireless client and an access point are temporary session keys.

- WPA uses *Temporal Key Integrity Protocol (TKIP)* for enhanced encryption. Although TKIP does rely on an IV, the IV is expanded from WEP's 24-bit IV to a 48-bit IV. Also, broadcast key rotation can be used, which causes a key to change so quickly that an eavesdropper would not have time to exploit a derived key. TKIP uses RC4 for the encryption algorithm, and the CompTIA Network+ exam may reference TKIP-RC4 in a discussion of wireless.

- TKIP leverages Message Integrity Check (MIC), which is sometimes referred to as *Message Integrity Code*, to confirm that data has not been modified in transit.

NOTE   Although the term *WPA* is not typically written as WPA1, when you see it, consider it to be WPA Version 1 (WPA1). WPA Version 2, however, is written as *WPA2*.

WPA2

The IEEE 802.11i standard, which was approved in 2004, requires stronger algorithms for encryption and integrity checking than those used with previous WLAN security protocols, such as WEP and WPA. The requirements set forth in the IEEE 802.11i standard are implemented in the WiFi Alliance's WPA Version 2 (*WPA2*) security standard. WPA2 uses Counter Mode with Cipher Block Chaining Message Authentication Code Protocol (CCMP) for integrity checking and *Advanced Encryption Standard (AES)* for encryption. On the Network+ exam, you might find this referenced as simply CCMP-AES. WPA2 that uses a centralized server for authenticating users is referred to as *WPA2 Enterprise* mode. An implementation of WPA2 that uses a configured password or PSK instead of a centralized server is referred to as *WPA2 Personal* mode.

Additional Wireless Options

Other wireless technologies, such as Bluetooth, infrared (IR), and Near Field Communication (NFC), which are often integrated into smartphones, can also provide connectivity for a personal area network (PAN) or other short-range networking applications. Many of these technologies help facilitate the Internet of Things (IoT).

Another interesting wireless technology is *geofencing*, which often uses the Global Positioning System (GPS) or radio frequency identification (RFID) to define geographic boundaries. Geofencing allows you to define triggers so that when a device enters (or exits) the boundaries defined by the administrator, an alert is issued.

Geofence virtual barriers can be active or passive. Active geofences require an end user to opt in to location services and require a mobile app to be open. Passive geofences are always on; they rely on WiFi and/or cellular data instead of GPS or RFID and can work in the background.

A practical application of geofencing might be a hospital with patient information on tablets that the hospital distributes to staff. If these tablets travel beyond the geofence, an administrative alert can trigger.

Real-World Case Study

Acme, Inc. hired an outside contractor that specializes in WiFi. The consultants came in and did a needs assessment and performed a wireless site survey. Recommendations were then made about the need for 15 access points in the headquarters office spaces and 3 access points at each of the remote branch offices. Three wireless LAN controllers, one for each office, will be used to manage the respective access points. The management of the access points through the wireless LAN controllers will be done primarily through the headquarters office, using the WAN that is connecting the branch offices to the headquarters office.

Because of the high number of other WiFi access points being used in the same building as the headquarters office, Acme, Inc. decided to use the 5GHz range (because of the reduced competition in that space) and to use 802.11ac.

For security, Acme, Inc. will use WPA2 in conjunction with a RADIUS server. Acme, Inc. will use Enterprise mode for authentication of each user before allowing users access on the wireless network(s). The RADIUS server is integrated with Microsoft Active Directory so that Acme, Inc. will not have to re-create every user account; the RADIUS server can check with the Active Directory server to verify user credentials and passwords.

Separate SSIDs were set up that map to the various VLANs and departments currently on the wired network. Also, a separate SSID was set up as a wireless guest network that has limited access but does provide Internet access for guest users.

Once all this was in place, a site survey was done again to verify the signal strengths and to identify any interference related to the wireless implementation. A heat map was provided to visually represent the signal strengths in the coverage areas in the respective office spaces.

Summary

Here are the main topics covered in this chapter:

- This chapter identifies various components, technologies, and terms used in WLANs.

- This chapter presents WLAN design considerations, such as the selection of WLAN standards, bands, and nonoverlapping channels. Potential sources of interference are also discussed.

- This chapter describes some of the security risks posed by a WLAN and the technologies available for mitigating those risks.

Exam Preparation Tasks

Review All the Key Topics

Review the most important topics from this chapter, noted with the Key Topic icon in the outer margin of the page. Table 12-4 lists these key topics and the page number where each is found.

Key Topic

Table 12-4 Key Topics for Chapter 12

Key Topic Element	Description	Page Number
Figure 12-1	Basic WLAN topology with a wireless router	323
Figure 12-2	Basic WLAN topology with a wireless access point	324
List	Antenna selection criteria	324
Figure 12-3	Omnidirectional antenna coverage	326
Figure 12-4	Unidirectional antenna coverage	326
Figure 12-5	Nonoverlapping channels in the 2.4GHz band	328
List	Spread-spectrum transmission methods	330
Table 12-3	Characteristics of 802.11 standards	333
Figure 12-6	Independent basic service set (IBSS) WLAN	334
Figure 12-7	Basic service set (BSS) WLAN	335
Figure 12-8	Extended service set (ESS) WLAN	336
List	Sources of interference	336
Figure 12-9	Coverage overlap in coverage areas for nonoverlapping channels	338
Figure 12-10	Nonoverlapping coverage cells for the 2.4GHz band	339
List	Wireless security threats	339
Figure 12-12	IEEE 802.1X security for a WLAN	342
List	Security standards and best practices	343

Complete Tables and Lists from Memory

Print a copy of Appendix C, "Memory Tables," or at least the section for this chapter and complete as many of the tables as possible from memory. Appendix D, "Memory Tables Answer Key," includes the completed tables and lists so you can check your work.

Define Key Terms

Define the following key terms from this chapter and check your answers in the Glossary:

802.11a, 802.11b, 802.11g, 802.11n, 802.11ac, 802.11ax, wireless band, wireless channel, channel bonding, service set identifier (SSID), basic service set (BSS), extended service set (ESS), independent basic service set (IBSS or ad hoc), roaming, omnidirectional antenna, unidirectional antenna, WiFi Protected Access (WPA), WPA2 Personal, Advanced Encryption Standard (AES), Temporal Key Integrity Protocol (TKIP), WPA2 Enterprise, code-division multiple access (CDMA), Global System for Mobile Communications (GSM), Long-Term Evolution (LTE), 3G, 4G, 5G, multiple input, multiple output (MIMO), multi-user MIMO (MU-MIMO)

Complete Chapter 12 Hands-On Labs in Network+ Simulator Lite

- Wireless Security Terminology
- Switching Terminology

Additional Resources

WiFi Standards: https://youtu.be/q64AZjPfa0Y

Fundamentals of WiFi 6: https://www.youtube.com/watch?v=V5qLv0BtBcM

Review Questions

The answers to these review questions are in Appendix A, "Answers to Review Questions."

1. What type of antenna, used in wireless APs and wireless routers in SOHO locations, radiates power equally in all directions?

   a. Unidirectional

   b. Yagi

   c. Parabolic

   d. Omnidirectional

2. When you're using the 2.4GHz band for multiple access points in a WLAN in the United States, which nonoverlapping channels should you select? (Choose three.)

   a. 0

   b. 1

   c. 5

    d. 6

    e. 10

    f. 11

    g. 14

3. What technology do WiFi devices use to decide when they gain access to the wireless media?

    a. SPF

    b. CSMA/CA

    c. RSTP

    d. DUAL

4. Which IEEE 802.11 variant supports a maximum speed of 54Mbps and uses the 2.4GHz band?

    a. 802.11a

    b. 802.11b

    c. 802.11g

    d. 802.11n

5. Which of the following does IEEE 802.11n use to achieve high throughput using multiple antennas for transmission and reception?

    a. MIMO

    b. DSSS

    c. FHSS

    d. LACP

6. A WLAN formed directly between wireless clients (without the use of a wireless AP) is referred to as what type of WLAN?

    a. Enterprise mode

    b. IBSS

    c. Personal mode

    d. BSS

7. When extending the range for a 2.4GHz WLAN, you can use nonoverlapping channels for adjacent coverage cells. However, there should be some overlap in coverage between those cells (using nonoverlapping channels) to prevent a connection from dropping as a user roams from one coverage cell to another. What percentage of coverage overlap is recommended for these adjacent cells?

   a. 5% to 10%

   b. 10% to 15%

   c. 15% to 20%

   d. 20% to 25%

8. If a WLAN does not need a user to provide credentials to associate with a wireless AP and access the WLAN, what type of authentication is in use?

   a. WEP

   b. SSID

   c. Open

   d. IV

9. WEP's RC4 approach to encryption uses a 24-bit string of characters added to transmitted data, such that the same plaintext data frame will never appear as the same WEP-encrypted data frame. What is this string of characters called?

   a. Initialization vector

   b. Chips

   c. Orthogonal descriptor

   d. Session key

10. Which standard developed by the WiFi Alliance implements the requirements of IEEE 802.11i?

   a. TKIP

   b. MIC

   c. WEP

   d. WPA2

11. Which security technique uses wireless technologies to create an invisible boundary around some point?

   a. WPA3

   b. LTE

   c. War driving

   d. Geofencing

This chapter covers the following topics related to Objective 3.1 (Given a scenario, use the appropriate statistics and sensors to ensure network availability) of the CompTIA Network+ N10-008 certification exam:

- Performance metrics/sensors
  - Device/chassis
    - Temperature
    - Central processing unit (CPU) usage
    - Memory
  - Network metrics
    - Bandwidth
    - Latency
    - Jitter
- SNMP
  - Traps
  - Object identifiers (OIDs)
  - Management information bases (MIBs)
- Network device logs
  - Log reviews
    - Traffic logs
    - Audit logs
    - Syslog
  - Logging levels/severity levels

- Interface statistics/status
  - Link state (up/down)
  - Speed/duplex
  - Send/receive traffic
  - Cyclic redundancy checks (CRCs)
  - Protocol packet and byte counts
- Interface errors or alerts
  - CRC errors
  - Giants
  - Runts
  - Encapsulation errors
- Environmental factors and sensors
  - Temperature
  - Humidity
  - Electrical
  - Flooding
- Baselines
- NetFlow data
- Uptime/downtime

CHAPTER 13

Ensure Network Availability

No one would argue with the statement that networks today are more critical than ever before for organizations. Fortunately, many tools and techniques are available to help us ensure that our networks are performing as we need them to and staying that way for as long as possible.

In this chapter you will learn about many metrics and statistics you can call upon to gauge the health of your network. These include simple metrics that indicate problems in the network as well as sophisticated logs that can be powerful sources of network operational information.

It is imperative to engage in careful and continuous network monitoring to create resources and reports that provide valuable information. For example, the primary network management protocol used by network management systems (NMSs) is Simple Network Management Protocol (SNMP), and this chapter discusses the various versions of SNMP. In addition, syslog servers and a variety of reports are considered.

Foundation Topics

Monitoring Tools

For several decades, Simple Network Management Protocol (SNMP)–based software packages dominated in the enterprise monitoring space. Fortunately, SNMP evolved over several versions to include security enhancements. Even with these advancements, as you'll learn later in this chapter, there are other methods and technologies to consider when it comes to monitoring a network. This section discusses some key performance metrics and sensors that you need to monitor.

Performance Metrics/Sensors

As networks have become more and more important to the organizations that host them, metrics have increasingly become available to carefully monitor and assess the health of network components. In fact, you need to be careful not to overwhelm yourself by trying to monitor too many metrics for your devices.

The following are some key metrics that help you monitor a device and the device's chassis:

- **Temperature:** Network equipment vendors make it very clear what temperature range is supported for inside the device chassis. Of course, you will not want the temperature to exceed or go too far below this recommended range. You might run into temperature problems, for example, if your network equipment was not installed following best practices and there is not adequate distance between a device and other objects. These other objects might be blocking air flow to the network device. Maybe the warm air that is supposed to be being pushed out of the chassis is getting caught and trapped inside the chassis. Sensors can provide metrics regarding the temperature inside network devices to help you pinpoint such issues. Later in this chapter, you will learn about tools called *environmental monitors* that are specialized for monitoring things like temperature, humidity, and more.

- **Central processing unit (CPU) usage:** The CPU is the "brains" of a computer, often navigating the tricky waters of the control plane processing requirements for you. It is very important to monitor CPU utilization consistently over the life of a network device. Doing so can help you identify network attacks and the busy times for network devices where performance is actually suffering. In addition, monitoring the CPU can help you see when components are beginning to fail and causing high CPU utilization.

- **Memory:** To improve the performance of network devices, data is taken from nonvolatile storage and placed in (much faster) volatile memory. Of course, you need to make sure you have enough memory available for this at all times. Monitoring the various memory metrics can help you track down lots of current and potential performance issues.

As you can imagine, it is important to carefully monitor these metrics for a network device and its chassis. In addition, you should also carefully monitor the network itself. The following are some of the basic metrics for monitoring a network:

- *Bandwidth:* The "plumbing" of your network is the connections between the devices. Remember that these connections might be physical media that you can see, and they might also be wireless media that you cannot see. Carefully measuring the bandwidth available and bandwidth consumed by specific applications or traffic forms is imperative. Watch out for bottlenecks in the network design, which often occur when a network designer fails to consider the aggregate bandwidth required. For example, say that you have 100 10Gbps ports, and you need to plan for busy times when those 100 really fast ports all have lots of data they want to send. You might require multiple 40Gbps connections upstream to handle the aggregate bandwidth needs.

- *Latency:* Latency (that is, delay) is a fact of life. When a network device sends packets, there will be serialization delay, propagation delay, processing delay, and probably even more types of delay. You need to take baseline measurements so you can understand the latency in your network. You should also pay attention to the requirements for certain technologies. For example, perhaps your organization wants to engage with the latest Cisco collaboration solutions, including voice and video over IP. Cisco will give you documentation on just the latency that the solutions can handle. Cisco might say something like, "For this solution to perform well, you must not exceed 120 ms of delay consistently over time." It is important to gather data on such metrics before you even consider rolling out a solution.

- *Jitter:* Jitter is what happens when you drink too much coffee, and it also refers to large variations in latency. Jitter is especially problematic for VoIP traffic. If the latency in a network is not predictable and fairly steady, it can be very difficult for VoIP quality to remain steady and satisfactory.

> **NOTE**   For all of the major metric categories, you should ensure that you perform baselining and properly store the results for future analytics. A *baseline* provides a look at the metrics and their values during "normal" operation. If your network tends to run at 45% capacity, then you would want to watch for this level of usage and then start capturing your metric information to create a baseline. This is incredibly important. Think about it: If you do not know what the metrics measure when everything is fast and brilliant and performing just as you need it to, how are you going to be able to identify when things are starting to go badly? Always keep baselines of metric data for your enterprise.

SNMP

The first Request for Comments (RFC) for *Simple Network Management Protocol (SNMP)* came out in 1988. Since then, SNMP has become the de facto standard for network management protocols. The original intent for SNMP was to manage network nodes, such as network servers, routers, and switches. SNMP Version 1 (SNMPv1) and SNMP Version 2c (SNMPv2c) specify three major components of an SNMP solution, as detailed in Table 13-1.

Key Topic

Table 13-1   Components of an SNMPv1 and SNMPv2c Network Management Solution

Component	Description
SNMP manager	An SNMP manager runs a network management application. This SNMP manager is sometimes referred to as a *network management system (NMS)*.
SNMP agent	An SNMP agent is a piece of software that runs on a managed device (for example, a server, router, or switch).
Management Information Base (MIB)	Information about a managed device's resources and activity is defined by a series of objects. The structure of these management objects is defined by a managed device's MIB. Interfaces and their details—such as errors, utilization, discards, packet drops, resets, speed and duplex, system memory, utilization of bandwidth, storage, CPU, and memory—can be monitored and reported via SNMP.

As illustrated in Figure 13-1, an SNMP manager (an NMS) can send information to, receive request information from, or receive unsolicited information from a managed device (a managed router, in this example). The managed device runs an SNMP agent and contains the MIB.

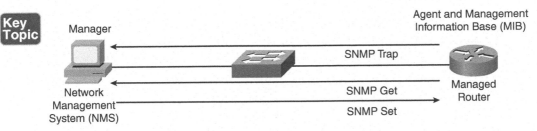

FIGURE 13-1   SNMPv1 and SNMPv2c Network Management Components and Messages

Clearly, the MIB is a critical component in the functionality of SNMP. It is a hierarchical collection of MIB variables that stores the data that SNMP relies on. But how are these MIB variables identified? This is done using a unique *object identifier (OID)* for each variable. The OIDs are organized in a hierarchical tree-like structure. SNMP is very efficient at scanning this tree and extracting the exact OIDs and values of these variables that are needed to monitor or even reconfigure a network device.

Multiple SNMP messages might be sent between an SNMP manager and a managed device, and there are three broad categories of SNMP message types:

- **Get:** An SNMP get message retrieves information from a managed device.

- **Set:** An SNMP set message sets a variable in a managed device or triggers an action on a managed device.

- *Trap*: An SNMP trap message is an unsolicited message sent from a managed device to an SNMP manager, which can notify the SNMP manager about a significant event that occurred on the managed device.

SNMP management software can make requests for each of the MIB objects from an SNMP agent. This can be referred to as an SNMP *walk* because the management software is logically "walking" the entire MIB (also often called the *tree*) to gather information from the agent. SNMP offers security against malicious users attempting to collect information from a managed device, change the configuration of a managed device, or intercept information being sent to an NMS. However, the security integrated with SNMPv1 and SNMPv2c is considered weak. Specifically, SNMPv1 and SNMPv2c use *community strings* to gain read-only access or read/write access to a managed device. You can think of a community string as a password. Also, be aware that multiple SNMP-compliant devices on the market today have the read-only community string set to *public* by default and have the read/write community string set to *private* by default. As a result, if such devices are left at their default SNMP settings, they could be compromised.

> **NOTE**   Notice that this section refers to SNMPv2c as opposed to SNMPv2. SNMPv2 contained security enhancements as well as other performance enhancements. However, few network administrators adopted SNMPv2 because of the complexity of the newly proposed security system. Instead, Community-Based Simple Network Management Protocol (SNMPv2c) gained widespread acceptance because it included the performance enhancements of SNMPv2 without using SNMPv2's complex security solution. Instead, SNMPv2c kept the SNMPv1 concept of community strings.

Fortunately, the security weaknesses of SNMPv1 and SNMPv2c are addressed in SNMPv3. To better understand these security enhancements, consider the concept of a security model and a security level:

- **Security model:** Defines an approach for user and group authentication (for example, SNMPv1, SNMPv2c, and SNMPv3).

- **Security level:** Defines the type of security algorithm performed on SNMP packets. The following are the three security levels discussed here:

  - **noAuthNoPriv:** The noAuthNoPriv (no authorization, no privacy) security level uses community strings for authorization and does not use encryption to provide privacy.

  - **authNoPriv:** The authNoPriv (authorization, no privacy) security level provides authorization using Hashed Message Authentication Code (HMAC) with Message Digest 5 (MD5) or Secure Hash Algorithm (SHA). However, no encryption is used.

  - **authPriv:** The authPriv (authorization, privacy) security level offers HMAC MD5 or SHA authentication and provides privacy through encryption. Specifically, the encryption uses the Cipher Block Chaining (CBC) Data Encryption Standard (DES) (DES-56) algorithm.

> **NOTE**   The security protocols originally featured in SNMPv3 are still considered strong enough for today's networks. Since then, additions to SNMPv3 have made it even more secure. These additions enable high-security environments to call on the latest and strongest security mechanisms for key functions, such as encryption, and feature protocols such as AES.

As summarized in Table 13-2, SNMPv3 supports all three security levels, and SNMPv1 and SNMPv2c support only the noAuthNoPriv security level.

Table 13-2 Security Models and Security Levels

Security Model	Security Level	Authentication Strategy	Encryption Type
SNMPv1	noAuthNoPriv	Community string	None
SNMPv2c	noAuthNoPriv	Community string	None
SNMPv3	noAuthNoPriv	Username	None
SNMPv3	authNoPriv	MD5 or SHA	None
SNMPv3	authPriv	MD5 or SHA	CBC-DES (DES-56)

Through the use of security algorithms, as shown in Table 13-2, SNMPv3 dramatically increases the security of network management traffic. Specifically, SNMPv3 offers three primary security enhancements over SNMPv1 and SNMPv2c:

- **Integrity:** Using hashing algorithms, SNMPv3 ensures that an SNMP message was not modified in transit.

- **Authentication:** Hashing allows SNMPv3 to validate the source of an SNMP message.

- **Encryption:** Using the CBC-DES (DES-56) encryption algorithm, SNMPv3 provides privacy for SNMP messages, making them unreadable by an attacker who might capture an SNMP packet.

In addition to its security enhancements, SNMPv3 differs architecturally from SNMPv1 and SNMPv2c. SNMPv3 defines SNMP entities, which are groupings of individual SNMP components. As shown in Figure 13-2, SNMP applications and an SNMP manager combine into an NMS SNMP entity, whereas an SNMP agent and an MIB combine into a managed node SNMP entity.

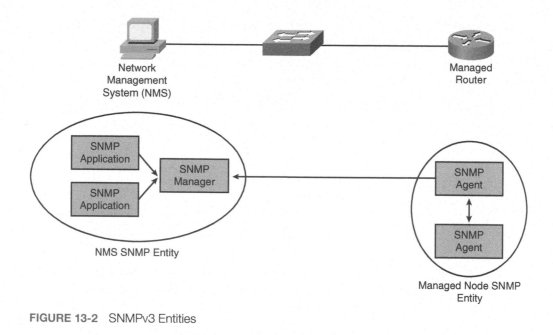

FIGURE 13-2 SNMPv3 Entities

Additional Monitoring Topics

Network administrators routinely monitor network resources and review reports to be proactive in their administration. For example, a potential network issue might be averted by spotting a trend such as increasing router CPU utilization or increasing bandwidth demand on a WAN link. Monitoring resources and reports come from various sources, such as a syslog server, an SNMP server, Event Viewer logs on a Microsoft Windows server, and packet captures from a network sniffer. Remember that monitoring is also critical in the area of network security. For example, security information and event management (SIEM) software products and services combine security information management (SIM) and security event management (SEM). This section introduces a number of resources for monitoring network information.

An organization should consistently conduct *log reviews*. A log review should include the following, at a minimum:

- *Traffic logs*: You can use a variety of traffic logging mechanisms, many of which are built in to devices. For example, many devices today support Net-Flow, which is a powerful traffic monitoring tool that can export traffic flow information to a central collector on a network. (NetFlow is covered in more detail later in this chapter.) Keep in mind that traffic logging vehicles differ based on the network environment. For example, while you might rely on NetFlow in an on-premises network, you might be using VPC Flow Logs in your AWS infrastructure as a service environment.

■ *Audit logs*: You might audit many actions in your network environment and record them in an audit log. For example, a network device might have a setting to log each time an administrator logs in to the system and uses admin powers. These logs can be very valuable in tracking and monitoring the admin activities in your network. AWS Cloud offers a tool called CloudTrail that can log every activity that takes place in your public cloud environment.

Syslog

A variety of network components (for example, routers, switches, and servers) can send their log information to a common *syslog* server. By having information for multiple devices in a common log and examining time stamps, network administrators can better correlate events occurring on one network device with events occurring on a different network device. Syslog messages and SNMP traps can be used to trigger notification messages that may be sent via email and SMS. A syslog logging solution consists of two primary components:

■ **Syslog server:** A syslog server receives and stores log messages sent from syslog clients.

■ **Syslog clients:** As shown in Figure 13-3, various types of network devices can act as syslog clients and send logging information to a syslog server.

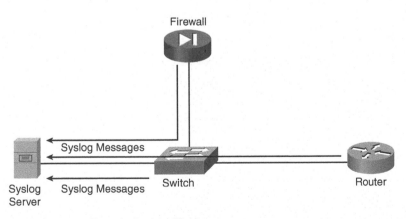

FIGURE 13-3   Sample Syslog Clients

Messages sent from a syslog client to a syslog server vary in their severity levels. Table 13-3 lists the eight severity levels of syslog messages. The higher the syslog level, the more detailed the logs. Keep in mind that more detailed logs require additional storage space on a syslog server.

Key Topic

Table 13-3 Syslog Severity Levels

Level	Name	Description
0	Emergencies	The most severe error conditions, which render the system unusable
1	Alerts	Conditions requiring immediate attention
2	Critical	A less-severe condition than an alert that should be addressed to prevent interruption of service
3	Errors	Notifications about error conditions within the system that do not render the system unusable
4	Warnings	Notifications that specific operations failed to complete successfully
5	Notifications	Non-error notifications that alert an administrator about state changes within a system
6	Informational	Detailed information about the normal operation of a system
7	Debugging	Highly detailed information (for example, information about individual packets) that is typically used for troubleshooting purposes

Figure 13-4 shows the format of a syslog message. The syslog log entries contain time stamps, which help you understand how one log message relates to another. The log entries also include severity level information, in addition to the text of the syslog messages.

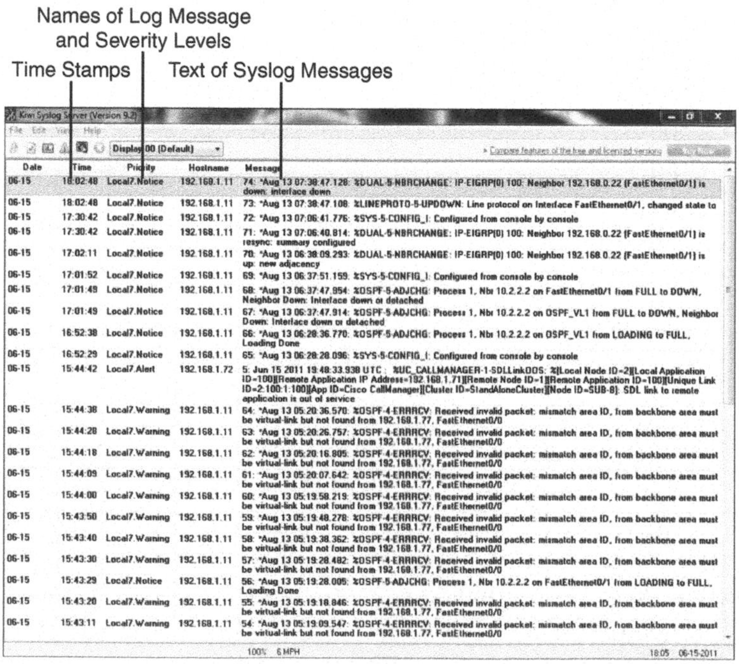

FIGURE 13-4   Structure of a Syslog Message

NOTE A variety of systems can act as syslog servers. You can download a free syslog utility from https://solarwinds.com/downloads.

Logs

In addition to logs generated by routers, switches, and other infrastructure gear, the operating systems powering network clients and servers generally have the capability to produce log output. Rather than containing general log information (that is, log information about all of a system's tracked components), Microsoft Windows incorporates the Event Viewer application, which allows you to view various log types, including application, security, and system logs. These logs can be archived for later review and can be used to spot network trends and provide data for creating baselines.

NOTE Logs are beneficial in your network management endeavors only if they are reviewed! Be sure to document standard operating procedures for periodic and careful review of the many logs incorporated into a network.

Application Logs

Microsoft Windows application logs contain information about software applications running on the underlying operating system. In Figure 13-5, notice the three levels of severity associated with the events in the log: Information, Warning, and Error. The events provide a collection of information about the event, such as the source (for example, the application) that caused the event, the severity level of the event, and a date/time stamp of the event.

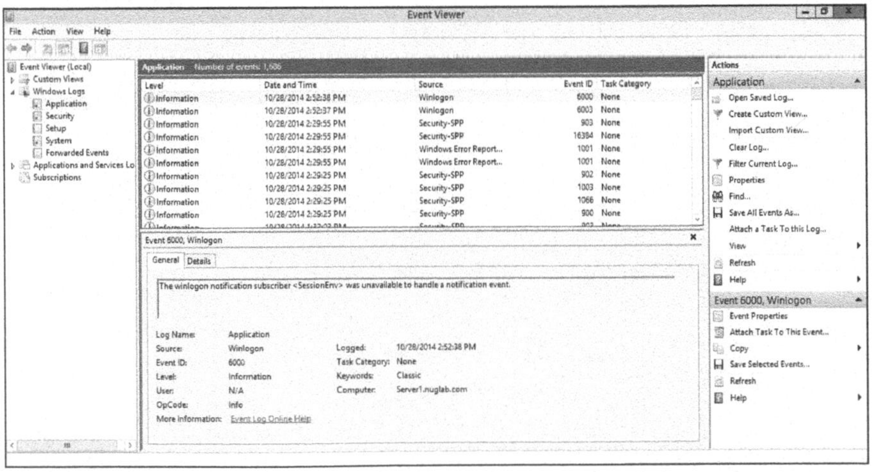

FIGURE 13-5 Application Log

Security Logs

Figure 13-6 shows an example of a Microsoft Windows security log, highlighting both successful and failed login attempts.

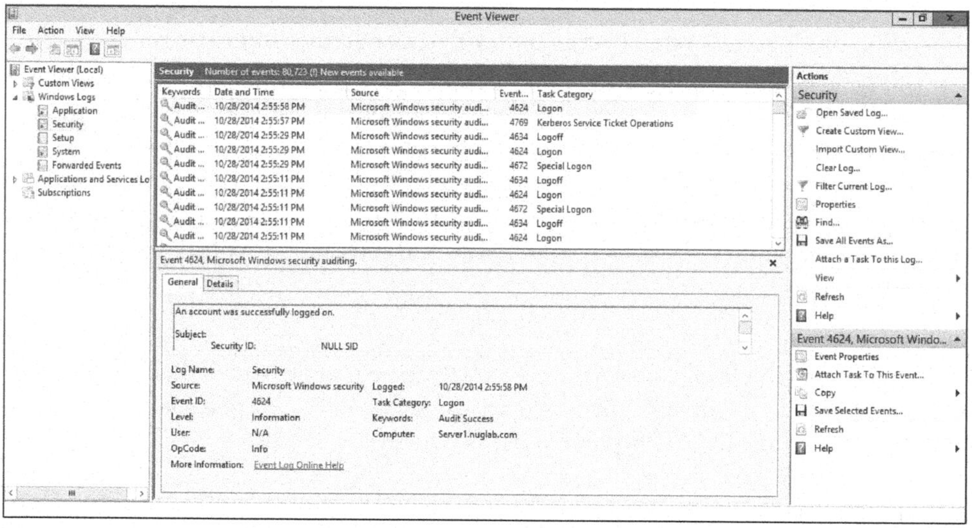

FIGURE 13-6   Security Log

System Logs

A Microsoft Windows system log, an example of which is shown in Figure 13-7, lists events generated by the underlying operating system.

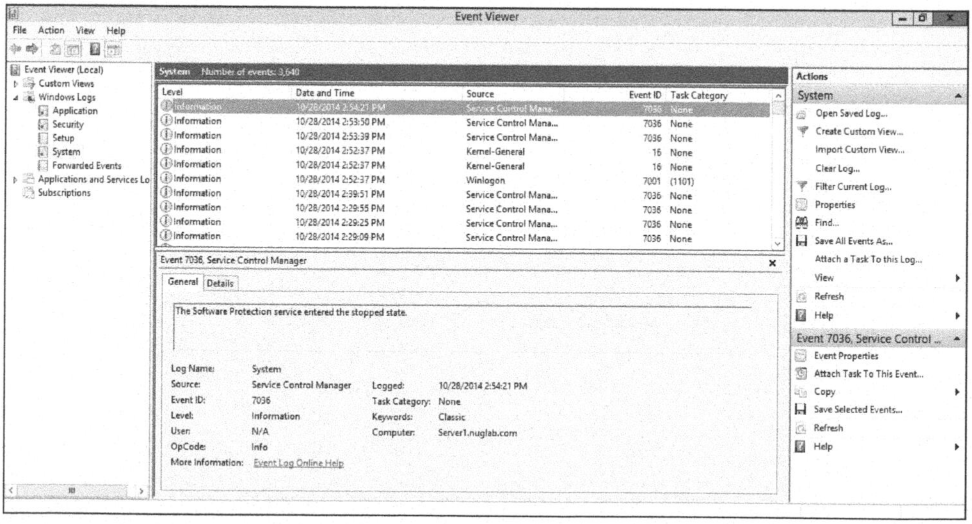

FIGURE 13-7   System Log

Environmental Monitor

Components making up a computer network (for example, routers, switches, and servers) are designed to operate within certain environmental limits. If the temperature rises too high in a server farm, for example—possibly because of an air-conditioning outage—components could begin to fail. To prevent such an occurrence, you can use *environmental monitors* to send an alert if the temperature in a room rises above or drops below administratively configured thresholds. With the appropriate personnel being alerted about a suspicious temperature variation before it becomes an issue, action can hopefully be taken to, for example, repair an air-conditioning unit or provide extra ventilation, thus preventing system failure. In addition to monitoring a room's temperature, you can use environmental monitors to check a room's humidity.

Environmental monitors, including power and temperature monitors, can alert appropriate personnel in a variety of ways. For example, as you learned earlier in this chapter, some environmental monitors can send alerts to a SNMP server. This type of alert is known as an *SNMP trap*. Another common notification option allows an environmental monitor to send an email or SMS text message to alert appropriate personnel about the suspect environmental condition.

Fault-tolerant power options—such as uninterruptible power supplies (UPSs), fault-tolerant power circuits into the building, generators, and appropriate converters or inverters for the critical network devices—can assist in preventing downtime in the event of a single power failure. Monitoring systems allow you to react and provide redundancy.

Devices should be placed in racks in such a way that air can properly flow through the systems in the racks. Racks may be two- or four-post racks organized into rows. Free-standing racks may also be used to hold network systems and devices. A rack-mounted server has rails on the side that allow it to be inserted into a rack. Environmental monitors can trigger alerts about potential damage if the humidity or temperature goes outside the values specified for network devices and servers.

Environmental monitors and sensors can also be used to detect water and send alerts when water is present in a network closet or datacenter. Whether you had water on the floor due to flooding or water coming from the ceiling due to excessive rain or structural damage to the building, you would want to be alerted to this unwelcome element as quickly as possible.

Interface Statistics/Status

Network device interfaces are a key component of a network environment. Fortunately, there are many mechanisms you can use to monitor these important network components. You can monitor the various statistics these interfaces have to offer, and you can also obtain at-a-glance status information when you are troubleshooting problems in a network. Figure 13-8 provides an example of monitoring physical characteristics, data link layer components, and interface statistics and status.

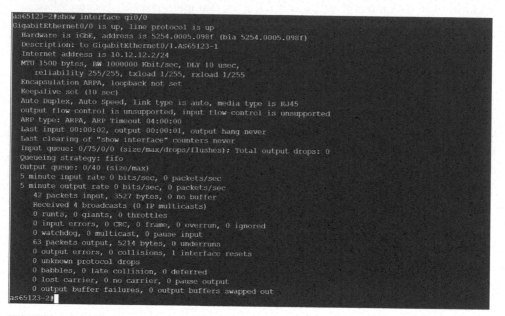

```
as65123-2#show interface gi0/0
GigabitEthernet0/0 is up, line protocol is up
  Hardware is iGbE, address is 5254.0005.098f (bia 5254.0005.098f)
  Description: to GigabitEthernet0/1.AS65123-1
  Internet address is 10.12.12.2/24
  MTU 1500 bytes, BW 1000000 Kbit/sec, DLY 10 usec,
     reliability 255/255, txload 1/255, rxload 1/255
  Encapsulation ARPA, loopback not set
  Keepalive set (10 sec)
  Auto Duplex, Auto Speed, link type is auto, media type is RJ45
  output flow-control is unsupported, input flow-control is unsupported
  ARP type: ARPA, ARP Timeout 04:00:00
  Last input 00:00:02, output 00:00:01, output hang never
  Last clearing of "show interface" counters never
  Input queue: 0/75/0/0 (size/max/drops/flushes); Total output drops: 0
  Queueing strategy: fifo
  Output queue: 0/40 (size/max)
  5 minute input rate 0 bits/sec, 0 packets/sec
  5 minute output rate 0 bits/sec, 0 packets/sec
     42 packets input, 3527 bytes, 0 no buffer
     Received 4 broadcasts (0 IP multicasts)
     0 runts, 0 giants, 0 throttles
     0 input errors, 0 CRC, 0 frame, 0 overrun, 0 ignored
     0 watchdog, 0 multicast, 0 pause input
     63 packets output, 5214 bytes, 0 underruns
     0 output errors, 0 collisions, 1 interface resets
     0 unknown protocol drops
     0 babbles, 0 late collision, 0 deferred
     0 lost carrier, 0 no carrier, 0 pause output
     0 output buffer failures, 0 output buffers swapped out
as65123-2#
```

FIGURE 13-8 Viewing Interface Statistics and Status

The following are just some of the statistics and statuses that you need to monitor:

- **Link state:** Is the interface up, is it down, or is it in some other status (such as suspended)? Notice in Figure 13-8 that Cisco likes to report the status for the physical layer and the data link layer health of an interface. In this example, you can see that the GigabitEthernet 0/0 interface is UP, and that the line protocol is UP.

- **Speed/duplex:** The output in Figure 13-8 also shows the speed and duplex setting of the interface. In the case of the router shown, the interface is configured for autonegotiation of both speed and duplex. If you connect 1Gbps-capable media and a 1Gbps remote port, you can enjoy gigabit bandwidth, and this rate is automatically configured thanks to the autonegotiation of speed for the ports involved.

- **Send/receive traffic:** Notice in Figure 13-8 that network devices can report on the amount of traffic sent and received.

- *Cyclic redundancy checks (CRCs)*: In Figure 13-8 notice the CRC field, which in this case displays 0. This value would increment if packets failed the CRC check. Remember that the CRC is a mathematical algorithm that is executed by each sender of packets. The network devices can compare the CRC values received and gather evidence that there was no corruption of the data in transit. CRC errors are an important metric to watch for.

- **Protocol/packet byte counts:** Network interfaces can often report on the types of protocols for which they are sending traffic as well as the number of packets per protocol type. Clearly this information is very valuable when you are monitoring a network for baseline operation.

The following are the specific network interface errors and alerts you should watch for, at a minimum:

- **CRC errors:** Watch for these errors to ensure that your media is functioning properly and that you do not have attackers attempting to corrupt data in transit.

- *Giants*: Giants are alerts that are reported when packets are larger than 1500 bytes. (Such packet sizes might be perfectly normal in your enterprise or datacenter.)

- *Runts*: Like giants, runts are alerts based on packet size. A runt is an Ethernet frame that is less than the IEEE 802.3's minimum length of 64 octets. Runts could be caused by collisions, malfunctioning network interface cards, buffer underruns, duplex mismatches, or software issues.

- **Encapsulation errors:** In Figure 13-8, you can see that Cisco reports on the status of Layer 1 and Layer 2. What type of error would produce a Layer 2 problem for a Cisco interface? A classic example would be an encapsulation error. Perhaps your interface is configured for PPP operation, and you are connected to a device that is not enabled for PPP. This mismatch would prevent the interface from functioning, and Cisco would report the interface as line protocol down.

NOTE Monitoring software can provide you with information about the overall uptime and downtime of your network interfaces, your network modules, and the network devices themselves. You should consider monitoring this valuable metric information in order to provide network assurance.

NetFlow

Cisco introduced *NetFlow* to the world around 1996. As discussed earlier in this chapter, NetFlow gives network administrators the ability to collect IP network traffic statistics as traffic exits or enters interfaces.

By analyzing the data provided by NetFlow, you can learn all kinds of valuable information about how your network is actually being used. NetFlow can also be a key tool for tracking down network bottlenecks, which tend to be somewhat inevitable. by using the data collected by NetFlow, you can often quickly determine root causes.

A typical implementation of NetFlow includes the following:

- **Flow exporter:** This component aggregates packets into flows and exports flow records toward one or more flow collectors.

- **Flow collector:** This component is responsible for reception, storage, and preprocessing of flow data received from a flow exporter.

- **Analysis application:** You use this application to analyze received flow data in various contexts. Perhaps you are most interested in performance issues during key times of the day. Or perhaps you are more concerned about security issues that NetFlow might be able to help pinpoint.

Real-World Case Study

Acme, Inc. has decided to improve their network and operations by improving the observability they can accomplish regarding their network. They have decided to employ NetFlow on many of the key network nodes so that these devices can share performance data with a central repository in the network.

Acme, Inc. is also going to start using Splunk Enterprise to make sense of the many logs and other machine data produced in the organization. Splunk permits the configuration of powerful dashboards and reports to assist the team at Acme, Inc. in being more proactive when it comes to supporting the network infrastructure.

Summary

Here are the main topics covered in this chapter:

- This chapter describes best practices for monitoring performance with metrics and sensors.

- The operation of SNMP is discussed, as are the security enhancements available in SNMPv3.

- This chapter describes the operation of syslog and the syslog message severity levels.

- This chapter discusses other types of log files.

- This chapter explains interface errors and alerts.

- This chapter discusses environmental factors and monitoring techniques.

- This chapter provides examples of logs collected by the Microsoft Windows Event Viewer application, including application, security, and system logs.

Exam Preparation Tasks

Review All the Key Topics

Review the most important topics from this chapter, noted with the Key Topic icon in the outer margin of the page. Table 13-4 lists these key topics and the page number where each is found.

Table 13-4   Key Topics for Chapter 13

Key Topic Element	Description	Page Number
Table 13-1	SNMP components	356
Figure 13-1	SNMP components and messages	357
Section	Syslog	361
Table 13-3	Syslog severity levels	362
List	Interface metrics	366

Complete Tables and Lists from Memory

Print a copy of Appendix C, "Memory Tables," or at least the section for this chapter and complete as many of the tables as possible from memory. Appendix D, "Memory Tables Answer Key," includes the completed tables and lists so you can check your work.

Define Key Terms

Define the following key terms from this chapter and check your answers in the Glossary:

bandwidth, latency, jitter, SNMP, trap, object identifier (OID), Management Information Base (MIB), traffic log, audit log, syslog, NetFlow, cyclic redundancy check (CRC), giant, runt, baseline

Complete Chapter 13 Hands-On Labs in Network+ Simulator Lite

- Wireless Antenna Placement
- Manually Configuring Wireless Signals on a Small Office/Home Office Router

Additional Resources

How Healthy Is Your Existing Network?: https://www.ajsnetworking.com/how-healthy-is-your-existing-network

SNMP Operation: https://www.youtube.com/watch?v=tg47MZdtcAE

Review Questions

The answers to these review questions appear in Appendix A, "Answers to Review Questions."

1. SNMP uses a series of objects to collect information about a managed device. What is the name of the structure, similar to a database, that contains these objects?

   a. RIB

   b. MIB

   c. Syslog

   d. Baseline

2. Which syslog level is the most severe?

   a. Informational

   b. Critical

    c. Errors

    d. Warnings

3. What are the main categories of SNMP message types? (Choose three.)

    a. Get

    b. Put

    c. Set

    d. Trap

4. What Microsoft Windows application enables you to view a variety of log types, including application, security, and system logs?

    a. Event Viewer

    b. Performance Monitor

    c. Microsoft Management Console

    d. Control Panel

5. As you monitor a key area of your network, you discover that the average latency spans a wide range. You are seeing some periods of 50 ms and others of 300 ms. What is the term for this type of variation in delay?

    a. CRC

    b. DSCP

    c. WRED

    d. Jitter

6. Which SNMPv3 security level is the equivalent of SNMPv2c?

    a. noAuthNoPriv

    b. authPriv

    c. authNoPriv

    d. noAuthPriv

7. What syslog level is used for informational messages?

    a. 0

    b. 8

    c. 7

    d. 6

8. Which network assurance tool would most likely feature the use of a collector?

    a. NetFlow

    b. SNMP

    c. nmap

    d. traceroute

9. Which of the following are reported when packets are larger than 1500 bytes?

    a. Encapsulation errors

    b. Giants

    c. Runts

    d. OIDs

10. How can you fix a duplex mismatch?

    a. Enable autonegotiation.

    b. Change the link state to up.

    c. Adjust the protocol and packet byte counts.

    d. Reduce the humidity level.

This chapter covers the following topics related to Objective 3.2 (Explain the purpose of organizational documents and policies) of the CompTIA Network+ N10-008 certification exam:

- Plans and procedures
  - Change management
  - Incident response plan
  - Disaster recovery plan
  - Business continuity plan
  - System life cycle
  - Standard operating procedures
- Hardening and security policies
  - Password policy
  - Acceptable use policy
  - Bring your own device (BYOD) policy
  - Remote access policy
  - Onboarding and offboarding policy
  - Security policy
  - Data loss prevention
- Common documentation
  - Physical network diagram

- Floor plan
- Rack diagram
- Intermediate distribution frame (IDF)/main distribution frame (MDF) documentation
- Logical network diagram
- Wiring diagram
- Site survey report
- Audit and assessment report
- Baseline configurations
- Common agreements
  - Non-disclosure agreement (NDA)
  - Service-level agreement (SLA)
  - Memorandum of understanding (MOU)

CHAPTER 14

Organizational Documents and Policies

If you are reading this text start to finish, you might have a newfound appreciation for how complex networking is today. Fortunately, there are many established policies and best practices you can use to help take much of the guesswork out of implementing and maintaining your network. This is especially beneficial in the complex and challenging area of network security.

This chapter begins by describing (in detail) policies you can consider for your own network. Keep in mind that some of these may not apply to your organization at all, but you should still take time to study them if you are preparing for the Network+ exam. For example, your organization may not have BYOD (bring-your-own-device) policies in place because it might forbid BYOD completely; however, this topic might show up on the exam. Do not make the mistake of assuming that information that does not apply in your organization will not be tested on the exam.

This chapter also covers many best practices you can implement, such as implementing non-disclosure agreements (NDAs) and using system life cycle approaches. Again, although some best practices may not be applicable to you, there is much to be gained by studying them.

Foundation Topics

Plans and Policies

Many important plans and policies have become fairly commonplace in networks today. While no one likes it when plans and policies are overly complex due to "red tape," you should consider many of them for your own organization. This section of the chapter lists some of the most critical plans and policies for your review.

Change Management

Have you ever made a simple little change to a system and been horrified to see the entire solution self-destruct? It can happen, and because of this, you should ensure that there is a well-thought-out *change management* and change control policy in place. You should also have a plan that includes the appropriate change management documentation. Oftentimes, it is necessary to make updates to existing documentation as part of the overall change management process.

Change management can help ensure that your network keeps running in good health. It can also ensure that your documentation reflects the true and current state of the objects it is describing. This is very important for many aspects of your operations, including security responses and troubleshooting operations. Change management documentation often includes the following:

- A documented reason for a change
- The actual change request
- The approval process
- The required maintenance window
- The change notification process

Incident Response Plan

Because security issues are inevitable in a network, it is critical to prepare a comprehensive incident response plan. Such a policy might outline various phases of incident response, including the following:

- **Prepare:** This often involves being able to identify the start of an incident, preparing a recovery plan, determining how to get everything back to normal, and creating established security policies.

- **Identify:** The focus here is on the precise identification of the actual security incident.

- **Contain:** Here, the main concern is often twofold: first, protecting and keeping available critical computing resources; second, determining the operational status of the infected computer, system, or network. The goal is to limit the spread of the security incident.

- **Eradicate:** This phase deals specifically with the removal of the attack or infection.

- **Recover:** This phase often includes service restoration as well as recertification of network devices and systems.

- **Review:** All phases should be analyzed in this review phase to gauge their effectiveness and modify the *incident response policy* as needed for the future.

Disaster Recovery and Business Continuity Policies

A business should have a *disaster recovery plan (DRP)* and *business continuity plan (BCP)* in place so that, in the event of any type of downtime (due to an attack or a natural disaster), the organization can be back up and running to maintain its business. Disaster recovery focuses on getting critical applications back online, and business continuity focuses on the tasks carried out by an organization to ensure that critical business functions continue to operate during and after a disaster. These plans should include training, identification, and roles of the first responders as well as practice drills to confirm that the plans are functional. An organization without these plans in place could fall victim to a permanent denial-of-service (DoS) attack, which could ultimately destroy the business if an attacker has damaged the hardware (by reflashing firmware, for example) with corrupt or defective images to such a point that it is no longer usable.

System Life Cycle

Your IT networking personnel should consider adhering to a well-planned *system life cycle* for the equipment and software in use. The system life cycle should provide valuable guidance on best practices throughout the organization concerning the network components.

Key Topic

Here are some examples of phases in a system life cycle:

- Conceptual design

- Preliminary system design

- Detail design and development

- Production and construction
- Utilization and support
- Phase-out
- Disposal

Hardening and Security Policies

Cybersecurity becomes a bigger challenge for organizations every day. In this section, we examine many important policies an organization can implement to vastly improve its security posture. Keep in mind that not only is it important to create these policies for most organizations, but employees also need to be properly trained in order to closely follow them.

Password Policy

Because more and more sensitive data is finding its way into storage on our networks, more security measures are required than ever before. Therefore, an organization needs to possess a well-crafted security policy that includes a comprehensive *password policy*. As you'll learn in this section, you should also provide detailed training on this part of the security policy.

Keep in mind that in addition to "simple" username and password combinations, many other powerful technologies used in modern networks are available for user authentication, including the following:

- One-time passwords (OTPs)
- Client certificates
- Smart cards
- Biometrics
- Multifactor authentication

Despite these additional security options, simple username and password combinations are still used by themselves in most networks. It is obvious by glancing at recent news headlines that user credentials represent a major area of attack.

Your password policy should include the following:

- Education for end users
- Strong password requirements, such as the following:
    - Minimum password lengths

- Restrictions on the use of proper names

- Password expiration

- No previously used passwords allowed

- No words spelled out completely within the password

- The use of characters from the following groups:

  - Uppercase letters
  - Lowercase letters
  - Numbers
  - Special characters

Your password policy might also detail the use of password management software, which stores passwords for different resources and can help users generate complex passwords across these resources. Of course, the software itself must be protected with a strong password that the user should memorize.

Security Policies

One of the main reasons security breaches occur within an organization is the lack of a security policy or, if a security policy is in place, failure to effectively communicate/ enforce the security policy to all concerned. A *security policy* is a continually changing document that dictates a set of guidelines for network use. These guidelines complement organizational objectives by specifying rules for how a network is used.

The main purpose of a security policy is to protect the assets of an organization. An organization's assets include more than just tangible items. Assets also include intellectual property (IP), processes and procedures, sensitive customer data, and specific server functions (for example, email or web functions).

Aside from protecting an organization's assets, a security policy serves other purposes, such as the following:

- Making employees aware of their obligations in regard to security practices

- Identifying specific security solutions required to meet the goals of a security policy

- Acting as a baseline for ongoing security monitoring

One of the most well-known components of a security policy is an *acceptable use policy (AUP)*. An AUP identifies what users of a network are and are not allowed to do on a network. For example, retrieving sports scores during working hours via an organization's Internet connection might be deemed inappropriate by an AUP. (AUPs are covered in more detail later in this chapter.)

Because an organization's security policy applies to various categories of employees (such as management, technical staff, and end users), a single document might not be sufficient. For example, managerial personnel might not be concerned with the technical intricacies of a security policy, whereas technical personnel might not be very concerned with why a policy is in place. Also, end users might be more likely to comply with the policy if they understand the reasoning behind the rules. Therefore, a security policy might be a collection of congruent yet separate documents. Figure 14-1 offers a high-level overview of these complementary documents.

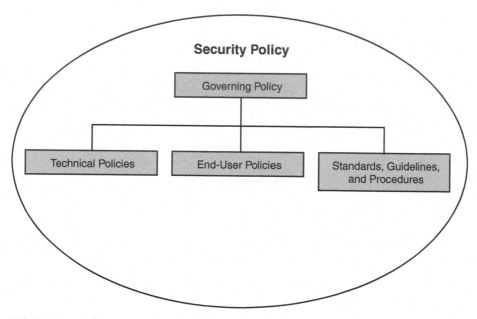

FIGURE 14-1   Components of a Security Policy

Data Loss Prevention

A comprehensive *data loss prevention (DLP) policy* focuses on accidental or malicious data losses. DLP policies consider internal and external users as well as define practices to guard against the loss or damage of sensitive data. The best DLP policies also cover wide network integration and are not limited to certain areas of networking, such as email.

Most DLP policies focus on the use of content-level scanning and deep content inspection (DCI) to identify sensitive data and protect it. DLP policies target activities at three levels:

- Client level (data in operation/processing)

- Network level (data in transit/motion)

- Storage level (data at rest)

You should take the following actions when designing a DLP policy for your organization:

- Consider any risk assessments your organization has performed.

- Incorporate key members of management from the various departments of your organization.

- Identify the organization's most sensitive data.

- Outline a phased implementation of DLP and incorporate guidelines for tracking success of the initiative.

- Attempt to minimize any negative impacts on the business caused by the policy implementation.

- Periodically review the DLP policy.

- Include the appropriate event-monitoring specifics as they apply to the policy.

Remote Access Policies

Remote access to corporate network resources presents unique challenges for organizations today. Of primary concern is the fact that the remote network might lack appropriate security controls or may even be currently compromised.

The following are some important considerations for a *remote access policy*:

- The scope of the policy should be clear and may include applicable targets, such as employees, contractors, vendors, and agents with organization-owned or personally owned computers or workstations used to connect to the corporate network. A remote access policy typically applies to remote connections to the organization itself, including reading or sending email and viewing intranet web resources. Such a policy also tends to cover every remote access option, including dial-up, VPN, and web portal access.

- It is important to clearly detail the requirements of the policy, which might include encryption and security standards as well as the acceptable areas of network access.

- An organization might want to include a section on compliance, which could include exceptions to the policy, how to measure compliance, and the consequences of noncompliance.

- You might want to include a section that indicates what other security policies for the network closely relate to this policy.

Bring-Your-Own-Device (BYOD) Policy

Closely related to a remote access policy is a *bring-your-own-device (BYOD) policy*. At the very least, this important policy should incorporate the following:

- An explicit and detailed list of what devices are permitted

- An explicit security policy for each device or device category

- An appropriate corporate support policy for each device or device category

- A clear delineation of what applications and data are owned by the corporation versus owned by the user and/or employee

- An explicit list of applications permitted in the BYOD environment

- An integration of the **BYOD policy** with the AUP

- A detailed presentation of the exit (offboarding) policies for employees as they relate to BYOD

Acceptable Use Policy (AUP)

An AUP, which is sometimes referred to as a *fair use policy*, seeks to provide restrictions and overall guidelines on how the network should be used. Such a policy can have tremendous legal implications for an organization in the event of problems with employee actions on the network. An organization might be able to protect itself in such legal situations if its employees have signed a detailed AUP during the onboarding process.

An AUP should have the following characteristics:

- It should be clear.

- It should be concise.

- It should be detailed regarding acceptable and unacceptable use of the network.

- It should be congruent with the associated overall security policies of the organization.

- It should be concrete regarding consequences of AUP violations.

Like many of the other policies in this section, the AUP should be reviewed and updated as required.

Safety Procedures

I am hesitant to install a light bulb in my own home, so I have great respect for the complexity of installing large, complex, and heavy network equipment and components within an organization. Sure enough, an organization should consider implementing safety policies and procedures for the networking equipment. Here are some areas that are commonly addressed in such policies:

- Following the installation and maintenance guides for the equipment as closely as possible

- Keeping all work areas as clean and organized as possible

- Wearing appropriate safety equipment

- Getting assistance when lifting heavy network objects

- Using caution when interacting with electricity

- Avoiding other risks of electric shock

Privileged User Agreement (PUA)

Because network administrators often require "God-like" power and access over the network and the data that flows through it, it is important to consider implementing a privileged user agreement (PUA) in an IT department. A PUA agreement might stipulate the following:

- Privileged access should be granted only to authorized individuals who read and sign the agreement.

- Privileged access may be used only to perform assigned job duties.

- If methods other than using privileged access will accomplish an action, those other methods must be used unless the burden of time or other resources required clearly justifies using privileged access.

- Privileged access may be used to perform standard system-related duties only on machines and networks for which the individual is assigned responsibility.

- Privileged access may be used to grant, change, or deny resources, access, or privilege to another individual only for authorized account management activities or under exceptional circumstances.

Onboarding/Offboarding Procedures

Another excellent best practice is to have detailed *onboarding/offboarding procedures* in place for the hiring and termination of employees. These procedures should address IT and the network.

Examples of typical onboarding functions might include the following:

- ID number and PIN assignment
- Username and password assignment
- ID card and access assignments
- Email mailbox setup
- Email client setup
- Workstation setup
- Workstation network access verification
- IT security and best practices training
- Phone and BYOD setup
- Time management and other HR software training
- Signing an AUP and an NDA

Of course, *offboarding* is the opposite of *onboarding*. This critical phase involves tasks such as the following:

- Disabling user identities
- Deleting user identities
- Gathering and examining former employees' computer equipment (mobile and non mobile) that belongs to the organization
- Wiping this computer equipment clean
- Disposing of or repurposing this computer equipment

Licensing Restrictions

You may need to provide training in the proper licensing and use of corporate hardware and software. As networks have become more complex (for example, incorporating public cloud technologies), so have licensing agreements. It is important that your users remain in compliance with all existing licensing agreements and restrictions.

International Export Controls

Another important best practice is to educate IT staff and end users on the international export rules your organization must observe. For example, specific U.S. government agencies regulate the transfer of information, commodities, technology, and software considered to be strategically important to the United States in the interest of national security, economic, and/or foreign policy concerns.

Your management must understand that noncompliance with export controls can result in severe monetary and criminal penalties against both an individual in your organization and the organization itself.

> **NOTE**   An important area of export regulations is cryptography. The "Additional Resources" section at the end of this chapter provides a link for more information about this important area.

Non-Disclosure Agreement (NDA)

It is a best practice for an organization to have individuals sign *non-disclosure agreements (NDAs)*. An NDA is a legal contract with the following common traits:

- It is between at least two parties.

- It outlines confidential material, knowledge, or information that the parties want to share with one another but want to restrict others from accessing.

- It creates a confidential relationship between the parties to protect any type of confidential and proprietary information or trade secret.

- It protects non public business information.

It has become quite common for all employees to sign NDAs during the onboarding process.

Common Documentation

I cannot stress enough the importance of up-to-date and accurate network documentation. Documentation is useful for proper network management tasks, and it is also critical in troubleshooting, security, optimization, and other key areas of networking today. Consider these important aspects of network documentation:

- *Physical network diagrams*: Many of the diagrams listed in the bullets that follow can be considered physical network diagrams. This umbrella term is used to describe many more specifically titled diagrams of specific parts of a network.

- **Floor plan:** This type of physical network diagram shows the layout of the office space and, often, the distribution of employee workstations.

- **Diagram symbols:** Your IT department should use standard templates to consistently represent network objects in diagrams; where needed, legends should clearly delineate one network device from another. The figures in this book demonstrate many of the standard diagram symbols for the most popular network objects.

- **Standard operating procedures (SOP)/work instructions:** Whenever possible, it is important to document the procedures your IT staff are to follow given certain network conditions. For example, steps for dealing with an Internet outage could aid staff members in taking quick action and minimizing disruptions.

- **Logical network diagrams versus physical diagrams:** Be sure to consider physical and logical topologies when diagramming. Remember, the logical and physical flows of data through the organization might result in very different diagrams.

- **Rack diagrams:** These days, thanks to the very small form factors of many network devices, we have more devices than ever before coexisting in a single rack in a datacenter. Therefore, rack diagrams are needed to assist in the management of all the various devices in the racks.

- **Change management documentation:** It is critical that an organization have change controls in place as well as careful documentation when changes actually take place. Such documentation helps ensure the accuracy of network information and can prove critical in security response and troubleshooting operations.

- **Wiring diagram and port locations:** Another key piece of documentation is a diagram showing wiring and port locations. This documentation allows you to track cable runs from switches and map them to actual wall jacks where users connect to your network; these connections might also represent trunks to additional network devices such as wireless access points.

- **Intermediate distribution frame (IDF)/main distribution frame (MDF) documentation:** Diagrams are also crucial for the IDF and the MDF. These distribution and core facilities house critical network data and devices, and proper documentation can aid in all forms of maintenance and security.

- **Labeling:** Proper labeling in diagrams as well as on physical equipment can ensure that such documentation is as useful as possible.

- **Network configuration and performance baselines:** You should document the base configurations for network devices as well as capture data utilization and bandwidth consumption during "normal" business operations; this might also include taking SLA measurements during such times. Without this baseline information, it can be nearly impossible to identify subtle performance problems.

- **Inventory management:** Another aspect of your documentation should be an inventory management system. Such a system should track spares (including hot spares) for inevitable hardware malfunctions and keep an inventory of software (including licenses).

- *Site survey report*: Site survey reports are critical during wireless site surveys. These site surveys (and their reports) attempt to describe the WiFi capabilities and potential risk points in an installation.

- *Audit and assessment report*: This report helps you identify and address critical issues that might be occurring in your network infrastructure. Such a report often identifies performance and security issues that need to be addressed in order to help ensure that the network continues to function as desired.

- *Baseline configurations*: When you need to return network equipment to the exact configurations that existed at a specific point in time, baseline configuration documentation can come to the rescue. Various stages of the network device life cycle can be captured in these baselines.

- *Service-level agreements (SLAs)*: It is important to have access to SLAs, which often outline the expected (and purchased) quality of connections or equipment accessed.

- *Memorandum of understanding (MOU)*: An MOU is an agreement between two parties that outlines the roles and responsibilities that each will play. MOUs often come up in IT business agreements.

Real-World Case Study

Acme, Inc. wants to ensure that it incorporates as many well-thought-through policies and best practices as possible in designing, operating, and maintaining its network. Therefore, the organization has assembled a team involving legal counsel and key department heads to draft important policy documents and best practices.

Acme now has a comprehensive network security policy that includes the following:

- A password policy

- A data loss prevention policy

- An incident response policy

- An acceptable use policy

- Onboarding and offboarding procedures

- A BYOD policy

- A mandatory NDA for all employees

- A detailed system life cycle for networking hardware and software

Also, administrators for Acme, having higher privileges on the network than standard users, are now required to sign a PUA before they are granted access to the administrative environment.

Acme has also planned for a consistent review of the documents and best practices as well as a procedure for their alteration.

Summary

Here are the main topics covered in this chapter:

- This chapter provides details on several common policies used in networks today, including password policies, data loss prevention policies, remote access policies, incident response policies, BYOD policies, acceptable use policies, and safety policies.

- This chapter also describes many best practice items, including privileged user agreements, onboarding and offboarding procedures, licensing restrictions, international export controls, non-disclosure agreements, and system life cycles.

Exam Preparation Tasks

Review All the Key Topics

Review the most important topics from this chapter, noted with the Key Topic icon in the outer margin of the page. Table 14-1 lists these key topics and the page number where each is found.

Table 14-1 Key Topics for Chapter 14

Key Topic Element	Description	Page Number
List	Typical phases of an incident response plan	376
List	Sample phases of a system life cycle	377
List	Typical elements of a password policy	378
List	Key elements of a data loss prevention policy	381
List	Important elements of a remote access policy	381
List	Important elements of a BYOD policy	382
List	Important aspects of network documentation	385

Define Key Terms

Define the following key terms from this chapter and check your answers in the Glossary:

password policy, data loss prevention (DLP) policy, remote access policy, incident response policy, BYOD policy, acceptable use policy (AUP), onboarding/offboarding procedures, non-disclosure agreement (NDA), system life cycle, change management, disaster recovery plan (DRP), business continuity plan (BCP), standard operating procedures (SOP), security policy, physical network diagram, floor plan, rack diagram, intermediate distribution frame (IDF)/main distribution frame (MDF) documentation, logical network diagram, wiring diagram, site survey report, audit and assessment report, baseline configuration, service-level agreement (SLA), memorandum of understanding (MOU)

Additional Resources

Information Security Policy Templates: https://www.sans.org/security-resources/policies

Overview of US Export Laws: https://research.ucdavis.edu/wp-content/uploads/Export-Control-Overview-of-Regulations.pdf

Review Questions

The answers to these review questions appear in Appendix A, "Answers to Review Questions."

1. Which of the following is not a typical best practice in a password policy?

   a. Expire passwords regularly

   b. Use of uppercase and lowercase letters only in passwords

   c. Require password uniqueness

   d. Ban use of proper names in passwords

2. Which of the following is not an area typically targeted by a data loss prevention policy?

   a. Cloud level

   b. Network level

   c. Client level

   d. Storage level

3. An incident response policy often ends with which phase?

   a. Prepare

   b. Contain

   c. Review

   d. Eradicate

4. What should you follow closely when installing new network equipment?

   a. YouTube videos

   b. Certified training courses

   c. Installation and maintenance guides

   d. IETF guidelines

5. Which agreement would need to be read carefully and signed by an end user in the Sales department regarding the technology they were granted access to?

   a. AUP

   b. SLA

   c. PUA

   d. Vacation policy

6. You are discussing a legally binding document that organizations might require of both their own employees and anyone else who comes into contact with confidential information. What is this document called?

   a. NDA

   b. DLP

   c. SOP

   d. MOU

7. What is often the last stage of a system life cycle used in a network?

   a. Phase-out

   b. Disposal

   c. Support

   d. Development

8. You have created written instructions that detail organizational procedures to be followed when an employee leaves the organization or is terminated. What type of document is this?

   a. Data loss prevention policy

   b. Service-level agreement

   c. Onboarding procedures

   d. Offboarding procedures

This chapter covers the following topics related to Objective 3.3 (Explain high availability and disaster recovery concepts and summarize which is the best solution) of the CompTIA Network+ N10-008 certification exam:

- Load balancing
- Multipathing
- Network interface card (NIC) teaming
- Redundant hardware/clusters
  - Switches
  - Routers
  - Firewalls
- Facilities and infrastructure support
  - Uninterruptible power supply (UPS)
  - Power distribution units (PDUs)
  - Generator
  - HVAC
  - Fire suppression
- Redundancy and high availability (HA) concepts
  - Cold site

- Warm site
- Hot site
- Cloud site
- Active-active vs. active-passive
  - Multiple Internet service providers (ISPs)/diverse paths
  - Virtual Router Redundancy Protocol (VRRP)/First Hop Redundancy Protocol (FHRP)
- Mean time to repair (MTTR)
- Mean time between failure (MTBF)
- Recovery time objective (RTO)
- Recovery point objective (RPO)
- Network device backup/restore
  - State
  - Configuration

CHAPTER 15

High Availability and Disaster Recovery

If you saw the movie *Field of Dreams*, you are familiar with the sentiment "If you build it, he will come." This idea has proven to be true in today's networks. Networks were once relegated to the domain of data but now carry voice and video. These additional media types, as well as mission-critical data applications, need a network to be up and available for users.

It is likely that your telephone service has been unavailable much less often than your data network. Unfortunately, data networks have traditionally been less reliable than voice networks; however, today's data networks often *are* voice networks, and this convergence has contributed to the increased demand for uptime. Unified voice services such as call control and communication gateways can be integrated into one or more network devices, leveraging the bandwidth available on the LAN and WAN.

In this chapter, we take a tour of key disaster recovery techniques and concepts. We also examine high availability and tools that can help ensure high availability in networks today.

High Availability

If a network switch or router stops operating correctly (meaning that a *network fault* occurs), communication through the network could be disrupted, resulting in the network becoming unavailable to its users. Therefore, network availability, called *uptime*, is a major design consideration. This consideration might, for example, lead you to add fault-tolerant devices and fault-tolerant links between those devices. This section discusses the measurement of high availability along with a number of high-availability design considerations.

High Availability (HA) Measurement

The availability of a network is measured by its uptime during a year. For example, if a network has *five nines* availability, it is up 99.999% of the time, which translates to a maximum of 5 minutes of downtime per year. If a network has *six nines* availability (meaning it is up 99.9999% of the time), it is down less than 30 seconds per year.

As a designer, one of your goals is to select components, topologies, and features that maximize network *availability* within certain parameters (for example, a budget). Be careful not to confuse *availability* with *reliability*. A *reliable* network, for example, does not drop many packets, whereas an *available* network is up and operational.

MTTR, MTBF, RTO, and RPO

The ***mean time to repair (MTTR)*** is the average time required to fix a failed component and return it to production status. This is also sometimes called mean time to recovery.

Mean time between failures (MTBF) is the average amount of time that passes between hardware component failures, excluding time spent repairing components or waiting for repairs.

Yet another important measure is *mean time to failure (MTTF)*. This is the length of time a device or product is expected to last in operation. It represents how long a product can reasonably be expected to perform, based on specific testing.

Another goal in your design might be to meet the requirements set forth in a service-level agreement (SLA). An SLA is an official commitment that exists between a service provider and a client. Aspects of the IT services provided—quality, availability, specific responsibilities—are agreed upon between the service provider and the service user. Strict SLAs are becoming increasingly common in networking today as more and more cloud services find their way into the IT landscape. A cloud provider is a specialized service provider, and a cloud consumer is the client.

Two other measures that an organization should consider are the *recovery time objective (RTO)* and the *recovery point objective (RPO)*. These two measurements might sound the same, but they are very different measures:

- **RTO:** The RTO is the time in the future when you expect to restore availability after some failure (or even a disaster) has rendered your IT services unavailable. The RTO value is a very important measure of how long you expect the network to be down.

- **RPO:** As important as the RTO is the RPO, which is the point in time to which you can recover the network. For example, say that your network system failed at 4 p.m. last Monday. Your RPO might be for that very point in time. Sometimes, unfortunately, the RPO will not be the exact point of failure. This is often the case with database systems. For example, a failure might occur at 4 p.m. on a Monday, but you might only be able to recover to 11 a.m. that Monday. This gap in your data might be a result of your disaster recovery plans. Perhaps your backup design can only restore your systems to that 11 a.m. point. An organization must ensure it can accept a particular amount of potential data and service loss.

> **NOTE** The RPO is the amount of data that will be lost or will have to be re-entered because of network downtime. The RTO is the amount of time that can pass before the disruption begins to seriously impede normal business operations.

Fault-Tolerant Network Design

Two important concepts to know when designing a fault-tolerant network are as follows:

- **Single points of failure:** If the failure of a single network device or link (for example, a switch, router, or WAN connection) would result in a network becoming unavailable, that single device or link is a potential single point of failure. To eliminate single points of failure from your design, you might include redundant links and redundant hardware. For example, some high-end Ethernet switches support two power supplies, and if one power supply fails, the switch continues to operate by using the backup power supply. Link redundancy, as shown in Figure 15-1, can be achieved by using more than one physical link. If a single link between a switch and a router fails, the network would not go down because of the link redundancy that is in place.

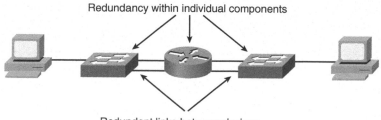

FIGURE 15-1   Redundant Network with Single Points of Failure

- **No single points of failure:** A network without a single point of failure contains redundant network-infrastructure components (for example, switches and routers). In addition, these redundant devices are interconnected with redundant links. Although a network host could have two network interface cards (NICs), each connecting to a different switch, such a design is rarely implemented because of the increased costs. Instead, as shown in Figure 15-2, a network with no single points of failure in the backbone allows any single switch or router in the backbone to fail or any single link in the backbone to fail while maintaining end-to-end network connectivity.

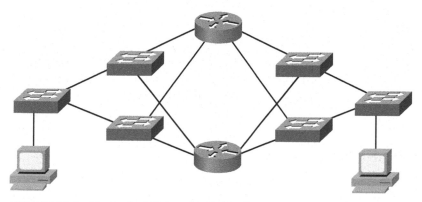

FIGURE 15-2   Redundant Network with No Single Point of Failure

Approaches to fault-tolerant network design can be used together to increase a network's availability even further.

NOTE   Creating multiple paths that data can take in a network is often simply termed *multipathing*. Routing protocols can make multiple paths very valuable to use since they can engage in equal-cost multipathing (ECMP). In fact, Enhanced Interior Gateway Routing Protocol (EIGRP) even provides the unique capability of load sharing between paths of unequal cost.

Hardware Redundancy

Having redundant route processors in a switch or router chassis improves the reliability of the chassis. If a multilayer switch has two route processors, for example, one of the route processors could be active, and the other route processor could be standing by to take over in the event that the active processor became unavailable.

An end system can have redundant NICs. There are two modes of NIC redundancy:

- **Active-active:** Both NICs are active at the same time, and each has its own MAC address. This makes troubleshooting more complex, while giving you slightly better performance than the active-passive approach.

- **Active-passive:** Only one NIC is active at a time. This approach allows the client to appear to have a single MAC address and IP address, even in the event of a NIC failure.

NIC redundancy is most often used in strategic network hosts, rather than in end-user client computers, because of the expense and administrative overhead incurred with redundant NIC configuration.

NOTE   Different vendors use different terms to refer to combining NICs for hardware redundancy. The two most commonly used terms are *network interface card (NIC) teaming* and *NIC bonding*. CompTIA prefers *NIC teaming*.

Another powerful method of hardware redundancy comes in the form of computer clustering. A computer cluster consists of a set of tightly connected computers that work together. In many respects, clients view them as a single system.

The servers in a cluster are usually connected to each other through fast local area networks, with each node running its own instance of an operating system. In most circumstances, all of the nodes use the same hardware and the same operating system, although in some setups, different operating systems—or even different hardware—can be used on each computer.

Computer clusters emerged as a result of the convergence of a number of computing trends, including the availability of low-cost microprocessors, high-speed networks, and software for high-performance distributed computing. They have a wide range of applicability and deployment, ranging from small business clusters with a handful of nodes to some of the fastest supercomputers in the world.

Clustering approach has also made its way to networking devices themselves. For example, today it is not uncommon for large enterprises and datacenters to feature clustered solutions for switches, routers, and firewalls.

Layer 3 Redundancy

End systems not running a routing protocol point to a default gateway. The default gateway is traditionally the IP address of a router on the local subnet. However, if the default gateway router fails, the end systems are unable to leave their subnet. There are four *First Hop Redundancy Protocol (FHRP)* technologies (which offer Layer 3 redundancy):

- **Hot Standby Router Protocol (HSRP):** HSRP is a Cisco-proprietary approach to first-hop redundancy. Figure 15-3 shows a sample HSRP topology.

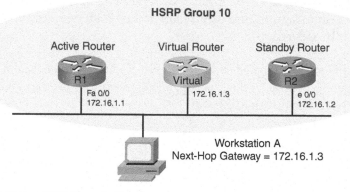

FIGURE 15-3   HSRP Sample Topology

In Figure 15-3, workstation A is configured with the default gateway (that is, the next-hop gateway) 172.16.1.3. To prevent the default gateway from becoming a single point of failure, HSRP enables routers R1 and R2 to each act as the default gateway, supporting the virtual IP address of the HSRP group (172.16.1.3), although only one of the routers will act as the default gateway at any one time. Under normal conditions, router R1 (that is, the *active router*) forwards packets sent to virtual IP address 172.16.1.3. However, if router R1 is unavailable, router R2 (that is, the *standby router*) can take over and start forwarding traffic sent to 172.16.1.3. Notice that neither router R1 nor R2 has a physical interface with IP address 172.16.1.3. Instead, a logical router (called a *virtual router*), which is serviced by either router R1 or R2, maintains the 172.16.1.3 IP address.

- **Common Address Redundancy Protocol (CARP):** CARP is an open-standard variant of HSRP.

- *Virtual Router Redundancy Protocol (VRRP):* VRRP is an IETF open standard that operates in a similar method to Cisco's proprietary HSRP. As with HSRP, with VRRP, many routers can operate in a group and ensure that there is always a router available for the hosts to use as a default gateway. Also as with HSRP, a virtual IP address is assigned to the hosts for their default gateway setting. The routers in the VRRP group can also respond (if needed) to that virtual IP address.

■ **Gateway Load Balancing Protocol (GLBP):** GLBP is another first-hop redundancy protocol that is proprietary to Cisco Systems.

With each of these technologies, the MAC address and the IP address of a default gateway can be serviced by more than one router (or multilayer switch). Therefore, if a default gateway becomes unavailable, the other router (or multilayer switch) can take over and still service the same MAC and IP addresses.

Another type of Layer 3 redundancy is achieved by having multiple links between devices and selecting a routing protocol that balances the load over the links. Link Aggregation Control Protocol (LACP) enables you to assign multiple physical links to a logical interface, which appears as a single link to a route processor. Figure 15-4 illustrates a network topology using LACP.

Gig 0/1-4   Gig 0/1-4

SW1   SW2

FIGURE 15-4   LACP Sample Topology

Finally, another important redundancy technique is to ensure that your default gateways can connect to multiple Internet service providers (ISPs) using diverse paths when redundant Internet connectivity is required. Note that such a solution protects against internal device failures as well as ISP failures that are beyond your control. Your network design can even incorporate periodic reachability tests to ensure that your ISPs are truly available and able to direct you to remote resources successfully.

Design Considerations for High-Availability Networks

When designing networks for high availability, it is important to consider the following questions:

■ Where will module and chassis redundancy be used? Module redundancy provides redundancy within a chassis by allowing one module to take over in the event that a primary module fails. Chassis redundancy means having more than one chassis, thus providing a path from the source to the destination even in the event of a chassis or link failure.

■ What software redundancy features are appropriate?

- What protocol characteristics affect design requirements?

- What redundancy features should be used to provide power to an infrastructure device—for example, using an *uninterruptible power supply (UPS)*, a *generator*, or dual power supplies?

- What redundancy features should be used to maintain environmental conditions (for example, dual air-conditioning units)?

- Will dual circuits be provided in the event of a loss of connection with one of the circuits?

- What backup strategy exists for infrastructure and user data? The main backup strategies are as follows:

  - **Full:** A full backup is a backup of all of the data set. Although this is the safest and most comprehensive way to ensure data availability, it can be time-consuming and costly.

  - **Incremental:** An incremental backup backs up only data that has changed since the previous incremental backup. An incremental backup is incomplete for full recovery without a valid full backup and all incremental backups since the last full backup.

  - **Differential:** A differential backup is similar to an incremental backup in that it starts with a full backup, and then subsequent backups contain only data that has changed. The difference is that whereas an incremental backup only includes the data that has changed since the previous backup, a differential backup contains all of the data that has changed since the last full backup.

  - **Snapshots:** A snapshot is a read-only copy of a data set that is frozen in a point in time. This type backup is often used with virtual machines and file system objects.

- What backup strategy exists for your network devices (both software images and configurations)? Are you backing up state information and configuration information from these devices?

High-Availability Best Practices

Key Topic

The following are the five best practices for designing high-availability networks:

- Examine technical goals.

- Identify the budget for funding high-availability features.

- Categorize business applications into profiles, each of which requires a certain level of availability.

- Establish performance standards for high-availability solutions.

- Define how to manage and measure the high-availability solution.

Although existing networks can be retrofitted to make them highly available, network designers can often reduce expenses by integrating high-availability best practices and technologies into the initial design of a network.

Content Caching

A *content engine* is a network appliance that can receive a copy of content stored elsewhere (for example, a video presentation located on a server at a corporate head-quarters) and serve that content to local clients, thus reducing the bandwidth burden on an IP WAN. Figure 15-5 shows a sample topology using a content engine as a network optimization technology.

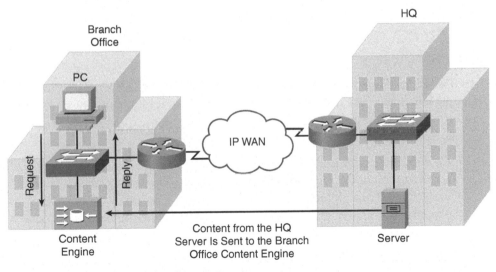

FIGURE 15-5   Content Engine Sample Topology

Load Balancing

Content switching allows a request coming into a server farm to be distributed across multiple servers containing identical content. This approach to **load balancing** lightens the load on individual servers in a server farm and allows servers to be taken out of the farm for maintenance without disrupting access to the server farm's data.

Figure 15-6 illustrates a sample content-switching topology that performs load balancing across five servers (containing identical content) in a server farm.

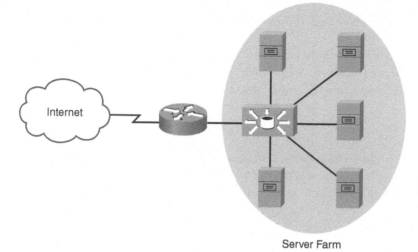

Server Farm

FIGURE 15-6   Content-Switching Sample Topology

Hardware Redundancy

It is possible to design site redundancy into your network infrastructure. Doing so requires redundant data and equipment located in geographically distant areas. How fast can your IT infrastructure be back up and running in the event that issues arise in your primary site? The following options are possible:

- *Cold site*: Recovery is possible but is difficult and time-consuming. A cold site is the weakest of the recovery site options but also the least costly. However, keep in mind that although a cold site may be the least costly when you're planning for disaster, after a disaster occurs, equipment purchased for a cold site might be expensive or difficult to obtain.

- *Warm site*: Recovery is possible fairly quickly, but it might the site might not have the resources and responsiveness of the original site. A warm site is a scaled-down version of a hot site. The recovery site is often only configured with power, phone, and network jacks. It may have computers and other resources, but they are not configured and ready to go.

- *Hot site*: Downtime is minimal, with a service level nearly identical to that of the organization's main site. This type of site is most expensive, and it functions like the original site and is equipped with all necessary hardware, software, network, and Internet connectivity fully installed, configured, and ready to go.

NOTE Today, thanks to advancements in public cloud computing, *cloud sites* are also possible. You can configure cloud sites as cold, warm, or hot sites, typically with ease. More and more, hot site configurations are capable thanks to cloud sites. This is due to the lowered costs and technological requirements made possible by cloud.

Real-World Case Study: SOHO Network Design

Based on what you have learned so far in this book, this section challenges you to create a network design to meet a collection of criteria. Because network design is part science and part art, multiple designs can meet the specified requirements. However, as a reference, this section presents one solution, against which you can contrast your solution.

While working through your design, consider the following:

- Meeting all requirements
- Media distance limitations
- Network device selection
- Environmental factors
- Compatibility with existing and future equipment

Case Study Scenario

The following are the design scenario and criteria for this case study:

- Company ABC leases two buildings (building A and building B) in a large office park, as shown in Figure 15-7. The office park has a conduit system that allows physical media to run between buildings. The distance (via the conduit system) between building A and building B is 1 km.

- Company ABC will use the Class B address 172.16.0.0/16 for its sites. You should subnet this classful network not only to support the two buildings (one subnet per building) but to allow as many as five total sites in the future, as Company ABC continues to grow.

- Company ABC needs to connect to the Internet, supporting a speed of at least 30Mbps, and this connection should come into building A.

- Cost is a primary design consideration, and performance is a secondary design consideration.

- Each building contains various WiFi client devices (for example, smartphones, tablets, and laptops).

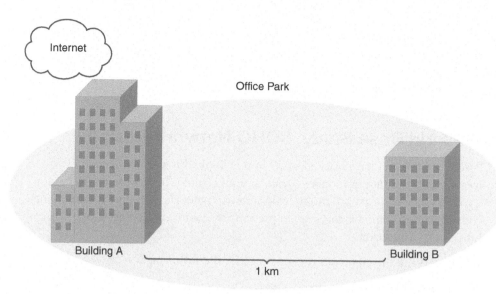

FIGURE 15-7 Case Study Topology

Table 15-1 identifies the number of hosts contained in each building and the number of floors in each building.

Table 15-1 Case Study Information for Buildings A and B

Building	Number of Hosts	Floors (and Wireless Coverage)
A	200	Three floors, each of which can be serviced by a single wireless access point
B	100	One floor, which can be serviced by a single wireless access point

Your design should include the following information:

- Network address and subnet mask for building A
- Network address and subnet mask for building B
- Layer 1 media selection
- Layer 2 device selection
- Layer 3 device selection
- Wireless design

- Any design elements based on environmental considerations
- An explanation of where cost savings were created from performance trade-offs
- A topological diagram of the proposed design

Use multiple sheets of paper to create your network design. After your design is complete, perform a sanity check by contrasting the listed criteria against your design. Finally, while keeping in mind that multiple designs could meet the design criteria, you can review the following suggested solution. In the real world, reviewing the logic behind other designs can often give you a fresh perspective for future designs.

Suggested Solution

This suggested solution begins with IP address allocation. Then, consideration is given to the Layer 1 media, followed by Layer 2 and Layer 3 devices. Wireless design decisions are presented. Design elements based on environmental factors are discussed. The suggested solution also addresses how cost savings were achieved through performance trade-offs. Finally, a topological diagram of the suggested solution is presented.

IP Addressing

Questions you might need to consider when designing the IP addressing of a network include the following:

- How many hosts do you need to support (now and in the future)?
- How many subnets do you need to support (now and in the future)?

From the scenario, you know that each subnet must accommodate at least 200 hosts. Also, you know that you must accommodate at least 5 subnets. In this solution, the subnet mask is based on the number of required subnets. Eight subnets are supported with 3 borrowed bits, and 2 borrowed bits support only four subnets, based on this formula:

Number of subnets = 2^s

where s is the number of borrowed bits

With 3 borrowed bits, you have 13 bits left for host IP addressing, which is much more than needed to accommodate 200 host IP addresses. These 3 borrowed bits yield the subnet mask 255.255.224.0. Because the third octet is the last octet to contain a binary 1 in the subnet mask, the third octet is the *interesting octet*.

The block size can be calculated by subtracting the subnet decimal value in the interesting octet from 256 (that is, 256 − 224 = 32). Because the block size is 32 and the interesting octet is the third octet, the following subnets are created with the 255.255.224.0 (that is, /19) subnet mask:

172.16.0.0 /19

172.16.32.0 /19

172.16.64.0 /19

172.16.96.0 /19

172.16.128.0 /19

172.16.160.0 /19

172.16.192.0 /19

172.16.224.0 /19

The first two subnets are selected for the building A and building B subnet, as shown in Table 15-2.

Table 15-2   Case Study Suggested Solution: Network Addresses

Building	Subnet
A	172.16.0.0 /19
B	172.16.32.0 /19

Layer 1 Media

Questions you might need to ask when selecting the Layer 1 media types of a network include the following:

- What speeds need to be supported (now and in the future)?
- What distances between devices need to be supported (now and in the future)?

Within each building, Category 6a (Cat 6a) unshielded twisted-pair (UTP) cabling is selected to interconnect network components. The installation is based on Gigabit Ethernet. However, 10-Gigabit Ethernet devices may be installed in the future, as Cat 6a is rated for 10GBASE-T for distances as long as 100 m.

The 1 km distance between building A and building B is too great for UTP cabling. Therefore, multimode fiber (MMF) is selected. The speed of the fiber link will be 1Gbps. Table 15-3 summarizes these media selections.

Table 15-3   Case Study Suggested Solution: Layer 1 Media

Connection Type	Media Type
LAN links within buildings	Cat 6a UTP
Link between building A and building B	MMF

Layer 2 Devices

Questions you might need to consider when selecting Layer 2 devices in a network include the following:

- Where will the switches be located?

- What port densities are required on the switches (now and in the future)?

- What switch features need to be supported (for example, STP or LACP)?

- What media types are used to connect to the switches?

A collection of Ethernet switches interconnect network devices within each building. Assume that the 200 hosts in building A are distributed relatively evenly across the three floors (with each floor containing approximately 67 hosts). Therefore, each floor will have a wiring closet containing 2 Ethernet switches: a 48-port switch and a 24-port switch. Each switch is connected to a multilayer switch located in building A using four connections logically bundled together using LACP.

NOTE   Link aggregation is also known as *port aggregation*. CompTIA prefers the term *port aggregation* to link aggregation.

Within building B, 2 Ethernet switches, each with 48 ports, and 1 Ethernet switch, with 24 ports, are installed in a wiring closet. These switches are interconnected in a stacked configuration, using 4 connections logically bundled together with LACP. One of the switches has an MMF port, which allows it to connect via fiber to building A's multilayer switch.

Table 15-4 summarizes the switch selections.

Table 15-4   Case Study Suggested Solution: Layer 2 Devices

Building	Quantity of 48-Port Switches	Quantity of 24-Port Switches
A	3	3
B	2	1

Layer 3 Devices

Questions you might need to consider when selecting Layer 3 devices for a network include the following:

- How many interfaces are needed (now and in the future)?

- What types of interfaces need to be supported (now and in the future)?

- What routing protocol (or protocols) needs to be supported?

- What router features (for example, HSRP or security features) need to be supported?

One Layer 3 device is used: a multilayer switch located in building A. All switches within building A home back to the multilayer switch using four LACP-bundled links. The multilayer switch is equipped with at least one MMF port, which allows a connection with one of the Ethernet switches in building B. The multilayer switch connects to a router via a 10Gbps Ethernet connection. This router contains a serial interface, which connects to the Internet via a T3 connection.

Wireless Design

Questions you might need to consider when designing the wireless portion of a network include the following:

- What wireless speeds need to be supported (now and in the future)?

- What distances need to be supported between wireless devices and wireless access points (now and in the future)?

- What IEEE wireless standards need to be supported?

- What channels should be used?

- Where should wireless access points be located?

Because the network needs to support various WiFi clients, the 2.4GHz band is chosen. Within building A, a wireless access point (AP) is placed on each floor of the building. To avoid interference, the nonoverlapping channels 1, 6, and 11 are chosen. The 2.4GHz band also allows compatibility with IEEE 802.11ac/ax.

Within building B, a single wireless AP accommodates WiFi clients. Table 15-5 summarizes the wireless AP selection.

Table 15-5   Case Study Suggested Solution: Wireless AP Selection

AP Identifier	Building	Band	Channel
1	A (1st floor)	2.4GHz	1
2	A (2nd floor)	2.4GHz	6
3	A (3rd floor)	2.4GHz	11
4	B	2.4GHz	1

Environmental Factors

Questions you might need to consider when considering environmental factors of a network design include the following:

- What temperature or humidity controls exist in the rooms containing network equipment?

- What power redundancy systems are needed to provide power to network equipment in the event of a power outage?

Because the multilayer switch in building A could be a single point of failure for the entire network, the multilayer switch is placed in a well-ventilated room, which can help dissipate heat in the event of an air-conditioning failure. To further enhance the availability of the multilayer switch, the switch is connected to a UPS, which can help the multilayer switch continue to run for a brief time in the event of a power outage. Protection against an extended power outage could be achieved with the addition of a generator. However, no generator is included in this design for budgetary reasons.

NOTE   Other common considerations in this area include the use of **power distribution units (PDUs)**, which are devices fitted with multiple outputs designed to distribute electric power. **Heating, ventilation, and air-conditioning (HVAC)** and **fire suppression systems** should also be analyzed to determine their power needs.

Cost Savings Versus Performance

When assimilating all the previously gathered design elements, you need to weigh budgetary constraints against network performance metrics. In this example, Gigabit Ethernet was chosen over 10-Gigabit Ethernet. In addition, the link between building A and building B could become a bottleneck because it runs at a speed of 1Gbps, although it transports an aggregation of multiple 1Gbps links. However, cost savings are achieved by using 1Gbps switch interfaces as opposed to 10Gbps interfaces or a bundle of multiple 1Gbps fiber links.

Topology

Figure 15-8 shows the topology of the proposed design based on design decisions described in this section.

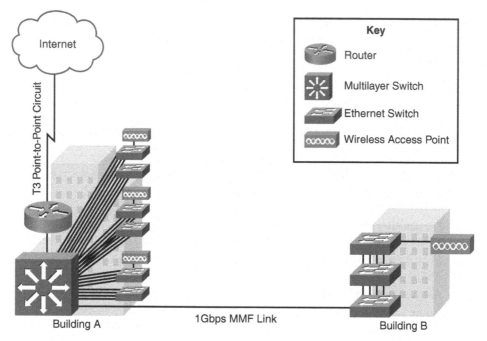

FIGURE 15-8   Case Study Proposed Topology

Real-World Case Study

The network design for Acme, Inc. includes fault tolerance at several points in the network. The uplinks that go to the wiring closets from the MDF downstairs are implemented as redundant pairs so that if a single pair fails or a single interface fails, the other fiber pair and associated interfaces can continue to forward traffic. The routing function is located downstairs, and each VLAN (and associated subnet) has a pair of routers acting as an HSRP group.

The firewalls that control traffic at the edge of the company's networks are also set up in an active-active failover pair.

A dedicated VLAN just for voice traffic on the wired network has been set up with the appropriate marking of traffic. Routers and switches have been configured to identify voice traffic based on its markings, and if congestion is present, the voice traffic will receive priority treatment for forwarding over the network.

The Active Directory servers that the company is using internally are running on a virtualized hardware platform using VMware's vSphere. VMware offers fault tolerance in the form of a backup copy of the Active Directory servers available in the event that the primary servers fail.

A VPN over the Internet will be used (via a second service provider) to connect the branch and headquarters offices in the event of the failure of the Multiprotocol Label Switching (MPLS) path over the primary WAN through the primary service provider.

Abnormally high levels of Internet Control Message Protocol (ICMP) packets that are heading to the headquarters site from the Internet will be rate-limited at the service provider. This will reduce the potential for an ICMP-based attack that is attempting to consume all the bandwidth available to the HQ site.

Summary

Here are the main topics covered in this chapter:

- This chapter discusses network availability, including how availability is measured and can be achieved through redundant designs.

- This chapter discusses performance optimization strategies, including the use of content caching, link aggregation, and load balancing.

- This chapter includes a case study that challenges you to design a network to meet a collection of criteria.

Exam Preparation Tasks

Review All the Key Topics

Review the most important topics from this chapter, noted with the Key Topic icon in the outer margin of the page. Table 15-6 lists these key topics and the page number where each is found.

Key Topic

Table 15-6   Key Topics for Chapter 15

Key Topic Element	Description	Page Number
Section	Two approaches to fault-tolerant networks	395
Section	Layer 3 redundancy	398
List	Design considerations for high-availability networks	399
List	High-availability best practices	400

Define Key Terms

Define the following key terms from this chapter and check your answers in the Glossary:

load balancing, multipathing, network interface card (NIC) teaming, uninterruptible power supply (UPS), power distribution units (PDUs), generator, heating, ventilation, and air-conditioning (HVAC), fire suppression systems, cold site, warm site, hot site, cloud site, Virtual Router Redundancy Protocol (VRRP), First Hop Redundancy Protocol (FHRP), mean time to repair (MTTR), mean time between failure (MTBF), recovery time objective (RTO), recovery point objective (RPO)

Complete Chapter 15 Hands-On Labs in Network+ Simulator Lite

- Identifying Network Performance Terminology
- Disaster Recovery/Business Continuity

Additional Resources

How to Prevent Network Outages: https://www.youtube.com/watch?v=DqCgkn2CDbc

Networking Design Best Practices: https://www.youtube.com/watch?v=sckuGYiHYRA

Review Questions

The answers to these review questions appear in Appendix A, "Answers to Review Questions."

1. If a network has five nines availability, how much downtime does it experience per year?

   a. 30 seconds

   b. 5 minutes

   c. 12 minutes

   d. 26 minutes

2. What mode of NIC redundancy has only one NIC active at a time?

   a. Publisher-subscriber

   b. Client-server

   c. Active-passive

   d. Active-subscriber

3. What performance optimization technology involves a network appliance that can receive a copy of content stored elsewhere (for example, a video presentation located on a server at a corporate headquarters) and serves that content to local clients, thus reducing the bandwidth burden on an IP WAN?

   a. Content engine

   b. Load balancer

   c. LACP

   d. CARP

4. What type of backup solution is a point-in-time, read-only copy of data?

   a. Differential

   b. Incremental

   c. Snapshot

   d. Virtual

5. What type of site provides a nearly identical level of service to the organization's main site, with virtually no downtime?

   a. Warm

   b. Cold

   c. Hot

   d. Remote

6. What capability of routing protocols allows them to help you use the bandwidth that you might have available in a multipathing design?

   a. ECMP

   b. Distance vector

   c. Link state

   d. Dual stack

7. In order to measure high availability (HA), you need to know the average amount of time that passes between hardware component failures. What is this called?

   a. MTTR

   b. RPO

   c. RTO

   d. MTBF

8. You are tasked with locating a backup facility for your organization to use in the event of a disaster. You have a slim budget, and the facility needs to include electricity, bathrooms, and space. Which type of recovery site suits your requirements?

   a. Hot site

   b. Cold site

   c. Warm site

   d. Cloud site

9. Which of the following statements are true regarding backups? (Select three.)

   a. The difference between incremental and differential backups is that a differential backup includes all data that has changed since the last incremental backup.

   b. A differential backup includes all data that has changed since the last full backup.

c. An incremental backup is incomplete for full recovery without a full backup and all incremental backups since the last full backup.

d. A full backup is the safest and most comprehensive way to ensure data availability, but it can be time-consuming and costly.

This chapter covers the following topics related to Objective 4.1 (Explain common security concepts) of the CompTIA Network+ N10-008 certification exam:

- Confidentiality, integrity, availability (CIA)
- Threats
  - Internal
  - External
- Vulnerabilities
  - Common vulnerabilities and exposures (CVE)
  - Zero-day
- Exploits
- Least privilege
- Role-based access
- Zero Trust
- Defense in depth
  - Network segmentation enforcement
  - Screened subnet [previously known as demilitarized zone (DMZ)]
  - Separation of duties
  - Network access control
  - Honeypot
- Authentication methods
  - Multifactor

- Terminal Access Controller Access Control System Plus (TACACS+)
- Single sign-on (SSO)
- Remote Authentication Dial-In User Service (RADIUS)
- LDAP
- Kerberos
- Local authentication
- 802.1X
- Extensible Authentication Protocol (EAP)
- Risk management
  - Security risk assessments
    - Threat assessment
    - Vulnerability assessment
    - Penetration testing
    - Posture assessment
  - Business risk assessments
    - Process assessment
    - Vendor assessment
- Security information and event management (SIEM)

CHAPTER 16

Common Security Concepts

Today's networks are increasingly dependent on connectivity with other networks. However, connecting an organization's trusted network to untrusted networks, such as the Internet, introduces security risks. Security risks exist even internally within an organization.

To protect your organization's data from malicious users, you need to understand the types of threats against which you might have to defend. Then you need to know your options for defending the network. A key security concept to understand is that you need multiple layers of security (defense in depth) for your network, not just a single solution, such as a firewall. You might, for example, combine user training, security policies, remote access security protocols, firewalls, VPNs, and intrusion prevention systems to provide overlapping layers of network protection.

This chapter begins by introducing the fundamentals of security, including a discussion of defense-in-depth strategies. This chapter also presents the most common authentication methods used in networks today, and it concludes with a look at risk management and as security information and event management (SIEM).

Foundation Topics

Core Security Concepts

This section examines several very important core security concepts that are critical for you to understand in the current cybersecurity landscape—starting with *confidentiality, integrity, and availability (CIA)*.

Confidentiality, Integrity, and Availability (CIA)

For most of today's corporate networks, the demands of e-commerce and customer contact require connectivity between internal corporate networks and the outside world. Today's corporate networks tend to be large and interconnected with other networks, and they typically run both standards-based and proprietary protocols. In addition, the devices and applications connecting to and using corporate networks are continually increasing in complexity. It would be unusual for a corporate network not to need network security.

CIA refers to the three primary goals of network security:

- Confidentiality

- Integrity

- Availability

The following sections explain these goals in more detail.

Confidentiality

Data confidentiality involves keeping data private by physically or logically restricting access to sensitive data or encrypting traffic traversing a network. A network that provides confidentiality would, for example, do the following:

- Use network security mechanisms, such as firewalls and access control lists (ACLs), to prevent unauthorized access to network resources.

- Require appropriate credentials (such as usernames and passwords) to access specific network resources.

- Encrypt traffic such that any traffic captured off the network by an attacker could not be deciphered by the attacker.

Confidentiality can be provided by using *encryption*. Encryption allows a packet to be encoded in such a way that it can be decoded by an intended party. However, a malicious user who intercepted an encrypted packet in transit would not be able to decrypt the packet. The way most modern encryption algorithms prevent decryption by a third party is through the use of a *key*. Because the encryption or decryption algorithm uses a key in its mathematical calculation, a third party who does not possess the key cannot interpret intercepted data that is encrypted.

Encryption has two basic forms: *symmetric encryption* and *asymmetric encryption*.

Symmetric Encryption

Symmetric encryption is faster than asymmetric encryption. The word *symmetric* in symmetric encryption implies that the same key is used by both the sender and the receiver to encrypt or decrypt a packet. Examples of symmetric encryption algorithms include the following:

- **DES:** Data Encryption Standard (DES) is an older encryption algorithm (developed in the mid-1970s) that uses a 56-bit key. It is considered weak by today's standards and has been deprecated.

- **3DES:** Triple DES (3DES), developed in the late 1990s, uses three 56-bit DES keys (for a total of 168 bits) and was originally considered a strong encryption algorithm. However, the security of 3DES varies based on the way it is implemented. Specifically, 3DES has three keying options: All three keys may be different (keying option 1), two of the three keys may be the same (keying option 2), or all three keys may be the same (keying option 3) to maintain backward compatibility with DES. Because of the high computational overhead of 3DES, many companies have moved directly to the much faster AES instead of using 3DES.

- **AES:** Advanced Encryption Standard (AES), released in 2001, is the preferred symmetric encryption algorithm. AES, which is a variant of the Rijndael family of symmetric ciphers, is available in 128-bit key, 192-bit key, and 256-bit key versions. This technology is being used more and more for many different applications, including wireless, mobile, VPNs, and web security implementations. It is popular because of its overall strength and its ability to provide various levels of security based on key length. For lower-security environments, you can use 128-bit key AES; a 256-bit key implementation is considerable almost unbreakable.

Figure 16-1 provides an example of symmetric encryption, where both parties have a shared key to be used during a session (called a *session key*).

NOTE   Another widely deployed encryption algorithm is Pretty Good Privacy (PGP), which is often used to encrypt email traffic. PGP uses both symmetric and asymmetric algorithms. A free variant of PGP is GNU Privacy Guard (GPG).

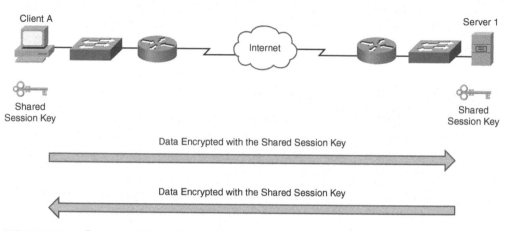

FIGURE 16-1   Symmetric Encryption Example

Asymmetric Encryption

Asymmetric encryption is slow compared to symmetric encryption but provides better security. As its name suggests, asymmetric encryption uses asymmetric (different) keys for the sender and the receiver of a packet. Because of its speed, asymmetric encryption is not typically used to encrypt large quantities of real-time data. Rather, asymmetric encryption might be used to encrypt a small chunk of data used, for example, to authenticate the other party in a conversation or to exchange a shared key to be used during a session (after which the parties in the conversation could start using symmetric encryption). One of the most popular asymmetric encryption algorithms in use today is RSA; its name comes from the last initials of its inventors: Ronald L. Rivest, Adi Shamir, and Leonard M. Adleman.

RSA is commonly used as part of a public key infrastructure (PKI) system. Specifically, PKI uses digital certificates and a certificate authority (CA) for authentication and encryption services.

For example, in the example shown in Figure 16-2, when client A wants to communicate securely with server 1, the following steps occur:

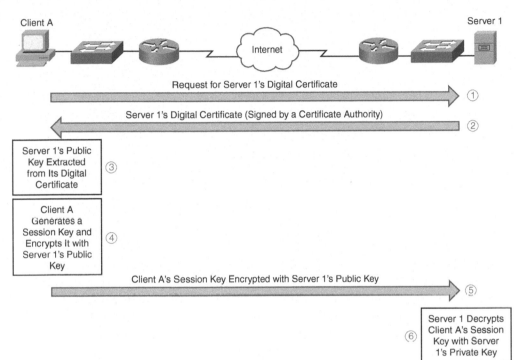

FIGURE 16-2 Asymmetric Encryption Example

Step 1.   Client A requests server 1's digital certificate.

Step 2.   Server 1 sends its digital certificate, and client A knows the received certificate is really from server 1 because the certificate has been authenticated (*signed*) by a trusted third party, called a *certificate authority*.

Step 3.   Client A extracts server 1's public key from server 1's digital certificate. Data encrypted using server 1's public key can only be decrypted with server 1's private key, which only server 1 has.

Step 4.   Client A generates a random string of data called a *session key*.

Step 5.   The session key is encrypted using server 1's public key and sent to server 1.

Step 6.   Server 1 decrypts the session key by using its private key.

At this point, both client A and server 1 know the session key, which can be used to symmetrically encrypt traffic during the session.

> **NOTE** Symmetric key algorithms are faster and are often used for bulk encryption of data. Asymmetric key algorithms are slower and are often used for initial security transactions such as authentication.

Integrity

Ensuring data *integrity* involves making sure data has not been modified in transit. Also, a data integrity solution might perform origin authentication to verify that traffic is originating from the source that should send the traffic.

Examples of integrity violations include the following:

- Modifying the appearance of a corporate website

- Intercepting and altering an e-commerce transaction

- Modifying financial records that are stored electronically

Hashing is one approach to providing integrity to data transmissions crossing a network. Specifically, hashing takes a string of data (such as a password) and runs it through an algorithm. The result of the algorithm is called a *hash* or a *hash digest*. If the sender of that data runs a hashing algorithm on the data and sends the hash digest along with the data, when the recipient receives the data, she can also run the data through the same hashing algorithm. If the recipient calculates the same hash digest, she might conclude that the data has not been modified in transit (that is, she has confirmed the integrity of the data). Note that a hashing algorithm produces hash digests of the same length, regardless of the size of the data being hashed.

Two hashing algorithms are commonly used:

- **Message Digest 5 (MD5):** Creates 128-bit hash digests

- **Secure Hash Algorithm 1 (SHA-1):** Creates 160-bit hash digests

Hashing by itself, however, does not guarantee data integrity because an attacker could intercept a string of data, manipulate it, and recalculate the hash value based on the manipulated data. The victim would then determine that the hash is valid based on the data. To overcome this limitation of pure hashing, Hashed Message Authentication Code (HMAC) uses an additional secret key in the calculation of a hash value. Therefore, an attacker would not be able to create a valid hash value because he would not know the secret key. Other variants of hashing algorithms, such as SHA-256, involve longer digests. In cryptography, a bigger digest implies better security.

NOTE   Challenge-Response Authentication Mechanism Message Digest 5 (CRAM-MD5) was a common variant of HMAC frequently used in email systems. Today, even this enhancement has been deprecated in favor of more secure technologies such as SSL and TLS.

Availability

The availability of data is a measure of the data's accessibility. For example, if a server were down only 5 minutes per year, the server would have an availability of 99.999% (that is, the *five nines availability*).

Here are a couple of examples of how an attacker could attempt to compromise the availability of a network:

- Send improperly formatted data to a networked device, resulting in an unhandled exception error.

- Flood a network system with an excessive amount of traffic or requests, which would consume a system's processing resources and prevent the system from responding to many legitimate requests. This type of attack is commonly referred to as a denial-of-service (DoS) attack.

Threats, Vulnerabilities, and Exploits

To effectively guard a network against attacks, you should be able to identify a number of security concepts within your own environment, as described in this section.

Threats

You should work with your team to carefully identify the realistic security ***threats*** that your enterprise could face. This might mean dealing with hypotheticals, but it is nonetheless a very important exercise. While the focus is often on external threats to an organization, you cannot forget that internal threats exist. In fact, a network often faces more internal threats than external ones.

Vulnerabilities

One of the reasons there are so many potential threats against organizations today is the fact that ***vulnerabilities*** are constantly discovered in networks and network components. New code installed on a network device (such as a router) might cause a vulnerability. For example, this code could introduce a new feature that creates a backdoor into the device for unauthorized persons.

Because vulnerabilities are a major issue for IT staff, a number of tools have been developed to deal with them. The **Common Vulnerabilities and Exposures (CVE)** system is free to use and can be incredibly helpful. This online resource provides excellent search tools and can leverage a large database of publicly known information security vulnerabilities and exposures. CVE, which was officially launched in September 1999, is sponsored by US-CERT within the U.S. Department of Homeland Security (DHS). The MITRE Corporation maintains a CVE dictionary at https://cve.mitre.org.

NOTE   The two catalogs of known vulnerabilities you should be familiar with are CVE and VCSS. CVE is a list of publicly known vulnerabilities containing an ID number, description, and reference for each vulnerability. The Common Vulnerability Scoring System (CVSS) provides a score from 0 to 10 that indicates the severity of a vulnerability. Also of great value is the Open Web Application Security Project (OWASP), which is a foundation that works to improve software security. Each year, OWASP publishes the OWASP Top 10 for web application security exploits. For more information, visit https://owasp.org.

NOTE   *Zero-day attacks* are cybersecurity attacks that use techniques or vulnerabilities that have not already been discovered by cybersecurity specialists or anti-malware companies. While it might sound hopeless, remember that today's sophisticated security appliances can typically prevent or mitigate damage from zero-day attacks by using machine learning (ML) to stop activities in a network that are outside the normal baseline activities.

Exploits

As mentioned earlier, when we discussed threats, we are typically talking about hypotheticals— events that might possibly occur in a network. When we discuss *exploits*, however, we are talking about facts. An exploit consists of a (hopefully detailed) description of what exactly occurred with a security breach. An exploit often describes the most likely attacker, the technology used, and any vulnerabilities or misconfigurations that made the attack possible.

Least Privilege

An important security best practice that you should implement everywhere possible in your network is *least privilege*. You and every other person who interacts with the network should always be using a user account that has the least number of privileges required to do a job. It is important to carefully audit the required permissions to complete tasks and then create accounts (or groups) that have just those permissions. Then, if a computer criminal manages to begin operating on the network using your account, the criminal will only be able to accomplish minimal tasks.

Implementing least privilege might sound easy, but human nature often opposes this commonsense measure. For example, an administrator might prefer to use an administrator or root account for all administrative tasks because switching between accounts can be tedious.

It can also be very easy to violate this best practice without even knowing it. This often happens in public cloud environments. An administrator may start a free tier Amazon Web Services (AWS) account using his email address. He may have not studied much about AWS and might not realize that there is a service called Identity and Access Management (IAM) designed for the creation of accounts and permissions in AWS. The administrator may continue to use that administrative account email address for day-to-day operations in AWS, even though AWS makes it clear that using such a high-level account is not safe. The only time you should use that high-level admin account is when you are performing some specific change that requires it, such as changing the credit card on the account or other billing configurations.

Role-Based Access

Most network device designers strive to implement *role-based access control (RBAC)* for administrators who must manage devices. In addition, more and more network access models for users are emphasizing RBAC for network access.

The idea with RBAC is to create permissions around roles that you can then assign to users. For example, you might use RBAC for guest access; to do so, you would create a guest role and assign that role to visitors to your organization when you want to give them limited privileges. Perhaps you just want such visitors to be able to access your public Internet connection for limited Internet access. You might also use RBAC to create network administrator accounts for users who need to have the ability access the network and also reconfigure it.

> **NOTE** A scalable method for assigning roles (permissions) to user accounts is to include those user accounts in roles (also called groups) that have the appropriate permissions assigned. The users inherit the permissions thanks to their group membership. On some network devices, RBAC is more limited, and you can only assign permissions to the user accounts themselves.

Zero Trust

Zero Trust is a relatively new security model that many corporations are starting to use. As the name indicates, this model seeks to reduce or eliminate security breaches for an organization by trusting absolutely nothing by default. In fact, the credo of this approach is "never trust; always verify."

Zero Trust was created by John Kindervag of Forrester Research. He realized that traditional security models operate on the silly assumption that everything inside an organization's network should be trusted. With models based on this assumption, once a network attacker has gained access, that user account is trusted. The Zero Trust model views trust as a vulnerability.

Zero Trust is implemented using many different technologies in a network, including the following:

- Segmenting the network
- Preventing lateral movement
- Providing Layer 7 threat prevention
- Simplifying granular user access control

Defense in Depth

Cisco Systems is one of the networking giants that helped to popularize the great idea of *defense in depth* for network security. Defense in depth involves striving to secure each layer of a solution. For example, you might use strong security on containers and virtual machines that provide software as a service (SaaS) for your organization. You can then use strong security controls for the host systems that provide these virtual servers. You can also have strong security controls in place on the network switch that connects to these hosts. This process continues, building layer after layer of security into the network and the systems that connect to it.

As with the Zero Trust security approach, there is no single technique that makes defense in depth what it is. This section describes just some of the security approaches you might employ when you are using a defense-in-depth approach.

Network Segmentation Enforcement

Logical segmentation of networks helps to enforce strong security designs. For example, VLANs can be used to constrain broadcasts and permit the definition of VLAN access control lists (ACLs) and router ACLs for controlling communication between VLANs.

Network segmentation enforcement can also help to minimize the effects of security attacks by limiting them to the local subnet.

At Layer 3, you can segment by using virtual routing and forwarding (VRF) tables for network devices. These tables, which are like virtual routers running within the main router, can be separate and distinct from the main routing table. The main routing table is termed the *global routing table*.

Screened Subnet

A *screened subnet*—previously called a *demilitarized zone (DMZ)*—often contains servers that should be accessible from the public Internet. With a screened subnet, for example, you could allow users on the Internet to initiate an email or web session coming into your organization's email or web server; however, you could block other protocols for those users.

Separation of Duties

A popular security best practice is to implement a *separation of duties* policy in the network. This policy ensures that user accounts in the network do not have too much power. You can also ensure that your IT staff are mapped to these various duties and even rotated through them. This helps to ensure that internal attacks against your network do not occur. It is important to include separation of duties when planning for security policy compliance. Without this separation, all areas of control and compliance could end up in the hands of a single individual.

Network Access Control

Network access control (NAC) involves using a set of protocols to ensure that users are identified immediately when they try to access the network. A NAC system might integrate automatic remediation processes to fix the issues with host systems so that they are brought in compliance with corporate security policies.

A common approach to building a NAC system is to incorporate 802.1X in the network. 802.1X is covered later in this chapter.

Honeypot

A *honeypot* acts as a distracter. Specifically, a system designated as a honeypot appears to be an attractive attack target. One school of thought on the use of honeypots is to place one or more honeypot systems in a network to entice attackers into thinking a system is real. The attackers then use their resources to attack the honeypot, and in doing so, they leave the real servers alone.

A honeypot can also be used to see what attackers are attempting to do on the system. A honeypot could, for example, be a UNIX or Linux-based system configured with a weak password. After an attacker logs in, surveillance software could log what the attacker does on the system. This knowledge could then be used to protect real servers in the network.

NOTE For larger networks, a network administrator might deploy multiple honeypots, forming a *honeynet*.

Authentication Methods

Because authentication is such an important part of network security, it is little surprise that, today, there are many different approaches you can use. This section describes several authentication methods.

Multifactor

Authentication that requires multiple factors is called ***multifactor authentication (MFA)***. Factors might include the following:

- Something you know (such as a passcode)
- Something you are (such as biometrics)
- Something you have/possess (such as a smart card)
- Something you must perform (such as connecting to a specific network)

Today, smartphones are often used in multifactor authentication. A smartphone is something you possess, and a network can take advantage of this by sending a one-time password (OTP) to your smartphone to make sure you are who you claim to be.

TACACS+

Terminal Access Controller Access Control System Plus (TACACS+) is a Cisco-proprietary TCP-based protocol. TACACS+ has three separate and distinct sessions or functions for authentication, authorization, and accounting (AAA). It is similar to Remote Authentication Dial-In User Service (RADIUS) but uses TCP instead of UDP as a transport method; it uses port 49 as the default port. TACACS+ takes a client/server model approach.

Single Sign-On

Single sign-on (SSO) allows a user to authenticate only once to gain access to multiple systems or applications, without requiring the user to independently authenticate with each system or application.

RADIUS

Remote Authentication Dial-In User Service (RADIUS) is a UDP-based protocol used to communicate with a AAA server. Unlike TACACS+, RADIUS does not encrypt an entire authentication packet; it encrypts only the password. However, RADIUS does offer more robust accounting features than TACACS+. Also, RADIUS is a standards-based protocol, whereas TACACS+ is a Cisco-proprietary protocol. RADIUS uses UDP port 1812 for authentication and authorization and UDP port 1813 for accounting.

LDAP

Lightweight Directory Access Protocol (LDAP) permits a set of standards for the storage and access of user account information. Many proprietary user stores support LDAP for ease of access, including Microsoft's Active Directory. By default, LDAP traffic is unsecured (over port 389). LDAP over TLS/SSL (LDAPS) is a secure form of LDAP with secured communications using port 636.

Kerberos

Kerberos is a client/server authentication protocol that supports mutual authentication between a client and a server. With Kerberos, a trusted third party (a key distribution center [KDC]) hands out tickets that are used instead of username and password combinations.

Here is a look at this process:

Step 1.   The client contacts a CA.

Step 2.   The CA creates a time-stamped session key with a limited duration (by default, eight hours) by using the client's key and a randomly generated key that includes the identification of the target service.

Step 3.   The CA sends this information back to the client in the form of a ticket-granting ticket (TGT).

Step 4.   The client submits the TGT to a ticket-granting server (TGS).

Step 5.   The TGS generates a time-stamped key encrypted with the service's key and returns both keys to the client.

Step 6.   The client uses its key to decrypt its ticket, contacts the server, and offers the encrypted ticket to the TGS.

Step 7.   The TGS uses its key to decrypt the ticket and verify that the time stamps match and the ticket remains valid.

Step 8.   The service contacts the KDC and receives a time-stamped session keyed ticket that it returns to the client.

Step 9.   The client decrypts the keyed ticket by using its key. When the client and the server agree that they are the proper accounts and that the keys are within their valid lifetimes, communication is initiated.

Local Authentication

Local authentication refers to a network device authenticating the user with a database of user account information stored on the device itself. This is often an important fallback authentication method used when another external method fails.

802.1X

IEEE *802.1X* is a type of NAC that involves permitting or denying a wireless or wired LAN client access to a network. If IEEE 802.1X is used to permit access to a LAN via a switch port, then IEEE 802.1X is being used for port security.

The device seeking admission to a network is called the *supplicant*. The device to which the supplication connects (either wirelessly or through a wired connection) is called the *authenticator*. The device that checks the supplicant's credentials and permits or denies the supplicant to access the network is called an *authentication server*. Usually, an authentication server is a RADIUS server.

EAP

Extensible Authentication Protocol (EAP) specifies how authentication is performed by IEEE 802.1X. A variety of EAP types exist, including Protected Extensible Authentication Protocol (PEAP), Extensible Authentication Protocol Flexible Authentication via Secure Tunneling (EAP-FAST), Extensible Authentication Protocol Transport Layer Security (EAP-TLS), and Extensible Authentication Protocol-Tunneled Transport Layer Security (EAP-TTLS).

In a typical 802.1X setup, EAP is used to carry the credential information provided by the supplicant to the authenticator. EAP is then encapsulated into RADIUS for transmission to the authentication server.

Risk Management and SIEM

Two final areas of cybersecurity that this chapter examines are risk management and security information and event management (SIEM). Every organization should consider risk management, and many would argue that every organization should also consider SIEM. Both of these areas can help an organization save money, save time, and, ultimately, be more secure.

Risk Management

It is important for an organization to take a formal approach to *risk management* in order to secure the organization and also help ensure that the organization is spending its time and resources on the best possible security solutions for the situation.

Risk management involves carefully identifying, evaluating, and prioritizing risks. It typically also involves the coordinated application of resources to minimize, monitor, and control the probability or impact of cybersecurity-related events.

Security Risk Assessments

Cybersecurity concerns continue to increase in number and importance. Fortunately, there are many assessments you can conduct to help improve the overall security of your network infrastructure. This section details some of the ones you should be familiar with.

Threat Assessment

Oftentimes, as part of risk management, you need to engage in *threat assessment*. This process involves evaluating the credibility and seriousness of potential threats and analyzing the probability that particular threats will become a reality.

Vulnerability Assessment

Another common part of risk management is *vulnerability assessment*. When you perform a vulnerability assessment, you identify, quantify, and prioritize the vulnerabilities in a system.

> **NOTE**   Vulnerability assessments can be performed for a wide variety of systems within an IT department and in a network as a whole.

Penetration Testing

Penetration testing can be an important part of the risk management processes for an organization. Penetration testing involves trying to find vulnerabilities and problems with the security settings of a network or network component. Penetration testing can help you find major problems with systems and mitigate the risk of cyberattack.

Posture Assessment

Another common part of risk management is *posture assessment*, which involves examining the state of a network and the network nodes from a security perspective. You can use the results of posture assessment to implement new security rules through an AAA system. With posture assessment, you can design requirements related to patch levels, software updates, or things like firewall rules. If an incoming system does not meet those requirements, you can deny it access to the network.

Business Risk Assessment

Thorough risk management processes might include business risk assessment. With this type of assessment, the focus may be on the business processes and vendors the organization has partnered with. Process and vendor assessment are just two of the many types of business risk assessment an organization might perform.

Process Assessment

A thorough *process assessment* can help determine the security-consciousness of the various business processes that an organization engages in. Process assessments often concentrate on many other areas beyond security. For example, an organization may find many inefficiencies in the business processes in use daily.

One of the many reasons that business process assessments are necessary is that companies can get complacent and fail to update their process documentation even though many small changes have been implemented over time.

Vendor Assessment

A *vendor assessment* is a type of risk assessment in which a team analyzes the many vendors an organization uses in its business processes. This type of assessment considers how much organizational data vendors have access to, and the security practices of the vendors. There are a number of issues you should consider in assessing the vendors your business relies on.

Security Information and Event Management (SIEM)

Key Topic

Monitoring is a critical part of network security. For example, *security information and event management (SIEM)* software products and services combine security information management (SIM) and security event management (SEM).

SIEM systems provides real-time analysis of security alerts generated by applications and network hardware. These systems can log security data and generate reports for compliance purposes.

A SIEM system can take many forms; it can be implemented as software, as appliances, or as managed services.

Here are just some of the focuses of various SIEM products:

- **Log management:** This aspect of the SIEM helps administrators back up and archive the many log files in the network, along with many other management tasks appropriate for this data.

- **Security information management (SIM):** SIM focuses on long-term storage as well as analysis and reporting of log data.

- **Security event manager (SEM):** SEM involves real-time monitoring, correlation of events, notifications, and console views.

- **Managed security service (MSS) or managed security service provider (MSSP):** The most common managed services are related to connectivity and bandwidth, network monitoring, security, virtualization, and disaster recovery.

- **Security as a service (SECaaS):** These security services often include authentication, antivirus, anti-malware/spyware, intrusion detection, penetration testing, and security event management, among others.

Real-World Case Study

Acme, Inc. is currently improving the security posture of the organization. As part of this effort, Acme, Inc. is training the IT team in the most common types of cybersecurity attacks that are likely to impact Acme, Inc.

The company is also implementing a well-regarded SIEM to assist with the day-to-day handling and detection of potential security exploits.

Finally, Acme, Inc. is also changing some of the authentication methods used in the enterprise network. Specifically, Acme, Inc. is planning to implement MFA for all users of the enterprise software.

Summary

Here are the main topics covered in this chapter:

- This chapter reviewed key security concepts that we should be aware of in networking today. This includes important concepts like CIA, symmetric and asymmetric encryption, and threats, vulnerabilities, and exploits.

- This chapter also examined the various authentication methods that are popular today. This includes technologies like MFA (multifactor authentication).

- Finally, this chapter concludes by examining risk management and SIEMs. These can be important aspects of the security operations for the organization.

Exam Preparation Tasks

Review All the Key Topics

Review the most important topics from this chapter, noted with the Key Topic icon in the outer margin of the page. Table 16-1 lists these key topics and the page number where each is found.

Table 16-1 Key Topics for Chapter 16

Key Topic Element	Description	Page Number
Section	Confidentiality, integrity, and availability (CIA)	418
Section	Symmetric encryption	419
Section	Asymmetric encryption	421
Section	Integrity	422
Section	Least privilege	425

Key Topic Element	Description	Page Number
Section	Zero Trust	426
Section	802.1X	430
Section	SIEM	433

Define Key Terms

Define the following key terms from this chapter and check your answers in the Glossary:

confidentiality, integrity, and availability (CIA), threat, vulnerability, Common Vulnerabilities and Exposures (CVE), zero-day attack, exploit, least privilege, role-based access control (RBAC), Zero Trust, defense in depth, network segmentation enforcement, screened subnet, demilitarized zone (DMZ), separation of duties, network access control (NAC), honeypot, multifactor authentication (MFA), Terminal Access Controller Access Control System Plus (TACACS+), single sign-on (SSO), Remote Authentication Dial-In User Service (RADIUS), Lightweight Directory Access Protocol (LDAP), Kerberos, local authentication, 802.1X, Extensible Authentication Protocol (EAP), risk management, threat assessment, vulnerability assessment, penetration testing, posture assessment, process assessment, vendor assessment, security information and event management (SIEM)

Complete Chapter 16 Hands-On Labs in Network+ Simulator Lite

- Network Vulnerabilities
- Secure Protocols vs. Unsecure Protocols
- Security Terminology and Descriptions
- Cryptographic Authentication Terminology
- Creating Network Users on a Domain Controller

Additional Resources

8 Most Common Cyber Security Attacks: https://www.youtube.com/watch?v=Dk-ZqQ-bfy4

10 Hacking Tactics You Should Know: https://www.youtube.com/watch?v=kOGSPHI-Ok4

Review Questions

The answers to these review questions appear in Appendix A, "Answers to Review Questions."

1. Which of the following is a symmetric encryption algorithm available in 128-bit, 192-bit, and 256-bit key versions?

   a. RSA

   b. 3DES

   c. AES

   d. TKIP

2. What aspect of modern cybersecurity focuses on ensuring that data has not been manipulated in transit?

   a. Integrity

   b. Confidentiality

   c. Authentication

   d. Availability

3. What security approach involves creating multiple accounts for your own access to the network and to its devices?

   a. 802.1X

   b. Least privilege

   c. Network access control

   d. SIEM

4. Which of the following is a device that is meant to attract security attacks?

   a. SIEM

   b. Next Generation Firewall

   c. IPS

   d. Honeypot

5. What security protocol is used in 802.1X to securely transport the credentials used in an exchange?

   a. IPsec

   b. EAP

   c. SSH

   d. HTTPS

6. Which of the following provides excellent search tools to leverage a large database of publicly known information security vulnerabilities and exposures?

   a. ACL

   b. AWS

   c. SHA-256

   d. CVE

7. Which of the following provides real-time analysis of security alerts generated by applications and network hardware and can log security data and generate reports for compliance purposes?

   a. SIEM system

   b. Screened subnet

   c. VRF instance

   d. Defense in depth

8. Which of the following is a client/server authentication protocol that supports mutual authentication between a client and a server and hands out tickets that are used instead of a username and password combination?

   a. TACACS+

   b. RADIUS

   c. Kerberos

   d. LDAP

9. You go to the store and put your bank card into an ATM and enter your PIN. Which of the following factors of multifactor authentication have you exhibited? (Choose two.)

   a. Something you are

   b. Something you have

   c. Something you know

   d. Somewhere you are

10. Which of the following would best help you ensure that all areas of control and compliance don't end up in the hands of a single individual?

    a. Role-based access control

    b. Zero Trust

    c. Posture assessment

    d. Separation of duties

This chapter covers the following topics related to Objective 4.2 (Compare and contrast common types of attacks) of the CompTIA Network+ N10-008 certification exam:

- Technology-based
  - Denial-of-service (DoS)/distributed denial-of-service (DDoS)
    - Botnet/command and control
  - On-path attack (previously known as man-in-the-middle attack)
  - DNS poisoning
  - VLAN hopping
  - ARP spoofing
  - Rogue DHCP
  - Rogue access point (AP)
  - Evil twin

- Ransomware
- Password attacks
  - Brute-force
  - Dictionary
- MAC spoofing
- IP spoofing
- Deauthentication
- Malware
- Human and environmental
  - Social engineering
    - Phishing
    - Tailgating
    - Piggybacking
    - Shoulder surfing

CHAPTER 17

Common Types of Attacks

Have you ever heard the expression "Know your enemy"? It is a very fitting expression for this chapter, which focuses on the attacks that are very common in today's networked environment. As you will see, most network attacks are divided into two major categories: those that involve technology and those that involve humans and/or the environment.

It is important to note that many of the successful security attacks carried out against a wide variety of organizations are successful because they involve using multiple attack types in strategic ways. Very successful cybercriminals realize that they can use specific attacks to achieve specific goals as part of an overall strategy.

Foundation Topics

Technology-Based Attacks

When you think about cybersecurity attacks, you are likely to think about attacks that make use of technology. After all, you are in the field of technology. But these are not the only attacks that affect networks. Social engineering attacks are also a major problem today and are often the first step in more sophisticated attacks that take place. Before we launch into a look at these human and environmental attacks, let us take a detailed look at a variety of common technology-based attacks.

Denial of Service

An attacker can launch a *denial-of-service (DoS) attack* on a system by sending the target system a flood of data or requests that consume the target system's resources. In addition, some operating systems and applications crash when they receive specific strings of improperly formatted data, and the attacker can leverage such OS/application vulnerabilities to render a system or an application inoperable. The attacker often uses IP spoofing to conceal his identity when launching a DoS attack, as illustrated in Figure 17-1.

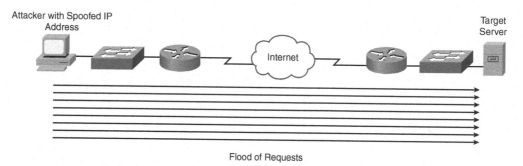

Flood of Requests

FIGURE 17-1   DoS Attack

DoS attacks are often categorized as follows:

- **Reflective:** A third-party system is used to help carry out this type of attack. Often this third party is not compromised, which makes a reflective attack very difficult to track down.

- **Amplified:** A DNS server is often used in an amplification attack, but other services could be used in such an exploit as well. With these attacks, legitimate servers are tricked into flooding responses at a target system; the forged request tends to be small but results in large responses hitting the target. It can be difficult to mitigate amplified attacks because the server involved (called the *reflector server*) is a legitimate device.

Distributed Denial of Service

Distributed denial-of-service (DDoS) attacks can increase the amount of traffic flooded to a target system. A DDoS attack is a coordinated attack. Specifically, an attacker compromises multiple systems and then instructs those compromised systems, called *zombies or bots*, to simultaneously launch a DDoS attack against a target system. The attacker uses **command and control** software to instruct the zombies to do their job. These zombies are even scarier than the ones in *The Walking Dead* because they are remotely controlled.

NOTE   A *botnet* is an entire network segment that is filled with bots.

A significant traffic spike (as compared to the baseline) could provide an early indication that an attack is taking place. An intrusion prevention system (IPS) is designed to recognize and alert when attacks or malicious traffic is present on a network.

NOTE   Remember that a DoS attack originates from a single system, whereas a DDoS attack originates from multiple systems simultaneously.

On-Path Attack (Formerly Known as Man-in-the-Middle Attack)

An attacker who can get in the direct path between a client and a server can then eavesdrop on the conversation between the client and the server; this type of attack is called an **on-path attack**. If cryptography is being used and the attacker fools the client and server both into building VPNs to the attacker instead of to each other, the attacker can see all the data in plaintext. On a local Ethernet network, methods such as Address Resolution Protocol (ARP) spoofing, ARP cache poisoning, Dynamic Host Configuration Protocol (DHCP) spoofing, and Domain Name System (DNS) spoofing and poisoning may be used to redirect a client's traffic through the attacker instead of directly to the server.

NOTE   The newer terminology on-path attack is much more accurate than the older term *man-in-the-middle attack*, which does not properly convey that the attacker can carry out an attack from any point on the path (not just the middle).

DNS Poisoning

Another potential for attacks against cybersecurity involves the DNS service and systems, and many advancements have therefore been made in DNS security mechanisms. One simple approach to DNS attacks is the injection of false entries into the DNS system, known as *DNS poisoning*. This might be done in order to deny service to systems or to redirect them to websites that might be designed to disseminate malware or collect credentials.

VLAN Hopping

802.1Q trunk links support a feature called Q-in-Q tunneling. This approach, which involves encapsulating 802.1Q traffic inside other 802.1Q traffic, can be very beneficial for service providers that might take trunk traffic from customers and need to tunnel that traffic through their own service provider trunks.

Unfortunately, the use of a native VLAN can be exploited with this Q-in-Q tunneling technology. Specifically, an attacker can use the combination of Q-in-Q tunneling and the native VLAN feature to send traffic into a VLAN that the attacker would not normally be able to send traffic into. This type of attack is called *VLAN hopping*.

Common security changes to prevent VLAN hopping attacks include ensuring that the native VLAN is set to a completely unused VLAN or, for switches that support it, tagging the native VLAN. Both measures eliminate VLAN hopping attacks.

ARP Spoofing

As you might expect, *ARP spoofing* involves falsifying identity. With ARP spoofing, the Layer 2 MAC address is misrepresented. An attacker might use MAC spoofing to bypass simple MAC-based security mechanisms, such as port security.

Rogue DHCP

Rogue DHCP servers might be accidental or malicious in a network. When they are malicious, the attacker is seeking to disrupt (or redirect) end-user traffic by providing false DHCP leased IP address information.

Today, DHCP snooping provides excellent protection against such attacks. This technology seeks to ensure that DHCP server traffic is legitimate in the network at all times.

Rogue Access Point

Rogue access points are unauthorized access points (APs) that prevent legitimate network access through intentional misconfiguration. This approach is very similar to the rogue DHCP server approach.

Evil Twin

An *evil twin* is a special type of rogue access point attack. An evil twin attack is designed to capture authentication information from an unsuspecting network user. This attack is so named because a rogue AP is configured in this scenario to appear just like the legitimate AP that the client should be connecting with.

Ransomware

Ransomware has been an extremely popular type of cybersecurity attack for the past several years. With this style of exploit, the attacker locks access to a system or files (often using encryption) or at least pretends to have locked access. The attacker asks the computer user to pay a ransom to get the system or files unlocked. Attackers commonly ask for the ransom in bitcoin or some other cryptocurrency to make the attack less traceable.

Password Attacks

For as long as computer systems have existed, *password attacks* have also existed. With this type of attack, the attacker seeks to gain access to systems or files by using the actual password required for that access. There are many different forms of password attacks, including the following:

- *Brute-force password attack*: In this type of attack, the attacker tries all possible password combinations until a match is made. For example, a brute-force attack might start with the letter a and go through the letter z, and then the attacker might attempt the letters aa through zz, continuing to try combinations until the password is determined. Using complicated passwords—with a mixture of upper- and lowercase letters as well as special characters and numbers—can help prevent brute-force attacks.

- *Dictionary password attack*: In this type of attack, the attacker tries multiple password guesses. However, a dictionary attack is based on a dictionary of commonly used words rather than trying all possible combinations, as in a brute-force attack. Picking a password that is not a common word helps thwart dictionary attacks.

MAC Spoofing

MAC spoofing is a simple attack in which a cybercriminal pretends to possess a different MAC address than is actually on the criminal's system. MAC spoofing is often the first step in a much larger and more sophisticated attack. Because MAC spoofing is relatively easy to accomplish, port security is not often viewed as a sophisticated and comprehensive defense in a network. More sophisticated security solutions, such as dynamic ARP inspection (DAI), are more robust and more effective mechanisms to mitigate issues like MAC spoofing in the network.

IP Spoofing

It did not take long in the history of TCP/IP and the Internet for attackers to realize that they could fool many IP security mechanisms by simply pretending to possess a different IP address. Think about how many security mechanisms (such as access control lists [ACLs]) focus on the IP address that a source of traffic is using. Faking this address is often all that is required to breach an IP address-based security solution.

It relatively easy to modify a source IP address, but there are many mechanisms you can use in modern networks to guard against *IP address spoofing*. One Cisco solution is IP Source Guard, which is a tool that relies on DHCP snooping and coordinates DHCP-assigned IP addresses to systems in a network based on the MAC addresses of those systems.

Deauthentication

In a *deauthentication* attack, the attacker sends a deauthentication frame to the victim to disconnect that client from the wireless LAN. While continuously disconnecting a client from WiFi would do a great job frustrating the end user (and the local help desk), it would not in and of itself cause much damage. Typically, the attacker carries out further attacks against the client. For example, an attacker who has installed an evil twin on the network might first carry out a deauthentication attack and then, when the client is reconnecting to the network, attempt to ensure that the end user connects to the evil twin.

Malware

Malware has become a catchall term for the various types of viruses, worms, spyware, Trojans, and other problematic and malicious software or code on a network. Malware can vary from a mere inconvenience to a catastrophic type of security incident. For example, after a single machine in an organization is compromised and is running malicious software, the attacker might use that single computer to proceed further into the internal network and use the compromised host as a pivot point.

Malware in your organization may have been implemented by an outside attacker or by an inside disgruntled employee. Antivirus and anti-malware software should be run on all systems, and users should be given very limited rights related to installation of any software on the computers they use.

Human and Environmental Attacks

Attacks that leverage human nature and human behavior are called *social engineering* attacks. These types of attacks are very common and are often the first step or steps in much larger attacks. The following are some specific types of social engineering attacks:

- *Phishing*: This variation of a social engineering attack involves sending an email to a user that appears to be legitimate in an attempt to have that user input authentication information that is then captured. For example, the email may ask the reader to click a website link to claim a package from FedEx. The attacker constructs a website at the false address that looks just like the actual FedEx website.

- *Tailgating*: With tailgating, the attacker physically follows a valid employee through a secured area of the organization. For example, the attacker might notice that a security badge swipe opens a door and that the door, once opened, does not lock again for 30 seconds. The attack will wait for a valid entry and then sneak into the area after that entry and before 30 seconds has elapsed.

- *Piggybacking*: Piggybacking is similar to tailgating and, in fact, the two terms are often used interchangeably. However, piggybacking is often distinguished from tailgating in that the valid employee knows and is cooperating with the cybercriminal. In addition, the term *piggybacking* is used to refer to a purely electronic transaction. In this form of piggybacking, data flows through some key point in the network, and while that channel is open, the criminal sneaks their data through.

- *Shoulder surfing*: In this classic form of social engineering attack, the cybercriminal simply watches over the shoulder of an authorized employee to learn passwords and other inputs to gain access at a later time. In addition, a shoulder surfer might look for sensitive information such as employees' Social Security numbers on the screen of an HR person.

Other Miscellaneous Attacks

Table 17-1 describes other miscellaneous types of attacks that you need to be familiar with in today's networked environment.

Table 17-1   Miscellaneous Attacks

Attack	Description
Packet capture	An attacker can use a packet capture (or *packet sniffing*) utility such as Wireshark (https://wireshark.org) to capture packets after placing a PC's network interface card (NIC) in promiscuous mode. Some protocols, such as Telnet and HTTP, are sent in plaintext, which means packets sent with these protocols can be read by an attacker, perhaps allowing the attacker to see confidential information.
Confidentiality attacks (ping sweep and port scan)	A confidentiality attack might begin with a scan of network resources to identify attack targets on a network. A ping sweep could be used to ping a series of IP addresses. Ping replies might indicate to an attacker that network resources were reachable at those IP addresses. After a collection of IP addresses is identified, the attacker might scan a range of UDP or TCP ports to see what services are available on the hosts at the specified IP addresses. Also, port scans often help attackers identify the operating system running on a target system. These attacks are also commonly referred to as *reconnaissance attacks*.
Dumpster diving	Many organizations throw away hard copies containing confidential information without properly shredding them, and attackers may rummage through an organization's trash in hopes of discovering information that could be used to compromise network resources.
Electromagnetic interference (EMI) interception	Data is often transmitted over wires (for example, unshielded twisted pair), and attackers can sometimes copy information traveling over a wire by intercepting the EMI *emanations* being emitted by the transmission medium. A government project called Tempest studied the ability to understand the data traveling through a network by listening to emanations. A Tempest room is designed to keep emanations contained within that room to increase the security of data communications happening there.
Wiretapping	An attacker who gains physical access to a wiring closet might physically tap into telephone cabling to eavesdrop on telephone conversations or might insert a shared media hub inline with a network cable to connect to the hub and receive copies of packets flowing through the network cable.
Information sent over overt channels	An attacker might send or receive confidential information over a network by using an *overt channel*. An example of using an overt channel is tunneling one protocol inside another (for example, sending instant-messaging traffic via HTTP). Steganography is another example of sending information over an overt channel. For example, an attacker might send a digital image made up of millions of pixels with secret information encoded in specific pixels, where only the sender and the receiver know which pixels represent the encoded information.

Attack	Description
Information sent over covert channels	An attacker might send or receive confidential information over a network by using a covert channel, which can communicate information as a series of codes/events. For example, an attacker could represent binary data by sending a series of pings to a destination. A single ping within a certain period of time could represent a binary 0, and two pings within that same time period could represent a binary 1.
FTP bounce	FTP supports a variety of commands for setting up a session and managing file transfers. An attacker may use one of these commands, the **port** command, to access a system that would otherwise deny the attacker. Specifically, an attacker connects to an FTP server by using the standard port 21. However, FTP uses a secondary connection to send data. The client issues a **port** command to specify the destination port and destination IP address for the data transmission. Normally, the client would send its own IP address and an ephemeral port number. The FTP server would then use the source port 20 and the destination port specified by the client when sending data to the client. However, an attacker might issue a **port** command specifying the IP address of a device to access, along with an open port number on that device. As a result, the targeted device might allow an incoming connection from the FTP server's IP address but reject a connection coming in from the attacker's IP address. Fortunately, most modern FTP servers do not accept the **port** command coming from a device that specifies a different IP address than the client's IP address.
Session hijacking	An attacker could hijack a TCP session, for example, by completing the third step in the three-way TCP handshake process between an authorized client and a protected server. An attacker who successfully hijacks the session of an authorized device might be able to maliciously manipulate data on the protected server.
Salami attack	A salami attack is a collection of small attacks that result in a larger attack when combined. For example, an attacker who has a collection of stolen credit card numbers could withdraw small amounts of money using each credit card, and the combination of the multiple small withdrawals would add up to a significant sum for the attacker.
Data diddling	Data diddling involves changing data before it is stored in a computing system. Malicious code in an input application or a virus could perform data diddling. For example, a virus, Trojan horse, or worm could be written to intercept keyboard input, and while the appropriate characters are displayed onscreen (so that the user does not see an issue), manipulated characters could be entered into a database application or sent over a network.

Attack	Description
Trust relationship exploitation	Different devices in a network might share a trust relationship. For example, a certain host might be trusted to communicate through a firewall using specific ports, while other hosts are denied passage through the firewall using those same ports. If an attacker were able to compromise the host that had a trust relationship with the firewall, the attacker could use the compromised host to pass normally denied data through a firewall.
Logic bomb	In this type of attack, malicious code is hidden in a system and can be triggered by the author or by another attacker. For example, a programmer might hide malicious code that starts deleting files if the programmer's employment is terminated.
TCP SYN flood	In this variant of a DoS attack, an attacker initiates multiple TCP sessions by sending SYN segments but then never completing the three-way TCP handshake. The attacker can send multiple SYN segments to a target system with false source IP addresses in the header of the SYN segments. Because many servers limit the number of TCP sessions they can have open simultaneously, a SYN flood can render a target system incapable of opening a TCP session with a legitimate user.
Buffer overflow	A computer program may be given a *buffer*, which is a dedicated area of memory to which it can write. If the program attempts to write more information than the buffer can accommodate, a buffer overflow may occur. If permitted to do so, the program can fill up its buffer and then have its output spill over into the memory area being used for a different program. This can potentially cause the other program to crash. Some programs are known to have this vulnerability (that is, be able to overrun their memory buffers), which can be exploited by attackers.
ICMP attack	Many networks permit the use of Internet Control Message Protocol (ICMP) traffic (for example, ping traffic) because pings can be useful for network troubleshooting. However, attackers can use ICMP for DoS attacks. One ICMP DoS attack variant, called the *ping of death*, uses ICMP packets that are too big. Another variant sends ICMP traffic as a series of fragments in an attempt to overflow the fragment reassembly buffers on the target device. Also, a *Smurf attack* can use ICMP traffic directed to a subnet to flood a target system with ping replies.
Electrical disturbance	At a physical level, an attacker may launch an availability attack by interrupting or interfering with the electrical service available to a system. For example, an attacker who gains physical access to a datacenter's electrical system might be able to cause a variety of electrical disturbances, such as power spikes, electrical surges, blackouts, and brownouts.

> **NOTE** The attack types listed in this chapter are just some of the many attacks types being used today. New attacks and even new categories of attacks are being created all the time. Also, keep in mind that many attacks are actually perpetrated by employees of an organization. They are called *insider attacks*.

Real-World Case Study

Acme, Inc. has decided to improve its security training for both staff members in IT and all the end users of the organization.

The decision has been made to focus on social engineering with the end users. IT staff are continuously receiving training, including training on the latest social engineering advancements.

The main concern for the end users at the moment is the increasing number of successful phishing attacks occurring in the enterprise. Therefore, phishing will be a large focus of the training in the first round.

Your IT staff will receive training on the latest advancements in DDoS attacks. One particular focus is the ability to detect such attacks at the network perimeter as quickly as possible.

Summary

Here are the main topics covered in this chapter:

- This chapter describes some of the most common technology-based security attacks.

- This chapter describes some of the most common human and environmental-based attacks.

- This chapter describes some of the common miscellaneous attacks that may be carried out against a network.

Exam Preparation Tasks

Review All the Key Topics

Review the most important topics from this chapter, noted with the Key Topic icon in the outer margin of the page. Table 17-2 lists these key topics and the page number where each is found.

Table 17-2 Key Topics for Chapter 17

Key Topic Element	Description	Page Number
Section	Denial of service (DoS)	440
Section	Distributed denial of service (DDoS)	441
Section	Social engineering	445

Define Key Terms

Define the following key terms from this chapter and check your answers in the Glossary:

denial-of-service (DoS) attack, social engineering, distributed denial-of-service (DDoS) attack, logic bomb, rogue access point, evil twin, phishing, ARP spoofing, botnet, command and control, brute-force password attack, deauthentication, dictionary password attack, DNS poisoning, IP address spoofing, MAC spoofing, malware, on-path attack, password attack, piggybacking, ransomware, rogue DHCP server, shoulder surfing, tailgating, VLAN hopping

Complete Chapter 17 Hands-On Lab in Network+ Simulator Lite

- Configuring a Small Office/Home Office Router—Network User Security Settings
- Network Security Appliance Terminology and Methods

Additional Resources

Cloud Security and Privacy: https://www.ajsnetworking.com/ccie-evolving-technologies-2

What are the Most Common Types of Cyberthreats?: https://www.cisco.com/c/en/us/products/security/common-cyberattacks.html

Review Questions

The answers to these review questions appear in Appendix A, "Answers to Review Questions."

1. Which type of attack exploits the native VLAN of 802.1Q?
   a. Evil twin
   b. Tailgating

    c. Deauthentication

    d. VLAN hopping

2. In what type of attack does the attacker compromise multiple systems and then instruct those compromised systems, called *zombies*, to simultaneously flood a target system with traffic?

    a. DoS attack

    b. TCP SYN flood attack

    c. Buffer overflow

    d. DDoS attack

3. Which of the following is an example of a social engineering attack?

    a. DDoS attack

    b. DoS attack

    c. Piggybacking

    d. On-path attack

4. In what type of attack does the attacker try all possible password combinations until a match is made?

    a. Dictionary attack

    b. MAC spoofing

    c. IP spoofing

    d. Brute-force attack

5. What type of attack often seeks payment in bitcoin or other cryptocurrency?

    a. Malware

    b. DDoS

    c. Ransomware

    d. DNS poisoning

This chapter covers the following topics related to Objective 4.3 (Given a scenario, apply network hardening techniques) of the CompTIA Network+ N10-008 certification exam:

- Best practices
  - Secure SNMP
  - Router Advertisement (RA) Guard
  - Port security
  - Dynamic ARP inspection
  - Control plane policing
  - Private VLANs
  - Disable unneeded switchports
  - Disable unneeded network services
  - Change default passwords
  - Password complexity/length
  - Enable DHCP snooping
  - Change default VLAN
  - Patch and firmware management

- Access control list
- Role-based access
- Firewall rules
  - Explicit deny
  - Implicit deny
- Wireless security
  - MAC filtering
  - Antenna placement
  - Power levels
  - Wireless client isolation
  - Guest network isolation
  - Preshared keys (PSKs)
  - EAP
  - Geofencing
  - Captive portal
- IoT access considerations

CHAPTER 18

Network Hardening Techniques

For a long time, many network vendors emphasized using a defense-in-depth strategy. And while they would still stand behind this approach, today plenty of other security initiatives are promoted, such as Zero Trust. If you think about the defense-in-depth concept for a moment, you'll realize the importance of network device hardening in this strategy. After all, it's wise to tightly secure the network devices themselves in an attempt to build a very secure network.

In addition, network (device) hardening is an excellent idea because many devices ship from the manufacturer with default configurations that can be quite dangerous. For example, you might receive a network router that has a web server process enabled inside it. This web server software might permit HTTP (not HTTPS) connections, and there may be no access control list or firewall of any kind protecting this web server. Perhaps this security vulnerability is meant to permit web-based management of the device. Your security policy probably does not permit such a vulnerability. Hardening this device by disabling or even eliminating that web server is an excellent idea. In fact, because you should always try to adhere to your security policy, in this scenario, the web server must be uninstalled or at least disabled.

Foundation Topics

Best Practices

While the hardening of a network through the hardening of its network devices can be a daunting task, the great news is that there are many standard best practices in this regard. Just remember that whenever you see a list like this, you should be prepared to encounter plenty of best practices that will not be applicable for your particular network or your particular network device.

The following is an impressive list of network hardening techniques you should at least consider:

- **Change default credentials:** At a very minimum, you should always do this step! The first thing an attacker is likely to do as an initial step in a larger-scale attack is try using default username and password credentials to access network devices. Plenty of websites provide lists of default username and password credentials for common systems from popular vendors. If you take none of the other steps described in this chapter, at least take this one as it is crucial.

- **Avoid using common passwords and usernames on devices:** Avoid using usernames like **admin** and passwords like **pasword123**. You also need to follow your own enforced password complexity and length policy. Today, it is recommended that passwords be at least 8 to 12 characters and include a certain combination of special characters, numbers, and upper- and lowercase letters.

> **NOTE**   Always be sure to keep up on the latest industry recommendations. For example, NIST's "Digital Identity Guidelines" includes the latest password recommendations. This document is available at https://pages.nist.gov/800-63-3/sp800-63b.html.

- **Upgrade firmware:** By installing updated firmware, you gain new functionality on a device, and oftentimes the device gets much-needed security patches and enhancements. Figure 18-1 shows the firmware upgrade process for a small office/home office (SOHO) wireless router.

- **Patch and update:** Just as your firmware needs consistent attention to patches and updates, so do your operating system and applications. Many network devices from popular vendors today are so sophisticated with their OS that they can run plug-in types of applications or even full-blown apps. Patches and updates might bring advanced features to a device.

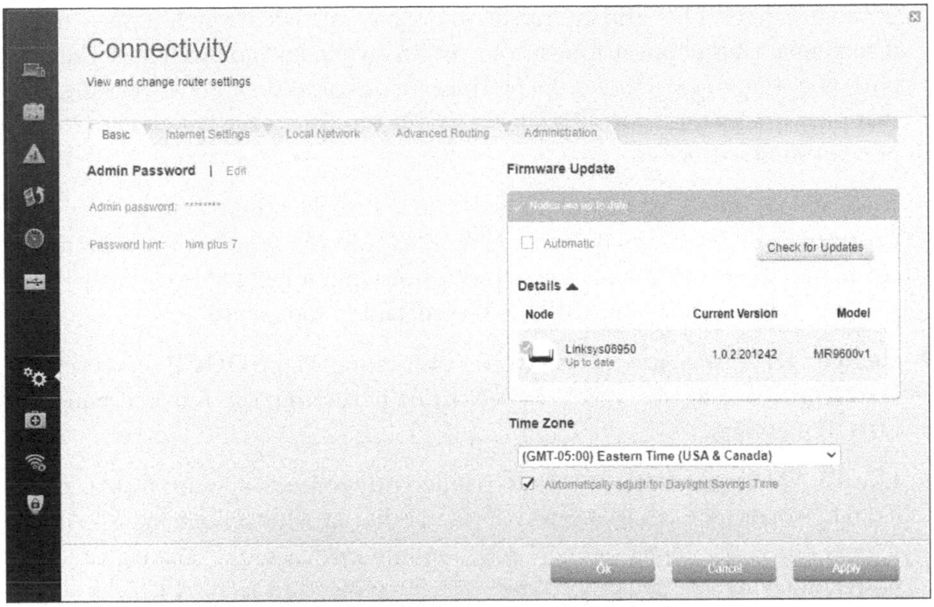

FIGURE 18-1 Upgrading the Firmware on a SOHO Wireless Router

- **Disable unneeded network services:** Modern network devices tend to have many network services enabled by default. To reduce the attack surface, you should trim off any unnecessary services by disabling them. Reducing the attack surface by not running services means that there is less that the attacker can target. Attackers commonly target Bluetooth and remote desktop services as methods of carrying out access for their subsequent attacks.

- **Use secure protocols:** Use secure protocols over unsecure protocols whenever possible. For example, use Secure Shell (SSH) rather than the insecure Telnet for remote management using terminals. Other unsecure protocols to remember include HTTP, SLIP, FTP, Trivial FTP (TFTP), and Simple Network Management Protocol Version 1/2 (SNMPv1/v2).

- **Secure SNMP:** Be sure to use the security features of the relatively new SNMP Version 3. "SNMP means Security is Not My Problem" does not apply to Version 3 of SNMP, which provides encryption.

- **Generate new keys/credentials:** Rotate, rotate, and then rotate again those important credentials that are used to guard your corporate systems and data. Also remember that responsible encryption key management is crucial to securing cryptographic keys.

- **Disable unneeded switch ports:** You might have a few, or you might have a ton of ports on switches that are not connected to anything. These ports need to be shut down. One primary reason to disable unneeded switch ports is that if someone gains physical access to a network switch and connects to a switch port, you want to ensure that the person cannot access the network through that port. You can use port blocking as well as physical security practices to prevent such access.

■ **Ensure spanning tree protections:** If you are stuck with Spanning Tree Protocol (STP) in your network, you need to be sure to use any protections offered by a network device. These protections might include Root Guard, Bridge Protocol Data Unit (BPDU) Guard, and Flood Guard.

■ **Enable *DHCP snooping*:** This involves preventing rogue DHCP servers and DHCP pool exhaustion attacks by restricting ports from accepting certain DHCP messages.

■ **Use VLAN segmentation:** Doing so inherently protects systems from accidental or malicious attacks from systems in other broadcast domains. VLAN segmentation also forces inter-VLAN communications to pass through a router, allowing you to easily enforce security policy and security checks on the traffic.

■ **Use *port security*:** Locking down switch ports to MAC addresses is a good first step in hardening a network. Doing so guards against MAC flood attacks nicely, but note that the network is still vulnerable to MAC spoofing attacks.

■ **Use *Router Advertisement (RA) Guard*:** This helps protect against attacks in IPv6 environments, where routers can advertise the network prefix information to end systems. These end systems can configure their own unique host IDs. Therefore, you can address end systems without requiring DHCP implementation. While these types of features are excellent, you need security controls such as RA Guard to make sure these features are not exploited.

■ **Use *dynamic ARP inspection (DAI)*:** This Layer 2 security mechanism guards against MAC address spoofing. It can pair nicely with port security.

■ **Use *control plane policing (CoPP)*:** CoPP is an excellent security feature that can control the rate of packets to and from the control plane of a network device. Think about life without CoPP: Attackers could easily cause denial of service (DoS) on a network device by simply flooding fake Border Gateway Protocol (BGP) updates to the device (or updates from another control plane protocol).

■ **Use *private VLANs*:** You will often implement networks for special types of deployments. For example, say that you are creating a network to be shared by a row of stores in a shopping mall. Each store needs to be segmented from every other store. Private VLANs are excellent for such a design. Each store can have its own private VLAN. All of these private VLANs can reach the Internet, but they cannot enter the other private VLANs. All of the VLANs in this case can be in the same IP subnet. This type of topology would confuse an attacker who is unaware of the private VLAN feature. The attacker would see that the systems are clearly in the same IP subnet, but they would be unable to communicate with each other. This would be very strange in a VLAN topology.

- **Change the *default VLAN*:** Most network devices that offer switch ports place all of these ports in a default VLAN. For example, Cisco Systems switches have all ports in VLAN 1 by default. Attackers know this and seek out ports in the default configuration to try to exploit them.

- **Use *access control lists (ACLs)*:** Use ACLs wherever possible to help strengthen security. For example, a network device might actually be using the built-in web server for network management. If this device offers an ACL feature to protect the internal web server from unauthorized access, you should take advantage of this feature.

- **Use role-based access:** Consider using role-based access control (RBAC) by creating groups or roles on network devices. You can map these groups to different permission levels. This would allow you to permit junior engineers read-only access to devices to help you with monitoring. At the same time, you can have groups with much higher levels of privileges to help with configuration and optimization.

- **Use firewall rules:** Many network devices have full-blown firewall services built in. It is important to consider how a firewall operates with traffic that does not match any permit statement in the firewall configuration. Does the device have an *implicit deny* rule for all of this traffic, or do you need to configure an *explicit deny* for this traffic? As traffic passes through the firewall rules, it is permitted or denied based on those rules. When it reaches the end of the explicitly stated rules, is it dropped due to an implicit deny? Or do you need to configure an explicit deny rule at the end? The most common configuration is to have an implicit deny in place for all the unmatched traffic in the firewall rules.

NOTE   For a firewall that consists of all DENY entries, you might need to add an explicit *permit all* entry at the end of the rules to override an implicit *deny all*.

Wireless Security and IoT Considerations

There are a number of security best practices to consider for wireless networks and the ever-growing *Internet of Things (IoT)*. Here are just a few of them:

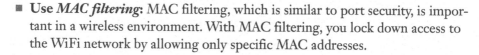

- **Use *MAC filtering*:** MAC filtering, which is similar to port security, is important in a wireless environment. With MAC filtering, you lock down access to the WiFi network by allowing only specific MAC addresses.

- **Consider *antenna placement*:** It often helps to place and direct WiFi antennas so that there is not a lot of overflow to the reach of the signal. For example, you might use a directional antenna to beam a signal as directly as possible to another system. This helps keep the signal strong, and it also prevents many potential devices from receiving the signal. You should also try to minimize the placement of WiFi antennas in unsecured network locations.

> **NOTE**   A professional site survey for WiFi environments can help you determine what access point (AP) placement approaches to use to address coverage areas and security concerns.

- **Adjust power levels:** A nice feature of wireless LAN controllers (WLCs) is that they can automatically adjust the power levels of APs and their antennas so that signals are not sent into areas where they are not wanted or not needed.

- **Use wireless client isolation:** Wireless client isolation is a security feature that prevents wireless clients from communicating with one another. This feature is useful for guest and BYOD wireless networks.

- **Use guest network isolation:** If you do not care if your guest WiFi nodes can reach each other, you might consider implementing isolation for the entire guest WiFi network. This is a very common practice. The guest WiFi permits the nodes inside it to access the public Internet, but it does not permit any of the network devices in the enterprise hosting the guest WiFi.

- **Rotate and secure the use of strong *preshared keys (PSKs)*:** If you are relying on PSKs in your WiFi security environment, be sure to rotate and protect these credentials just as you do with the more traditional passwords for user accounts in your enterprise.

- **Use *Extensible Authentication Protocol (EAP)*:** EAP has become the de facto standard for carrying security credentials in a WiFi network. In the case of the popular 802.1X, the EAP client (called the *supplicant*) sends the security credentials to the WLC wrapped in an EAP packet. The WLC wraps this packet in a RADIUS packet and sends the information to an authentication server on the network. This system checks the security credentials and then instructs the WLC whether it should permit the device or user on the network.

- **Use *geofencing* where needed:** This technology often uses the Global Positioning System (GPS) or radio frequency identification (RFID) to define geographical boundaries. Geofencing allows you to define triggers so that when a device enters (or exits) the boundaries defined by the administrator, an alert is issued. Geofence virtual barriers can be active or passive. An active geofence requires an end user to opt in to location services and requires a mobile app to be open. Passive geofences are always on; they rely on WiFi and/or cellular data instead of GPS or RFID and can work in the background. For example, say that a hospital keeps patient information on tablets that the hospital distributes to staff. If these tablets travel beyond the geofence, an administrative alert can trigger.

- **Use *captive portals*:** As you will read in Chapter 19, "Remote Access Methods," captive portals can obtain information about guests that are attempting to access guest networks or other network resources. With this approach, you send the user to a web page to enter credential information and/or accept agreements on usage. Most public networks, including WiFi hotspots, use a *captive portal*, which requires users to agree to some condition before they use the network or Internet.

- **Control IoT access:** You need to be concerned about breaches of security in your IoT infrastructures, which often rely on your WiFi (or at least portions of it). Therefore, many of the other best practices listed in this section are appropriate for IoT infrastructures. It is a good idea to consistently update your IoT devices for the new security enhancements that inevitably come. You should also segment the IoT traffic as much as possible in the enterprise.

Real-World Case Study

Acme, Inc. has decided to perform a security audit of the network. As part of this audit, they are finding many improvements that can be made very easily. Most of these center around network and device hardening.

Acme, Inc. has identified many services running on network nodes that can safely be disabled. They also identified an area of the organization where the password policy in effect was not appropriately following best practices.

Finally, Acme, Inc. is changing a portion of the network design where in-band network management traffic was discovered. This traffic, if captured, would have revealed several parameters regarding the network configuration that are considered private.

This management traffic is now flowing through an encrypted tunnel so that the chance of a man-in-the-middle attack is now greatly reduced.

Summary

Here are the main topics covered in this chapter:

- This chapter covers best practices for hardening a network and network devices.

- This chapter discusses best practices for hardening a wireless network and wireless devices.

- This chapter covers common issues related to network hardening in IoT access environments.

Exam Preparation Tasks

Review All the Key Topics

Review the most important topics from this chapter, noted with the Key Topic icon in the outer margin of the page. Table 18-1 lists these key topics and the page number where each is found.

Table 18-1   Key Topics for Chapter 18

Key Topic Element	Description	Page Number
List	Network hardening best practices	454
List	Hardening for wireless and IoT networks	458

Define Key Terms

Define the following key terms from this chapter and check your answers in the Glossary:

Router Advertisement (RA) Guard, port security, dynamic ARP inspection (DAI), control plane policing (CoPP), private VLAN, DHCP snooping, default VLAN, access control list (ACL), MAC filtering, preshared key (PSK), Extensible Authentication Protocol (EAP), geofencing, captive portal, Internet of Things (IoT)

Complete Chapter 18 Hands-On Labs in Network+ Simulator Lite

- Network Security Appliance Terminology and Methods
- Configuring a Small Office/Home Office Router – Network User Security Settings
- Configuring a Small Office/Residential Router – Network User Security Settings
- Folder Sharing and Security
- Using Encrypting File System (EFS) to Encrypt Data Files

Additional Resources

Network Device Hardening: https://media.defense.gov/2020/Aug/18/2002479461/-1/-1/0/HARDENING_NETWORK_DEVICES.PDF

RBAC: https://digitalguardian.com/blog/what-role-based-access-control-rbac-examples-benefits-and-more

Review Questions

The answers to these review questions appear in Appendix A, "Answers to Review Questions."

1. Your primary concern when hardening your network is the fact that you are vulnerable to several DoS attacks that involve your IGP and EGP protocols. What hardening technique addresses this challenge most directly?

    a. Control plane policing

    b. Geofencing

    c. SNMP

    d. Dynamic ARP inspection

2. What protocol makes 802.1X possible?

    a. SSH

    b. Telnet

    c. SNMPv3

    d. EAP

3. What device hardening technique might be found in a row of stores in a shop-ping mall to ensure that the different stores are segmented from each other?

   a. Default VLAN

   b. DHCP snooping

   c. Private VLAN

   d. Dynamic ARP inspection

4. Which of the following is not a network hardening best practice?

   a. Use SNMPv3

   b. Disable unneeded services

   c. Implement role-based access

   d. Change to default passwords

5. Which of the following means that if you have not been explicitly granted access, then access is denied?

   a. Implicit deny

   b. Explicit deny

   c. Allow

   d. BPDU

6. What do most public networks, including WiFi hotspots, use to require users to agree to some condition before they use the network or Internet?

   a. PSKs

   b. Proper antenna placement

   c. Appropriate signal power levels

   d. Captive portalssw

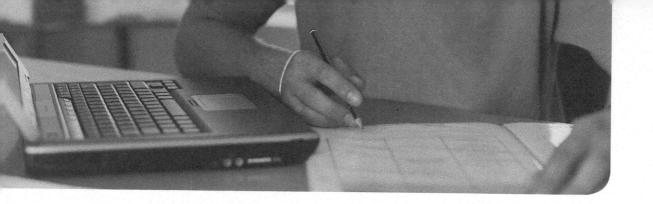

This chapter covers the following topics related to Objective 4.4 (Compare and contrast remote access methods and security implications) of the CompTIA Network+ N10-008 certification exam:

- Site-to-site VPN
- Client-to-site VPN
  - Clientless VPN
  - Split tunnel vs. full tunnel
- Remote desktop connection
- Remote desktop gateway
- SSH
- Virtual network computing (VNC)
- Virtual desktop
- Authentication and authorization considerations
- In-band vs. out-of-band management

CHAPTER 19

Remote Access Methods

It is inevitable: If you haven't already, you will need remote access at some point in your IT career. After all, one of the defining characteristics of cloud (according to the NIST) is broad network access. Fortunately, there are more options than ever before in this regard. Advancements in WAN technologies (such as SD-WAN) are making it easier than ever before to create and manage remote access connections for a wide variety of purposes. This chapter discusses the most common remote access solutions in networking today.

Foundation Topics

Virtual Private Networks (VPNs)

Much of today's workforce is located outside a corporate headquarters location. In fact, as I write this, we are still in the grips of the global pandemic due to the COVID-19 virus. The vast majority of workers globally are working from home. Many of these employees might never return to a traditional office as even reluctant employers have seen how well their employees can continue to be productive when working from home.

But even before the pandemic, some employees worked in remote offices, and others telecommuted. Remote employees can connect to their main corporate network by using a variety of WAN technologies, such as leased lines or high-speed fiber connections. However, these WAN technologies typically cost more than widely available broadband technologies, such as cable, which might also offer faster speeds, or at least comparable speeds.

Virtual private networks (VPNs) support secure communication between sites over an untrusted network (for example, the Internet). The two primary categories of VPNs are site-to-site and client-to-site VPNs:

- **Site-to-site VPN:** A site-to-site VPN interconnects two sites, as an alternative to a leased line, at a reduced cost. Figure 19-1 shows an example of a site-to-site VPN.

- **Client-to-site VPN:** A client-to-site VPN (also known as a *remote access VPN*) interconnects a remote user with a site, as an alternative to dial-up or ISDN connectivity, at a reduced cost. Figure 19-2 shows an example of a client-to-site VPN.

Although a VPN tunnel might physically pass through multiple service provider routers, the tunnel appears to be a single router hop from the perspective of the routers at each end of the tunnel.

A client-to-site VPN allows a user with software on a client computer to connect to a centralized VPN termination device, and a site-to-site VPN interconnects two sites without requiring the computers at those sites to have any specialized VPN software installed. Client-to-site VPNs could be implemented using a VPN-compatible device, such as a router, a firewall, or a special-purpose device called a *VPN concentrator* that is custom-built for handling remote access client-to-site VPN connections. It is also possible, with the correct software, for two computers to connect to each other directly using a host-to-host IPsec VPN connection.

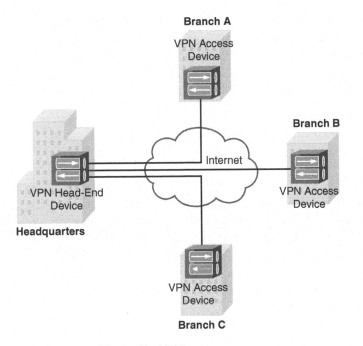

FIGURE 19-1   Site-to-Site VPN

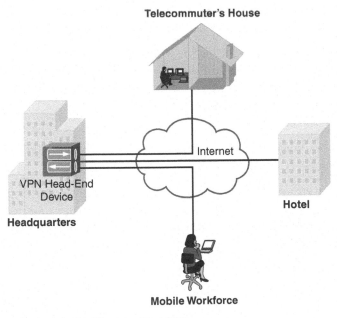

FIGURE 19-2   Client-to-Site VPN

One very popular option in client-to-site VPNs is a ***clientless VPN*** (although this is a bit of a misnomer). With a clientless VPN, there is a client software piece, but it is not a separate piece of software; rather, the client's web browser acts as the VPN client software. This type of VPN connection leverages the SSL/TLS capabilities of the modern Internet and web browsers to provide a secured connection.

Another important consideration when it comes to VPN configuration is whether you will be using a split tunnel or full tunnel configuration:

- With a ***full tunnel*** configuration you have all the end-user traffic go through the VPN tunnel.

- With a ***split tunnel*** configuration, you don't have all the end-user traffic go through the VPN tunnel. For example, you might choose to have just the traffic that needs to access the corporate network sent through the VPN tunnel, while allowing traffic destined for the Internet (perhaps Office 365 traffic) to bypass the tunnel. Split tunneling is often an advantageous configuration because the bandwidth required by the VPN connection (and the overhead associated with it) can be minimized.

Overview of IPsec with IKEv1

Broadband technologies, such as cable, in addition to other VPN transport mechanisms, often traverse an untrusted network, such as the Internet. Therefore, a primary concern with using a broadband technology as a VPN transport is security.

VPN technologies such as IP Security (IPsec), Generic Routing Encapsulation (GRE), Layer 2 Tunneling Protocol (L2TP), and Layer 2 Forwarding (L2F) offer a variety of features, but IPsec VPNs offer strong security features. Specifically, IPsec offers CIA protection for traffic. Recall from Chapter 16, "Common Security Concepts," the components of the CIA triad:

- **Confidentiality:** Data confidentiality is provided by encrypting data. A third party who intercepts the encrypted data will not be able to interpret it.

- **Integrity:** Data integrity ensures that data is not modified in transit. For example, routers at each end of a tunnel can calculate a checksum value or a hash value for the data, and if both routers calculate the same value, the data has most likely not been modified in transit.

- **Authentication:** Data authentication allows parties involved in a conversation to verify that the other party is the party they claim to be.

IPsec also scales to a wide range of networks. IPsec operates at Layer 3 of the OSI model (the network layer). As a result, IPsec is transparent to applications, which means that applications do not require any sort of integrated IPsec support.

IKE Modes and Phases

IPsec uses a collection of protocols to provide its features. One of the primary protocols that IPsec uses is Internet Key Exchange (IKE). Specifically, IPsec can provide encryption between authenticated peers using encryption keys that are periodically changed. IKE, however, allows an administrator to manually configure keys.

As outlined in Table 19-1, IKE can use three modes of operation to set up a secure communicate path between IPsec peers.

Table 19-1   IKE Modes

Mode	Description
Main mode	Main mode involves three exchanges of information between the IPsec peers:
	Exchange 1: The responder selects a proposal it received from the initiator.
	Exchange 2: Diffie-Hellman (DH) is used to securely establish a shared secret key over the unsecured medium.
	Exchange 3: An Internet Security Association and Key Management Protocol (ISAKMP) session is established. This secure session is then used to negotiate an IPsec session.
	One peer, called the *initiator*, sends one or more proposals to the other peer, called the *responder*. The proposals include supported encryption and authentication protocols and key lifetimes. In addition, the proposals indicate whether perfect forward secrecy (PFS) should be used. PFS ensures that a session key remains secure, even if one of the private keys used to derive the session key becomes compromised.
Aggressive mode	Aggressive mode more quickly achieves the same results as main mode, using only three packets. The initiator sends the first packet, which contains all the information necessary to establish a security association (SA)—that is, an agreement between the two IPsec peers about the cryptographic parameters to be used in the ISAKMP session. The responder sends the second packet, which contains the security parameters selected by the responder (the proposal, the keying material, and its ID). The responder uses this second packet to authenticate the session. The third and final packet, which is sent by the initiator, finalizes the authentication of the ISAKMP session.
Quick mode	Quick mode negotiates the parameters (the SA) for the IPsec session. This negotiation occurs within the protection of an ISAKMP session.

The IKEv1 modes reflect the two primary phases of establishing an IPsec tunnel. For example, during IKE Phase 1, a secure ISAKMP session is established, using either main mode or aggressive mode. During IKE Phase 1, the IPsec endpoints establish transform sets (which are collections of encryption and authentication protocols), hash methods, and other parameters needed to establish a secure ISAKMP session (sometimes called an ISAKMP tunnel or an IKE Phase 1 tunnel). This collection of parameters is called a *security association* (*SA*). With IKE Phase 1, the SA is bidirectional, which means that the same key exchange is used for data flowing across the tunnel in either direction.

IKE Phase 2 occurs within the protection of an IKE Phase 1 tunnel, using the previously described *quick mode* of parameter negotiation. A session formed during IKE Phase 2 is sometimes called an *IKE Phase 2 tunnel* or simply an *IPsec tunnel*. However, unlike IKE Phase 1, IKE Phase 2 performs unidirectional SA negotiations, which means that each data flow uses a separate key exchange.

Although an IPsec tunnel can be established using just IKE Phase 1 and IKE Phase 2, an optional IKE Phase 1.5 can be used. IKE Phase 1.5 uses the Extended Authentication (XAuth) protocol to perform user authentication of IPsec tunnels. Like IKE Phase 2, IKE Phase 1.5 is performed within the protection of an IKE Phase 1 tunnel. The user authentication provided by this phase adds a layer of authentication for VPN clients. Also, parameters such as IP, WINS, and DNS server information can be provided to a VPN client during this optional phase. A newer version called IKEv2 combines many of the same functions of IKEv1 and uses an initial IKEv2 tunnel (instead of IKEv1 phase 1) and child security associations (SAs/tunnels) for the IPsec tunnels instead of calling them IKE Phase 2 tunnels.

Authentication Header and Encapsulating Security Payload

In addition to IKE, which establishes the IPsec tunnel, IPsec relies on either the Authentication Header (AH) protocol (IP protocol number 51) or the Encapsulating Security Payload (ESP) protocol (IP protocol number 50). Both AH and ESP offer origin authentication and integrity services, which ensure that IPsec peers are who they claim to be and that the data was not modified in transit.

However, the main distinction between AH and ESP is encryption support. ESP encrypts the original packet, whereas AH does not offer encryption. As a result, ESP is much more popular on today's networks.

Both AH and ESP can operate in one of two modes: transport mode or tunnel mode. Figure 19-3 illustrates the structure of an ESP transport mode packet versus an ESP tunnel mode packet.

NOTE You might be concerned that transport mode allows the IP address of the IPsec peers to remain visible during transit because the original packet's IP header is used to route a packet. However, IPsec is often used in conjunction with the *Generic Routing Encapsulation (GRE)* tunneling protocol. With transport mode, the original IP packet is encapsulated inside a GRE tunnel packet, which adds a new GRE tunnel header. The GRE packet is then sent over an IPsec tunnel. Even if the IPsec tunnel were running in transport mode, the original packet's IP header would still not be visible. Instead, the GRE packet's header would be visible.

Transport Mode

ESP Auth	ESP Trailer	Payload	ESP Header	Original IP Header

Tunnel Mode

ESP Auth	ESP Trailer	Payload	Original IP Header	ESP Header	New IP Header

FIGURE 19-3   Transport Mode Versus Tunnel Mode

Following is a detailed description of these two modes:

- **Transport mode:** Uses a packet's original IP header, as opposed to adding an additional tunnel header. This approach works well in networks where increasing a packet's size might cause an issue. Also, transport mode is often used for client-to-site VPNs, where a PC running VPN client software connects back to a VPN termination device at a headquarters location.

- **Tunnel mode:** Unlike transport mode, tunnel mode encapsulates an entire packet. As a result, the encapsulated packet has a new header (an IPsec header). This new header has source and destination IP address information that reflects the two VPN termination devices at different sites. Therefore, tunnel mode is often used in an IPsec site-to-site VPN.

One reason a GRE tunnel might be used with an IPsec tunnel is as a limitation on the part of IPsec. Specifically, an IPsec tunnel can only transmit unicast IP packets. The challenge is that large enterprise networks might have a significant amount of broadcast or multicast traffic (for example, routing protocol traffic). GRE can take any traffic type and encapsulate the traffic in a GRE tunnel packet, which is a uni-cast IP packet that can then be sent over an IPsec tunnel. Take, for example, a multicast packet used by a routing protocol. Although IPsec cannot directly transport the multicast packet, if the packet is first encapsulated by GRE, the GRE packet can then be sent over an IPsec tunnel, thereby securing the transmission of the multicast packet.

The Five Steps in Setting Up and Tearing Down an IPsec Site-to-Site VPN Using IKEv1

The process of establishing, maintaining, and tearing down an IPsec site-to-site VPN consists of five primary steps, which are illustrated in Figure 19-4 and described in detail in the list that follows:

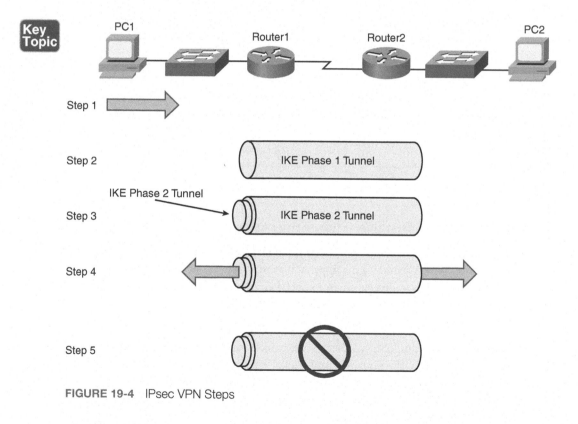

FIGURE 19-4 IPsec VPN Steps

Step 1. PC1 sends traffic destined for PC2. Router1 classifies the traffic as "interesting" traffic, and this classification initiates the creation of an IPsec tunnel.

Step 2.   Router1 and Router2 negotiate an SA used to form an IKE Phase 1 tunnel, which is also known as an ISAKMP tunnel.

Step 3.   Within the protection of the IKE Phase 1 tunnel, an IKE Phase 2 tunnel is negotiated and set up. An IKE Phase 2 tunnel is also known as an IPsec tunnel.

Step 4.   After the IPsec tunnel is established, interesting traffic (for example, traffic classified by an ACL) flows through the protected IPsec tunnel. Note that traffic not deemed interesting can still be sent between PC1 and PC2. However, the noninteresting traffic is transmitted outside the protection of the IPsec tunnel.

Step 5.   After no interesting traffic is seen for a specified amount of time, the IPsec tunnel is torn down and the IPsec SA is deleted.

This example describes an IPsec site-to-site VPN, but the procedure is similar for a client-to-site VPN. IPsec is typically deployed using IKEv1, with its two phases (Phase 1 and Phase 2).

IKEv2

The latest version IKE, IKE Version 2 (IKEv2) offers many great improvements over IKEv1. IKEv2 uses fewer packets in setting up the SAs between VPN peers and does not use the terms *Phase 1* and *Phase 2*. Instead, the initial tunnel is called the *IKEv2 SA*, and the IPsec SA is referred to as a *child tunnel* (instead of being called an IKE Phase 2 tunnel).

Additional features that are integrated into IKEv2 include the following:

- EAP
- NAT traversal (that is, the ability to detect NAT in the path between the peers)
- The ability to validate the tunnel

IKEv1 requires additional configuration and vendor add-ons to implement similar types of features.

Other VPN Technologies

Although IPsec VPNs are popular for securely interconnecting sites or connecting a remote client to a site, you need to be aware of other VPN protocols, examples of which are provided in Table 19-2.

Key Topic

Table 19-2 Examples of VPN Protocols

Protocol	Description
SSL	Secure Socket Layer (SSL) provides cryptography and reliability for the upper layers (Layers 5–7) of the OSI model. SSL, which was introduced in 1995, has largely been replaced by Transport Layer Security (TLS). However, recent versions of SSL (for example, SSL 3.3) have been enhanced to be more comparable with TLS. Both SSL and TLS provide secure web browsing via Hypertext Transfer Protocol Secure (HTTPS).
L2TP	Layer 2 Tunneling Protocol (L2TP) is a VPN protocol that lacks security features, such as encryption. However, L2TP can still be used for a secure VPN connection if it is combined with another protocol that does provide encryption.
L2F	Layer 2 Forwarding (L2F) is a VPN protocol designed (by Cisco Systems) with the goal of providing a tunneling protocol for PPP. Like L2TP, L2F lacks native security features.
PPTP	Point-to-Point Tunneling Protocol (PPTP) is an older VPN protocol (which supported the dial-up networking feature in older versions of Microsoft Windows). Like L2TP and L2F, PPTP lacks native security features. However, Microsoft's versions of PPTP bundled with various versions of Microsoft Windows were enhanced to offer security features.
TLS	Transport Layer Security (TLS) has largely replaced SSL as the VPN protocol of choice for providing cryptography and reliability to upper layers of the OSI model. For example, when you securely connect to a website using HTTPS, you are probably using TLS.
SSTP	Secure Socket Tunneling Protocol (SSTP) is a VPN tunnel that transports PPP traffic through an SSL/TLS channel. SSL/TLS provides transport-level security. SSTP's use of SSL/TLS over TCP port 443 allows SSTP to pass through virtually all firewalls and proxy servers.
OpenVPN	OpenVPN is a software VPN system that creates secure point-to-point or site-to-site connections in routed or bridged configurations and remote access facilities. It implements both client and server applications.

Other Remote Access Technologies

When it comes to remote access solutions, it is not surprising that varying amounts of security are possible today and can be implemented in a wide variety of ways. Your organization might require the strongest possible protections over one remote access connection, while another might require the mildest possible security treatment. Fortunately, remote access technologies abound today, and these varying degrees of security can be accommodated with no problem.

Although ACLs can be used to permit or deny specific connections flowing *through* a router (or switch), you also need to control connections *to* network devices (for example, routers, switches, or servers). Table 19-3 summarizes many of these remote access technologies.

Table 19-3   Remote Access Technologies

Method	Description
RRAS	Microsoft Routing and Remote Access Server (RRAS) is a Microsoft Windows Server feature that allows Microsoft Windows clients to remotely access a Microsoft Windows network. This product is often used in Windows-centric corporate networks. This is partly due to the fact that RRAS is included in Windows Server 2016 (or higher). To make this solution even more accessible to Windows systems, Windows 10 features a built-in VPN client that works well in conjunction with RRAS. When comparing RRAS to the other technologies in this section, just remember that we are talking about a very Windows-centric environment. To be fair, however, the RRAS server could easily provide VPN service for a wide variety of operating systems using VPN software set to common standards.
RDP	Remote Desktop Protocol (RDP) is a Microsoft protocol that allows a user to view and control the desktop of a remote computer. RDP uses port 3389. This solution, which has been around a long time, permits simple desktop sharing over an Internet or other network connection. This product has widespread use because (once again) it is technology that is built in to Windows systems. Thankfully, RDP access to your local Windows 10 device is not enabled by default. Today, RDP usage has leveled off because a wide variety of best-selling software applications do the same thing (desktop sharing) but also offer many advanced features. These applications include LogMeIn, TeamViewer, and Splashtop. Once again, RDP is a Windows-centric solution. However, you can run the Windows Remote Desktop Client in a wide variety of operating systems, so you can access your Windows desktop from a Mac or Linux machine.
Remote desktop connection	When you have a user accessing a system remotely using RDP (or a similar remote desktop technology), this is called a *remote desktop connection (RDC)*.
Remote desktop gateway	The *remote desktop gateway* feature is a service available in Windows Server systems. It is a very clever use of the RDP protocol in which the server becomes a gateway to permit access to the server for management purposes for administrators who need to connect. These administrators can use *Secure Shell (SSH)* for secure remote access. This is a common practice that administrators perform with non-Windows systems, so now they can feel right at home when managing Windows servers.

Method	Description
Virtual network computing (VNC)	VNC can be thought of as a platform-independent version of Microsoft's RDP. Just like RDP, it seeks to provide an easy-to-use graphical user interface–driven remote desktop experience.
	VNC is used with Mac and Linux operating systems that do not have desktop sharing software built in (as is the case with Windows and RDP). This certainly makes sense in the case of Linux because many Linux administrators prefer the command line Linux environment and do not use a GUI-based front end.
Virtual desktop	Virtual desktop technology is growing at a fast pace, thanks in large part to the adoption of cloud technologies and increased bandwidth between datacenters and end users. Using this approach, a user accesses a desktop that is housed on a server in the datacenter. The user might not even realize that the operating system is not hosted on the local PC or laptop.
	Note that the virtual desktop concept discussed here is different from other types of virtual desktops in IT. For example, in both Windows and macOS systems, you can create virtual desktops. These are just running "spaces" on the local system that have different windows and programs running within them, which makes it easier to multitask. Notice how very different this technology is from the virtual desktops we are referencing here.
PPP	Point-to-Point Protocol (PPP) is a common Layer 2 protocol that offers features such as multilink interface, looped link detection, error detection, and authentication.
PPPoE	Point-to-Point Protocol over Ethernet (PPPoE) is a protocol commonly used between a DSL modem in a home (or business) and a service provider. Specifically, PPPoE encapsulates PPP frames within Ethernet frames. This approach allows an Ethernet connection to leverage features of PPP, such as authentication.
ICA	Independent Computing Architecture (ICA) is a Citrix-proprietary protocol that allows an application running on one platform (for example, Microsoft Windows) to be seen and controlled from a remote client, independent of the client platform (for example, UNIX or Linux).
SSH	Secure Shell (SSH) is a protocol used to securely connect to a remote host (typically via a terminal emulator). Secure Shell has enjoyed such widespread success that it is even used as the basis for several other security protocols and techniques. For example, SCP calls on SSH for some of its functionality. SSH uses port 22.
	As mentioned earlier, Linux administrators often prefer to use the command line for all operation and work in the operating system, and SSH is a perfect secure remote access tool for such users. Administrators can use the CLI to connect securely with SSH, and then they can operate in a BASH CLI environment to manage or work within the system.

Method	Description
Kerberos	Kerberos is a client/server authentication protocol that supports mutual authentication between a client and a server. Kerberos uses the concept of a trusted third party (a key distribution center) that hands out tickets that are used instead of username and password combinations. Kerberos is covered in depth in Chapter 16.
AAA	Authentication, authorization, and accounting (AAA, pronounced "triple A") allows a network to have a single repository of user credentials. A network administrator can, for example, supply the same credentials to log in to various network devices (for example, routers and switches). RADIUS and TACACS+ are protocols commonly used to communicate with a AAA server.
RADIUS	Remote Authentication Dial-In User Service (RADIUS) is a UDP-based protocol used to communicate with a AAA server. Unlike TACACS+, RADIUS does not encrypt an entire authentication packet; rather, it encrypts only the password. However, RADIUS does offer more robust accounting features than TACACS+. Also, RADIUS is a standards-based protocol, whereas TACACS+ is a Cisco-proprietary protocol.
TACACS+	Terminal Access Controller Access-Control System Plus (TACACS+) is a Cisco-proprietary TCP-based AAA protocol. TACACS+ has three separate and distinct sessions or functions for authentication, authorization, and accounting.
NAC	Network access control (NAC) can be used to permit or deny access to a network based on characteristics of the device seeking admission rather than just checking user credentials. For example, a client's operating system and version of antivirus software could be checked against a set of requirements before allowing the client to access a network. This process of checking a client's characteristics is called *posture assessment*.
IEEE 802.1X	IEEE 802.1X is a type of NAC that can permit or deny a wireless or wired LAN client access to a network. If IEEE 802.1X is used to permit access to a LAN via a switch port, then IEEE 802.1X is being used for port security. While covered elsewhere in this text, to summarize, in 802.1X, the device seeking admission to the network is called the *supplicant*. The device to which the supplication connects (either wirelessly or through a wired connection) is called the *authenticator*. The device that checks the supplicant's credentials and permits or denies the supplicant to access the network is called an *authentication server*. Usually, an authentication server is a RADIUS server.
CHAP	Challenge-Handshake Authentication Protocol (CHAP) performs one-way authentication for a remote access connection. However, authentication is performed through a three-way handshake (challenge, response, and acceptance messages) between a server and a client. The three-way handshake allows a client to be authenticated without sending credential information across a network. Password Authentication Protocol (PAP) is an unencrypted plaintext method of password exchange that should be avoided.

Method	Description
MS-CHAP	Microsoft Challenge-Handshake Authentication Protocol (MS-CHAP) is a Microsoft-enhanced version of CHAP that offers a collection of additional features not present with CHAP, including two-way authentication.
EAP	Extensible Authentication Protocol (EAP) specifies how authentication is performed by IEEE 802.1X. A variety of EAP types exist: Extensible Authentication Protocol-Flexible Authentication via Secure Tunneling (EAP-FAST), Extensible Authentication Protocol-Message Digest 5 (EAP-MD5), and Extensible Authentication Protocol-Transport Layer Security (EAP-TLS). EAP is covered in Chapter 16.
Two-factor authentication	Two-factor authentication (TFA) requires two types of authentication from a user seeking admission to a network. For example, a user might have to *know* something (for example, a password) and *have* something (such as a specific fingerprint, which can be checked with a biometric authentication device).
Multifactor authentication	Multifactor authentication requires two or more types of successful authentication factors before granting access to a network.
Single sign-on	Single sign-on (SSO) allows a user to authenticate only once to gain access to multiple systems rather than needing to independently authenticate with each system.
Local authentication	Local authentication refers to a network device authenticating the user with a database of user account information stored on the device itself; this is often an important fallback method of authentication used when another external method fails.
LDAP	Lightweight Directory Access Protocol (LDAP) permits a set of standards for the storage and access of user account information. Many proprietary user stores (including Microsoft's Active Directory) support LDAP for ease of access. LDAP uses port 389.
Captive portal	A captive portal is a web page that appears before a user is able to access the network resource; this web page accepts the credentials of the user for authentication and presents them to the authentication server.

Authentication and Authorization Considerations

There is a strong emphasis in IT on *authentication* and *authorization* for remote access as this area continues to explode in popularity and usage. For example, multifactor authentication is currently surging in popularity due to its ability to help secure networks and their data.

The following are some of the options for components of multifactor authentication:

- Something you know (such as a passcode or pin)

- Something you have (such as a smart card or badge)

- Something you are (such as a fingerprint or retinal scan)

- Something you do (such as a swipe pattern or puzzle completion)

- Somewhere you are (such as a geolocation or IP address)

To ensure that you understand the simplicity and beauty of multifactor authentication, consider this simple example: John goes to the store and puts his bank card into an ATM and enters his PIN. What examples of multifactor authentication has he exhibited?

An automated teller machine (ATM) provides a common example of a multifactor authentication system, requiring both of the following:

- A "something you have" physical key (your ATM card)

- A "something you know" personal identification number (PIN)

Technology has also progressed in the specific area of authorization. New technologies such as data loss prevention (DLP) enable mechanisms for the protection of data throughout its lifetime and use in all locations related to the enterprise. This type of technology is especially useful in heavily mobile environments. In fact, DLP functions are often a key aspect of mobile device management (MDM) solutions.

DLP systems are designed to detect and prevent unauthorized use and transmission of confidential information based on one of the three states of data:

- In use

- In motion

- At rest

A well-designed DLP strategy allows control over sensitive data, reduces the cost of data breaches, and achieves greater insight into organizational data use.

In-Band vs. Out-of-Band Management

One reason for the explosion in remote access technologies and their adoption is the growing number of solutions emphasizing out-of-band management. *Out-of-band management* means that the network management traffic never mingles with the user data traffic. Your network device can have a separate network interface for this purpose. This separate network interface connects to a separate WAN connection, and this separate connection is used only for the network management traffic. Consider the advantages of out-of-band versus *in-band network management*. With in-band management, security issues are possible because the network management traffic shares the same path. There is also a contention for bandwidth in this scenario.

While out-of-band management may sound like the de facto answer and solution you should implement, keep in mind that not all designs are optimal for all different topologies, technologies, and solutions. There are plenty of in-band management solutions that run securely and optimally. In fact, well-designed network management solutions tend to involve low bandwidth consumption as part of their excellent design.

Real-World Case Study

Acme, Inc. has implemented a new site-to-site VPN between the main HQ location and a large branch office that has just been brought online. Acme, Inc. decided on a site-to-site VPN because of the high volume of sensitive corporate data that needs to be sent frequently between these two locations. Having the VPN always available for these transfers is a major requirement.

Acme, Inc. has also decided to implement out-of-band network management traffic whenever possible. This includes the conversion of several types of management traffic from the current use of in-band management traffic.

An important exception to this new rule has been established. The IT Support Team will still be permitted to use SSH to several key systems using the main data network. Note that this only permitted due to the strong encryption that is used with SSH.

Summary

Here are the main topics covered in this chapter:

- This chapter discusses VPN technologies in general.

- This chapter discusses client-based and site-to-site based VPNs.

- This chapter covers a wide variety of remote access technologies and approaches.

Exam Preparation Tasks

Review All the Key Topics

Review the most important topics from this chapter, noted with the Key Topic icon in the outer margin of the page. Table 19-4 lists these key topics and the page number where each is found.

Table 19-4 Key Topics for Chapter 19

Key Topic Element	Description	Page Number
List	Two primary categories of VPNs	466
Figure 19-3	Transport mode versus tunnel mode	471
Figure 19-4	IPsec VPN steps	472
Table 19-2	Examples of VPN protocols	474
Table 19-3	Remote access technologies	475

Complete Tables and Lists from Memory

Print a copy of Appendix C, "Memory Tables," or at least the section for this chapter and complete as many of the tables as possible from memory. Appendix D, "Memory Tables Answer Key," includes the completed tables and lists so you can check your work.

Define Key Terms

Define the following key terms from this chapter and check your answers in the Glossary:

site-to-site VPN, client-to-site VPN, clientless VPN, split tunnel, full tunnel, remote desktop connection (RDC), remote desktop gateway, Secure Shell (SSH), virtual network computing (VNC), virtual desktop, authentication, authorization, in-band management, out-of-band management

Complete Chapter 19 Hands-On Lab in Network+ Simulator Lite

- Configuring a Small Office/Home Office Router—Network User Security Settings
- WAN Terminology
- Configuring a VPN Client

Additional Resources

Remote Desktop Software and an SSL VPN: https://www.youtube.com/watch?v=NOytvWA0ZQwIPsec

Virtual Private Networks: https://www.youtube.com/watch?v=FpKLc56VFc8

Review Questions

The answers to these review questions appear in Appendix A, "Answers to Review Questions."

1. What type of VPN might feature the use of a clientless VPN solution?

   a. Site-to-site

   b. Client-to-site

   c. Client-to-client

   d. Server-to-server

2. Which of the following is often considered a multiplatform solution that is similar to the approach taken by RDP?

   a. VNC

   b. SSH

   c. Telnet

   d. MDM

3. What remote access technology is considered a secure alternative to Telnet for making a secure connection to a remote network device and operating at the CLI?

   a. SCP

   b. SFTP

   c. SSH

   d. SSL

4. Sally has been issued a new corporate laptop. This laptop requires a fingerprint followed by a pin code in order to access the desktop. What examples of MFA are in use here? (Choose two.)

   a. Something she is

   b. Something she has

   c. Something she knows

   d. Somewhere she is

5. A user clicks Accept, views an advertisement, provides an email address, or performs some other required action, and the network grants access to the user. Which of the following is being described here?

   a. Virtual network computing (VNC)

   b. Remote desktop connection (RDC)

   c. SSH

   d. Captive portal

This chapter covers the following topics related to Objective 4.5 (Explain the importance of physical security) of the CompTIA Network+ N10-008 certification exam:

- Detection methods
  - Camera
  - Motion detection
  - Asset tags
  - Tamper detection
- Prevention methods
  - Employee training
  - Access control hardware
    - Badge readers
    - Biometrics
  - Locking racks
  - Locking cabinets
  - Access control vestibule (previously known as a mantrap)
  - Smart lockers
- Asset disposal
  - Factory reset/wipe configuration
  - Sanitize devices for disposal

CHAPTER 20

Physical Security

Have you ever had (the rather depressing) thought that all the hard work you have done in Cisco IOS on a network device to secure it is worthless if an attacker gains physical access to your device? Someone who has physical access to a device might press a reset button in order to reset the device to factory defaults (allowing them to log in and reconfigure the device) or they might just take a less sophisticated approach and smash the device using a sledgehammer. If an attacker has access to your network equipment, you are in trouble.

This chapter provides some common examples of physical security tools and techniques to help ensure that you can protect your network equipment from physical (Layer 1) types of attacks. Just as with many other areas of network security, detection and prevention are both important to physical security. This chapter also discusses the important area of asset disposal.

Foundation Topics

Detection Methods

When you think about detecting an attack against your network, you likely envision monitoring packets traveling into and out of your network devices. When you think about physical security, you can think in similar terms. You will certainly need to monitor the flow of humans into and out of the area where the network devices exist.

Today, there are many affordable options in the physical security detection realm of network security. Here are just some of the ones you should be aware of:

- *Motion detection*: Using either mechanical or electronic methods, you can install motion detection devices that alert you when objects change position in a physical network location.

- *Cameras*: Cameras allow you to view key network areas by using video surveillance. Video footage is often recorded and stored locally or in the cloud. Modern camera systems have been combined with more advanced intelligence to detect weapons and other threats.

- *Asset tracking tags*: You can use various wireless technologies to track the physical locations of network objects and personnel by using tag technologies attached to the entities. For example, radio frequency identification (RFID) uses electromagnetic fields and allows one-way communication of information from a chip to an RFID reader.

- *Tamper detection*: You can take steps to ensure that network equipment is not tampered with. For example, you might place key network cable runs in clearly viewable conduits and make appliances readily viewable through glass enclosures. You could also use IP camera systems to send alerts when certain areas containing hardware are infiltrated and tamper panels to detect when the cover of an all-in-one system or computer case is opened or tampered with.

Prevention Methods

There are many options you can use to assist in the area of physical attack prevention.

Many security professionals today will beg you to accept the fact that the most important prevention method you can take is complete and thorough *employee training*. One of the reasons for this common opinion is that many attacks cannot be carried out without user intervention. For example, social engineering requires a user to give sensitive information (such as username and password credentials) to an attacker in order for the attacker to access the user's account. As a result, a number of potential cybersecurity-related attacks can be thwarted through effective user training. For instance, users could be trained on using policies such as the following:

- Never give out your password to anyone, even if that person claims to be from IT.

- Do not open email attachments from unknown sources.

- Select strong passwords, consisting of at least 8 to 12 characters and containing a mixture of alphabetic (upper- and lowercase), numeric, and special characters.

- Do not visit unauthorized websites.

- Report suspicious activity.

- Do not run or install any applications not provided directly by the company.

- Change your passwords monthly.

This list is only an example, and you should develop a collection of best practices for your users based on your network's specific circumstances. Users should also know whom to contact in the event of a suspected data breach or compromise of the computers and systems the users are responsible for. Users should also know never to run penetration testing tools or other network discovery tools that may unintentionally lead to denial of service (DoS) or other harm to the network and its devices. Technical controls such as web/content filtering, port filtering, IP filtering, and access control lists (ACLs) that deny specific traffic can be used to assist in the enforcement of the policies agreed to by the users.

As part of user training and for the safety of human life, emergency procedures should also be communicated and verified with each user, including the

- Building layout

- Fire-escape plan

- Safety and emergency exits

- Doors that automatically fail closed or fail open based on their purpose to contain or allow access

- Emergency alert systems

- Fire suppression systems

- Heating, ventilation, and air conditioning (HVAC) operations

- Emergency shutoff procedures

In a datacenter, procedures for safety related to electrostatic discharge (ESD), grounding, rack installation, lifting, tool safety, and the correct placement of devices should also be planned, communicated, and verified. If there are dangerous substances in or near the work area, a material safety data sheet (MSDS) should be created to identify procedures for handling and working with those substances.

While employee training is undeniably important, keep in mind that it transcends just physical security concerns. Here are just some of the additional prevention methods you can engage in for physical security:

- **Badge readers**: Identification badges assist with physical security regarding employees. Badge readers are specialized hardware devices that read identification badges, and the data they collect is valuable for physical security. Whereas identification might be limited to name and photo, more sophisticated approaches can include electronic swipes and asset tags.

- **Biometrics**: Although at one time biometrics were reserved for the most sophisticated of environments, now using a thumbprint reader, facial recognition, or a retina scan is a reality with such common devices as cell phones.

> **NOTE** It is common to refer to badge readers and biometrics as belonging to a category of devices called *access control hardware*.

- **Smart cards:** A smart card looks like a credit card but possesses circuitry that allows it to authenticate a user against network systems; this aids security and is known as multifactor authentication (MFA) because the user must possess something (the smart card) and know something (the password). This MFA approach has worked well for ATMs in the banking system for decades.

- **Key fobs:** A key fob is an electronic attachment to a key ring that might provide access to a network system or might simply lock or unlock a secure door.

- **Locks:** Sometimes the simplest of security mechanisms are the most effective; this is often the case with locks on network areas and equipment. Your enterprise might feature racks for network equipment that have locking cages over them. These are often simply referred to as *locking racks*. You can also use *locking cabinets* for physical security.

- **Smart lockers:** It is always wonderful when one technology can assist another. This is certainly the case with smart lockers. These lockers might look like typical lockers from the outside, but they include network connectivity intelligence and might even be configured for Internet access. Smart lockers can accurately log user access and provide a level of security never before seen with basic lockers.

- *Access control vestibule* **(formerly called a mantrap):** As you learned in Chapter 17, "Common Types of Attacks," there are at least two forms of social engineering attacks—tailgating and piggybacking—that require an attacker to follow an authorized user through a secured entrance or exit. An access control vestibule (formerly known as a mantrap), which is a small entry area with two interlocking doors, provides assurance that these forms of social engineering cannot take place.

Asset Disposal

Early in the development of networking, there were many infamous tales of sensitive data being retrieved from networking assets that were disposed of. Perhaps the engineering team thought (rather foolishly) that no one would be interested in fishing through the large Dumpster behind headquarters to find the hard drives nestled inside the decade-old PCs being disposed of. These same engineers might have felt very secure in this disposal if they had taken the additional step of formatting the hard drives before disposal.

Unfortunately, data can be recovered from a disk that has been formatted, and, of course, attackers would be happy to dig through a Dumpster (that is, Dumpster dive) to retrieve these drives. In fact, attackers would be thrilled to have such an easy way to obtain an organization's data.

Today there are many excellent techniques for proper and safe asset disposal. The following are some examples:

- *Factory reset*: One step in ensuring that a device does not contain information that can be used against an organization is a factory reset. Such a reset can often ensure that a networking device contains no data or settings that are specific to the organization.

- *Wipe configuration*: In many organizations, it is standard procedure to wipe the configuration from a networking device when disposal is needed. In fact, in many bring-your-own-device (BYOD) environments, mobile devices are programmed so that it is possible to automatically wipe their configurations if they are reported stolen.

- *Sanitize devices for disposal*: In high security environments, there is often a process in place for completely sanitizing a device of all existing data before disposal of the device. This might involve degaussing, which involves passing powerful magnets over the surface of storage to ensure that the data can never be recovered. In other environments, even degaussing might not even be considered enough, and physical destruction or shredding of the component might be required to erase data permanently.

> **NOTE**   Some legislation, including HIPAA (which applies to medical records), requires that paper records be properly disposed of due to privacy concerns and regulations. In fact, many government agencies require a signed certificate of disposal after data disposal.

Real-World Case Study

Networking is expanding its operations, and it is planning to revamp the physical security posture of the organization. There is a main datacenter location that needs surveillance cameras and motion detection. There are also asset tags needed at the main employee location.

In addition to the detection improvements, AJSnetworking has planned some major enhancements to the prevention areas of physical security. Specifically, AJSnetworking will begin some detailed training courses that will be mandatory for all employees. This security training will include key points regarding physical security. AJSnetworking is also going to be using Splunk to better analyze badge reader data and smart locker data. The plan is to be much more aware of anomalies that are occurring in this data that can point to potential physical security issues.

Summary

Here are the main topics covered in this chapter:

- This chapter covers some of the most common methods and tools for detecting physical security attacks, including cameras, motion detection, asset tags, and tamper detection.

- This chapter covers some of the most common methods for preventing physical attacks, including employee training and the use of badge readers, biometrics, locking racks and cabinets, access control vestibules, and smart lockers.

- This chapter covers some of the most common methods for asset disposal, including factory resets/wipes and sanitization of devices for disposal.

Exam Preparation Tasks

Review All the Key Topics

Review the most important topics from this chapter, noted with the Key Topic icon in the outer margin of the page. Table 20-1 lists these key topics and the page number where each is found.

Table 20-1 Key Topics for Chapter 20

Key Topic Element	Description	Page Number
List	Common physical security detection methods	486
List	Common physical security prevention methods	488
List	Common physical security asset disposal methods	489

Define Key Terms

Define the following key terms from this chapter and check your answers in the Glossary:

camera, motion detection, asset tracking tag, tamper detection, employee training, badge reader, biometrics, locking cabinet/rack, access control vestibule, smart locker, factory reset, wipe configuration, sanitize device

Additional Resources

What is Network Security?: https://www.cccouncil.org/network-security/

What Is Asset Disposition?: https://whatis.techtarget.com/definition/IT-asset-disposition-ITAD

Review Questions

The answers to these review questions appear in Appendix A, "Answers to Review Questions."

1. Which of the following is not a common physical security prevention method?

   a. Motion detection

   b. Employee training

   c. Locking racks

   d. Access control vestibule

2. Which of the following is not a common physical security detection method or tool?

    a. Camera

    b. Asset tag

    c. Tamper detection

    d. Biometrics

3. Which two of the following are common techniques used when disposing of assets in an enterprise environment? (Choose two.)

    a. Factory reset

    b. Baselining

    c. Configuration backup

    d. Configuration wipe

4. Which of the following are applied to physical network assets to permit location monitoring for these devices?

    a. Badge readers

    b. Locking racks

    c. Asset tags

    d. ACLs

5. Which of the following are terms for a small entry area with two interlocking doors that prevents tailgating/piggybacking? (Choose two.)

    a. Smart locker

    b. Access control vestibule

    c. Mantrap

    d. Configuration wipe

This chapter covers the following topics related to Objective 5.1 (Explain the network troubleshooting methodology) of the CompTIA Network+ N10-008 certification exam:

- Identify the problem
  - Gather information
  - Question users
  - Identify symptoms
  - Determine if anything has changed
  - Duplicate the problem, if possible
  - Approach multiple problems individually
- Establish a theory of probable cause
  - Question the obvious
  - Consider multiple approaches
    - Top-to-bottom/bottom-to-top OSI model
    - Divide and conquer
- Test the theory to determine the cause
  - If the theory is confirmed, determine the next steps to resolve the problem
  - If the theory is not confirmed, reestablish a new theory or escalate
- Establish a plan of action to resolve the problem and identify potential effects
- Implement the solution or escalate as necessary
- Verify full system functionality and, if applicable, implement preventive measures
- Document findings, actions, outcomes, and lessons learned

CHAPTER 21

A Network Troubleshooting Methodology

As you perform your day-to-day tasks of administering a network, a significant percentage of your time will be dedicated to resolving network issues. Whether the issues you are troubleshooting were reported by an end user or were issues you discovered, you need an effective plan to respond to them. Specifically, you need a systematic approach to clearly articulate an issue, gather information about the issue, hypothesize the underlying cause of the issue, validate your hypothesis, create an action plan, implement that action plan, observe results, and document your resolution. Without a plan, your efforts might be inefficient, as you try one thing after another, possibly causing other issues in the process.

Although your troubleshooting efforts can most definitely benefit from a structured approach, realize that troubleshooting is part art and part science. Specifically, your intuition and instincts play a huge role in isolating an issue. Of course, those skills are developed over time and come with experience and exposure to more and more scenarios.

To help you start developing or continue honing your troubleshooting skills, this chapter presents a troubleshooting methodology that can act as a guide for addressing almost any network issue. This chapter also presents a collection of common network issues to consider in your real-world troubleshooting efforts (and issues to consider as you prepare for the Network+ exam).

The common network issues in this chapter are broken down into the following categories: physical layer issues, data link layer issues, network layer issues, and wireless network issues.

Foundation Topics

Troubleshooting Basics

Troubleshooting network issues is implicit in the responsibilities of a network administrator. Such issues could arise as a result of human error (for example, a misconfiguration), equipment failure, software bugs, or traffic patterns (for example, high utilization or a network being under attack by malicious traffic).

Many network issues can be successfully resolved using a variety of approaches. This section begins by introducing you to troubleshooting fundamentals and then presents a structured troubleshooting methodology you should know for the Network+ exam.

Troubleshooting Fundamentals

The process of troubleshooting, at its essence, is the process of responding to a problem report (sometimes in the form of a *trouble ticket*), diagnosing the underlying cause of the problem, and resolving the problem. Although you normally think of the troubleshooting process beginning when a user reports an issue, through effective network monitoring, you might detect a situation that could become a troubleshooting issue and resolve that situation before it impacts users.

After an issue is reported, the first step toward resolution is clearly defining the issue. After you have a clearly defined troubleshooting target, you can begin gathering information related to that issue. Based on the information collected, you might be able to better define the issue. Then you can hypothesize the likely causes of the issue. Evaluation of these likely causes leads to the identification of the suspected underlying root cause of an issue.

After a suspected underlying cause is identified, you define approaches to resolve an issue and select what you consider to be the best approach. Sometimes the best approach to resolving an issue cannot be implemented immediately. For example, a piece of equipment might need to be replaced. However, implementing such an approach during working hours might disrupt a business's workflow. In such situations, a troubleshooter might use a temporary fix until a permanent fix can be put in place.

As a personal example, when helping troubleshoot a connectivity issue for a resort hotel at a major theme park, my coworkers and I discovered that a modular Ethernet switch had an issue causing Spanning Tree Protocol (STP) to fail, resulting in a Layer 2 loop. This loop flooded the network with traffic, preventing the hotel from issuing keycards for guest rooms. The underlying cause was clear: The Ethernet switch had a bad module. However, the issue was pinpointed around 4 p.m., a peak time for guest registration. So, instead of immediately replacing the faulty module, we disconnected one of the redundant links, thus breaking the Layer 2 loop. The logic was that it was better to have the network function at this time without STP than for the network to experience an even longer outage while the bad module was replaced. Late that night, someone came back to the switch and swapped out the module, resolving the underlying cause while minimizing user impact.

Figure 21-1 provides a simplified model of the troubleshooting steps just described, which consists of three steps:

Step 1. Problem report

Step 2. Problem diagnosis

Step 3. Problem resolution

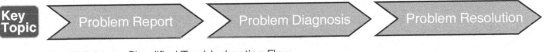

FIGURE 21-1 Simplified Troubleshooting Flow

Of these three steps, the majority of a troubleshooter's efforts are spent in the *problem diagnosis* step. Table 21-1 describes key components of this diagnosis step.

Table 21-1 Steps to Diagnose a Problem

Step	Description
Gather information.	Because a typical problem report lacks sufficient information to give a troubleshooter insight into a problem's underlying cause, the troubleshooter should collect additional information, perhaps using network maintenance tools or interviewing impacted users.
Duplicate the problem, if possible.	Testing to see if you can duplicate the problem is often a key step in problem diagnosis.
Question users.	Although it can be difficult to gather information from your end users, doing so is often critical in correctly pinpointing the exact problem. Oftentimes, finding out user actions prior to the problem is critical.
Identify symptoms.	What symptoms has the problem has created?
Determine if anything has changed.	Perhaps your end users will provide valuable clues if they accurately indicate what changes they might have made to systems.
Approach multiple problems individually.	Unfortunately, you might discover that there are multiple issues. Be sure to approach each one individually.

Structured Troubleshooting Methodology

Troubleshooting skills vary from administrator to administrator. Therefore, although most troubleshooting approaches include the collection and analysis of information, elimination of potential causes, hypothesis of likely causes, and testing of the suspected cause, different troubleshooters might spend different amounts of time performing these tasks.

If a troubleshooter does not follow a structured approach, the temptation is to move between the previously listed troubleshooting tasks in a fairly random way, often based on instinct. Although such an approach might well lead to problem resolution, it can become confusing to remember what you have tried and what you have not tried. Also, if another administrator comes to assist you, communicating to that other administrator the steps you have already gone through could be challenging. Therefore, following a structured troubleshooting approach not only helps prevent you from trying the same thing more than once and inadvertently skipping a task but also aids in communicating to someone else the possibilities you have already eliminated.

You might encounter a variety of structured troubleshooting methodologies in networking literature. However, for the Network+ exam, the methodology shown in Figure 21-2 is the one you should memorize.

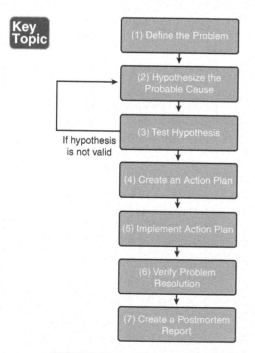

FIGURE 21-2   Structured Troubleshooting Approach

Key Topic

The following is an elaboration on this seven-step methodology:

Step 1.   **Identify the problem.** Effective troubleshooting begins with a clear problem definition. This definition might include specific symptoms. Here's an example: "User A's computer is unable to communicate with server 1 (as verified by a ping test). However, user A can communicate with all other servers. Also, no other user seems to have an issue connecting to server 1." This problem definition might come from questioning the impacted user(s) and doing your own testing (for example, seeing if you can ping from user A's computer to server 1). If possible, determine whether anything has changed in the network (or in the computer) configuration. Also, find out whether this is a new installation that has failed to work in the past.

Step 2.   **Establish a theory of probable cause.** This is the point in the troubleshooting process where your experience and intuition can be extremely helpful because it is when you brainstorm a list of possible causes. As you brainstorm, be sure to question the obvious. Also, think in terms of *top-to-bottom troubleshooting* (moving from top to bottom within the OSI model) or *bottom-to-top troubleshooting*. Alternatively, you could use a *divide-and-conquer troubleshooting* approach. When examining your collected data (for example, output from the **ipconfig /all** command), question everything. For example, you might think that the issue described in step 1 could result from causes such as an ACL blocking traffic to or from the PC, a connectivity issue with the PC or server, or an incorrect IP address configuration on the PC. From your list of possible causes, select the one you consider the most likely. From the previous list, you might believe that an incorrect IP address configuration on the PC is the most likely cause of the problem. Specifically, you might conclude that the issue is not related to connectivity because other PCs can get to the server, and user A's PC can get to other servers. Also, you might conclude that it is more likely that user A's PC has a bad IP address configuration than that an ACL has been administratively added to the router to block traffic only between user A's PC and server 1.

Step 3.   **Test the theory to determine the cause.** Before taking action on what you consider to be the most likely cause of a problem, do a *sanity check* on your theory. Would your hypothesized cause lead to the observed symptoms? In the example presented in the preceding steps, you might examine the subnet mask assigned to user A's computer and determine that it is incorrect. Specifically, the subnet mask makes user A's computer think that server 1 is on the same subnet as user A's computer. As a result, user A's computer does not forward traffic to its default gateway when attempting to reach server 1. If your hypothesis is technically sound, you can proceed to step 4. However, if you notice a flaw in your logic, you need to formulate an alternate hypothesis. The formation of an alternate hypothesis might involve escalating the problem to someone more familiar with the device(s) in question.

Step 4.   **Establish a plan of action to resolve the problem and identify potential effects.** Once you have confirmed that your theory makes sense technically, you need to develop an action plan. If time permits, you should document your action plan. The documentation of your action plan can be used as a *back-out plan* if your hypothesis is incorrect. In the example we have been building on throughout these steps, an action plan might be to change the subnet mask on user A's computer from 255.255.0.0 to 255.255.255.0.

Step 5.   **Implement the solution or escalate as necessary.** Based on your documented plan of action, you should schedule an appropriate time to implement the action plan. The selection of an appropriate time is a balance between the severity of a problem and the impact your action plan will have on other users. Sometimes, when attempting to implement an action plan, you realize that you do not have sufficient administrative privileges to perform a task in your action plan. In such cases, you should escalate the issue to someone who has appropriate administrative rights. In this example, changing the subnet mask on one computer should not impact any other devices. So, you might immediately make the configuration change on user A's computer.

Step 6.   **Verify full system functionality and, if applicable, implement preventive measures.** After implementing an action plan, you need to verify that the symptoms listed in your original problem definition are gone. You also need to attempt to determine whether your action plan has caused any other issues on the network. A mistake many troubleshooters make at this point is believing that the issue has been resolved because the specific symptom (or symptoms) they were looking for is gone. However, the user who originally reported the issue might still be having a problem. Therefore, troubleshooters should live by the mantra "A problem isn't fixed until the user believes it's fixed." You should get confirmation from the person reporting an issue that, from her perspective, the reported issue has indeed been resolved. In this example, you could attempt to ping server 1 from user A. If the ping is successful, you can check with user A to see whether she agrees that the problem is resolved.

Step 7. **Document findings, actions, outcomes, and lessons learned.** A *post-mortem* report is a document that describes the reported issue, its underlying causes, and what was done to resolve the issue. This report might be useful when troubleshooting similar issues in the future.

Keep in mind when working your way through the previous steps that you might encounter an issue that you do not have sufficient information to solve. When that happens, you might need to further research the issue yourself. However, if time is of the essence, you might need to immediately escalate the issue to someone else within your organization, to an equipment vendor, or to an outside consultant.

Real-World Case Study

Networking is analyzing the efficiency of the support desk. During this analysis, it was discovered that the previous attempts at an enforcement of a troubleshooting methodology were not being followed. The methodology also had several weaknesses to it that did not warrant following to begin with.

Networking is implementing training on a new methodology and is introducing several new software tools that will make it easier to follow and more effective overall.

Summary

Here are the main topics covered in this chapter:

- This chapter covers the basics of troubleshooting and looks at the fundamentals of this vast subject.

- This chapter describes a structured troubleshooting methodology.

Exam Preparation Tasks

Review All the Key Topics

Review the most important topics from this chapter, noted with the Key Topic icon in the outer margin of the page. Table 21-2 lists these key topics and the page number where each is found.

Table 21-2   Key Topics for Chapter 21

Key Topic Element	Description	Page Number
Figure 21-1	Simplified troubleshooting flow	497
Table 21-1	Steps to diagnose a problem	497
Figure 21-2	Structured troubleshooting approach	498
Step list	Steps in the CompTIA Network+ structured troubleshooting methodology	499

Complete Tables and Lists from Memory

Print a copy of Appendix C, "Memory Tables," or at least the section for this chapter and complete as many of the tables as possible from memory. Appendix D, "Memory Tables Answer Key," includes the completed tables and lists so you can check your work.

Define Key Terms

Define the following key terms from this chapter and check your answers in the Glossary:

top-to-bottom troubleshooting, bottom-to-top troubleshooting, divide-and-conquer troubleshooting

Complete Chapter 21 Hands-On Labs in Network+ Simulator Lite

- Troubleshooting Practice

Additional Resource

A **Guide to Network Troubleshooting:** https://www.comptia.org/content/guides/a-guide-to-network-troubleshooting

Review Questions

The answers to these review questions appear in Appendix A, "Answers to Review Questions."

1. Which of the following is often the first step in a structured troubleshooting methodology?

    a. Hypothesize the probable cause.

    b. Create an action plan.

    c. Create a postmortem report.

    d. Define the problem.

2. Which of the following comprise a simplified troubleshooting flow? (Choose three.)

    a. Problem resolution

    b. Problem monitoring

    c. Problem diagnosis

    d. Problem report

3. What step is most likely to follow the "create an action plan" step in a structured troubleshooting methodology?

    a. Verify problem resolution.

    b. Test the hypothesis.

    c. Define the problem.

    d. Hypothesize the possible cause.

4. Which networking troubleshooting methodology step would include establishing a new theory or escalating if the theory is not confirmed?

    a. Step 1: Identify the problem.

    b. Step 4: Establish a plan of action to resolve the problem and identify potential effects.

    c. Step 2: Establish a theory of probable cause.

    d. Step 3: Test the theory to determine the cause.

5. You have verified full system functionality and implemented preventive measures. What should you do next?

    a. Question the obvious and duplicate the problem.

    b. Create a differential backup plan.

    c. Document findings, actions, outcomes, and lessons learned.

    d. Gather information and create a baseline.

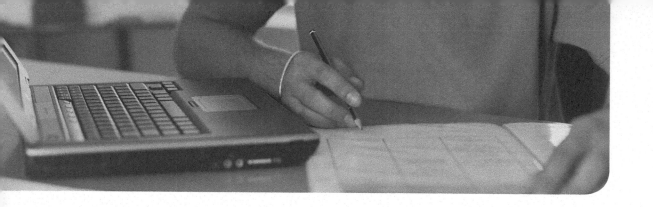

This chapter covers the following topics related to Objective 5.2 (Given a scenario, troubleshoot common cable connectivity issues and select the appropriate tools) of the CompTIA Network+ N10-008 certification exam:

- Specifications and limitations
  - Throughput
  - Speed
  - Distance
- Cable considerations
  - Shielded and unshielded
  - Plenum and riser-rated
- Cable application
  - Rollover cable/console cable
  - Crossover cable
  - Power over Ethernet
- Common issues
  - Attenuation
  - Interference
  - Decibel (dB) loss
  - Incorrect pinout
  - Bad ports
  - Open/short
  - Light-emitting diode (LED) status indicators
  - Incorrect transceivers

- Duplexing issues
- Transmit and receive (TX/RX) reversed
- Dirty optical cables
- Common tools
  - Cable crimper
  - Punchdown tool
  - Tone generator
  - Loopback adapter
  - Optical time-domain reflectometer (OTDR)
  - Multimeter
  - Cable tester
  - Wire map
  - Tap
  - Fusion splicers
  - Spectrum analyzers
  - Snips/cutters
  - Cable stripper
  - Fiber light meter

CHAPTER 22

Troubleshoot Common Cabling Problems

A lot can go wrong when it comes to the physical media (cables) that make up a network. But the great news is that there are more tools and techniques than ever before to proactively head off physical layer issues.

This chapter ensures that you understand the common problems to watch out for, as well as the tools that the best in the industry commonly use to solve these many potential issues.

Foundation Topics

Specifications and Limitations

There are some very basic requirements when it comes to thinking about the physical layer media of your infrastructure. You need to focus on at least these three aspects of the specifications and limitations for the media:

- *Throughput*: This is a measure of the total amount of data that media can send over a given time period.

- *Speed*: This is a measure of the data send rate; for example, Cat 6 media supports a maximum speed of 10Gbps.

- *Distance*: For both wired and wireless media, as you get farther away from the sender over the media, you start to suffer the effects of attenuation (that is, a weakening of the signal over distance). You need to pay attention to the maximum distances supported by various physical layer media options. For example, Cat 6 has become the minimum standard for new network cable installations. And while the speed of Cat 6 (10Gbps) is exciting, Cat 6 supports distances only up to 55 meters.

Cable Considerations and Applications

The following are some considerations you should keep in mind when considering physical cable:

- *Shielded* versus *unshielded*: Physical cable often needs to be twisted or shielded (or both) in order not to suffer from electromagnetic interference (EMI). For example, in shielded twisted-pair (STP) cables, a metallic shielding covers the twisted pair inside the cable. This shielding helps protect against EMI, but it does so at a cost: These types of cables can be much more expensive than unshielded cables due to the shielding.

With unshielded twisted-pair (UTP), the twists in the cable are tighter to reduce EMI. This eliminates the need for the expensive shielding.

- *Plenum* and *riser rated*: If a twisted-pair cable is to be installed under raised flooring or in an open-air return, fire codes must be considered. For example, imagine that a fire breaks out in a building. If the outer insulation of a twisted-pair cable catches fire or starts to melt, it could release toxic fumes. If those toxic fumes were released in a location such as an open-air return, those fumes could be spread throughout a building, posing a huge health risk.

To mitigate the concern of pumping poisonous gas throughout a building's heating, ventilation, and air-conditioning (HVAC) system, plenum-rated cabling can be used. The outer insulation of a plenum twisted-pair cable is fire retardant; in addition, some plenum cabling uses a fluorinated ethylene polymer (FEP) or a low-smoke polyvinyl chloride (PVC) to minimize dangerous fumes.

NOTE   Check your local fire codes before installing network cabling.

A *riser* is a vertical area that passes from one floor to another floor inside a building. Riser-rated cables are cables that run through risers; they should be fire-proof to prevent flames from traveling up the cable. However, the fire rating requirements for riser areas are less strict than the requirements for plenum areas.

You should also consider the following physical cable applications:

- *Rollover cable/console cable*: The flattened cable that comes with a network device from the factory is called a *rollover cable*. Because you typically use these cables to make console connections to devices, these cables are often referred to as *console cables*.

- *Crossover cable*: The concern about whether you need a crossover cable versus a straight-through Ethernet cable is quickly fading from our concerns due to Auto-MDIX technology, which permits a port to adjust to the type of cable that is connected. Before this technology came along, administrators had to be careful to use crossover cables to connect like devices. For example, connecting two switches together (to form a trunk) required a crossover cable.

- *Power over Ethernet (PoE)*: Power over Ethernet (PoE) is a technology that makes it simple to connect devices such as cameras and access points to the network and have these devices get power from the single network connection. This prevents you from having to find an outlet for plugging in a number of smart devices. For PoE to work, you need to use Cat 5e or better media.

Common Issues

To be an effective troubleshooter, it helps to understand the types of things that commonly go wrong in networks so that you can become more proficient in recognizing and solving these issues. Here are just some of the things you need to be on the lookout for with cabling in a network:

- *Attenuation*: As mentioned earlier in this chapter, distance is the enemy of cabling. The longer the signal travels through the media, the more it weakens. It is very important to know the maximum distances for the various media in your enterprise network. Attenuation is measured in decibels (dB), which is covered shortly.

■ *Interference*: While they are not as sensitive to interference as wireless media, cables can suffer from EMI and other types of interference. Just as with wireless networks, you need to do proper testing for interference issues before deploying physical media. In addition, to reduce interference, you should follow the recommendations of the cable manufacturer.

■ *Decibel (dB) loss*: If physical cable has lots of different splits or splices in it, there might be a great deal of dB loss. This loss is also more prone to happen as the signal needs to go farther and farther in the media.

■ **Bad cables, incorrect pinouts, or bent pins**: Faulty cables (with electrical characteristics preventing successful transmission) or faulty connectors (which do not properly make connections) can prevent successful data transmission at Layer 1. A bad cable could simply be an incorrect category of cable being used for a specific purpose. For example, using a Cat 5 cable (instead of a Cat 6 or higher cable) to connect two 1000BASE-TX devices would result in data corruption. Bent pins in a connector or incorrect pinouts could also cause data to become corrupted.

■ *Bad ports*: A physical port on a network device might be bad. You can often easily confirm whether a port is bad by looking at the network connection LED and status indicators.

■ *Open/short*: An *open* is a broken strand of copper that prevents current from flowing through a circuit. A *short* occurs when two copper connectors touch each other, resulting in current flowing through that short rather than through the attached electrical circuit because the short has lower resistance.

■ *Light-emitting diode (LED) status indicators*: Many network devices are very specialized and require special types of indicators. Oftentimes, indicators are implemented in the form of special LED status indicators. Thanks to such indicators, with a single glance, a network administrator can ascertain whether there is a problem with the network device. For example, a solid green LED for a network card normally indicates that the card is connected or receiving a signal. If there are no lights present or if the lights are orange or red, the network may not be connected properly or may be receiving a signal from the network.

■ *Incorrect transceivers*: A *transceiver* is a device that is able to both send and receive analog or digital signals. You must be sure to select transceivers carefully. The transceiver you select for a network device must match the cable type used and the wavelengths that are in use on the network.

■ **Speed and duplex issues**: Speed and duplex mismatches can be tricky to troubleshoot in a network, especially considering that connectivity is often maintained (although at unacceptable levels).

■ **Transmit and receive reversed**: Some Ethernet switches support *media-dependent interface crossover* (MDIX), which allows a switch port to properly configure its leads as transmit (Tx) or receive (Rx) leads. You can interconnect such switches by using a straight-through cable (as opposed to a crossover cable). However, if a network device does not support MDIX, it needs a crossover cable in order for its Tx leads to connect to the Rx leads on a connected device and vice versa. Therefore, you must take care when selecting cable types for interconnecting network components.

■ **Dirty optical cables**: An often-overlooked aspect of fiber-optic media care and maintenance is keeping the fiber-optic connector end faces clean. A dirty fiber connection can either slow down or completely inhibit network traffic. One method to clean optical cables is to use a combination of wet and dry cleaning approaches. For example, you might use a small amount of solvent on a wiping material and immediately dry the surface.

Common Tools

While a number of issues related to physical layer cables can cause problems for you, the great news is that there are many tools you can use to attack these problems and even prevent them from occurring. Here are just some of these tools:

Key Topic

■ *Cable crimper*: A crimper, as pictured in Figure 22-1, can be used to attach a connector (for example, an RJ45 connector) to the end of a UTP cable. To accompany a crimper, you might want to purchase a spool of cable (for example, Category 6 or higher UTP cable) and a box of RJ45 connectors. You will then be equipped to make your own Ethernet patch cables, which might be less expensive than buying pre-terminated UTP cables. Making your own is also convenient when you need a patch cable of a nonstandard length or when you need a nonstandard pinout on the RJ45 connectors (for example, when you need a T1 crossover cable). Many crimpers have a built-in wire stripper and wire snip function as well.

■ *Punchdown tool*: When terminating wires on a punchdown block (for example, a 110 block), you insert an insulated wire between two contact blades. These blades cut through the insulation and make electrical contact with the inner wire. As a result, you do not have to strip off the insulation. However, if you attempt to insert the wire between the two contact blades using a screwdriver, for example, the blades might be damaged to the point where they will not make a good connection. Therefore, you should use a punchdown tool, which is designed to properly insert an insulated wire between the two contact blades without damaging the blades.

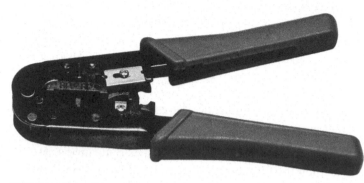

FIGURE 22-1   Crimper

- **Tone generator**: If you are working on a punchdown block and attempting to identify which pair of wires connect back to an end user's location (for example, someone's office), you can use a toner probe. A toner probe allows you to place a tone generator at one end of a connection (for example, someone's office) and use a probe on a punchdown block to audibly detect to which pair of wires the tone generator is connected. A toner probe, therefore, comes in two pieces: the tone generator and the probe. Another common name for a toner probe is a fox and hound, where the tone generator is the fox, and the probe (which searches for the tone) is the hound. Some network devices have built-in troubleshooting tools; for example, a voice-enabled Cisco router can produce test tones.

- **Loopback plug**: When troubleshooting a network device, you might want to confirm that a network interface is functional (for example, ensure that it can transmit and receive traffic). One way to perform such a test is to attach a loopback plug to a network interface and run diagnostic software designed to use the loopback plug. A loopback plug takes the transmit pins on an Ethernet connector and connects them to the receive pins, such that everything that is transmitted is received back on the interface. Similarly, a fiber-optic loopback plug, as shown in Figure 22-2, interconnects a fiber connector's transmit fiber with a connector's receive fiber. The diagnostic software can then transmit traffic out of a network interface and confirm its successful reception on that same interface.

FIGURE 22-2   Fiber-Optic Loopback Plug (Photo Courtesy of Digi-Key Corporation, http://www.digikey.com)

■ *Optical time-domain reflectometer (OTDR) and time-domain reflectometer (TDR)*: Suppose that you have been troubleshooting a network cable (either copper or fiber optic), and you determine that there is a break in or physical damage to the cable. Identifying exactly where a break or damage exists in a long length of cable can be problematic. Fortunately, you can use a time-domain reflectometer (TDR) for copper cabling or an optical time-domain reflectometer (OTDR) for fiber-optic cabling to locate a cable fault. Both light and electricity travel at speeds approaching 3×10^8 meters per second (approximately 186,000 miles per second), although the speeds are a bit slower and vary depending on the media. A TDR can send an electrical signal down a copper cable or an OTDR can send light down a fiber-optic cable, and when the electrical signal or light encounters a cable fault, a portion of the electric signal or light reflects back to the source. Based on the speed of electricity or light in the medium and the amount of time required for the reflected electric signal or light to be returned to the source, a TDR or an OTDR can mathematically determine where the cable fault lies. Figure 22-3 shows an example of an OTDR.

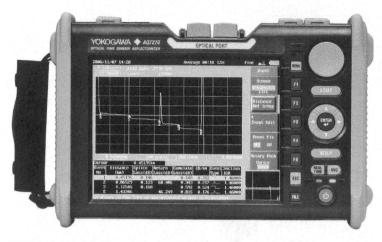

FIGURE 22-3   Optical Time Domain Reflectometer (Photo Courtesy of Coral-i Solutions, http://www.coral-i.com)

- ***Multimeter***: When working with copper cabling (as opposed to fiber-optic cabling), you can use a multimeter to check a variety of electrical characteristics in a cable, including resistance (in ohms), current (in amps), and voltage (in volts). Figure 22-4 shows an example of a multimeter.

FIGURE 22-4   Multimeter

For example, you could use the ohmmeter function of a multimeter (the resistance feature) to check the continuity of an Ethernet cable. If you connect the two leads of a multimeter to two pins of a cable, the resulting resistance is approximately 0 ohms if those two pins are connected, and the resulting resistance approaches an infinite number of ohms if the pins do not connect with one another.

Another common use of a multimeter is for measuring voltage. For example, you could check the leads of an Ethernet cable to see whether DC voltage is being applied to a device requiring PoE.

- *Cable tester*: A cable tester can test the conductors in an Ethernet cable. By connecting the two parts of a cable tester to the ends of a cable under test, you can check the wires in the cable for continuity (that is, check to make sure there are no opens, or breaks, in a conductor). In addition, you can verify an RJ45 connector's pinouts (that is, ensure that wires are connected to the appropriate pins on an RJ45 connector).

- *Wire map tester*: Wire map testing enables you to determine whether a wire has continuity and whether each conductor of a four-pair cable is correctly connected to the corresponding pin at the far end. Wire map testing tests for open, shorts, reversed pairs, crossed pairs, and split pairs.

- *Traffic access point (TAP)*: A traffic access point (also called a test access point) is a hardware device inserted at a specific point in a network where data can be accessed for testing or troubleshooting purposes. Network TAPs are mainly used to monitor the network traffic between two points in a network infrastructure.

- *Fusion splicer*: Fusion splicing is a way to join two fibers by using heat. Prepared fiber ends are placed in the splicer and automatically aligned and then fused together. Fusion splicing ensures greater reliability with less light being scattered or reflected back by the splice. If you follow the instructions for a fusion splicer, you should end up with an optical cable that is as strong as the original cable.

- *Spectrum analyzer*: A spectrum analyzer measures the magnitude of an input signal versus frequency within the full frequency range of the instrument. The primary use is to measure the power of the spectrum of known and unknown signals.

- *Snips/cutters*: As a network administrator, you often need to precisely cut or snip cables and cabling accessories. It is important that you have a pair of well-maintained snips or cutters in your supply bag at all times.

- *Cable stripper*: Cable strippers, which allow you to remove the plastic shielding from cables, are often built in to cable crimpers.

- *Fiber light meter*: A fiber light meter is a device used to measure the power in an optical signal. It is a device for testing average power in fiber-optic systems.

Real-World Case Study

You are just starting as an intern at a local IT support firm. You are going to be starting in a department where you will be attending remote service calls with a senior technician. You have been provided with a toolkit that includes cable crimpers, and various diagnostic testers. There is also safety equipment in the set of equipment. Finally, you have a multipurpose tool for snipping, cutting, and striping cable. You are very excited to learn to use these tools effectively in the field!

Summary

Here are the main topics covered in this chapter:

- This chapter covers cabling considerations and common issues.

- This chapter also covers common tools used in order to support the network media.

Exam Preparation Tasks

Review All the Key Topics

Review the most important topics from this chapter, noted with the Key Topic icon in the outer margin of the page. Table 22-1 lists these key topics and the page number where each is found.

Table 22-1 Key Topics for Chapter 22

Key Topic Element	Description	Page Number
List	Common issues	507
List	Common tools	509
Figure 22-4	Multimeter	512

Define Key Terms

Define the following key terms from this chapter and check your answers in the Glossary:

throughput, speed, distance, shielded, unshielded, plenum, riser rated, rollover cable, console cable, crossover cable, Power over Ethernet (PoE), attenuation, interference, decibel loss, open, short, Light-emitting diode (LED) status indicator, incorrect transceiver, cable crimper, punchdown tool, tone generator, loopback plug, optical time domain reflectometer (OTDR), multimeter, cable tester, wire map, traffic access point (TAP), fusion splicer, spectrum analyzer, snip, cutter, cable stripper, fiber light meter

Additional Resources

Network Cable Testers: https://www.flukenetworks.com/expertise/learn-about/cable-testing

How to Use a Multimeter: https://www.youtube.com/watch?v=ts0EVc9vXcs

Review Questions

The answers to these review questions appear in Appendix A, "Answers to Review Questions."

1. What type of cable must be used for PoE with network devices?

    a. Cat 5e or greater

    b. Cat 3 or greater

    c. Cat 5 or greater

    d. Cat 4 or greater

2. Which of the following can be a major issue for fiber-optic media?

    a. Incorrect pin outs

    b. Dirty optical media

    c. EMI

    d. dB loss

3. What type of cable testing device permits a network device to communicate with itself in order to test its ability to send and receive traffic?

   a. Cable tester

   b. Loopback plug

   c. Cable crimper

   d. Fusion splicer

   e. Tone generator

4. Which types of cables would you install to meet most building codes today and prevent fires and poisonous gases from spreading? (Choose two.)

   a. UTP rated

   b. Rollover rated

   c. Plenum rated

   d. Riser rated

5. Which of the following terms are directly related to the weakening or loss of a signal as it travels farther down the network media? (Choose two.)

   a. Attenuation

   b. Throughput

   c. OTDR

   d. Interference

   e. Decibel (dB) loss

6. You need to connect two older switches that do not have auto-MDIX ports. What should you use?

   a. Console cable

   b. Crossover cable

   c. PoE cable

   d. Loopback adapter

7. You have a link between two network interfaces (devices) that is operating inefficiently. What would most likely be the cause of this problem?

   a. Incorrect pinout

   b. Bad ports

   c. Duplex mismatch

   d. Failed NIC

This chapter covers the following topics related to Objective 5.3 (Given a scenario, use the appropriate network software tools and commands) of the CompTIA Network+ N10-008 certification exam:

- Software tools

  - WiFi analyzer

  - Protocol analyzer/packet capture

  - Bandwidth speed tester

  - Port scanner

  - iperf

  - NetFlow analyzers

  - Trivial File Transfer Protocol (TFTP) server

  - Terminal emulator

  - IP scanner

- Command line tool

  - ping

  - ipconfig/ifconfig/ip

- nslookup/dig

- traceroute/tracert

- arp

- netstat

- hostname

- route

- telnet

- tcpdump

- nmap

- Basic network platform commands

  - show interface

  - show config

  - show route

CHAPTER 23

Network Software Tools and Commands

Troubleshooting your network and proactively stopping issues before they become trouble tickets are made much easier for you by a wide variety of software tools and command line tools that you can use with ease.

In this chapter, you will learn about a number of software tools that can make maintenance and troubleshooting of your network much easier. This chapter also covers the most popular command line tools. Finally, this chapter reviews several commands that are very important on common network devices.

Foundation Topics

Software Tools

A number of software tools are designed to help with managing networks. This section provides an excellent starting point, introducing you to some of the commonly used tools—many of these which are freely available.

WiFi Analyzer

A *WiFi analyzer* is software that runs on a general-purpose computer or on a specialized device that can perform wireless analysis of WiFi signals. This type of tool would be used as part of a wireless site survey after WiFi has been implemented to create a heat map of the wireless airspace.

Protocol Analyzer/Packet Capture

If you understand the characteristics of the protocols running on your network (such as the fields in a protocol's header), a *protocol analyzer* (also known as a *network sniffer or simply packet capture tool*) can be a tremendous troubleshooting asset. A protocol analyzer can be a standalone device or software running on a laptop or other mobile computer. You can use a protocol analyzer to capture traffic flowing through a network switch, using the port mirroring feature of the switch. By examining the captured packets, you can discern the details of communication flows (sessions) as they are being set up, maintained, and torn down. The examination of these captured packets, referred to as *traffic analysis*, provides an administrator with valuable insights about the nature of traffic flowing through a network.

Protocol analyzers come with a wide range of features and at a variety of price points. Wireshark is a free software program that can make your laptop act like a protocol analyzer. Protocol analyzers can assist in identifying details such as top talkers, top destinations, top protocols in use, and quantity of traffic on the network. You can download a free copy of Wireshark from https://www.wireshark.org. Figure 23-1 shows the Wireshark application.

Bandwidth Speed Tester

Many *bandwidth speed testers* are available to assist you in verifying throughput from a local computer to an Internet site. One example is https://www.speedtest.net. Using sites such as this can assist you in determining whether an overall connection to the Internet is slow or whether just a specific site or server is slow to respond.

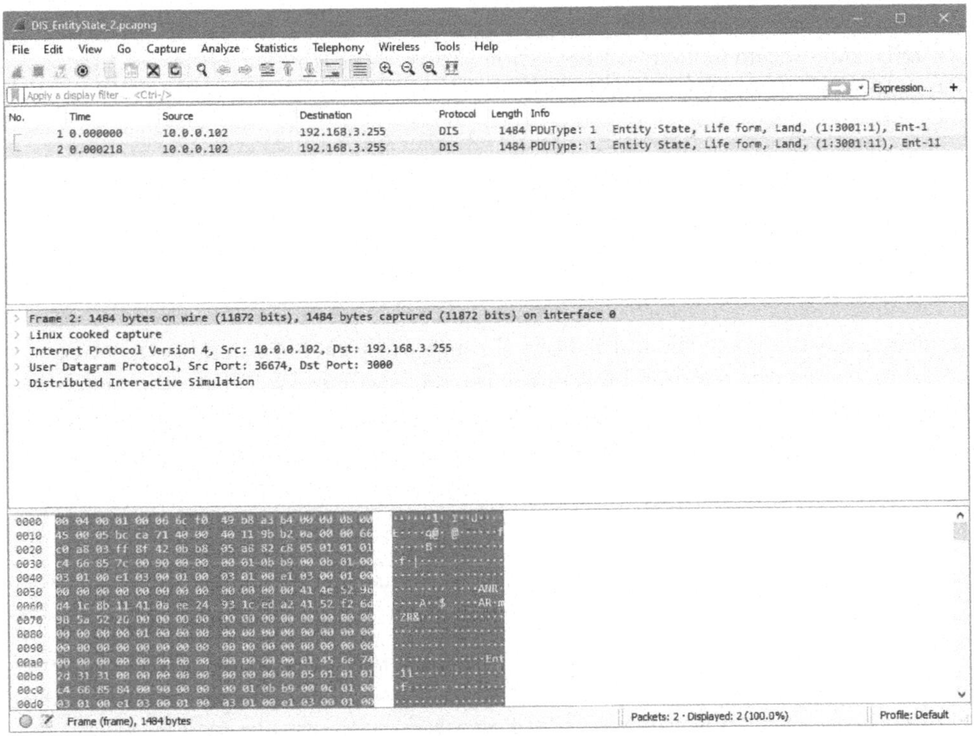

FIGURE 23-1 Wireshark Protocol Analyzer Software

Port Scanner

A *port scanner* is a useful software tool that probes a network device to determine which ports are open on the device. A port scanner can send port scans to a single device, or it can perform a port sweep, where it checks for open ports on a number of network devices at one time.

Many port scanners today are considered IP scanners. IP scanners are superb at running port sweeps against entire subnets of IP addressed network hosts or systems.

In addition to being helpful to network administrators, port scanners can be used to carry out harm. Computer criminals might use port scanners in launching attacks on open ports.

iperf

iperf is a software tool for networking that obtains active measurements of the maximum bandwidth available on IP networks. This software tool supports tuning of various parameters related to timing, buffers, and protocols. The protocols you can tune include Transmission Control Protocol (TCP), User Datagram Protocol (UDP), and Stream Control Transmission Protocol (SCTP) with Internet Protocol Version 4 (IPv4) and Version 6 (IPv6).

iperf reports on bandwidth, packet loss, and other important network parameters. A nice feature of iperf is that it can be run in Linux and Windows environments.

NetFlow Analyzers

NetFlow, which is a software component included in many network devices today, collects statistics about the traffic flows through a device. However, the data that NetFlow collects is not useful unless you can analyze it and see it in a way that makes sense. You can use *NetFlow analyzers* (often also called *collectors*) to examine NetFlow collections and get valuable and insightful representations of the data.

TFTP Server

For network maintenance, it is helpful to have a *Trivial File Transfer Protocol (TFTP) server* or two on your network. These low-overhead-producing servers allow you to store backups of software images that power network devices, as well as backup and baseline configurations. Many network devices today can install their software or configurations from a TFTP server directly over the network.

Terminal Emulator

A software tool you are likely to find yourself using all the time is a *terminal emulator*. This program allows you to access a command line interface to monitor and configure devices, which is often a very efficient way to carry out these networking tasks.

IP Scanner

Many tools can provide IP address information for systems in a network, but *IP scanners* can do this precise function better than any alternative. IP scanners can acquire information more accurately and faster than the alternatives. Many IP scanners can also provide additional information from nodes, such as operating system, software application, and physical resource usage information.

Command Line Tools

You will often find yourself firing open a terminal emulator to access a command line interface when you are maintaining or troubleshooting a network. This section ensures that you are very familiar with many of the command line tools in use today.

ping

The *ping* command is one of the most commonly used command line commands. You can use it to check IP connectivity between two network devices. Multiple platforms (for example, routers, switches, and hosts) support the **ping** command.

The **ping** command uses Internet Control Message Protocol (ICMP), which is a Layer 4 protocol. If you issue a **ping** command from your PC, your PC sends an ICMP echo message to the specified destination host. If the destination host is reachable, the host responds with an ICMP echo reply message. Other ICMP messages can be returned to your PC, from your PC's default gateway, to indicate that a destination host is unreachable, that an ICMP echo timed out, or that a Time-to-Live (TTL) value (which is decremented by 1 at each router hop) has expired (that is, has been decremented to a value of 0).

The syntax of the **ping** command, along with some of its commonly used options, is as follows:

```
ping [-t] [-n count] [-l size] [-f] [-i TTL] [-S srcaddr] target_name
```

Table 23-1 explains these command options.

Table 23-1 Parameters for the Windows **ping** Command

Parameter	Purpose
-t	This option repeatedly sends pings (ICMP echo messages) until you stop it by pressing Ctrl+C.
-n count	This option specifies the number of pings to send.
-f	This option sets the "don't fragment" bit in a packet's header. If the packet tries to cross a router that attempts to fragment the packet, the packet is dropped, and an ICMP error message is returned.
-i TTL	This option sets the TTL value in a packet's header. The TTL value is decremented for each router hop. A packet is discarded when its TTL value reaches 0.
-S srcaddr	If the PC from which you are issuing the **ping** command has more than one IP address, this option allows you to specify the source IP address from which the ICMP echo messages should be sent.
target_name	This option specifies the name or the IP address of the device to which you are sending ICMP echo messages.

A Windows **ping** command specifying only the *target_name* parameter sends four ICMP echo messages to the specified target, as shown in Example 23-1. In the output, notice that none of the packets were dropped.

Key Topic

Example 23-1   Sample Output from the Windows **ping** Command

```
C:\> ping 192.168.1.2
Pinging 192.168.1.2 with 32 bytes of data:
Reply from 192.168.1.2: bytes=32 time=2ms TTL=64
Reply from 192.168.1.2: bytes=32 time=1ms TTL=64
Reply from 192.168.1.2: bytes=32 time=1ms TTL=64
Reply from 192.168.1.2: bytes=32 time=1ms TTL=64

Ping statistics for 192.168.1.2:
    Packets: Sent = 4, Received = 4, Lost = 0 (0% loss),
Approximate round trip times in milli-seconds:
    Minimum = 1ms, Maximum = 2ms, Average = 1ms
```

If the specified target address is unreachable, output from the **ping** command indicates that the target cannot be reached, as shown in Example 23-2.

Example 23-2   Windows **ping** Command Indicating an Unreachable Destination

```
C:\> ping 192.168.1.200

Pinging 192.168.1.200 with 32 bytes of data:
Reply from 192.168.1.50: Destination host unreachable.
Reply from 192.168.1.50: Destination host unreachable.
Reply from 192.168.1.50: Destination host unreachable.
Reply from 192.168.1.50: Destination host unreachable.

Ping statistics for 192.168.1.200:
    Packets: Sent = 4, Received = 4, Lost = 0 (0% loss),
```

ping with IPv6

Depending on the operating system, **ping** can natively work to test connectivity using IPv6 when an IPv6 destination address is part of the **ping** command. On some systems, the command **ping -6** *IPv6-destination-address*, **ping6** *IPv6-destination-address*, or some variant specific to that operating system may be available for testing IPv6 connectivity.

ipconfig

You can use the *ipconfig* command to display IP address configuration parameters on a Windows PC. In addition, if the PC uses Dynamic Host Configuration Protocol (DHCP), you can use the **ipconfig** command to release and renew a DHCP lease, which is often useful when troubleshooting.

The syntax of the **ipconfig** command, along with some of its most commonly used parameters, is as follows:

```
ipconfig [/all | /renew | /release | /renew6 | /release6]
```

Table 23-2 describes the parameters for the **ipconfig** command.

Table 23-2 Parameters for the Windows **ipconfig** Command

Parameter	Purpose
/all	The **ipconfig** command entered by itself displays summary information about a PC's IP address configuration. This parameter gives more verbose information, including DNS, MAC address, and IPv6 address information.
/release and **/release6**	These options release a DHCP lease for an IPv4 and IPv6 address, respectively.
/renew and **/renew6**	These options renew a DHCP lease for an IPv4 and IPv6 address, respectively.

Example 23-3 shows the **ipconfig** command, without any parameters, being issued on a PC. The PC contains an Ethernet network interface card (NIC) and a wireless NIC. From the output, you can conclude that one of the NICs has the IP address 172.16.202.129, and the other NIC has the IP address 172.16.202.128. Also, you can see that these two NICs share the common default gateway 172.16.202.2.

Key Topic

Example 23-3 Sample Output from the Windows **ipconfig** Command

```
C:\> ipconfig
Windows IP Configuration
Ethernet adapter Local Area Connection 3:
    Connection-specific DNS Suffix .   : localdomain
    Link-local IPv6 Address . . . . . : fe80::5101:b420:4354:d496%20
    IPv4 Address. . . . . . . . . . . : 172.16.202.129
    Subnet Mask . . . . . . . . . . . : 255.255.255.0
    Default Gateway . . . . . . . . . : 172.16.202.2
Ethernet adapter Local Area Connection:
    Connection-specific DNS Suffix .   : localdomain
    Link-local IPv6 Address . . . . . : fe80::a10f:cff4:15e4:aa6%11
    IPv4 Address. . . . . . . . . . . : 172.16.202.128
    Subnet Mask . . . . . . . . . . . : 255.255.255.0
    Default Gateway . . . . . . . . . : 172.16.202.2
OUTPUT OMITTED...
```

Example 23-4 shows the **ipconfig /all** command being issued on a PC. Notice the additional output from this command beyond what is shown for the ipconfig command in Example 23-3. For example, in Example 23-4 you can see the MAC address (labeled as the *physical address*) for each NIC and the DNS server's IP address, 172.16.202.2.

Example 23-4 Sample Output from the Windows **ipconfig /all** Command

```
C:\> ipconfig /all
Windows IP Configuration
    Host Name . . . . . . . . . . . . : WIN-OD1IG7JF47P
    Primary Dns Suffix . . . . . . . :
    Node Type . . . . . . . . . . . . : Hybrid
    IP Routing Enabled. . . . . . . . : No
    WINS Proxy Enabled. . . . . . . . : No
    DNS Suffix Search List. . . . . . : localdomain
Ethernet adapter Local Area Connection 3:
    Connection-specific DNS Suffix . : localdomain
    Description . . . . . . . . . . . : Intel(R) PRO/1000 MT Network
Connection #2
    Physical Address. . . . . . . . . : 00-0C-29-3A-21-67
    DHCP Enabled. . . . . . . . . . . : Yes
    Autoconfiguration Enabled . . . . : Yes
    Link-local IPv6 Address . . . . . : fe80::5101:b420:4354:d496%20
(Preferred)
    IPv4 Address. . . . . . . . . . . : 172.16.202.129(Preferred)
    Subnet Mask . . . . . . . . . . . : 255.255.255.0
    Lease Obtained. . . . . . . . . . : Saturday, May 29, 2021 6:28:08 PM
    Lease Expires . . . . . . . . . . : Saturday, May 29, 2021 9:28:08 PM
    Default Gateway . . . . . . . . . : 172.16.202.2
    DHCP Server . . . . . . . . . . . : 172.16.202.254
    DHCPv6 IAID . . . . . . . . . . . : 419433513
    DHCPv6 Client DUID. . . . . . . . : 00-01-00-01-14-A6-11-77-00-0C-
                                        29-3A-21-5D
    DNS Servers . . . . . . . . . . . : 172.16.202.2
    Primary WINS Server . . . . . . . : 172.16.202.2
    NetBIOS over Tcpip. . . . . . . . : Enabled
Ethernet adapter Local Area Connection:
    Connection-specific DNS Suffix . : localdomain
    Description . . . . . . . . . . . : Intel(R) PRO/1000 MT Network
Connection
```

```
   Physical Address. . . . . . . . . : 00-0C-29-3A-21-5D
  DHCP Enabled. . . . . . . . . . . : Yes
  Autoconfiguration Enabled . . . . : Yes
  Link-local IPv6 Address . . . . . : fe80::a10f:cff4:15e4:aa6%11
(Preferred)
  IPv4 Address. . . . . . . . . . . : 172.16.202.128(Preferred)
  Subnet Mask . . . . . . . . . . . : 255.255.255.0
  Lease Obtained. . . . . . . . . . : Saturday, May 29, 2021 6:27:56 PM
  Lease Expires . . . . . . . . . . : Saturday, May 29, 2021 9:28:08 PM
  Default Gateway . . . . . . . . . : 172.16.202.2
  DHCP Server . . . . . . . . . . . : 172.16.202.254
  DHCPv6 IAID . . . . . . . . . . . : 234884137
  DHCPv6 Client DUID. . . . . . . . : 00-01-00-01-14-A6-11-77-00-0C-
                                      29-3A-21-5D
  DNS Servers . . . . . . . . . . . : 172.16.202.2
  Primary WINS Server . . . . . . . : 172.16.202.2
  NetBIOS over Tcpip. . . . . . . . : Enabled
OUTPUT OMITTED...
```

If you are troubleshooting a PC and suspect that IP addressing might be an issue, you can release the PC's current DHCP lease by issuing the **ipconfig /release** command, as shown in Example 23-5. Then you can renew the DHCP lease with the **ipconfig /renew** command, as shown in Example 23-6.

Example 23-5   Sample Output from the Windows **ipconfig /release** Command

```
C:\> ipconfig /release
Windows IP Configuration
Ethernet adapter Local Area Connection 3:
   Connection-specific DNS Suffix . :
   Link-local IPv6 Address . . . . . :   fe80::5101:b420:4354:d496%20
   Default Gateway . . . . . . . . . :
Ethernet adapter Local Area Connection:
   Connection-specific DNS Suffix . :
   Link-local IPv6 Address . . . . . :   fe80::a10f:cff4:15e4:aa6%11
   Default Gateway . . . . . . . . . :
OUTPUT OMITTED...
```

Example 23-6   Sample Output from the Windows **ipconfig /renew** Command

```
C:\> ipconfig /renew
Windows IP Configuration
Ethernet adapter Local Area Connection 3:
   Connection-specific DNS Suffix .  :  localdomain
   Link-local IPv6 Address . . . . . :  fe80::5101:b420:4354:d496%20
   IPv4 Address. . . . . . . . . . . :  172.16.202.129
   Subnet Mask . . . . . . . . . . . :  255.255.255.0
   Default Gateway . . . . . . . . . :  172.16.202.2
Ethernet adapter Local Area Connection:
   Connection-specific DNS Suffix .  :  localdomain
   Link-local IPv6 Address . . . . . :  fe80::a10f:cff4:15e4:aa6%11
   IPv4 Address. . . . . . . . . . . :  172.16.202.128
   Subnet Mask . . . . . . . . . . . :  255.255.255.0
   Default Gateway . . . . . . . . . :  172.16.202.2
OUTPUT OMITTED...
```

ifconfig

The rough equivalent in the UNIX/Linux world for the **ipconfig** utility is *ifconfig*. Example 23-7 demonstrates the use of this command to learn IP address information configured on an interface.

Example 23-7   Sample Output from the Linux **ifconfig** Command

```
anthony@DESKTOP-91165JO:~$ ifconfig
eth0: flags=4163<UP,BROADCAST,RUNNING,MULTICAST>  mtu 1500
        inet 192.168.86.29  netmask 255.255.255.0  broadcast
192.168.86.255
        inet6 fe80::6044:94be:583f:4f82  prefixlen 64  scopeid
0xfd<compat,link,site,host>
        ether 84:8f:69:f5:5f:3d  (Ethernet)
        RX packets 0  bytes 0 (0.0 B)
        RX errors 0  dropped 0  overruns 0  frame 0
        TX packets 0  bytes 0 (0.0 B)
        TX errors 0  dropped 0 overruns 0  carrier 0  collisions 0
lo: flags=73<UP,LOOPBACK,RUNNING>  mtu 1500
        inet 127.0.0.1  netmask 255.0.0.0
        inet6 ::1  prefixlen 128  scopeid 0xfe<compat,link,site,host>
        loop  (Local Loopback)
```

```
         RX packets 0   bytes 0 (0.0 B)
         RX errors 0   dropped 0   overruns 0   frame 0
         TX packets 0   bytes 0 (0.0 B)
         TX errors 0   dropped 0 overruns 0   carrier 0   collisions 0
anthony@DESKTOP-91165JO:~$
```

NOTE   This might sound crazy, but I captured Example 23-7 on my Windows 10 desktop PC. It is simple now to run Linux inside Windows. You install the Windows Subsystem for Linux by using the Apps option in Settings. You can then install many variations of Linux from the Microsoft Store.

ip

Many Linux systems are moving to the *ip* command instead of even preloading the **ifconfig** command. The powerful **ip** command functions with many additional keywords, including the **address** keyword, which displays the same information as **ifconfig**.

nslookup

Although the *nslookup* command offers various command options, this section focuses on the most common use for the command: resolving a fully qualified domain name (FQDN) to an IP address. This can, for example, help you determine whether a DNS record is correct and verify that your DNS server is operating.

The **nslookup** command can be issued along with an FQDN, or it can be used in an interactive mode, where you are prompted to enter command parameters. The syntax of this command can be summarized as follows:

```
nslookup [fqdn]
```

In noninteractive mode, you issue the **nslookup** command followed by an FQDN to display the IP address corresponding to the FQDN. To illustrate, consider Example 23-8, where the **nslookup** command is issued to resolve the IP address of the website ajsnetworking.com, which appears to be 172.31.194.74.

NOTE   A private IP address is used here for illustrative purposes. In a real-world example, a public IP address would be displayed.

Key Topic

Example 23-8 Sample Output from the Windows **nslookup** Noninteractive Command

```
C:\> nslookup cbtnuggets.com
Server: UnKnown
Address: 192.168.1.1

Non-authoritative answer:
Name: ajsnetworking.com
Address: 172.31.194.74
```

In interactive mode, you enter the **nslookup** command and then, from the > prompt, enter command parameters. Example 23-9 shows cbtnuggets.com entered at the prompt to see the IP address corresponding to that FQDN. Also, notice that entering a question mark (**?**) displays a help screen that shows command options. By entering **quit**, you exit interactive mode.

Example 23-9 Sample Output from the Windows **nslookup** Interactive Command

```
C:\> nslookup
Default Server: UnKnown
Address: 192.168.1.1

> cbtnuggets.com
Server: UnKnown
Address: 192.168.1.1

Non-authoritative answer:
Name: cbtnuggets.com
Address: 172.31.194.74

> ?
Commands:    (identifiers are shown in uppercase, [] means optional)
NAME           - print info about the host/domain NAME using default
server
NAME1 NAME2      - as above, but use NAME2 as server
help or ?        - print info on common commands
set OPTION       - set an option
   all                      - print options, current server and host
   [no]debug                - print debugging information
   [no]d2                   - print exhaustive debugging information
   [no]defname              - append domain name to each query
```

```
    [no]recurse               - ask for recursive answer to query
    [no]search                - use domain search list
    [no]vc                    - always use a virtual circuit
    domain=NAME               - set default domain name to NAME
    srchlist=N1[/N2/.../N6]   - set domain to N1 and search list to
N1,N2, etc.
    root=NAME                 - set root server to NAME
OUTPUT OMITTED...
> quit
C:\>
```

dig

As you have seen here, the Windows **nslookup** command is used to resolve a given FQDN to its IP address. UNIX has a similar **nslookup** command, which you can also use for FQDN-to-IP-address resolution.

You can also use the *dig* command to resolve FQDNs to IP addresses. Unlike the **nslookup** command, however, the **dig** command is entirely a command line command. (That is, **dig** lacks the interactive mode of the **nslookup** command.)

Example 23-10 compares the output of the **nslookup** and **dig** commands. Notice that the **dig** command offers more information than the **nslookup** command. For example, the *A* in the QUESTION SECTION part of the output of the **dig** command identifies the DNS record type (an A record, which is an alias record). If you peruse the output, you can find a few other pieces of information present in the dig command output that are not available in the **nslookup** command output; however, the **dig** command is rarely used to glean these more subtle pieces of information. Rather, many UNIX administrators use the **dig** command simply as an alternative way of resolving FQDNs to IP addresses. Notice in Example 23-10 that both the **nslookup** and **dig** commands indicate that the IP address corresponding to the FQDN www.pearsonitcertification.com is 64.28.85.25.

Key Topic

Example 23-10   *Comparing Output from the Windows **nslookup** and UNIX **dig** Commands*

```
C:\> nslookup www.pearsonitcertification.com
Server: 192.168.1.1
Address: 192.168.1.1#53

Non-authoritative answer:
```

```
Name: www.pearsonitcertification.com
Address: 64.28.85.25


HOST# dig www.pearsonitcertification.com

; <<>> DiG 9.6.0-APPLE-P2 <<>> www.pearsonitcertification.com
;; global options: +cmd
;; Got answer:
;; ->>HEADER<<- opcode: QUERY, status: NOERROR, id: 10821
;; flags: qr rd ra; QUERY: 1, ANSWER: 1, AUTHORITY: 0, ADDITIONAL: 0

;; QUESTION SECTION:
;www.pearsonitcertification.com. IN A

;; ANSWER SECTION:
www.pearsonitcertification.com. 10791 IN A 64.28.85.25

;; Query time: 5 msec
;; SERVER: 192.168.1.1#53(192.168.1.1)
;; WHEN: Mon May 30 13:36:11 2011
;; MSG SIZE rcvd: 64
```

traceroute

You can use the UNIX command *traceroute* to determine which router hop along the path from a source device to a destination device is having issues. Also, based on the round-trip response time information reported for each hop, you can better determine which network segment might be causing excessive delay due to congestion. Example 23-11 provides sample output from the **traceroute** command, which is identifying the 13 router hops a UNIX host must transit to reach pearsonitcertification.com.

Example 23-11   Sample Output from the UNIX **traceroute** Command

```
HOST# traceroute www.pearsonitcertification.com
traceroute to pearsonitcertification.com (64.28.85.25), 64 hops max,
52 byte packets
 1  192.168.1.1 (192.168.1.1) 3.480 ms 2.548 ms 2.404 ms
 2  cpe-76-177-16-1.natcky.res.rr.com (76.177.16.1) 22.150 ms 11.300
ms 9.719 ms
```

```
 3   gig2-0-0.rcmdky-mx41.natcky.rr.com (65.28.199.205) 9.242 ms 19.940
ms 11.735 ms
 4   tge0-2-0.chcgileq-rtr1.kc.rr.com (65.28.199.97) 38.459 ms 38.821
ms 36.157 ms
 5   ae-4-0.cr0.chi10.tbone.rr.com (66.109.6.100) 41.903 ms 37.388 ms
31.966 ms
 6   ae-0-0.pr0.chi10.tbone.rr.com (66.109.6.153) 75.757 ms 46.287 ms
35.031 ms
 7   if-4-0-0.core1.ct8-chicago.as6453.net (66.110.14.21) 48.020 ms
37.248 ms 45.446 ms
 8   if-1-0-0-1878.core2.ct8-chicago.as6453.net (66.110.27.78) 108.466
ms 55.465 ms 87.590 ms
 9   63.243.186.25 (63.243.186.25) 64.045 ms 63.582 ms 69.200 ms
10   cr2-pos-0-8-0-3.nyr.savvis.net (208.173.129.29) 64.933 ms 65.113
ms 61.759 ms
11   hr1-tengig-13-0-0.waltham2bo2.savvis.net (204.70.198.182) 71.964
ms 65.430 ms 74.397 ms
12   das3-v3038.bo2.savvis.net (209.202.187.182) 65.777 ms 64.483 ms
82.383 ms
13   blhosting.bridgelinesw.com (64.14.81.46) 63.448 ms !X * 68.879 ms
     !X
```

The Windows *tracert* command can be used for the same purpose as the UNIX **traceroute** command.

traceroute for IPv6

You can verify the IPv6 path through a network by using **traceroute** for IPv6. Depending on the vendor and platform, this may be done by using **traceroute** *destination-IPv6-address*, **traceroute6** *destination-IPv6-address*, **traceroute -6** *destination-IPv6-address*, or some variant specific to the vendor and product being used.

arp

You can use the *arp* command to view the MAC address to IP address name resolution that has succeeded and been entered in the ARP cache. In addition, you can use the **arp** command to statically add a MAC-address-to-IP-address mapping to a PC's Address Resolution Protocol (ARP) MAC address lookup table.

The syntax of the **arp** command is as follows:

```
arp -s inet_addr eth_addr [if_addr]
arp -d inet_addr [if_addr]
arp -a [inet_addr] [-N if_addr] [-v]
```

Table 23-3 describes the **arp** command's *switches* (for example, *-s*, *-d*, and *-a*) and *arguments* (for example, *inet_addr* and *if_addr*).

Table 23-3 Parameters for the Windows **arp** Command

Parameter	Purpose
-a or **-g**	These options display current entries in a PC's ARP table.
-v	This option, which stands for *verbose*, includes any invalid and loopback interface entries in an ARP table.
inet_addr	This option is a specific IP address.
-N *if_addr*	This option shows ARP entries learned for a specified network.
-d	This option, in combination with the *inet_addr* parameter, can delete an ARP entry for a host. With the wildcard character *, it can delete all host entries.
-s	This option, used in conjunction with the *inet_addr* and *eth_addr* parameters, statically adds a host entry to the ARP table.
eth_addr	This parameter is a 48-bit MAC address.
if_addr	If a host has multiple interfaces, an ARP entry might be associated with a specific interface. This option can be used to statically add or delete an ARP entry in a specified interface.

Example 23-12 shows the **arp -a** command being issued on a PC. The output shows what MAC addresses have been learned for the listed IP addresses. The dynamically learned addresses have *dynamic* listed in the *Type* column, and statically configured addresses (which are addresses configured by a user or the OS) are listed with *static* in the *Type* column. From the output, you can determine, for example, that the network device with the IP address 172.16.202.1 has the MAC address 00-50-56-c0-00-08, which could alternatively be written as 0050.56c0.0008. Also, you can determine from the output that this information was dynamically learned, as opposed to being statically configured.

Key Topic

Example 23-12 Sample Output from the Windows **arp -a** Command

```
C:\> arp -a
Interface: 172.16.202.128 --- 0xb
    Internet Address        Physical Address        Type
    172.16.202.1            00-50-56-c0-00-08        dynamic
    172.16.202.2            00-50-56-fd-65-2c        dynamic
```

```
    172.16.202.254          00-50-56-e8-84-fc        dynamic
    172.16.202.255          ff-ff-ff-ff-ff-ff        static
    224.0.0.22              01-00-5e-00-00-16        static
    224.0.0.252             01-00-5e-00-00-fc        static
    255.255.255.255         ff-ff-ff-ff-ff-ff        static


Interface: 172.16.202.129 --- 0x14
    Internet Address        Physical Address         Type
    172.16.202.1            00-50-56-c0-00-08        dynamic
    172.16.202.2            00-50-56-fd-65-2c        dynamic
    172.16.202.254          00-50-56-e8-84-fc        dynamic
    172.16.202.255          ff-ff-ff-ff-ff-ff        static
    224.0.0.22              01-00-5e-00-00-16        static
    224.0.0.252             01-00-5e-00-00-fc        static
    224.0.1.60              01-00-5e-00-01-3c        static
    255.255.255.255         ff-ff-ff-ff-ff-ff        static
```

From a troubleshooting perspective, keep in mind that static ARP entries tend to be more problematic than dynamic entries. For example, a static entry might be added to a laptop computer, and the computer might later connect to a different network. If a PC then attempts to reach the IP address specified in the static ARP entry, the Layer 2 frame would have the incorrect destination MAC address (which should then be the MAC address of the PC's default gateway) in its header.

netstat

You can use the *netstat* command to display various information about IP-based connections on a PC. For example, you can view information about current sessions, including source and destination IP addresses and port numbers. You can also display protocol statistics, which might be useful for troubleshooting purposes. For example, you might issue the **netstat** command and see that your PC has sessions open to an unknown host on the Internet. These sessions might prompt further investigation to determine why the sessions are open and if they might be resulting in performance issues on the PC or possibly posing a security risk.

The following is the syntax for the **netstat** command and some of its commonly used options:

```
netstat [-a] [-b] [-e] [-f] [-p proto] [-r] [-s]
```

Table 23-4 explains these command options.

Table 23-4   Parameters for the Windows **netstat** Command

Parameter	Purpose
-a	This option displays all of a PC's active IP-based sessions, along with the TCP and UDP ports of each session.
-b	This option shows the name of the program that opened a session.
-e	This option shows statistical information for an interface's IP-based traffic, such as the number of bytes sent and received.
-f	This option displays FQDNs of destination addresses appearing in a listing of active sessions.
-p *proto*	This option displays connections for a specific protocol, which might be **icmp, icmpv6, ip, ipv6, tcp, tcpv6, udp,** or **udpv6**.
-r	This option displays a PC's IP routing table. (Note that **netstat** with this option generates the same output as the **route print** command.)
-s	This option displays statistical information for the following protocols: ICMPv4, ICMPv6, IPv4, IPv6, TCPv4, TCPv6, UDPv4, and UDPv6.

The **netstat** command issued without any options lists source and destination IP addresses and port numbers for all IP-based sessions. Example 23-13 shows sample output from this command.

Key Topic

Example 23-13   Sample Output from the Windows **netstat** Command

```
C:\> netstat
OUTPUT OMITTED...
  TCP  127.0.0.1:27015        LIVE-DELIVERY:1309          ESTABLISHED
  TCP  192.168.1.50:1045      172.16.224.200:https        CLOSE_WAIT
  TCP  192.168.1.50:1058      THE-WALLACES-TI:microsoft-ds ESTABLISHED
  TCP  192.168.1.50:1079      tcpep:https                 ESTABLISHED
  TCP  192.168.1.50:1081      174:http                    ESTABLISHED
  TCP  192.168.1.50:1089      by2msg4020609:msnp          ESTABLISHED
  TCP  192.168.1.50:1111      HPB81308:netbios-ssn        ESTABLISHED
  TCP  192.168.1.50:1115      10.65.228.81:https          ESTABLISHED
  TCP  192.168.1.50:1116      10.65.228.81:https          ESTABLISHED
  TCP  192.168.1.50:1117      10.65.228.81:https          ESTABLISHED
  TCP  192.168.1.50:1118      10.65.228.81:https          ESTABLISHED
  TCP  192.168.1.50:1126      10.65.228.81:https          ESTABLISHED
  TCP  192.168.1.50:1417      vip1:http                   CLOSE_WAIT
```

```
  TCP    192.168.1.50:1508      208:https                CLOSE_WAIT
  TCP    192.168.1.50:1510      208:https                CLOSE_WAIT
  TCP    [::1]:2869             LIVE-DELIVERY:1514       TIME_WAIT
  TCP    [::1]:286              LIVE-DELIVERY:1515       ESTABLISHED
OUTPUT OMITTED...
```

You might notice an open connection using a specific port and be unsure what application opened that connection. As you can see in Example 23-14, the **netstat -b** command shows which application opened a specific connection. In this example, Dropbox.exe, iTunex.exe, firefox.exe, and OUTLOOK.exe are applications that have currently open connections.

Example 23-14   Sample Output from the Windows **netstat -b** Command

```
C:\> netstat -b
Active Connections
OUTPUT OMITTED...
  Proto          Local Address       Foreign Address        State
  TCP            127.0.0.1:1068      LIVE-DELIVERY:19872    ESTABLISHED
[Dropbox.exe]
  TCP            127.0.0.1:1309      LIVE-DELIVERY:27015    ESTABLISHED
[iTunes.exe]
  TCP            127.0.0.1:1960      LIVE-DELIVERY:1961     ESTABLISHED
[firefox.exe]
  TCP            192.168.1.50:1115   10.1.228.81:https      ESTABLISHED
[OUTLOOK.EXE]
  TCP            192.168.1.50:1116   10.1.228.81:https      ESTABLISHED
[OUTLOOK.EXE]
OUTPUT OMITTED...
```

hostname

The *hostname* command is available on both UNIX/Linux and Windows systems. On a Linux system, you use this command to change the computer name or the domain name of the system. When you run the command on a Windows system, the command simply displays the computer name.

route

The *route* command can display a PC's current IP routing table. In addition, you can use the **route** command to add or delete entries in the routing table. The syntax of the **route** command, with a collection of commonly used options, is as follows:

```
C:\>route [-f] [-p] command [destination] [mask netmask] [gateway]
[metric metric] [if interface]
```

Table 23-5 explains these command options.

Table 23-5   Parameters for the Windows **route** Command

Parameter	Purpose
-f	This option clears gateway entries from the routing table. If this option is used with another option, the clearing of gateways from the routing table occurs before any other specified action.
-p	This option can be used with the **add** command to make a statically configured route persistent, which means the route will remain in a PC's routing table even after a reboot.
command	Supported commands include **print, add, delete,** and **change.** The **print** command lists entries in a PC's routing table. The **add** command adds a route entry. The **delete** command removes a route from the routing table, and the **change** command can modify an existing route.
destination	This option specifies the destination host or subnet to add to a PC's routing table.
mask netmask	This option, used in conjunction with the *destination* option, specifies the subnet mask of the destination. If the destination is the IP address of a host, the *netmask* parameter is 255.255.255.255.
gateway	This option specifies the IP address of the next-hop router used to reach the specified destination.
metric	This option specifies the cost to reach a specified destination. If a routing table contains more than one route to reach the destination, the route with the lowest cost is selected.
if interface	This option forwards traffic to a specified destination out a specific interface.

Example 23-15 illustrates the use of the **route print** command, which displays the contents of a PC's routing table. Notice that the output identifies a listing of the PC's interfaces, along with IPv4 routes and IPv6 routes. From the output, you can see that the 10.0.0.0 255.0.0.0 network is reachable via two gateways (192.168.1.77 and 192.168.1.11). Also, notice that there is a persistent route (a route entry that survives a reboot) to act as a default gateway for the PC, which is 192.168.1.1.

Example 23-15   Sample Output from the Windows **route print** Command

```
C:\> route print
===========================================================================
Interface List
 11...00 24 81 ee 4c 0e ......Intel(R) 82566DM-2 Gigabit Network
Connection
  1...........................Software Loopback Interface 1
 12...00 00 00 00 00 00 00 e0 Microsoft ISATAP Adapter
 13...00 00 00 00 00 00 00 e0 Teredo Tunneling Pseudo-Interface
===========================================================================


IPv4 Route Table
===========================+===============================================
Active Routes:
Network Destination     Netmask          Gateway        Interface  Metric
          0.0.0.0  0.0.0.0          192.168.1.1    192.168.1.50  276
         10.0.0.0  255.0.0.0        192.168.1.77   192.168.1.50   21
         10.0.0.0  255.0.0.0        192.168.1.11   192.168.1.50   21
        127.0.0.0  255.0.0.0        On-link        127.0.0.1     306
        127.0.0.1  255.255.255.255  On-link        127.0.0.1     306
  127.255.255.255  255.255.255.255  On-link        127.0.0.1     306
       172.16.0.0  255.255.0.0      192.168.1.1    192.168.1.50   21
      192.168.0.0  255.255.255.0    192.168.1.11   192.168.1.50   21
      192.168.1.0  255.255.255.0    On-link        192.168.1.50  276
     192.168.1.50  255.255.255.255  On-link        192.168.1.50  276
    192.168.1.255  255.255.255.255  On-link        192.168.1.50  276
        224.0.0.0  240.0.0.0        On-link        127.0.0.1     306
        224.0.0.0  240.0.0.0        On-link        192.168.1.50  276
  255.255.255.255  255.255.255.255  On-link        127.0.0.1     306
  255.255.255.255  255.255.255.255  On-link        192.168.1.50  276
===========================================================================
Persistent Routes:
  Network Address     Netmask      Gateway Address   Metric
        0.0.0.0         0.0.0.0     192.168.1.1       Default
===========================================================================


IPv6 Route Table
===========================================================================
Active Routes:
 If   Metric  Network Destination      Gateway
```

```
13    58 :      :/0                                    On-link
1     306 :     :1/128                                 On-link
13    58        2001::/32 On-link
13    306       2001:0:4137:9e76:10e2:614f:b34e:ea84/128
                                                       On-link
11    276       fe80::/64                              On-link
13    306       fe80::/64                              On-link
13    306       fe80::10e2:614f:b34e:ea84/128
                                                       On-link
11    276       fe80::f46d:4a34:a9c4:51a0/128
                                                       On-link
1     306       ff00::/8                               On-link
13    306       ff00::/8                               On-link
11    276       ff00::/8                               On-link
=====================================================================
Persistent Routes:
  None
```

Say that you want to remove one of the route entries for the 10.0.0.0 255.0.0.0 network. Example 23-16 shows how one of the two entries (specifically, the entry pointing to 192.168.1.11) can be removed from the routing table. Notice from the output that after the **route delete 10.0.0.0 mask 255.0.0.0 192.168.1.11** command is issued, the route no longer appears in the routing table.

Key Topic

Example 23-16   Sample Output from the Windows **route delete** Command

```
C:\> route delete 10.0.0.0 mask 255.0.0.0 192.168.1.11
  OK!
C:\> route print
OUTPUT OMITTED...
IPv4 Route Table
=====================================================+++=================
Active Routes:
Network Destination     Netmask         Gateway         Interface       Metric
0.0.0.0                 0.0.0.0         192.168.1.1     192.168.1.50    276
10.0.0.0                255.0.0.0       192.168.1.77    192.168.1.50    21
127.0.0.0               255.0.0.0       On-link         127.0.0.1       306
127.0.0.1               255.255.255.255 On-link         127.0.0.1       306
127.255.255.255         255.255.255.255 On-link         127.0.0.1       306
```

```
172.16.0.0          255.255.0.0        192.168.1.11  192.168.1.50  21
192.168.0.0         255.255.255.0      192.168.1.11  192.168.1.50  21
192.168.1.0         255.255.255.0      On-link       192.168.1.50  276
192.168.1.50        255.255.255.255    On-link       192.168.1.50  276
192.168.1.255       255.255.255.255    On-link       192.168.1.50  276
224.0.0.0           240.0.0.0          On-link       127.0.0.1     306
224.0.0.0           240.0.0.0          On-link       192.168.1.50  276
255.255.255.255     255.255.255.255    On-link       127.0.0.1     306
255.255.255.255     255.255.255.255    On-link       192.168.1.50  276
========================================================================

OUTPUT OMITTED...
```

You can add a route by using the **route add** command. Example 23-17 shows and confirms the addition of a route pointing to the 10.2.1.0 255.255.255.0 network, with the next-hop route (gateway) 192.168.1.1.

Example 23-17   Sample Output from the Windows **route add** Command

```
C:\> route add 10.2.1.0 mask 255.255.255.0 192.168.1.1
 OK!
C:\> route print
OUTPUT OMITTED...
IPv4 Route Table
========================================================================
Active Routes:
Network            Netmask            Gateway         Interface     Metric
Destination
0.0.0.0            0.0.0.0            192.168.1.1     192.168.1.50  276
10.0.0.0           255.0.0.0         192.168.1.77    192.168.1.50  21
10.2.1.0           255.255.255.0     192.168.1.1     192.168.1.50  21
127.0.0.0          255.0.0.0         On-link         127.0.0.1     306
127.0.0.1          255.255.255.255   On-link         127.0.0.1     306
127.255.255.255    255.255.255.255   On-link         127.0.0.1     306
172.16.0.0         255.255.0.0       192.168.1.11    192.168.1.50  21
192.168.0.0        255.255.255.0     192.168.1.11    192.168.1.50  21
192.168.1.0        255.255.255.0     On-link         192.168.1.50  276
192.168.1.50       255.255.255.255   On-link         192.168.1.50  276
192.168.1.255      255.255.255.255   On-link         192.168.1.50  276
224.0.0.0          240.0.0.0         On-link         127.0.0.1     306
```

```
224.0.0.0         240.0.0.0          On-link        192.168.1.50  276
255.255.255.255   255.255.255.255    On-link        127.0.0.1     306
255.255.255.255   255.255.255.255    On-link        192.168.1.50  276
===============================================================================
OUTPUT OMITTED...
```

telnet

For many years, *telnet* was the command line tool of choice for making remote access connections to systems for management. Today, this command is frowned upon as the Telnet protocol offers no security for the information transmitted. Telnet is now found only in lab and practice environments. Secure Shell (SSH) is the technology of choice today for remote access to systems because it is secure.

tcpdump

You can use the *tcpdump* command to print out the headers of packets on a network interface that match a Boolean expression. You can also run the command with the **-w** flag to save the packet data to a file for later analysis and/or with the **-r** flag to read from a saved packet file rather than to read packets from a network interface. The syntax and options for the **tcpdump** command are as follows:

```
tcpdump [ -adeflnNOpqRStuvxX ] [ -c count ] [ -C file_size ]
[ -F file ]
   [ -i interface ] [ -m module ] [ -r file ]
   [ -s snaplen ] [ -T type ] [ -U user ] [ -w file ]
   [ -E algo:secret ] [ expression ]
```

nmap

The *nmap* command (short for Network Mapper) is an open-source and very versatile tool for UNIX network administrators. You use **nmap** to explore networks, perform security scans, create network audits, and find open ports on remote machines. The tool can scan for live hosts, operating systems, packet filters, and open ports. Here is an example of the syntax for this command:

```
nmap [Scan Type(s)] [Options] {target specification}
```

Basic Network Platform Commands

Although the Network+ exam is vendor neutral, you need to be aware of several Cisco network device commands that are incredibly popular and used on equipment from a number of vendors:

- *show interface*: The **show interface** command allows you to examine the statistics and the status of the interfaces on a network system.

- *show config*: The **show config** command (or some variation of it) is used to examine the configuration of a network device. For example, on a Cisco router, the **show running-configuration** command permits you to see the current configuration of the device, which is stored in the RAM of the device. To view the saved configuration that is loaded when the system is rebooted, you can use the **show startup-configuration** command.

- *show route*: The **show route** command (or some variation of it) is used to view the routing table configuration of the network device. On a Cisco router, you can use **show ip route** to view the IPv4 routing table.

Real-World Case Study

Acme, Inc. has invested in several new software packages to help support the network. These include Enterprise-level versions of protocol analyzers and port scanners.

Acme, Inc. is also providing training to the junior technicians that includes command line tool training. This training includes common network device command line working, including the monitoring commands used in the wide array of Cisco and Juniper network devices in use.

Summary

The main topics covered in this chapter are the following:

- This chapter covers many different software tools that can assist greatly in the support of the network. This includes tools such as WiFi analyzers and port scanners.

- This chapter describes command line tools that you can use to help troubleshoot and maintain modern networks. These include the commonly used tools like ipconfig and traceroute.

- This chapter also covers some basic commands found on some network devices.

Exam Preparation Tasks

Review All the Key Topics

Review the most important topics from this chapter, noted with the Key Topic icon in the outer margin of the page. Table 23-6 lists these key topics and the page number where each is found.

Table 23-6   Key Topics for Chapter 23

Key Topic Element	Description	Page Number
Figure 23-1	Wireshark protocol analyzer software	521
Example 23-1	Sample output from the Windows **ping** command	524
Example 23-3	Sample output from the Windows **ipconfig** command	525
Example 23-8	Sample output from the Windows **nslookup** noninteractive command	530
Example 23-10	Comparing output from the Windows **nslookup** and UNIX **dig** commands	531
Example 23-12	Sample output from Windows **arp –a** command	532
Example 23-13	Sample output from the Windows **netstat** command	534
Example 23-14	Sample output from the Windows **netstat -b** command	536
Example 23-15	Sample output from the Windows **route print** command	539
Example 23-16	Sample output from the Windows **route delete** command	540

Complete Tables and Lists from Memory

Print a copy of Appendix C, "Memory Tables," or at least the section for this chapter and complete as many of the tables as possible from memory. Appendix D, "Memory Tables Answer Key," includes the completed tables and lists so you can check your work.

Define Key Terms

Define the following key terms from this chapter and check your answers in the Glossary:

WiFi analyzer, protocol analyzer, packet capture, bandwidth speed tester, port scanner, iperf, NetFlow analyzer, Trivial File Transfer Protocol (TFTP) server, terminal emulator, IP scanner, ping, ipconfig, ifconfig, ip, nslookup, dig, traceroute/tracert, arp, netstat, hostname, route, telnet, tcpdump, nmap, show interface, show config, show route

Complete Chapter 23 Hands-On Labs in Network+ Simulator Lite

- Identifying Troubleshooting Commands to use for various tasks
- Matching Command Output to Commands
- Verify a Data Link Connection from a Computer to a Network
- Using ipconfig to Discover Network Settings
- Using ping to Troubleshoot Connectivity
- Using Extended Ping (Command Switches) to Troubleshoot Connectivity
- Using ipconfig, ping, arp, and tracert, to Troubleshoot Connectivity
- Using basic Linux troubleshooting commands
- IPv6 Troubleshooting

Additional Resource

11 Networking Commands Every Windows Admin Should Use: https://techgenix.com/top-11-networking-commands/

Review Questions

The answers to these review questions appear in Appendix A, "Answers to Review Questions."

1. Consider the following output:

```
C:\> arp -a
Interface: 172.16.202.128 --- 0xb
Internet Address Physical Address Type
```

```
172.16.202.2 00-50-56-fd-65-2c dynamic
172.16.202.255 ff-ff-ff-ff-ff-ff static
224.0.0.22 01-00-5e-00-00-16 static
224.0.0.252 01-00-5e-00-00-fc static
255.255.255.255 ff-ff-ff-ff-ff-ff static
```

In this example, what is the MAC address corresponding to the IP address 172.16.202.2?

- a. ff-ff-ff-ff-ff-ff
- b. 00-50-56-fd-65-2c
- c. 01-00-5e-00-00-16
- d. 01-00-5e-00-00-fc

2. What option would you specify after the **ipconfig** command to display the IP address of a Windows PC's DNS server?

- a. No option is needed because **ipconfig** displays DNS server information by default.
- b. **/full**
- c. **/fqdn**
- d. **/all**

3. What protocol is used by the **ping** command?

- a. IGMP
- b. PIM
- c. ICMP
- d. RTP

4. Which of the following commands is used on a UNIX host to generate information about each router hop along the path from a source to a destination?

- a. **ping -t**
- b. **tracert**
- c. **ping -r**
- d. **traceroute**

5. Which of the following UNIX commands can be used to check FQDN-to-IP address resolution? (Choose three.)

- a. **nslookup**
- b. **netstat**

   c. **dig**

   d. **host**

6. What command produced the following snippet of output?

```
OUTPUT OMITTED...
;; global options: +cmd
;; Got answer:
;; ->>HEADER<<- opcode: QUERY, status: NOERROR, id: 62169
;; flags: qr rd ra; QUERY: 1, ANSWER: 1, AUTHORITY: 0, ADDITIONAL: 0
;; QUESTION SECTION:
;pearsonitcertification.com. IN A
;; ANSWER SECTION:
pearsonitcertification.com. 10800 IN A 64.28.85.25
;; Query time: 202 msec
;; SERVER: 192.168.1.1#53(192.168.1.1)
;; WHEN: Wed Jun 1 20:41:57 2011
;; MSG SIZE rcvd: 60
OUTPUT OMITTED...
```

   a. **traceroute -d pearsonitcertification.com**

   b. **dig pearsonitcertification.com**

   c. **netstat -a pearsonitcertification.com**

   d. **nbtstat pearsonitcertification.com**

7. Which tool would be used as part of a wireless site survey and produces a heat map?

   a. Bandwidth tester

   b. WiFi analyzer

   c. port scanner

   d. iperf

8. What command is used to view the routing table configuration of a network device?

   a. **show config**

   b. **show interface**

   c. **show route**

   d. **show tcpdump**

This chapter covers the following topics related to Objective 5.4 (Given a scenario, troubleshoot common wireless connectivity issues) of the CompTIA Network+ N10-008 certification exam:

- Specifications and limitations
  - Throughput
  - Speed
  - Distance
  - Received signal strength indication (RSSI) signal strength
  - Effective isotropic radiated power (EIRP)/power settings
- Considerations
  - Antennas
    - Placement
    - Type
    - Polarization
  - Channel utilization
  - AP association time
  - Site survey

- Common issues
  - Interference
    - Channel overlap
  - Antenna cable attenuation/signal loss
  - RF attenuation/signal loss
  - Wrong SSID
  - Incorrect passphrase
  - Encryption protocol mismatch
  - Insufficient wireless coverage
  - Captive portal issues
  - Client disassociation issues

CHAPTER 24

Troubleshoot Common Wireless Issues

Troubleshooting wireless might be a close second to supporting local network printers—although typically it is not as labor intensive. Wireless has become an expected part of the enterprise network that is a fairly consistent source of troubleshooting for you and your department. This chapter ensures that you know the basics of this common area of troubleshooting in today's enterprise networks.

Foundation Topics

Specifications and Limitations

Chapter 12, "Wireless Standards," examines wireless standards. As you should recall from that chapter, there are big differences in the 802.11 standards when it comes to the specifications and limitations of each standard.

Key Topic

This section reviews just some of the key values and concepts that you need to be concerned about when troubleshooting WLAN deployments:

- **Speed:** Typically, when the speed of the wireless technology is described, it is actually the theoretical maximum speed that is actually being described. For example, the speed of 802.11n is typically said to be 300Mbps. But is this true? In short, the answer is no. A more accurate way to describe how a WLAN is actually performing is to look at throughput, described next.

- *Throughput:* This term is typically used to indicate the amount of data you are able to send on the network media. In this case, of course, the media is the radio frequencies that power wireless. Although the stated speed of 802.11n is 300Mbps, when you actually test the throughput, you might discover that the network is averaging 225Mbps. This actual throughput measurement provides a much more accurate picture of the capabilities of the network segment.

- **Distance:** Attenuation is a fact of life with network media. As the signal gets farther and farther away from the source, the signal weakens, and speed (and throughput) suffer. Notice that in a wired infrastructure, the effect of distance can be much easier to predict. When you are troubleshooting wireless environments, it's important to keep in mind that all distances are not created equal. For example, there might be only half the distance between your access point (AP) and your client as between your AP and another client in your network. If there is a large source of WLAN interference in the shorter path, this might be the much more problematic client system.

> **NOTE** There are actually many places in the wireless infrastructure where attenuation can be an issue. A careful analysis of the WiFi design might find attenuation/signal loss resulting from the antenna cable in use. This might add to the existing and known problems of *RF attenuation* and *signal loss*.

- *Received signal strength indication (RSSI) signal strength*: When you are performing site surveys or just performing typical wireless troubleshooting, it is important to use metric information that you can trust and interpret accurately. The RSSI might be presented in different formats, depending on the software you are working with, but comparing your internal testing results can make this measurement extremely valuable. No matter how exactly you see the value, the RSSI is a measure of the power level being received by the local client you are testing with. In most software packages, the greater the RSSI value, the stronger the signal, and the better the chances for higher throughput.

■ ***Effective isotropic radiated power (EIRP)/power settings:*** Another very valuable metric used with wireless today, EIRP, measures the maximum amount of power that could be radiated from an antenna. Of course, this value must incorporate the antenna gain and the transmitter power of the RF system. You most often see EIRP presented as decibels over isotropic, or dBi.

Considerations

Troubleshooting wireless networks might seem overwhelming compared with troubleshooting wired infrastructures. As described in the following sections, there are certainly many unique considerations when troubleshooting WiFi networks. However, through study and practice, you will soon be as efficient at troubleshooting WiFi as you are at troubleshooting a pesky network printer.

Antennas

As discussed in Chapter 12, antenna choices are often critical for the proper functioning of a wireless LAN. You need to ensure that the most critical design goals were met:

■ Double-check distances from the clients and APs.

■ Test the coverage area of the antenna type and form factor selected.

■ Test both the indoor and outdoor coverages.

■ Test for interference with other APs.

Recall from Chapter 12 that there are multiple types of wireless antennas, and they fall into two broad categories, based on coverage area:

■ **Omnidirectional:** The signal is spread in nearly a 360-degree radius around the antenna.

■ **Unidirectional:** The signal is projected in a single, relatively precise direction.

NOTE   The direction in which an antenna emits signal is termed ***polarization***.

Frequencies and Channels

Keep in mind these key facts regarding frequencies and channels when troubleshooting wireless networks:

- WLANs use frequencies in the 2.4GHz–2.5GHz range or in the 5.725GHz–5.875GHz range.

- Within each band are specific frequencies (or *channels*) at which wireless devices operate.

- To avoid *interference*, nearby wireless APs should use frequencies that do not overlap with one another.

- In the 2.4GHz band, channel frequencies are separated by 5MHz (with the exception of channel 14, which has 12MHz of separation from channel 13).

- A single channel's transmission can spread over a frequency range of 22MHz. As a result, five consecutive channels tend to overlap one another. In the United States, the nonoverlapping channels are 1, 6, and 11.

- More and more 802.11ax (WiFi 6) devices are becoming available. This technology extends WiFi into the 6GHz band.

Other Considerations

An exhaustive list of WLAN considerations is beyond the scope of this book, but there are a few more you might encounter in a network and on the Network+ exam:

- *AP association time*: In larger enterprise environments, wireless LAN controllers (WLCs) often provide the control plane intelligence that APs lack. Key metrics to consider in this environment are how long it takes for a typical client to properly associate with an AP and is the length of time it takes an AP to associate with a WLC. These are both points of latency as well as potential failures.

- *Site survey*: There is no substitute for a thorough, well-planned, well-documented site survey when it comes to planning and deploying wireless successfully. When implementing a production WLAN, planning is a much better option than simply trying and failing. A proper site survey can set you up for great success. It will help you determine where to place antennas and what types of antennas you need, and it will help you learn about potential sources of interference and other enemies of the WLAN. Fortunately, there are many options to choose from when it comes to site survey blueprints and software packages.

In a site survey, you use WiFi and other wireless analyzers to understand and map out the wireless infrastructure. One output is a wireless heat map, which provides a visual method for understanding coverage and signal strength.

Common Issues

Network engineers are consistently thinking about what can go wrong. Fortunately, this type of doomsday thinking can be very valuable in networking. The following are some of the common issues you need to be aware of when it comes to wireless networking:

Key Topic

- **Interference:** Wireless communication can be interrupted due to radio frequency interference (RFI). Common RFI sources that impact wireless networks include 2.4GHz cordless phones, microwave ovens, baby monitors, and gaming consoles.

- **Signal strength:** The RSSI value measures the power of a wireless signal. RSSI values vary based on distance from a wireless antenna and physical objects interfering with line-of-sight communication with a wireless antenna (for example, drywall, metal filing cabinets, elevator shafts). Some wireless networks automatically drop their wireless transmission rate when an RSSI value drops below a certain value.

- **Misconfiguration of wireless parameters:** For communication to occur, a variety of wireless parameters must match between a wireless client and a wireless AP. For example, the client needs to be using a wireless standard supported by the wireless AP (for example, IEEE 802.11a/b/g/n/ac/ax). Wireless channels must also match. However, a wireless client usually automatically sets its channel based on the wireless AP's channel. Encryption standards must match. For example, a wireless client using WPA would not successfully communicate with a wireless AP using WPA2. In addition, the service set identifier (SSID) of a wireless AP must be selected by the wireless client. In many cases, a wireless AP broadcasts its SSID, and a wireless client can select that SSID from a list of visible SSIDs. In other cases, a wireless AP does not broadcast its SSID, and a wireless client must have a matching SSID manually configured.

- **Latency:** Wireless networks may experience more delay than their wired counterparts. One reason for the increased delay is the use of carrier-sense multiple access with collision avoidance (CSMA/CA) in WLANs; CSMA/CA introduces a random delay before data is transmitted in an attempt to avoid collisions. Another reason for the increased delay is the fact that all wireless devices associated with a single wireless AP are in the same collision domain, introducing the possibility of collisions (retransmissions), which can increase delay.

- **Multiple paths of propagation:** An electromagnetic waveform cannot pass through a perfect conductor. Admittedly, perfect conductors do not exist in most office environments. However, very good conductors, such as metal filing cabinets, are commonplace in offices. As a result, if the waveform of a wireless transmission encounters one of these conductive objects, most of the signal bounces off the object, creating multiple paths (modes) of propagation. These multiple modes of propagation can cause data (specifically, bits) to arrive at uneven intervals, possibly corrupting data. This problem is similar to multimode delay distortion, which occurs in multimode fiber-optic cabling.

- **Incorrect AP placement:** Wireless APs should be strategically located in a building to provide sufficient coverage to all desired coverage areas. However, the coverage areas of wireless APs using overlapping channels should not overlap. To maintain coverage between coverage areas, you should have overlapping coverage areas among wireless APs using nonoverlapping channels (for example, channels 1, 6, and 11 for wireless networks using the 2.4GHz band of frequencies). A common design recommendation is that overlapping coverage areas (using nonoverlapping channels) should have an overlap of approximately 10% to 15%. Keep in mind that the 5GHz band and the 6 GHz band of WiFi 6e offer many more nonoverlapping channels.

- **Captive portal issues:** Many wireless network environments make use of a captive portal. A captive portal is a web page that often presents an acceptable use policy (AUP) that the user must accept in order to access the Internet via a wireless connection. The web page also typically collects profile information from end users. It might even market products to wireless users. The captive portal is a key element of the wireless association process, and so it must perform as expected. Most wireless networks fail closed, which means if the captive portal or any other step of the process is not functioning, the wireless network remains inaccessible to new clients.

- **Client disassociation issues:** Clients appreciate a wireless network much more if they are able to remain connected. While you might be able to immediately rule out many categories of issues that could cause disassociation, there are plenty that might require additional inspection and analysis. Remember that there is an entire category of attacks that target client disassociation, and these attacks are often initial steps in much larger attacks; an attacker may disassociate a client and then associate it to a rogue device.

Wireless Network Troubleshooting

As a practice troubleshooting scenario for wireless networks, consider Figure 24-1. Based on this topology, can you spot a design issue with the wireless network?

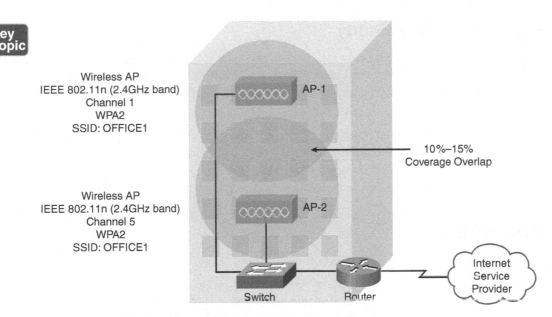

Wireless AP
IEEE 802.11n (2.4GHz band)
Channel 1
WPA2
SSID: OFFICE1

AP-1

10%–15%
Coverage Overlap

Wireless AP
IEEE 802.11n (2.4GHz band)
Channel 5
WPA2
SSID: OFFICE1

AP-2

Internet
Service
Provider

Switch   Router

FIGURE 24-1   Wireless Network Troubleshooting: Sample Topology

Wireless Network Troubleshooting Solution

The wireless network presented in Figure 24-1 includes two wireless APs. Although these wireless APs have a matching wireless standard, encryption type, and SSID, the channels being used (channels 1 and 5) interfere with one another. Recall from Chapter 12 that channels in the 2.4GHz band need at least five channels of separation (for overlapping coverage areas), but the channels used in this example have only four channels of separation. A fix for this *channel overlap* issue is to assign AP-2 to channel 6, thus providing five channels of separation between AP-1 and AP-2.

A wireless analyzer may be needed to identify problems such as signal loss, overlapping or mismatched channels, unacceptable signal-to-noise ratios, rogue APs, and power levels. Breaking down a problem into smaller pieces allows you to identify the fault domain or the area that is causing the problem. For example, if a user cannot access the wireless network, the pieces involved may be the user connecting to an incorrect SSID or problems with the AP, the switch, the WLC, the RADIUS server, the Active Directory (AD) server, or the user account and password. By testing the individual components, where possible, you can isolate the problem and then correct it.

Real-World Case Study

Networking is improving the wireless use in the main Enterprise campus location. As part of these improvements, the IT team is performing an analysis of the existing WiFi signals. A big metric in this study is the RSSI and EIRP values throughout the location.

Another big aspect of the redesign is the replacement of several access points and the introduction of a new and improved Wireless LAN Controller (WLC). Networking is also ensuring their new IT team members are properly trained in supporting and understanding the WiFi infrastructure.

Summary

Here are the main topics covered in this chapter:

- This chapter describes some of the important metrics associated with specifications and limitations in wireless networking.

- This chapter examines several important considerations that are critical in wireless troubleshooting.

- This chapter concludes by examining some of the most common issues in wireless networks today.

Exam Preparation Tasks

Review All the Key Topics

Review the most important topics from this chapter, noted with the Key Topic icon in the outer margin of the page. Table 24-1 lists these key topics and the page number where each is found.

Table 24-1 Key Topics for Chapter 24

Key Topic Element	Description	Page Number
List	Specifications and limitations	550
List	Key facts for frequencies and channels	552
List	Common issues for wireless networking	553
Figure 24-1	Wireless network troubleshooting sample topology	555

Define Key Terms

Define the following key terms from this chapter and check your answers in the Glossary:

throughput, received signal strength indication (RSSI) signal strength, effective isotropic radiated power (EIRP)/power settings, polarization, AP association time, site survey, interference, channel overlap, RF attenuation, signal loss

Complete Chapter 24 Hands-On Labs in Network+ Simulator Lite

- Matching Wireless Standards and Terminology

Review Questions

The answers to these review questions appear in Appendix A, "Answers to Review Questions."

1. Which of the following is a value measuring the power of a wireless signal?

   a. RSSI

   b. SSID

   c. RFI

   d. CSMA/CA

2. Which of the following are the most common sources of radio frequency interference (RFI) in a wireless network? (Choose three.)

   a. Gaming consoles

   b. Fax machines

   c. Microwave ovens

   d. Baby monitors

   e. Bluetooth

3. Which metric provides the best idea of how a wireless network is actually performing?

    a. Throughput

    b. Speed

    c. Relative jitter

    d. Availability

4. A satellite dish antenna is an example of what type of wireless antenna?

    a. Omnidirectional

    b. Integrated

    c. Beam-formed

    d. Unidirectional

5. What is the name for a web page that is presented to wireless clients seeking access to a network?

    a. Authentication server

    b. Captive portal

    c. Self-registration gateway

    d. Supplicant client

6. Which of the following should you consider conducting before designing and deploying a high-performance WLAN infrastructure?

    a. Site survey

    b. Reconnaissance

    c. Nmapping

    d. Port scan

7. A target wireless client has been disconnected from the company AP and associated with a rogue device. What has most likely occurred?

    a. Disassociation

    b. Propagation

    c. Incorrect AP placement

    d. Misconfigured parameter

8. To maintain coverage between areas, you need to have overlapped coverage areas among wireless APs using nonoverlapping channels. In the United States, what channels in the 2.4GHz band of frequencies should you use?

   a. CSMA/CA channels

   b. 1, 6, and 11

   c. EIRP channels

   d. 2, 7, and 12

This chapter covers the following topics related to Objective 5.5 (Given a scenario, troubleshoot general networking issues) of the CompTIA Network+ N10-008 certification exam:

- Considerations
  - Device configuration review
  - Routing tables
  - Interface status
  - VLAN assignment
  - Network performance baselines
- Common issues
  - Collisions
  - Broadcast storm
  - Duplicate MAC address
  - Duplicate IP address
  - Multicast flooding
  - Asymmetrical routing
  - Switching loops
  - Routing loops
  - Rogue DHCP server
  - DHCP scope exhaustion

- IP setting issues
  - Incorrect gateway
  - Incorrect subnet mask
  - Incorrect IP address
  - Incorrect DNS
- Missing route
- Low optical link budget
- Certificate issues
- Hardware failure
- Host-based/network-based firewall settings
- Blocked services, ports, or addresses
- Incorrect VLAN
- DNS issues
- NTP issues
- BYOD challenges
- Licensed feature issues
- Network performance issues

CHAPTER 25

Troubleshoot General Network Issues

As you perform your day-to-day tasks of administering a network, a significant percentage of your time will be dedicated to resolving network issues. Whether the issues you are troubleshooting were reported by an end user or were issues you discovered, you need an effective plan to respond to them. Specifically, you need a systematic approach to clearly articulate an issue, gather information about the issue, hypothesize the underlying cause of the issue, validate your hypothesis, create an action plan, implement that action plan, observe results, and document your resolution. Without a plan, your efforts might be inefficient, as you try one thing after another, possibly causing other issues in the process.

Although your troubleshooting efforts can definitely benefit from a structured approach, it is important to realize that troubleshooting is part art and part science. Specifically, your intuition and instincts play a huge role in isolating an issue. Of course, those skills are developed over time and come with experience and exposure to more and more scenarios.

This chapter details many of the general network issues you are likely to encounter today, why they occur, and what you can often do about them.

Foundation Topics

Considerations for General Network Troubleshooting

How much can go wrong in a network today? *A lot!* In fact, the list of potential issues grows all the time as new services and data types are provided by networks. Fortunately, there are some common considerations that can help you greatly as you approach this vast and challenging topic. Here are some common considerations and best practices that you should keep in mind:

Key Topic

- **Device configuration:** You should be consistently reviewing the configurations of network devices to ensure that your network is not suffering from *configuration drift* (that is, configurations gradually changing from their original documented defaults for a network). Many software packages and tools, such as Ansible, can assist you in making sure all your network devices remain in a constant, stable, and known configuration state.

- *Routing tables:* It is important to carefully monitor and analyze the routing tables of Layer 3 devices. Forwarding decisions are critical to the operation of a network, and you want to ensure that packets are flowing exactly as you want and expect them to.

- *Interface status:* One embarrassing network issue that you do not want to experience is the administratively downed interface scenario. In this scenario, you try desperately to reach a key network device, only to discover that you failed to enable the interface that you are trying to contact. Remember that there are simple commands you can use, and even GUI-based web pages that can give you status information on your critical network interfaces. Knowing which are healthy and which are not can be critical in network troubleshooting.

NOTE   Often the status of an interface in a network is contingent on the network layer settings. The physical and data link layer settings might be fine (that is, Cisco displays this status as UP/UP), but if the IP settings are incorrect, the physical and data link layer health of the interface are not of great benefit to you. The following settings typically must be perfect:

- Default gateway IP address
- Subnet mask
- IP address
- DNS address

Think about the symptoms you might see for each of these potential misconfigurations. For example, if your default gateway IP address is incorrect, you might be able to communicate with your local subnet peers just fine, but you will not be able to successfully reach any remote destinations—which would not be good!

■ **VLAN assignment:** Ensuring that the right interfaces are in the correct VLANs is really important. Remember that VLANs are IP subnets, so it makes perfect sense that if you have two machines in the 192.168.1.0/24 network, these machines must be in the same VLAN to properly communicate with one another.

■ **Network performance baselines:** As you have probably noticed throughout this book, it is critical that you know the details about how your network performs under "normal" conditions and what its speeds and throughput really are. (How can you know that you are having a problem if you do not even know what your network should be performing like when there are no problems?) Fortunately, as this book has discussed, there are many tools and techniques for capturing accurate and detailed network performance baselines and using the data you collect to keep tabs on the network.

Common Issues

The following list of common general network issues may be a bit intimidating, and it is not even an exhaustive list. As a network administrator and as a candidate for the Network+ certification, you need to understand the following common issues:

■ **Duplicate IP address:** Hosts on a subnet should have unique IP addresses. If two hosts are configured with the same IP address, unpredictable traffic patterns can occur for those hosts. One reason (of many) this might happen is because a DHCP server is inadvertently leasing out an address that has been statically assigned on the network. These statically assigned addresses should be excluded from the DHCP scope.

■ **Duplicate MAC address:** Although it's rarer than a duplicate IP address on a network, a MAC address could be duplicated. A MAC address on a network is typically taken from the address that is "burned in" to the hardware by the device vendor. To ensure uniqueness between vendors, each network device vendor is assigned a MAC prefix, and the vendor can control the remaining bits. Therefore, when a MAC address is duplicated on a network, it is most often a human error that occurs when MAC addresses are software defined to override the hardware addresses that are burned in.

- **Expired IP address:** Perhaps a leased DHCP address has expired for a workstation. This might be the case, for example, if the lease duration has been set to a small value, perhaps because of an IP address shortage in a particular area of the network.

- *DHCP scope exhaustion:* If your end user network device population has grown, you might have issues with DHCP scope exhaustion that are innocent in nature. DHCP scope exhaustion refers to the scope being completely out of IP addresses that it can lease to clients. If your population is outgrowing your design, a redesign is expected, and you should not be surprised by this. DHCP scope exhaustion attacks can be very disruptive because you will not know it is coming. Suddenly, clients in your network cannot communicate properly as they have lost their IP address configuration.

- *Rogue DHCP server:* This security concern could certainly cause troubleshooting headaches on a network due to the incorrect IP configurations that could result. When rogue DHCP servers appear on a network, it is often because users have brought in their own devices, either maliciously or accidentally.

- **Untrusted SSL certificate:** If you are using certificates for authentication, you might have an issue with an SSL certificate preventing such authentication. Perhaps a certificate is invalid due to time, or perhaps it has been manually revoked for some reason.

- **Incorrect time:** Because many network configurations rely on the correct time, you might have problems in a network due to a workstation, server, or network appliance having the wrong time set. Remember that you should strongly consider using Network Time Protocol (NTP) or a competing technology to help ensure that your network devices are all set to the correct time.

- **Blocked TCP/UDP ports, services, or addresses:** A trouble ticket may be about blocked TCP or UDP ports. This type of blockage is often the result of misconfigured security devices in the network path. There might be other security mechanisms that are blocking specific IP addresses or services. These are all worthy of inspection when you are experiencing unexpected connectivity issues in a network.

- **Incorrect firewall settings:** Host-based firewall settings and network-based firewall settings may cause problems. Firewalls are great, but you need to make sure they are not blocking traffic that you need to pass through the network.

- **Incorrect access control list (ACL) settings:** ACLs can have effects on network traffic, and if their settings are incorrect, you could end up with trouble tickets.

■ **Unresponsive service:** Services that have failed in a network are common sources of problems.

■ *Collisions:* You should not see any collisions taking place if you have built a network using modern techniques and standards. Remember that microsegmentation of a network means keeping single devices in collision domains so that you do not experience collisions on the network. Often, if you are seeing collisions on a network, it is an indicator that you have a misconfiguration or a hardware device that is malfunctioning.

■ *Broadcast storms:* It might sound crazy, but it is possible to go to a Layer 2 switch and turn off Spanning Tree Protocol (STP). This is *never* recommended. Even in cases where you don't need STP because you have used technologies like port channels, you need to make sure STP is still enabled and running in the background. If STP isn't running, a broadcast storm may occur as a result of a Layer 2 loop. You might experience broadcast storms for other reasons as well, such as a NIC malfunctioning and flooding the network with erroneous broadcast frames.

■ *Multicast flooding:* You need to be concerned about broadcast, unknown unicast, and multicast (BUM) traffic in your network. This is the traffic that Layer 2 switches must flood. You want to minimize the amount of traffic flooding your network must perform, and you therefore often need to closely analyze the amount of BUM traffic flooding. In addition, you can use protection mechanisms such as network storm control to guard against excessive amounts of BUM traffic hampering network operations.

■ *Asymmetrical routing:* Sometimes packets take very different paths back to you than they took toward the destination. This situation, called asymmetrical routing, is not always a bad thing, and sometimes you even engineer it to happen for some specific reason. Often, however, asymmetrical routing is not wanted and can cause issues.

■ *Switching loops:* If STP is not running correctly—or not running at all—it will not be long before you have broadcast storms and switching loops. These are the enemies that STP is engineered to protect you from.

■ *Routing loops:* The dynamic routing protocols in use today do an excellent job of protecting themselves against loops. In fact, a loop could never get terribly bad because of the Time-to-Live (TTL) mechanism at Layer 3, which prevents a packet from circulating on the network endlessly in a loop. Layer 3 can still happen, though, especially when redistribution between routing protocols is configured incorrectly, and they are still awful. Be very careful when performing redistribution.

- **Missing route:** When a user indicates that a remote destination must be down, be sure to run through your methodical troubleshooting steps; in many cases you may discover that the issue is simply a missing route in the local routing table. Remember that networks change, and you need to ensure that our dynamic routing protocols (or even static routes) are being updated properly.

- **Hardware failure:** Network devices or parts sometimes fail, and components can burn out. Such failures are rare, but you need to consider them in your troubleshooting flow.

- **Low optical link budget:** A fiber-optic link budget, also known as a *loss budget*, indicates the total acceptable amount of optical power loss (expressed in decibels) that a fiber-optic link can withstand. Such power loss results from cables, connectors, splices, and couplers in the installed system.

- **BYOD challenges:** Perhaps the investigation of a trouble ticket reveals that an end user is trying to interact with your network by using a tablet she brought in from home. Whether or not your ***bring your own device (BYOD) policy*** allows this type of use and how you control this potential nightmare—such as through a mobile device management (MDM) policy—is an area of networking that deserves your attention.

- **Licensed feature issues:** Sometimes a network does not function properly because the organization lacks the appropriate licensing. Licensing of network devices can get quite complicated. You might need a license for a network device itself, and then you might also need additional licenses for certain features or levels of scalability.

- **Network performance issues:** Sometimes you know exactly why a network is not performing well. For example, you might have to fail over to another service provider and a very slow backup WAN link when the main service provider is down for maintenance. It is always an excellent idea to inform end users about these kinds of issues up front to prevent the disruption that would be caused by a flood of trouble tickets.

Real-World Case Study

To be better prepared for network issues, Acme, Inc. has introduced a training program for their support team that focuses on common issues that have been occurring in the network. This training focuses on the following areas:

- Multicast flooding
- Asymmetrical routing

- Missing routes
- Hardware failures

This training includes basic troubleshooting, but most importantly, it implements new guidelines for documentation and problem escalation procedures and techniques.

Summary

Here are the main topics covered in this chapter:

- This chapter focuses on the considerations you frequently need to make while engaged in general network troubleshooting.

- This chapter examines many common problematic issues in networks today.

Exam Preparation Tasks

Review All the Key Topics

Review the most important topics from this chapter, noted with the Key Topic icon in the outer margin of the page. Table 25-1 lists these key topics and the page number where each is found.

Table 25-1   Key Topics for Chapter 25

Key Topic Element	Description	Page Number
List	Common considerations for general network troubleshooting	562
List	Common issues in modern networks	563

Define Key Terms

Define the following key terms from this chapter and check your answers in the Glossary:

routing table, interface status, collision, broadcast storm, multicast flooding, asymmetrical routing, switching loop, routing loop, rogue DHCP server, DHCP scope exhaustion, bring your own device (BYOD) policy

Complete Chapter 25 Hands-On Labs in Network+ Simulator Lite

- Reordering Troubleshooting Steps
- Using NSLookup for DNS Troubleshooting
- DNS Troubleshooting Simulation
- Exploring Troubleshooting using PowerShell
- Using tracert to Troubleshoot Connectivity
- Using the route print Command
- Using netstat to Troubleshoot Connectivity

Additional Resources

Troubleshooting with Speed and Confidence - https://www.youtube.com/watch?v=9kqRGecITxA

Review Questions

The answers to these review questions appear in Appendix A, "Answers to Review Questions."

1. What might you want to investigate if you can reach a web server by using its IP address but not its name?

   a. NTP

   b. DHCP

   c. DNS

   d. ARP

2. What device would most likely be unreachable if your default gateway IP address is misconfigured on the client?

   a. A remote web server

   b. A local printer

   c. Your neighbor's laptop

   d. Your loopback

3. In the absence of STP, what issues might result from a Layer 2 loop in a network? (Choose two.)

   a. A router interface's MTU decrementing

   b. MAC address table corruption

   c. Broadcast storms

   d. Packet fragmentation

4. If you successfully ping from host A to host B, what can you conclude about host A?

   a. OSI Layers 1–4 are functional.

   b. OSI Layers 1–3 are functional.

   c. OSI Layers 1–7 are functional.

   d. You must have a fully functional default gateway.

5. What configuration on a Layer 2 switch is used to define broadcast domains where they would not exist naturally on their own?

   a. ARP

   b. STP

   c. VTP

   d. VLAN

6. To what subnet does a host with the IP address 172.16.155.10/18 belong?

   a. 172.16.0.0 /18

   b. 172.16.96.0 /18

   c. 172.16.128.0 /18

   d. 172.16.154.0 /18

CHAPTER 26

Final Preparation

The first 25 chapters of this book cover the technologies, protocols, design concepts, and considerations you need to understand for the CompTIA Network+ N10-008 exam. This chapter details a set of tools and a study plan to help you complete your preparation for the CompTIA Network+ N10-008 exam.

This brief chapter has three main sections. The first section lists exam preparation tools. The second section provides a suggested study plan you can use now that you have completed all the earlier chapters in this book. The third section describes some strategies that can help you take the exam.

Tools for Final Preparation

The digital resources associated with the book are available on the book's companion website. To access the companion website, follow these steps:

Step 1. Go to **http://www.pearsonitcertification.com/register.**

Step 2. Either log in to your account (if you have an existing account) or create a new account.

Step 3. Enter the ISBN of your book (**9780137449941**) and click **Submit**.

Step 4. Answer the challenge questions to validate your purchase.

Step 5. On your account page, click the **Registered Products** tab and then click the **Access Bonus Content** link.

Resources available on the companion website include the following:

- Interactive glossary flash card application
- Interactive exam essentials appendix
- Performance-based exercises
- CompTIA Network+ Hands-on Lab Simulator software
- The Pearson Test Prep practice test software

- Video training on key exam topics

- Memory table review exercises and answer keys

- A study planner tool

- Your Network+ certification exam voucher, which provides a 10% discount on the exam

Video Training

The companion website for this book makes available 10 training videos that address a couple of the most misunderstood concepts in the CompTIA Network+ curriculum—specifically the OSI model and IP addressing:

- **Video 1:** Introduction to the OSI Model

- **Video 2:** Layer 1—The Physical Layer

- **Video 3:** Layer 2—The Data Link Layer

- **Video 4:** Layer 3—The Network Layer

- **Video 5:** Layer 4—The Transport Layer

- **Video 6:** Layers 5–7—The Upper Layers

- **Video 7:** IP Addressing—Part 1 (Binary Numbering Review)

- **Video 8:** IP Addressing—Part 2 (Basic Subnetting)

- **Video 9:** IP Addressing—Part 3 (Advanced Subnetting)

- **Video 10:** IP Addressing—Part 4 (Introduction to IPv6)

These training videos are presented by Kevin Wallace, who is a dear friend and industry great. You can find more of his great work at his training company website, https://www.kwtrain.com.

Memory Tables

Like most other *Cert Guides* from Pearson IT Certification, this book purposefully organizes information into tables and lists for easier study and review. Rereading these tables and lists can be very useful before the exam. However, it is easy to skim over tables without paying attention to every detail, especially when you remember having seen the table's contents when reading the chapter.

To help you more effectively learn the information in the tables throughout this book, the companion website provides two appendixes:

■ Appendix C, "Memory Tables," lists partially completed versions of many of the tables in this book. You can open Appendix C and print the appendix. For review, you can attempt to complete the tables.

■ Appendix D, "Memory Tables Answer Key," which is also a PDF, lists the completed tables so that you can check your answers. You can also just refer to the tables printed in the book.

Simulations and Performance-Based Exercises

The CompTIA Network+ exam contains more than just multiple-choice questions. It also contains performance-based questions (PBQs) that test your understanding of exam topics and hands-on skills in interactive ways. CompTIA makes some sample PBQs available on its website, so you might want to check them out prior to taking your exam. You can find these sample PBQs at https://www.comptia.org/testing/testing-options/about-comptia-performance-exams/performance-based-questions-explained.

This book comes with a set of hands-on practice labs to help you practice and develop your hands-on skills in the CompTIA Network+ N10-008 Hands-on Lab Simulator software. This software is available for you to download from the companion website. The book also comes complete with a set of 40 performance-based exercises that mimic the PBQs on the exam.

You should practice *all* the simulations, PBQs, and hands-on activities included as part of this book as you work through each chapter—and it may be useful for you to repeat the labs again when you have finished the book to make sure you have a firm grasp of these hands-on concepts. The hands-on practice with these simulations will assist you in preparing for any simulations you may encounter in the certification exam and will help you learn skills that you can apply in a live environment.

End-of-Chapter Review Tools

Chapters 1–25 all have several features in the "Exam Preparation Tasks" and "Review Questions" sections at the end of the chapter. You might have already worked through these tools in each chapter. However, it can help to use them again as you make your final preparations for the exam.

Suggested Plan for Final Review and Study

This section lists a suggested study plan from the point at which you finish reading Chapter 25 until you take the CompTIA Network+ exam. You can ignore this plan, use it as is, or modify it to better meet your needs.

The plan involves five steps:

Step 1.   **Review key topics.** You can use the table at the end of each chapter that lists the key topics of the chapter, or you can just flip through the pages looking for key topics icons.

Step 2.   **Complete memory tables.** Open Appendix C on the companion website, print the entire appendix, and then complete the tables.

Step 3.   **Study the "Review Questions" sections.** Go through the "Review Questions" section at the end of each chapter to identify areas in which you need more study. All of these questions are available to you in the Pearson Test Prep software. Simply select the Book Questions exam bank to run a practice exam using just these questions from the book.

Step 4.   **Use the Pearson Test Prep practice test engine to practice.** You can use the Pearson Test Prep practice test engine to study using a bank of unique exam-realistic questions available only with this book. Run through the questions the first time in study mode and assess your areas of weakness. Then work through the questions again in practice exam mode to assess your exam readiness. Go through the questions a final time in flash card mode to really challenge yourself to answer the questions without being able to see the multiple-choice answers.

Step 5.   **Use the simulations and performance-based exercises to practice.** These exercises can help confirm your knowledge and how to apply that knowledge.

The database of questions used by the Pearson Test Prep software was created specifically for this book. You can use the Pearson Test Prep practice test engine either in study mode, practice exam mode, or flash card mode, as follows:

- **Study mode:** Study mode is most useful when you want to use the questions for learning and practicing. In study mode, you can select options such as randomizing the order of the questions and answers, automatically viewing answers to the questions as you go, and testing on specific topics.

- **Practice exam mode:** Practice exam mode presents questions in a timed environment, providing you with an exam-realistic experience. It also restricts your ability to see your score as you progress through the exam and view answers to questions as you are taking the exam. These timed exams not only allow you to study for the actual CompTIA Network+ exam but help you simulate the time pressure that can occur during an exam.

■ **Flash card mode:** Flash card mode simply removes the multiple-choice answers, challenging you to answer each question in your head, without the benefit of seeing the possible answers. Using this mode is a great way to drill on topics in which you are particularly weak. Note that in this mode, you will not be able to record questions as right or wrong, and a grade report is not available; you will have to assess yourself on your own when you view the correct answers.

When doing your final preparation, you can use study mode, practice exam mode, and flash card mode. However, after you have seen each question a few times, you are likely to remember the questions, and the usefulness of the exam database might decrease. Therefore, consider the following options when using the exam engine:

■ Use the exam bank 1 question database for review. Use study mode to study the questions by chapter, just as with the other final review steps listed in this chapter. When you are ready to do final review, use the other exam bank that you have not seen before.

■ Save the question database by not using it during your review of each part of this book so that you will not have seen the questions before. Then, use practice exam mode to simulate the exam.

Picking the correct mode from the exam engine's user interface is straightforward. The following steps show you how to move to the screen where you can select the mode:

Step 1.   Click the **My Products** tab if you are not already in that screen.

Step 2.   From the list of available products, select the product you want to use.

Step 3.   Click the **Exams** button.

You can then choose study mode, practice exam mode, or flash card mode. When in study mode or flash card mode, you can further choose the book chapters, thus limiting the questions to those explained in the specified chapters of this book.

The Pearson Test Prep software also allows you to mark questions, thus creating a custom database of questions for topics on which you might need extra review. It also allows you to enter notes on questions and review those notes.

Strategies for Taking the Exam

Are you ready for some strategy tips for your Network+ exam attempt? This section provides several of them. Of course, you can apply many of these to other certification exams as well:

- You can use one of two overall strategies for scheduling your exam. One approach is to schedule for an exam slot when you are fully ready; this is my favorite approach. You might have to wait as much as a week if all of the exam slots at your desired time are full, but typically if you are near a large city, you can find a slot for the very next day. The other approach is to schedule for several months out and then study, study, study to be ready for the exam slot you booked. Some people need to use this strategy to avoid procrastinating. If you adopt this strategy, be sure to check into the cancelation or rescheduling policy just in case your life gets in the way of your studies!

- Schedule the exam for a time that works great for you. If you are not a morning person, do not schedule the exam for early morning! Instead, schedule the exam for a time slot that works for you, even if it means waiting an extra day or two.

- Plan for and get a good night's rest before the exam. Also be sure to eat a good meal (breakfast or lunch) before the exam. Drink plenty of water to stay hydrated. Your mind will perform better when your body has what it needs. With that said, be sure not to experiment the day of the exam. I have talked to students who decided to suddenly try consuming a bunch of caffeine before the exam. They had a terrible exam experience because they were doing something their bodies were not used to.

- Map out where the testing center is and ensure that you know how to get there and how long the trip takes.

- Bring the proper identification required for the exam.

- Plan to arrive 30 minutes before your exam time, anticipate the traffic, and adjust your plan accordingly. Take a few moments before signing in at the testing center to relax and take several healthy breaths to increase your ability to do well on the exam. You might want to use the restroom before taking the exam so that your focus can be in the correct place during the exam.

- Manage your time in the exam. It is hard to answer a question correctly if you have run out of time and never see that question! If you have questions that you are unsure about, or if there is a simulation or lengthy question that may take several minutes, consider marking that question for review and come back to it after you have had an opportunity to answer the other questions. Often, other questions will refresh your memory and provide insight into questions that you have previously marked for review.

- Get ready for the performance-based questions to be grouped together and to be near the front of the exam. CompTIA has stuck to this formula pretty consistently. Doing this gives the students a little better chance at proper time management because these performance-based questions tend to take a bit more time than the multiple-choice questions.

- Smile at questions that are puzzling to you. The exam may give you an opportunity to learn a couple new things, and smiling when you see a tricky question can assist you in staying positive while you continue to answer the other questions that you know. It is likely that you will want to mark any puzzling questions for review and come back to them.

- Use your scratch paper in the exam to note the topics of questions that you are forced to take a best guess at. If you don't pass the exam, memorize this list of topics. These are areas you should spend extra time on in your preparation for your second (and hopefully final!) attempt. Focusing on these areas, repeat the preparation steps outlined in this chapter.

- Have fun with this process. If you are enjoying the journey, everything regarding this certification process will go much more smoothly.

Summary

The tools and suggestions listed in this chapter are designed with one goal in mind: to help you develop the skills required to pass the CompTIA Network+ exam. This book has been developed from the beginning to not just present you with a collection of facts but to help you learn how to apply those facts. Regardless of your experience level before reading this book, it is our hope that the broad range of preparation tools and the structure of the book will help you pass the exam with ease. We wish you success with your exam and hope that our paths will cross again as you continue to grow in your networking career.

Glossary of Key Terms

Numerics

3G The third generation of wireless mobile telecommunications technology.

4G The fourth generation of wireless mobile technology, which was designed as a complete replacement for earlier 3G technology. The first 4G networks were widely deployed starting in 2009.

5G The fifth generation of wireless mobile technology, which seeks to eventually replace 4G technology. This technology enhances performance once again and began to be deployed in 2019.

10BASE-T An Ethernet standard that transmits at 10Mbps over twisted wire pairs (telephone wire).

10GBASE-LR A 10-Gigabit Ethernet standard specified to transmit data over long distance through single-mode fiber. (The letters "LR" stand for "long range.")

10GBASE-SR A multimode fiber-optic medium. (The letters "SR" stand for "short range.")

10GBASE-T A type of Ethernet signaling providing speeds over twisted-pair cabling that go beyond 1Gbps for distances up to 100 meters.

40GBASE-T 40-Gigabit Ethernet over copper twisted-pair cabling.

66 block A block traditionally used in corporate environments for cross-connecting phone system cabling. As 10Mbps LANs started to grow in popularity in the late 1980s and early 1990s, these termination blocks were used to cross-connect Category 3 UTP cabling. The electrical characteristics (specifically, crosstalk) of a 66 block, however, do not support higher-speed LAN technologies, such as 100Mbps Ethernet networks.

100BASE-FX A version of Fast Ethernet over optical fiber.

100BASE-SX A version of Fast Ethernet over optical fiber standardized in TIA/EIA-785-1-2002. It is a lower-cost, shorter-distance alternative to 100BASE-FX.

100BASE-TX   The predominant form of Fast Ethernet, which runs over two wire pairs inside a Cat 5 or later cable. Each network segment can have a maximum cabling distance of 100 meters.

110 block   A block that can be used to terminate a cable (such as a Category 5 cable) used for high-speed LANs.

802.11a   A standard, ratified in 1999, that supports speeds as high as 54Mbps. Other supported data rates (which can be used if conditions are not suitable for the 54Mbps rate) include 6Mbps, 9Mbps, 12Mbps, 18Mbps, 24Mbps, 36Mbps, and 48Mbps. The 802.11a standard uses the 5GHz band and the OFDM transmission method.

802.11ac   An IEEE wireless networking standard that operates in the 5GHz range and provides increased throughput compared to previous WiFi IEEE standards.

802.11ax   A modern high-speed WLAN technology that uses the 6GHz spectrum in addition to the 2.4GHz and 5GHz bands. Also known as WiFi 6.

802.11b   A standard, ratified in 1999, that supports speeds as high as 11Mbps. However, 5.5Mbps is another supported data rate. The 802.11b standard uses the 2.4GHz band and the DSSS transmission method.

802.11g   A standard, ratified in 2003, that supports speeds as high as 54Mbps. As with 802.11a, other supported data rates include 6Mbps, 9Mbps, 12Mbps, 18Mbps, 24Mbps, 36Mbps, and 48Mbps. However, like 802.11b, 802.11g operates in the 2.4GHz band, which allows it to offer backward compatibility to 802.11b devices. 802.11g can use either the OFDM or DSSS transmission method.

802.11n   A standard, ratified in 2009, that supports a variety of speeds, depending on the implementation. Although the speed of an 802.11n network could approach 300Mbps (through the use of channel bonding), many 802.11n devices on the market have speed ratings in the 130Mbps–150Mbps range. An 802.11n WLAN can operate in the 2.4GHz band, the 5GHz band, or both simultaneously. 802.11n uses the OFDM transmission method.

802.1X   A type of NAC that can permit or deny a wireless or wired LAN client access to a network. If IEEE 802.1X is used to permit access to a LAN via a switch port, then IEEE 802.1X is being used for port security.

1000BASE-LX   An optical-fiber Gigabit Ethernet standard specified in IEEE 802.3 to work over a distance of up to 5 km over 10 μm single-mode fiber.

1000BASE-SX   An optical-fiber Gigabit Ethernet standard for operation over multimode fiber up to a distance of 220 to 550 meters, depending on the type of multimode fiber.

1000BASE-T   A standard for Gigabit Ethernet over copper wiring designed to work over a maximum length of 100 meters.

A

acceptable use policy (AUP)   A policy that identifies what users of a network are and are not allowed to do on that network. For example, retrieving sports scores during working hours via an organization's Internet connection might be deemed inappropriate by an AUP.

access control list (ACL)   Rules typically applied to router interfaces to specify permitted and denied traffic.

access control vestibule   A small entry area with two interlocking doors that prevents tailgating/piggybacking. Formerly called a mantrap.

access layer   A layer in the three-tier network design that is concerned with permitting end users fast and secure access to the network.

access point (AP)   In wireless networks, a device that permits wireless clients to access the network. Access points tend to fall into two categories: lightweight and autonomous. A lightweight AP cannot perform control plane functions and requires a wireless LAN controller (WLC) for the control plane. An autonomous AP does not require a WLC.

address (A)   A DNS record that maps a hostname to an IPv4 address.

Address Resolution Protocol (ARP) request   A broadcast asking for the MAC address corresponding to a known IP address. An ARP reply contains the requested MAC address.

administrative distance (AD)   A routing protocol's index of believability. Routing protocols with a smaller AD are considered more believable than routing protocols with a higher AD.

Advanced Encryption Standard (AES)   A symmetric block cipher implemented in hardware and software that protects sensitive or confidential data through encryption. AES offers various levels of strength.

angled physical contact (APC)   A type of fiber connector that minimizes back reflection due to a 5° to 15° angle-polish applied to end faces

anycast   A communication that has a one-to-nearest (from the perspective of a router's routing table) flow.

AP association time   The amount of time it takes to associate a client with an AP. This can also be a measure of the delay when the AP is associating to a wireless LAN controller.

application layer   In software-defined networking, the logical layer that that presents the applications to the network manager. These applications allow simple control over the environment, permitting the engineer to configure and monitor the network as needed.

application layer (OSI model)   The application layer is Layer 7 of the OSI model. This top layer of the model provides applications access to network services.

arp   A command that can be used in either a Microsoft Windows or UNIX environment to see what Layer 2 MAC addresses correspond to Layer 3 IP addresses.

ARP spoofing   An attack that involves falsifying a Layer 2 MAC address in order to bypass simple MAC-based security mechanisms, such as port security.

asset tag   A tag applied to a physical network asset to permit the monitoring of the location of this device.

asymmetrical routing   A type of routing in which an exit path does not match an entry path of traffic. This is sometimes very undesirable and can cause issues for applications.

attenuation   The weakening of a signal as a result of distance between two network devices.

audit and assessment report   A report that helps identify and address critical issues that might be occurring in the network infrastructure. This report often identifies performance and security issues that need to be addressed to help ensure that the network continues to function as desired.

audit logs   Log files that contain records of actions that were performed in the network. For example, audit logs could contain records of the user accounts that successfully (or unsuccessfully) tried to access a key network resource.

auditing (AAAA)   A DNS IPv6 address record that maps a hostname to an IPv6 address.

authentication   In a network, the process in which a device attempts to prove its identity to another device.

Authentication Header (AH)   An IPsec protocol that provides authentication and integrity services but that does not provide encryption services.

authentication server   In a network using 802.1X user authentication, a server (typically, a RADIUS server) that checks a supplicant's credentials. If the credentials are acceptable, the authentication server notifies the authenticator that the supplicant is allowed to communicate on the network. The authentication server also gives the authenticator a key that can be used to securely transmit data during the authenticator's session with the supplicant.

authenticator   In a network using 802.1X user authentication, a device called an authenticator forwards a supplicant's authentication request on to an authentication server. After the authentication server authenticates the supplicant, the authenticator receives a key that is used to communicate securely during a session with the supplicant.

authorization   In a network, a definition of what users are permitted to do. Note that authorization often follows an authentication phase.

Automatic Private IP Addressing (APIPA)   A feature that allows a networked device to self-assign an IP address from the 169.254.0.0/16 network. Note that this address is usable only on the device's local subnet (meaning that the IP address is not routable).

automation   The automated completion of a task or tasks.

available leases   The number of remaining IP addresses available to be leased to clients in a DHCP scope.

B

backbone   Another name for the core layer of the classic three-tier network design. This is also the name given to area 0 in OSPF.

badge reader   A device used to read ID badges worn by employees of an organization to assist with physical security.

bandwidth   The measure of network throughput possible on network media or a network path.

bandwidth speed tester   Software or hardware that is designed to test the true speed of a link, which will vary from the advertised theoretical maximum bandwidth of the technology.

baseline configuration documentation   Documentation that makes it possible to return network equipment to the exact configurations that existed at a specific point in time. Various stages of the network device life cycles can be captured in baselines.

baseline   A collection of data portraying the characteristics of a network under normal operating conditions. Data collected while troubleshooting can be contrasted against baseline data.

basic service set (BSS) WLAN   A WLAN that has just one AP. BSS WLANs are said to run in infrastructure mode because wireless clients connect to an AP, which is typically connected to a wired network infrastructure. BSS networks are often used in residential and SOHO locations, where the signal strength provided by a single AP is sufficient to service all of the WLAN's wireless clients.

bidirectional wavelength-division multiplexing (WDM)   The transmission of optical channels on a fiber propagating simultaneously in both directions. This is accomplished by use of either a wavelength division multiplexing (WDM) technique on a single fiber, or unidirectional transmission over two fibers.

biometrics   The use of unique characteristics of the human body to provide access credentials and security. For example, a thumbprint can be used to access a mobile device.

block size   The number of IP addresses in a subnet, including the subnet's address and the subnet's directed broadcast address.

Bootstrap Protocol   A legacy broadcast-based protocol used by networked devices to obtain IP address information.

Border Gateway Protocol (BGP)   A path-vector routing protocol that can use as its metric the number of autonomous system hops that must be transited to reach a destination network, as opposed to the number of required router hops. BGP is the only EGP in widespread use today, and it is considered to be the routing protocol that runs the Internet.

borrowed bits   Bits added to a classful subnet mask.

botnet/command and control   A collection of compromised systems used in a distributed denial-of-service (DDoS) attack. The attacker uses command and control software to control the compromised systems.

bottom-to-top troubleshooting   A troubleshooting methodology in which the engineer starts at the physical layer of the OSI model and works up the stack, trying to determine the problem.

bridge   The predecessor technology to switches. Bridges could connect different types of networks. While this was important so that the two networks could communicate, it also ended up creating additional broadcast domains.

bring your own device (BYOD) policy   A policy that specifies the types of permitted devices, security, data, and applications as well as offloading procedures when an employee leaves a company.

broadcast storm   A problem that results when excessive broadcast packets flood a network area. It might be caused by an issue with Spanning Tree Protocol (STP), which is designed to protect against broadcast storms due to redundancy in the design.

brute-force A form of password attack in which the attacker tries all possible password combinations until a match is made.

Building Industry Cross-connect (Bix) A commonly used networking panel that terminates 25 pairs (50 wires) that are punched down to one side of a wafer. The wafer is then inserted into the metal frame with the punched-down side against the wall, so only the unused side is visible.

bus topology A topology that typically uses a cable running through the area requiring connectivity; devices to be networked can tap into that cable.

business continuity plan (BCP) A comprehensive policy that includes a disaster recovery plan. It may be broken down into supporting plans and policies that encompass topics such as business resumption plans and incident management.

C

cable Broadband Internet connection provided by a cable TV company. This infrastructure might include either coaxial or fiber-optic cabling—or both.

cable crimper A tool used to attach a connector (for example, an RJ45 connector) to the end of an unshielded twisted-pair (UTP) cable.

cable modem A device that attaches to the same coaxial cable (typically in a residence) that provides television programming. A cable modem can use predetermined frequency ranges to transmit and receive data over that coaxial cable.

cable stripper A tool that is often built in to cable crimpers. The cable stripping capability of a tool permits the plastic shielding to be removed from cables.

cable tester A tool that can check the conductors in an Ethernet cable. It contains two parts. By connecting these parts of the cable tester to each end of a cable under test, it is possible to check the wires in the cable for continuity (that is, check to make sure that there are no opens, or breaks, in a conductor). In addition, it is possible to verify an RJ45 connector's pinouts (which are wires connected to the appropriate pins on an RJ45 connector).

camera A device that permits the viewing of key network areas using video surveillance. Video footage is often recorded and stored locally or in the cloud. Modern camera systems have been combined with more advanced intelligence and even have the ability to detect weapons and other threats.

campus area network (CAN) An interconnection of networks located in nearby buildings (for example, buildings on a college campus).

canonical name (CNAME)   A DNS canonical name record that aliases an existing record, thus allowing multiple DNS records to map to the same IP address.

captive portal   Typically, a web page designed to collect the username and password of a user trying to gain access to a network or an application. Such a portal might require the user to agree to an acceptable use policy (AUP).

carrier-sense multiple access with collision detection (CSMA/CD)   A media access control method used on an Ethernet network to help prevent collisions from occurring and to recover if collisions do occur. CSMA/CD is only needed on half-duplex connections.

Cat 5   Category 5 twisted-pair cable. Supports 10BASE-T, 100BASE-TX (Fast Ethernet), 1000BASE-T (Gigabit Ethernet), 2.5GBASE-T, and 5GBASE-T.

Cat 5e   Category 5e twisted-pair cable. Supports Gigabit Ethernet (10/100/1000Mbps).

Cat 6   Category 6 twisted-pair cable. Supports 10G Ethernet (10/100/1000/10000Mbps) and reduces crosstalk for more reliable connections at Gigabit speeds.

Cat 6a   Category 6a twisted-pair cable. Support frequencies up to 500MHz and speeds up to 10Gbps.

Cat 7   Category 7 twisted-pair cable used in high-speed Ethernet based computer networks of 1Gbps or higher.

Cat 8   Category 8 twisted-pair cable. Differs greatly from the previous cables in that it supports a frequency of up to 2GHz (2000MHz) and is limited to a 30-meter two-connector channel. Supports speeds of 25Gbps or even 40Gbps.

change management (CM)   In networking, careful planning and policy creation to accommodate thoughtful and warranted changes to the network infrastructure and configurations.

channel bonding   A process in which two wireless bands are logically bonded together, forming a band with twice the bandwidth of an individual band. Some literature calls channel bonding 40MHz mode, which refers to the bonding of two adjacent 20MHz bands into a 40MHz band.

channel overlap   A wireless issue in the 2.4GHz band that causes interference. In order to avoid this issue, adjacent WLAN segments should be placed on nonoverlapping channels—that is, channels 1, 6, and 11 in the 2.4GHz band. Notice channel overlap is not an issue in the 5 GHz band.

classful mask   The default subnet mask applied to Class A, B, and C IPv4 networks. Specifically, Class A networks have the classful mask 255.0.0.0, Class B networks have the classful mask 255.255.0.0, and Class C networks have the classful mask 255.255.255.0.

classless interdomain routing (CIDR)   A process that involves shortening a classful subnet mask by removing right-justified 1s from a classful mask. As a result, CIDR allows contiguous classful networks to be aggregated. This process is sometimes called *route aggregation*.

client   With NTP, a network device that consumes the correct time from an NTP server system.

client/server network   A network in which a dedicated server (for example, a file server or a print server) provides shared access to a resource (for example, files or a printer). Clients (for example, PCs) on the network with appropriate privilege levels can gain access to those shared resources.

client-to-site virtual private network (VPN)   Also known as a remote-access VPN, a virtual network that interconnects a remote user with a site. The remote user is typically using a broadband Internet connection and software running in the OS that configures and maintains the VPN connection.

clientless virtual private network (VPN)   A virtual network that has a client software piece that is not a separate piece of software. In this arrangement, the client's web browser acts as the VPN client software. This type of VPN connection leverages the SSL/TLS capabilities of the modern Internet and web browsers in order to provide a secured connection.

cloud site   A recovery site in the cloud that can be configured for cold, warm, or hot behavior, typically with ease. Cloud sites offer lower costs and relaxed technological requirements compared to physical recovery sites.

coaxial/RG6   A network cable that is composed of two conductors. One of the conductors is an inner insulated conductor. This inner conductor is surrounded by another conductor. This second conductor is sometimes made of a metallic foil or woven wire. RG6 is used to distribute HDTV signals in a home or office. RG6QS uses quad shielding for better signal quality over long runs. Also known as coax.

code-division multiple access (CDMA)   A technology that allows several transmitters to send information simultaneously over a single communication channel so that several users can share a band of frequencies. CDMA is used as the access method in many mobile phone standards.

cold site   A barebones redundant site for a network that requires time and effort to bring online.

collision   A problem that occurs when two devices on an Ethernet network simultaneously transmit frames. Because an Ethernet segment cannot handle more than one frame at a time, both frames in a collision become corrupted.

Common Vulnerabilities and Exposures (CVE)   A free online resource that provides excellent search tools to leverage a large database of publicly known information security vulnerabilities and exposures.

community cloud   Cloud services used by individuals, companies, or entities with similar interests. The community cloud is typically a partnership between many different cloud vendors or organizations.

confidentiality, integrity, and availability (CIA)   A security principle that helps in securing a network. It entail using confidentiality (often using encryption), integrity (often using hashing algorithms), and availability with a wide variety of security mechanisms.

connection-oriented   Refers to transport protocols that provide reliable transport, in that if a segment is dropped, the sender can detect that drop and retransmit the dropped segment. Specifically, a receiver acknowledges segments that it receives. Based on those acknowledgments, a sender can determine which segments were successfully received.

connectionless   Refers to transport protocols that are sent unreliably. There is no session created in which flow control and error checking types of behaviors take place. UDP is the connectionless transport protocol of the transport layer of the OSI model.

console cable   A cable used to make a console connection to a network device such as router.

control layer   In software-defined networking, the layer of abstraction that defines the control plane operations, which might include a centralized controller and both southbound and northbound APIs.

control plane policing (CoPP)   An implementation of policing for the control plane of a network device that protects the device from many different potential DoS attacks targeting control plane protocols such as OSPF and BGP.

core layer   S layer in the three-layer network design that is concerned with speed.

course wavelength division multiplexing (CWDM)   A technology that allows up to 18 channels to be connected over a dark fiber pair.

crossover cable   A cable that can be used to directly connect two devices—such as two computer systems—or as a means to expand networks that use devices such as hubs or switches. A traditional crossover cable is a UTP cable in which the wires are crossed for the purposes of placing the transmit line of one device on the receive line of the other.

current state modulation   A way to electrically or optically represent binary digits by using a binary 1 for the presence of voltage on a copper cable or the presence of light on a fiber-optic cable and using a binary 0 for the absence of light or voltage.

cutter   A tool used to cut cables and other cabling accessories.

cyclic redundancy check (CRC)   A mathematical algorithm that is executed on a data string by both the sender and the receiver of the data string. If the calculated CRC values match, the receiver can conclude that the data string was not corrupted during transmission.

D

data as a service (DaaS)   A cloud-based service that uses software tools for working with data. Of course, all of these software tools are cloud-based.

data link layer   Layer 2 of the OSI model, which is concerned with packaging data into frames and transmitting those frames on a network, performing error detection/correction, uniquely identifying network devices with an address, and handling flow control.

data loss prevention   The practice of detecting and preventing data breaches, exfiltration, or unwanted destruction of sensitive data in an organization.

deauthentication   A type of attack in which the attacker sends a deauthentication frame to the victim in order to disconnect the user from the wireless LAN. Such an attack is usually followed up with another form of attack, such as an evil twin.

decibel (dB) loss   A loss of signal power. If a transmission's dB loss is too great, the transmission cannot be properly interpreted by the intended recipient.

default gateway   The IP address of a router (or multilayer switch) to which a network device sends traffic destined for a subnet other than the device's local subnet.

default static route   An administratively configured entry in a router's routing table that specifies where traffic for all unknown networks should be sent.

default VLAN   The VLAN assigned to interfaces on a device when no explicit VLAN assignment has been made.

defense in depth   A technique that involves striving to secure each layer of a solution.

demarcation point (demarc)   The point in a telephone network where the maintenance responsibility passes from a telephone company to a subscriber (unless the subscriber purchased an inside wiring plan). This demarc is typically a box mounted to the outside of a customer's building (for example, a residence).

denial-of-service (DoS)   A type of attack that floods a system with an excessive amount of traffic or requests, consuming the system's processing resources and preventing the system from responding to many legitimate requests.

dense wavelength-division multiplexing (DWDM)   An optical multiplexing technology used to increase bandwidth over existing fiber networks. DWDM works by combining and transmitting multiple signals simultaneously at different wavelengths on the same fiber.

designated port   In an STP topology, a single port on a network segment that is closest to the root bridge, in terms of cost. All ports on a root bridge are designated ports.

DHCP relay   A device (often a router or a server) that can convert broadcast DHCP DISCOVER messages to unicast packets so that they can be forwarded to a DHCP server on another TCP/IP subnet. Normally these broadcast messages would be dropped by a router on a segment.

DHCP scope exhaustion   A situation that occurs when there are no available IP addresses to lease out to clients.

DHCP snooping   The process of securing a network against a rogue DHCP server attack or other types of DHCP security attacks.

DHCPv6   The IPv6 version of Dynamic Host Configuration Protocol (DHCP).

dictionary   An attack, similar to a brute-force password attack, that uses commonly used words (rather than every combination) to determine a password.

dig   A command that can resolve an FQDN to an IP address on UNIX hosts.

digital subscriber line (DSL)   A group of technologies that provide high-speed data transmission over existing telephone wiring. DSL has several variants that differ in terms of data rates and distance limitations.

disaster recovery plan (DRP)   A documented process to execute an organization's disaster recovery processes. A DRP is designed to help recover and protect IT infrastructure in the event of a disaster.

distance   In reference to wired and wireless media, how far a signal can travel over media before it weakens and suffers from the effects of attenuation.

distance-vector   A type of routing protocol that determines the best route for data packets based on distance.

distributed denial-of-service (DDoS)   An attack that can increase the amount of traffic flooded to a target system. Specifically, an attacker compromises multiple systems, and those compromised systems, called zombies, can be instructed by the attacker to simultaneously launch a DDoS attack against a target system.

distribution layer   A layer in the three-tier network design that is concerned with routing traffic to remote destinations.

divide-and-conquer troubleshooting   A troubleshooting methodology in which an engineer starts at a precise layer of the OSI model based on information collected. The engineer might move up or down from that layer after discovering more information.

DMZ   *See* screened subnet.

DNS caching   A process that keeps the name-to-IP address mapping in memory for subsequent usage. A DNS TTL ensures that entries time out after some time period, which helps ensure that cached information has not gone stale.

DNS poisoning   The introduction of false data into the DNS system.

DNS record types   DNS records stored in a database that include the actual DNS names and appropriate associated IP addresses.

DNS server   A server that resolves a domain name (for example, www.ciscopress.com) to a corresponding IP address (for example, 10.1.2.3).

DNS Time-to-Live (TTL)   The amount of time DNS clients or servers are permitted to cache resolution entries for quick recall when needed on the network. The shorter the DNS TTL, the more current the DNS information that is available, but this might come at the cost of more "cache misses," where the information cannot be quickly recalled from system memory.

Domain Name System (DNS)   A system that resolves a domain name (for example, www.ciscopress.com) to a corresponding IP address (for example, 10.1.2.3).

dotted-decimal notation   A method of writing an IPv4 address or subnet mask, where groups of 8 bits (called octets) are separated by periods.

DSL modem   A local device that makes data transfers possible in DSL WAN environments. DSL is a relatively high-speed WAN (Internet) option that operates over the POTS.

dual stack   The ability of a network interface to run multiple protocols, such as IPv4 and IPv6.

Dynamic ARP Inspection (DAI)   A feature that ensures that MAC addresses coordinate to the Layer 3 addresses as they should.

dynamic assignment   The automatic assignment of IP address information in a network. In a TCP/IPv4 environment, this is most often accomplished with DHCP.

Dynamic Host Configuration Protocol (DHCP)   A protocol that dynamically assigns IP address information (for example, IP address, subnet mask, DNS server's IP address, and default gateway's IP address) to network devices.

dynamic routing   The process of distributing network prefix information through a network so that traffic can be forwarded to network destinations. The opposite approach to dynamic routing is static routing, where an administrator trains a network device how to reach network destinations.

E

east–west traffic flow   The flow of traffic in a datacenter, where the traffic moves horizontally between devices.

effective isotropic radiated power (EIRP)/power settings   A value that seeks to measure the maximum amount of power that could be radiated from an antenna. This value must incorporate the antenna gain and the transmitter power of the RF system.

elasticity   Refers to the ability of a cloud solution to grow and shrink as needed.

employee training   A proactive way to ensure that employees are aware of company policies and educated on cybersecurity threats such as social engineering.

Encapsulating Security Payload (ESP)   An IPsec protocol that provides authentication, integrity, and encryption services.

enhanced form-factor pluggable (SFP+)   A compact, hot-swappable transceiver designed to support 100/1000Mbps Ethernet, 10Gbps Ethernet, Fibre Channel, and SONET, among other communication standards.

Enhanced Interior Gateway Routing Protocol (EIGRP)   A Cisco-proprietary protocol that is popular in Cisco-only networks but less popular in mixed-vendor networks. Like OSPF, EIGRP is an IGP with very fast convergence and high scalability. EIGRP is considered to be an advanced distance-vector or a hybrid routing protocol.

enhanced quad small form-factor pluggable (QSFP+)   A compact, hot-swappable transceiver that supports Ethernet, Fibre Channel, InfiniBand, and SONET/SDH standards with different data rate options.

Ethernet   A Layer 1 technology developed by Xerox that encompasses a variety of standards that specify various media types, speeds, and distance limitations.

EUI-64   A method used to automatically configure IPv6 host addresses.

evil twin   A device that is postured to appear like a legitimate access point on a network to carry out a wireless attack.

exclusion range   A range of IP addresses that are not assigned to clients of a network. It is often necessary to configure these ranges to avoid inadvertently leasing out IP addresses that are already statically assigned to servers or key routers in an organization.

exploit   A detailed description of what exactly occurred with a security breach. An exploit often describes the most likely attacker, the technology used, and any vulnerabilities or misconfigurations that made it possible.

extended service set (ESS) WAN   A WLAN containing more than one AP. Like BSS WLANs, ESS WLANs operate in infrastructure mode. With more than one AP, it is important to prevent one AP from interfering with another. Specifically, nonoverlapping channels (that is, channels 1, 6, and 11 for the 2.4GHz band) should be selected for adjacent wireless coverage areas.

Extensible Authentication Protocol (EAP)   A security protocol for networking that expands the authentication methods used by the early Point-to-Point Protocol (PPP). EAP is used on encrypted networks to provide a secure way to send identifying information to provide network authentication.

Exterior Gateway Protocol (EGP)   A routing protocol that operates between autonomous systems, which are networks under different administrative control. Border Gateway Protocol (BGP) is the only EGP in widespread use today.

external DNS server   A DNS server that is external to an organization (most often located on the Internet). An organization might not control (at all) the external DNS servers.

F

F-type connector   A connector used for cable, satellite, and fixed wireless Internet and TV service. F-connectors can be crimped or attached via compression to coaxial cable.

factory reset   The process of restoring a network device to factory settings to ensure that it contains no data or settings that are specific to the organization.

fiber distribution panel   A networking panel used for accommodating fiber cable terminations, connections, and patching.

fiber light meter   A device used to measure the power in an optical signal. The term usually refers to a device for testing average power in fiber-optic systems.

File Transfer Protocol (FTP)   A protocol capable of transferring files over a network.

firewall   Primarily a network security appliance that can protect a trusted network (for example, a corporate LAN) from an untrusted network (for example, the

Internet) by allowing the trusted network to send traffic into the untrusted network and receive the return traffic from the untrusted network while blocking traffic for sessions that were initiated on the untrusted network.

First Hop Redundancy Protocol (FHRP)   A protocol that permits redundancy for the Layer 3 gateway function. There are several protocols to choose from in this category.

floor plan   A drawing to scale, typically showing a view from above, of the relationships between rooms, spaces, traffic patterns, and other physical features at one level of a structure.

forward lookup   A standard DNS query in which the client has the name of the network resource and it is requesting the IP address associated with this name.

full tunnel VPN   A VPN in which all traffic is sent down the VPN connection. Contrast this to a split tunnel VPN.

full-duplex   A connection that allows a device to simultaneously transmit and receive data.

full-mesh topology   A network topology that directly connects every site to every other site.

fusion splicer   A tool used to join two fibers together by using heat.

G

generator   A device that converts motive power (mechanical energy) into electrical power for use in an external circuit. Sources of mechanical energy include steam turbines, gas turbines, water turbines, internal combustion engines, wind turbines, and even hand cranks.

Generic Routing Encapsulation (GRE)   A tunneling protocol used to encapsulate a wide variety of network layer protocols inside virtual point-to-point links or point-to-multipoint links over an IP network.

geofencing   A virtual perimeter of a geographic area. For example, a wireless geofence boundary around a datacenter could send an alarm if equipment leaves the perimeter.

giants   A packet larger than 1500 bytes.

global DNS hierarchy   In the DNS database system, the strict hierarchy in domain naming or in servers that make up the DNS system.

Global System for Mobile Communications (GSM)   A standard developed by the European Telecommunications Standards Institute (ETSI) to describe the protocols for second-generation digital cellular networks used by mobile devices such as tablets.

H

half-duplex   A connection that allows a device to either receive or transmit data at any one time. However, a half-duplex device cannot simultaneously transmit and receive.

heating, ventilation, and air conditioning (HVAC)   Technology used for indoor and vehicular environmental control of temperature and air quality.

hold-down timer   A timer that can speed the convergence process of a routing protocol. After a router makes a change to a route entry, the hold-down timer prevents subsequent updates for a specified period of time. This approach can help stop flapping routes (which are routes that oscillate between being available and unavailable) from preventing convergence.

honeypot   A system that appears to be an attractive attack target to entice attackers into thinking the system is real. The attackers then use their resources to attack the honeypot and leave the real servers alone.

hostname   On a Windows system, the command that simply displays the computer name. On a Linux system, a command used to change the computer name or the domain name of a system.

hot site   A redundant datacenter location that is ready to replace a failed datacenter with little to no time or effort.

hub   An older technology used to interconnect network components, such as clients and servers. Hubs vary in the number of available ports. A hub does not perform inspection of the traffic it passes. Rather, a hub simply receives traffic in a port and repeats that traffic out all of its other ports.

hub-and-spoke topology   A network topology used to interconnect multiple sites (for example, multiple corporate locations) via WAN links, with a WAN link from each remote site (a spoke site) to the main site (the hub site).

HVAC sensor   A sensor that facilitates connectivity of an HVAC system to a network for maintenance and configuration purposes.

hybrid cloud   An environment that features private cloud services, some of which interact with public clouds.

hybrid routing protocol   A routing protocol that features aspects of different routing protocol techniques. For example, EIGRP has aspects that are taken from both the distance-vector and link-state routing protocol approaches.

Hypertext Transfer Protocol (HTTP)   An insecure protocol for retrieving HTML (and other files) over an IP network. HTTP is the basis for the Internet as we know it today.

Hypertext Transfer Protocol over SSL (HTTPS)   A protocol for securing web traffic over the Internet by using Secure Socket Layer and Transport Layer Security technology.

hypervisor   Software that makes the virtualization of underlying hardware possible. Hypervisors are divided into Type 1 and Type 2 variants. Type 1 hypervisors install directly on "bare metal," and Type 2 hypervisors install within an OS.

I

ifconfig   A command used to display IP address configuration parameters on a UNIX/Linux system.

IMAP over SSL   The secure version of IMAP, which uses SSL for security, much as HTTPS uses SSL.

in-band management   Management traffic that is sent on the same paths and equipment as data traffic.

incident response policies   Policies designed to deal with any encountered security issues, typically consisting of the following phases: prepare, identify, contain, eradicate, recover, and review.

incorrect transceiver   A transceiver selected for a network device that does not match the cable type used and the wavelengths in use in a network.

independent basic service set (IBSS) ad hoc   A WLAN that is created without the use of an AP. Such a configuration, called an IBSS, is said to work in an ad hoc fashion. An ad hoc WLAN is useful for temporary connections between wireless devices. For example, it might be necessary to temporarily interconnect two laptop computers to transfer a few files.

industrial control system (ICS)/supervisory control and data acquisition (SCADA)   A system that is used to control remote equipment and to monitor that equipment. It may be part of an ICS that is used to manage a power plant or water treatment facility.

infrastructure as code (IaC)   A cloud capability that makes it possible to easily automate, and even orchestrate, common networking tasks that used to take weeks or months to carry out on physical servers.

infrastructure as a service (IaaS)   A cloud service model in which the company rents virtualized servers (which are hosted by a service provider) and runs specific applications on those servers.

infrastructure layer   In software-defined networking, the layer where the networking devices are defined.

interface status   An indication of the operational and administrative characteristics of an interface. For example, on a multilayer switch, part of the interface status can be whether the port will function as a router port (Layer 3) or a switch port (Layer 2).

interference   In networking, the disruptive modification of a signal as it travels along a communication channel between source and receiver. The term is often used to refer to the addition of unwanted signals during a useful and expected signal. A common example is radar impacting a WiFi LAN that receives the unwanted radar signals.

Interior Gateway Protocol (IGP)   A routing protocol that operates within an autonomous system, which is a network under a single administrative control. OSPF and EIGRP are popular examples of IGPs.

intermediate distribution frame (IDF)/main distribution frame (MDF) documentation   Documentation specific to the IDF and MDF facilities of an organization. These distribution and core facilities house critical network data and devices, and proper documentation can aid in all forms of maintenance and security.

internal DNS server   A DNS server that is part of an organization's network and equipment.

Internet Control Message Protocol (ICMP)   A transport layer protocol used by utilities such as **ping** and **traceroute**.

Internet layer   The layer of the TCP/IP stack that maps to Layer 3 (the network layer) of the OSI model. Although multiple routed protocols (for example, IPv4 and IPv6) may reside at the OSI model's network layer, the Internet layer of the TCP/IP stack focuses on IP as the protocol to be routed through a network.

Internet Message Access Protocol (IMAP)   A protocol that retrieves email from an email server. It is only one option of many for the retrieval of email from such servers. IMAP uses TCP port 143 in its operation.

Internet of Things (IoT)   A network of physical objects (things) that possess embedded sensors, software, and other technologies for the purpose of exchanging data with other devices and systems. Often, the connectivity is with devices over the Internet. These devices are often called smart devices.

Internet Protocol Security (IPsec)   A complex suite of protocols that are used to create secured connections between network systems.

intrusion detection system (IDS) device   An system that seeks to recognize attack traffic and prevent that traffic from entering a network or devices.

intrusion prevention system (IPS)   A system that seeks to alert administrators regarding a cybersecurity attack but that typically does not prevent the attack through its own actions.

ip   A command used to assign an address to a network interface or configure network interface parameters in Linux systems. It replaces the **ifconfig** command in modern Linux versions.

IP address spoofing   Falsifying the IP address information in a packet.

IP header   Information at the beginning of an Internet Protocol (IP) packet that enables proper addressing and routing.

IP helper/UDP forwarding   A DHCP relay agent, which can forward DHCP DISCOVER messages as unicast packets to the DHCP server housed on a remote subnet.

IP scanner   A tool that is designed to efficiently gather IP address information for the nodes in a network.

ipconfig   A Microsoft Windows command that can be used to display IP address configuration parameters on a PC. In addition, if the PC uses DHCP, the **ipconfig** command can be used to release and renew a DHCP lease, which can be useful during troubleshooting.

iperf   A tool for network performance measurement and tuning. It is a cross-platform tool that can produce standardized performance measurements for any network.

iterative lookup   A DNS lookup in which the client indicates it will accept the answer, or a referral to another DNS server that might have the answer.

J–K–L

jitter   The uneven arrival of packets.

Kerberos   A client/server authentication protocol that supports mutual authentication between a client and a server. Kerberos uses the concept of a trusted third party (a key distribution center) that hands out tickets to be used instead of a username and password combination.

Krone   A proprietary European alternative to 110 block. Krone is used in data environments and also television broadcasting.

latency   A measure of the delay in a network.

Layer 2 switch   A transparent switch that is not capable of routing. This switch tends to be lower cost and is designed for access layers in networks.

Layer 3–capable switch   *See* multilayer switch.

lease time   The amount of time that a DHCP client gets to maintain its DHCP-learned information before it must surrender or renew this information.

leased line   Typically a point-to-point connection interconnecting two sites. All the bandwidth on that dedicated leased line is available to those sites. Often referred to as a dedicated leased line.

least privilege   An important security best practice that dictates that every user who interacts with the network should always be using a user account that has the least privileges possible.

LED status indicators   Indicators on a networking device that signal whether operations are functioning as expected.

Lightweight Directory Access Protocol (LDAP)   An open standard for storing directory information for the network such as usernames and passwords and other user and computer parameters.

Lightweight Directory Access Protocol over SSL (LDAPS)   A secure version of LDAP in which SSL provides protection.

link aggregation   As defined by the IEEE 802.3ad standard, a process that allows multiple physical connections to be logically bundled into a single logical connection.

link-local   A nonroutable IP address that is usable only on a local subnet.

link-state   A category of routing protocol that maintains a topology of a network and uses an algorithm to determine the shortest path to a destination network.

link-state advertisement (LSA)   A message is sent by a router in a network to advertise the networks the router knows how to reach. Routers use LSAs to construct a topological map of a network. The algorithm run against this topological map is Dijkstra's shortest path first algorithm.

load balancer   A networking device that distributes traffic from clients (or other sources) to multiple nodes to increase performance and availability.

load balancing   The process of distributing client requests among different network resources that can provide the same service or data.

local area network (LAN)   A network that interconnects network components within a local region (for example, within a building).

local authentication   The process in which a network device authenticates a user with a database of user account information stored on the device itself; this is often an important fallback method of authentication used when another external method fails.

local connector (LC)   A terminating device used with fiber-optic cabling.

locking cabinets/racks   Cabinets or racks for network equipment that have locking cages over them to assist with physical security.

logic bomb   An attacker's malicious code that resides in a software system and will be triggered when certain conditions are met.

logical network diagram   A diagram that focuses on how information flows through a network infrastructure. Such diagrams tend to omit details used in physical network diagrams as the concern is with the overall information flows through many underlying network devices.

logical topology   A topology of the network that is based on the flow of traffic.

Long-Term Evolution (LTE)   A standard for wireless broadband communication for mobile devices based on the GSM/EDGE and UMTS/HSPA technologies. It increases capacity and speed by using a different radio interface together with core network improvements.

loopback   An logical (virtual) interface on a network device that is often used for testing purposes.

loopback plug   A device that connects the transmit pins on an Ethernet connector to the receive pins, such that everything that is transmitted is received back on the interface.

M

MAC filtering   A security method in which the MAC address assigned to each network card is used to determine access to the network. It is often used as an additional security measure in WiFi environments.

MAC spoofing   An attack in which the cybercriminal pretends to possess a different MAC address from what they actually have on their system. This is often the first step in a much larger and more sophisticated attack.

mail exchange (MX)   A DNS mail exchange record that maps a domain name to an email (or message transfer agent) server for that domain.

malware   A catchall term for the various types of viruses, worms, spyware, Trojans, and other malicious software or code on a network.

Management Information Base (MIB)   A database of variables that exist on an SNMP-managed device.

management layer   In software-defined networking, the layer used to describe the various network management protocols that might be in use to manage the various other layers of the solution.

maximum transmission unit (MTU)   The largest packet size supported on an interface.

mean time between failures (MTBF)   The predicted elapsed time between inherent failures in a mechanical system.

mean time to repair (MTTR)   The predicted time it takes to repair a network or network object.

mechanical transfer (MT)   A connector used for fiber-optic cables.

media converter   A device that connects different types of network devices together, such as a fiber-optic device that needs to communicate with a twisted-pair device in a network segment OR An adapter used to facilitate connectivity in an environment with a wide variety of copper and fiber cabling used by different network devices.

memorandum of understanding (MOU)   An agreement between two parties that outlines the roles and responsibilities that each will play.

metric   A value assigned to a route. Lower metrics are preferred over higher metrics.

metro-optical   The optical-based based WAN portion of a metropolitan area network. This is often implemented with SONET.

metropolitan area network (MAN)   A network that interconnects locations scattered throughout a metropolitan area.

motion detection   A physical security approach that involves using sensors to detect motion in a secured area.

multi-user MIMO (MU-MIMO)   A technology for wireless communication that relies on multiple users or terminals, each radioing over one or more antennas to communicate with one another.

multicast   A one-to-many communication flow.

multicast flooding   The process of sending a multicast packet to all ports of a VLAN.

multifactor   A type of authentication that requires two or more types of successful authentication before access to a network is granted.

multilayer switch   A switch that can make traffic forwarding decisions based on Layer 3 information. These powerful devices are often modular, so it is possible to equip them with the "perfect" number of interfaces for Layer 2 and Layer 3 functionality.

multimeter   A tool used to check the electrical characteristics of cabling, including resistance (in ohms), current (in amps), and voltage (in volts).

multimode   A type of fiber-optic cabling that has a core with a diameter large enough to permit the injection of light at multiple angles. The different paths (that is, modes) that light travels can lead to multimode delay distortion, which causes bits to be received out of order because the pulses of light representing the bits traveled different paths (and therefore different distances).

multipathing   The process of creating multiple paths that data can take in a network. Routing protocols can make these multiple paths very valuable to use since they can engage in what is called equal-cost multipathing (ECMP).

multiple-input multiple-output (MIMO)   A technology that uses multiple antennas for transmission and reception. These antennas do not interfere with one another, thanks to the use of spatial multiplexing, which encodes data based on the antenna from which the data will be transmitted. Both reliability and throughput can be increased with MIMO's simultaneous use of multiple antennas.

Multipoint Generic Routing Encapsulation (mGRE)   A version of the GRE encapsulation protocol that permits a local device to make multiple GRE connections to various remote devices. This technology is a key ingredient in the Cisco DMVPN solution.

multiprotocol label switching (MPLS)   A WAN technology popular among service providers that performs label switching to forward traffic within an MPLS cloud by inserting a 32-bit header (which contains a 20-bit label) between a frame's Layer 2 and Layer 3 headers and making forwarding decisions based on the label within an MPLS header.

multitenancy   A situation in which physical servers in the public cloud infrastructure are hosting workloads for many different customers.

MySQL   An open-source relational database management system (RDBMS) based on a client/server model.

N

name server (NS)   A DNS record that delegates a DNS zone to use the given authoritative name servers.

neighbor discovery   A process whereby network elements can discover each other on the network. In the case of EIGRP, hello packets are used, for example.

NetFlow   A software system that seeks to collect key network traffic information (statistics) and, most commonly, send these statistics to a central network collector.

NetFlow analyzer   Software that can consume NetFlow data from remote systems and provide analysis of the information.

netstat   A command that can display a variety of information about IP-based connections on a Windows or UNIX host.

network access control (NAC)   A process that uses a set of protocols to ensure that users are identified immediately when they try to access the network. A NAC system might integrate automatic remediation processes that can fix issues with host systems so that they are brought into compliance with the corporate security policies.

Network Address Translation (NAT)   A technology that allows private IP addresses (as defined in RFC 1918) to be translated into Internet-routable IP addresses (that is, public IP addresses).

network function virtualization (NFV)   A process for virtualizing aspects of a network such as security, storage, compute, and monitoring services.

network interface card (NIC) teaming   A technology that permits multiple network interface cards to function as a single interface to the network. NIC teaming provides excellent redundancy.

network interface layer   The layer of the TCP/IP stack (also known as the network access layer) that encompasses the technologies addressed by Layers 1 and 2 (that is, the physical and data link layers) of the OSI model.

network layer   Layer 3 of the OSI model, which is primarily concerned with forwarding data based on logical addresses.

network segmentation enforcement   A process that enforces strong security design. For example, VLANs can be used to constrain broadcasts and permit the definition of VLAN access control lists (ACLs) and router ACLs for controlling communication between VLANs.

Network Time Protocol (NTP)   A protocol that strives to ensure that network devices (including client systems) have the correct time and date. NTP uses port 123.

next-hop IP address   An IP address on the next router to which traffic should be forwarded.

nmap   A management tool that permits the scanning of a network for hosts and services.

non-disclosure agreement (NDA)   A legal contract used to create a confidential relationship between two parties to protect any type of confidential and proprietary information or trade secret.

nondesignated port   In STP terms, a port that blocks traffic to create a loop-free topology.

north–south traffic flows   The flow of data in a datacenter, where the user traffic flows from the top layer of the hierarchy to the bottom layer and vice versa.

nslookup   A command that can resolve an FQDN to an IP address on Microsoft Windows and UNIX hosts.

O

object identifier (OID)   A unique identifier for an SNMP MIB variable. OIDs are organized in a tree-like hierarchy within a database.

octet   A grouping of 8 bits. An IPv4 address consists of four octets (that is, a total of 32 bits).

omnidirectional antenna   An antenna that radiates power at relatively equal power levels in all directions (somewhat similar to the theoretical isotropic antenna). Omnidirectional antennas are popular in residential WLANs and SOHO locations.

on-path attack   An attack in which an attacker attempts to get in the direct path between a client and a server in order to eavesdrop. If cryptography is being used and the attacker fools the client and server both into building VPNs to the attacker instead of to each other, the attacker can see all the data in plaintext. Formerly known as man-in-the-middle attack.

onboarding/offboarding procedures   Procedures for the hiring and termination of employees that relate to IT and the network.

open   A broken strand of copper that prevents current from flowing through a circuit.

Open Shortest Path First (OSPF)   A link-state routing protocol that uses the metric cost, which is based on the link speed between two routers. OSPF is a popular IGP because of its scalability, fast convergence, and vendor interoperability.

Open Systems Interconnection (OSI) reference model   A seven-layer model that categorizes various network technologies. Commonly referred to as the OSI model or the OSI stack.

optical time-domain reflectometer (OTDR)   A device that detects the location of a fault in a fiber cable by sending light down the fiber-optic cable and measuring the time required for the light to bounce back from the cable fault. The OTDR can then mathematically calculate the location of the fault.

orchestration   The scheduling and monitoring of many different automations.

out-of-band management   Management traffic that is sent outside the networks used for data traffic. It tends to be more secure than in-band management.

P

packet capture   Refers to software (or possibly hardware) that obtains packets or copies of packets for analysis.

partial-mesh topology   A hybrid of a hub-and-spoke topology and a full-mesh topology that can be designed to provide an optimal route between selected sites, while avoiding the expense of interconnecting every site to every other site.

password attack   An attack that aims to compromise a password in order to gain access to systems and files.

password policy   A policy that stipulates the required complexity (length, mix of uppercase/lowercase letters, symbols, duration before expiration, and so on) of passwords in order to ensure security.

patch panel/patch bay   A box designed as a junction point for twisted-pair (TP) cable and fiber-optic cable used in networks.

payload   A simple and generic method of describing data itself, which is separate and distinct from any of the other information required for proper transmission.

peer-to-peer network   A network that allows interconnected devices (for example, PCs) to share their resources (such as files or printers) with one another.

penetration testing   A type of testing that tries to find vulnerabilities and problems with the security settings of a network or network component. Penetration tests can help find major problems with systems and mitigate those risks before they are the subject of cyberattack.

personal area network (PAN)   A network with a smaller scale than a LAN. A connection between a PC and a digital camera via a USB cable is an example of a PAN.

phishing   An attack that uses email or other messages to attempt to capture authentication information (or other information) from an end user.

physical access control device   A device used to enforce the security of the physical resources that make up a network and infrastructure.

physical layer   Layer 1 of the OSI model, which is concerned with the transmission of bits on a network.

physical network diagram   A diagram of specific parts of a network, which typically includes documentation of physical device names, locations, and ports.

physical topology   A network topology (typically a diagram) based on how the components are physically interconnected.

piggybacking   Following an authorized employee through a security checkpoint. It is similar to tailgating except that the two individuals moving through the checkpoint are cooperating with each other.

ping   One of the most commonly used command line commands, which can check IP connectivity between two network devices. Multiple platforms (for example, routers, switches, and hosts) support the **ping** command.

platform as a service (PaaS)   A cloud service model that can provide a development platform for companies that are developing applications and want to focus on creating the software without having to worry about the servers and infrastructure being used for that development.

plenum   Fire-retardant cable that minimizes toxic fumes if it catches on fire. Local fire codes often require plenum cabling in raised flooring or in open-air return ducts.

pointer (PTR)   A DNS record that points to a canonical name. A PTR record is commonly used when performing a reverse DNS lookup, which is a process used to determine what domain name is associated with a known IP address.

poison reverse   A feature of a distance-vector routing protocol that causes a route received on one interface to be advertised back out that same interface with a metric that is considered to be infinite.

polarization   The direction in which an antenna radiates wavelengths. This direction can be vertical, horizontal, or circular.

POP3 over SSL   A secure version of POP3 that uses SSL for security.

Port Address Translation (PAT)   A variant of NAT in which multiple inside local IP addresses share a single inside global IP address. PAT can distinguish between different flows based on port numbers.

port scanner   Software that seeks to discover port states (that is, open or closed) on a network device. In this case, ports can be TCP or UDP ports.

port security   802.1X protection of a port or a Layer 2 security mechanism that can lock down a port to learning specific MAC addresses.

Post Office Protocol Version 3 (POP3)   A protocol used to retrieve email from an email server.

posture assessment   The process of examining the state of a network and network nodes from a security perspective.

power distribution unit (PDU)   A device fitted with multiple outputs designed to distribute electric power.

Power over Ethernet (PoE)   A network feature defined by IEEE 802.3af and 802.3at that allows an Ethernet switch to provide power to an attached device (for example, a wireless access point, security camera, or IP phone) by applying power to the same wires in a UTP cable that are used to transmit and receive data.

Power over Ethernet plus (PoE+)   A network feature defined IEEE 802.3at that offers as much as 32.4W of power, enabling PoE to support a wider range of devices than PoE.

prefix notation   A method of indicating how many bits are in a subnet mask. For example, /24 is prefix notation for a 24-bit subnet mask. Prefix notation is also known as slash notation.

pre-shared keys (PSKs)   A method of performing authentication in a network environment in which each device has a complex string configured and stored locally that must match the string on the remote device.

presentation layer   Layer 6 of the OSI model, which is responsible for the formatting of data being exchanged and securing the data with encryption.

private cloud   Cloud services that include systems that only have interactions and communications with other devices inside that same private cloud or system.

private IP addresses   A range of Class A, B, and C addresses that are designed for private use. Although these networks are routable within an organization, service providers do not route these private networks over the public Internet.

private VLAN   A sub-VLAN within a main VLAN in a LAN, which can have special rules regarding access. For example, an isolated sub-VLAN cannot communicate with any other private VLAN members.

process assessment   An assessment that looks for flaws in common business processes for an organization. Process assessments often concentrate on many other areas beyond security. For example, an organization may find many inefficiencies in the business processes in use daily.

protocol analyzer   A software (or perhaps hardware) tool that captures packets and analyzes protocol information from that captured data.

protocol data unit (PDU)   Data at different layers of the OSI model. Specifically, a Layer 4 PDU is a segment, a Layer 3 PDU is a packet, a Layer 2 PDU is a frame, and a Layer 1 PDU is a bit.

proxy server   A server that intercepts requests being sent from a client and forwards those requests to their intended destination. The proxy server then sends any return traffic to the client that initiated the session. This provides address hiding for the client. Also, some proxy servers conserve WAN bandwidth by offering a content-caching function. In addition, some proxy servers offer URL filtering to, for example, block users from accessing social networking sites during working hours.

public cloud   Cloud services that interact with devices on public networks such as the Internet and potentially other public clouds.

punchdown block   A mechanism used to cross-connect sets of wires through a metal peg system in a local area network (LAN).

punchdown tool   A tool that is designed to properly insert an insulated wire between two contact blades in a punchdown block without damaging the blades.

Q–R

quad small form-factor pluggable (QSFP)   A compact, hot-pluggable transceiver also used for data communications applications.

quality of service (QoS)   An approach to ensuring that network traffic receives the correct treatment by network devices to foster high performance.

rack diagram   A two-dimensional elevation drawing showing the organization of specific equipment on a rack. It is often drawn to scale and typically shows the layout of components from both the front and the back of the rack.

ransomware   An exploit in which the attacker locks out access to a system or to files (often using encryption) or at least pretends to have locked out access. The attacker then asks the computer user for a ransom to unlock the system or the files.

Rapid Spanning Tree Protocol (RSTP)   An enhancement to the original STP standard that improves convergence time and adds other operational improvements. It is defined in IEEE 802.1W.

received signal strength indication (RSSI) signal strength   A measure of the power level being received by a local client.

recovery point objective (RPO)   The point in time to which an organization can recover a network.

recovery time objective (RTO)   The time in the future when an organization expects to restore availability after some failure (or even a disaster) has rendered IT services unavailable.

recursive lookup   A DNS lookup in which the client instructs the DNS server that it must provide an answer, and if it cannot, it should not respond with a referral to another DNS server.

registered jack (RJ)   A connector found in most networks that is either RJ45 (for Ethernet) or RJ11 (for telephony).

remote access policy   A policy that typically applies to remote connections to an organization, including reading or sending email and viewing intranet web resources. Such a policy also tends to cover every remote access option, including dial-up, VPN, and web portal access.

Remote Authentication Dial-In User Service (RADIUS)   A UDP-based protocol used to communicate with an AAA server. Unlike TACACS+, RADIUS does not encrypt an entire authentication packet; it encrypts only the password. However, RADIUS offers more robust accounting features than TACACS+. Also, RADIUS is a standards-based protocol, whereas TACACS+ is a Cisco-proprietary protocol.

remote desktop connection   A connection to a remote system using RDP (or a similar remote desktop technology).

remote desktop gateway   A service available in Windows server systems. It is a very clever use of RDP in which the server becomes a gateway to permit access to the server for management purposes for administrators who need to connect.

Remote Desktop Protocol (RDP)   A protocol that permits remote access to OS desktop remotely from another device on the network. For example, this is the default solution for accessing a Windows system hosted in the cloud via Amazon Web Services (AWS).

repeater   *See* hub.

reverse lookup   A DNS query in which the client has the IP address of the resource and is trying to resolve to the name that the IP address is associated with.

RF attenuation   The weakening of radio frequencies over distance.

RFC 1918   A document that defines the range of private IP addresses.

ring topology   In network topology in which traffic flows in a circular fashion around a closed network loop (that is, a ring). Typically, a ring topology sends data, in a single direction, to each connected device in turn, until the intended destination receives the data.

riser-rated   Cable that is designed to pass from one floor to another floor inside a building.

risk management   A process that involves carefully engaging in the identification, evaluation, and prioritization of risks. It is typically followed by a coordinated application of resources to minimize, monitor, and control the probability or impact of cybersecurity-related events.

RJ11   A telephone interface that uses a cable of twisted wire pairs and a modular jack with two, four, or six contacts. RJ-11 is the common connector for plugging a telephone into a wall and a handset into a telephone.

RJ45   The most common Ethernet cable, which connects network interface cards on PCs to network switches and SOHO routers.

roaming   A feature in modern WLANs that permits users to move throughout an organization without losing WiFi access as they transition to different WiFi cells and equipment.

rogue access point   An access point that is not permitted on a network.

rogue DHCP   An attack in which the attacker seeks to disrupt (or redirect) end-user traffic by providing false DHCP-leased IP address information.

rogue DHCP server   A server that is not authorized to exist on a network.

role-based access control (RBAC)   An approach that involves creating permissions around roles that are then assigned to users. An excellent example of the use of RBAC is with guest access.

rollover cable   A flattened cable that comes with a network device from the factory. Also called a console cable.

root DNS server   An authoritative DNS server for a root domain in the DNS system. Root DNS servers are located all over the public Internet to ensure proper resolution of the root domains.

root port   In an STP topology, the port on a switch that is closest to the root bridge, in terms of cost. Every nonroot bridge has a single root port.

route   A command that can add, modify, or delete routes in the IP routing tables of Microsoft Windows and UNIX hosts. In addition, the **route** command can be used to view the IP routing tables of Microsoft Windows hosts.

route redistribution   A process that allows routes learned by one routing protocol to be injected into the routing process of another routing protocol.

routed protocol   A protocol with an addressing scheme (for example, IP) that defines different network addresses.

router   A Layer 3 device that makes forwarding decisions based on logical network addresses.

router advertisement   A message that a router sends to advertise its presence together with various link and Internet parameters, either periodically or in response to a router solicitation message.

Router Advertisement (RA) Guard   A feature that can filter IPv6 router advertisement messages that the protocol uses to simplify IPv6 address assignments such as the default gateway address.

Routing Information Protocol (RIP)   A distance-vector routing protocol that uses hop count as the metric. The maximum number of hops between two routers in an RIP-based network is 15. Therefore, a hop count of 16 is considered to be infinite. RIP is considered to be an IGP.

routing loop   A problem that occurs when routers send packets to each other endlessly. The TTL in a Layer 3 packet is one guard against this behavior.

routing protocol   A protocol (such as RIP, OSPF, or EIGRP) that advertises route information between routers to describe how to reach specified destination networks.

routing table   A table that stores the routing entries that dictate how traffic is forwarded through a network.

runt   An Ethernet frame that is smaller than the IEEE 802.3's minimum length of 64 octets.

S

sanitize a device   To purge a device of all existing data before disposing of the device. This might involve passing powerful magnets over the surface of the storage to ensure that the data can never be recovered.

satellite   A device that provides WAN access to sites where terrestrial WAN solutions are unavailable. Satellite WAN connections can suffer from long round-trip delay (which can be unacceptable for latency-sensitive applications) and are susceptible to poor weather conditions.

scalability   Refers to a solution's ability to grow with need or demand.

scope   An address pool assigned by a DHCP server.

scope options   In DHCP, various additional pieces of information or settings that can be applied to clients of that scope.

screened subnet   A subnet that often contains servers that should be accessible from the public Internet. This approach allows users on the Internet to initiate an email or web session coming into an organization's email or web server, but other protocols are blocked. Previously known as DMZ.

Secure File Transfer Protocol (SFTP)　A protocol that provides FTP file transfer service over an SSH connection.

Secure Shell (SSH)　A cryptographic network protocol for operating network services securely over an unsecured network. SSH is used for remote login to computer systems.

security information and event management (SIEM)　Software products and services that combine security information management (SIM) and security event management (SEM). SIEM systems provide real-time analysis of security alerts generated by applications and network hardware. SIEM systems can log security data and generate reports for compliance purposes.

security policy　A continually changing document that dictates a set of guidelines for network use. These guidelines complement organizational objectives by specifying rules for how a network is used.

separation of duties policy　A network policy that ensures that user accounts do not have too much power. It may also ensure that IT staff are mapped to these various duties and even rotated through them to help prevent internal attacks against the network.

server　With NTP, a device that provides the correct time to NTP clients. The most common servers these days are located regionally on the Internet.

Server Message Block (SMB)　A protocol used by Microsoft clients to share files, printers, and other network resources.

service (SRV)　A generalized service location record that is used for newer protocols instead of creating protocol-specific records such as MX.

service set identifier (SSID)　A string of characters that identifies a WLAN. APs participating in the same WLAN can be configured with identical SSIDs. An SSID shared among multiple APs is called an extended service set identifier (ESSID).

service-level agreement (SLA)　Important documentation that outlines the expected (and purchased) quality of connections or equipment accessed.

Session Initiation Protocol (SIP)　A VoIP signaling protocol that is used to set up, maintain, and tear down VoIP phone calls.

session layer　Layer 5 of the OSI model, which is responsible for setting up, maintaining, and tearing down sessions.

shielded twisted-pair (STP)　Cabling that is shielded to prevent the wires in the cable from acting as an antenna, which might receive or transmit EMI. STP cable might have a metallic shielding, similar to the braided wire that acts as an outer conductor in a coaxial cable.

short   A problem that occurs when two copper connectors touch each other, resulting in current flowing through the short rather than through the attached electrical circuit because the short has lower resistance.

shoulder surfing   A social engineering attack in which a cybercriminal watches over the shoulder of an authorized employee to learn information that can be used at a later time.

show config   A command used to examine the configuration of a network device.

show interface   A command that permits the examination of the statistics and the status of the interfaces on a network system.

show route   A command used to view the routing table configuration of a network device.

signal loss   A condition that occurs when a wireless device is suffering from interference or other issues, in which the RF signals are not strong enough to allow association or data transfers.

Simple Mail Transfer Protocol (SMTP)   A protocol used for sending email throughout a network.

Simple Network Management Protocol (SNMP)   A protocol used to monitor and manage network devices, such as routers, switches, and servers.

single sign-on (SSO)   A process that allows a user to authenticate once to gain access to multiple systems without requiring the user to independently authenticate with each system.

single-mode fiber (SMF)   Cabling that has a core with a diameter large enough to permit only a single path for light pulses (that is, only one mode of propagation). By having a single path for light to travel, SMF eliminates the concern of multimode delay distortion.

site survey   An analysis of an area where wireless is to be deployed. A site survey can identify major issues supporting wireless, such as interference from certain objects, devices, and/or technologies.

site survey report   A report that describes the WiFi capabilities and potential risk points in a given installation. Site survey reports are critical during wireless site surveys.

site-to-site VPN   A VPN that connects to another organization site (for example, a headquarters location connecting to a remote branch).

slash notation   *See* prefix notation.

small form-factor pluggable (SFP)   A compact, hot-pluggable network interface module used for both telecommunication and data communications applications.

smart locker   A locker that accurately logs user access to provide increased security.

smartjack   A network interface device that adds circuitry for features as converting between framing formats on a digital circuit (for example, a T1 circuit), supporting remote diagnostics, and regenerating a digital signal.

SMTP TLS   A method of securing SMTP traffic through the use of TLS.

snips   A tool used to cut cables and other cabling accessories.

social engineering   A technique (which often leverages people's desire to be helpful) that attackers use to obtain confidential information. For example, an attacker might pose as a member of an IT department and ask a company employee for her login credentials in order for the IT staff to test the connection.

software as a service (SaaS)   A cloud service model in which the details of the servers are hidden from the customer, and the customer's experience is similar to using a web-based application.

software-defined networking (SDN)   An approach to computer networking that allows network administrators to programmatically initialize, control, change, and manage network behavior dynamically via open interfaces and provide abstraction of lower-level functionality.

software-defined wide area network (SD-WAN)   An overlay solution for a traditional WAN that provides more flexibility, visibility, and manageability to the enterprise WAN.

Spanning Tree Protocol (STP)   Defined by the IEEE 802.1D standard, a protocol that allows a network to have redundant Layer 2 connections while logically preventing loops, which could lead to symptoms such as broadcast storms and MAC address table corruption.

spectrum analyzer   A tool used to measure the magnitude of an input signal versus frequency within the full frequency range of the instrument.

speed   A measure of the data send rate; for example, Cat 6 media supports a maximum speed of 10Gbps.

spine and leaf   A newer network topology that consists of just two layers: a spine layer and a leaf layer.

split horizon A feature of a distance-vector routing protocol that prevents a route learned on one interface from being advertised back out that same interface.

split tunnel A type of VPN design that has some traffic (only the required traffic) sent to another enterprise location and the remainder of traffic sent out an Internet connection (or other destination).

SQLnet Oracle's networking software, which allows remote data access between programs and the Oracle database or among multiple Oracle databases.

standard operating procedures (SOP) A set of step-by-step instructions compiled by an organization to help workers carry out routine operations.

star topology A network topology that has a central point (for example, a switch) from which all attached devices radiate.

start of authority (SOA) A DNS record that provides authoritative information about a DNS zone, such as email contact information for the zone's administrator, the zone's primary name server, and various refresh timers.

state transition modulation An approach of representing binary digits in which the transition between a voltage level (for example, going from a state of no voltage to a state of voltage, or vice versa, on a copper cable) or the transition of having light or no light on a fiber-optic cable is represented as a binary 1; having no transition in a voltage level or light level from one time period to the next is represented as a binary 0.

static assignment Manual assignment of IP address information for servers or hosts. *See also* dynamic assignment.

storage area network (SAN) A specialized network for the storage of data.

straight tip (ST) A connector used with fiber-optic cables that utilizes a bayonet-style plug and socket.

stratum An important value in NTP operations. It is like a hop count and measures how far the client is from the accurate time source. The larger the stratum value, the more chance that time on the client is inaccurate because it is more hops away from the accurate time source.

Structured Query Language (SQL) A language used to run powerful queries against the data stored in local or remote databases.

subinterface A virtual interface on a single physical interface.

subnet mask A 32-bit value (in IPv4) that indicates what portion of the IP address is the network ID versus what portion is the host ID.

subscriber connector (SC)   A fiber-optic connector with a push-pull latching mechanism that provides quick insertion and removal while ensuring a positive connection.

supplicant   In a network using 802.1X user authentication, the device that wants to gain access to a network.

switch   A network device that learns which devices reside off which ports, interrogates traffic to see where it's destined, and forwards the traffic out the appropriate port and not out all the other ports.

switching loop   A problem that occurs when switches forward frames endlessly back and forth. Spanning Tree Protocol (STP) was designed to permit switches to eliminate switching loops caused by redundancy.

syslog   A logging solution that consists of two primary components: syslog servers (which receive and store log messages sent from syslog clients) and syslog clients (which can be a variety of network devices that send logging information to a syslog server).

system life cycle   A model that provides valuable guidance on best practices throughout an organization concerning the network components from design through disposal.

T

tailgating   A social engineering attack in which the attacker follows a valid employee through a secured area of an organization.

tamper detection   The use of a device to sense when an active attempt to compromise the device integrity or the data associated with the device is in progress; the detection of the threat may enable the device to initiate appropriate defensive actions.

TCP flag   A field in TCP headers used to indicate a particular connection state or provide additional information. It is often used for troubleshooting purposes or to control how a particular connection is handled.

TCP header   A data packet header that contains 10 mandatory fields totaling 20 bytes (or octets). The header holds information about the connection and the data currently being sent.

TCP/IP stack   A four-layer model (as opposed to the seven-layer OSI model) that targets the suite of TCP/IP protocols. Also known as the DoD model.

tcpdump   A common packet analyzer run at the command line. It allows the user to display TCP/IP and other packets being transmitted or received over a network to which the computer is attached.

Telnet   A method of remote access for network devices that does not provide any security mechanisms.

Temporal Key Integrity Protocol (TKIP)   A security protocol used in the IEEE 802.11 wireless networking standard that was designed to make improvements over security flaws in WEP. TKIP is no longer considered secure and was deprecated in the 2012 revision of the 802.11 standard.

Terminal Access Controller Access Control System Plus (TACACS+)   A TCP-based protocol used to communicate with an AAA server. Unlike RADIUS, TACACS+ encrypts an entire authentication packet rather than just the password. TACACS+ is a Cisco-proprietary protocol.

terminal emulator   A computer program that emulates a video terminal within some other display architecture.

text (TXT)   A DNS record that was originally meant for arbitrary human-readable text. Since the early 1990s, however, this record has carried machine-readable data.

threat   A realistic attack that might possibly occur against a network. Threats often target network vulnerabilities.

threat assessment   The process of evaluating the credibility and seriousness of potential threats. A threat assessment involves analyzing the probability that a threat will become a reality.

three-tiered architecture   A classic network design that consists of a core layer, a distribution layer, and an access layer.

throughput   A measure of the successful data send rate between systems.

TIA/EIA-568A   A wiring standard that uses the following wires from pin 1 to 8: green stripe, green, orange stripe, blue, blue stripe, orange, brown stripe, brown.

TIA/EIA-568B   A wiring standard that uses the following wires from 1 to 8: orange stripe, orange, green stripe, blue, blue stripe, green, brown stripe, brown.

time-division multiplexing (TDM)   A method of transmitting different communication sessions (for example, different telephone conversations in a telephony network) on the same physical medium by allowing sessions to take turns. For a brief period of time, defined as a time slot, data from the first session is sent, followed by data from the second session. This continues until every session has had a turn, and the process repeats.

Time-to-Live (TTL)   A field in an IP header that is decremented once for each router hop. If the value in a TTL field is reduced to 0, a router discards the frame and sends a time exceeded Internet Control Message Protocol (ICMP) message back to the source.

tone generator   A tool that is used in conjunction with a toner probe on a punchdown block to audibly detect to which pair of wires the tone generator is connected.

top-of-rack switching   A form of datacenter switching in which the switching occurs at the top of each rack of servers.

top-to-bottom troubleshooting   A troubleshooting methodology in which the engineer starts at the application layer of the OSI model and works down, trying to determine the problem.

traceroute/tracert   A UNIX (**traceroute**) or Windows (**tracert**) command that displays every router hop along the path from a source host to a destination host on an IP network. Information about the router hop can include the IP address of the router hop and the round-trip delay of that router hop.

traffic access point (TAP)   A hardware device inserted at a specific point in a network where data can be accessed for testing or troubleshooting purposes. Also called a test access point.

traffic log   A log file in a network that details traffic statistics for key areas of the infrastructure.

traffic policing/shaping   Tools that make it possible to limit available bandwidth.

transceiver   A device that makes it possible to uplink one Ethernet switch to another if different connectors (for example, MMF, SMF, or UTP) for different installations are required.

Transmission Control Protocol (TCP)   A connection-oriented transport protocol that provides reliable transport, in that if a segment is dropped, the sender can detect that drop and retransmit that dropped segment. Specifically, a receiver acknowledges segments that it receives. Based on those acknowledgments, a sender can determine which segments were successfully received.

transport layer (OSI model)   Layer 4 of the OSI model, which acts as a dividing line between the upper layers and the lower layers. Specifically, messages are taken from the upper layers (Layers 5–7) and encapsulated into segments for transmission to the lower layers (Layers 1–3). Similarly, data streams coming from lower layers are decapsulated and sent to Layer 5 (the session layer) or some other upper layer, depending on the protocol.

transport layer (TCP/IP stack)   Layer 4 of the OSI model, which acts as a dividing line between the upper layers and the lower layers. Specifically, messages are taken from the upper layers (Layers 5–7) and encapsulated into segments for transmission to the lower layers (Layers 1–3). Similarly, data streams coming from lower layers are decapsulated and sent to Layer 5 (the session layer) or some other upper layer, depending on the protocol.

Transport Layer Security (TLS)   A security protocol designed to ensure privacy between communicating client/server applications.

traps   An unsolicited SNMP message sent from a managed device to an SNMP manager that notifies the SNMP manager about a significant event that occurred on the managed device.

Trivial File Transfer Protocol (TFTP)   A file transfer protocol that does not have the security or error checking of FTP. TFTP uses UDP as a transport protocol and therefore is connectionless.

trunk   (1) In the context of an Ethernet network, a single physical or logical connection that simultaneously carries traffic for multiple VLANs. (2) In the context of telephony, an interconnection between telephone switches.

tunneling   The process of transmitting traffic with additional encapsulation.

twinaxial   A type of cable similar to coaxial cable but with two inner conductors instead of one.

twisted-pair   Today's most popular media type, in which individually insulated copper strands are intertwined into a twisted-pair cable. Two categories of twisted-pair cable are shielded twisted pair (STP) and unshielded twisted pair (UTP).

U

UDP header   In a UDP datagram, a header that contains four fields (source port, destination port, length, and checksum) totaling 8 bytes.

ultra-physical contact (UPC)   A style of fiber-optic connector with back reflection around –55 dB.

unicast   A one-to-one communication flow.

unidirectional antenna   A style of WiFi antenna that directs the signal in a specific direction. *See also* omnidirectional antenna.

uninterruptible power supply (UPS)   An appliance that provides power to networking equipment in the event of a power outage.

unshielded twisted pair (UTP)   Cabling that blocks EMI from the copper strands making up a twisted-pair cable by having more tightly twisted strands (that is, more twists per centimeter). Because these strands are wrapped around each other, the wires insulate each other from EMI.

User Datagram Protocol (UDP)   A connectionless transport protocol that provides unreliable transport, in that if a segment is dropped, the sender is unaware of the drop, and no retransmission occurs.

V

variable-length subnet masking (VLSM)   The process of assigning various subnetwork IDs in a network to issue the appropriate number of IP addresses.

vendor assessment   An assessment in which a team analyzes the many vendors the organization might use in their business processes. It considers how much data of the organization the vendors have access to and what security practices the vendors follow.

virtual desktop   A solution that allows a user to store data in a centralized datacenter rather than on the hard drive of the local computer. With appropriate authentication credentials, the user can access his data from various remote devices (for example, his smartphone or another computer).

virtual IP address   In load-balancing environments, an address that is used to provide a single IP address for accessing a shared resource.

virtual LAN (VLAN)   A single broadcast domain, representing a single subnet. Typically, a group of ports on a switch is assigned to a single VLAN. For traffic to travel between two VLANs, that traffic needs to be routed.

virtual network computing (VNC)   An alternative to RDP that allows the access of a desktop from another system on the network.

virtual network interface card (vNIC)   A virtualized network interface that permits virtual machines to connect to virtual and physical networks beyond the local host.

virtual private network (VPN)   A set of security protocols that, when implemented by two devices on either side of an insecure network such as the Internet, can allow the devices to send data securely. VPNs provide privacy, device authentication, anti-replay services, and data integrity services.

Virtual Router Redundancy Protocol (VRRP)   A protocol that increases availability by providing automatic assignment of available IP routers to hosts.

VLAN hopping   An attack in which the attacker uses Q-in-Q tunneling in conjunction with the native VLAN feature to send packets into a VLAN from an unauthorized VLAN.

voice gateway   Often considered the most critical component in a VoIP network, a gateway that connects the VoIP of an enterprise to the global public telephone network.

voice over IP (VoIP)   Convergence of voice (telephone) traffic and the data networks of today. VoIP introduces new and exciting features for communication that were not possible under the legacy voice networks.

VPN headend   A network device typically found in the headquarters of an enterprise network that terminates VPN connections from remote clients and/or branch offices.

vSwitch   A virtual switch that performs Layer 2 functions (for example, VLAN separation and filtering) between various server instances running on a single physical server.

vulnerability   A weakness in a component of software that might be exploited by an attacker. New code might be installed on a network device (a router, for example), and this code could cause a vulnerability. For example, the code could introduce a new feature that permits a backdoor into the device for unauthorized persons.

vulnerability assessment   An assessment that seeks to identify, quantify, and prioritize the vulnerabilities in a system. Vulnerability assessments can be performed for a wide variety of systems within the IT department and the network as a whole.

W

warm site   A redundant site that can be brought online with minimal time and effort.

wide area network (WAN)   A network that interconnects geographically separated network components.

WiFi analyzer   Software that runs on a general-purpose computer or on a specialized device that can perform wireless analysis of WiFi signals. This type of tool can be used as part of a wireless site survey after WiFi has been implemented to create a heat map of the wireless airspace.

WiFi Protected Access (WPA)/WPA2 Personal   A security standard developed by WiFi Alliance (a nonprofit organization formed to certify interoperability of wireless devices) to address the weaknesses of Wired Equivalent Privacy (WEP). This new security standard was called WiFi Protected Access (WPA) Version 1. WPA2 Uses Counter Mode with Cipher Block Chaining Message Authentication Code Protocol (CCMP) for integrity checking and Advanced Encryption Standard (AES) for encryption. These algorithms enhance the security offered by WPA.

wipe configuration   The standard procedure used to wipe the configuration from a networking device when disposal is needed. In some cases, this can be done remotely for a device that is lost or stolen.

wire map testing   A type of testing used with cables to find opens, shorts, reversed pairs, crossed pairs, and split pairs.

wireless bands   The specific frequencies that are capable of carrying modern WiFi. The IEEE 802.11 uses various frequency bands, including the 2.4GHz, 5GHz, 6GHz, and 60GHz bands.

wireless channel   An indication of how the WiFi frequency bands are divided up in order to carry the WiFi signal. Countries apply their own regulations to the available channels to allow users and maximum power levels within these frequency ranges.

wireless LAN controller (WLC)   A specialized network device that permits the central control and management of large numbers of lightweight access points.

wireless local area network (WLAN)   A wireless network that interconnects network components that are geographically separated.

wiring diagram   A key piece of documentation that details wiring and port locations. This documentation makes it possible to track cable runs from switches and map them to the wall jacks where users connect to the network; these connections might also represent trunks to additional network devices such as wireless access points.

WPA/WPA2/WPA3 Enterprise   WPA configurations used in organizations that feature stronger security mechanisms than the personal configurations available.

X–Z

Zero Trust   A relatively new security model that many corporations are starting to follow. This model seeks to reduce or eliminate security breaches for an organization by trusting absolutely nothing by default. In fact, the credo of this approach is "never trust; always verify."

zero-day   Cybersecurity attacks that take advantage of techniques or vulnerabilities that have not already been discovered by cybersecurity specialists or anti-malware companies.

Zeroconf   A technology that performs three basic functions: assigning link-local IP addresses, resolving computer names to IP addresses, and locating network services.

zone transfer   A process by which different DNS servers can sync their databases. Zone transfers are often performed when a primary DNS server updates one or more secondary (backup) DNS servers.

Answers to Review Questions

Chapter 1

1. **Answer: d.** The data link layer of the OSI model is the only layer of the famous model that is typically divided into sublayers (the MAC and LLC sublayers).

2. **Answer: b.** Baseband technology uses the entire medium to transmit. In contrast, broadband technology can divide the medium into different channels. A great example of broadband is the use of the coaxial cable you might have in your home, which carries cable television signals as well as high-speed Internet.

3. **Answer: c.** The transport layer offers TCP and UDP. With TCP, a connection-oriented protocol, windowing can be used to dictate how much data is sent at one time.

4. **Answer: a.** An IP address is a typical ingredient at the network layer (Layer 3) of the OSI model. Routers use these addresses to route traffic through an internetwork.

5. **Answer: c.** User Datagram Protocol (UDP) sacrifices reliability for speed and efficiency in the transport of data.

6. **Answer: b.** The maximum transmission unit (MTU) is the network interface setting that defines the largest packet that may be sent onto the network.

7. **Answer: b.** The well-known port numbers are all below 1024. An example would be HTTP (WWW) at port 80.

8. **Answer: b.** HTTPS uses TCP port 443 in its operation. Contrast this to HTTP (that offers no security) and used port 80.

9. **Answer: c.** The TTL value of the IP packet is decremented for each router hop. This is a loop prevention mechanism.

10. **Answer: d.** The connection-oriented TCP uses several techniques to ensure reliability in the communications. Windowing is one of those.

11. **Answer: b.** As data moves down through the OSI model layers (on a host), it is encapsulated with a header added to the beginning and a trailer to

the end. When the data arrives at the receiving host, it moves up the model and is decapsulated in that the header and trailer are stripped off as it moves up though the OSI layers.

12. **Answer: d.** The data link layer is concerned with packaging data into frames and ensuring that frames do not exceed the maximum transmission unit (MTU) of the physical media.

Chapter 2

1. **Answer: b.** ADSL has a distance limitation of 18,000 feet between a DSL modem and its DSLAM. Remember that ADSL features different upload and download speeds.

2. **Answer: d.** An HFC distribution network typically features multiple media types.

3. **Answer: d.** Virtualization is possible with servers thanks to specialized software called a hypervisor. The hypervisor is used to manage multiple virtual machines (VMs) existing on one host.

4. **Answer: b.** *SD-WAN* makes many of the principles that make cloud computing SD-WAN brings cloud computing advantages to the WAN at the WAN level. This is done by adopting a virtual WAN architecture leveraging a combination of transport services (MPLS, 5G, LTE, broadband, and so on) to securely connect users to applications.

5. **Answer: d.** A metropolitan area network is superb for connecting various buildings in a citywide area. Metro Ethernet is one example of connectivity technology for this design.

6. **Answer: c.** A personal area network features fewer nodes than are typically found in a LAN. This design also features a small geographic area, such as a car or a single-room office.

7. **Answer: c.** The star topology is common today in switched LANs. However, it does feature quite a bit of cabling, as the switches require media to each and every node (wired) that needs to communicate. There are also typically trunk connections between the switches for an extended star topology, and this means even more cabling.

8. **Answer: a.** The full-mesh topology might be complex and expensive to implement, but it does provide excellent levels of redundancy. In the event that one or more links fail, it is often possible to reroute traffic around the failures.

9. **Answer: b.** The formula for the number of connections required for the full-mesh topology is $n(n-1)/2$, where n is the number of nodes. So, in this case, $5(5-1)/2$ is 10.

10. **Answer: a, c.** The hub and spoke is actually a form of a partial-mesh topology. This topology has the advantage of being less complex, less costly, and, overall, more scalable than a full-mesh design.

11. **Answer: c.** A peer-to-peer (P2P) network features clients sharing information directly with each other.

12. **Answer: b.** P2P networks are often celebrated for their simplicity and low cost. Unfortunately, these networks are not scalable and can actually cause administrative nightmares when scaling is required.

13. **Answer: d.** The storage area network (SAN) assists when large amounts of data must be stored in the network and transferred efficiently from various nodes to other nodes.

Chapter 3

1. **Answer: b, c.** Cat 5e and Cat 6 are often used for Fast Ethernet networks.

2. **Answer: b.** Plenum cable is a special type of cable for use in the plenum spaces.

3. **Answer: b.** The RJ45 connector uses eight pins and is the most common connector used in Ethernet networks.

4. **Answer: b, d.** The two major categories of fiber-optic media are single-mode and multimode.

5. **Answer: b.** Fast Ethernet operates at 100Mbps.

6. **Answer: a.** A fiber distribution panel is often used in the fiber media environment for terminating media.

7. **Answer: c.** Cat 5e is an enhanced version of Cat 5. Cat 5e was the first standard for 1Gbps Ethernet.

8. **Answer: c.** An F-connector, or F-type connector, is often used for cable TV (including cable modem) connections.

9. **Answer: b, d.** To define industry-standard pinouts and color coding for twisted-pair cabling, the TIA/EIA-568 standard was developed. The first iteration of the TIA/EIA-568 standard has come to be known as the *TIA/EIA-568A* standard, and since then, an updated standard called *TIA/EIA-568B* has been released. *TIA/EIA-568B* is the more commonly used standard in the United States today.

10. **Answer: a.** 1000BASE-LX uses single-mode fiber (SMF), has a bandwidth capacity of 1Gbps, and has a distance limitation of 5 km.

Chapter 4

1. **Answer: b.** The binary representation of 117 is 01110101 (based on 117 = 64 + 32 + 16 + 4 + 1).

2. **Answer: d.** 10110100 is the equivalent of 180 because 128 + 32 + 16 + 4 = 180.

3. **Answer: a.** Because the decimal value 10 appears in the first octet, this is a Class A address.

4. **Answer: d.** 239.1.2.3 is an example of a multicast IP address. You use multicast to send a single packet to groups of systems that have "subscribed" to this address.

5. **Answer: a, d.** Notice that a key to this question is "routable IP addresses." Only BOOTP and DHCP are valid options in this case.

6. **Answer: a.** There are 5 bits left here for host address assignment, and 2 raised to the fifth power is 32. You then subtract 2 for the network ID and broadcast address. That is, $2^5 - 2 = 30$.

7. **Answer: c.** /28 is the prefix notation for 255.255.255.240. Notice that the mask consists of 8 bits + 8 bits + 8 bits + 4 bits.

8. **Answer: c.** Using a /27 mask gives you 3 bits for subnetting. This permits the creation of eight subnets and satisfies your requirement of seven subnets and gives you the most possible host addresses per subnet.

9. **Answer: a.** This host address and subnet mask combination references the following subnet of usable addresses: 172.16.0.1–172.16.63.254.

10. **Answer: c.** Remember, you can drop the leading zeros in any field, and one time within an address, you can use the shorthand symbol :: to represent continuous sections of zeros.

11. **Answer: b.** EUI-64 in IPv6 permits the automatic generation of host portions of addresses.

12. **Answer: A.** The IP address assigned to the physical outside interface is the IP address that is often the basis for the PAT configuration. Many different internal IP addresses (inside) can be translated into this single address.

13. **Answer: d.** A very similar concept to the virtual IP address is the subinterface. This handy interface capability, which is supported by most router and switch manufacturers, allows you to create many virtual interfaces out of a single physical interface.

14. **Answer: b.** Network Address Translation (NAT) allows private IP addresses (as defined in RFC 1918) to be translated into Internet-routable IP addresses (public IP addresses).

15. Answer: a. IPv6 networks use *stateless address autoconfiguration (SLAAC)* to assign IP addresses. With SLAAC, a device sends the router a request for the network prefix, and then the device uses the prefix along with its own MAC address to create an IP address.

Chapter 5

1. Answer: b. The Secure Shell (SSH) protocol allows you to make secure remote connections to network systems. This protocol is specialized for terminal connections. For graphical user interface connections, you can use technologies such as Remote Desktop Protocol (RDP) and VNC Viewer.

2. Answer: d. Dynamic Host Configuration Protocol is used to dynamically assign IP address information to network systems (typically end-user devices).

3. Answer: d. Domain Name System (DNS) is a global hierarchy system that resolves names to IP addresses.

4. Answer: a, c. HTTPS uses TCP port 443 in its operation.

5. Answer: b, d. Syslog produces machine data that you can use to monitor and understand the state of services on a device. Syslog runs on UDP port 514.

6. Answer: c. ICMP is used by many troubleshooting and monitoring tools. ping and traceroute are two such ICMP-based utilities.

7. Answer: a, b. Using POP3 over SSL (port 995) or IMAPS (port 993) allows the incoming data from the client to be encrypted because these protocols use SSL/TLS sessions. Answer c is incorrect because Simple Mail Transfer Protocol (SMTP) (port 25) is for outgoing email. Answer d is incorrect because one of the biggest security issues with plain POP (and IMAP as well) is that login credentials are transmitted in plaintext over unencrypted connections.

8. Answer: b. Secure Shell (SSH) establishes a session between the client and host computers using an authenticated and encrypted connection over port 22. SSH requires encryption of all data, including the login portion. Answer a is incorrect because SSH is the secure replacement for Telnet. Using Telnet is ill advised because a Telnet session is not encrypted. Answers c and d are incorrect. Lightweight Directory Access Protocol (LDAP) is a directory services protocol for use on IP networks. By default, LDAP traffic is unsecured. LDAP over SSL (LDAPS) is a method to secure LDAP by enabling communication over SSL/TLS.

Chapter 6

1. **Answer: c.** The DHCP DISCOVER message is the first step in the four-way DHCP process. A client broadcasts these messages on the local subnet in an attempt to find a DHCP server.

2. **Answer: b.** You often use the scope options in DHCP to set things like lease duration, as well as other pieces of IP configuration information that the client might need.

3. **Answer: a.** A pointer record in DNS points to a canonical name. This record type is typically used to perform reverse lookups when required.

4. **Answer: d.** The DNS TTL (time to live) dictates how long devices can cache the results of name resolutions.

5. **Answer: b, e.** NTP relies on UDP port 123 in its operation.

6. **Answer: b.** The stratum is a value used in NTP to provide an indicator of how many hops a client is from the NTP server.

Chapter 7

1. **Answer: d.** The core layer is most concerned with raw speed.

2. **Answer: b.** The distribution/aggregation layer is most concerned with QoS, security, and setting policy.

3. **Answer: b.** Each leaf device connects to each and every spine device to provide a full mesh of all the leafs for every spine.

4. **Answer: b.** In SDN, a great example of east-to-west traffic flow is container-to-container (or VM-to-VM) traffic in the datacenter.

5. **Answer: d.** The Fibre Channel over Ethernet (FCoE) technology is the unifying technology described here. This approach encapsulates Fibre Channel traffic in Ethernet frames for transport over the converged network infrastructure.

6. **Answer: b.** Border Gateway Protocol is an exterior gateway protocol used to share prefixes across the Internet. It can also be used to route internally for very large organizations, and it is an example of a control layer/plane technology.

Chapter 8

1. **Answer: a.** A public cloud provider services many clients from a single large infrastructure.

2. **Answer: c.** Platform as a service (PaaS) is targeted at developers. This cloud service seeks to provide everything the developers need to test and deploy applications.

3. **Answer: b.** Elasticity refers to the ability to scale resources based on demand. For example, virtual machines might be dynamically added to a pool of servers or removed, based on demand at different times.

4. **Answers: b, c.** Companies that are concerned about data security as they send and receive data from the cloud often use a VPN or a direct private connection to provide strong security for the transfer of this data.

5. **Answer: b.** Multitenancy refers to physical servers in the public cloud infrastructure hosting workloads for multiple customers.

Chapter 9

1. **Answer: c.** SIP is a control protocol for VoIP that is responsible for call maintenance tasks.

2. **Answer: b.** The best answer here is switch because, unlike a multilayer switch, this device must use MAC addressing for frame forwarding.

3. **Answer: d.** Routers make their forwarding decisions using IP addresses at Layer 3 of the OSI model. Specifically, the destination IP address is the key piece of information used by default.

4. **Answer: a, c.** Bridges are slower than switches (typically) and tend to lack the port density of switches.

5. **Answer: d.** A router creates a broadcast domain on each of the router (Layer 3) ports.

6. **Answer: d.** A switch creates a collision domain on each port by default.

7. **Answer: b.** ANT+ is an IoT technology that is specialized wireless for monitoring sensor data. Garmin helped create this technology.

8. **Answer: d.** An intrusion prevention system (IPS) typically uses signatures to identify common network attacks.

9. **Answer: c.** A proxy server caches content and improves performance. It can also include permit and deny lists for Internet locations.

10. **Answer: b.** A stateful firewall has the ability to examine outbound connections and dynamically permit the appropriate inbound responses.

Chapter 10

1. **Answer: b.** Note that the destination IP address does not change in the packet. However, as the router sends the frame out the exit interface heading toward the destination, it will update the destination MAC address to the next hop/device.

2. **Answer: d.** ARP is one of the many name resolution protocols we deal with. In this case, the names are Layer 2 and Layer 3 addresses.

3. **Answer: d.** The default route is 0.0.0.0/0.

4. **Answer: c.** The better the administrative distance, the more believable the protocol. Lower is better for the AD score.

5. **Answer: b, c.** Split horizon and poison reverse are critical loop preventions for early routing protocols.

6. **Answer: c.** RIP cannot be used in large networks due to a maximum hop count of 15.

7. **Answer: a.** BGP is the protocol that makes the Internet a reality.

8. **Answer: c.** Jitter is how we describe this unpredictable variation in delay.

9. **Answer: b.** IntServ features the use of RSVP.

10. **Answer: b.** Traffic shaping seeks to smooth traffic volumes by buffering excess packets.

Chapter 11

1. **Answer: a.** A 1000BASE-T Ethernet network has a distance limitation of 100 m.

2. **Answer: d.** A random back-off timer is used in a CSMA/CD network when a collision is detected.

3. **Answer: b.** 100GBASE-SR10 Ethernet uses multimode fiber.

4. **Answer: a, b.** VLANs are also IP subnets. A router must route between these subnets. The VLAN is also a broadcast domain.

5. **Answer: a.** The 802.1Q native VLAN is the only VLAN in a Layer 2 domain that is not tagged.

6. **Answer: b.** The designated port is forwarding, and there must be one on every network segment. Remember that all root ports are designated by default.

7. **Answer: b.** 802.3ad is the open-standard version of link aggregation.

8. **Answer: b.** The IEEE 802.3af standard specifies 15.4W as the maximum amount of power a switch is allowed to provide per port.

9. **Answer: c.** Port mirroring permits frame analysis in a switched network.

10. **Answer: b.** 802.1X features a supplicant, an authentication server, and an authenticator. The authentication server is responsible for actually checking the credentials.

Chapter 12

1. **Answer: d.** The key to this question is the fact that power is being radiated in all directions relatively equally.

2. **Answer: b, d, f.** The nonoverlapping channels in the United States are 1, 6, and 11.

3. **Answer: b.** WLANs use carrier-sense multiple access with collision avoidance.

4. **Answer: c.** This scenario describes 802.11g.

5. **Answer: a.** Multiple input, multiple output is the technology described here.

6. **Answer: b.** An independent BSS (IBSS) is formed directly between wireless clients.

7. **Answer: b.** The recommended amount of overlap is 10% to 15%.

8. **Answer: c.** Open authentication permits the use of the wireless LAN with no credentials. This is useful in a public, free Wi-Fi hotspot or in a guest area in an enterprise.

9. **Answer: a.** The string of characters is an initialization vector (IV).

10. **Answer: d.** The IEEE 802.11i requirements are found in WPA2.

11. **Answer: d.** Geofencing permits the creation of a boundary for administrative alerts and actions.

Chapter 13

1. **Answer: b.** The Management Information Base (MIB) is a database filled with variables that represent the metrics of the managed network devices.

2. **Answer: b.** The Critical syslog level is Level 2, the most severe level.

3. **Answer: a, c, d.** The put method is used with HTTP. SNMP uses get, set, and trap messages—among others.

4. **Answer: a.** Event Viewer is a classic Windows tool that is still used today to view the log information for the Windows system. It includes application, security, and system log information.

5. **Answer: d.** Jitter, which is variation in delay, can be a large problem for VoIP networks.

6. **Answer: a.** The noAuthNoPriv security level of SNMPv3 is like the community string approach of SNMPv2c.

7. **Answer: d.** Syslog level 6 is for informational messages. Note that the lowest level, level 7, is used for debugging messages.

8. **Answer: a.** NetFlow often uses a flow collector, which can be a single-purpose device on a network for storing, backing up, and making logs available to the authorized staff.

9. **Answer: b.** Giants are reported when packets are larger than 1500 bytes. Note that these large packets might be perfectly normal in your enterprise or datacenter.

10. **Answer: a.** You can fix a duplex mismatch by either enabling autonegotiation or forcing the same settings on both connecting interfaces.

Chapter 14

1. **Answer: b.** A strong password should include uppercase letters, lowercase letters, numbers, and special characters.

2. **Answer: a.** Data loss prevention policies typically categorize activities at the client, network, and storage levels.

3. **Answer: c.** Typical phases of incident response include prepare, identify, contain, eradicate, recover, and review.

4. **Answer: c.** For the highest degree of safety, you should always follow the vendor instructions.

5. **Answer: c.** A privileged user agreement (PUA) targets administrators and others who have elevated levels of access on the network.

6. **Answer: a.** A non-disclosure agreement (NDA) is a legally binding document that organizations might require of both their own employees and anyone else who comes into contact with confidential information, including vendors, consultants, and contractors. The purpose of an NDA is to protect an organization's intellectual property and trade secrets.

7. **Answer: b.** Typical life cycle phases are conceptual design, preliminary system design, detailed design and development, production and construction, utilization and support, phase-out, and disposal.

8. **Answer: d.** When employees leave the organization, offboarding procedures need to be in place to ensure that in addition to all access being removed, equipment and data are returned. The process should be clear regarding expectations, particularly those related to confidential or internal-use-only data.

Chapter 15

1. **Answer: b.** Five nines availability means 99.999% uptime and translates into about 5 minutes of downtime per year.

2. **Answer: c.** The active-passive design uses one NIC that is actually active and able to pass traffic. The other NIC is in a passive (often called standby) state.

3. **Answer: a.** A content engine permits the caching of key data to which clients need low-latency access.

4. **Answer: c.** A snapshot is typically a complete point-in-time read-only copy of data.

5. **Answer: c.** A hot site is often the ultimate goal of a disaster recovery design. A hot site would be able to provide full-service levels with virtually no downtime after a disaster occurs.

6. **Answer: a.** Equal-cost multipathing (ECMP) enables routing protocols to distribute traffic among different available paths in the network. This is very advantageous, especially compared to classic Layer 2 designs that feature STP, which blocks redundant paths in order to prevent loops.

7. **Answer: d.** The mean time between failure (MTBF) is the average amount of time that passes between hardware component failures, excluding time spent repairing components or waiting for repairs.

8. **Answer: b.** A cold site is the weakest of the recovery sites but also the least costly. (However, although a cold site may be the least costly when you're planning for disaster, after a disaster occurs, equipment purchased for a cold site might be expensive or difficult to obtain.) Electricity, bathrooms, and space are about the only facilities a cold site contract provides.

9. **Answer: b, c, d.** The difference between incremental and differential backups is that differential backups include all data that has changed since the full backup. Therefore, answer a is the only false statement.

Chapter 16

1. **Answer: c.** Advanced Encryption Standard (AES) permits the configuration of various strength levels, including 128-, 192-, and 256-bit key versions.

2. **Answer: a.** Integrity involves ensuring that data has not been manipulated in transit.

3. **Answer: b.** The principle of least privilege involves giving a user account the fewest possible permissions required to do a job.

4. **Answer: d.** A honeypot is a network device that tries to attract security attacks, allowing a network administrator to analyze the attackers and their strategies.

5. **Answer: b.** EAP is a security protocol that carries the credentials of a system (supplicant) that is trying to access a network.

6. **Answer: d.** The Common Vulnerabilities and Exposures (CVE) system is a free online resource that provides excellent search tools to leverage a large database of publicly known information security vulnerabilities and exposures.

7. **Answer: a.** Security information and event management (SIEM) systems provide real-time analysis of security alerts generated by applications and network hardware. SIEM systems can log security data and generate reports for compliance purposes.

8. **Answer: c.** Kerberos is a client/server authentication protocol that supports mutual authentication between a client and a server. With Kerberos, a trusted third party (a key distribution center) hands out tickets that are used instead of username and password combinations.

9. **Answer: b, c.** An automated teller machine (ATM) provides a common example of a multifactor authentication system. It requires both a "something you have" physical key (your ATM card) and a "something you know" personal identification number (PIN).

10. **Answer: d.** It is important to include separation of duties when planning for security policy compliance. Without this separation, all areas of control and compliance could end up in the hands of a single individual.

Chapter 17

1. **Answer: d.** A VLAN hopping attack leverages two technologies in its operation: Q-in-Q tunneling and the native VLAN feature.

2. **Answer: d.** A distributed denial-of-service (DDoS) attack involves many systems to compromise the availability of a system.

3. **Answer: c.** Piggybacking is a social engineering attack in which an authorized user permits an unauthorized user to access an area or systems. The unauthorized user may follow closely behind the authorized user through some type of security checkpoint.

4. **Answer: d.** In a brute-force password attack, the attacker tries all possible password combinations until a match is made. For example, a brute-force attack might start with the letter a and go through the letter z, and then the attacker might attempt the letters aa through zz, continuing to try combinations until the password is determined. Using complicated passwords—with a mixture of upper- and lowercase letters as well as special characters and numbers—can help prevent brute-force attacks.

5. **Answer: c.** Ransomware is an attack that involves the demand of a ransom (often in cryptocurrency) for access to files or systems to be restored.

Chapter 18

1. **Answer: a.** Control plane policing (CoPP) can help in this situation. Because your IGP and EGP routing protocols are part of the control plane, you can use CoPP to watch the amount of traffic that is permitted to your CPU. In this way, you can prevent many different types of DoS attacks that target the control plane.

2. **Answer: d.** Extensible Authentication Protocol (EAP) is a flexible solution that is used in many network environments to support a wide variety of authentication and authorization scenarios. EAP is the featured technology of 802.1X.

3. **Answer: c.** Private VLANs add segmentation capabilities beyond what is typical for VLAN communication. You can create segmentation within an IP subnet by using this technology.

4. **Answer: d.** Network hardening best practices include using SNMPv3 instead of earlier versions, disabling unneeded ports and unneeded services, and changing default passwords to something other than the known default passwords.

5. **Answer: a.** An implicit deny clause (in a firewall rule) means that if the proviso in question has not been explicitly granted, then access is denied.

6. **Answer: d.** A public network or a WiFi hotspot may use a captive portal, which requires users to agree to some condition before they can use the network or Internet.

Chapter 19

1. **Answer: b.** The client-to-site VPN type often features the use of a client system and its web browser and SSL/TLS to make a VPN connection. This is often considered "clientless" because the web browser is built in to the operating system, and there is no need for any separate client software installation.

2. **Answer: a.** Virtual network computing (VNC) is a multiplatform solution for remote desktop access. It is a very similar approach taken by Microsoft Remote Desktop Protocol (RDP).

3. **Answer: c.** The Secure Shell (SSH) protocol is the secure replacement technology for Telnet. Unlike Telnet, SSH offers strong security mechanisms that are in wide use today.

4. **Answer: a, c** In this example, Sally is using something she is (her fingerprint) along with something that she knows (the pin code).

5. **Answer: d.** Captive portals are common in public places such as airports and coffee shops. The user simply clicks Accept, views an advertisement, provides an email address, or performs some other required action, and the network then grants access to the user and no longer holds the user captive to that portal.

Chapter 20

1. **Answer: a.** Motion detection can certainly help with physical security, but it is a technique used in detection, not prevention.

2. **Answer: d.** Biometrics is an excellent form of a physical security control; however, this control is considered a prevention method and not a detection method.

3. **Answer: a, d.** Factory resets and configuration wipes are common asset disposal physical security controls. They are often used in combination.

4. **Answer: c.** You can use various wireless technologies to track the physical locations of network objects and personnel by using tag technologies attached to the entities.

5. **Answer: b, c.** An access control vestibule (formerly known as a mantrap) is a small entry area with two interlocking doors that prevents the tailgating and piggybacking forms of social engineering from taking place.

Chapter 21

1. **Answer: d.** Identifying or defining the problem is often the first step in a troubleshooting methodology.

2. **Answer: a, c, d.** Identifying, fixing, and reporting the problem are often the three steps in a simplified troubleshooting flow.

3. **Answer: a.** One of the final steps in a structured troubleshooting methodology would be to verify problem resolution. This would follow the creation and implementation of an action plan.

4. **Answer: d.** Step 3 is "Test the theory to determine the cause." This step includes a number of substeps: If the theory is confirmed, determine the next steps to resolve the problem. If the theory is not confirmed, establish a new theory or escalate. If you answered this question correctly, you have a solid grasp of the CompTIA network troubleshooting methodology!

5. **Answer: c.** After you have verified full system functionality and implemented preventive measures (Step 6), you should complete the final step (Step 7) by documenting findings, actions, outcomes, and lessons learned.

Chapter 22

1. **Answer: a.** In order to use PoE, your physical media must be Cat 5e or higher.

2. **Answer: b.** You need to ensure that you do not allow dirt to enter fiber-optic cable or cable connectors.

3. **Answer: b.** Using a loopback plug is a simple method of testing a network device's ability to send and receive traffic.

4. **Answer: c, d.** To mitigate the concern of pumping poisonous gas throughout a building's heating, ventilation, and air-conditioning (HVAC) system, you can use plenum-rated cabling. The outer insulation of a plenum twisted-pair cable is fire retardant; in addition, some plenum cabling uses a fluorinated ethylene polymer (FEP) or a low-smoke polyvinyl chloride (PVC) to minimize dangerous fumes. Cables that run through risers should also be fire-proof to prevent flames from traveling up the cable.

5. **Answer: a, e.** Attenuation is the weakening of a signal with greater distance between two devices on network media. Attenuation is measured in decibels (dB). dB loss is also more prone to happen as the signal needs to go farther and farther in the media.

6. **Answer: b.** Auto-MDIX technology on newer devices permits a port to adjust to the type of cable that is connected. Before this technology existed, it was necessary to use crossover cables to connect like devices. For example, connecting two switches required a crossover cable.

7. **Answer: c.** Duplex mismatches can cause links between devices to run inefficiently. A common scenario is one device operating in half-duplex while the other operates in full-duplex. You can check this setting in Windows 10 for a NIC, for example. Open Device Manager and right-click on the suspect network adapter. Select **Properties** and then **Speed & Duplex** and look at the **Value** setting.

Chapter 23

1. **Answer: b.** The **arp** command permits you to see the IP-address-to-MAC-address mappings. You can read them from left to right.

2. **Answer: d.** You can use the **/all** switch to learn many additional details about the IP configuration, including DNS details.

3. **Answer: c.** The **ping** command uses ICMP.

4. **Answer: d.** You use **traceroute** in UNIX to follow the hop-by-hop path that a packet takes.

5. **Answer: a, c, d.** You can use the UNIX commands **nslookup**, **dig**, and **host** to verify DNS operations.

6. **Answer: b.** This output is an example of output from the **dig** command.

7. **Answer: b.** A WiFi analyzer is a tool that would be used as part of a wireless site survey after WiFi has been implemented to create a heat map of the wireless airspace.

8. **Answer: c.** The **show route** command is used to view the routing table configuration of a network device.

Chapter 24

1. **Answer: a.** Received signal strength indication (RSSI) is an excellent metric for measuring the strength of the received wireless signal.

2. **Answer: a, c, d.** Fax machines and Bluetooth are the technologies in this list that are least likely to cause interference with wireless networks. Gaming consoles, microwaves, and baby monitors are the most common sources of RFI in wireless networks.

3. **Answer: a.** Speed is the theoretical maximum data rate for wireless. Throughput is a measure of the actual data that can be sent through the network.

4. **Answer: d.** A unidirectional antenna directs the bulk of its signal in a specific direction. In contrast, an omnidirectional antenna sends the signal in a 360-degree coverage area around the antenna.

5. **Answer: b.** A captive portal is a web page that asks clients seeking access to agree to organizational policies and typically captures information from clients.

6. **Answer: a.** A site survey can be a critical aid in implementing wireless network infrastructure. During a site survey, key issues can be tested for, such as excessive interference in certain areas.

7. **Answer: a.** Disassociation is often an initial step in a much larger attack. Once the client is disassociated, it can be associated to a rogue device.

8. **Answer: b.** The coverage areas of wireless APs using overlapping channels should not overlap. To maintain coverage between coverage areas, you should have overlapping coverage areas among wireless APs using nonoverlapping channels (for example, channels 1, 6, and 11 for wireless networks using the 2.4GHz band of frequencies).

Chapter 25

1. **Answer: c.** This problem sounds like it could be related to DNS-based name resolution.

2. **Answer: a.** A misconfigured default gateway address can lead to issues with reaching remote destinations.

3. **Answer: b, c.** STP protects against three main issues: MAC address table corruption, broadcast storms, and loops at Layer 2.

4. **Answer: b.** Being able to successfully ping another host is a simple method of confirming that Layers 1 through 3 of the OSI model are working.

5. **Answer: d.** The configuration of VLANs permits the creation of additional broadcast domains.

6. **Answer: c.** This IP address and subnet mask combination means that this host lives on the 172.16.128.0 subnet.

CompTIA Network+ (N10-008) Cert Guide Exam Updates

Over time, reader feedback allows Pearson to gauge which topics give our readers the most problems when taking the exams. To assist readers with those topics, the authors create new materials clarifying and expanding on those troublesome exam topics. As mentioned in the Introduction, the additional content about the exam is contained in a PDF on this book's companion website, at http://www.pearsonitcertification.com/title/9780137449941.

This appendix is intended to provide you with updated information if CompTIA makes minor modifications to the exam upon which this book is based. When CompTIA releases an entirely new exam, the changes are usually too extensive to provide in a simple update appendix. In those cases, you might need to consult the new edition of the book for the updated content. This appendix attempts to fill the void that occurs with any print book. In particular, this appendix does the following:

- Mentions technical items that might not have been mentioned elsewhere in the book

- Covers new topics if CompTIA adds new content to the exam over time

- Provides a way to get up-to-the-minute current information about content for the exam

Always Get the Latest at the Book's Product Page

You are reading the version of this appendix that was available when your book was printed. However, given that the main purpose of this appendix is to be a living, changing document, it is important that you look for the latest version online at the book's companion website. To do so, follow these steps:

Step 1. Browse to **www.pearsonitcertification.com/title/9780137449941.**

Step 2. Click the **Updates** tab.

Step 3. If there is a new Appendix B document on the page, download the latest Appendix B document.

> **NOTE** The downloaded document has a version number. Comparing the version of the print Appendix B (Version 1.0) with the latest online version of this appendix, you should do the following:
>
> - **Same version:** Ignore the PDF that you downloaded from the companion website.
>
> - **Website has a later version:** Ignore this Appendix B in your book and read only the latest version that you downloaded from the companion website.

Technical Content

The current Version 1.0 of this appendix does not contain additional technical coverage.

Index

U

To receive your 10% off
Exam Voucher, register
your product at:

www.pearsonitcertification.com/register

and follow the instructions.